# BIBLICAL THEOLOGY

OF THE

# NEW TESTAMENT

BY
REVERE FRANKLIN WEIDNER,

*Doctor and Professor of Theology, Author of "Studies in the Book," "Commentary on Mark," "Biblical Theology of the Old Testament," "Theological Encyclopædia," "An Introduction to Dogmatic Theology," "New Testament Greek Method," "Christian Ethics," Etc.*

TWO VOLUMES BOUND IN ONE

WIPF & STOCK · Eugene, Oregon

Wipf and Stock Publishers
199 W 8th Ave, Suite 3
Eugene, OR 97401

Biblical Theology of the New Testament
By Weidner, Revere Franklin
Softcover ISBN-13: 978-1-7252-9021-1
Hardcover ISBN-13: 978-1-7252-9020-4
eBook ISBN-13: 978-1-7252-9022-8
Publication date 10/30/2020
Previously published by Fleming H. Revell Company, 1891

This edition is a scanned facsimile of the original edition published in 1891.

# BIBLICAL THEOLOGY

OF THE

# NEW TESTAMENT

BY

REVERE FRANKLIN WEIDNER,

*Doctor and Professor of Theology, Author of "Studies in the Book," "Commentary on Mark," "Biblical Theology of the Old Testament," "Theological Encyclopædia," "An Introduction to Dogmatic Theology," "New Testament Greek Method," "Christian Ethics," Etc.*

VOL. I.

PART I. THE TEACHING OF JESUS.
PART II. THE PETRINE TEACHING.

WIPF & STOCK · Eugene, Oregon

TO

THE VENERABLE

JOSEPH A. SEISS, D. D., LL. D.,

A PRINCE

AMONG PULPIT ORATORS,

WHOSE FRIENDSHIP AND CONFIDENCE HAVE BEEN

THE INSPIRATION OF MY LITERARY LIFE,

THIS WORK, AS A

TOKEN OF AFFECTION AND ESTEEM,

IS

RESPECTFULLY DEDICATED.

# PREFACE.

An attempt is here made to present, in a concise and yet full form, the teaching of the New Testament with reference to all its most important doctrines and duties. The aim is to investigate, in an exact and historical manner, the teaching of each single writer in the New Testament. There is no discipline of theological science which is more important than Biblical Theology, and on which more depends. Of late, with many, Christain Dogmatics or Systematic Theology has fallen into disrepute, and more stress is laid upon Biblical Theology. We are told that in Church doctrine and Systematic Theology we have the deductions and speculations of men, while in Biblical Theology we have the pure teaching of the Word of God. But Systematic Theology is not necessarily unbiblical, and the nature of the Biblical Theology which is thus taught depends altogether on the standpoint from which it is written. It may be evangelical or rationalistic, theistic or pantheistic.

Believing that the Bible is the Word of God, truly Divine and yet truly human, the absolute rule of our faith, and the infallible guide of our daily life, the writer has simply sought to reproduce the thoughts of the Sacred writers, taking the statements of Scripture as the basis. The great question which must be answered in all cases is, What is written? What does Jesus, or Peter, or Paul, or John truly teach? The exegetic function required is of the highest kind. No one is able to present such a teaching of what the New Testament contains, in its fullness and scientific precision, unless he has repeatedly gone over all the books of the Bible, with this special object in view. It implies a critical study of the original texts, both of the Old and New Testaments, together with a thorough acquaintance with ecclesiastical and speculative dogmatics. For any one, who in his ignorance or temerity, attempts to expound the Bible without reference to what has been done towards its elucidation in the past, and without being guided by the development of doctrine, is exactly as foolish as the man who would undertake to take up any branch of science without regard to what has been done before.

The writer does not claim to have attained this high ideal; but he has sought, with all the power and gifts that God has bestowed upon him, guided by His Spirit, clearly and simply to set forth the true meaning of God's Word. The foundation for a careful and exact study of the Bible was laid seventeen years ago, when the writer began the *systematic* study of the Word of God in its original languages, with the help of the commentaries of Delitzsch and Keil on the Old Testament, and of the commentaries of Ellicott, Lightfoot, and Meyer on the New. The systematic study of the Bible, thus begun, has never ceased, and has led to a careful investigation in the original text, of every statement of God's Word.

When, in 1882, the writer was providentially called to the chair of Dogmatics and Exegesis in a Theological Seminary, these studies began to take a definite shape, although the direction towards which they were tending can be judged from a "Commentary on Mark"

(1881), which contained the statement, "This volume is the first of a series intended to embrace the whole New Testament." In 1883, in addition to preparation of lectures on Dogmatics and on Exegesis of the New Testament, a thorough investigation of the Theology of the Old Testament was begun, which resulted in the rewriting of Oehler's great work for his students, under the title, "Biblical Theology of the Old Testament" (1886). But the preparation of lectures on Dogmatics led the writer daily more deeply into the New Testament, and ere long the material was at hand for a presentation of the Theology of the New Testament; for, after all, Biblical Theology is nothing else than the exegetical foundation for Dogmatic Theology, and no treatment of the latter can be satisfactory which is not based upon Holy Scripture.

Already, in the fall of 1886, a special investigation of this science was commenced under the guidance of the well-known works of Schmid, Neander, Van Oosterzee, Lechler, and Weiss. The writer was especially drawn to Bernhard Weiss by his clearness of statement, his lucid arrangement, and his scientific treatment, without, however, accepting his peculiar aberrations, or being drawn aside by his remarkable idiosyncrasies. These latter peculiarities, indeed, have been the means of provoking to a still closer and deeper study of God's Word; and although, in Biblical Theology, stress is laid upon the manifold forms of doctrine, the result has been that, by laying stress upon the exact and positive meaning of each passage of Scripture, and then comparing with other passages, the unity of Biblical truth has been established, in the writer's mind, clearer than ever before.

So scientific and lucid is the arrangement of Weiss's

work, that his system, in the main, has been followed. There was even a strong temptation to put on the title-page, "Based on Weiss;" but this would not in any way have expressed the relation of this work to his. It would have been unjust to that learned author; for this book is by no means a reproduction of Weiss's Biblical Theology, although the writer is indebted to him, directly or indirectly, for what is best in this presentation of the subject.

There is nothing polemic in the following pages, and no attempt has been made to attack the interpretations of the rationalistic school of critics, by whatever name they may be known. The writer simply presents what he believes to be the plain, simple teaching of Scripture; and what has been written he holds to be the truth of God's Word, as he now understands it.

The first writing of this work was finished two years ago; but, so important is the subject, that the writer felt it his duty to study anew the whole New Testament, in an inductive way, and to develop again the teaching of each book separately. The result of these studies appeared, during the last year, in three volumes, under the general title of "Studies in the Book." In the meanwhile, transverse sections of the topics under discussion were developed, some of which have been delivered in the form of lectures at Chautauqua, and other Assemblies. Special attention also was given to all the most important treatises relating to the entire subject, published in English, German and Swedish, during the last decades. On the basis of these preliminary studies the whole work has been entirely rewritten during the last year, and some parts even three times.

In order that this work may be used advantageously as a text-book by private students, and also by intelligent readers of the Bible, an analysis has been appended at the close of each section. A full index, both alphabetical and analytical, will be given at the close of the second volume, which is already in press.

And now I send these pages forth with the earnest prayer that they may be blessed to aid the cause of truth and righteousness, and be the means of opening to many the rich treasures of God's Word.

R. F. W.

AUGUSTANA THEOLOGICAL SEMINARY.
ROCK ISLAND, ILL., *February* 11, 1891.

# LIST OF AUTHORITIES.

*The following are some of the books and editions which have been constantly used and referred to in the preparation of this work:*

Alexander. *Isaiah.* 2 vols. New York, 1846-47.
—— *Psalms.* Edinburgh, 1864.
Alexander. *Witness of the Psalms to Christ.* Second ed. New York, 1879.
Alexander. *Bible Truth.* Philadelphia, 1846.
Alford. *Greek Testament.* Seventh edition. 4 vols. Boston, 1880.
Auberlen. *Daniel and Revelation.* Edinburgh, 1856.

Baumgarten. *Acts of the Apostles.* From the German. 3 vols. Edinburgh, 1854.
Beck. *Leitfaden der Christ. Glaubenslehre.* 2 vols. Stuttgart, 1862.
—— *Biblical Psychology.* Edinburgh, 1877.
Beecher. *Scriptural Doctrine of Retribution.* New York, 1878.
Beet. *Romans.* Third ed. New York, 1883.
—— *Corinthians.* London, 1882.
—— *Galatians.* New York, 1885.
Bengel. *Gnomon.* Second ed. Tübingen, 1759. English translation. Fourth ed. 5 vols. Edinburgh, 1860.
Bennett. *Theology of the Early Christian Church.* London, 1855.
Bernard. *Progress of Doctrine in New Testament.* New York.
Beste. *Luther's Glaubenslehre.* Halle, 1845.
Binnie. *The Church.* Edinburgh, 1882.
Bleek. *Introduction to New Testament.* 2 vols. Edinburgh, 1869.
Boehl. *Zwölf Messianische Psalmen.* Basel, 1862.
Bonar. *Leviticus.* Third ed. London, 1852.
—— *Christ and His Church in the Psalms.* London, 1859.
Briggs. *Biblical Study.* New York, 1883.
Broadus. *Matthew.* Philadelphia, 1886.
Bruce. *Humiliation of Christ.* New York, 1887.

Bruce. *Kingdom of God.* In *Monthly Interpreter.* Also published separately. 1888.
Bruder. *Concordantiæ.* Leipsic, 1867.
Buttmann. *New Testament Grammar.* Andover, 1876.

Cadman. *Christ in the Gospels.* Chicago, 1885.
*Cambridge Bible Commentary.* 22 vols.
Candlish. *Doctrine of God.* Edinburgh.
—— *Work of Holy Spirit.* Edinburgh.
Caspari. *Introduction to Life of Christ.* From the German. Edinburgh, 1876.
Conybeare and Howson. *Life and Epistles of Paul.* 2 vols. London, 1861.
Cremer. *Lexicon of New Testament Greek.* From the second German ed. Edinburgh, 1880.
—— Sixth German ed. Gotha, 1889.
—— *Eschatologische Rede Jesu Christi.* Stuttgart, 1860.
—— *Beyond the Grave.* New York, 1886.
Crippen. *History of Christian Doctrine.* Edinburgh, 1883.

Davidson. *Hebrews.* Edinburgh, 1882.
Delitzsch. *Genesis.* Translation from Fifth German ed. 2 vols. New York, 1889.
—— *Psalms.* Translation from Fourth German ed. 3 vols. New York, 1887.
—— *Isaiah.* 2 vols. Edinburgh, 1877.
—— *Hebrews.* 2 vols. Edinburgh, 1882.
—— *Biblical Psychology.* Edinburgh, 1869.
—— *Biblisch-prophetische Theologie.* Leipsic, 1845.
—— *Old Testament History of Redemption.* Edinburgh, 1881.
—— *Messianic Prophecies.* Edinburgh, 1880.
Doren. *Luke.* 2 vols. 1881.
Dorner. *System of Christian Doctrine.* 4 vols. Edinburgh, 1880-82.

## LIST OF AUTHORITIES.

Eadie. *Thessalonians.* London, 1877.
Ebrard. *Gospel History.* Edinburgh, 1869.
—— *Epistles of John.* Edinburgh, 1860.
Ellicott. *Life of Christ.* Boston, 1874.
—— *Epistles to the Thessalonians.* Third ed. London, 1866.
—— *Galatians.* Fourth ed. London, 1867.
—— *First Corinthians.* London, 1887.
—— *Ephesians.* Fourth ed. London, 1868.
—— *Philippians, Colossians, Philemon.* Fourth ed. London, 1875.
—— *Pastoral Epistles.* Boston, 1867.
—— *Revision of New Testament.* New York, 1873.
Elliott. *Horæ Apocalypticæ.* Third ed. 4 vols. London, 1847.
*Encyclopædia Britannica.* Ninth ed. 24 vols.
*Expositor.* Third series. 10 vols. 1885-89.

Fairbairn. *Pastoral Epistles.* Edinburgh, 1874.
Farrar. *Life of Christ.* 2 vols. New York, 1875.
—— *Life of Paul.* 2 vols. New York.
—— *Early Days of Christianity.* New York, 1883.
Fausset. *Bible Cyclopædia.* Philadelphia, 1878.
Field. *Handbook of Christian Theology.* New York, 1887.
Fischer. *Bibl. Psychologie, Biologie, etc.* Gotha, 1889.

Gebhardt. *Doctrine of the Apocalypse.* Edinburgh, 1878.
Gebhardt. *Novum Testamentum Græce et Germanice.* Leipsic, 1881.
Geikie. *Life of Christ.* 2 vols. New York, 1880.
Gerhard. *Erklar. der beiden Art. von der heiligen Taufe und dem heil. Abendmahl.* Berlin, 1868.
Gess. *Scripture Doctrine of Person of Christ.* Translated by Reubelt. Andover, 1876.
Glassius. *Philologia Sacra.* Leipsic, 1743.
Godet. *Luke.* New York, 1881.
—— *John.* 2 vols. New York, 1886.
—— *Romans.* New York, 1883.
Göschel. *Der Mensch nach Leib, Seele und Geist, desseits und jenseits.* Leipsic, 1856.
Goodwin. *Greek Moods and Tenses.* Boston, 1882; also edition of 1890.
Grau. *Bibl. Theol. des N. T.* In Zöckler's *Handbuch.*
Green. *Handbook to Grammar of Greek Testament.* Revised ed. London, 1886.
—— *Apostle Peter.* London.
Green. *Grammar of New Testament.* London, 1862.
—— *Developed Criticism.* London.

Hackett. *Acts.* Boston, 1858.
Harless. *Ephesians.* Stuttgart, 1858.
Herzog. *Encyclopædia.* First ed. 21 vols.
Hodge. *Theology of the Shorter Catechism.* New York, 1888.
—— *Outlines of Theology.* New York, 1882.
Hofmann. *Schriftbeweis.* First ed. 3 vols. Nord., 1852-55.
—— *Ephesians.* Nordlingen, 1870.
Hollazius. *Exam. Theol.* Leipsic, 1741.
Hopkins. *Scriptural Idea of Man.* London, 1883.
Hovey. *Biblical Eschatology.* Philadelphia, 1888.
Huidekoper. *Christ's Mission to the Underworld.* New York, 1882.
Humphrey. *Acts.* Second ed. London, 1854.

Jacobs. *Book of Concord.* 2 vols. Philadelphia, 1882-83.
Jennings and Lowe. *Psalms.* 3 vols. London, 1875-77.
Jukes. *Law of the Offerings.* London, 1848.
—— *Differences of Four Gospels.* Fourth ed. London, 1867.

Keil. *Peter and Jude.* Leipsic, 1883.
—— *Pentateuch.* 3 vols. Edinb., 1869.
—— *Daniel.* Edinburgh, 1872.
—— *Minor Prophets.* Leipsic, 1866.
Kellogg. *Are Pre-Millennialists Right?* Chicago.
Kern. *Burk's Rechtfertigung und Versicherung.* Stuttgart, 1854.
Kitto. *Biblical Cyclopædia.* Third ed., by Alexander. 3 vols. Philadelphia, 1866.
Kliefoth. *Christliche Eschatologie.* Leipsic, 1886.
Köstlin. *Der Glaube.* Gotha, 1859.
Krauth. *Conservative Reformation.* Philadelphia, 1871.
Kurtz. *Christliche Religionslehre.* Eighth ed. Mitau, 1863.
—— *Sacred History.* Phila., 1869.

Laidlaw. *Bible Doctrine of Man.* Edinburgh, 1879.
Langbein. *Der Christl. Glaube.* Leipsic, 1873.
Lange. *Isaiah.* New York, 1884.
—— *Minor Prophets.* New York, 1875.
—— *Matthew.* New York, 1867.
—— *Acts.* New York, 1873.
—— *Corinthians.* New York, 1870.
—— *James, Peter, John, Jude.* New York, 1868.
Lechler. *Apostolic and Post-Apostolic Times.* Third ed. 2 vols. Edinburgh, 1886.
Lee. *Book of Revelation.* In Speaker's Commentary.
Lewin. *Life and Epistles of Paul.* Fourth ed. 2 vols. London, 1878.

## LIST OF AUTHORITIES.   xiii

Liddon. *Our Lord's Divinity.* London, 1871.
Lightfoot. *Galatians.* Andover, 1870.
—— *Colossians and Philemon.* London, 1879.
Lightfoot. *Philippians.* London, 1869.
—— *Revision of New Testament.* New York, 1873.
Lillie. *Thessalonians.* New York, 1860.
—— *Epistles of Peter.* New York, 1873.
Lowe. *Zechariah.* London, 1882.
Loy. *Justification.* Columbus, 1869.
Luthardt. *John's Gospel.* From the German. 3 vols. Leipsic, 1876.
—— *Kompendium der Dogmatik.* Seventh ed. Leipsic, 1886.
—— *Lehre von den letzten Dingen.* Third ed. Leipsic, 1885.

Macdonald. *Life and Writings of John.* New York, 1877.
Maitland. *Apostles' School of Prophetic Interpretation.* London, 1849.
Manly. *Bible Doctrine of Inspiration.* New York, 1888.
Martensen. *Christian Dogmatics.* Edinburgh, 1866.
—— *Christian Ethics.* 3 vols. Edinburgh, 1879-82.
McClellan. *The Four Gospels.* London, 1875.
Meyer. *New Testament Commentary.* 11 vols. New York.
Milligan and Moulton. *John.* New York, 1883.
*Monthly Interpreter.* 4 vols. Edinburgh, 1885-86.
Morison. *Matthew.* Boston, 1884.
—— *Mark.* Third ed. London, 1882.
Morris. *Is There Salvation After Death?* New York, 1887.
Moule. *Outlines of Christian Doctrine.* New York, 1889.
Müller. *Christian Doctrine of Sin.* 2 vols. Edinburgh, 1868.

Neander. *History of Planting and Training of the Christian Church.* Edited by Robinson. New York, 1864.
—— *Memorials of Christian Life.* London, 1852.
—— *History of Christian Dogmas.* 2 vols. 1878.
Norris. *Rudiments of Theology.* New York, 1876.

Oehler. *Theology of the Old Testament.* New York, 1883.
Oosterzee, Van. *Christian Dogmatics.* 2 vols. New York, 1874.
—— *Theology of New Testament.* London, 1871.
Orelli. *Old Testament Prophecy.* Edinburgh, 1885.

Passmore. *Compendium of Theology.* New York, 1876.

Pearson. *On the Creed.* Chevallier's ed. Cambridge, 1859.
Perowne. *Psalms.* 2 vols. Andover, 1879.
Philippi. *Kirchliche Glaubenslehre.* 9 vols. Gütersloh, 1868-1883.
—— *Romans.* From Third German ed. 2 vols. Edinburgh, 1878.
*Premillennial Essays.* Chicago, 1879.
*Prophetic Studies.* Chicago, 1887.
Pusey. *Minor Prophets.* 2 vols. New York, 1885.
—— *Daniel.* New York, 1885.
—— *What is Faith as to Everlasting Punishment?* Third ed. London, 1880.

Rinck. *Zustand nach dem Tode.* Second ed. Ludwigsburg, 1866.
—— *Zeichen der letzten Zeit.* Second ed. Basel, 1880.

Sadler. *Second Adam and the New Birth.* Fifth ed. London, 1876.
—— *Church Doctrine, Bible Truth.* Fourth ed. New York, 1869.
Schaff. *Matthew.* New York, 1882.
—— *Companion to Greek Testament.* Third ed. New York, 1888.
—— *Person of Christ.* Boston, 1865.
—— *Apostolic Church.* New York, 1856.
—— *Apostolic Christianity.* New York, 1882.
Schlottmann. *Bibl. Theologie des Alt. und N. T.* Leipsic, 1889.
Schmid. *Biblical Theology of New Testament.* From Fourth German ed. Edinburgh, 1870.
Schmid. *Doctrinal Theology of Lutheran Church.* Second ed. Philadelphia, 1889.
Scrivener. *Greek Testament.* Editio Major. Cambridge, 1887.
—— *Introduction.* Second ed. Cambridge, 1874. Also Third ed. Cambridge, 1883.
*Second Advent.* Discussion by Fausset, Godet, Beet, Brown, etc. New York, 1888.
Seiss. *Holy Types.* Second ed. Philadelphia, 1870.
—— *Apocalypse.* 3 vols. 1872-80.
Shedd. *History of Christian Doctrine.* 2 vols. New York, 1872.
—— *Dogmatic Theology.* 2 vols. New York, 1885.
Smith. *Dictionary of the Bible.* 4 vols. New York, 1873.
Smyth. *Dorner on the Future State.* New York, 1883.
*Speaker's (Bible) Commentary.* 10 vols. New York.
Splittgerber. *Tod, Fortleben und Auferstehung.* Fourth ed. Halle, 1885.
—— *Schlaf und Tod.* 2 vols. Halle, 1881.

## LIST OF AUTHORITIES.

Steinmeyer. *Miracles of our Lord.* Edinburgh, 1875.
Strong. *Systematic Theology.* Rochester, 1886.
Stuart. *Future Punishment.* Philadelphia, 1867.

Thayer. *Greek-English Lexicon of New Testament.* New York, 1887.
Tholuck. *Sermon on the Mount.* From the Fourth German ed. Philadelphia, 1860.
Thomasius. *Colossians.* Erlangen, 1869.
—— *Christliche Dogmengeschicte.* 2 vols. Erlangen, 1874-76.
—— *Christi Person und Werk.* Third ed. 2 vols. Erlangen, 1886.
Thompson. *Theology of Christ.* New York, 1873.
Tischendorf. *Novum Testamentum Græci.* Eighth Major ed. 2 vols. Leipsic, 1869-72.
—— *Wann wurden unsere Evangelien verfaszt?* Leipsic, 1866.
Trench. *Parables.* New York, 1876.
—— *Miracles.* New York, 1875.
—— *Synonyms of New Testament.* Seventh ed. London, 1871.
—— *Authorized Version.* New York, 1873.
—— *Epistles to the Seven Churches.* New York, 1872.
Tulloch. *Christian Doctrine of Sin.* New York, 1876.

Ullman. *Sinlessness of Jesus.* From Sixth German ed. Edinburgh, 1858.
Urwick. *Servant of Jehovah.* Edinburgh, 1877.

Vaughan. *Romans.* Fifth ed. London, 1880.
Vilmar. *Dogmatik.* 2 vols. Gütersloh, 1874.

Walther. *Kirche und Amt.* Erlangen, 1865.
Webster and Wilkinson. *Greek Testament.* 2 vols. London, 1855-61.

Weidner. *Mark.* Second ed. 1888.
—— *Biblical Theology of Old Testament.* Chicago, 1886.
—— *Studies in the Book.* 3 vols. Chicago, 1890.
Weiss. *Biblical Theology of New Testament.* From Third German ed. 2 vols. Edinburgh, 1882.
—— *Lehrbuch der Bibl. Theologie des Neuen Testaments.* Third ed. Berlin, 1880.
—— *Same.* Fifth German ed. Berlin, 1888.
—— *Introduction to New Testament.* 2 vols. New York, 1889.
Westcott and Hort. *Greek Testament.* 2 vols. New York, 1881-82.
Westcott. *Introduction to the Study of the Gospels.* Boston, 1872.
—— *John.* In Speaker's Commentary.
—— *Epistles of John.* London, 1883.
—— *Hebrews.* London, 1889.
—— *Canon of the New Testament.* Fifth ed. London, 1881.
—— *Christus Consummator.* In *Expositor.* Also published separately.
Whitelaw. *Divinity of Jesus.* London, 1883.
Wiescler. *Chronological Synopsis of Four Gospels.* Cambridge, 1864.
Winer. *New Testament Grammar.* Andover, 1877.
—— *Bibl. Realwörterbuch.* Third ed. 2 vols. Leipsic, 1847.
Wordsworth. *Greek Testament.* 2 vols. London, 1877.
Wright. *Zechariah and His Prophecies.* New York, 1879.
Wünsche. *Joel.* Leipsic, 1872.
—— *Hosea.* Leipsic, 1868.

Young. *Analytical Concordance.* Edinburgh, 1881.
Young. *Christ of History.* New York, 1857.

Zezschwitz. *Christenlehre im Zusammenhang.* 3 vols. Leipsic, 1883-84.
Zöckler. *Handbuch der Theol. Wissenchaften.* Third ed. 4 vols. Nördlingen, 1889.

# CONTENTS.

## INTRODUCTION.

| SECTION | PAGE |
|---|---|
| 1. Definition of the Science | 13 |
| 2. Relation to Other New Testament Branches | 14 |
| 3. The Methodology and Divisions of Biblical Theology | 16 |
| 4. Investigation of Sources | 19 |
| 5. The Origin of the Science | 20 |
| 6. Earlier Works on Biblical Theology | 22 |
| 7. The More Recent Works | 22 |
| 8. Auxiliary Labors | 25 |

## PART I.

### THE TEACHING OF JESUS.

#### INTRODUCTION.

| | |
|---|---|
| 9. The Life and Teaching of Jesus in their Relation to Biblical Theology | 31 |
| 10. Sources for the Representation of the Teaching of Jesus | 33 |
| 11. Critical Presuppositions for the use of the Three Synoptic Gospels | 36 |
| 12. The Discourses of Jesus in John's Gospel | 38 |

#### SECTION I.

##### THE TEACHING OF JESUS ACCORDING TO THE THREE SYNOPTISTS.

| | |
|---|---|
| 13. General Divisions | 40 |

#### CHAPTER I.

##### THE MESSAGE REGARDING THE KINGDOM OF GOD.

| | |
|---|---|
| 14. The Kingdom of God and the Messiah | 41 |
| 15. The Kingdom of God and the Disciples | 45 |
| 16. The Kingdom of God in its Consummation | 47 |

## CHAPTER II.

### THE TESTIMONY OF JESUS TO HIMSELF AS THE MESSIAH.

| | |
|---|---:|
| 17. The Son of Man | 48 |
| 18. The Son of God | 50 |
| 19. The Purpose of the Incarnation | 54 |
| 20. The Anointed One | 55 |
| 21. The Son of David and the Exalted Messiah | 57 |

## CHAPTER III.

### THE MESSIANIC ACTIVITY.

| | |
|---|---:|
| 22. The New Revelation of God | 60 |
| 23. Repentance | 61 |
| 24. The Messianic Salvation | 64 |
| 25. The Victory Over Satan | 67 |

## CHAPTER IV.

### THE RIGHTEOUSNESS OF THE KINGDOM OF GOD.

| | |
|---|---:|
| 26. Righteousness and the Law | 70 |
| 27. The Greatest Commandment | 72 |
| 28. Righteousness as Disposition | 74 |

## CHAPTER V.

### THE ANTHROPOLOGY OF CHRIST.

| | |
|---|---:|
| 29. The Anthropology of Christ | 77 |

## CHAPTER VI.

### THE MESSIANIC CHURCH.

| | |
|---|---:|
| 30. The Calling | 82 |
| 31. Discipleship | 84 |
| 32. The Elect | 85 |
| 33. The Apostles and the Church | 89 |

## CHAPTER VII.

### THE ESCHATOLOGY OF JESUS.

| | |
|---|---:|
| 34. Death in General | 91 |
| 35. The Doctrine of Recompense | 92 |
| 36. Bodily Death | 94 |
| 37. The State of the Soul After Death | 95 |

## CONTENTS.

38. The Second Coming of Christ . . . . . . 102
39. The General Resurrection of All Men . . . . 108
40. The Final Judgment . . . . . . . . 111
41. The End of the World . . . . . . . 114
42. Eternal Life . . . . . . . . . . 116
43. Eternal Death . . . . . . . . . 118

### SECTION II.

#### THE TEACHING OF JESUS ACCORDING TO JOHN.

44. General Divisions . . . . . . . . 124

### CHAPTER VIII.

#### CHRISTOLOGY.

45. The Sending of the Only-Begotten Son . . . . 125
46. The Heavenly Origin of the Son of Man . . . 126

### CHAPTER IX.

#### THE SALVATION IN CHRIST.

47. Christ the Life of the World . . . . . . 129
48. Christ the Light of the World . . . . . 130
49. Christ the Saviour of the World . . . . . 131

### CHAPTER X.

#### THE APPROPRIATION OF SALVATION.

50. Faith and Fellowship With Christ . . . . . 132
51. Fellowship With God . . . . . . . 134
52. Keeping the Commandments of God . . . . 134

### CHAPTER XI.

#### THE HISTORICAL REALIZATION OF SALVATION.

53. The Preparatory Revelation of God . . . . . 136
54. Victory Over the Devil . . . . . . . 137
55. The Church of the Disciples . . . . . . 140

### CHAPTER XII.

#### THE CONSUMMATION OF SALVATION.

56. The Sending of the Holy Spirit . . . . . 143
57. The Fellowship of Believers . . . . . . 145

## PART II.

### THE PETRINE TEACHING.

#### INTRODUCTION.

| | |
|---|---|
| 58. The Petrine Type of Doctrine | 49 |
| 59. The Discourses of Peter in the Acts | 149 |
| 60. The First Epistle of Peter | 151 |
| 61. The Epistle of James | 152 |
| 62. The Second Epistle of Peter and the Epistle of Jude | 153 |
| 63. The Evangelists Matthew and Mark | 154 |

### SECTION I.

#### THE DISCOURSES OF PETER IN THE ACTS.

##### CHAPTER I.

###### THE PROCLAMATION OF THE MESSIAH AND THE MESSIANIC TIME.

| | |
|---|---|
| 64. The Fulfillment of Prophecy in the Earthly Life of Jesus | 156 |
| 65. The Exalted Messiah | 158 |
| 66. The Coming of the Messianic Time | 159 |

##### CHAPTER II.

###### THE MOTHER CHURCH AND THE QUESTION OF THE GENTILES.

| | |
|---|---|
| 67. The Church and the Apostles | 161 |
| 68. The Conversion of the Whole of Israel | 164 |
| 69. The Position of the Gentile Christians in the Church | 165 |
| 70. Lechler's Presentation of the Discourses in Acts | 167 |

### SECTION II.

#### THE FIRST EPISTLE OF PETER.

##### CHAPTER III.

###### THE BEGINNING OF THE MESSIANIC CONSUMMATION IN THE CHRISTIAN CHURCH.

| | |
|---|---|
| 71. The Elect Race | 171 |
| 72. The Peculiar People and the Calling | 173 |
| 73. The New Birth and the Nourishment of the New Life | 175 |
| 74. Christian Social Life | 177 |

## CHAPTER IV.

### THE MESSIAH AND HIS WORK.

| | |
|---|---|
| 75. Jesus the Messiah | 180 |
| 76. The Saving Significance of the Suffering of Christ | 180 |
| 77. The Descent of Christ into Hades | 184 |
| 78. The Resurrection as the Ground of Christian Hope | 196 |
| 79. The Apostle of Hope | 198 |
| 80. Lechler's Presentation | 200 |

## SECTION III.

### THE EPISTLE OF JAMES.

## CHAPTER V.

### CHRISTIANITY AS THE PERFECT LAW.

| | |
|---|---|
| 81. The Word of Truth | 202 |
| 82. Justification | 204 |
| 83. Election | 207 |

## CHAPTER VI.

### THE DIVINE CLAIM AND THE DIVINE RECOMPENSE.

| | |
|---|---|
| 84. The Divine Claim | 208 |
| 85. Human Sin | 210 |
| 86. Recompense and Judgment | 211 |

## SECTION IV.

### THE SECOND EPISTLE OF PETER AND THE EPISTLE OF JUDE.

## CHAPTER VII.

### CHRISTIAN HOPE AND CHRISTIAN STRIVING AFTER VIRTUE.

| | |
|---|---|
| 87. The Object of Christian Knowledge | 214 |
| 88. The Striving After Christian Virtue | 216 |
| 89. The Destruction of the World and the Consummation of Salvation | 217 |

## SECTION V.

### THE EVANGELISTS MARK AND MATTHEW.

## CHAPTER VIII.

### THE MESSIAH OF THE JEWS.

| | |
|---|---|
| 90. The Gospel of Mark | 220 |
| 91. The Gospel of Matthew | 223 |

## SECTION VI.

### SUMMARY OF PETRINE TEACHING.

#### CHAPTER IX.

##### THE PETRINE CHRISTOLOGY.

92. The Pre-Incarnate Existence of Jesus . . . . 227
93. Christ Truly Divine . . . . . . . 228
94. Christ Truly Human . . . . . . . . 228

#### CHAPTER X

##### THE PETRINE ESCHATOLOGY.

95. Method of Presenting the Petrine Eschatology . . 229
96. The Teaching Concerning Death . . . . . 229
97. The Conversion of Israel . . . . . . . 230
98. The Second Coming of Christ . . . . . 231
99. The Resurrection of the Dead . . . . . . 233
100. The Day of Judgment . . . . . . 233
101. The End of the World . . . . . . . 235

# BIBLICAL THEOLOGY

## OF THE

# NEW TESTAMENT.

### INTRODUCTION.[1]

§ 1. *Definition of the Science.*

Biblical Theology of the New Testament has for its task the scientific representation, in a summary form, of the religious ideas and doctrines contained in the canonical books of the New Testament. Within its province there can be no distinction between Dogmatics and Ethics, because, from the stand-point of the New Testament writers, faith and life are not only united, but one. As it seeks to investigate, in a purely historical manner, the teaching of each single writer of the New Testament, it is a historical science, and is one of the branches of Historical Theology.[2]

As the New Testament was written by different authors and at different times, a variety of religious ideas and doctrines is to be looked for in it. The revelation of God in Christ did not consist, as to its nature, in the communication of a *sum* of religious ideas and

---

[1] This Introduction is based upon *Bernhard Weiss*, without however accepting his methods or adopting all his views.

[2] See my *Theological Encyclopædia: Vol. II. Historical and Systematic Theology*, §§ 8–10. (F. H. Revell: Chicago, 1889.)

doctrines, given *all at once*, but the religious consciousness and life which were produced by the revelation in Christ assumed different forms in its different leading representatives, and at the different stages of its development. And it is the task of New Testament Theology to represent the individually and historically conditioned manifoldness of the New Testament forms of doctrine, and clearly to set them forth in their unity and harmony.

[ANALYSIS: 1) Aim of the science; 2) is a historical science; 3) revelation is progressive.]

## § 2. *Relation to Other New Testament Branches.*

Biblical Theology of the New Testament, as a science, stands in close connection with "New Testament Introduction." This latter science precedes, and to it we leave all critical investigations as to the authenticity, authorship, and integrity of the New Testament writings. New Testament Theology also assumes that the normative character of the writings of the New Testament has been established. It is not within the province of our science to prove the Inspiration of the Bible, for this belongs to the science of Apologetics, or rather of Dogmatics. The writer, however, accepts the doctrine of the Plenary Inspiration of the Bible—believes, not simply that the Bible *contains* the Word of God, but that it *is* the Word of God. The divine and the human, employed in its composition, are so combined as to produce one undivided and indivisible result. Notwithstanding the exercise of human agency in writing the Bible, it is all alike Divine, and notwithstanding the Divine agency employed in its composition, it is all alike human. The Divine and the human elements together constitute a theanthropic book. For the Bible is absolutely Divine in its spirit, yet truly human in its body. It is God's Word mediated through man.

The science of Biblical Theology also stands in close connection with Exegesis, or the science of Interpretation, because its aim is to reproduce the thoughts of the Sacred writers, taking the statements of Scripture as its basis. But the exegetic function which it performs is of the highest and most advanced kind. It ascertains the ideas and doctrines conveyed by a whole body of didactic discourses and passages, by taking a comprehensive view of its different portions in their relation to one another. It is not contented with isolated ideas and propositions, but, taking an aggregate of doctrinal ideas and dogmas, it presents both their unity and their variety in a life-like doctrinal whole.

The relation in which our science stands to Dogmatic Theology is somewhat different, being introductory to it. Biblical Theology has been frequently understood to mean nothing else than a certain kind of positive divinity, which, without regard to ecclesiastical interpretations, is founded mainly upon the New Testament alone. Nevertheless, although its aim certainly is a systematic summary of its subject-matter, it is essentially distinct from dogmatics proper, by reason of its historical character. It is still further removed from ecclesiastical, speculative, or descriptive dogmatics. It is nothing else than the exegetical foundation for Dogmatic Theology. It is the material with which this latter science builds. The exegetical function of Dogmatic Theology has been often very unsatisfactorily performed. Some speculative systems are supported merely by a few quotations from Scripture. No treatment of Dogmatic Theology can be satisfactory which is not based upon Holy Scripture—not on the mere letter, but on the spirit which is contained in it. Biblical Theology must therefore furnish the material, and is not limited to isolated exegesis or to the furnishing of a mere biblical commentary, but it must develop the entire biblical systems of thought as they lie before us in the New Testament. It must set forth the different systems of thought in their unity and manifold variety, and show us how their total result presents a united record of the Divine Word. It is in this way that Biblical Theology opens the way for that use of the Scriptures which has become a necessity to Dogmatic Theology.[1]

[ANALYSIS : 1) Its relation to New Testament Introduction; 2) it assumes the Inspiration of Scripture; 3) its relation to the science of Interpretation; 4) to Dogmatic Theology; 5) its task.]

§ 3. *The Methodology and Divisions of Biblical Theology.*

As Biblical Theology of the New Testament has to give a separate representation of the doctrinal systems of the individual books of the New Testament, or of the authors by whom several of these books have been written, we must have some special method of treatment. Not only does our science borrow from historico-critical introduction the results regarding the authors and dates of the separate books, in order that it may be able to decide what books it has to regard as sources of a definite doctrinal system, and in what connection it has to exhibit these systems, but it must also borrow from the history of the Apostolic Age—to which it itself affords the material for the representation of its inner development—the knowledge of the circumstances and tendencies of the time in accordance with which it arranges the individual doctrinal systems.

[1] See Schmid's *Biblical Theology of the New Testament*, § 1.

## METHODOLOGY AND DIVISIONS.

As Biblical Theology has to do with the variety of the biblical forms of teaching, the representation of the several doctrinal systems will have to start from the central point around which the doctrinal view of each individual writer moves; and from that point, following the lines of thought which are found in the writer himself, it will have to describe the whole circle of his ideas and doctrines. The method must trace the manner of the origination of the different ideas and their development; it must be chronological, tracing the inner process of development of one and the same writer, as St. Paul; it must be analytical, for the synthesis has no value unless the analysis has been true.[1] The investigations must be thorough, exact, complete, impartial, and truth-loving, begun and continued in a truly prayerful and believing spirit. Faith here also leads to a better and truer knowledge, and knowledge thus gained will lead us to a still deeper faith. (1 John 5:13.)

A close investigation enables us to distinguish *four* types of doctrine under which the doctrinal systems of the New Testament writings may be discussed:

I. The teaching of Jesus: 1) according to the three Synoptists; 2) according to John.

II. The Petrine type of Doctrine: 1) according to the Acts of the Apostles; 2) according to 1 Peter; 3) according to James; 4) according to 2 Peter and Jude; 5) according to the type of doctrine represented by Matthew and Mark.

III. Paulinism in its various stages of development: 1) according to the Acts of the Apostles and the two Epistles to the Thessalonians; 2) according to the four great doctrinal and controversial Epistles (Galatians, 1

---

[1] See Van Oosterzee's *Theology of the New Testament*, § 3.

and 2 Corinthians, Romans); 3) according to the four Epistles of the First Captivity (Colossians, Philemon, Ephesians, Philippians); 4) according to the Pastoral Epistles (1 Timothy, Titus, 2 Timothy); 5) according to the Evangelist Luke; 6) according to the Epistle to the Hebrews.

IV. The Theology of St. John: 1) according to the Apocalypse; 2) according to the Gospel and Epistles.

For the right understanding of our science, we ought to distinguish between Biblical Theology proper and Biblical Dogmatics. As the former is a historical, the latter is more of a systematic science; as the former has to do with the variety of biblical forms of teaching, the latter has to do with the unity of the truth which is recorded in them. Some would separate the two disciplines altogether, but it is better to treat both of these branches in one work. After presenting the historical part (Biblical Theology proper) of the teaching of Jesus, of Peter, of Paul, or of John, it is also advisable to discuss in a summary, in a systematic manner (Biblical Dogmatics), the various doctrines taught by each representative writer. As all the doctrinal truths revealed in God's Word naturally gather around *seven* great centres,[1] we may speak of the Theology, Anthropology, Christology, Soteriology, Pneumatology, Ecclesiology, and Eschatology, of Jesus, of Peter, of Paul, and of John, respectively.

[ANALYSIS: 1) There must be a proper arrangement of the doctrinal systems; 2) the central doctrine of each writer must be developed; 3) attention must be paid to the inner process of development; 4) four types of doctrine may be distinguished; 5) distinction be-

---

[1] The doctrine of God, or Theology proper; 2) the doctrine of Man, or Anthropology; 3) the doctrine of the Person of Christ, or Christology; 4) the doctrine of the Work of Christ, or Soteriology;

tween Biblical Theology proper and Biblical Dogmatics; 6) Biblical Dogmatics may be included in one treatment; 7) the seven centres of Christian doctrine.]

### § 4. *Investigation of Sources.*

As a historical science, New Testament Theology is referred only to the circle of religious ideas in which the writers of the New Testament stand historically, and in which they have grown up. Now, since the Old Testament is the principal source of this circle of ideas, it is mainly from it that, in all doubtful cases, the meaning which they connect with their expressions is to be elucidated. In ascertaining, however, the ideas and teachings of the New Testament we are limited mainly to the books of the New Testament which lie before us. The essential import of every idea will have to be ascertained from the heterogeneous context of all the passages in which it occurs, from its connection with other ideas which are already known, from the characteristic individuality of the authors, and their place in the history of the Apostolic Age. It follows that, in ascertaining the ideas of a book, we are referred, in the first place, exclusively to that book itself, or to the books which belong to the same author. It is only when these are not sufficient that we are referred, in the second place, to the books which belong to a kindred tendency and to the same time; and, in the third place, to earlier books of the New Testament, especially if we can prove or assume that they were known to the author whose ideas we are investigating. Of course, New Testament Theology cannot be satisfied with having found one proof passage for a doctrine; it must examine every passage

5) the doctrine of the Work of the Holy Spirit, or Pneumatology; 6) the doctrine of the Church, or Ecclesiology; 7) the doctrine of the Last Things, or Eschatology.

in which it appears, in the light of the peculiar connection of thought in which it stands, in order that it may discover, as completely as possible, the threads by means of which it is connected with other ideas and doctrines.

As a preliminary condition of this there is need of grammatico-historical exegesis, which, however, must continue in constant reciprocal action with Biblical Theology.

[ANALYSIS: 1) Our first source, the books of the New Testament; 2) then those of the Old Testament; 3) all passages must be examined; 4) first, the individual book; 5) then books by the same author; 6) then books of kindred tendency and same time; 7) finally, earlier books of New Testament; 8) not satisfied with one proof passage; 9) our science rests on a grammatico-historical exegesis.]

§ 5. *The Origin of the Science.*

So long as the theology of the Church was conscious of its unity with the theology of the Bible, no need was felt of a scientific representation of the latter. But the more tradition asserted itself, as a rule of doctrine alongside of Scripture, so much the more did the theology of the Church deviate, in its further development, from that which is contained in the Bible. No doubt there were never lacking men who, in opposition to the dominant Church doctrine, pointed to the pure teaching of the Word; but the Reformation first brought the difference between the doctrine of the Church and the Bible into clear consciousness, and demanded a renovation of theology in accordance with its formal principle—the sole authority of Holy Scripture.

The first impulse to such a scientific representation was given by a separate exegetico-dogmatic discussion of the biblical proof passages (the so-called *dicta probantia*), which theologians had up to this time annexed, within dogmatics itself, to the several *loci* as proofs.[1] In these works the representation of the doctrinal matter of the Bible is only a means, not an end; the arrangement is determined altogether by the *dogmatic loci*, and the exegesis of the individual passages has quite a dogmatic character. The case remained the same when Rationalism employed this form of treatment in order to master the dogmatics of the Church upon its own soil, and in the interest of their system the collected proof passages were now misinterpreted or emptied of their real contents (see especially the works of Teller, Semler, and Hufnagel).

This naturally led to the attempt to arrange, in an independent manner, the results so obtained alongside of the dogmatics of the Church, either as its support or as its corrective. In this connection we must refer to the influence of Spener (1635–1705) and of Bengel (1687–1751). Pietism attempted to represent the teaching of the Bible in a manner which was simpler and more in keeping with the Bible itself, without breaking essentially with the doctrine of the Church.

But John Philip Gabler, in his academic oration, *De justo discrimine theologiæ biblicæ et dogmaticæ*, Altdorf, 1789 (reprinted in his minor theological writings, 1831, vol. 2), was the first who asserted the purely historical character of Biblical Theology, in the manner in which it has since his time been almost universally acknowledged.

[ANALYSIS: 1) The influence of the Reformation; 2) separate treatment of biblical proof passages; 3) Rationalism; 4) Pietism; 5) the work of Gabler.]

[1] Compare Sebastian Schmidt's *Collegium Biblicum:* Strassburg, 1671, 3d ed., 1689; Joh. Huelsemann's *Vindiciæ S. S. per loca classica Syst. Theol.:* Leipsic, 1679; Joh. Guil. Baier's *Analysis et vindicatio illustrium Script. dictorum*, etc.: Altorf, 1716.

## § 6. Earlier Works on Biblical Theology.

The attempt of George Lorenz Bauer (1755–1806) to carry out Gabler's conception of our science was still too much under the influence of rationalistic dogmatism. The works of W. M. L. de Wette (*Biblische Dogmatik des A. und N. T.*, Berlin, 1813, 2nd ed., 1830), L. J. Rueckert (*Christliche Philosophie*, 2 vols., Leipsic, 1825), and Dan. v. Coelln (*Biblische Theologie*, edited by David Schulz; Leipsic, 1836), are far more scientific, although even in them justice is not done to the historical character of Bible Theology. In the work of L. F. O. Baumgarten-Crusius (*Grundzüge der biblischen Theologie:* Jena, 1828), the right point of view which had already been gained for the treatment of Biblical Theology is again, for the most part, surrendered.

[ANALYSIS: 1) The work of Bauer; 2) De Wette; 3) Rueckert; 4) Von Coelln; 5) Baumgarten-Crusius.]

## § 7. The More Recent Works.

A new impulse to the deeper conception and more thorough performance of the problem assigned to our science was given by Augustus Neander (1789–1850), who, in his *History of the Planting and Training of the Christian Church by the Apostles* (4th German ed., 1847; best English edition by Robinson: New York, 1865), represented the teaching of the Apostles separately.[1]

---

[1] We most heartily recommend this work. It is one of the best guides to the study of Dogmatic Theology, but must be read with care. Neander divides his subject into six Books:

1) The Christian Church in Palestine previous to its introduction among the heathen nations.

2) The first spread of Christianity among heathen nations.

3) The spread of Christianity . . . by the instrumentality of Paul.

4) A review of the labors of James and Peter during the period described in book third,

Inspired by Neander, Christian Friedrich Schmid (1794–1852), in his *Biblical Theology of the New Testament* (4th German edition, 1868; abridged English translation, Edinburgh, 1870), sought to develop the manifoldness of New Testament types of doctrine from the religious individuality of the writers, and has found many followers. He obtains a fourfold possibility of types of doctrine, which, according to him, has left its imprint in the four Apostolic personalties. James (compared with the Gospel of Matthew) represents Christianity as the fulfilled law; Peter (compared with the Gospel of Mark), the fulfilled promise; Paul (compared with the historical books written by Luke, and with the Epistle to the Hebrews) represents Christianity in its contrast to the law; and John, in his writings, in its contrast to law and prophecy. In comparing the Epistle of James with that of Jude, Schmid maintains that the latter forms a transition to the Petrine system (compare 2 Peter). This work of Schmid is distinguished by its union of the historic sense and the thoughts of organic development with the most decided faith in the absolute revelation in Christ. It will long maintain its present high position.[1]

In close dependence upon Neander and Schmid, H. Messner, in his *Lehre der Apostel* (Leipsic, 1856), has treated of the several doctrinal systems (those of the smaller books, however, in greater detail than they), and has, with great care, sought to develop each of

5) The Apostle John and his ministry at the closing point of the Apostolic Age.

6) The Apostolic Doctrine.

*a*) The Pauline Doctrine; *b*) the doctrine of the Epistle to the Hebrews; *c*) the doctrine of James; *d*) the doctrine of John.

[1] We have made continual use of this excellent work.

them in its inner connection, and to compare it with the other. G. V. Lechler's work (*The Apostolic and Post-Apostolic Times*, translated from the third German ed., 2 vols.: Edinburgh, 1886), follows the same method, though far less thoroughly. He prefixes to the Pauline doctrinal system the representation of the preaching of the original Apostles, and follows it up with the doctrines of James, Peter, and John, in the shape which they assumed in the period after Paul.

The handbook of J. J. van Oosterzee (*The Theology of the New Testament*, London and New York, various editions; 2nd original Dutch edition, Utrecht, 1869), though far from independent and lacking in scientific definiteness, still has considerable value. The author, besides discussing the theology of Jesus Christ (according to the Synoptists, and according to John), gives us a full presentation of the Petrine, Pauline, and Johannean theologies.

If, since Neander, the diversity of the New Testament types of doctrine was traced back to the religious individuality of the several writers, the Tübingen school regarded the historical development of Christianity as the gradual reconciliation of the original opposition between the Jewish Christianity of the original Apostles and the anti-Judaism of Paul. Inspired by this school, A. Ritschl (in his work, *Entstehung der altkath. Kirche*, 2nd ed., Bonn, 1857) and E. Reuss (in his *History of Christian Theology in the Apostolic Age*, 3rd French edition, Strassburg, 1864; English translation, 2 vols., London, 1872-74) have represented the several doctrinal systems in connection with the history of the Apostolic Age. F. C. Baur, the founder of the famous "Tübingen School," in his *Vorlesungen ueber N. T. Theologie* (Leipsic, 1864), brings to light all the advantages, but also all the defects, of the method employed by that school. Dr. A. Immer, in his *Theologie des N. T.* (Berne, 1877), follows in the footsteps of the Tübingen school. Notwithstanding exact exegesis on the whole, and a diffuseness which is often very wearisome, a precise expression is scarcely anywhere given to the several ideas and lines of thought discussed by him.

The most important addition, so far, to the science of Biblical Theology is the work of Bernhard Weiss[1] (*Biblical Theology of the New Testament*, 2 vols.: Edinburgh, 1882; translated from the third German edition, Berlin, 1880), on which to a certain extent, with respect to scientific statement of results, but not as to principles or method, this present work is based.

[ANALYSIS: 1) The work of Neander; 2) of Schmid; 3) of Messner; 4) of Lechler; 5) of Van Oosterzee; 6) the Tübingen school; 7) Ritschl; 8) Reuss; 9) Baur; 10) Immer; 11) the work of Weiss.]

## § 8. *Auxiliary Labors.*

The attempts to represent a connected system of biblical doctrine are of assistance to Biblical Theology in proportion as they enter into the reproduction of the lines of thought of the several writers. In this sense J. T. Beck[2] (in his *Christliche Lehrwissenschaft nach den bibl. Urkunden*, Stuttgart, 1841) has worked up the doctrinal material of the Old and New Testaments into a whole; while J. Chr. K. v. Hofmann (in his *Schriftbeweis*, Nördlingen, 1852–55, 2nd ed., 1857–59), although

---

[1] Fifth German edition, Berlin, 1888.

[2] See also Beck's *Einleitung in das System der Christ. Lehre*, 2nd ed., Stuttgart, 1870; and his *Leitfaden der Christ. Glaubenslehre*, Stuttgart, 1862.

strongly opposed to every assumption of different biblical types of doctrine, establishes in its several parts the system with which he commences in such a manner that he advances from the Old Testament to the New, and from the sayings of Jesus to those of His Apostles. In his later great work on the New Testament (*Die heilige Schrift neuen Testaments zusammenhängend untersucht*, 7 vols., Nördlingen, 1862–76), Hofmann carried out his exceedingly original exegesis through almost all the Epistles of the New Testament. R. Kuebel (in his *Christliche Lehrsystem nach der heiligen Schrift*, Stuttgart, 1873) expressly distinguishes his task from the historical or descriptive task of Biblical Theology. Although, in many doctrines, this author enters into the diversities of the several types of teaching, yet the prevailing tendency is to obtain a system which is derived from the testimony of Scripture in its various forms—a testimony which is full of life, and given in accordance with experience, and therefore in the form of intuition—and developed in the form of discursive scientific knowledge.

Biblical Theology is still more directly assisted by the representation of particular doctrinal systems of the New Testament, such as the Pauline, Petrine, and Johannean systems, or by dissertations on particular ideas and doctrines of these systems. The different works will be considered more particularly when we come to these several systems.

Dissertations on particular fundamental doctrines of theology also furnish much acceptable material in proportion as they enter, somewhat in detail, into the teaching of Scripture. They are, as it were, transverse sections through the whole of our discipline; and although they are always somewhat defective, inasmuch as no individual doctrine can be fully appreciated outside of the connection of the system in which it is found, yet they have their peculiar value in this, that the relationship of the various systems comes out more directly in a definite point than in the complete representation given by our discipline.

Lastly, the lexicography of the New Testament cannot possibly avoid entering into biblico-theological investigations. Just as certainly as it has a purely philological side, so certainly it cannot, from that side, meet all the requirements of its task. Of New Testament lexicographers, S. C. Schirlitz (in his *Griechish-deutsches Wörterbuch zum N. T.*, 3rd ed., Giessen, 1868) and H. Cremer (in his *Biblico-Theological Lexicon of New Testament Greek*, Edinburgh, 1880; translation of second German edition; 6th German edition, Gotha, 1889) have purposely aimed to furnish us aid in the science of Biblical Theology. To the English student we would especially recommend Thayer's *Greek-English Lexicon of the New Testament* (being Grimm's Wilke's *Clavis Novi Testamenti*, translated, revised, and enlarged): New York, 1887.

[ANALYSIS: 1) The writings of Beck; 2) of Hofmann; 3) of Kuebel; 4) the presentation of particular doctrinal systems; 5) the lexicography of the N. T.; 6) the works of Cremer and Thayer.]

# PART I.

THE TEACHING OF JESUS.

# PART I.

## THE TEACHING OF JESUS.

### INTRODUCTION.

**§ 9.** *The Life and Teaching of Jesus in their Relation to Biblical Theology.*[1]

It is neither methodically permissible nor conducive to the aim of our science to admit into it a historical representation of the life of Jesus, as Schmid has done. If we were to give such a representation, we should go far beyond the boundaries of our discipline. Even as regards method, the scientific representation of the life of Jesus demands investigations of a totally different kind. It presupposes a historico-critical examination of sources which is of a totally different nature from the method of Biblical Theology. The latter has only to inquire what are the ideas and doctrines of the writings before us; the former inquires critically concerning the origin, the connection, and the value of these books.

It is not only what the Evangelists knew of the facts of the life of Jesus, but also what in these facts was regulative for their view of the significance of His Person and of His manifestation, and therefore for the forming of their religious ideas and doctrines, that is important for Biblical Theology. And this science not only inquires how we, in consequence of the complete testimony of

---

[1] Compare *Weiss*, § 9.

the Gospels, have to conceive the character of the facts of this life as a revelation, but also how it was conceived by the earliest preachers of the Gospel.

This conception, however, was conditioned by the teaching of Jesus, inasmuch as it gave the authentic explanation of the significance of His Person and of His manifestation; and hence the representation of the teaching of Jesus must precede in every delineation of doctrine. It is not to be supposed, however, that the whole riches of the self-testimony of Jesus had already passed over into the comprehension and the proclamation of the earliest witnesses; and, still further, Jesus, in His activity as a teacher (and therefore also in His self-testimony) was restrained, partly by the pedagogic regard to the inability of His hearers to comprehend the revelation which was making its first appearance in the world,[1] and partly by regard to the circumstance which belongs to the history of salvation, that the facts of salvation were but tending towards their completion, and that therefore the full comprehension of their significance was still unattainable.

There are some who maintain that what the Evangelists ascribe to Jesus Himself as His own teaching, is in truth nothing but the doctrine of the Apostles in a later state of development; but, as we shall see later on, the doctrine of Jesus, as transmitted to us by the Evangelists, really bears the same relation to the apostolical doctrine of the other New Testament writers as the foundation does to a finished building. What has been handed down to us as the teaching of Jesus in the Gospels is in fact of such a nature as to serve as the foundation of all other doctrine; and the apostolical

---

[1] John 16:12. "I have yet many things to say unto you, but ye cannot bear them now."

teaching in the other books of the New Testament is obviously the offshoot and development of this. In the didactic discourses of Jesus we have the pregnant germ and kernel, the root, the simple yet solid groundwork; in the apostolical doctrine, as presented in the other books, we have the shoots and branches, the plant developed from the germ, the finished building resting on that simple but firm foundation.[1]

As teaching was the characteristic feature of the life of Christ, no true understanding of His mission can be had without a knowledge of what He taught as the truth of God. The message which He brings comprises not only the rules of practical morality, but the truths and doctrines of a positive theology. So far as the very Words of Christ have been preserved, we have the very essence of Christianity. To preach Christ is to preach the doctrines that He taught and that are the substance of His message.[2]

[ANALYSIS: 1) We need not give a historical representation of the life of Christ; 2) our aim is to outline the ideas and doctrines of the recorded sayings of Jesus; 3) this naturally precedes in every system of Biblical Theology; 4) we can even mark a progress in the revelation as made by Christ; 5) the Sayings of Jesus are historical; 6) the foundation of all apostolical teaching; 7) the Words of Christ are the very essence of Christianity.]

§ 10. *Sources for the Representation of the Teaching of Jesus.*[3]

Biblical Theology does not ask for as complete a collection of the Sayings of Jesus as is possible, but it only asks what are the Sayings and Teachings of Jesus with which the earliest writers of the New Testament were

[1] See *Schmid*, § 1.
[2] See *Thompson's* "Theology of Christ," pp. 2-5.
[3] Compare *Weiss*, § 10.

acquainted, and what is the conception of His teaching which comes out from the form in which they possessed these sayings. Although tradition makes us acquainted with some so-called unwritten sayings of our Lord,[1] and we have single contributions in other parts of the New Testament (Acts 20:35; 1 John 1:5; 4:21), nevertheless the Four Gospels remain the principal source.

We here have to do only with the teaching of Christ as reported by the Evangelists, the statements of the Evangelists themselves belonging to a later development of doctrine.

In dealing with the teaching of Jesus, the difference between the utterances of the Lord in the three Synoptists and those in the Gospel of John is at once evident. This distinction is perceptible to every eye and has been recognized in every age; and yet, as we shall see, unless we allow ourselves to be misled by mere form, notwithstanding all differences, essential unity underlies them. The Synoptists are distinguished from John by describing our Lord's ministry in Galilee only, extending their account subsequently to Peræa and the final scene at Jerusalem. John, on the other hand, records principally the sayings of Christ in Judea. In John the discourses are more central; in the Synoptists, less so.[2] From the sixth chapter onwards, John gives for the most part the direct testimony of Jesus Himself as to His person and work; in the Synoptists the discourses are mainly preparatory to this.[3]

[1] Compare Westcott: *Introduction to the Study of the Gospels.* Appendix C.: Boston, 1872.

[2] See *Schmid*, § 3.

[3] The characteristics of the Four Gospels, as evincing the clear individuality of each one of the Inspired records, may be presented in the following excellent summary, given by Ellicott in his *Historical*

## SOURCES FOR REPRESENTATION.

[ANALYSIS: 1) The Sayings of Jesus are recorded in the Four Gospels; 2) the statements of the Evangelists themselves belong to a later period; 3) a distinction can be drawn between the teaching of Jesus as recorded by the three Synoptists, and by John; 4) marks of distinction; 5) the various characteristics of the Four Gospels according to Ellicott; 6) according to Bernard.]

*Lectures on the Life of our Lord Jesus Christ* (*Note* 1, p. 46). Boston, 1874.

1. "In regard of the *External Features and Characteristics*, we are perhaps warranted in saying that *a*) the *point of view* of the first Gospel is mainly Israelitic; of the second, Gentile; of the third, universal; of the fourth, Christian;—that *b*) the general *aspect* and, so to speak, *physiognomy*, of the first mainly is Oriental; of the second, Roman; of the third, Greek; of the fourth, spiritual;— that *c*) the *style* of the first is stately and rhythmical; of the second, terse and precise; of the third, calm and copious; of the fourth, artless and colloquial;—that *d*) the most striking *characteristic* of the first is symmetry; of the second, compression; of the third, order; of the fourth, system;—that *e*) the *thought and language* of the first are both Hebraistic; of the third, both Hellenistic; while in the second, the thought is often Occidental, though the language is Hebraistic and in the fourth the language Hellenistic, but the thought Hebraistic.

2. "In respect of *subject-matter and contents* we may say perhaps that *a*) in the first Gospel we have narrative; in the second, memoirs; in the third, history; in the fourth, dramatic portraiture;— that *b*) in the first we have often the record of events in their accomplishment; in the second, events in their details; in the third, events in their connection; in the fourth, events in relation to the teaching springing from them;—that thus *c*) in the first we more often meet with the notice of impressions; in the second, of facts; in the third, of motives; in the fourth, of words spoken;—and that, lastly, *d*) the record of the first is mainly collective and often antithetical; of the second, graphic and circumstantial; of the third, didactic and reflective; of the fourth, selective and supplemental.

3. "We may conclude by saying that in respect, of the *Portraiture of our Lord*, the first Gospel presents Him to us mainly as the Messiah; the second, mainly as the God-Man; the third, as the Redeemer; the fourth, as the Only-begotten Son of God."

With this may also be compared the presentation by Bernard in his *Progress of Doctrine in the New Testament* (Amer. ed., pp. 65–

## § 11. *Critical Presuppositions for the Employment of the Three Synoptic Gospels.*

The relation which the three Synoptical Gospels bear to one another has given rise to the widest differences of opinion. The writer adopts the view that all three Evangelists drew from a common source, which constitutes the foundation of our first three Gospels, and that this source was the oral teaching of the Apos-

70): "If the Synoptic Gospels are taken by themselves, we observe certain orderly steps of advance. Each of these narratives has its own *prevailing* character, whereby it makes its proper contribution to the complete portrait of the Lord; each also has its own *historical associations*, whereby it represents a separate stage in the presentation of Christ to the world. . . . The record of St. Matthew, ever recognized as the Hebrew Gospel, is the true *commencement* of the New Testament showing how it grows out of the Old. . . . It founds itself on the ideas of the old covenant. It is a history of *fulfillment*, presenting the Lord as the fulfiller of all righteousness. It corresponds to that period in the historical course of events when the Word was preached to none but to the Jews only.

"The Gospel of St. Mark is traditionally connected with St. Peter, who first opened the door of Faith to Gentiles. . . . It is the Gospel of *action*—rapid, vigorous, vivid. . . . It occupies an intermediate position between those of St. Matthew and St. Luke.

"The preface of St. Luke's Gospel, addressed to a Gentile convert, shows us at the outset that we have passed from Jewish associations to a stage in the history of the world when its purpose of expansion has been proved, and its character of universality established. The whole tone of this Gospel constitutes it pre-eminently a Gospel for the Gentiles, specially adapted to the Greek mind. Its internal character thus accords with its historical position as the Gospel of St. Paul, written by his close companion, and circulated, we cannot doubt, in the Churches which he founded.

"If in traversing the Synoptic Gospels we march in the line of a historical advance, it is still more plain that we do so when we pass to the teaching of St. John. One Apostle, the first and the last of the 'Glorious Company,' was chosen as the chief instrument for settling human thought, defeating the wiles of the Devil, and certifying the Witness of God. There was but one moment in which the con-

tles, which, on account of its sincerity and simplicity, immediately received a fixed form; and there are strong reasons for supposing that of the three Synoptists, Mark exhibits the oral tradition of the official life of our Lord in its earliest extant form.[1] The fact that the first (Matthew) and third Gospels (Luke) are two writings which are altogether independent of one another is of the greatest consequence in the further investigation of the sources of the Synoptists. Where Matthew and Luke agree as to language, without the intervention of Mark, we have the very words of the Apostolic source which was used by them.

Matthew in his Gospel, no doubt, faithfully reports the tradition which had become current in his own immediate apostolic circle (Matthew, James), using his early Hebrew Gospel mentioned by Papias, which consisted to a very great extent of longer discourses and sayings of the Lord, but which also contained narrative portions. Mark gives us more especially the Petrine Gospel, while Luke (though Pauline in his tendencies) expressly says in his introduction that he has followed the tradition of eye-witnesses, and appeals to previous works of an analogous nature (Luke 1:1-4). The sources of Luke, therefore, must either have been of

---

ditions for such a production could co-exist. . . . Such a moment was secured by the Providence which ordained that John should live till the first heresies had shaped themselves. The disciple who first came to Jesus, who followed Him most closely, who lay in his bosom, who stood by His Cross, who believed when others were confounded, who saw with more penetrating eye the glory which they all beheld, was reserved to complete the written statement of the Person of Christ, in a record which has been designated from ancient days as 'the Gospel according to the Spirit.'" (*Condensed.*)

[1] For a fuller presentation, see my *Commentary on Mark*, second edition, 1888.

direct apostolic origin, or they must have been drawn directly out of apostolic tradition.

[ANALYSIS: 1) The three Synoptists are based on the Oral Gospel; 2) their relation to one another; 3) their distinction from one another.]

## § 12. *The Discourses of Jesus in John's Gospel.*

The words of Jesus in the Fourth Gospel bear such peculiar character that a separate treatment is not only desirable but necessary.[1] Not only are the most connected and fullest of the discourses of Jesus presented in this Gospel, but we are in a position to show that it is quite possible to exhibit separately the Apostle John's system of doctrine and that of Jesus as here set forth.

Some, indeed, maintain that we do not hear Jesus as He truly spoke, but only as St. John represents Him as speaking; but if John was truly the bosom friend of

---

[1] *Van Oosterzee:* "Even without in general entering into a consideration of the differences between the Fourth Gospel and the three others, it is seen at once that here, even when we hear the Lord Himself speak, we are moving in an entirely different circle of thoughts.

"Not only is the theatre upon which we here meet Him, the form of His discourses, and the impression which is thereby made, different, but even the substance, compared with that of the Synoptical Gospels, offers important points of distinction. *There* the Kingdom of Heaven is presented, *here* it is the King himself; *there* the human, *here* the Divine side of the Person of the Redeemer; *there* the blessedness of salvation on the other side of the grave is brought into the foreground; *here* the blessedness on this side. . . . In the Lord's words, as presented by John, these words bear in the highest sense a Christo-centric character—in other words, His own Person and His own work is the great centre around which all moves. In a certain degree this is also to be observed in the discourses of the Synoptists, but what was there an element of the Gospel of the Kingdom has here manifestly become the main theme." (§ 17.)

Jesus, and had received into his own breast the deepest impression and image of that unique Personality, and more than others had penetrated into the Spirit of the Messiah, it is entirely inconceivable that he should have placed in his Master's lips words which were never spoken by Him.

We need not seek far to find a reason why St. John reported these particular sayings of Christ. St. John wrote this Gospel when the traditions respecting the history of Christ, oral and written, had already been in circulation for a long time, and hence would give only such a selection from the evangelical history as had not been given, and which appeared to him precisely the best fitted to represent Jesus as the Son of God, from whom alone men could receive eternal life. That he made exactly this selection from the sayings and works of Christ in order to lead men to this faith, and to aid, strengthen, and uphold them in maintaining it, is positively declared by the Apostle himself, when at the close of his Gospel he says: "Many other signs did Jesus in the presence of the disciples, which are not written in this book; but these are written, that ye may believe that Jesus is the Christ, the Son of God, and that believing ye may have life in his name" (John 20:30, 31).

[ANALYSIS: 1) The teaching of Jesus according to John can be presented separately; 2) distinctions as drawn by Van Oosterzee; 3) the Sayings of Christ in John are historical; 4) the reason why John selected these particular discourses of Christ; 5) the aim of his Gospel ]

# SECTION I.

## THE TEACHING OF JESUS ACCORDING TO THE THREE SYNOPTISTS.

### § 13. *General Divisions.*

The representation of the teaching of Jesus will have to begin with the message regarding the Kingdom of God as the historical central point of His preaching. Bernhard Weiss presents the discussion under the following heads:

1. The Kingdom of God is present in the Messiah;
    *a*) The Messianic Self-testimony.
    *b*) The Messianic Activity.
2. The Kingdom of God is realized in the company of the disciples;
    *a*) The Righteousness of the Kingdom of God.
    *b*) The Messianic Church.
3. The Messianic Consummation.[1]

Van Oosterzee, in his presentation of the theology of Christ according to the Synoptical Gospels, follows this order most closely.[2] His divisions are: 1) The Kingdom of God; 2) Its Founder; 3) The King of Kings; 4) The Subjects; 5) Salvation; 6) The Way of Salvation; 7) The Completion.

Following very closely the system of Weiss, it probably will be best to present the teaching of Jesus according to the three Synoptists, as follows:

---

[1] Compare *Weiss*, §§ 12-34.
[2] See his *Theology of the New Testament*, pp. 61-128.

1) The Message regarding the Kingdom of God (Ecclesiological);

2) The testimony of Jesus to Himself as the Messiah (Christological);

3) The Messianic Activity (Soteriological);

4) The Righteousness of the Kingdom of God (Theological);

5) The Anthropology of Jesus.

6) The Messianic Church (Pneumatological and Ecclesiological);

7) The Eschatology of Jesus.

[ANALYSIS: 1) The arrangement adopted by Weiss; 2) by Van Oosterzee; 3) in the present work.]

## CHAPTER I.

### THE MESSAGE REGARDING THE KINGDOM OF GOD.[1]

§ 14. *The Kingdom of God and the Messiah.*[2]

The central point of the preaching of Jesus was the glad tidings (*gospel, evangelion*) that the Kingdom of God was at hand, because the time was fulfilled in which its coming was expected.

This preaching of Jesus was a *proclamation*, an announcing (*kerússein*, Mark 1:14, 38, 39), which Jesus Himself, with a plain allusion to Isa. 61:1, characterizes as a message of joy to the poor[3] (Matt. 11:5; Luke 7:22).

---

[1] This chapter largely bears upon the doctrine of the Church, or Ecclesiology.

[2] Compare *Weiss*, § 13.

[3] Not simply the literally "poor" in the narrower sense, nor simply the spiritually "poor" in the religious sense; but rather the whole nation in its oppression and national wretchedness.

With special frequency Mark makes Jesus describe His proclamation as a message of joy (*gospel, evangelion*, Mark 1:15; 8:35; 10:29; 13:10; 14:9). Christ appears on the scene of His ministry with the message, "the kingdom of God is at hand" (Mark 1:15), and with this same message He sent forth His disciples on their probationary mission (Matt. 10:7; Luke 10:9). What this Kingdom of God is, is nowhere expressly said; but the idea is regarded as one quite familiar to the people. No one in Israel would understand anything else than a kingdom in which the will of God is fulfilled as perfectly upon earth as by the angels in heaven (Matt. 6:10). The message assumes that the coming of this Kingdom was expected after the lapse of a divinely appointed time, and announces that "the time is fulfilled" (Mark 1:15), and that therefore the advent of the Kingdom of God is immediately at hand.

The prophets, who spoke in the Holy Spirit (Mark 12:36), had promised the realization of this ideal Kingdom of God in the Messianic time, and therefore the message regarding the fulfillment of the time stated that this promised Messianic time was come.

Prophecy assumes throughout that the completion of the theocracy, which is to begin at the Messianic time, will take place under the forms of the commonwealth of Israel, whether, as in the earlier prophets, it is conceived of as a restoration of the old splendor, and a supreme glorification of the Davidic kingdom, or as in Dan. 7:13, 14, as the founding of an everlasting kingdom, which makes an end of all the kingdoms of the world. In this sense the people greet in the Messiah the coming kingdom of His father David (Mark 11:10) —in this sense they expect the appearing of the Kingdom of God (Mark 15:43; Luke 17:20; 19:11), or the restoration of the kingdom of Israel (Acts 1:6). For there can be no question that, at the time of Christ, the expectation of a personal Messiah in the form of the Promised Son of David was diffused among the people.

It was only in the sense of this expectation that the people could understand the message of Jesus regarding the Kingdom of God. That which is new in it is, therefore, simply the proclamation of the joyful fact that the time is come in which the promised and expected completion of the theocracy is to begin.

In His activity Jesus exhibited the signs of the promised time of salvation which the Last and Greatest of the Messengers of God must introduce. When John the Baptist inquires whether He is the expected One, Jesus refers him to the fact that the signs of the Messianic time, foretold in Isa. 35:5, 6, appear in His miracles of healing (Matt. 11:3–5 ; Luke 7:19–22). He also declared the Baptist to be the messenger of God foretold in Mal. 3:1, who was to prepare the way of the Messiah (Matt. 11:10 ; Luke 7:27). He also called him His Elijah (Mark 9:12, 13 compared with Mal. 4:5). With the appearing of Jesus there has commenced a time of joy for His disciples, which (Mark 2:19, 20) He compares with the joy of the companions of the bridegroom who have assembled to the marriage feast. Nevertheless, He forbade the demons who recognized Him as the Messiah (Mark 1:25, 34; 3:11, 12), and even His disciples (Mark 8:30), to proclaim His Messiahship publicly. The proneness of the people to make Him the hero of the Messianic revolution in the sense of their expectation, which conceived political emancipation as a preliminary condition of the theocratic consummation, compelled Him to refrain from directly proclaiming His Messiahship.

The more, however, the approaching catastrophe of His life relieved Jesus from all reserve, so much the more openly did He profess to be the Messiah promised by the prophets and expected by the people. At Jericho he no longer refuses the popular invocation as the Son of David (Mark 10:47), and when he enters Jerusalem He allows Himself to be hailed as the Messianic King (Mark 11:8-10). Before the priests he declares Himself to be the corner-stone of the theocracy spoken of in Ps. 118:22 (Mark 12:10, 11); before His disciples He declares Himself to be the Shepherd promised in Zech. 13:7 (Mark 14:27); and before the tribunal He solemnly avows His Messianic dignity (Mark 14:62 ; 15:2). He has also pointed to the fact that everything which stands written of the Messiah must be accomplished in His own fate (Mark 12:10, 11 ; 14:21, 27, 49), and that the disciples have found in Him what the prophets and pious men of the Old Testament longed to see (Matt. 13:17; Luke 10:24).[1]

[ANALYSIS: 1) The Kingdom of God is at hand; 2) this a message of joy; 3) a kingdom in which the will of God is done; 4) the Messianic Kingdom spoken of by the prophets; 5) introduced by the Personal Advent of Jesus Christ; 6) who exhibits the signs of the Messianic times; 7) but before the time was ripe forbids His disciples to proclaim His Messiahship, yet in due time allows Himself to be hailed as the Messianic King; 8) who fulfills all the prophecies pertaining to the Messiah.]

---

[1] *Van Oosterzee:* "The Gospel which the Lord proclaims is the Gospel of the Kingdom; and the kingdom itself is a religious-moral institution, which, boundless in extent and everlasting in duration, in its design to unite, sanctify and save humanity, embraces heaven and earth. The Kingdom is *a)* something new (Matt. 4:17; Luke 10:23, 24); *b)* something essentially present (Luke 17:20, 21); *c)* something spiritual (Matt. 20:25-28; 18:3; Luke 12:13, 14); *d)* something unlimited, being universal (Matt. 5:13, 14; 8:11, 12); *e)* without end, bounded neither by time nor space (Matt. 24:14; 26:13;

## § 15. *The Kingdom of God and the Disciples.*[1]

The aim of the mission of the Messiah, the realization of the dominion of God in Israel, begins to be fulfilled when a company of disciples gathers around Jesus, in whose midst is the Kingdom of God. The Kingdom of God not only comes in the Person of the Messiah, but this same Kingdom must also exist somehow or other outside His person. The possession of the Kingdom of Heaven is immediately bestowed upon those who are qualified for it (Matt. 5:3, 10 ; Mark 10:14), and can be received in this present life, if sought for in the right manner (Mark 10:15). There are some who already go into the Kingdom of God (Matt. 21:31), while others are already therein (Matt. 11:11 ; Luke 7:28).

In the Parable of the Sower Jesus represents His activity in the founding of the Kingdom (Matt. 13:3–9) as of a spiritual nature—the preaching of the Word (Mark 4:14). The mystery of the Kingdom of God, which the parable unveils, lies in this, that the founding of the Kingdom does not take place in the manner in which the popular expectation assumed (a political restoration of the theocracy accomplished by employing physical force). The Kingdom is realized only where the spiritual activity of the Messiah succeeds.

Although the Kingdom of God is certainly existing in His disciples, nevertheless it is as certainly not yet perfectly realized even in them ; for Jesus teaches His disciples still to strive after the Kingdom of God (Matt. 6:33), to pray for its coming, and to surrender every

28:20) ; *f*) something growing (Matt. 13:31–33; Mark 4:26–29); *g*) something incomparably glorious and blessed (Matt. 13:44–46; 6:33)." (*Condensed.*)

[1] Compare *Weiss*, § 14.

other possession for this *highest good* (Matt. 13:44, the Parable of the Hidden Treasure; Matt. 13:45, 46, the Parable of the Pearl of Great Price). In general, the Kingdom of God, which is established so far as regards its vital germs, must grow with an inherent productiveness until the day comes which brings its completion. Its realization cannot be limited to the small circle of the present disciples of Jesus, for these have been chosen for the express purpose of bestowing upon others what they themselves possess (Mark 3:14; Matt. 10:26, 27). The Kingdom of God must spread over the whole nation (the Parable of the Mustard Seed, Matt. 13:31, 32); it must permeate the whole national life (the Parable of the Leaven, Matt. 13:33). Although there is no indication in these parables that the Kingdom will extend beyond the limits of Israel, neither, on the other hand, is the development of the Kingdom so described as to limit it to the national fellowship of Israel.

In the Parable of the Tares (Matt. 13:24–30) and of the Draw-net (Matt. 13:47–50), Jesus teaches that the sin which exists in the world mixes as a disturbing influence, not only during the development of the Kingdom of God in the world, but even at its foundation. It is not only impossible, but also inadmissible, to cast out all impure elements; not till the close of this development can the separation of the genuine members of the Kingdom of God be undertaken: then, however, it will be effected.

[ANALYSIS: 1) Beginning of the Kingdom; 2) must also exist outside of the Person of Christ; 3) entrance into it takes place in this life; 4) is a spiritual kingdom, not political; 5) not yet perfectly realized; 6) must grow until its day of completion; 7) is not limited to any one period of time; 8) must become universal; 9) in its development in this world contains impure elements].

## § 16. *The Kingdom of God in its Consummation.*[1]

Although the Kingdom of God is already existent in the Person of the Messiah, and is in the act of coming in the circle of His disciples, the advent of the Messianic judgment at its close points to a future in which its consummation first appears.

With the manifestation of the Messiah, prophecy had always connected the idea of a future glorious form of the kingdom of Israel, in which all the promised salvation should be realized. The fact that it is the nature of the Kingdom of God to develop gradually from the time of its being founded to its completion, gives us a solution of the contradiction between the prophetic description and the present condition of the Kingdom of God. All the prophets have made the fulfillment of their promises dependent upon the behavior of the people, and so the realization of the Kingdom depends upon the attitude of the people to the proclamation of Jesus regarding the Kingdom.

As soon as only the nature of the Kingdom of God is rightly conceived (as a Kingdom in which the will of God is fulfilled as perfectly upon earth as by the angels in Heaven, Matt. 6:10), it is self-evident that it exists at every stage of its realization, and that, therefore, the promised future time of salvation has really commenced with the appearing of the Messiah. The pledge of the consummation of the Kingdom of God is given with the manifestation of the promised Messiah.

[ANALYSIS: 1) The Kingdom has a consummation; 2) develops gradually; 3) consummation depends upon the attitude of men towards the Kingdom; 4) exists at every stage of its development; 6) had its beginning at the appearance of the Messiah.]

---

[1] Compare *Weiss*, § 15.

## CHAPTER II.

### THE TESTIMONY OF JESUS TO HIMSELF AS THE MESSIAH.[1]

§ 17. *The Son of Man.*[2]

Most frequently Jesus calls Himself the Son of Man (some eighty times; without reckoning parallels, about fifty times)—an expression used only by Christ Himself, excepting in Luke 24:7; John 12:34, and Acts 7:56. This name contained a revelation fitted to instruct His contemporaries, if not as to His absolute Divinity, at least as to His perfect humanity. From Matt. 16:13, we infer that this name was not one of the current designations of the Messiah. Not until Jesus Himself, by His use of this name, led them to remember Dan. 7:13, could it be regarded as such.[3]

By the title, "the Son of Man," Jesus designates, at once, His close relation to humanity and His distinctness from it, even as man. He was, in a special sense, one and alone among His brethren, a definite Son of Man, whose uniqueness required no explanation for His hearers.

All the sayings of Jesus concerning Himself as the

---

[1] This chapter bears upon the doctrine of the Person of Christ, or Christology.

[2] Compare *Weiss*, § 16.

[3] Three different passages from the Old Testament have been specified as affording a probable basis for the origin of the term, "Son of Man,"—1) Gen. 3:15; so Godet and Gess; 2) Ps. 8:4-6; so Schmid; 3) Dan. 7:13, 14; so most commentators.

## THE SON OF MAN. 49

Son of Man point to His unique calling, whose duties, powers, and Divinely appointed destiny characterize it clearly enough as the Messianic. He is that Man who distinguishes Himself from others, on the one side, through His Heavenly origin, His peculiar affinity with God, His sovereign position in the universe, and, on the other side, through the inwardness of the bond which unites Him with humanity.

The Son of Man appears as a man among men, and is described as having neither property nor home (Matt. 8:20; Luke 9:58); He eats and drinks (Matt. 11:19; Luke 7:34); He can forgive sins (Matt. 9:6; Mark 2:10; Luke 5:24); He is Lord of the Sabbath (Matt. 12:8; Mark 2:28; Luke 6:5); He is come to save (Matt. 18:11; Luke 19:10), and to minister (Matt. 20:28; Mark 10:45). Sin against Him shall be forgiven (Matt. 12:32; Luke 12:10); the sign of Jonah is fulfilled in Him (Matt. 12:40; Luke 11:30); He must suffer, be rejected, betrayed by the kiss of a Judas (Luke 22:48), and delivered up into the hands of sinners, ill-treated and crucified (Mark 8:31; 9:12, 31; 10:33, etc.); but He will rise again (Mark 9:9, 31, etc.); and a great future with the Father, and a return in glory for the establishment of His kingdom and for judgment, is in store for Him (Matt. 16:27; Mark 8:38; Matt. 25:31; 26:64; Luke 22:69).

There can be no doubt that in our Lord's own utterances respecting His person He makes definite allusion to the Son of Man in Dan. 7:13 (Matt. 24:30; Mark 13:26; Luke 21:27; Matt. 26:64; Mark 14:62, etc.). In these passages Jesus says that the Son of Man shall come in or upon the clouds of heaven; wherein we have this twofold assertion about the coming King—1) that He is like a son of man, and 2) that He comes in the clouds of heaven. Our Lord here evidently intends His hearers to recall to mind Dan. 7:13, and also to regard himself as there indicated.[1]

Two points are always implied in the expression Son of Man—1) that, although veritably the Son of Man, He was at the same time something much higher still; and 2) that, exalted as He was, in the strict sense of the word He was still a man—a man in all human lowliness, and yet in the highest perfection. Cremer[2] maintains that "the Son of Man" was a Messianic name given to Jesus by Himself, chosen and adopted by Him on account of the relation in which He stands as the promised "seed of the woman" to His brethren.

An antithesis is hinted at in the expression, Son of Man; and this is easily accounted for if we remember that He frequently calls Himself the Son of God.

[ANALYSIS: 1) Title "Son of Man" not a current designation of the Messiah; 2) meaning of title; 3) points to his unique office as the Messiah; 4) utterances of Christ concerning himself as the Son of Man; 5) definite allusion to Dan. 7:13; 6) deeper meaning of title; 7) antithesis implied.]

§ 18. *The Son of God.*

In the Old Testament the expression "Son of God" is used in a theocratic sense. Already the inspired writers were familiar with the idea of a Heavenly Family of God, in which the angels appear as the sons of God (Job 38:7; Ps. 29:1; 89:6). Upon the earth, however, Israel is the Son of Jehovah (Ex. 4:22; Hos. 11:1), in virtue of His election (Deut. 14:1, 2); and hence individual members of this nation are children of the covenant of God. Jesus did not limit Himself to the theocratic idea, but rather ascribed to Himself,

---

[1] Compare the discussion on this subject in Schmid's *Bibl. Theol. of the N.T.*, pp. 107-115. The treatment of Weiss is very unsatisfactory.
[2] In his *Lexicon of N. T. Greek*.

as the Son of God, such attributes and such a relation to the Father, that the title, although based historically on the theocratic idea, acquired a much higher significance. He calls Himself not merely Son of Man, but Son of God, and is the son of David only in the sense of being at the same time the Son of God.

Jesus calls upon the Lord of Heaven and earth (Matt. 11:25–27; Luke 10:21), the Almighty (Mark 14:36), as His Father (compare Luke 23:34, 46); He speaks very frequently of God as His Father (Matt. 7:21; 10:32, 33; 15:13; 16:17; 18:19, 35; 25:34; Mark 8:38). He speaks of *being sent by God* (Matt. 10:40; Luke 9:48; Mark 9:37). In Matt. 11:27; Luke 10:22, Jesus calls Himself the Son, and ascribes to Himself exclusively as the Son adequate knowledge of the Father, affirming that to Him everything was delivered by the Father, thus expressing His unique personal relationship to God—a relationship not simply of inward intimacy, but also of essence.[1] De-

---

[1] The expression "Son of God" has been variously interpreted by different schools, as pointing to a Sonship either—1) physical, with reference to His supernatural birth (Beyschlag); or 2) ethical, as marking the exceptional perfection of His moral nature (Strauss, Hase, Baur, Ewald, and others); or 3) official, signalizing the God-Man as the Messiah (Weiss), the relationship originating at the Incarnation (Moses Stuart, Adam Clarke), at the exaltation of the God-Man (Pfleiderer). But it is better to interpret these passages as bearing on the *metaphysical* relation to the Trinity rather than physical, ethical, or official, and as descriptive of the *essential* relationship subsisting between the divine and pre-existent nature of the Son of God and the Deity (so Gess, Godet, Luthardt, and others). That this is so can be seen from the passage known as the Great Sonship Confession (Keim): " No one knoweth the Son, save the Father; neither doth any know the Father, save the Son, and he to whomsoever the Son willeth to reveal Him " (Matt. 11:25–27; Luke 10:21, 22). That these words alluded to a Sonship, which was not merely temporal, official, and external, but eternal, personal, and essential, everything about them declares. The similarity of the language

cisive for Christ's absolute equality with God is His claim which He frequently makes to perform, in His own name as well as by His own authority and power, works which

shows that the passage ought to have the same interpretation as John 10:15; the "all things" of Matt. 11:27 points to equality with the Father in respect of power, and this power which the Son of God possessed from eternity has also been given to Him according to His human nature; the mutual knowledge which the Father and Son possess of each other is such as could only spring from community of nature and essence; in both the knowledge is complete, absolute, perfect, in extent no less than in depth (the Greek verb is *epiginósko*). He who speaks like Christ knows and feels himself not merely a God in the moral sense of the word, but also a Son of God in the supernatural sense of the word—as one who is of heavenly origin, and has appeared on earth to fulfill the Divine Counsel.

Although in the Fourth Gospel the self-witness of Jesus, as to His *pre-existence* as the Son of God, possesses a richness and fullness which are wanting in the three Synoptists, yet even in the latter we have clear statements to prove to us that Christ believed Himself to have existed antecedently to His coming to the earth. The statement in Luke 4:43 ("for therefore was I sent") must be interpreted in the same way as John 16:28, of a coming forth from the Father and coming into the world. Along with this may be conjoined the various utterances in which He speaks of having come (Matt. 5:17; 10:34, 35; Mark 2:17; Luke 12:49, 51); of the Son of Man as having come (Matt. 20:28; Mark 10:45; Luke 19:10); and of His having been sent by God (Matt. 10:40; 15:24; Mark 9:37; Luke 9:48). The question, "If David then calleth Him Lord, how is He his Son?" (Matt. 22:45; Mark 12:37; Luke 20:44), could only point to His supernatural origin and His pre-existence, since, if David in the Spirit called Him Lord, he must at least in David's time have already been in existence. The true meaning of this passage is, that Christ according to His human nature is the Son of David, and, according to His Divine nature, the Son of God.

Christ also avowed Himself the Son of God before the high priest (Matt. 26:63, 64; Mark 14:61; Luke 22:70). After Whitelaw's *How is the Divinity of Jesus Depicted in the Gospels and Epistles*, pp. 12-15, 41-46, compare also Beyschlag's *Die Christologie des Neuen Testaments*, pp. 61, 62; Gess' *Christi Person und Werk*, pp. 128, 177, 217, etc.

God alone can perform, as—1) to control the powers of nature (Matt. 8:26, 27) and of the spirit world (Matt. 12:28; etc.); 2) to raise the dead (Matt. 9:24, 25; etc.); 3) to forgive sin (Matt. 9:6; Luke 5:24; 7:48); 4) to impart to men salvation and eternal life (Matt. 11:28; Mark 10:30), etc. Furthermore, the position Christ assigns Himself in the baptismal formula (Matt. 28:19), placing His own name of "Son" exactly between that of the Father and the Spirit, shows that He regarded Himself as One in essence with the Father; for He certainly could not have done this if he had been a mere man. So, likewise, in Mark 13:32, Christ calls Himself *the Son* in contrast with angels and men, indicating that the Son could claim an acquaintance with the highest Divine decrees as no other person could claim.

The expression "the Son of God" is, therefore, that title of the Messiah which denotes His relation to God. Jesus adopts this designation of His Messianic dignity in Matt. 26:64, over against the other title, *the Son of Man;* and the adoption of this by Him was regarded as blasphemy. Two thoughts are implied in the title *the Son of God*—1) that the *Man* Christ Jesus is the Messiah, elect and chosen of God, and 2) that a relationship of the Son to God, previous to His incarnation, lies at the foundation of His Messiahship.[1]

[ANALYSIS : 1) The Old Testament usage of the expression, "Son of God;" 2) Jesus ascribes this title to Himself ; 3) various interpretations of its meaning ; 4) the true meaning; 5) the passage in Matt. 11:25-27; 6) the pre-existence of the Son of God; 7) the passage in Matt. 22:45; 8) Christ claims to perform works

---

[1] The treatment of Weiss is very unsatisfactory. Compare Schmid's *Biblical Theology of New Testament*, pp. 115-140, and Cremer's *Lexicon of New Testament Greek*.

which God alone can do; 9) the testimony of the baptismal formula); of Mark 13:32; 11) the true significance of the title "Son of God."]

### § 19. *The Purpose of the Incarnation.*[1]

According to the three Synoptists, our Saviour represents the purpose of His incarnation as principally twofold:

1) To save men from the condemnation of sin, for the Son of Man came to seek and to save that which was lost (Luke 19:10); to call sinners to repentance (Luke 5:32); for Jesus was the True Physician (Matt. 9:12, 13), the True Shepherd seeking that which is lost (Luke 15:4–6).

2) To make atonement by dying as a sacrifice for sin, thus satisfying the justice of God. Seven times *at least* does Christ allude to His death in the utterances regarding Himself as recorded by the three Evangelists:[2] *a*) In His conversation with John's disciples about the taking away of the Bridegroom (Matt. 9:15; Mark 2:20; Luke 5:35), and in His remarks to the Scribes and Pharisees about the sign of the prophet Jonas (Matt. 12:39, 40; Luke 11:30); repeated also later in the region of Magadan (Matt. 16:4); *b*) in the last year of His ministry, when, in the neighborhood of Cæsarea Philippi, Christ had explicitly announced to His disciples that He must be killed and on the third day be raised up (Matt. 16:21; Mark 8:31; Luke 9:22); *c*) still later, in the autumn of the same year, while in Galilee He repeats the announcement (Matt. 17:22, 23; Mark 9:30–32; Luke 9:43–45); *d*) later still, about a month before His death, on the way to Jerusalem, He repeats the announcement with

---

[1] See my "Studies in the Book," *First Series*, p. 97.

[2] Compare Whitelaw's *How is the Divinity of Jesus Depicted*, etc., pp. 143, 144.

still greater fullness of detail (Matt. 20:17-19; Mark 10:32-34; Luke 18:31-34);[1] *e*) in His next reference (near Jericho) Christ first speaks of His death as a vicarious death, as a propitiation, as a ransom which He was to give instead of the many who could not provide a ransom for themselves ("for the Son of Man came . . . to give His life a ransom for many," Matt. 20:28; Mark 10:45); *f*) during Passion-week we also have various references (Matt. 26:2, 12, 24, 39-42, and parallel passages); *g*) especially clear is our Saviour's statement with reference to the expiatory character of His death, as given in the institution of the Lord's Supper. His blood "was shed for many," to effect their deliverance from the guilt of sin ("unto remission of sins") (Matt. 26:26-28; Mark 14:22-24; Luke 22:19, 20).

[ANALYSIS: 1) Christ came to save men from the condemnation of sin; 2) to make atonement for sin; 3) His death a vicarious death.]

### § 20. *The Anointed One*.[2]

The very name Messiah points to the *anointing* which consecrated the King of Israel to his calling (1 Sam. 10:1; 24:6), and which must not be lacking in the case of the Ideal King of the completed theocracy (Ps. 2:2; 45:7). It continued to be the real technical designation of Him who was looked for, in consequence of prophecy, to bring about that completion—THE CHRIST (Mark 8:29; 14:61).

Jesus characterized His activity as that of the Anointed One which is described in Isa. 61:1 (Luke 4:18, 21; Matt. 11:5). Some have contended that it

---

[1] See *Harmony of Gospels*, in my *Commentary on Mark*, second edition, 1888.

[2] Compare *Weiss*, § 18.

was not until a late period that Jesus fully comprehended Himself as the Messiah (Matt. 16:21). Although Jesus in the beginning of His ministry always speaks with the greatest reserve as to the Messianic idea, nowhere, however, from the very first does He decline to acknowledge His Messiahship, but rather admits it on every occasion (Matt. 8:10–13, 29–32; 9:18–26, 27–29; 12:23–30). From the very first He gives Himself out as the Messiah, most decidedly in the Sermon on the Mount (note especially the emphasis laid on His own Person in Matt. 5:11; 7:21–24), and in the discourse about John (Matt. 11:12–15). Moreover, His further ministry, His prescriptions to His disciples, His teaching, and His miracles, are not all these the very things which He Himself characterized as Messianic? (Matt. 11:5.) Jesus Himself regards His healing of the sick (Matt. 11:5; Luke 13:32) and His expulsion of the devils (Matt. 12:28) as essential parts of His Messianic activity; He describes them as mighty works, whose impression He reckons so great that they could have led Tyre and Sidon, as well as Sodom and Gomorrah, to repentance (Matt. 11:21, 23).

At His baptism Jesus was anointed to be the Messiah (Matt. 3:16; Mark 1:10), and the Spirit which was bestowed upon Him qualified Him for His Messianic activity. The name Messiah points not only to a peculiar equipment, but also to a peculiar dignity. He is exalted above the kings and prophets of the Old Testament (Matt. 12:41, 42). David has called the Messiah his Lord (Mark 12:36, 37); the Messiah is greater than the Temple, which forms the holiest central point of the Old Testament theocracy (Matt. 12:6). In Him Jehovah Himself comes to His people (Luke 1:17, 76); whoever, therefore, receives Him receives God Himself

(Matt. 10:40). Blessed is he who is not offended in Christ (Matt. 11:6), who is persecuted (Matt. 5:11) and loses his life (Matt. 10:39) for Jesus's sake. Only he who confesses Him will stand before the judgment-seat of God (Matt. 10:32, 33). In all this it is implied that THE CHRIST is more than a man; that He is the *Messiah*, in whom is present the Kingdom of God, and who alone can secure unto men participation in the blessedness of the Kingdom.

[ANALYSIS: 1) The Messiah of the Old Testament; 2) Jesus is conscious of His Messiahship from the very first; 3) ascribes to Himself the works of the Messiah; 4) assumes the official office at His baptism; 5) meaning of the term.]

### § 21. *The Son of David and the Exalted Messiah.*[1]

The *personal* name of our Redeemer was JESUS—the name by which He was known as a man among men; His *official* designation was THE CHRIST, the Messiah of the Old Testament, the hope of Israel; His special title was the *Son of God*. By His birth Jesus became David's Son, but before His birth He was already the Son of God. His relation to God could be known only by Divine revelation, but His relation to David was known from His parentage. In all their cavils the Jews never questioned the Davidic descent of Jesus, for ample proof was given by the genealogies recorded at Jerusalem and at Bethlehem. Considering the great stress which the Jews laid upon the Davidic descent of the Messiah, the objection would surely have been raised if it had been otherwise, and if the proof had been inadequate.

He was recognized by the people as the Son of David (Matt. 9:27; Mark 10:47), and He was expected to mount

---

[1] Compare *Weiss*, § 19.

the throne of His father David (Mark 11:10; Luke 1:32, 33). Jesus has never controverted this expectation, which was directly suggested by prophecy; but very early in His ministry He indicates that it was through death and resurrection that He would be exalted to His position of royal dominion (Mark 2:20; 8:31, 32). The ultimate exaltation of God's Anointed to royal glory could not be hindered by His cruel persecution and death. The violent slaying of the Messiah could only furnish the occasion for God to glorify Him by His wonderful deliverance from Hades, and thus to give the nation the last and greatest token that He was the Elect One (Matt. 12:39, 40). Christ always connected with the prophecy of His violent death the allusion to His resurrection after three days (Mark 8:31; 9:31; 10:34). Jesus is not, like other men, raised up at the Last Day, but after a very brief interval, which is proverbially (Hos. 6:2; Mark 15:29; Luke 13:32) described by the *after three days*. His resurrection forms the transition to His heavenly exaltation, in which is now fulfilled that which was prophesied in Ps. 110:1, of Jehovah's Anointed. Henceforth the Son of Man sits at God's right hand—*i. e.*, He shares in the Divine honor and sovereignty of the world. Now He has entered into the full sovereign dignity which was appointed the Messiah; but it is not the throne of His father David which He has ascended—it is the world-throne of His Father in Heaven.

As the partaker of the Divine honor and sovereignty of the world, Jesus is now removed from the sphere of human and earthly existence. As a Divine being Jesus can promise His Divine omnipresence to His disciples (Matt. 18:20). It is in the future that the prophecy of Daniel has its perfect fulfillment (Dan. 7:13)—that prophecy in consequence of which the Son of Man, who has been intrusted with sovereignty over the completed Kingdom of God, comes as Jehovah Himself, with the clouds of heaven (Mark 14:62). And He returns to the earth in order to discharge the Divine function of judging the world (Matt. 25:31), with great might and glory (Matt. 24:30), which is described in Mark 8:38 as the glory of His Father. He comes accompanied by the angels, the specific servants of Jehovah, who are now His servants (Mark 8:38; Matt. 25:31); He Himself now sends them forth to execute His commands, on which account Matthew calls them His angels (Matt. 24:31). Only a Divine being can be exalted over the angels.

[ANALYSIS: 1) JESUS, the personal name of our Redeemer; 2) CHRIST, His official name; 3) from eternity, the Son of God; 4) by human birth, the Son of David; 5) His Davidic descent never questioned; 6) recognized by the Jews; 7) Jesus teaches that through death and the resurrection He shall become the exalted Messiah; 8) His resurrection forms the transition; 9) His sovereignty as the Exalted Messiah.]

## CHAPTER III.

### THE MESSIANIC ACTIVITY.[1]

§ 22. *The New Revelation of God.*[2]

As the Messiah, Jesus announces the dawn of the day of salvation, in which He is the Mediator of a new revelation of God. This message presupposes a deed performed by God, in which Jehovah Himself comes to His people in the person of the Promised Messiah, in order to bring about the completion of the theocracy, and, consequently, the fulfillment of all the promises. The Messiah alone can be the Mediator of this last and highest revelation of God, because He by whom the Divine decrees of salvation are accomplished must also have the most perfect insight into them, and is therefore able to reveal them as such to the people. Jesus represents His activity as the Messiah under this point of view: "All things have been delivered unto me of my Father: and no one knoweth the Son, save the Father; neither doth any know the Father, save the Son, and he to whomsoever the Son willeth to reveal him" (Matt. 11:27).

This new revelation of God is a revelation of His Fatherly love, which is graciously manifested to the members of the Kingdom in caring for and protecting their earthly life, as well as in hearing their prayers (Matt. 7:9–11). This Fatherly Love naturally finds its realiza-

---

[1] This chapter bears largely on the doctrine of the work of Christ, or Soteriology.

[2] Compare *Weiss*, § 20.

tion only in the Kingdom of God which is founded by Jesus (Matt. 6:1, 9). It is only as members of the Kingdom that they can be certain that God knows and satisfies their needs, and thereby frees them from the anxiety of the Gentiles (Matt. 6:31-33), and that He takes under His protection even that which is most insignificant in their life (Matt. 10:29, 30). He desires their prayers, but He promises also to the prayer of faith an assured answer (Matt. 7:7-11 ; Luke 11:9-13 ; Mark 11:23-24 ; Luke 17:6), provided it be very persevering, and does not become faint (Luke 11:5-8 ; 18:1-7).

In the Kingdom of God as founded by Jesus there is realized the filial relationship which, in the theocracy of Israel, could be realized only imperfectly. Each individual who now by grace belongs to the Kingdom of God, can call upon God as his Father. The Messianic activity of Jesus consists not only in His teaching, but also in His doing; in the latter, also, the new revelation of God must be given. Wherever Jesus came the sick were healed, the hungry fed, the threatening waves of the sea had to be still. Hence He could point to His miracles of healing as signs that the time of the expected salvation was come (Matt. 11:5) ; hence He bade His disciples accompany the preaching of the nearness of the Kingdom of God with the same signs (Matt. 10:8).

[ANALYSIS: 1) Jesus as the Messiah is the Mediator of the last and highest revelation of God ; 2) which is a revelation of the Fatherly love of God to members of the new Kingdom ; 3) in which the members are regarded as Sons; 4) this new revelation is displayed by deeds as well as by teaching.]

§ 23. *Repentance.*[1]

As the Messiah, Jesus has not only to announce the coming of the Kingdom of God, but He has also to found

[1] Compare *Weiss*, § 21.

it, and for this the preaching of repentance is required. It is His task to realize among the people the Kingdom of God, in which God's will is done perfectly upon earth (Matt. 6:10). Jesus assumes it as self-evident that men are evil (Matt. 7:11), and that they differ only in the degree of wickedness (Luke 13:2–5). The call to repentance, therefore, with which Jesus makes His appearance (Mark 1:15), and with which He sends forth His disciples (Mark 6:12), is addressed to all without distinction. An unwillingness to accept His teaching is characterized as a want of readiness to repent (Matt. 11:20; 12:41; 21:32; Luke 13:3–5). When Jesus says: "I came not to call the righteous, but sinners" (Mark 2:17), He says it in such general terms that it is plain that He feels Himself to be the Physician of sinners with respect to the whole of mankind; and it is from this very fact that He derives the right to call to Himself even the most depraved, who need Him most. Without repentance, however, sinners cannot participate in the Kingdom of God.

But the Message of Jesus is not merely a resumption of the prophetic teaching of repentance; He does not merely demand, but also promises, the indispensable Divine renewal. For when, in the Sermon on the Mount, Jesus calls blessed the spiritually poor—those who are mourning because of their poverty, and those who are hungering after righteousness (Matt. 5:3, 4, 6) —it is implied that He comes, not in the first place, to demand, but to bring something; and it is expressly promised them that they shall be filled with righteousness. Thus righteousness appears, not as something demanded, but as a gift; and it is as a gift that they have already been led to expect it by Messianic prophecy (Isa. 61:10; 45:24; Jer. 33:16). Rest for souls laboring under the burden of the law is found only when the way is pointed out which leads to righteousness (Matt. 11:28–30).

This new revelation of God spontaneously works the repentance which Jesus demands. God does not demand that man should meet Him; He Himself meets man with graciousness, and thereby makes man capable of the repentance in which He has His greatest joy (Luke 15:4–10). God works this conversion by the revelation of His grace. He comes in the Person of the Messiah, and brings the time of the completion of salvation. Whosoever now accepts the joyous message concerning the Kingdom of God is a member of the Kingdom; he knows himself to be a child of the Heavenly Father; and with this knowledge there is implanted in him a totally new principle for his religious moral life. The member of the Kingdom has not yet to *become* a child of God; he *is* a child of God, and *therefore* he cannot but always *will* to become so more and more in perfect moral likeness to Him.

But, even here, the Messianic activity of Jesus consists not only in His teaching, but also in His doing. What the children of God are yet more and more to become, that the Son of God already is in a perfect manner. Accordingly, those are His nearest relatives who do the will of God as He Himself does it (Matt. 12:50). He is come to fulfill the law (Matt. 5:17); He yields Himself unreservedly to the will of God (Mark 14:36); in Him and in His life the will of God is always perfectly realized. The whole of His moral bearing is exemplary in an absolute sense (Matt. 11:29; Mark 10:45). In Him the child of God beholds the ideal of moral likeness to God realized every moment. It does not present itself to the believer as a legal demand, but it brings him the blessed assurance, that what he *wills* to become, that he also *can* become in fellowship with Jesus. Thus, to follow Him, to learn of Him, is an easy yoke and a light burden; and this is the way which leads to the rest of souls (Matt. 11:28–30), to full satisfaction with righteousness (Matt. 5:6).

[ANALYSIS: 1) Jesus assumes that all men are evil; 2) therefore, all are called to repent; 3) without repentance no entrance into the Kingdom; 4) the Gospel works the repentance which Jesus demands; 5) whoever accepts the message is a member of the Kingdom; 6) a new principle of life is implanted; 7) Christ is the ideal life.]

### § 24. *The Messianic Salvation.*[1]

Jesus as the Messiah also brings salvation to the members of the Kingdom by means of the forgiveness of sins. He is come as the Son of Man to seek and to save the lost sheep of the house of Israel (Luke 19:10; Matt. 10:6; 15:24). If this is effected by sinners being led to repentance, it is also necessary that the guilt of the past be removed from them by the forgiveness of sins. Such a forgiveness they were led in many ways to anticipate in the Messianic time (Isa. 43:25; 44:22; Jer. 33:8; Zech. 3:9; Dan. 9:24). Accordingly, Jesus promises the comfort of forgiveness to those who were mourning because of sin (Matt. 5:4). As the Son of Man He claims power to proclaim upon earth the forgiveness of sins, which God bestows in Heaven (Matt. 9:2, 6), and bequeaths this power to His Church (Matt. 18:18), in order thereby to insure to it one of the most essential blessings of the Kingdom of God (Luke 24:47).

The Parable of the Prodigal Son (Luke 15:11–32) shows how it is in keeping with the Fatherly Love of

---

[1] Compare *Weiss,* § 22.

God joyfully to receive every repenting son (such an one is every member of the Kingdom), and pardon him of all his sins. The Parable of the Unmerciful Servant (Matt. 18:23–27) takes, for granted, that to every member of the Kingdom of God there has been remitted an infinite debt, and the Lord's Prayer teaches them to pray for forgiveness in the same way as for daily bread (Matt. 6:12). The present day of salvation, however, is the time when reconciliation with the creditor is still possible by means of the forgiveness which is proffered by the Messiah. It is necessary to use this time, before the judgment draws on, from which there is no escape (Luke 12:58, 59). Every sin can still be forgiven—even the most heinous, the blasphemy against the Son of Man. Only he who persistently denies the power of God, and so blasphemes against the Holy Ghost, has committed a sin which cannot be forgiven, because it is the sign of enduring hardness of heart (Matt. 12:31, 32). If the child of God must resemble his father, this is especially true of the forgiving love which he shows to his enemies (Matt. 5:44–48). Where the forgiveness which has been experienced does not produce the readiness to forgive thy fellow-servant, which according to its nature it ought to produce, then that forgiveness can only be withdrawn (see Parable of the Unmerciful Servant, Matt. 18:23–35).

But the Messiah does not only proclaim the forgiveness of sins, but by means of His atoning death He also secures it, and so establishes the new covenant of grace and forgiveness. Here also the Messianic activity of Jesus consists not only in His teaching, but also in His doing. If in Mark 8:36, 37, Jesus asserts that no man, even although he should gain the whole world, possesses anything which would be of sufficient value in God's sight to redeem his soul (compare Ps. 49:7–9), which, on account of sin, is forfeited to destruction; nevertheless, in Mark 10:45, He regards the fulfillment of His calling, which is accomplished in the surrender of His life, as a work which is of such value in God's sight that it avails as a ransom which He gives instead of the many who were not in a position to provide it themselves. Hereby is given the solution of the death of Christ, inasmuch as it is represented as the means of delivering the many ("to give His life a ransom for *many*," Matt. 10:45—*i.e.*, unquestionably all the members of the Kingdom) from the destruction to which they must have been delivered over in death because of their sins. The same thought is expressed, when, on the occasion of the Last Supper, Jesus calls His blood "the blood of the covenant which was shed for many" (Mark 14:24). As the institution of the old covenant required a covenant-sacrifice, whose blood was sprinkled purifyingly (Heb. 9:22) upon the people (Ex. 24:8), so now also a covenant-sacrifice was required. Only the atoning blood of the covenant-sacrifice (Lev. 17:11), shed, as is rightly explained in Matt. 26:28, for the remission of sins, can purify the people, so that it may be capable of entering into the covenant fellowship with God, in which it can then be always certain of the pardoning Love of the Father. If we consider the saying regarding the ransom (Mark 10:45; Matt. 20:28) as laying emphasis on the God-pleasing performance of Jesus, which secures the salvation of the members of the Kingdom, then Christ's violent and bloody death appears as a suffering which was appointed Him according to the counsel of God, because it was indispensable to the carrying out of the purpose of salvation.

[ANALYSIS: 1) Guilt of the past must be removed by forgiveness ; 2) Jesus claims power to forgive sins; 3) lesson of the Parable of the Prodigal Son ; 4) of that of the Unmerciful Servant ; 5) forgiveness to be had only in this life ; 6) all sins to be forgiven save one ; 7) the believer must have a forgiving spirit ; 8) forgiveness secured by the death of Christ ; 9) no man can redeem his soul ; 10) Christ's death avails for the ransom of all ; 11) without the shedding of blood no forgiveness ; 12) the death of Christ the fulfillment of the counsel of God.]

## § 25. *The Victory Over Satan*.[1]

So long as the Kingdom of God is not set up upon earth, Satan rules as the prince of this world; as the tempter to sin he has power over the kingdoms of the world. The great enemy of God is called by Jesus *the Satan*, *the Adversary* (Mark 4:15 ; Luke 10:18, 13:16 ; 22:31 ; Matt. 4:10) ; *the devil* (Matt. 13:39 ; 25:41), the *slanderer*, because he slanders God to man (Gen. 3:4, 5), and man to God (Job. 1:9–11 ; 2:4–5 ; Rev. 12:10) ; also *the evil one* (Matt 13:19, 38). When Jesus speaks of Satan and his kingdom (Matt. 12:26 ; Luke 11:18), He refers to the company of spirits or demons who are in his service (Matt. 12:28) In the history of the Temptation (Matt. 4:1–11), Satan appears as the ruler of the world ; for his offer of all the kingdoms of the world to Jesus (Matt. 4:9) is correctly explained, in Luke 4:6, to mean that power over these kingdoms has been given to him.

In particular, by means of the unclean spirits, Satan exerts his power over the sick who are possessed by them (Matt. 12:43–45 ; Luke 11:24–26). These unclean spirits are also called *demons* by Jesus (Matt. 10:8 ; 11–18 ; 12:27, 28). According to Matt. 12:43, the unclean spirits dwell in the desert (compare Mark

[1] Compare *Weiss*, § 23.

5:10); and in Matt. 12:45 the possibility is assumed of a possession by several spirits, such as occurs in Mark 5:9. It appears that the possession of a human, or, at least, of an animal soul (Matt. 8:31) is indispensable to them, and they shun the purely spiritual form of existence. Jesus heals those possessed by them by commanding the spirits to come forth (Mark 1:25; Matt. 8:32). He gives His disciples the same power (Matt. 10:8), and speaks of their success (Luke 10:20). He expressly distinguishes these expulsions of the demons from His other cures of the sick (Luke 13:32), and in these demons Jesus sees the Satanic power active (Matt. 12:26).

In His disciples' expulsions of the demons Jesus sees the headlong overthrow of the Satanic power (Luke 10:18); but it is He Himself who has given them power to fight so victoriously against His enemy (Luke 10:19). By the expulsion of the demons He brings about the sovereignty of God upon earth (Matt. 12:28); but it is only because Jesus has previously overcome Satan himself (Matt. 12:29). This victory over Satan was achieved at the time of Christ's Temptation, at the very beginning of His Messianic activity. Inasmuch as the adversary of God did not succeed in leading into sin the Messiah who was to bring about the completion of the Kingdom of God, this completion is secured. Jesus is thus always extending the sovereignty of God into the domain of Satan; and the demons who recognize in Jesus the Messiah (Mark 1:34; 3:11), know that He has come to destroy them (Mark 1:24), and that they cannot escape this destruction and the torment into which it brings them at the appointed time (Matt. 8:29);—for eternal fire is prepared for the devil and his angels (Matt. 25:41).

[ANALYSIS: 1) Satan prince of this world ; 2) called adversary, slanderer, the evil one ; 3) his kingdom consists of evil angels, or demons ; 4) who possess the souls of men ; 5) are expelled by Christ and His disciples ; 6) overthrow of Satan began at the Temptation ; 7) Christ is always extending the sovereignty of God into the domain of Satan ; 8) who finally, with his angels, shall be cast into eternal fire.]

## CHAPTER IV.

### THE RIGHTEOUSNESS OF THE KINGDOM OF GOD.[1]

§ 26. *Righteousness and the Law.*[2]

Righteousness, the perfect fulfilling of the will of God, which is revealed in the law and the prophets, is an essential part of the Kingdom of God, which is to be founded by the Messiah. If the will of God is to be done perfectly in the Kingdom of God (Matt. 6:10), then the characteristic quality of the members of the Kingdom must be righteousness. It is the wedding-garment, without which no one can share in the completed Kingdom of God (Matt. 22:11, 12); the striving after righteousness and after the Kingdom of God (Matt. 6:33) are most intimately connected, as are the promises of the Kingdom of God and of satisfaction with righteousness (Matt. 5:3–6). It is only he who does the will of God that is related to the Messiah (Matt. 12:50), and can enter the Kingdom of God (Matt. 7:21, 24). The will of God, however, is revealed in the law and the prophets (Matt. 5:17; 7:12; 22:40). In so far as the Scribes and the Pharisees sit on Moses's seat—*i. e.*, teach his law—Jesus fully recognizes their authority (Matt. 23:2, 3).

The fulfillment of the law which was customarily taught and practiced was a very imperfect one. Jesus first fulfilled it, and taught that it was to be fulfilled, according to the rule of the perfect will of God which

[1] This chapter bears largely on the doctrine of God, or Theology.
[2] Compare *Weiss*, § 24.

was revealed by Him. Accordingly, Jesus does not merely contend against Pharisaic additions or interpretations; but neither will He complete or improve the law. He will only fulfill it and teach it to be fulfilled, according to the rule of the perfect will of God, which is already contained in the law itself. This is the meaning of the exposition which Christ gives to a series of commandments in the Sermon on the Mount (Matt. 5, 21–47). From the husk of the Old Testament law He unfolds its kernel; He not only teaches, but also practices, its fulfillment (Matt. 5:17), and here also shows, in His life, that the ideal which is striven after in the Kingdom of God is already realized.

If not even the least of the commandments in the law is to remain unfulfilled (Matt. 5:18), then the so-called ceremonial law cannot be excluded from this fulfillment. Accordingly, Jesus has nowhere drawn a distinction between a ceremonial and a moral law; His recognition and fulfillment of the law refers to it as a whole.

In the promise that He, in whom God Himself had come to His people, would always remains in the midst of His own (Matt. 18:20), there lay the germ of the knowledge that God would one day dwell among His people in a more perfect way than in the Temple. If His blood, as atoning sacrificial blood, qualified His own for the fellowship of the new covenant (Mark. 14:24), then the atoning sacrifices of the old covenant must ultimately appear unnecessary after their object was fully attained.

[ANALYSIS: 1) Righteousness the characteristic quality of the members of the Kingdom; 2) Jesus fulfilled all righteousness; 3) the religious worship of the Old Testament abolished; 4) God dwells among His people in a more perfect way than in the Temple.]

## § 27. *The Greatest Commandment.*[1]

In the Old Testament the demand of likeness to God is the principle of the law: "Be ye holy, for I am holy" (Lev. 11:44). In the new revelation of God this demand of likeness to God is confirmed and modified into the demand of love. It is the task of the children of God to imitate the essential perfection of their Father in Heaven, which consists in His all-embracing Love (Matt. 5:45, 48). Accordingly, immediately alongside of love to God, to love one's neighbor is the greatest commandment (Matt. 22:37–40). The inwardness and exclusiveness of this demand, "with all thy heart," cannot be expressed in stronger terms than it is expressed here. Jesus expressly assigns as His reason for giving prominence to these commandments, that all the demands of God, as they are proclaimed in the law and the prophets, are dependent upon one or other of these commandments, and are therefore either a demand of love to God or to our neighbor. The unselfishness which manifests itself in the love of enemies, and the readiness to make sacrifices, which is shown in forgiving injuries, in meekness and peaceableness, are essential elements of love. It is only by the greatness of the sacrifice which it makes that the real character of love can be estimated (Mark 12:41–44). To the question, Who is the neighbor whom the law commands us to love?—the Parable of the Compassionate Samaritan gives the answer: Whoever requires our assistance, his distress is the duty of compassionateness to relieve (Luke 10:29–35). It is in such compassionate love to our enemies that our love becomes similar to the all-embracing love to God (Matt. 5:44, 45). As the Fatherly Love of

---

[1] Compare *Weiss*, § 25. This section treats largely of Ethics.

God reveals itself through the Messiah as forgiving love, so also the forgiving love of the children of God, which is thereby produced, must know no limits, not only as regards the offenses of brethren (Matt. 18:21, 22), but also as regards those of men in general (Matt. 6:12)—especially as forgiving love is the foundation of all love of enemies after the example of God (Matt. 5:44, 45). For this is required the meekness (Matt. 5:5) which is not roused to wrath or invective by any offense of one's neighbor (Matt. 5:22), but is always ready to endure something worse (Matt. 5:39); and there is also required the peaceableness which is always the first to offer the hand of reconciliation (Matt. 5:23, 24), and rather yields to the most unreasonable request than commences strife (Matt. 5:40, 42).

Neither the gentle nor the ministering love, however, can exist without humility, in which Jesus Himself has given the grandest example (Matt. 11:29). In Mark 9:36, 37, Jesus shows by His own example how no one should count himself too high to condescend in love to the very lowliest. Pride is an abomination in the sight of God (Luke 16:15). This pride leads to the high-minded judging and reforming of others which overlooks one's own far greater faults and weaknesses (Matt. 7:1-5). It leads to Pharisaic boasting before God, and to contempt for one's neighbor (Luke 18:9-14). The modest estimate of self forbids also the striving after rank and titles, which does prejudice to brotherly equality as well as to men's position with respect to God (Matt. 23:7-10), and the striving after dominion, which is characteristic of the worldly life (Matt. 20:25). In the Kingdom of God each one is to seek His greatness in service (Matt. 20:26-28), which is not possible without self-humiliation (Mark 9:33-35). It is precisely in this humble service of love that Jesus has given the most perfect example (Mark 10:45).

[ANALYSIS: 1) Likeness to God required; 2) fulfilled in love to God and to one's neighbor; 3) the essential elements of love; 4) Jesus the example of ministering love and humility.]

§ 28. *Righteousness as Disposition.*[1]

In the Parables of the Treasure and the Pearl, the Kingdom of God is represented as the *highest good* (Matt. 13:44-46), because in it the fulfillment of the Divine will or righteousness is realized. It is righteousness, therefore, which is striven after in the Kingdom of God as the highest good. This striving after righteousness, this service of God, must be an exclusive devotion. Hence, Jesus says: "No man can serve two masters" (Matt. 6:24; Luke 16:13). It is this service of God which is often represented as a working in God's vineyard (Matt. 20:1-7; 21:28-30); in the Kingdom of God there is no other work than this striving after righteousness; its results are the fruits which the Lord of the vineyard expects of the husbandmen (Matt. 21:34, 43).

Every other aim must give place to this striving; even the noblest and dearest possessions must be sacrificed if they stand in its way. Though riches can be used, with true wisdom, in the service of love, and therefore in the service of righteousness (Luke 16:1-9), still, according to experience, wealth, because it so easily draws away the heart from the highest interests, is one of the greatest obstacles in the way of the Kingdom of God (Mark 10:23-25), as the parable in Luke 16:19-31 shows, and must therefore, if need be, be sacrificed with decisiveness (Mark 10:21, 22). That which is true of riches is true, however, also of every other good. In

[1] Compare *Weiss*, § 26. This section also treats of Ethics.

Matt. 5:29, 30, the right eye and the right hand are undoubtedly symbols of the dearest and most indispensable goods, which, as soon as they make us falter in the right way, must likewise be sacrificed. In this sense Jesus regards it as justifiable, if one abstains from marriage for the sake of the Kingdom of God (Matt. 19:10–12). The same applies also to the holiest family bonds, if they hinder us from recognizing and striving after the Kingdom of God (Matt. 10:37; Luke 14:26); it applies even to our own life, when the striving after its maintenance hinders us in obtaining salvation (Matt. 10:39; Mark 8:35–37). That the Kingdom of God is the *highest good* appears also from this, that, notwithstanding the apparent renunciations which it costs, man nevertheless really provides best even for his own well-being by striving after it.

If the true fulfillment of the Divine will consists in this exclusive seeking after righteousness, then all fulfillment of the Divine will in detail is valueless. No act can ever be well-pleasing to God, unless it proceeds from the right disposition, which has its seat in the heart. God, however, who sees in secret (Matt. 6:4, 6, 18), knows the hearts (Luke 16:15); therefore, He inquires also how matters stand in this the inmost and most secret ground. Love to Him (Matt. 22:37), as well as forgiveness (Matt. 18:35), must be from the heart; it is as necessary to be lowly in heart (Matt. 11:29) and pure in heart (Matt. 5:8); and adultery in the heart is already adultery in the sight of God (Matt. 5:28).

How everything depends upon the heart, upon its fundamental disposition, cannot be more strongly expressed than in Matt. 6:21, "for where thy treasure is, there will thy heart be also." Here it is plainly assumed, as undoubted, that everything depends upon giving the heart the right bent, and that the bent of the heart towards heaven is the right one. In heaven, however, the will of God is done perfectly (Matt. 6:10); and the bent of the heart thither is, accordingly, the disposition which strives after righteousness as the *highest good*.

[ANALYSIS: 1) Righteousness the highest good; 2) striving after the true service of God; 3) everything must be sacrificed which stands in the way; 4) everything depends upon giving the heart the right bent.]

## CHAPTER V.

### THE ANTHROPOLOGY OF CHRIST.

§ 29. *The Anthropology of Christ.*[1]

This is the most suitable place for explaining the anthropological and psychological ideas to which many of the sayings of Jesus refer. Since these ideas are the same in the whole of the New Testament, we shall here take into account the whole of the writings of the New Testament save those of Paul.

That which distinguishes man from the immaterial spiritual beings is flesh. The New Testament speaks of unclean spirits or demons, who also appear as fallen angels (Rev. 12:7, 9; Jude 6; 2 Pet. 2:4), and of the angels who are ministering spirits (Heb. 1:14)—that is, it speaks of evil and good angels. Man differs from these spiritual beings in that he has flesh, for a spirit has not flesh and bones (Luke 24:39). The flesh is the corporeal part of man, the substance of the body. It mediates and brings about man's connection with nature. It denotes human nature in and according to its corporeal manifestation (1 John 4:2; Heb. 12:9); it is exposed to external defilement (1 Pet. 3:21; Jude 8; Heb. 9:13), and defilement proceeds from it (Jude 23). The flesh is subject to death (1 Pet. 3:18; John 6:51) and corruption (Acts 2:31).

The flesh of living man, however, is flesh possessed of a soul, and the soul has its seat in the blood. The soul is, therefore, in the first place, the bearer of the

[1] Compare *Weiss*, § 27.

bodily life, which is prolonged by nourishment (Matt. 6:25; Luke 12:19); for so long as the soul is in man he lives (Acts 20:10). In death it is taken away from man (Luke 12:20), and is, in a certain sense, lost (Matt. 10:39); for it requires the body for its own perfect life. In voluntary death the soul is laid down (John 10:11, 15, 17, 18) or surrendered (Mark 10:45; Acts 15:26). According to the Old Testament view, however, the soul has its seat in the blood (Gen. 9:4; Lev. 17:11), by which all living flesh is permeated, in which its life, as it were, pulsates. Hence, human nature, as distinguished from the Divine, can be described as *flesh* and *blood* (*sarx* and *haima*) (Matt. 16:17), and the blood can be conceived of as the principle of the propagation of the bodily life (John 1:13). If the blood is shed, the soul departs (Matt. 23:35; Mark 14:24; Acts 22:20). The soul of the flesh is the subject of every sensuous feeling—*i. e.*, of every feeling which is owing to the body (Luke 12:19); through it even the animated flesh itself becomes susceptible to sensuous impressions (Mark 14:38), capable of suffering (1 Pet. 4:1); the subject of sensuous appetites (John 1:13) and lusts (1 Pet. 2:11; 2 Pet. 2:18). While, however, the flesh, as that which is purely material, is that which is common to men, the soul forms the central point of the life of the individual.

The soul has originated in consequence of the Divine breath of life which was breathed into the earthly material (Gen. 2:7), and it is therefore also the bearer of the spiritual life in man which is independent of his corporeity. The New Testament does not teach, any more than does the Old Testament, that there is a *trichotomy* of the human being in the sense of *body, soul and spirit* as being originally three co-ordinate elements of man; *body* and *spirit* are of distinct natures, but the soul is of one nature with the spirit. The spirit is the inbreathing of the Godhead, and the soul is the outbreathing of the spirit. The spirit is the life-centre provided for the body, as the object of its endowment with soul, and the soul is the raying forth of this centre of life. The inward being of the soul is the spirit, and the external nature of the spirit is the soul.

If the spirit quits the body, man is dead (Matt. 27:50; Acts 7:59); if it returns, he becomes alive again (Luke 8:55); without spirit, the body is dead (James 2:26).

This spirit (*pneuma*), however, is not only the principle of the bodily life in man, but also of the higher spiritual life. It therefore forms the antithesis of the flesh (*sarx*), which is determined by sensuous impressions (Mark 14:38); growth in spirit is the antithesis of bodily growth (Luke 1:80). That which is not perceptible to the senses is perceived in the spirit (Mark 2:8). It is in the spirit that purposes are formed (Acts 19:21; 20:22); it is in the spirit that zeal dwells (Acts 18:25), as well as meekness (1 Pet. 3:4).

Now, since this spirit (*pneuma*) has begotten the human soul, this latter is not only the bearer of the bodily sensuous life, but also of the higher spiritual life. The spirit is the inward being of the soul, and the soul is the external nature of the spirit. As the bearer of the Christian life the soul is strengthened (Acts 14:22) and exhausted (Heb. 12:3); it is endangered by sensuous lusts (1 Pet. 2:11; 2 Pet. 2:8, 14); it is subverted by heresy (Acts 15:24); it is guarded (1 Pet. 2:25; 4:19; Heb. 13:17) and purified (1 Pet. 1:22). For this very reason it does not die at death (Matt. 10:28); it is only separated from the body. The souls which are separated from the body (Rev. 6:9; 20:4) are pure spiritual essences—*pneumata* (1 Pet. 3:19; Heb. 12:23). At the death of the body and their separation from it their final fate is decided, whether they fall a prey to destruction, and are therefore definitively lost (Matt. 10:28, 39; Mark 8:36, 37); or whether they are delivered from destruction, and therefore gained (Matt. 10:39; Luke 21:19; 1 Pet. 1:9; Heb. 10:39; John 12:25).

The central organ within man is the heart, which is conceived of as the seat of the whole spiritual life (1 Pet. 3:4; James 5:8; Heb. 13:9). It is in the heart that thoughts dwell (Matt. 9:4; Luke 2:35; etc.); it is the seat of self-consciousness and of consciousness of truth (Heb. 10:22; 1 John 3:19–21; James 1:26). It is the spiritual eye, which, illuminated by the light of the truth (2 Pet. 1:19), gives light to the whole man (Matt. 6:22, 23). Where man does not accept the truth, the reason is to be found in the unsusceptibility of the heart (Matt. 13:15; Mark 3:5; 6:52; Acts 7:51; Heb. 3:8, 15; etc.). In the heart that which is heard is understood (Acts 16:14; 28:27; John 12:40); kept and pondered (Matt. 13:19; Luke 1:66; 8:15; 21:14); in the heart doubt (Luke 24:38) and unbelief (Luke 24:25; Heb. 3:12) have their root. It is also the seat of all feelings, joyous (Acts 2:26, 46; John 16:22) as well as painful (Acts 2:37; 7:54; John 16:6), of all inclinations and emotions (Luke 1:17; 24:32; Acts 4:32; 7:39; 1 Pet. 1:22, etc.), of all lusts (Mark 7:21–23; James 5:5; 2 Pet. 2:14) and resolutions (Acts 5:3, 4; 7:23; John 13:2, etc). That, however, which is in the heart is hidden (Luke 16:15; Acts 1:24; 1 Pet. 3:4), and cannot be perceived from without; it is only by that which proceeds from the heart that its nature is known, as the tree is known by the fruit (Matt. 7:15–20; 12:33–35). Therefore the disposition, as that which is purely inward and as contrasted with every expression by which it is perceived, has its seat in the heart (Luke 1:51 ; Heb. 4:12 ; 10:22 ; 1 Pet. 3:15 ; Acts 8:21, 22).

[ANALYSIS : 1) Man as distinguished from the angels ; 2) flesh the substance of the body ; 3) the soul the bearer of bodily life, and has its seat in the blood ; 4) distinction between flesh and soul ; 5) organ of the soul ; 6) body, soul, and spirit ; 7) the spirit the principle of the bodily and spiritual life; 8) begets the soul ; 9) the functions of the soul ; 10) the soul is separated from the body at death ; 11) the fate of the soul decided at death ; 12) the heart the seat of spiritual life ; 13) the functions of the heart.]

## CHAPTER VI.

### THE MESSIANIC CHURCH.[1]

§ 30. *The Calling.*[2]

The founding of the Kingdom of God begins with the calling of the individuals by the Messiah (Mark 2:17). In Luke 5:32, this call is conceived of as a summons to repentance; in Matt. 20:1–7, as a summons to work in God's vineyard—which summons, however, presupposes a thorough repentance. As the Kingdom of God is the highest good, it is also represented as an invitation to a feast (Luke 14:16; Matt. 22:2). Inasmuch as salvation is brought by the Messiah, this calling is also described as a seeking of the lost (Luke 19:10, compared with the Parables of the Lost Sheep and the Lost Piece of Money (Luke 15:3–10). In every case, however, the point in question is not, as in the Old Testament, the calling of the nation as a nation (Isa. 42:6; 48:12), but of its individual members.

The success of this calling is conditioned by the nature of the hearts of the men whom it reaches. The good ground upon which the Word is sown are such as hear the Word and accept it (Mark 4:20). Wherein this susceptibility consists is stated more precisely in the Beatitudes of the Sermon on the Mount, which specify the conditions of participating in the

---

[1] The sections of this chapter bear largely on the work of the Holy Spirit, or Pneumatology, and on the doctrine of the Church, or Ecclesiology.

[2] Compare *Weiss,* § 28.

already present Kingdom of God, and in its saving blessings (Matt. 5:39). The invitation is given to the weary and heavy-laden, to those who long for rest, and are willing to learn of Christ (Matt. 11:28, 29). It is to the simple (Matt. 11:25); to those of an humble and child-like spirit (Mark 10:14, 15), that the mystery of the Kingdom of God is made known.

In the Parable of the Sower (Mark 4:2–20; Matt. 13:1–23), the chief hindrances which oppose the calling in men's hearts are plainly described as stupidity, levity, and worldliness. The parable shows that, under certain circumstances, at least, levity and worldliness permit a kind of success to the calling, though not a success which is lasting. Selfishness, impenitence, and stupidity render the heart, however, altogether unsusceptible. No effect is possible if men resemble selfish children, who are always demanding that all the others dance as they pipe (Matt. 11:16, 17 ; Luke 7:32). The case is the same wherever there is no disposition to repent (Matt. 11:20; 12:41 ; Luke 13:3, 5). In the Parable of the Great Supper (Luke 14:16–24), we have an illustration of the stupidity of those who despise the call on account of their worldly interests. The condition in which every susceptibility is extinguished, Jesus describes also as death (Matt. 8:22). Though Jesus was not sent but unto the lost sheep of the house of Israel (Matt. 15:24), He, nevertheless, not only plainly warned the Jews of their rejection, and the calling of the Gentiles if they refused to accept His message (Luke 13:28, 29 ; Matt. 8:11, 12), but also in several parables clearly taught the calling of the Gentiles, instead of the Jews (See the Parable of the Marriage of the King's Son, Matt. 22:1–14 ; the Parable of the Great Supper, Luke 14:16–24 ; the Parable of the Wicked Husbandmen,

Matt. 21:33–46; Mark 12:1–12; Luke 20:9–18.) There is nothing said, however, as to the manner in which the Gentiles shall obtain this participation in the Kingdom, or the manner in which they are called.

[ANALYSIS : 1) Different aspects of the calling ; 2) success of calling is conditioned by the nature of the heart ; 3) chief hindrances which oppose the calling ; 4) Jesus taught the calling of the Gentiles.]

### § 31. *Discipleship.*[1]

He who is susceptible to the calling listens eagerly to the preaching of Jesus, and becomes His disciple. If Jesus calls, he comes to Him (Matt. 11:28); he hears His Word (Matt. 13:9), accepts it (Mark 4:20), and keeps it (Luke 11:28). To such eager listeners Jesus opens up the mysteries of the Kingdom of God, inasmuch as to them He explains the parables, which remain unintelligible to the unsusceptible people (Mark 4:11, 12, 34). This hearing, however, awakens the desire for further hearing ; they attach themselves to Jesus, and follow Him in His journeys (Mark 8:34).

As Christ declares Himself to be not merely a messenger of God in general, but the Messiah, His disciples must confess Him as such (Matt. 10:32). Such as see in Him the One that was looked for, and believe, in accordance with His message, that the Kingdom of God has come with Him (Matt. 11:11), they are already in the Kingdom.

Faith appears, primarily, as that trust in God to which the hearing of prayer is promised (Matt. 17:20). In particular, it stands also for trust in the miraculous power of Jesus to help (Matt. 8:10 ; 9:2). In this respect the story of the healing of the woman who had

[1] Compare *Weiss*, § 29.

an issue of blood is specially characteristic (Matt. 9:20–22). But this trust in His power to work miracles of healing already involved the belief that in Him the day of salvation or the Kingdom of God was come. Such a faith, however, imperfect it might be, Jesus demanded as a condition of His working miracles (Matt. 9:28, 29; 15:28; Mark 6:5, 6); for the blessings of the Kingdom of God, among which are also the miracles of healing, can be shared in only by the members of the Kingdom. The idea of faith receives another application, when it denotes the trust with which one receives as true the word of another (Matt. 21:32; Mark 11:31).

The success of the calling is regarded as a working of God, but this success is conditioned by human susceptibility. Flesh and blood does not reveal to us a knowledge of Christ as our Saviour (Matt. 16:17). Man has to thank God alone for the knowledge which brings salvation (Matt. 11:25). From Mark 10:27, we learn that it is the work of God even to produce the susceptibility to receive salvation. For if it is still more difficult for a rich man to enter into the Kingdom of God than for a camel to go through the eye of a needle (Mark 10:25), then, of course, it is absolutely impossible for human strength.

[ANALYSIS: 1) He whose heart is susceptible hears the Word; 2) hearing awakens desire for further hearing; 3) faith is trust in God; 4) the success of the calling a work of God; 5) the susceptibility of the heart to receive salvation a work of God.]

## § 32. *The Elect.*[1]

The participation of the individual in the Kingdom of God, which commences with discipleship, does not

[1] Compare *Weiss*, § 30.

attain its completion without making ever new and heavy demands upon the disciples of the Kingdom. In consequence of its inherent productive power, the Kingdom of God will grow, not only on the whole (Mark 4:26-28), but also in each individual. The preaching of Jesus is the energizing principle of a new God-like life; and the Kingdom of God must develop, spontaneously as it were, towards its completion, in the case of those who have once received the Word of Jesus as His disciples. This process demands, on man's part, a free acquiescence in the transformation of his whole life and character, which is being affected in him. As this transformation is a continual annihilation of the natural bent of man's life, it demands a protracted self-denial (Mark 8:34), and the readiness to make even the greatest sacrifices (Matt. 5:29, 30). It demands that the disciple of Jesus take up His Cross continually (Matt. 10:38), and willingly submit to the affliction which grows out of the enmity of the world, and continue therein with patience (Matt. 10:22). It is because of these demands that the gate is so narrow which leads to the completion of the Kingdom of God (Matt. 7:13, 14); and not every one who becomes a disciple of Jesus realizes the whole difficulty of his task, and considers whether he is fully resolved to submit to all its demands (Luke 14:28-33).

By reason of sin, however, the development of disciple life is threatened with many disturbances, for the overcoming and avoidance of which there is need of *prayer*, *watchfulness*, and *fidelity*. Conscious of his shortcomings, even the disciple of Jesus has always *to pray* for forgiveness of sins; and, conscious of his inability to fulfill the demands of the Kingdom, he has to pray for preservation against temptation, and for de

## THE ELECT.

liverance from the power of evil (Matt. 6:12, 13). There is need of prayer, also, in order that the help of God may be obtained (Mark 9:29; 11:24). For the conservation of discipleship is no more possible without Divine aid than is its beginning; but here, also, there must be a susceptibility to Divine help, and this susceptibility is manifested in prayer, which shows that the disciple feels his own weakness and hopes to obtain Divine help. In Mark 14:38, *watchfulness* appears joined with prayer. There must be a spiritual preparedness, which, in view of the return of the Messiah, who comes to prove the demeanor of His disciples, seeks to hold itself always ready, or to put itself in a state of readiness, for that event (Matt. 24:42–44; 25:1–13). But to live continually in the clear consciousness of His return, and in a state of constant readiness for it, is nothing else than to adhere faithfully to the bond of discipleship which unites the disciples to the Exalted Messiah. Accordingly, in Matt. 24:45–51, this is expressly described as *fidelity*. Above all, the Parable of the Talents (Matt. 25:14–30) shows that, in the Kingdom of God, that which is of the greatest importance is the *fidelity* which the disciple manifests in the administration of the goods intrusted to him.

The completion of salvation is not attained by all who have accepted the calling and become disciples. There may be a denial in time of persecution, through fear of man (Matt. 10:28–33), or there may be lacking that self-denial without which discipleship itself becomes something altogether worthless (Luke 14:34). It may happen that the one who confesses Christ as his Lord neither proves his discipleship to be real by obedience to His word (Matt. 7:21; 24:27), nor manifests fidelity to Him in his service (Matt. 25:24–28;

24:48–51), nor shows love to Him in loving the brethren (Matt. 25:42–45), and is therefore surprised by his Lord's unexpected return, and not found in the condition of the true disciples (Matt. 25:8–12). He who does not use the gift he has received loses even that which he has had (Matt. 25:29); he who does not advance goes backward and ends in apostasy. It is only when it is manifest from one's demeanor that the forgiveness of sins which was granted him has not wrought that which it necessarily works in the children of the Kingdom, that it is recalled (Matt. 18:32–35).

In Matt. 22:14, it is said that only a few of the many who are called are chosen. The *elect* are those in whom God's saving purpose of free Love is realized, and who by faith have renounced all merit, and thus have entered upon the state of reconciliation intended for them—who are selected out of the number of the disciples as genuine disciples, and are, therefore, counted worthy of the consummation of the Kingdom of God. It is His selected disciples whom Jesus will gather together, in order that He may bring them into His Kingdom (Matt. 24:31); they are the blessed of God, for whom the Kingdom has been prepared since the foundation of the world (Matt. 25:34); and that not because they are predestinated for the Kingdom, but because, according to the Divine counsel, the Kingdom is appointed only for the small flock of true disciples (Luke 12:32). This does not forbid that, even during their earthly life, God knows these His elect ones, hears their prayers (Luke 18:7), and on their account shortens the troubles of the last time (Matt. 24:22). The genuine disciple of Jesus, however, knows that as such his name is written in heaven (Luke 10:20); he knows that he is appointed to be a member of the Kingdom of God; and, accordingly, so long as he adheres closely to the bond of this discipleship, he can be certain of his salvation.

[ANALYSIS: 1) The Kingdom must grow in each individual; 2) demands self-denial; 3) prayer; 4) watchfulness; 5) fidelity; 6) not all the called are saved; 7) the grace of God may be lost; 8) the elect are the genuine disciples; 9) for whom the Kingdom has been prepared since the foundation of the world; 10) the true believer can be certain of his salvation as long as he is faithful.]

## § 33. *The Apostles and the Church.*[1]

In order that His proclamation may continue its calling activity even after His death, Jesus chose and sent out the twelve Apostles, upon whom He also conferred the full dignity of ambassadors (Matt. 10:40). Since the calling was addressed, in the first place, to the nation of the Twelve Tribes, Jesus therefore chose twelve of them, with evident reference to the work for which they were appointed (Matt. 19:28). They are the Fishermen who gather men into the net of the Kingdom of God (Mark 1:17); the laborers who, upon the field of the world, gather into the Kingdom the harvest of God, which grows up out of the preaching of Jesus (Matt. 9:37, 38).

By means of the Apostles, Peter taking a prominent part in the work, the fellowship of His disciples was to be gathered together into a separate community. In Matt. 16:18, Jesus designates the separate community of His disciples as the Church. The Church of Christ, in a certain sense, is certainly built on the Apostles (1 Cor. 3:10, 11; Eph. 2:20; Rev. 21:14), inasmuch as they were the first believers, and the rest have been added through their labors; and in Peter Jesus saw

[1] Compare *Weiss*, § 31.

that one among the Apostles whose activity would give the Church its greatest stability and consistency.[1]

To His Church Jesus has bequeathed the authority to announce and deny the forgiveness of sins (Matt. 16:17-19; 18:15-18); for Matt. 16:18, when rightly interpreted, cannot speak of a primacy of Peter in the sense of a special dignity.

He has also constituted the congregation of the Messianic Church the heir of the grandest promises given to Israel. As Jehovah promised to be in the midst of Israel in Messianic time (Joel 2:27), so the Exalted Messiah is now in the midst of His Church (Matt. 18:19, 20); as once the sanctuary of Israel had been the holy place, where Jehovah came to His people to bless them (Ex. 20:24), so Jesus consecrates the congregation of the Messianic Church as the place of blessing, where He will be near with His gracious Presence, which secures the hearing of prayer; for, along with the forgiveness of sins, the hearing of prayer is one of the Messianic blessings of salvation which is given, immediately and perpetually, with the new revelation of God in the Messiah.

[ANALYSIS: 1) The office of the Twelve Apostles; 2) the Church; 3) the office of the keys intrusted to the Church; 4) the Church constituted the heir of the promises given to Israel.]

---

[1] This is the natural interpretation of this much-discussed passage; but this, by no means, is a concession to the false claims of the Papacy.

# CHAPTER VII.

### THE ESCHATOLOGY OF JESUS.

§ 34. *Concerning Death in General.*

For the sake of clearness and simplicity, we will present the teaching of Jesus concerning "The Last Things," according to the three Synoptists, and according to John, together under each separate topic.

Our Saviour speaks of three kinds of death—spiritual,[1] bodily,[2] and eternal.[3] Two of these three are referred to when Christ says to one of His disiciples, "Leave the dead to bury their own dead" (Matt. 8:22)—*i. e.*, leave those spiritually dead to bury the bodies of their own dead. These spiritually dead are the lost for which

---

[1] John 5:24. "He that heareth my word, and believeth him that sent me, hath eternal life, and cometh not into judgment, but hath passed out of death into life."

John 6:53, "Except ye eat the flesh of the Son of Man and drink of his blood, ye have not life in yourselves."

Luke 15:24, "For this my son was dead, and is alive again; he was lost, and is found."

[2] Luke 12:20, "Thou foolish one, this night is thy soul required of thee."

John 9:4, "The night cometh, when no man can work."

John 10:11, 17, 18, "The good shepherd layeth down his life for the sheep. . . . I lay down my life, that I may take it again. No one taketh it away from me, but I lay it down of myself. I have power to lay it down, and I have power to take it again."

[3] Matt. 7:13; 10:28; 18:8; 23:33; 25:30, 41, 46; Mark 9:43, 45, 47, 48; John 3:16; 5:29.

It is likewise to this *eternal* death that Jesus refers in John 8:51 and 11:26, "If a man keep my word, he shall never see death;" "And whosoever liveth and believeth on me shall never die."

the Son of Man came to seek and to save (Luke 19:10). This spiritual death (John 5:24) is a state of sin and darkness (John 3:19, 20), on which the wrath of God abides (John 3:36). It is this state of sin and darkness into which all flesh is born (John 3:5, 6), which is the cause of spiritual death (John 3:19; 12:46).

These *three* forms of death have a close connection with one another; for *spiritual* death leads to *bodily* death, and unless spiritual death is overcome by faith in Christ,[1] it will end in *eternal* death. In John 8:44 Christ distinctly names the Devil as the cause of death, for "he was a murderer from the beginning."

[ANALYSIS: 1) Three kinds of death; 2) spiritual; 3) bodily; 4) eternal.]

### § 35. *The Doctrine of Recompense.*[2]

To serve God is the characteristic righteousness of the members of the Kingdom (Matt. 6:24), who are frequently represented in the parables as the servants of God (Matt. 18:23) or of His Son (Matt. 24:44, 45). In the Parable of the Laborers in the Vineyard (Matt. 20:1–16), this relation is expressly conceived of as a relation which is regulated by contract, and therefore involves the idea of reward; and yet this same parable teaches expressly that, notwithstanding the greatest *quantitative* difference in the service, the reward in the Kingdom of

---

[1] John 5:24; 5:40, "Ye will not come to me, that ye may have life."
6:51, "I am the living bread which came down out of heaven; if any man eat of this bread, he shall live forever."
8:24, "I said therefore unto you, that ye shall die in your sins; for except ye believe that I am he, ye shall die in your sins."
3:36, "He that believeth on the Son hath eternal life; but he that believeth not the Son shall not see life, but the wrath of God abideth on him."

[2] Compare *Weiss*, § 32.

God is the same to all—for they that were hired about the eleventh hour received as much as those who had borne the burden of the day.

Strange as it may at first sight appear, this reward is, on the one hand, equivalent to the service, and, on the other, it is the same to all. This equivalence is not to be conceived of as if it were a *quantitative* weighing of the reward according to the measure of the service, for the reward is a great one;[1] it is manifold,[2] and altogether disproportionate to the service. He who has been faithful over a few things is set over many things (Matt. 25:21-23; 24:46, 47). But this equivalence of reward is to be conceived of as *qualitative*. The reward for every individual consists of a participation in the completed Kingdom of God in heaven. The reward is immediately bestowed on the members of the Kingdom, but it is in heaven (Matt. 5:12; 6:1), as a heavenly treasure (Matt. 6:20; Mark 10:21), to be received in the future.

As the reward was equivalent to the service, so the punishment is equivalent to the guilt. The fundamental law of the equivalence of guilt and punishment is very clearly expressed by Christ.[3] Here, too, the greatness of the guilt is not to be measured quantitatively; it depends upon the greatness of the motive,[4]

---

[1] Matt. 5:12, "For great is your reward in heaven."

[2] Matt. 19:29, "They shall receive a hundred fold, and snall inherit eternal life."

[3] Matt. 7:2, "With what judgment ye judge, ye shall be judged; and with what measure ye mete, it shall be measured unto you."

Matt. 10:33, "Whosoever shall deny me before men, him will I also deny before my Father which is in heaven."

Matt. 18:35, "So shall also my heavenly Father do unto you, if ye forgive not every one his brother from your hearts."

[4] Matt. 12:41, 42; 11:22-24.

and of the opportunity which the individual had to avoid sin and do the will of God.[1] Here, too, the punishment at last is one and the same—exclusion from the completed Kingdom of God,[2] to which every one is condemned who cannot be acknowledged as righteous in the Day of Judgment.[3] He who has not striven after the Kingdom of God as a true disciple of Jesus cannot reach that Kingdom (Matt. 25:31-46).

[ANALYSIS: 1) Service involves the idea of reward; 2) this reward equivalent to the service, and yet the same to all; 3) the equivalence of reward not quantitative but qualitative; 4) the reward is immediately bestowed, and yet is still future; 5) punishment is equivalent to the guilt, and yet the same to all; 6) guilt is not to be measured quantitatively, but according to its quality.]

### § 36. *Bodily Death.*

Christ speaks of bodily death as a falling asleep (Matt. 9:24; John 11:11), because the body shall again be awakened (John 5:28, 29). That this is not a sleep of the soul can be seen from the Parable of the Rich Man and Lazarus (Luke 16:19-31). The body dies, but the soul and spirit, separated from the body, outlast the corruption of the body. The earth receives the body; but the soul, united to the spirit, descends into the kingdom of death, either into Hades proper, as

---

[1] Luke 12:47, 48, "That servant which knew his lord's will, and made not ready, nor did according to his will, shall be beaten with many stripes; but he that knew not, and did things worthy of stripes, shall be beaten with few stripes. And to whomsoever much is given, of him shall much be required; and to whom they commit much, of him will they ask the more."

[2] Matt. 8:12; 22:13, 25:12.

[3] Matt. 12:36, 37, "Every idle word that men shall speak, they shall give account thereof in the day of judgment. For by thy words thou shalt be justified, and by thy words thou shalt be condemned.

the place of torment (Luke 16:23),[1] or into that part of Hades known as Paradise (Luke 23:43),[2] the place of honor and comfort (Luke 16:22, 25).[3]

From Matt. 10:28,[4] we learn—1) that while the body dies the soul does not die; 2) that while the body dies at death, and is separated from the soul, there is to be a reunion of the two again; and 3) that thus united they may be cast into Gehenna, the place of eternal punishment for body and soul.

[ANALYSIS: 1) Sleep an image of death; 2) this does not imply a sleep of the soul; 3) the change at death; 4) teaching of Matt. 10:28.]

§ 37. *The State of the Soul after Death.*

In the Parable of the Rich Man and Lazarus (Luke 16:19–31), we have the clearest revelation in the New Testament of the state of the dead before Christ's death and resurrection. Whether a change took place in the condition of the dead at the time of Christ's resurrection (Acts 2:31) and descent unto the spirits in prison (1 Pet. 3:19, 20, 4:6); wrought by Christ's triumph over death and over Satan, will have to be decided later, when we examine the teaching of the Apostles. All that we can now affirm is, that in

[1] "In Hades he lifted up his eyes, being in torments."

[2] "To-day shalt thou be with me in Paradise."

[3] Let us bear in mind that this is Christ's presentation of the condition of the souls of the departed before His death, before His resurrection and triumph over Satan and death, before His ascension into heaven; for it was not until the ascension of Christ into heaven that heaven, the Paradise above the earth, was opened for believers, and has become the place of the general "assembly and church of the first-born" (Heb. 12:23).

[4] "Be ye not afraid of them which kill the body, but are not able to kill the soul; but rather fear him which is able to destroy both soul and body in Gehenna."

this parable we have a clear and definite presentation, by one who knows, of the condition of souls after death, before Christ Himself, the speaker, died, arose from the dead, and ascended into Heaven. In the interpretation of the parable, we must be careful not to literalize what is purely symbolical; but, at the same time, we must not forget that there is a literal truth underlying the symbolical. Figures, after all, imply literal verities.

This parable teaches, or at least implies—

1) That there is a particular judgment of each soul at death, the moment of the separation of the body and soul, for "it came to pass that the beggar died, and that he was carried away by the angels into Abraham's bosom; and the rich man also died, and was buried. And in Hades he lifted up his eyes, being in torments" (*vers.* 22, 23).[1] Probation ends at death. The night cometh when no man can work (John 9:4). This same truth is the lesson taught by Jesus in His Parable of the Foolish Man which built his house upon the sand (Matt. 7:26, 27), is the keynote of His exhortation to self-denial in Mark 8:34–38,[2] and the burden of his warning, in Luke 13:23–25.

That the eternal state of the soul is finally decided at death is not only the distinct teaching of Christ, but it is everywhere implied. In fact, although Christ speaks continually of the Last Judgment as something

---

[1] Compare, also, *vers.* 24, 25, "Father Abraham, have mercy on me, and send Lazarus, that he may dip the tip of his finger in water, and cool my tongue; for I am in anguish in this flame. But Abraham said, Son, remember that thou in thy lifetime receivedst thy good things, and Lazarus in like manner evil things; but now he is comforted, and thou art in anguish."

[2] Compare especially *ver.* 36, "For what doth it profit a man, to gain the whole world, and forfeit his soul?"

future, yet He also, especially in John, speaks of a judgment belonging already to the present time. His language is very exact, and there need be no misunderstanding of His meaning. There is already an *internal* judgment in this life. This judgment depends on the relation of the individual to Christ. " He that believeth not hath been judged already, because he hath not believed on the name of the Only-begotten Son of God" (John 3:18); and " he that heareth my word, and believeth him that sent me, hath eternal life, and cometh not into judgment, but has passed out of death into life" (John 5:24). What remarkable and important truths are here taught! Christ is THE JUDGE. The dividing already begins in this life. Our relation to Christ and His revelation decides our lot even in this life, and, though our relation to Christ may be changed at any time before our death, the particular judgment at death is but a continuation, a step of development of the same state or condition in which the soul finds itself at death.

The *unbeliever*, even now, in this life, " hath one that judgeth him,"[1] " hath been judged already " (John 3:18), " shall not see life, but the wrath of God abideth on him" (John 3:36); and the particular judgment that overtakes him at death (Luke 16:23, 24) is but a development of that same judgment already passed upon him, and at the Last Day he shall rise again "unto the resurrection of judgment" (John 5:29), and the word of Christ shall judge him in the last day " (John 12:48).

The *believer*, while yet on earth, even in this life, " hath eternal life, and cometh not into judgment, but

[1] John 12:48, "He that rejecteth me, and receiveth not my sayings, hath one that judgeth him."

hath passed out of death into life" (John 5:24), and at death Christ receives him unto Himself in glory, and at the Last Day Christ will raise him up (John 6:40, 54); and this our Saviour calls "the resurrection of life" (John 5:29).

This particular judgment at death differs from the general judgment which shall take place at the Last Day, especially in this, that the latter is an official confirmation of what has already taken place at death, and not only has reference to the whole individual, body and soul reunited, but involves the comprehensive exposition of all the dealings of God with mankind as a race. The Last Judgment is the grand and final completion of a process begun in the case of each individual here on earth, and definitely determined at the moment of his death.

2) This parable teaches that the entrance on the condition of joy or of woe is immediate upon death; for the rich man, immediately after death, was "in torments," "in anguish," in "this place of torment," while Lazarus was in "Abraham's bosom," "comforted." The condition or state of the rich man and of Lazarus was not indeterminate, but their lot was forever decided. Lazarus received his reward immediately at death, and so did the rich man immediately enter upon his punishment. There need be no question about the truth of this (see *vers.* 22, 23, 25). We have no right to suppose that the rich man was still in a state of probation, with character and condition undetermined. That immediately after death the soul enters upon its state of joy or of woe is also taught when Christ says to the thief on the Cross, "To-day shalt thou be with me in Paradise" (Luke 23:43).

3) This parable also controverts the doctrine that

## STATE OF THE SOUL AFTER DEATH. 99

the soul sleeps between death and the resurrection. Jesus here teaches that the soul consciously exists between death and the resurrection. His promise to the dying thief also implies such a conscious existence after death, and the whole argument of Christ in Matt. 22: 31, 32,[1] is evidence, conclusive, that the patriarchs not only existed, but existed in full consciousness.

4) This parable teaches that there is no annihilation of the wicked at death. The rich man was "in torments," "in anguish." Nor does Christ know of an annihilation of the wicked at the Final Judgment. Instead of this, He speaks of a destruction of both soul and body in Gehenna (Matt. 10:28), of a being "cast into Gehenna, where their own worm dieth not, and the fire is not quenched" (Mark 9:47, 48); and He speaks of an "eternal fire" for the wicked, and of an "eternal punishment" (Matt. 25:41, 46).

5) Christ also teaches us in this parable that there are gradations of bliss and dignity in Heaven; for Abraham's bosom is a place and condition of supreme dignity and joy, to which Lazarus, a child of Abraham by faith, is borne by the angels. The image of Abraham's bosom is that of a banquet, at which the highest place is that taken by Abraham; and the place of peculiar dignity is that next to him, in his bosom, referring to the manner in which the guests at an ancient banquet reclined at table, each with his neighbor next below him in his bosom.

That there shall be degrees of reward in the life to come is also distinctly taught by Christ in the Parable

[1] "But as touching the resurrection of the dead, have ye not read that which was spoken unto you by God, saying, I am the God of Abraham, and the God of Isaac, and the God of Jacob? God is not the God of the dead, but of the living."

of the Pounds (Luke 19:11–27), and in the Parable of the Talents (Matt. 25:14–30).

Equally explicit is Christ's teaching with reference to different degrees of punishment.[1]

6) We can also infer from this parable that Abraham's bosom, or the place where Abraham was, is not Hades in its specific sense as the place and state of the condemned, but that it is that part of the generic Hades, known as Paradise, where the thief on the Cross, immediately after death, met Jesus (Luke 23:43).

7) We also learn that Hades in its specific sense, as the place of torment, is far from the home of Abraham and of the pious in Paradise. There is a chasm or impassable gulf between them (*ver.* 26). It is so great that those who would pass from either side to the other cannot. No language could express more strongly that the specific Hades and Abraham's bosom, or Paradise, are not one place. All we can grant is that the specific Hades as the place of misery, which received all the souls of the wicked, and Abraham's bosom, or Paradise, as the place of joy and comfort, which received all the souls of the pious, are two parts of one place, generically known in the Old Testament as *Sheol*, and in the New Testament as *Hades*. But two parts of one place, the one the lower, the other the upper, if we speak exactly, are not one place.

8) Christ also teaches that the joy of the one place is as unchangeable as is the misery of the other. There is

---

[1] Matt. 11:24, "It shall be more tolerable for the land of Sodom in the day of judgment, than for thee."

Luke 12:47, 48, "He shall be beaten with many stripes;" "he shall be beaten with few stripes."

Matt. 23:15, "Ye make him twofold more a son of Gehenna than yourselves."

no transition from the one place or condition to the other. Christ represents Abraham as saying: "Besides all this, between us and you there is a great gulf fixed, that they which would pass from hence to you may not be able, and that none may cross over from thence to us" (*ver.* 26). Whatever character the soul has at death, whatever its relation to the Kingdom of God, that decides its condition after death, and there can be no change of character or condition after death.

9) This parable gives us no information with reference to the possibility of any communication with the spiritual world. When the rich man implores that Lazarus should be sent to his five brethren on earth, to testify unto them, lest they also come into that place of torment, Abraham does not say that the thing is either possible or impossible, but only that it would be attended by no results to justify it.

10) The inference that men, in the lower part of Hades, the place of torment, could talk with men in Paradise, or with Abraham himself, may not be warranted; but, if it were, it would prove nothing as to locality, for we know not through what range of space the communications of the eternal world may take place. The parable couches truth under certain suppositions as to what men would say, if they could. Disembodied spirits have not tongues and fingers; these touches belong to the drapery of the parable, but the body of the parable seems clearly to warrant us in drawing the inferences we so far have done.

[ANALYSIS: 1) Teaching of the Parable of the Rich Man and Lazarus; 2) there is a particular judgment at death; 3) probation ends at death; 4) there is already an internal judgment in this life; 5) in case of both unbeliever and believer; 6) the distinction between the particular judgment at death and the Last Judgment; 7) the entrance on the condition of joy or of woe is immediate at death;

8) the soul does not sleep between death and the resurrection; 9) there is no annihilation of the wicked at death, nor at the Final Judgment; 10) there are gradations of bliss and reward in Heaven; 11) as well as degrees of punishment for the wicked; 12) Abraham's bosom is not the specific Hades, but Paradise; 13) the specific Hades, as a place of torment, far from Paradise; 14) the joy of Paradise is as unchangeable as the misery of Hades; 15) this parable does not teach that we can have any communication with the spiritual world; 16) nor can we infer that there is communication between Paradise and Hades.]

## § 38. *The Second Coming of Christ.*

All the teachings of Christ point to His Second Coming, and to the marvelous events which shall attend that Great Day.

With reference to the *time* of the *Parousia*, God the Father has reserved it to Himself alone to determine the day and the hour of His return.[1] On the basis of three kinds of passages,[2] some maintain that Christ distinctly teaches that His Second Coming will occur in

---

[1] Matt. 24:36, "But of that day and hour knoweth no one, not even the angels of heaven, neither the Son, but the Father only;" *ver.* 42, "Watch therefore: for ye know not on what day your Lord cometh;" *ver.* 44, "For in an hour that ye think not the Son of Man cometh;" *ver.* 50, "The lord of that servant shall come in a day when he expecteth not, and in an hour when he knoweth not."

Matt. 25:13, "Watch therefore, for ye know not the day nor the hour."

Mark 13:32, "But of that day or that hour knoweth no one, not even the angels in heaven, neither the Son, but the Father;" *ver.* 33, "Take ye heed, watch and pray: for ye know not when the time is;" *ver.* 35, "Watch therefore: for ye know not when the lord of the house cometh."

See also Luke 12:40, 46; 21:34–36.

[2] *a*) Matt. 10:23, "Ye shall not have gone through the cities of Israel, till the Son of Man be come."

Matt. 16:28, "There be some of them that stand here, which shall in no wise taste of death, till they see the Son of Man coming in his Kingdom,"

the immediate future. In all these passages the coming of the Son of Man at the destruction of Jerusalem is a type of the final coming of the Lord.

In Matt. 10:23, the true interpretation is: think not that the Kingdom of Heaven will so soon be established in the hearts of men. It will take a long time; Israel will not be converted, " Till the Son of Man be come." Christ here speaks of a *coming* at some future time. Whether by this coming He refers to His coming in judgment at the destruction of Jerusalem, or, which is more likely, to His Second, Final Coming, we may not be able to decide, but Israel itself—even to this day— has not yet received the Gospel; nor has Christ come the second time, in His personal, visible appearance. The Kingdom of God came indeed at the resurrection of Christ, and at the outpouring of the Holy Ghost on the day of Pentecost, and in a more especial manner, the Son of Man came in His Kingdom with power, at the destruction of Jerusalem (70 A. D.); and there were some of those who had heard Christ speaking these words, still living at the time, for only about forty years had elapsed. That present generation (Matt. 24:34) was still living when "all these things"[1] pertaining to

Mark 9:1, "There be some here of them that stand by, which shall in no wise taste of death, till they see the kingdom of God come with power."

Luke 9:27, "There be some of them that stand here, which shall in no wise taste of death till they see the kingdom of God."

b) Matt. 24:34, "This generation shall not pass away, till all these things be accomplished." See also Mark 13:30; Luke 21:32.

c) Matt. 26:64, "Henceforth ye shall see the Son of Man sitting at the right hand of power, and coming on the clouds of heaven." See also Mark 14:62; Luke 22:69.

[1] Compare Matt. 24:33, where "All these things" cannot refer to the predictions in Matt. 24:29-31, which describe the very end itself (for our Saviour assuredly does not say that when "they shall see

the destruction of Jerusalem were accomplished. There is, in fact, no ground for maintaining that Christ teaches that His Second Coming in a personal, visible appearance will occur in the immediate future, although we must infer that the Apostles themselves, before the outpouring of the Holy Ghost, expected a speedy coming, and restoration of the Kingdom of Israel.[1] It may occur at any time, " in an hour that ye think not" (Matt. 24:44), " For ye know not when the time is" (Mark 13:33), and there may also be an unexpected long delay.[2] Those who maintain that Jesus, in the passages quoted, represents His personal return as an event to be looked for during that present generation, and who here speak of an "error" on the part of Jesus, altogether misconceive the nature of biblical

the Son of Man coming on the clouds of heaven with power and great glory," that then "ye know that he is nigh, even at the doors"), but to "all these things" which are "the beginning of travail" (Matt. 24:8), and which began with the destruction of Jerusalem.

[1] Matt. 24:3, "Tell us, when shall these things be? and what shall be the sign of thy coming, and of the consummation of the age?"

Acts 1:6, 7, "Lord, dost thou at this time restore the kingdom of Israel? And he said unto them, It is not for you to know times or seasons, which the father hath appointed within his own authority."

[2] Matt. 24:48, "But if that evil servant shall say in his heart, My Lord tarrieth."

Matt. 25:5, "Now while the bridegroom tarried."

Mark 13:35, "For ye know not when the lord of the house cometh, whether at even, or at midnight, or at cock-crowing, or in the morning."

Compare also the Parable of the Unrighteous Judge, Luke 18: 2–8.

Matt. 25:19, "Now after a long time the lord of those servants cometh."

Luke 21:24, 27, "And Jerusalem shall be trodden down of the Gentiles until the times of the Gentiles be fulfilled. . . . And then shall they see the Son of Man coming."

prophecy, which, so far as regards its fulfillment, always remains dependent on the historical development. In this development, however, the relation of man to the Kingdom of God forms an essential factor, in conformity with which the Father, who guides this development, alone determines the time and the hour. In a certain sense there was a coming of Christ at the destruction of Jerusalem, and the beginning of the judgment upon Israel; but this was but a type of His final coming in His own Glorified Person, with His holy angels (Matt. 16:27; Mark 8:38).

Jesus warns His disciples not to be deceived by false Christs;[1] He warns them not to be led astray by premature announcements of His return, since it will everywhere manifest itself visibly and unmistakably, like the lightning which comes down from heaven (Matt. 24:26-28; Luke 17, 23, 24); He warns them not to take the beginning of the travail for the end itself (Matt. 24:6-8).

As *signs* of His return, Jesus speaks—1) of great wars between nations and kingdoms, of famines and earthquakes, as the beginning of travail (Matt. 24:6-8; Mark 13:8). There shall also be terrors and great signs from heaven (Luke 21:10, 11). 2) The Gospel must first be preached unto all the nations (Matt. 24:14; Mark 13:10). 3) Great judgments must fall upon Israel and Jerusalem (Matt. 24:15-20; Mark 13:14, 16; Luke 21:20-22); then shall be great tribulation, such as hath not been from the beginning of the world until now (Matt. 24:21; Mark

---

[1] Matt. 24:5, "For many shall come in my name, saying, I am the Christ, and shall lead many astray;" *ver*. 24, "For there shall arise false Christs, and false prophets, and shall show great signs and wonders: so as to lead astray, if possible, even the elect." See also Mark 13:21-23.

13:19); with the destruction of Jerusalem the judgment of God already begins, and Jerusalem shall be trodden down of the Gentiles, until the times of the Gentiles be fulfilled (Luke 21:24). 4) Immediately before the end, "the sun shall be darkened, and the moon shall not give her light, and the stars shall fall from heaven, and the powers of the heavens shall be shaken; and then shall they see the Son of Man coming in clouds with great power and glory" (Matt. 24:29, 30; Mark 13:24–26).[1]

When Jesus returns, the great mass of men have not become His disciples. He will find men as little prepared for His judgment as on the occasion of His First gracious coming; for men will live in the same carnal security as in the days of the Flood, eating and drinking, marrying and giving in marriage. "As were the days of Noah, so shall be the Coming of the Son of Man" (Matt. 24:37–41; Luke 17:26–30).

The significance and *object* of His coming is to gather the harvest,[2] to gather together his elect,[3] to deliver His children from their great tribulation,[4] to receive them

---

[1] Luke 21:25, 26, "And there shall be signs in sun and moon and stars. And upon the earth distress of nations, in perplexity for the roaring of the sea and the billows; men fainting for fear, and for expectation of the things which are coming on the world, for the powers of the heavens shall be shaken."

[2] Matt. 13:30, 39, "Let both grow together until the harvest; and in the time of the harvest I will say to the reapers, Gather up first the tares and bind them in bundles to burn them; but gather the wheat unto my barn. . . . And the harvest is the end of the world; and the reapers are angels."

[3] Matt. 24:31, "And he shall send forth his angels with a great sound of a trumpet, and they shall gather together his elect from the four winds, from one end of heaven to the other."

[4] Luke 21:28, "But when these things begin to come to pass, look up, and lift up your heads; because your redemption draweth nigh."

unto Himself,[1] to celebrate the marriage feast with His faithful servants (Luke 12:35-40), to make a reckoning with His servants,[2] to requite the unfaithful,[3] to raise up all the believing dead,[4] both the evil and the good[5]—even to render unto every man according to his deeds (Matt. 16:27; 24:30, 51; 25:31-46), and to sever the wicked from among the righteous, and to cast them into the furnace of fire (Matt. 13:41, 42, 49, 50).

Jesus also describes the *manner* of His coming and of His appearance. He comes of His own free-will (John 14:3), not in a state of humiliation, but in His glory (Matt. 25:31)—in the glory of His Father with the Holy angels (Matt. 16:27, Mark 8:38), with the clouds of heaven (Mark 14:62), with great power (Mark 13:26) and great glory (Luke 21:27). With reference to those who are yet dwelling on earth at His coming, it will be as unexpectedly as a thief in the night (Matt. 24:43; Luke 12:39)—suddenly as a snare (Luke 21:34, 35), as

---

[1] John 14:3, "And if I go and prepare a place for you, I come again, and will receive you unto myself; that where I am, there ye may be also."

[2] Matt. 25:19, "Now after a long time the lord of those servants cometh, and make a reckoning with them."

[3] Luke 12:46, "The lord of that servant shall come in a day when he expecteth not, and in an hour when he knoweth not, and shall cut him asunder, and appoint his portion with the unfaithful."

[4] John 6:39, 40, "And this is the will of him that sent me, that of all that which he hath given me I should lose nothing, but should raise it up at the last day. For this is the will of my Father, that every one that beholdeth the Son and believeth on him, should have eternal life; and I will raise him up at the last day."

[5] John 5:28, 29, "For the hour cometh, in which all that are in the tombs shall hear his voice, and shall come forth; they that have done good, unto the the resurrection of life; and they that have done ill unto the resurrection of judgment."

the lightning cometh forth from the east, and is seen even unto the west (Matt. 24:27; Luke 17:24).

[ANALYSIS: 1) The time of the Second Coming the Father has reserved for Himself; 2) Christ nowhere teaches that it shall be in the immediate future; 3) all the passages cited for this view refer to the destruction of Jerusalem, which is a type of the Final Coming; 4) there may be an unexpected long delay; 5) there was no error on the part of Jesus; 6) the true nature of biblical prophecy; 7) Jesus warns His disciples not to be deceived; 8) the signs of His return; 9) at His return the great mass of men are still unconverted; 10) the object of His coming; 11) the manner of His coming.]

§ 39. *The General Resurrection of All Men.*

That there is a resurrection from the dead, Christ distinctly teaches in His answer to the Sadducees (Matt. 22:23–32; Mark 12:18–27; Luke 20:27–38).[1]

The *time* of the resurrection of believers is designated as "the Last Day."[2]

When the Final Coming of Christ shall take place the last day of the present age of the world shall dawn, and then shall the resurrection of the dead take place. This is also implied in John 5:27–29,[3] where it is connected with the Judgment.

---

[1] Matt. 22:29–32, "Ye do err not knowing the Scriptures nor the power of God. For in the resurrection they neither marry, nor are given in marriage, but are as angels in heaven. But as touching the resurrection of the dead, have ye not read that which was spoken unto you by God, saying, I am the God of Abraham, and the God of Isaac, and the God of Jacob? God is not the God of the dead, but of the living."

[2] John 6:39, 40, 44, 54, "And I will raise him up at the last day."

[3] John 5:27, 28, "And he gave him authority to execute judgment, because he is the Son of Man. Marvel not at this; for the hour cometh, in which all that are in the tombs shall hear his voice, and shall come forth."

## GENERAL RESURRECTION OF MEN. 109

Jesus teaches that believers will arise on the Last Day.[1]

Equally clear is Christ's teaching concerning the resurrection of unbelievers. "He that rejecteth me, and receiveth not my sayings, hath one that judgeth him: the word that I spake, the same shall judge him in the last day" (John 12:48). Hence Christ says, in John 5:28, 29, "For the hour cometh, in which all that are in the tombs shall hear his voice, and shall come forth; they that have done good, unto the resurrection of life; and they that have done ill, unto the resurrection of judgment." Believers are not raised *unto* judgment, for "he that believeth on him is not judged" (John 3:18), "they come not *into* judgment" (John 5:24), but they shall come forth "unto the resurrection of life" (John 5:29), inasmuch as they have already received eternal life by faith (John 5:24). Unbelievers do not attain "unto the resurrection of life," but they come forth "unto the resurrection of judgment" (John 5:29); for Christ distinctly says that "he that believeth not hath been judged already" (John 3:18), for "he that believeth not the Son shall not see life, but the wrath of God abideth on him" (John 3:36). This resurrection of evil-doers (John 5:29) is to be understood as a delivering over to eternal punishment and misery (Matt. 25:41, 46), and is compared by Christ to the fire which consumes the cut-away branches.[2]

---

[1] John 6:40, "For this is the will of my Father, that every one that beholdeth the Son, and believeth on him, should have eternal life; and I will raise him up at the last day." Compare also John 6:44, 54; 11:23-26; Luke 14:14.

[2] John 15:6, "If a man abide not in me, he is cast forth as a branch, and is withered; and they gather them, and cast them into the fire, and they are burned."

With reference to the *nature of the resurrection bodies* of believers, Christ gives us this additional information, that "they neither marry, nor are given in marriage" (Matt. 22:30), "neither can they die any more: for they are equal unto the angels, and are sons of God, being sons of the resurrection" (Luke 20:36).

Jesus ascribes the *Cause* and *Author* of the resurrection to "the power of God" (Matt. 22:29), to the Father and the Son, "for as the Father raiseth the dead and quickeneth them, even so the Son also quickeneth whom he will" (John 5:21); "and this is the will of him that sent me that of all that which he hath given me I should lose nothing, but should raise it up at the last day" (John 6:39), "and I will raise him up at the last day" (*vers.* 40, 44), "for the hour cometh in which all that are in the tombs shall hear the voice of the Son of God, and shall come forth" (John 5:28, 29).

Although Christ distinguishes between the resurrection of believers and unbelievers (John 5:28, 29), and between the judgment that overtakes them both (Matt. 25:31–46), He nowhere speaks of two resurrections, the one of the good, the other of the evil, separated by a longer or shorter period of time. There is indeed an order of resurrection; but He speaks of only one event, which appears to be a simultaneous event (John 5:28, 29), at a certain definite time, "the last day" (John 6:39, 40), at the Day of Judgment, in the Last Day (John 12:48), when the Son of Man shall come in His glory, and before Him shall be gathered all the nations (Matt. 25:31–33). We may have occasion to modify this statement, as there are two passages (Luke 14:14; 20:35, 36) which have to be more fully discussed with the doctrine of the first resurrection, as taught by John.

[ANALYSIS: 1) There is to be a resurrection of the dead; 2) the time is distinctly stated as the Last Day; 3) believers shall attain unto the resurrection of life; 4) unbelievers shall come forth unto the resurrection of judgment; 5) the nature of the risen bodies of believers; 6) the Cause and Author of the resurrection; 7) Christ makes a distinction of order, but not of time, between the resurrection of believers and of unbelievers.]

## § 40. *The Final Judgment.*

At Christ's Second Coming, the Last Judgment, which is looked forward to by prophecy, shall take place.[1] No distinction, save that of order, is drawn by Christ in the description of the wonders of the Last Day. According to His statements, His Second Coming, the resurrection of the dead, and the Last Judgment, shall all occur at one period, and not at several periods; and this period is defined as the Last Day, as the end of the world.[2]

It is the Triune God who comes to *judge*. Sometimes it is described as the act of God the Father,[3]

---

[1] Matt. 25:31, 32, "But when the Son of Man shall come in his glory, . . . before him shall be gathered all the nations; and he shall separate them one from another."

Matt. 11:22, "It shall be more tolerable for Tyre and Sidon in the day of judgment than for you."

Matt. 12:36, "And I say unto you, that every idle word that men shall speak, they shall give account thereof in the day of judgment."

[2] Matt. 13:39-43, "The harvest is the end of the world; and the reapers are angels. As therefore the tares are gathered up and burned with fire; so shall it be in the end of the world. The Son of Man shall send forth his angels, and they shall gather out of his kingdom all things that cause stumbling, and them that do iniquity, and shall cast them into the furnace of fire. . . . Then shall the righteous shine forth as the sun in the Kingdom of their Father."

[3] Matt. 18:35, "So shall also my heavenly Father do unto you, if ye forgive not every one his brother from your hearts."

sometimes as the act of the Son of Man,[1] unto whom the Father hath given "authority to execute judgment, because he is the Son of Man" (John 5:27); "for neither doth the Father judge any man, but He hath given all judgment unto the Son, that all may honor the Son, even as they honor the Father" (John 5:22, 23). This judgment of the Son is "*righteous*, because I seek not mine own will, but the will of Him that sent me" (John 5:30), and His judgment is *true*, for I am not alone, but I and the Father that sent me" (John 8:16).

This judgment is *universal*. All men shall be divided into two classes—the righteous on the right hand, and the wicked on the left hand (Matt. 25:33, 34, 41). *Believers* shall attain "the resurrection of life" (John 5:29), and shall appear *at the judgment*, but shall not come *into judgment* (John 5:24), and to them Christ shall say: "Come ye blessed of my Father, inherit the kingdom prepared for you from the foundation of the world. . . . And the righteous shall go away into eternal life" (Matt. 25:34, 46). *Unbelievers* shall come forth "unto the resurrection of judgment" (John

---

Matt. 22:11, 13, "But when the king came in to behold the guests, he saw there a man which had not on a wedding garment. . . . Then the king said to the servants, bind him hand and foot, and cast him out into the outer darkness."

Luke 18:7, "Shall not God avenge his elect, which cry to him day and night."

[1] Matt. 25:31, 32, "When the Son of Man shall come in his glory, . . . then shall he sit on the throne of his glory; and before him shall be gathered all the nations; and he shall separate them one from another."

Matt. 13:41, "The Son of Man shall send forth his angels."

Matt. 24:44, 50, 51, "For in an hour that ye think not the Son of Man cometh, . . . and shall cut him asunder, and appoint his portion with the hypocrites."

## THE FINAL JUDGMENT. 113

5:29); and to them Christ shall say: "Depart from me, ye cursed, into the eternal fire which is prepared for the devil and his angels. . . . And these shall go away into eternal punishment" (Matt. 25:41, 46).

Christ also clearly states what the great *principle* of judgment is, which decides the lot of every one appearing before the Throne of His Glory" (Matt. 25:31). It is faith in Jesus Christ as the Son of God, whom the Father hath sent to give life unto the world.[1]

He that *believeth* on the Son hath eternal life" (John 3:36), hath it already in this life, and at death in the particular judgment that visits him, still hath this eternal life, and his soul enters upon a state of joy with Christ, and waits for the Second Coming of Christ, at the Last Day, to attain "unto the resurrection of life" (John 5:29), then to appear before the judgment seat of Christ, but not to come into judgment, for the believer hath already in this life passed out of death into life (John 5:24).

"He that *believeth not* the Son shall not see life" (John 3:36), hath not passed out of death into life (John 5:24), "but the wrath of God abideth on him" (John 3:36), in this life, and in the life of the soul

---

[1] John 6:29, "This is the work of God, that ye believe on him whom he hath sent;" *ver.* 27, "Work for the meat which abideth unto eternal life, which the Son of Man shall give you;" *ver.* 33, "for the bread of God is that which cometh down out of heaven, and giveth life unto the world ;" *vers.* 50, 51, "This is the bread which cometh down out of heaven, that a man may eat thereof, and not die. I am the living bread, which came down out of heaven; if any man eat of this bread, he shall live forever ; yea and the bread which I will give is my flesh, for the life of the world."

John 5:40, "Ye will not come to me, that ye may have life."

John 8:24 "Except ye believe that I am he, ye shall die in your sins."

after death is waiting for the Last Day of Judgment; and at the judgment, when the unbeliever shall arise " unto the resurrection of judgment," then because he hath not on the wedding-garment (faith in Christ), "the king shall say to his servants, bind him hand and foot, and cast him out into the outer darkness " (Matt. 22:11–13; compare also Matt. 25:31–46).

The *rule* or *norm* of judgment is the Word of Christ, for " the word that I spake, the same shall judge him in the last day" (John 12:48).

Christ also speaks of the angels as being present at the Day of Judgment, for the Son of Man "shall send forth his angels with a great sound of a trumpet, and they shall gather together his elect from the four winds, from one end of heaven to the other" (Matt. 24:31), "and they shall gather out of his Kingdom all things that cause stumbling, and them that do iniquity, and shall cast them into the furnace of fire" (Matt. 13:41, 42), and sever the wicked from among the righteous" (*ver.* 49).

[ANALYSIS: 1) This occurs at the Last Day; 2) an act of the Triune God; 3) this Judgment is universal; 4) the great principle of Judgment; 5) the norm of Judgment; the service of the angels.]

## § 41. *The End of the World.*

The Final Judgment shall take place "in the last day" (John 12:48). The harvest is "the end of the world," "at the consummation of the age" (Matt. 13:39, 40). We are not so to limit the expression "the last day," as to embrace of necessity only twelve or twenty-four hours; nor, on the other hand, is it to be stretched out over a vague, indeterminate series of ages. We cannot compute the time necessary for its wonders from the data of the natural. The Last Day

## THE END OF THE WORLD.

brings about "the end of the world;" then the completion of the age takes place, and with this consummation is linked the Coming of Christ, the resurrection of the dead, and the Judgment.

The Evangelists represent Christ as using four different Greek words (*æon, ge, oikoumene, kosmos*), all of which we can translate by the word "world."

1) Christ says there is to be "the end of the *æon*" (Matt. 13:39-41), "the consummation of the age." This word *æon* contemplates the world as a thing relating to time, and has sometimes the force of age. The world is called an "*æon*," as existing in time, in contrast with the fleeting things upon it. Man passes away, but the *æon*, the world, abideth. Its true meaning in this connection, with reference to Christ's expressions concerning the end of the world, and with reference to the question of the disciples, "What shall be the sign of thy *Parousia*," and "of the consummation of the age?" (Matt. 24:3), is, that this word *æon* refers to the period or age preceding Christ's return. This *æon* began with Christ's first coming; it is this age, or *æon*, which is now progressing. This same age or *æon* shall have its consummation. This world or time as it now exists, or this world as time, shall pass away, and introduce the world to come" (Mark 10:30; Luke 18:30)—"the coming age"—which shall dawn at Christ's Second Coming.

2) This *ge, earth*, the world as a thing of land, in space (in contradistinction to *æon*, which contemplates the world as a thing of time), shall also pass away. With heaven, the term *ge, earth*, constitutes a term for the whole universe. This solid earth shall pass away. "Heaven and *earth* shall pass away, but my words shall not pass away" (Matt. 24:35).

3) Christ does not say that the *oikumene, the inhabited earth*, is to come to an end. On it the terrors accompanying Christ's Second Coming are to descend (Luke 21:26). The inhabited earth, however, ceases to be the habitation of man, as it now is; for this *ge, earth*, shall pass away.

4) The word *kosmos* designates the universe as a world of order. It includes this earth, the heavens, and the heavenly bodies. Christ does not say that the *kosmos* will come to an end, but it shall be changed and greatly disturbed by the events of the Last Day. "The sun shall be darkened, and the moon shall not give her light, and the stars shall fall from heaven, and the powers of the heavens shall be shaken" (Matt. 24:29; Mark 13:24, 25; Luke 21:25, 26). It is worthy of notice, that while the stars are here represented as falling from heaven, the powers of heaven are represented as shaken. This may imply, that while the whole universe comes to its consummation, the disturbances will not be equally great throughout the whole.

[ANALYSIS: 1) Significance of the term "the last day;" 2) then takes place the consummation of the age; 3) four Greek words are used in the New Testament to designate "the world;" 4) this *æon*, as a world of time, shall pass away; 5) this *ge*, as a world of space, shall pass away; 6) on this *oikumene*, inhabited world, the terrors of the Second Coming are to descend; 7) this *kosmos*, as a world of order, shall be changed.]

## § 42. *Eternal Life.*

Although eternal life begins even in this present time (John 3:36; 5:24), its fullness is only reached in the completed Kingdom of God, for "eternal life" forms the contrast to "this world" (John 12:25). The

## ETERNAL LIFE. 117

expected inheritance is described as eternal life (Matt. 19:29; 25:34). Jesus always connects His return with the absolute consummation of all things, and never with an earthly realization of the Kingdom of God. There is, indeed, no word whatever, on the part of Jesus, of a restoration of the Kingdom of Israel. If "heaven and earth shall pass away" (Matt. 5:18; 24:35), then " in the regeneration when the Son of Man shall sit on the throne of His glory " (Matt. 19:28), when the faithful shall eat and drink at the table of the Lord in His Kingdom (Luke 22:30), the earth will no longer find itself in its present condition. What takes place, Christ nowhere says, but the contrast between earth and heaven is abolished.

That this final consummation is a heavenly one, Christ everywhere teaches. As Christ came from heaven (John 3:31), so He has gone to heaven, and comes to take His own thither (John 14:2, 3). Thither the unbelievers cannot follow Him (John 8:21). But He has promised His own that they are to be where He is (John 12:26; 17:24). Jesus, accordingly, describes the life of the risen as a life which is similar to that of the angels—a life which belongs to the heavenly world, and is raised above the conditions of earthly life (Mark 12:25), a life, however, which is still conceived of as being in a corresponding corporeity, because otherwise there could be no mention made of a resurrection. If those who are made perfect see God (Matt. 5:8), it is evident also from this that, in the completed Kingdom of God, the contrast between heaven and earth is abolished, and God makes His abode in the midst of His sons (Matt. 5:9).

Believers, with body and soul reunited, shall not simply exist, but they have life—the true life, the life of spotless holiness, of pure joy, and of unspeakable glory. It is *eternal* life, associated with joys which are *perpetual*, without intermission or cessation, and which do not end. No one has ever questioned that the joy and glory of the risen believer shall ever have an end. The body, soul, and spirit shall enter upon the full fruition of this eternal life. When Christ says, in Matt. 25:46, "and the righteous shall go into eternal life," it is implied that the risen and glorified *body* shall enter upon a new form of existence, in which the perfected body, free from pain, from sickness, change, natural limitations and death, shall forever abide the perfect organ of the purified soul and spirit. It is implied that the *soul*, redeemed from all error, purified from all sin, possessed of the most perfect and most delightful knowledge, illumined by the direct vision of God, has entered upon its eternal and perpetual inheritance. It is implied that the *Spirit* of Man is now in perfect fellowship with the Triune God; that the will is perfect in its freedom, filled with supreme love to God, all its desires in perfect consonance with the Divine will, and in conformity with the Divine holiness. It is a complete fellowship with Christ (John 14:3)—a beholding of the glory of Christ (John 17:24). It is a glorious participation in the Kingdom of God (Matt. 25:34).

[ANALYSIS: 1) The fullness of eternal life attained after the resurrection; 2) this final consummation is a heavenly one; 3) the contrast between heaven and earth is abolished; 4) it is life, perpetual, and without end; 5) the glory of the body; 6) of the soul; 7) of the spirit.]

## § 43. *Eternal Death.*

Christ clearly teaches a twofold character of eternity. He marks eternal life as the portion of one class, and eternal punishment the portion of the other. The same adjectives qualify both. Especially emphatic are Matt. 25:41, 46, "Depart from me, ye cursed, into the eternal fire which is prepared for the Devil and his angels;" "and these shall go away into eternal punishment." If this term, *aionios*, translated *eternal*, allows us to think that punishment can have an end, it allows us to think that the joys of heaven can have an end; if the joy of the pious and the elect is eternal, without end, it means that the anguish of the godless is eternal, without end; for the same adjective is used to describe their respective conditions (Matt. 25:46).

The word *aionios*, *eternal*, occurs *thirty* times in the Gospels, twenty-five times in the sayings of Jesus. Once Christ uses the word of our eternal habitations in heaven (Luke 16:9), once of eternal punishment (Matt. 25:46), once of eternal sin (Mark 3:29), twice of eternal fire (Matt. 18:8; 25:41), and twenty times of eternal life. [Twice in Matthew,[1] once in Mark (10:30), once in Luke (18:30), and sixteen times in John.[2]] The word is always used by Him with reference to the future, and refers either to eternal life or to eternal punishment. Men may theorize and speculate as they please as to the meaning of *aionios*. No distinction can be drawn between the meaning of the word as applied to the blessedness of the righteous, and to the misery of the wicked; for if the punishment is not eternal, perpetual, unceasing, then eternal life is also not eternal, not perpetual, but will also cease. Christ sees clearly and distinctly into the future; it lies open before His vision. For the believer there is an eternity of life, and for the unbeliever

---

[1] Matt. 19:29; 25:46.
[2] John 3:15, 16, 36; 4:14, 36; 5:24, 39; 6:27, 40, 47, 54; 10:28; 12:25, 50; 17:2, 3.

there is an eternity of sin (Mark 3:29), and a perpetuity of punishment (Mark. 9:43).

Christ speaks of a *gehenna*, hell, "the unquenchable fire" (Mark 9:43, 45), "where their worm dieth not, and the fire is not quenched" (*vers.* 47, 48). The worm that preys upon the body is an image of the gnawing worm of conscience, and the fire that consumes is but a faint emblem of the misery which consumes but cannot annihilate the lost, and which is to continue without end. The expression "Gehenna of fire" occurs in Matt. 5:22; 18:9. *Gehenna* is represented as the place of the destruction of the body (Matt. 5:29, 30)—as a place of destruction to both soul and body (Matt. 10: 28); as the place of wickedness for the children of hell (Matt. 23:15). It is represented as the place of damnation (Matt. 23:33); and God is represented as that Supreme Being who has power to cast into Gehenna, and who will assign to it the wicked (Matt. 10:28; Luke 12: 5; Matt. 23:33).

There is no misunderstanding of the difference between inheriting the Kingdom of God (Matt. 25:34), and being cast into the Gehenna of fire. *Gehenna* is the Greek representative for *Ge-Hinnom*—more fully, *Ge-ben-Hinnom*, the name of a valley lying to the south of Jerusalem, where the idolatrous Israelites had formerly burned their children in the rites celebrated in honor of Moloch (Jer. 7:31). Afterwards, to mark the abhorrence of these cruel rites, this valley was polluted with every kind of filth; the carcasses of animals and the dead bodies of criminals were thrown into it, and, in order to avoid the pestilence which would otherwise have broken forth, fires were kept continually burning. Hence, the Valley of Hinnom, Gehenna, furnished one of the most obvious, vivid, and terrible natural symbols to designate the abode of all horror, pollution and shame. This name, *Gehenna* of fire, was therefore very naturally transferred to that place or condition, where the wicked after the resurrection, will suffer punishment. The Hades in which the rich man of Luke 16:23 found himself is the foretaste, the fore-hell, where the souls of the wicked, " in torments " and " anguish " (Luke 16:23, 24, 25), await the Day of Judgment, and then, after the resurrection and the publishing of the judgment, " shall the wicked go away into eternal punishment " (Matt. 25:46), to be cast into Gehenna, the hell proper, the place and condition of the lost after the resurrection, where body and soul reunited shall enter upon the lot of the unfaithful (Luke 12:46).

One of the most constant of images, under which the misery and torments of the lost is represented, is that of fire. Fire is the symbol of the Divine judgment of wrath (Matt. 5:22), the terrors of which are made vivid by this image. In Matt. 3:10, the godless are represented as a tree, hewn down and cast into the fire. In Matt. 3:12, the chaff, the godless, separated with the winnowing fan of Divine judgment, is burned with unquenchable fire. In Matt. 13:42, the wicked are said to be cast into the furnace of fire. In all these cases fire is a most vivid symbol of the Divine judgment, for the end of sinners is more dreadful than the most dreadful death (Matt. 18:6).

But fire is not the only image under which the misery of the lost is presented. Light is a thing of beauty, and the cutting off of all light around us would be the cutting off of all joy. Darkness is therefore used, as a symbol of evil and terror, to designate the sad estate of the lost. Those who are excluded from the Kingdom of God are cast into the outer darkness (Matt. 8: 12; 22:13; 25:30). In both these images of fire and darkness, it is implied that the godless are delivered up to a fate to whose terrors they are by no means unsusceptible—a fate which they feel, rather, "with weeping and gnashing of teeth." It is wonderful with what a steady and awful reiteration and emphasis the terrible effect is described. Seven times these terms are found in combination.[1] It is always our Lord who utters them. The terms are always the same, and always refer to the misery and torments of the lost.

That there are to be degrees of punishment, according to the quality and measure of sins, is clearly taught by Christ (Matt. 11:24; Luke 12:47, 48; Matt. 23:15).[2]

The destruction and misery of the wicked after the resurrection cannot be thought of as complete *annihilation;* for, in that case, it would not be *better* for the wicked if they had never been born (Mark 14:21), and the very idea of *eternal, unquenchable* fire (Matt. 25:41; Mark 9:43, 48) shows that it does not consume the objects of punishment, because, if so, it would cease to burn for them. The eternity of the punishment in hell is the necessary correlate of the idea that the decision in the Messianic judgment is the final one. Where there is a sin which can never be forgiven (Matt. 12:32), and is eternal (Mark 3:29), there must also be an eternal punishment (Matt. 25:46).

We have thus traced the teaching of Jesus concerning the Last Things through all its different bearings upon the life of the individual and upon the end of the world. We have sought simply to present the fundamental truths and doctrines which He taught on this

---

[1] Matt. 8:12; 13:42, 50; 22:13; 24:51; 25:30; Luke 13:28.
[2] See § 37, p. 100.

important topic. In our succeeding discussion, we will see in how far the Apostles built upon this same doctrine, and wherein the different phases of the doctrine are more fully developed.

[ANALYSIS: 1) Christ clearly teaches a twofold character of eternity ; 2) the same adjective qualifies both conditions ; 3) the term *aionios* ; 4) Christ speaks of a *Gehenna* of unquenchable fire ; 5) the meaning of Gehenna ; 6) fire as a symbol of eternal death ; 7) darkness as a symbol of eternal death ; 8) there are degrees of punishment ; 9) Christ knows of no annihilation of the wicked ; 10) where there is eternal sin, there is also eternal punishment.]

# SECTION II.

## THE TEACHING OF JESUS ACCORDING TO JOHN.

### § 44. *General Divisions.*

As in the contemplation of the utterances of Christ according to the Synoptists, so also here it is of the greatest importance to observe the central thought by which the Lord's words, as presented by John, are dominated, in order thereby to gain light upon the separate parts. On close examination it cannot be denied that the doctrine of His own Person and Work is the principal theme of the speeches of Christ as recorded in this Gospel, and it is therefore best to represent the testimony of Jesus under the following heads:

1) Christology, or the doctrine of His Person;
2) The salvation which is to be found in Him (Soteriology);
3) The appropriation of salvation (Pneumatology);
4) The historical realization of salvation;
5) The consummation of salvation.[1]

Van Oosterzee follows this order most closely.[2] His divisions are: 1) The Son of God in the flesh; 2) In His relation to the Father; 3) in His relation to the world; 4) in relation to His disciples; 5) in relation to His future.

[ANALYSIS: 1) Importance of tracing the central thought; 2) teaching to be presented under five heads; 3) the divisions of Van Oosterzee.]

---

[1] Compare *Weiss*, §§ 143–157.
[2] See his *Theol. of New Testament*, pp. 135–174.

# CHAPTER VIII.

### CHRISTOLOGY.

§ 45. *The Sending of the Only-begotten Son.*[1]

Jesus grounds His claim for the Messianic character of His mission on the fact that He has been sent as the Only-begotten Son of the Father (John 17, 3, 8, 21, 23, 25; 5:38; 6:29). He everywhere implies that, in the truest and completest sense, He has been sent by God; that He fulfills all the duties, and can claim all the rights, of One so sent. He has not assumed this calling of His own will (7:28; 8:42), but He has come in His Father's name (5:43). As His messenger, God has commissioned Him with what He is to say (12:49), and Jesus speaks only what God gave Him (12:50; 8:16, 26, 40). It is the purpose of His life to do the will of God (6:38; 4:34), and to finish the work which He who sent Him gave Him to do (9:4). For this the Father helps Him (8:29), and authenticates Him as His messenger by works which, without His help, none can do (11:42).

His relation to God's other messengers is expressly characterized in this way, that THE FATHER hath consecrated Him and sent Him (10:36). He is the Only-begotten Son (3:16, 18), sent by God, that whosoever believeth on Him should not perish, but have eternal life.

The Father has intrusted Him with full Messianic authority (17:2, 4); He has committed to Him the Messianic works of raising the dead and of judgment (5:21,

---

[1] Compare *Weiss*, § 143.

22), as also the gift of the Spirit promised for Messianic times (15:26; 16:7). These works are but the type and prelude of those works which He will execute one day in bringing about the final consummation (5:24-29). These miracles testify that the Father has sent Jesus (5:36); that He is the Son of God, and that the Father has honored Him as such before all the world (8:54).

By these miracles it is shown that the Father is in the Son and works in Him as the perfect organ of His working on earth, inasmuch as He abides continually in Him (14:10), the actual centre of His life and of His works (17:23, "thou in me"). As the Father has life in Himself, so has He given to the Son to have life in Himself (5:26).

Jesus and the Father are One (10:30, 38), and He knows that those who are made partakers of the Messianic salvation are as safe in His hand as in the Almighty Hand of the Father (10:28, 29). Any separate working of the Father and the Son is excluded, as both are One in their working (14:9, 10).

[ANALYSIS: 1) Jesus claims that He has been sent as the Only-begotten Son of the Father; 2) that He speaks only what God commissioned Him; 3) that the Father helps Him; 4) who has committed to Him Messianic works; 5) which testify that He is the Son of God; 6) He claims further that the Father is in Him and works in Him; 7) that He and the Father are One, and One in their working.]

### § 46. *The Heavenly Origin of the Son of Man.*[1]

Jesus claims for Himself that He perfectly knows the Father (10:15; 17:25); and He is conscious that this knowledge is not to be traced to any point in His earthly life, but He describes it as a seeing of the Father unapproachable to every other (6:46; 3:11, 32),

[1] Compare *Weiss*, § 144.

which He has had with the Father Himself (8:38). He points thereby to a prehistorical existence with the Father, and He speaks of the glory which He had with the Father before the foundation of the world, which He hopes to receive as the God-Man at His exaltation (17:5). Jesus knew Himself from eternity to be the Son of God, because the Father loved Him before the foundation of the world (17:24).

The Father, from whom He is, has sent Him; and so He has come into the earthly world (8:42), although He was not of this world, but from above (8:23). To this heavenly origin Jesus points back, when His historical coming into the world (3:19; 9:39; 12:46) is preceded by His going out from the Father (16:27, 28; 17:8).

He has come down from heaven to earth, because His Messianic calling required His appearing upon earth, to fulfill the will of Him who sent Him; and this will of God was directed to the Messianic blessing of men—a blessing which finds its consummation in the resurrection (6:38–40); as also in the execution of the Messianic Judgment, which the Father has committed to the Son (5:22–29), just because He is the Son of Man (*ver.* 27). He must appear as Man among men, in order to tell them the truth (8:40), which brings life. Just because He thereby offers them salvation, He can also execute judgment on them, when they have decided either for or against it.

Even in John, Jesus very frequently designates Himself as the Son of Man (1:51; 3:13, 14; etc.); and as the Son of man He awaits for His exaltation, which will serve the purpose of making Him known even to the world itself as He is, according to His original being (8:28).

In consequence of His entrance on the earthly historical life, Jesus, as a true man, is put under the Divine law (8:55; 15:10), which tells Him what He is to do (14:31) and what He is to suffer (10:17, 18; 18:11). Although, in virtue of His original existence with the Father, He possessed Divine glory and power, He lays aside their use while in the state of humiliation (17:24, 4, 5; 13:31, 32); and although He possesses full knowledge of God, which enables Him at any time to proclaim the truth, yet He always speaks what He has heard of the Father (12:49, 50; 8:26, 28; 15:15). It is clear, from His own testimony, that Jesus realized in His earthly life His relation to the Father as the God-Man.

Although, as the Son of God, He was from eternity the object of Divine love, as the Son became Man He must earn this love ever afresh by His own loving obedience (8:29; 10:17, 18; 15:10). Only as the incarnate Son can He designate the Father as the greater (14:28). The Son, who, in His heavenly existence with the Father, was equal to God in glory, claims that all who really love Him are to rejoice at His return, as the God-Man, to the Father, as He Himself rejoices (17:13), because His going to the Father, throned in glory, makes Him, as the God-Man, a partaker of that glory (17:5, 24).

[ANALYSIS: 1) The pre-existence of Jesus as the Son of God; 2) His glory from eternity; 3) His Heavenly Origin; 4) appeared on earth to fulfill the Messianic calling; 5) designates Himself the Son of Man; 6) as a true man is put under the law; 7) though possessing Divine power and knowledge, does not always exercise them; 8) as the incarnate Son He obeys the law; 9) and as the God-Man returns to the Father, becoming a partaker of His glory also according to His human nature.]

# CHAPTER IX.

### THE SALVATION IN CHRIST.[1]

### § 47. *Christ the Life of the World.*[2]

With John, also, Jesus begins His work with the proclamation that the Kingdom of God is at hand, and that it is necessary to fulfill the conditions under which only one can have a share in it (3:3, 5). The Kingdom of God (so also in the Synoptists) is not only future, but already present, for the believer *has* eternal life (3:36; 5:24; 6:47, 54); he has already passed from death to life (5:24). Bodily death cannot stop the continuance of this life (11:25); death does not in any way interfere with it (6:50, 51, 58; 8:51, 52; 11:26); resurrection unto life is not the condition, but the result, of this eternal life which the believer already possesses (6:40, 54).

Eternal life consists in the living, contemplative knowledge of God, as Christ has had it from eternity; for this is life eternal to know the only true God, and Jesus Christ, whom He did send (17:3). In the Son is this eternal life, and through Him do we receive this life (5:26; 6:57). Christ calls Himself The Life (11:25; 14:6); and this was the object of His mission, that He might communicate life to those who believe in His name (6:40; 3:15). As the simplest means of nourishment which supports the physical life is bread, Christ calls Himself the bread necessary for life (6:35, 48)—the

---

[1] This chapter deals mainly with the work of Christ, or Soteriology.

[2] Compare *Weiss*, § 146.

bread which gives life to the world (6:33, 50, 58). He is the Living Bread (6:51), inasmuch as the Living Father has given Him, with a view to His mission as the God-Man, to have life in Himself (6:57; 5:26). The means of revelation which procures for the world the true knowledge of God is His Word, which He calls the Living Water (4:10, 14; 7:37, 38), the Imperishable Food (6:27). As He is Himself the Author of life (11:25; 14:6), so are His Words life (6:63), and His preaching eternal life (12:49, 50).

[ANALYSIS: 1) The Kingdom of God is already present; 2) for the believer has already eternal life; 3) in what eternal life consists; 4) Christ calls Himself The Life; 5) and the Bread; 6) as He is the Author of life, so His Words are life.]

### § 48. *Christ the Light of the World.*[1]

Christ, as the One who brings the true knowledge of God, is the Light of the World (8:12; 9:5; 12:35, 36, 46). Whoever enters into connection with this Light-Giver has his whole being thereby laid bare (3:19–21); whoever follows Him does not walk in darkness, because he has a light which shows him the way (8:12), and is a child of Light (12:36).

Christ is the Truth (14:6); and to this end, indeed, did He come into the world, that He should bear witness unto the truth (18:37; 8:40). The truth of God in Christ has the power to deliver from the bondage of sin (8:32, 34, 36), and to work a life consecrated to God (17:17).

But Christ also brings a new revelation of God, which is especially designated as the love of God (3:16, 17). This love is an object of Christian knowledge; and those who will not know Christ as the Only-begotten Son sent from the Father have no knowledge of God, nor of His love (7:28; 8:19, 55; 15:21; 16:3).

[1] Compare *Weiss*, § 147.

[ANALYSIS: 1) Christ the Light of the World; 2) whoever follows Him is a child of Light; 3) Christ is the Truth; 4) and has revealed the Love of God.]

## § 49. *Christ the Saviour of the World.*[1]

The other side of the Messianic work is salvation from the destruction into which the world, on account of sin, falls at death. For the Messiah had to bring not only the consummation of salvation, but also deliverance from destruction (John 3:17; 12:47; 5:34; 10:9). Whoever dies in his sins is lost (8:21, 24). Believers even now pass out of death into life (5:24), and shall be raised up unto eternal life at the Last Day (6:39, 40).

As, according to the Synoptists, Jesus gives His life to be a *ransom*, so does He as the Good Shepherd (10:11, 14) lay down His life for the good of the sheep, that they may not become the prey of the wolf, and lose their soul in death (12:25). In this sense Jesus gives His flesh (in death) for the life of the world (6:51). As meat and drink sustain life, so His flesh and blood become the means by which the world, which has fallen under abiding death, is maintained in life (6:55). It is only because we have been delivered from death by His giving up His life, and our believing on Him, that we can receive eternal life in the other world (6:27, 29, 33, 40, 54).

Eternal life is obtained for us only by the death of Christ (3:14, 16); and though we shall not enter upon its full possession until after the resurrection (6:40), nevertheless whosoever believeth on Him already possesses it in this life (3:15).

[ANALYSIS: 1) Christ delivers us from destruction; 2) He is the Good Shepherd who lays down His life for His sheep; 3) by His death He has procured eternal life for us; 4) which can be ours already in this life.]

---

[1] Compare *Weiss*, § 148.

# CHAPTER X.

### THE APPROPRIATION OF SALVATION.[1]

§ 50. *Faith and Fellowship with Christ.*[2]

The subjective condition on which the obtaining of eternal life (3:15; 6:47) as well as deliverance from death depends (8:24), is designated as faith. The word *faith* is used, in the first place, to denote the confidence with which the word of another is accepted as true. Christ is *believed* when what He says is regarded as true (3:12; 4:21; 5:38; 8:45, 46; 10:37, 38; 14:11). If this faith refers to the facts which His Word announces, then it is the confident persuasion of the truth of those facts (3:12; 11:26; compare 9:18; 20:8). Thus Jesus demands faith in His Divine mission (11:42; 17:8, 21), in His coming from the Father (16:27), in His origin from above (8:23, 24), in His Oneness with the Father (14:10, 11), in His Messiahship (13:19). Faith is connected directly with the Person of Jesus ("believe on me"). Faith in the Son of God (3:16; 18:36; 6:40) is, according to 9:35–38, nothing else than the confident persuasion that Jesus is the Son of God (6:29), the Christ (9:22; 12:42).

Jesus is to be believed for the sake of His own Word (4:41); and we will believe Him, if we are not to render ourselves guilty of an unpardonable sin (12:48; 15:22). The hearing of His Word can lead but to faith and love (5:24), but it by no means leads to this necessarily. Only to those who are willing to hear His Word or His

---

[1] This chapter bears mainly on the work of the Holy Ghost, or Pneumatology.

[2] Compare *Weiss*, § 149.

testimony and receive it come faith and knowledge (17:8; 3:11, 12).

The believer, by the knowledge of God through Christ, receives a life rooted in Christ, and becomes conscious of being in Christ; and the important thing now is to continue in Christ. Christ must be personally appropriated by faith, and the true believer is in Christ, as the branch is rooted in the vine-stock (15:1, 5). Every believer is in Christ; but faith in Christ and being in Christ are as different as belief in the light (12:36) and being in the light. Being in Christ comes only as the blessed result of faith; it is the eternal life which Christ communicates to the believer. Being in Christ can abide only in so far as it is a conscious and willing act; as it realizes itself ever afresh in steady, personal self-surrender to Him from whom the believer has received his new life. Hence, Jesus exhorts to abide in Him (15:4). Whoever does not abide in Him has burst the bond which bound him to Christ, and falls under condemnation (15:6). This personal surrender to Christ, in which the new relation to Christ brought about by faith is perfected, is designated as love to Christ (14:15, 21, 23, 24; 16:27).

If the believer abides in Christ, then Christ promises to abide in him (15:4–6). Abiding in Christ is the condition of the continuance of eternal life, because only on this condition abides He in us, and gives us ever afresh the life of the true knowledge of God (6:56, 57). He only who abides in Christ can bring forth fruit (15:4), because then Christ abides in us and works this fruit (15:5).

[ANALYSIS: 1) Faith is the confident persuasion that Jesus is the Son of God; 2) the Christ; 3) it is sin not to believe His testimony; 4) hearing the Word leads to faith and knowledge; 5) faith in Christ leads to fellowship with Christ; 6) this fellowship continues as long as we abide in Christ; 7) is perfected by love to Christ; 8) and leads to the bringing forth of good fruit.]

### § 51. *Fellowship with God.*[1]

When we by faith appropriate Christ we have fellowship with Him, and, at the same time, a fellowship with the Father (John 17:21). This fellowship with the Father is constantly brought about by the mystical, living fellowship with Christ, and by the revelation of God given in it (17:23). That our whole moral life may be formed according to the will of God, there must be a divinely constituted beginning of it, which gives to it its specific character as a life born of God, just as the bodily birth gives character to the bodily life (3:3, 6).

[ANALYSIS: 1) Fellowship with God; 2) the new life.]

### § 52. *Keeping the Commandments of God.*[2]

He who loves Jesus will keep His Word (8:51), which is the same as the Word of the Father (14:23, 24; 17:6); he will keep His commandments (14:15, 21), which is at the same time a keeping of the commandments of God (15:10). Although love is the necessary effect of the perfect revelation of God, yet Jesus announces it as a new commandment (13:34; 15:12, 17), the fulfillment of which is a sign of discipleship (13:35). As fulfilling the commandments of Jesus is the result of love to Him (14:21), so the fulfilling of the Divine commandments is the result of love to God. If one looks at the Christian life from the ideal point of view, the believer has eternal life when he is born of God; for the new life is perfected all at once. He lives, therefore, no longer in sin. For in the Christian life there must be

---

[1] Compare *Weiss*, § 150.  [2] Compare *Weiss*, § 151.

a constant fulfilling of the Divine will, and there must be a development of the new life. The believer is again and again exhorted to continue in Christ and in God (15:4), to continue in love (15:17); he needs ever to be reminded of his Christian duty (13:14, 15), and Jesus has to pray the Father to keep His disciples from evil (17:11, 15).

And still the believer is regarded as yet sinning, for even the fruit-bearing branch requires further cleansing (15:2). As there is a danger of the believer falling away again into sin, our Saviour offers a motive why we should appropriate salvation. He promises His love to us as the reward of our love to Him when proved by obedience (14:21 ; 15:10, 14)—a gracious love to us, which brings about the highest gift of the Spirit (14:15, 16), and the love of the Father (14:21, 23), which assures us of the hearing of prayer (16:23, 26, 27).

As abiding in Christ or love to God proves itself by keeping His commandments, Jesus sets before the individual, at the resurrection, a destiny corresponding to His works (5:29); and he who does not shrink from self-sacrifice for Christ's sake shall receive an equivalent reward in his being honored by the Father (12:25, 22).

[ANALYSIS : 1) He who loves God will keep his commandments ; 2) the development of the new life ; 3) the motive why we should appropriate salvation lies in the love of Christ ; 4) and in the eternal glory promised by Christ.]

## CHAPTER XI.

### THE HISTORICAL REALIZATION OF SALVATION.

§ 53. *The Preparatory Revelation of God.*[1]

Israel possessed a revelation of God in prophecy, the last bearer of which was John the Baptist. It had indeed no direct vision of God, such as the Son had with the Father (6:46), and as Christians can have by Him; yet the Word of God came to individuals (10:35), or they saw the form of God (5:37) in vision or in a theophany. Though the Jews possessed a knowledge of God, in comparison with which that of the Samaritans is designated as a not knowing of God (4:22), nevertheless it was a mistake if they thought that by the possession of the Law and the Prophets, they already had eternal life (5:39, 40)—*i. e.*, the real saving blessing, as it was given only by the perfected revelation of God; and if on that account they would not come to Christ in order to receive it from Him alone (5:40). For these Old Testament writings had their essential significance only in this, that they testify of Christ (5:39, 46). The perfect revelation of God and the Messianic times come only with the incarnation of the Logos.

It is not merely to unbelieving Jews that Jesus points to the fact that the Scriptures testify of Him, but He shows even to the disciples how the Scriptures are fulfilled in His fate (13:18; 15:25; 17:12); and He does it with the express design, that they may be led thereby to believe that it is He of whom the Scriptures

[1] Compare *Weiss*, § 152.

prophesy (13:19). Jesus Himself takes it for granted that the blessings of the Messianic times prophesied in the prophets have come (6:45 ; 7:38), and he reveals himself to the Samaritan woman as the looked-for Messiah (4:25, 26, 29). When the Jews ask of Him a plain confession of His Messiahship (10:24), He evidently proclaims Himself to be the Son of God—the Promised Messiah (10:36). On the occasion of his Messianic triumphal entrance into Jerusalem, He allows Himself to be saluted by the people as King of Israel (12:13), and in the presence of Pilate He admits His Messianic Kingdom (18:37).

The law, as well as prophecy, was a preparatory revelation of God ; for those who do the truth are in God (3:21) and from God (8:47). The law works that inner state of mind which alone makes one receptive of the revelation of God in Christ. As Israel was the place for the revelation of God which was given in prophecy and in the law, so the earthly activity of Christ was by a Divine destination connected with Israel; only after His death could his glorification begin among the Gentiles; only when He has been exalted would He draw *all* men unto Him (12:32).

[ANALYSIS : 1) God had revealed Himself to Israel by prophecy; 2) this was not the perfected revelation of God ; 3) in Christ the Old Testament Scriptures are fulfilled ; 4) and He plainly confesses His Messiahship ; 5) the law was also a preparatory revelation ; 6) Christ's earthly activity was limited to Israel.]

§ 54. *Victory Over the Devil.*

God sent His Son into the world to save all men, that whosoever believeth on Him should not perish (3:16, 17). To gain the souls of men is the final aim of

---

[1] Compare *Weiss*, § 153.

Christ's prayer (17:21, 23). And humanity as a whole needs salvation, because men are sinful and need light (8:12; 9:5), life (6:33, 51), and deliverance (3:17; 12:47).

The reason lies in this, that the Devil rules men as a whole (14:30). Hence, the Devil is designated as "the prince of this world" (12:31; 16:11); and the world, in so far as it is ruled by him, is called "this world" (8:23; 12:31). It is the power of the Devil by which men are ruled when sin enslaves them (8:34); and this slavery to sin is the result of men's fleshly birth (3:3, 6).

The Devil is the author of sin, and he seduced men to sin to bring them to destruction. He is a murderer of men from the beginning (8:44), because he brought about death, spiritual, temporal, and eternal, and all the result of sin. The names given to this enemy of God and man describe his character ("Devil"—slanderer, 8:44; "Satan"—Adversary, 13:27; "the Evil One," 17:15).

Although the Devil is the ruler of the world, yet he has not the same influence by any means on all men. For as believers are under his influence only so far as they have sin, but otherwise in their deepest nature are ruled by God, so there are those also who, in their deepest being, allow themselves to be ruled by the Devil (8:37, 40, 44, 55). He who allows himself to be ruled by the Devil cannot hear the Words of God (8:47), neither understand and come to knowledge (8:43), much less believe on Christ (12:39). From 15:22-25 we learn that the hatred of the Jews toward Christ was inexcusable, and therefore self-condemned sin. Even in the betrayal of Judas, a Divine purpose had to be executed (13:18; 17:12); and yet that deed abides a work of the Devil (13:2, 27), which Judas did because he had made himself the organ of the Devil (6:70). Jesus explicitly states that a Divine judgment of hardening comes upon men who continue in their sins (9:39, 41). If those who do not wish to be convicted of their sins hate the light that has come into the world, and flee from it, then that is their judgment (3:19, 20), inasmuch as it is therewith decided in their case that they cannot attain to faith, and thereby to salvation (3:18).

If the Son gives life to whom He will (5:21), and if in complete harmony with the Divine will (6:40), He gives it only to those who hear His voice and believe (5:24, 25), then does He in that case exercise His power as a Judge (5:27), in that He condemns those who hear not His voice to exclusion from salvation.

Christ, however, has broken the power of the Devil, and those who believe on the Son conquer him. Jesus does not in the least belong to the world of which the Devil is prince (8:23 ; 17:14, 16). Jesus has conquered the world that was hostile to Him (16:33), in that He, in spite of all its opposition and the power of the Devil, has organized a fellowship of disciples, who no more belong to the world, as the territory ruled by the Devil (15:19; 17:14), and has preserved them from the Devil and the destruction which he brings (17:12). Jesus brings the light, and although the darkness produced by the ruler of darkness sets itself in hostile opposition to destroy His work (12:35), yet it cannot overcome the light. The world, on the other hand, does not know Christ(17:25), inasmuch as it has surrendered itself to the dominion of the Devil and hates Jesus, who brings its sin to its consciousness (7:7).

While Jesus, in the free obedience of love, goes to face death (14:30, 31), and through death returns to the Father and is proved to be the Righteous One (16:10), the Devil is judged because he has slain the Righteous

One (16:11), but not in such a sense as though the Devil had even now ceased to rule the world. For the world, in its antagonism to the community of the disciples, so far as it is and continues to be the world, remains his kingdom (14:17, 19; 15:18, 19; 16:8; 17:9, 14–16). And the Evil One ever seeks even yet to destroy the children of God; but God keeps His children safe at Christ's intercession (17:15).

[ANALYSIS: 1) Christ has come to save all men; 2) all men need salvation; 3) because the Devil rules men as a whole; 4) the names given to this arch-enemy describe his character; 5) his influence not the same over all men; 6) the Divine judgment of hardening of heart; 7) leads to the Final Judgment; 8) the power of the Devil overcome for the believer; 9) the Devil is already judged; 10) but he still rules the world, so far as it is sinful.]

### § 55. *The Church of the Disciples.*[1]

No man can come to Christ if the Father does not draw him (6:44); but this drawing takes place through the Word, which produces faith (6:45). All such as do not reject the message, God gives to Christ (17:6, 9), that He may give them eternal life and keep them from destruction (17:2; 10:28, 29). Those who believe are taken out of the whole world of men to which they once belonged (17:6), so that they now no longer belong to it (15:19). No doubt all believers are given by God to Christ, and chosen by Him, but that this choosing is not irrevocable can be seen from the fact that even Judas was a chosen one (6:70; 13:18; 17:12).

The Twelve are the representatives of believers generally; they are the first circle of the disciples. By them the salvation brought by Christ is to be historically realized more widely in the world. Jesus, therefore, sends them out into the world as the Father has

---

[1] Compare *Weiss*, § 154.

## THE CHURCH OF THE DISCIPLES. 141

sent Him (17:18; 20:21). By their word the world is to be brought to believe (17:20), but their activity will be much more comprehensive than was His own during His earthly life. They will reap what He has sown (4:37, 38); they will even do greater works than He has done (14:12). His earthly activity was confined to Israel; only after His death will His activity extend to all men (12:24, 32); only then can the gathering together of the scattered children of God begin (11:52).

To enable the disciples to fulfill the task appointed for them, Jesus promises that after His death they would see Him alive again, and He them (16:16, 22). This promise was fulfilled after His resurrection, when Jesus again resumes His body (10:17, 18), and appears bodily to the disciples (20:20, 27). The joy on this account, once kindled (20:20), could no more be taken from them (16:22). They could now no more feel desolate, as orphans (14:18), because the union with Christ, as the Risen One, was exalted above the limits of finiteness, and was subject to no change nor to any separation.

The appearance of the Risen One was not to restore any more their earlier intercourse with Jesus, in which the disciples with all their cares came pleading to Him, but now they can turn directly to the Father, who will give to them in His stead (16:23). They must henceforth ask of the Father in His name (15:16; 14:13, 14); but this asking in Christ's name can naturally begin only when His earthly work is ended (16:24). Jesus promises a hearing of such prayer, whether it be that the Father hears and answers directly (15:16), or whether Christ mediates it for them (14:13, 14).

For the advancement of the great work of the Kingdom it is important not only that new believers be won

(17:20, 21), but that they be kept in faith. Since fresh sins are ever occurring, even in believers, which threaten to destroy their possession of salvation, there must be the grace of forgiveness. For this end has the risen Christ given to the Apostles, and through them to the Church,[1] the Holy Spirit, that His ministers may be able to announce the forgiveness of sins, or refuse it (20:22, 23).

[ANALYSIS: 1) The Father draws men to Christ through the Word; 2) believers are chosen of Christ; 3) the Twelve Disciples are to preach the Kingdom; 4) Jesus prepares them for their work by His resurrection; 5) He promises to hear their prayers; 6) the power of absolution given to the Twelve.]

---

[1] This section treats mainly of topics belonging to Ecclesiology.

# CHAPTER XII.

## THE CONSUMMATION OF SALVATION.

§ 56. *The Sending of the Holy Ghost.*[1]

When Christ had finished His work on earth and had gone to the Father, the final epoch of the history of salvation begins with the sending of the Spirit (16:7). As long as Jesus was seen on earth, He had not yet gone home to His Father (20:17). Jesus promises that He will send the Spirit (16:7) from the Father (15:26), which the Father will send at His request (14:16, 26). The Spirit is to carry forward the work begun by Christ during His earthly life, as His substitute, who needs to be replaced no more by a new one, as the Spirit of Truth will abide forever with and in the disciples (14:16, 17).

As Christ's substitute, the Spirit is throughout represented by Christ as a person, just as much as Christ represents Himself as a person. He is the other advocate, or *paraclete*, whom the Father, after Christ's departure, gives to believers as their abiding help (14:16), or sends (14:26); He proceeds from the Father (15:26), and comes to the disciples (16:7, 13), as does the Son (16:28); He is received (14:17) as Christ is (13:20), and is in them (14:17) as Christ is in them. He proclaims (16:13–15), testifies (15:26), and teaches (14:26), like the Son; nay, His teaching depends on a hearing and receiving (16:13, 14), as do the Words of Christ. Jesus

[1] Compare *Weiss*, § 155. This section bears mainly on the Doctrine of God, or Theology proper.

speaks of the Holy Ghost throughout as of a person who carries forward His work in believers, and who stands in a position of complete equality with Him.

The Spirit is Christ's substitute, because He is the Spirit of Truth (14:17; 15:26; 16:13), as Christ Himself was (14:6). He can have, therefore, but the task to communicate further to believers the revelation of God which appeared in Christ. He reminds the disciples of all that Jesus had said (14:26); and, since abiding in Christ depends on keeping the Words of Christ (15:7, 10), so the continuance of salvation given in Christ is secured only by the Spirit. But the Spirit is not only to preserve Christ's work in believers—He is to advance and perfect it. Jesus had yet many things to say unto them, but they were not able to bear it (16:12), but the Spirit will teach them all things (14:26), will guide them into all the truth (16:13). Not as though Christ's work were in that way reduced to an imperfect work. All enlightenment of the Spirit will help only towards this: to glorify Christ, while it teaches to know Him ever more perfectly (16:14). If the Spirit carries forward the work of Christ, then the whole activity of the Spirit is to be regarded as the maintaining and perfecting of the revelation of God given in Christ.

Inasmuch as the coming of Christ to the heart is conditioned by faith, so the coming of the Spirit has no immediate relation to the unbelieving world. When Jesus says that the Spirit will convict the world of three things—"of sin, of righteousness, and of judgment" (16:8, 11)—this can only take place through the Apostolic word, in that the Spirit is in believers and testifies by them. The sin of which the world is to be convicted is, that it does not believe on Christ (16:9, 15; 22:24); the world shall be convinced of the righteousness of Christ (16:10), for His exaltation to Heaven, His going to the Father, is but a confirmation that He is the Son of God, the Christ—an acknowledgment that He is the Redeemer of the world (6:62). The world is to be convinced of judgment, and also of what judgment awaits it so long as it remains under the prince of this world; because the display of Christ's righteousness, which serves for the condemnation of the world, and for the salvation of those who believe on Him, has received its contrast in the judgment which is passed upon the prince of this world (16:11; 12:31). And Jesus expressly says that in consequence of the gift of the Spirit (7:38, 39), streams of living waters shall come from believers, and a life-giving proclamation shall go forth by their testimony.

[ANALYSIS: 1) The sending of the Spirit; 2) the substitute for Christ; 3) personality of; 4) work of the Spirit in the heart of believers; 5) relation to the unbelieving world.]

## § 57. *The Fellowship of Believers.*[1]

The fellowship of believers forms a living unity, in virtue of their fellowship with God and Christ. Believers, won by the truth, join themselves to this community (17:11, 20, 21, 23). This unity is a unity of life which corresponds to the living unity of the Father and the Son (17:11, 22). The more their fellowship with the Father and the Son is realized, the more completely is their unity with one another perfected (17:23), and the joy of believers becomes thereby more perfect (15:11; 17:13). We have here a characterization of the *Church*[2] as to her inner nature; for the community of believers

---

[1] Compare *Weiss*, § 156.

[2] This section bears on Ecclesiology, or the Doctrine of the Church.

is the vine-stock which God has planted (15:1), the flock of God, whose Shepherd is Christ (10:1–15).

In the fellowship of believers, love as Christian, brotherly love, is realized, without being exhausted therein. But the Love which Jesus demands from His disciples is, after His example, self-sacrificing love towards one another (13:34, 35; 15:12, 17).

The world, or humanity, remaining in unbelief, stands in sharpest opposition to the fellowship of the children of God, who, like Christ Himself, no longer really belong to the world (17:14, 16). As the world hated Christ (15:18, 25), so it will hate and persecute His servants (15:19, 20; 17:14), even to death (16:2); and the world threatens believers not only with its enmity, but even more with its temptation (17:15).

In spite of the sharp contrast between the world and the Church, the Spirit is ever seeking, by means of believers as His organs, to lead the world from its sin of unbelief, and to testify to it of Christ. And according to John, Christ certainly does not teach an *Apokatastasis*. In the passage 12:32, it is simply said that Christ's death avails for all men who come unto Him, and as little as the *drawing* of the Father (6:44) does the drawing of the Son attain its end in all. The world, as such, remains unbelieving; and the contrast between the Kingdom of God and the kingdom of the world remains, until all the enemies of Christ are put under His feet.

[ANALYSIS: 1) The community of Saints; 2) the inner characterization of the Church; 3) Christian brotherly love; 4) sharp contrast between the world and the Kingdom of God; 5) this contrast is to abide.]

# PART II.

## THE PETRINE TEACHING.

# PART II.

## THE PETRINE TEACHING.

### INTRODUCTION.

§ 58. *The Petrine Type of Doctrine.*

It is natural to discuss the Petrine theology immediately after the presentation of the teaching of Jesus, both on account of the prominence that Peter occupied in the history of the Apostolic Church, and because he is the representative of the original Apostolic type of doctrine previous to the time of Paul. The first source of Petrine doctrine we find in the Acts of the Apostles, especially in that portion which treats of the history of the founding of the Church, and in the Epistles of Peter. To this type of Christianity the Jewish Christians attached themselves, and we find that James and Jude occupy the same doctrinal position as Peter. The same may be said of the doctrinal views presupposed or expressed in the Gospels according to Matthew and Mark.

[ANALYSIS: 1) Peter represents the original Apostolic type or doctrine; 2) sources of Petrine doctrine.]

§ 59. *The Discourses of Peter in the Acts of the Apostles.*[1]

The Acts form the chief source of information as to the nature of the teaching of the Apostles (Acts 2:42),

---
[1] Compare *Weiss*, § 35.

during the first ten years after the founding of the Church, before Paul began his successful career. Besides the great Pentecostal Sermon of the Apostle Peter (Acts 2:14-40), this book contains a sermon of his delivered in the Temple to the people (Acts 3:12-26), and also the Missionary Sermon delivered in the house of Cornelius (Acts 10:34-43). Since all three sermons have the expressed purpose of leading the hearers to believe in Jesus, they are peculiarly fitted to make us acquainted with the sum of the earliest Apostolic preaching. But we must also include the shorter apologies before the Sanhedrim (Acts 4:8-12, 19, 20; 5:29-32), the prayers of the Church (Acts 1:24, 25; 4:24-30), the discourse in which Peter suggests the choice of a twelfth Apostle to succeed Judas (Acts 1:16-22), and the transactions of the Apostolic Council regarding the Gentiles (Acts 15:7-29). It is Peter who speaks on these occasions, and we are justified in recognizing him as the leader of the Twelve, and in deducing from his words what the belief of the Church was. The discourse of Stephen (Acts 7:2-53) is of special importance, inasmuch as it refers, apologetically and polemically, to the first conflict that the preaching of the Gospel had with the national attachment to the law.

It is seldom that the discourses of the Acts of the Apostles have received in Biblical Theology the consideration which their significance deserves. Lechler is the first who has given an independent representation of the original preaching[1] of the Apostles as contained in the book of Acts. That which makes a separate representation of the views which these discourses contain desirable is, not so much on account of any peculiar sys-

---

[1] *The Apostolic and Post-Apostolic Times*, vol. 1, pp. 266-288.

tem of doctrine, but rather because they bring before us a special aspect of the preaching of the Apostles—namely, its ingathering and apologetic aspect—and allow us also to obtain a glimpse into the religious life of the Mother Church, and into the questions which stirred it in the earliest age.

[ANALYSIS: 1) The Pentecostal Sermon; 2) the Sermon in the Temple; 3) in the house of Cornelius; 4) shorter apologies before the Sanhedrim; 5) speech of Stephen; 6) Lechler discusses them separately; 7) separate presentation desirable.]

## § 60. *The First Epistle of Peter.*[1]

The principal source for the Petrine system of doctrine is the First Epistle of Peter. His Second Epistle, because it was not so widely diffused in the early Church, and on account of its close relation to the Epistle of Jude, will be discussed separately. The date of the composition of 1 Peter is still in question [Weiss dates it as early as 54 A. D.]; but it is highly probable that it was written about 63 A. D. It was written to the believers who were sojourners of the Dispersion in Asia Minor; but without doubt these Churches were mixed, composed of Jewish and Gentile Christians, and probably contained a large majority of converted heathen (3:6; 4:3). Its expressed purpose is hortatory, but the exhortation receives its coloring from the circumstances which surrounded these Churches, and is based throughout upon the saving facts of Christianity. Its peculiar leading idea appears to be the insoluble connection and succession of suffering and glory in the life of the believing Christian (3:17; 4:13; 5:10). The Epistle unites with its hortatory aim the other aim of establishing its readers, by means of its Apostolic testimony, in the

[1] Compare *Weiss*, § 36.

truth of the proclamation which had reached them (1 Pet. 5:12).

The peculiarities of the Petrine system which is contained in this Epistle are—1) its Jewish-Christian character; 2) its predominant tendency to direct attention to Christian hope; 3) the directness of its attachment to the life and sayings of Jesus; and 4) the way in which the sufferings and resurrection of Jesus are spoken of.

In the previous representations of this system of doctrine, these peculiarities have not yet, in many respects, received due recognition. Schmid was the first to give a thorough representation of the doctrine of Peter, and Messner has substantially followed him. By these it is reckoned among those types of doctrine which exhibit the Gospel in its unity with the Old Testament; and it is stated to be its more special peculiarity that it regards the Gospel as the fulfillment of Old Testament promise. The Tübingen school, which holds it to be spurious, regards our Epistle as a monument of a later phase of Paulinism. Van Oosterzee gives an exposition of the theology of Peter—1) as the Apostle of Jesus Christ; 2) as the Apostle of the Circumcision, and 3) as the Apostle of Hope.

[ANALYSIS: 1) 1 Peter the principal source of Petrine doctrine; 2) date of composition; 3) to whom written; 4) aim of Epistle; 5) peculiarities of Epistle; 6) treatment of Van Oosterzee.]

### § 61. *The Epistle of James.*[1]

A third source of the Petrine type of doctrine is the Epistle of James. This Epistle was written by James, the half-brother of our Lord, who did not become a believer until after the resurrection of Jesus (John 7:5). In consequence, however, of the position which he assumed at the head of the Mother Church in Jerusalem after the

[1] Compare *Weiss*, § 37; *Schmid*, § 56.

departure of Peter (Acts 12:17), he gained an almost Apostolic authority in the early Church, especially in the Jewish-Christian portion of it. Though the date of the composition of this Epistle is as yet an unsolved problem, it is probably the oldest of the epistles of the New Testament. The whole character of the Epistle, which is addressed to the Jews of the Dispersion in general (James 1:1) is purely practical, and is directed not so much against errors of doctrine as against errors of life, and there is no direct or indirect reference to the teaching of Paul.

The Jewish-Christian type is stamped upon his Epistle, as well as upon the First Epistle of Peter. In fact, his whole manner of writing is plainly modeled upon that of the Prophetical Books and the Proverbs of the Old Testament. Like Peter, he also often attaches himself directly to the sayings of Jesus.

[ANALYSIS: 1) The author of the Epistle; 2) probably the oldest of the Epistles of the New Testament; 3) addressed to the Jews of the Dispersion; 4) of a practical character; 5) of the Petrine type of doctrine.]

### § 62. *The Second Epistle of Peter and the Epistle of Jude.*[1]

We accept the genuineness of the Second Epistle of Peter, and it was probably written about 65 to 67 A.D.[2] Its whole doctrinal method is Judæo-Christian, moving in Old Testament images, histories and ideas; and it exhibits, in all its fundamental lines, manifold affinities with the First Epistle of Peter. The Epistle is addressed to the essentially Gentile churches of Asia Minor (2 Pet. 1:1; 3:1), which had been founded by Paul's activity. He knows of Paul's Epistles (3:15, 16),

---

[1] Compare *Weiss*, § 112.
[2] Compare my "Studies in the Book," vol. 1, pp. 85–89.

and probably is acquainted with the letters of the first captivity.

The Second Epistle is hortative, as is the First. That great corruption of morals, which, as we shall see in the Pastoral Epistles of St. Paul, threatened the Church, has already in part begun. The rise of libertinism in its fundamental principles, as also the beginning of complaints, as to the delay of the Advent, form the historical background for the exhortations of the Epistle. The everlasting Kingdom of Jesus Christ, " His power and coming " (2 Pet. 1:16; 3:4–13), is the great object which the Apostle has in view. The " word of prophecy " (1:19–21) to Peter shines with so peculiar a splendor that it may be said that Christianity appears in this Epistle as the fulfillment of Old Testament prophecy. Generally speaking, we shall find that the didactic purport of this Epistle assumes the same standpoint as that of the First Epistle, and of Peter's discourses in the Acts. We also accept the genuineness of the Epistle of Jude, which seems to have been written some time after the Second Epistle of Peter (comparing 2 Pet. 2:1–3 with Jude 4). The author describes himself as the brother of James, doubtless of the best known and most distinguished of the name, and therefore a half-brother of the Lord. The Epistle is not addressed to the Christians of any particular place, but to all believers generally who had remained true and faithful, and yet the author may have sent it to one or more churches. After the death of James, Jude, his younger brother, was doubtless one of the most distinguished Christians in the Church of Palestine, and had every right to come forward with warnings against the heresies that were creeping in.[1]

---

[1] Compare *Schmid*, § 61.

As this Epistle is connected very closely with the Second Epistle of Peter, both in time and subject-matter, it seems suitable to treat of the two together.

[ANALYSIS: 1) The peculiarities of 2 Peter; 2) of a hortative character; 3) closely related to 1 Peter; 4) Epistle of Jude written later.]

## § 63. *The Evangelists Matthew and Mark.*

There can be no doubt that the first two Gospels, which bear the names of Matthew and Mark, in so far as they delineate the representations and views of the Evangelists themselves, are to be looked upon as witnesses for the original Apostolic or Petrine type of doctrine. Not only are their authors acknowledged to have been Jewish Christians, but the Gospel of Mark rests on a Petrine tradition, while Matthew in his Gospel faithfully reports the tradition which had become current in his own immediate Apostolic circle (Matthew, James, Jude). No doubt Matthew, as an Apostle, had delivered the purport of his Gospel by word of mouth many times before he communicated it to writing in Aramaic and Greek; for, according to the unanimous tradition of Christian antiquity, the Gospel had also been written in Aramaic, but there is no sufficient ground for not regarding our present Greek text as a genuine original. The Gospels according to Matthew and Mark were probably written a short time before the destruction of Jerusalem.[1]

[ANALYSIS: 1) Matthew's own presentation belongs to the original Apostolic type; 2) Mark is Petrine; 3) Matthew wrote both in Aramaic and Greek; 4) date of the Gospels of Matthew and Mark.]

---

[1] See my "Studies in the Book," vol. 1, pp. 39, 48.

# SECTION I.

## The Discourses of Peter in the Acts.

### CHAPTER I.

#### THE PROCLAMATION OF THE MESSIAH AND THE MESSIANIC TIME.

§ 64. *The Fulfillment of Prophecy in the Earthly Life of Jesus.*[1]

The Apostles not only proclaim that theirs are the days of which all the prophets have spoken, and therefore that the Messianic time has commenced (Acts 3:24), but in their preaching they lay special stress upon the proclamation of the fact that the Promised Messiah, in the Person of Jesus of Nazareth, has already come.

Even in His earthly life He had been, like Moses, the Promised Prophet, whom God Himself had approved by mighty works and wonders and signs, and the Anointed Servant of God, of whom the prophets had spoken (Deut. 18:15; Acts 3:22; 7:36, 37). In these miracles Peter sees the proof that Jesus of Nazareth had been anointed with the Holy Ghost (Acts 10:38). Prophecy, moreover, knew of a servant of God who was anointed with the Spirit of God (Isa. 42:1; 61:1), through whom God was to bring to the people the glad tidings of the commencement of the Messianic time (Isa. 52:7). Jesus

---

[1] Compare *Weiss*, § 38. This section bears on the doctrine of the Person of Christ, or Christology.

## THE FULFILLMENT OF PROPHECY. 157

was therefore this Anointed Servant of God (Acts 4:27; 3:13, 26); and through the anointing with the Holy Ghost this Servant has become the Holy Servant of God (Acts 4:27, 30), or the Holy One of God (Acts 2:27), of whom Ps. 16:10 spoke. But prophecy also had characterized the Servant of God simply as the Righteous One (Isa. 53:11); and since the whole life of Jesus was an exhibition of this spotless righteousness which corresponded to the will of God, they saw in Him the coming of the Righteous One (Acts 7:52) which the prophets had before announced (Acts 22:14).

According to prophecy, even the Messiah's shameful end had been foreordained by God. From Isa. 53, even the idea of a suffering Messiah might not be altogether unfamiliar to a profounder view of prophecy (Luke 2:34, 35; John 1:29); yet this certainly was not the form in which they conceived its fulfillment to be possible. It was necessary, therefore, to show that even this end had been already looked forward to by prophecy. Ps. 2:2 had already foretold a rebellion of the princes of this world against the Lord's Anointed (Acts 4:25-28). Nay, the Divine decree referred even to the shameful manner in which Jesus was delivered into the hands of His enemies by one of His disciples; for in Ps. 69:25; 109:8, Peter found the fate of the betrayer already foretold (Acts 1:16, 20). Everything was foreordained by God's power and counsel (Acts 4:28); everthing had taken place in accordance with His determinate counsel and foreknowledge (Acts 2:23).

[ANALYSIS: 1) Jesus of Nazareth the Promised Messiah; 2) the Promised Prophet foretold by Moses; 3) the Anointed Servant of God spoken of in the Old Testament; 4) the Righteous One; 5) a Suffering Messiah.]

## § 65. *The Exalted Messiah.*[1]

The decisive proof of the Messiahship of Jesus was furnished by His resurrection on the third day, which the Apostles proclaimed, as His chosen witnesses.

This fact of Christ's resurrection was the real central point of the Apostolic testimony (Acts 2:32; 3:15; 4:10; 5:30; 10:40, 41). He was the Messiah of whom prophecy spoke (Acts 2:25–32, compared with Ps. 16:10; 2 Sam. 7:12), because it was not possible that He should be holden of death (Acts 2:24).

In consequence of the promise of Jesus, and the outpouring of the Spirit, they could also proclaim His exaltation to the Right Hand of God (Acts 2:33–35; 5:31, 32). Through this exaltation God had invested Jesus with the full sovereignty which was appropriate to the Messiah. It is now that Christ has first become the corner-stone of the completed theocracy (Acts 4:11), the Prince—to which position God has exalted Him (Acts 5:31). But He is designated not only the Lord of the theocracy or of believers, but also simply *the Lord* (Acts 2:36; 11:23, 24), *the Lord Jesus* (Acts 1:21; 4:33; 11:20; 15:11), as only Jehovah Himself is named. The Messiah, who is exalted to this *lordship* or *dominion* must, of the very nature of the case, be a Divine being.

But not until He comes from Heaven the second time can Jesus appear to the nation as the Messianic Finisher and Judge. It is assumed in Acts 3:20, as self-evident, that the time will come when God will send this Jesus as the Messiah appointed for the nation, in His full Messianic glory, to bring to the people the times of the Messianic consummation. That no other

---

[1] Compare *Weiss*, § 39. This section contains matters bearing on Soteriology as well as Christology.

one than this Jesus will one day come as the Messiah; and that, too, not only as the accomplisher but also as the Judge of the world, ordained of God (Acts 10:42),—this it is that the proclamation of His Messiahship is meant to prove.

[ANALYSIS: 1) The resurrection of Christ a proof of His Messiahship; 2) His exaltation to the Right Hand of God; 3) Divine names ascribed to Him; 4) the Judge of the world.]

## § 66. *The Coming of the Messianic Time*.[1]

With the appearance of Christ, there has commenced the Messianic time to which all the prophets had pointed (Acts 3:24)—as the last days in which all the decrees of Jehovah must be accomplished (Gen. 49:1; Micah 4:1; Isa. 2:2; Acts 2:17 compared with Joel 2:28, 29). If, however, this is the case, then with it essential blessings of salvation must also already be given. Now, as such a blessing, the prophecy in Joel 2:28, 29, names a universal outpouring of the Spirit. This has taken place on the Day of Pentecost (Acts 2:16–21), and is ever repeated afresh in the case of those who believe in the Messiah (Acts 2:38). The Baptist had already stated that the Messiah would baptize with the Holy Ghost (Matt. 3:11), and the disciples of Jesus are conscious of having received this gift through their Exalted Lord (Acts 2:33). The other essentially Messianic blessing of salvation is the forgiveness of sins, which was promised by all the prophets for the Messianic time; and which, like the communication of the Spirit, is also secured through the mediation of the Messiah (Acts 10:43). This can now be offered to every one on occasion of his entrance into the Church of Christ (Acts

[1] Compare *Weiss*, § 40. This chapter bears largely on the work of Christ, or Soteriology.

2:38; 3:19; 5:31), in consequence of the authority which was bestowed upon it by Jesus.

Participation in these Messianic blessings depends, however, on the fulfillment of certain conditions. The Apostles demand repentance (Acts 2:38; 8:22) and a change in men's moral walk, and make this the condition of obtaining the forgiveness of sins (Acts 3:19; 5:31; 8:22). As the proclamation of Jesus not only demanded repentance, but also effectively called it into existence, so also the preaching of the Apostles. Through repentance, those who participate in the Messianic salvation enter into fellowship with God and become His true servants (Acts 4:29; 2:18), walking in the fear of the Lord and in the comfort of the Holy Ghost (Acts 9:31).

This repentance manifests itself, first of all, in the believing acceptance of the Apostolic message, and in the recognition of Jesus as the Messiah (Acts 8:12; 10:43; 15:11). As the immediate sequel of this end of the times which has already commenced, the Messianic judgment is to be looked for, from which only the Messiah can deliver all who call upon His name. For there is no other name, given among men whereby men can be saved, than the name of Jesus Christ (Acts 4:10–12). As the Messiah who is ordained to be the Judge (Acts 10:42), He has naturally also to determine who shall be delivered from this judgment.

[ANALYSIS: 1) The Messianic time begins with the First Coming of Christ; 2) the blessings offered are an outpouring of the Spirit and the forgiveness of sins; 3) conditions required are repentance and faith; 4) salvation in Jesus Christ alone.]

## CHAPTER II.

### THE MOTHER CHURCH AND THE QUESTION OF THE GENTILES.

§ 67. *The Church and the Apostles*.[1]

The Church was founded by the outpouring of the Spirit and the institution of the rite of baptism, to the reception of which, participation in the forgiveness of sins and in the gift of the Spirit is henceforth attached (Acts 2:38). There was now a Church of Christ—*the Church* (Acts 5:11; 8:1, 3), not bound together by peculiar religious ceremonies, but by the Divine gift of the Spirit, the bestowal of which declared its members to be the true servants of Jehovah (Acts 2:18; 4:29), in whose midst the completed theocracy with all its blessings must be realized. But those who wished to connect themselves with the Church had to be baptized in the name of Jesus Christ unto the remission of their sins (Acts 2:38, 41; 8:12; 10:48; 18:8). The symbolical act of John's baptism of repentance had in the Church become Christian baptism—a washing of regeneration, a sacrament, the vehicle of supernatural gifts of grace. Peter could, therefore, describe baptism as the way which leads to the Messianic salvation (Acts 2:40), inasmuch as, by its reception, they entered into the Church which the Messiah had founded.

The Church continued bound together by their participating in the teaching of the Apostles, by the realization of brotherly fellowship with one another, by the

[1] Compare *Weiss*, § 41. This section bears largely on the doctrine of the Church, or Ecclesiology.

sacred rite of the breaking of bread, and by common prayer (Acts 2:42). This brotherly fellowship found its expression in their compassionate provision for the widows (Acts 6:1), and naturally, also, for the poor in general; for this purpose not a few well-to-do members of the Church sold all their possessions (Acts 4:37)—without this, however, being regarded as a duty (Acts 4:5).

In consequence of the growth of the Church, the ministering of provision for the poor became more arduous; and so seven men, qualified by the Spirit's gift of wisdom to undertake this difficult task, were chosen in place of the Apostles, who had up to this time received and administered the gifts of Love (Acts 4:37; 5:2; 6:1–6). Although these seven men are not styled *deacons*, still it is a *diakonia* (service, ministration) which they undertake (Acts 6:2). The narrative in the Acts implies that this office of the *diakonate* thus created was entirely new. The narrative offers no hint that it was either a continuation of the order of Levites or an adaptation of an office in the synagogue. Their office was essentially a "serving of tables," as distinguished from the higher function of preaching and instruction. But partly from the circumstances of their position, partly from the personal character of those first appointed, the deacons at once assume a prominence which is not indicated in the original creation of the office. The devout zeal of a Stephen or a Philip would turn their great opportunities of moving freely among the poorer heathen to the best account; and thus, without ceasing to be dispensers of alms, they became also ministers of the Word.[1]

[1] See J. B. Lightfoot's *Dissertation on the Christian Ministry*, in his *Commentary on Philippians*.

When the Sacred historian first mentions the presbyters, he introduces them without preface, as though the institution were a matter of course. The reason of Luke's silence is evident. Over every Jewish synagogue, whether at home or abroad, a council of "elders" presided. It was not unnatural therefore that, when the Christian congregation took its place by the side of the Jewish synagogues, a similar organization should be adopted with such modifications as circumstances required; and thus the name "elder," familiar under the old dispensation, was retained under the new; and so a body of elders or presbyters would be chosen whenever a church was organized to direct the religious worship, and partly also to watch over the temporal well-being of the society. The two persecutions of which St. Stephen and St. James were respectively the chief victims, mark two important stages in the internal organization of the Church, as well as two stages in the diffusion of the Gospel. With the first persecution is connected the establishment of the *diakonate;* with the second, that of the presbytery. For this later persecution was the signal for the dispersion of the Twelve on a wider mission. At all events, now for the first time we read of "presbyters" or "elders" in connection with the Christian brotherhood at Jerusalem (Acts 11:30). From this time forward, all official communications with the Mother Church are carried on through their intervention; and on their very first missionary journey the Apostles Paul and Barnabas are described as appointing presbyters in every Church (Acts 14:23).

The Apostles now devote themselves wholly and diligently to prayer and the ministry of the Word (Acts 6.4). The prominent position which Peter assumes in the Church is a result of his peculiar qualifications, in consequence of which he throughout takes the lead in word and in deed. It is not a position which is officially fixed. Alongside of him, the sons of Zebedee, James and John must have been specially prominent (Acts 12:2; 3:1, 3, 4, 11; 4:13, 19; 8:14). After Peter's imprisonment, James, the brother of our Lord, takes his place, although we hear nothing as to any express determination of the matter (Acts 12:17; 15:13; 21:18).

[ANALYSIS: 1) The grace of Christian baptism; 2) the Lord's Supper; 3) provision for the poor; 4) appointment of the seven; 5) office of *deacon;* 6) of presbyters or elders; 7) the office of the Apostles; 8) Peter, the spokesman of the Apostles.]

§ 68. *The Conversion of the Whole of Israel.*[1]

The mission of the Apostles to Israel is only the resumption of the evangelizing and converting activity of Jesus; through the complete conversion of Israel, it is to render the return of Jesus, and therewith the coming of the consummation of all things possible.

Through Jesus, God had sent the glad tiding to the children of Israel (Acts 10:36); but the nation had killed its Messiah. After Christ's resurrection and exaltation, the Apostles were once more sent to the people of Israel (Acts 10:42) with the message regarding the Messiahship of Jesus, and with the demand of repentance. Jesus must now remain in Heaven until the times of the general conversion of which Malachi had prophesied (Acts 3:21; Mal. 4:5, 6). That it is of this that the *restoration of all things* is to be understood is shown by Mark 9:12, and confirmed by the context.

[1] Compare *Weiss*, § 42. This section treats largely of the Last Things, or Eschatology.

To bring about the repentance and conversion of Israel, so that the promised times of refreshing may come is the mission of the Apostles to Israel (Acts 3:19–21).

There remains, therefore, a Messianic salvation appointed for the people of Israel (Acts 2:39). That the rejection of the nation which was threatened by Jesus is still suspended for a time; that it can still be averted by the nation's repentance—this is the presupposition of the whole of the missionary preaching of the Apostles  Peter explicitly proclaims to the people that even the lawless slaying of the Messiah is still to be regarded as committed "in ignorance" (Acts 3:17), and may still be forgiven in consequence of a penitent conversion (Acts 3:19). But whoever does not now listen to the prophet promised by Moses, shall be utterly destroyed from among the people (Acts 3:23). Accordingly, a time of grace is still granted to the nation.

Even the renewed threatening prophecy of Stephen does not pronounce the eventual rejection of the nation (Acts 7:2–53). His speech is only a sharp castigatory sermon for the purpose of leading them to repentance; and it is pure arbitrariness to assume, with some, that, if Stephen had not been interrupted in his discourse, he would have pronounced the rejection of the nation.

[ANALYSIS: 1) The message was first to Israel; 2) the conversion of Israel must take place before Christ's Second Coming; 3) the speech of Stephen.]

§ 69. *The Position of the Gentile Christians in the Church.*[1]

Although, even from the first, there was reserved for the Gentiles an ultimate participation in the Messianic

[1] Compare *Weiss*, § 43.

salvation, yet the manner in which this was to be accomplished was left to God. God sent His Servant, first of all, to Israel, in order to effect its conversion (Acts 3:26) ; yet the promise of salvation belongs not only to the Jews, but also to those who are afar off Acts 2:39); and, according to Isa. 49:1, 12 ; 57:19, these are undoubtedly the Gentiles. The prophetic descriptions of the manner in which the Gentiles would, in the Messianic time, obtain a share in the salvation of Israel, had never conceived, however, of an actual mission to them. It was rather the Gentiles who, attracted by the glory of Israel, would of their own accord set out to attach themselves to the completed theocracy (Micah 4:1, 2 ; Isa. 2:2, 3 ; 60:4, 5 ; Jer. 3:17). This completion of the theocracy, however, could be brought about only by the conversion of Israel, upon which Jeremiah (4:1, 2) expressly makes the salvation of the Gentiles depend.

As the first indication given by God, that even before the complete conversion of Israel, uncircumcised persons were to be brought into the Church, we have the conversion of the Centurion Cornelius (Acts 10). But not until God had shown, by the outpouring of the Spirit, that He makes no difference between Gentile and Jewish believers, but has cleansed the hearts of the former by the faith wrought in them, did Peter allow Cornelius and his household to be received by baptism into the fellowship of believing Israel, to whom the promise belongs (Acts 10:44–48). In the newly converted Gentiles the Mother Church, however, could see only such as God had brought, before the time, to participation in the Messianic salvation, which was to be realized first of all in Israel, and to whom, therefore, they could and must allow an exceptional position.

At the Apostolic Council, the freedom of the converted Gentiles from the law was expressly recognized, in opposition to the Zealots, who demanded that they should pass through Judaism, and only precautions were taken that this recognition should not damage the mission to Israel. These precautions were that the Gentiles should abstain from things sacrificed to idols, and from blood, and from things strangled, and from fornication (Acts 15:20, 29).

[ANALYSIS: 1) The promise of salvation was also to the Gentiles; 2) teaching of prophecy; 3) conversion of Cornelius; 4) decision of the Apostolic Council at Jerusalem.]

## § 70. *Appendix: Lechler's Presentation of the Discourses in Acts.*[1]

Lechler discusses the doctrine of the early Apostolic time, during the first ten years before Paul began his successful course as Apostle of the Gentiles under the general heading of "The Speeches in the Acts." This presentation is so suggestive that we herewith present an outline of it.

The *resurrection of Jesus* appears, in primitive Christian preaching, as the fundamental fact—the Alpha and the Omega of Apostolic announcement (Acts. 1:22; 2:32; 3:15; 4:10; 5:30). The resurrection of Jesus is the beginning of His exaltation and glorification. The dogma based upon this fact is that *Jesus is the Messiah and the Lord* (2:36; 10:36).

The *Person* of Jesus is so described that He appears unmistakably as a *man*—"Jesus of Nazareth, a man approved" (2:22); an actual descendant of David (2:30),

[1] Compare his *Apostolic and Post-Apostolic Times*, vol. 1, pp. 266–288.

but "the Holy and Righteous One" (3:14). A relation to God is here indicated, which is still more plainly referred to by Peter, when, applying Old Testament language, he calls Jesus the "Holy One" of God (2:27).

We find the *dignity* of Jesus depicted in such a way as to make Him both Lord and Christ (2:36; 4:27; 10:36, 38). He is become the corner-stone of the building of God (4:11). God exalted Him to be a Prince and a Saviour (5:31). Connected with the resurrection of Jesus, the Apostles emphasize His ascension and exaltation to the Right Hand of God, as the facts by which His dignity is consummated (2:32-34).

Jesus, who was raised up after His crucifixion and exalted by God (3:13), is He in whom alone salvation is to be found (4:12). He is the SAVIOUR (5:31). This salvation in Christ is, in the first place, negative—rescue from impending judgment and ruin, by means of moral separation from a crooked generation (2:40); and on the other hand, positive—the fullness of the long-promised blessing through Jesus as the Messiah. For Jesus is the Prince or Author of life (3:15), the Herald and Giver of all true life. Peter, however, lays special emphasis on the *forgiveness of sins* and the gift of the Holy Spirit as the greatest blessings that salvation can bestow on man, and those which the believer shall actually attain through faith in Jesus (10:43; 2:38; 3:19; 10:36). The *gift of the Holy Ghost* is the positive supplement to the forgiveness of sins.

A change of heart and faith are demanded as the condition of participating in this salvation offered in Jesus of Nazareth. The reception of baptism is manifestly connected with a confession of faith in Jesus, and therefore a change of mind, or repentance and faith, are named as conditions of forgiveness (2:38; 3:16, 19, 26; 5:31; 8:22; 11:17, 18). Moreover, baptism is not merely a confessional act on the part of man, but also an act of God, by which He effects and imparts forgiveness of sin (2:38), and with which the gift of the Spirit is connected. We must, however, also observe the distinction, that the gift of the Holy Spirit may *follow* baptism as an effect (2:38), or *go before* it as a foundation (10:44-47).

But *for whom* is this salvation in Jesus ordained? The Apostles turn to the people of Israel, in which respect they follow the command that the Lord Himself gave (10:36, 42). They consider Jesus especially as the Deliverer of His people (5:31). Peter seems to take it for granted that Israel must first be converted before the blessing is transferred to the heathen peoples (3:26). That salvation is also for the heathen world, if they repent and believe, is directly and unequivocally stated in Peter's discourse on the day of Pentecost: "For to you is the promise, and to your children, and *to all that are afar off*, even as many as the Lord our God shall call unto Him" (2:39). This statement may be divided into three distinct propositions—1) the promise concerns *you*, the Israelites; 2) it is not limited to the present time or generation, but is lasting and permanent—*to your children*, to the future families of Israel; 3) it has a still more comprehensive destination—*to all* the nations *that are afar off*, namely, the heathen. (Compare also 10:34, 35.)

The *return of Jesus* as the Judge of the living and the dead is an important article of faith with the Apostles, according to the Acts (10:42; 3:19-21). Great prominence is given, in these primitive Apostolic testimonies, to the expectation of Christ's return and to the doctrine of the Last Things.

[ANALYSIS : 1) Great stress laid upon the resurrection of Jesus; 2) Jesus a true man; 3) exalted as Lord; 4) the Prince of life; 5) salvation is both negative and positive; 6) the conditions of salvation; 7) baptism; 8) salvation is also offered to the Gentiles; 9) the doctrine of the Last Things.]

# SECTION II.

## THE FIRST EPISTLE OF PETER.

### CHAPTER III.

#### THE BEGINNING OF THE MESSIANIC CONSUMMATION IN THE CHRISTIAN CHURCH.

§ 71. *The Elect.*[1]

The Apostle does not begin by proving that prophecy has been fulfilled in Jesus, but the basis of his exhortation is the fact that in the Christian Church the realization has commenced of that which was set before the theocratic nation as the highest ideal, and which was to be realized in the Messianic time, which has now come. Ye are an elect race, Peter writes to the Christian Churches of Asia Minor (1 Pet. 2:9). It is plain from the context that only the believers in Israel (*ver.* 7)—those who are not disobedient to the Word (*ver.* 8)—belong to the elect race, in which the ideal of the theocracy is being realized; only the believing company of Jews in Babylon is elect, together with his readers (1 Pet. 5:13).

Their election to participation in the completed salvation is accomplished in baptism, in which God makes them a holy nation by equipping them with His Spirit, and granting them the full forgiveness of sin. As in Acts 2:38, the obtaining of forgiveness of sins is the

---

[1] Compare *Weiss*, § 44. This section treats largely of Predestination, which belongs under the Doctrine of God, or Theology proper.

design of baptism, so here also the election which is accomplished in baptism (1 Pet. 1:2, for here, undoubtedly, the act of baptism is to be thought of, in which and by means of which the gift of the Spirit is given) appears as having in view the (purifying) sprinkling with the blood of Christ (1:2); and in 1 Pet. 3:21 baptism is expressly described as a washing, which does not, as in the case of an ordinary ablution, aim at the washing away of the filth which cleaves to the flesh, but at the cleansing of the conscience from the consciousness of guilt.

All Israelites who would not obey the demands of the message of salvation are excluded from the elect race. To them the Messiah has become the stone of stumbling and the rock of offense, as is said in 1 Pet. 2:8, with an express allusion to prophecy (Isa. 8:14). These no longer belong to the elect race, and have therefore no part in the completion of the theocracy which is brought about by the Messiah (1 Pet. 2:6, 9). Obstinate disobedience to the message of salvation, which demands its believing acceptance (1 Pet. 2:8; 4:17), and which is nothing else than disobedience to the Messiah Himself, is regarded as the presumptuous sin of godlessness (4:18)—a sin that cannot be forgiven, because through the Messiah the consummation is brought about, and disobedience to Him surely condemns.

Wherever individual Gentiles are received into the Church through baptism, they are joined to the elect race—the believing Israelites, who are the real stem, the substance of the Church.

[ANALYSIS: 1) Believers are the elect of God; 2) baptism bestows the gift of the Spirit and forgiveness of sins; 3) unbelieving Israel is excluded from the elect race; 4) believing Gentiles are joined to the elect race.]

## THE PECULIAR PEOPLE. 173

### § 72. *The Peculiar People and the Calling.*[1]

Although, according to Deut. 7:6, God has chosen Israel that it may be a people of His possession, yet, as appears from Ex. 19:5, the realization of this ideal remained dependent upon the obedience of the people. Faithless Israel is no longer the people of God; but it can become so again, if it is converted in the Messianic time (Hos. 2:23). Believing Israel is described by Peter as the people which has been taken to be God's own possession, the people which has now again become the people of God (1 Pet. 2:9, 10). The prophets declare that in the Messianic time Jehovah will dwell in the midst of His people (Ezek. 37:27), and this promise has now been fulfilled (1 Pet. 2:5); the Christian Church has itself become the House of God (1 Pet. 4:17), in which He dwells. They have now returned to God, their Shepherd and Overseer (Ezek. 34:10-19; 1 Pet. 2:25), and so form a Flock of God, over which He has set His chosen shepherds, and chief among these the Messiah (Ezek. 34:20-31; 1 Pet. 5:2-4).

God's peculiar people are assured of all blessings and of protection. As the people of God, they have also become the object of His Merciful Love (1 Pet. 2:10). In 1 Pet. 2:9, the incomparable happiness to which the members of the elect race are called out of the darkness of their misery, is represented under the symbol of a marvelous light; and, in 1 Pet. 5:10, the eternal glory of God Himself is named as the ultimate end of their calling. They appear as stewards of the manifold grace of God (1 Pet. 4:10), by which is meant the gracious gifts of the Spirit, with which God equips the members of the elect race for His service. And although there

[1] Compare *Weiss*, § 45. This section treats largely of the Doctrine of the Church, or Ecclesiology.

is still wished for them an increase of grace (1 Pet. 1:2), 1 Pet. 5:10 shows that with the calling given in Christ to the greatest salvation, there is at the same time given the certainty of all further gifts of grace, by means of which God leads them to the salvation of the consummation.

Christians are the true servants of God (1 Pet. 2:16; 4:10), whose fundamental obligation is described as the fear of God (1 Pet. 2:17; 3:15), which urges them to the fulfilling of every other duty (2:18; 3:2). Those who fear God will live unto righteousness (2:24), even if they should suffer for its sake (3:14); they are the righteous who do good and avoid evil (3:12; 4:18). To this well-doing, Christians have been called (2:21; 3:9); by the right use of their gifts (4:11) as well as by the manner in which they bear the Christian name under all their afflictions (4:16), they are to glorify God and make known the glorious attributes of the God who has called them (2:9). The whole Christian Church is a holy priesthood (2:5), and it is also called a royal priesthood (2:9), because it serves Jehovah as its King. All the privileges, which in the Old Testament belonged exclusively to the Levitical priesthood, have now passed over to the whole Christian Church. According to 1 Pet. 3:18, Christ has brought us nigh to God—has led us to Him from whom we were separated by our want of holiness. According to 1 Pet. 2:5, it appears as the task of the holy priesthood to offer acceptable sacrifices to God.

In the Old Testament, Jehovah is the God and Father of His people; Israel is His people and His Son. So Peter takes it for granted that Christians are the children of God, and that they call on God as their Father (1:14, 17), just as in 2:17 and 5:9 they are also regarded as a brotherhood. The calling to salvation is conceived of as a calling to Sonship, and as children of obedience (1:14); and this obedience is made to consist essentially in this, that the child conforms himself to his father, and becomes like the God who has called him to Sonship.

[ANALYSIS: 1) Faithless Israel no longer the people of God; 2) the Christian Church has become the House of God; 3) the blessings bestowed upon His Church; 4) the privileges and obligations of Christians; 5) the whole Christian Church is a royal priesthood; 6) Christians are the children of God; 7) and form a brotherhood.]

## § 73. *The New Birth and the Nourishment of the New Life.*[1]

The message of salvation is proclaimed in the power of the Holy Spirit sent down from Heaven (1 Pet. 1:12), and everything that is spoken by those endowed with the Spirit is to be regarded as a word which comes from God (4:11). This imperishable Word of God is a living and powerful working Word, by means of which Christians are begotten again to a new life (1:23); and through this Word God Himself works the new birth. When, in 1 Pet. 1:3, the resurrection of Christ is named as the means which God employs, in the background lies the fact that it was only through the preaching of the Gospel that the fact was made known to his readers (1:12). Similarly every preservation, strengthening, and furthering of the life of the Christian is traced back to God (1 Pet. 1:5; 5:10). And this working of Divine Grace is also conceived of as effected pre-eminently by means of the Word.

By means of the new birth, believers have been set free from their sinful lusts, and can now, in obedience

---

[1] Compare *Weiss*, § 46. This section treats largely of the work of the Holy Spirit, or Pneumatology.

to the Truth, purify their souls (1:22); and thus the holiness which was obtained in baptism by the work of the Holy Spirit in their hearts is ever more and more realized in all their walk (1:2, 14, 15), and the good conscience which they received in baptism (3:21) becomes their abiding possession (3:16). In such a case, the place of the life in the lusts is taken by the walk in the fear of God (1:17); in which fear they abstain from the fleshly lusts because they endanger the salvation of the soul (2:11), since they becloud the mind, and so rob men of the clearness of spirit and sobriety without which they cannot maintain the watchfulness demanded by Christ[1] (4:7; 5:8).

The nourishment of the new life—a nourishment which is supplied by the Word, and is to become more and more precious to Christians—is Christ Himself. Because it was but a short time since the Christians, to whom Peter writes, had become Christians, and had been born again, he calls them new-born babes (1 Pet. 2:2), whose thriving growth depends upon their desiring pure nourishment. The Word which begets Life is distinguished from the nourishment which is afforded in the Word; and the nourishment itself (2:3) is called Christ, of whom it is said that, if we have once tasted

---

[1] This Epistle illustrates the Lord's Prayer in a remarkable way: Our (1:4) Father (1:3, 17), who art in heaven (1:4, 12); hallowed be Thy name (1:15, 16); Thy Kingdom come (2:9); Thy will be done on earth as it is in heaven (2:15; 3:17; 4:2, 19); give us this day our daily bread (5:7); and forgive us our trespasses as we forgive those who trespass against us (4:1, 8); and lead us not into temptation (4:12); but deliver us from evil (4:13); for Thine is the kingdom (5:11), and the power (1:5; 4:11), and the glory (1:11, 21; 4:11, 14; 5:1, 10), forever and ever (4:11; 5:11). Amen (4:11; 5:11). (See my "Studies in the Book," vol. 1, p. 81, where also the Theology and Soteriology of this Epistle are fully developed.)

how sweet He is, we shall continually long for this nourishment.

[ANALYSIS: 1) The new birth is wrought by the Spirit, through the Word; 2) all grace is wrought by means of the Word; 3) the new birth the beginning of the Christian life; 4) Christ Himself is the nourishment of the new life.]

## § 74. *Christian Social Life.*[1]

Since Christians call one another brethren (1 Pet. 5:12), and form a brotherhood (2:17; 5:9), their specific duty to one another appears to be that love which Christ has called the greatest commandment. In 1:22, *brotherly love* is described as the most immediate aim of purification of heart, and its specific characteristic is derived from the nature of the new birth. The essence of love is described, in 3:8, as consisting in similarity of disposition, in sympathy, and compassionateness. Alongside of love, however, there stands *humility* (3:8; 5:5). As regards God, this consists in acquiescing patiently in His ways, and in bowing under His Almighty Hand (5:6). As regards our neighbor, it consists in giving to each man the honor which belongs to him (2:17; 3:7). Alongside of humility there stands, on the one hand, as in Matt. 11:29, the *meekness* (1 Pet. 3:4, 15) which patiently bears the injustice and enmity of others, which is not driven to violence by these wrongs; and, on the other hand, as in Matt. 20:25–28, the *humble serving* wherein each one subordinates himself to the other (1 Pet. 5:5).

In 1 Pet. 5:2, 3, Peter specially discusses the duties of the *elders*, to whom the office of pastors over the churches has been committed. This oversight of the

[1] Compare *Weiss*, § 47. This section treats mainly of Christian duties, or Ethics.

Church (the office of bishop) is also to be a service of love, which is to be performed voluntarily and readily; not merely from the constraint of duty, nor with a desire to obtain gain or lordship; it is to be performed in that humility which only seeks to give an example to others, and thereby to urge them to follow. Peter does not yet know of a second ecclesiastical office in the Churches to which he writes. As in the Church at Jerusalem, those who are younger in years, in accordance with their age, perform the external services of the Church without any special official position, and they are therefore admonished to be subject to the elders or presbyters (1 Pet. 5:5).

To the subjection to human ordinances which the Apostle demands for God's sake (1 Pet. 2:13), there belong especially obedience and honor to the authorities (2:13, 14, 17); but at the same time Peter does not fail to point out, by putting side by side their duty to God and the king, after the manner of Mark 12:17, that the fulfillment of the latter must not in any way prejudice the fulfillment of the former (1 Pet. 2:17).

There belongs to it, likewise, the patient endurance of the wrongs which slaves had often to suffer innocently (1 Pet. 2:18–21); and under the same point of view the Apostle places the relation of Christian wives to their still unbelieving husbands (1 Pet. 3:1–6). It is only incidentally that the Apostle glances at Christian marriages, and demands of the husbands intelligent discernment in their intercourse with the weaker vessel, and the due recognition of the Christian dignity of their wives, since it is only in this way that their joint prayer, which he seems to regard as the real crown of Christian married life, can receive its full blessing (1 Pet. 3:7).

Lastly, Peter demands, in general, that Christians, by their behavior, shall refute the calumnies of the Gentiles (1 Pet. 2:12, 15; 3:16), and become the means of blessing even to their enemies (3:9, 16–18). He who suffers dishonor because of Christs' name need not be ashamed of it, since he glorifies God by the manner of life that he leads (1 Pet. 4:14, 16).

[ANALYSIS: 1) Brotherly love is the specific duty of the Christian brotherhood; 2) joined to humility; 3) meekness; 4) and service; 5) the duties of elders; 6) Peter knows of no distinction between bishops and presbyters; 7) Christians must be subject to the authority of the State; 8) and be patient under oppression; 9) the responsibility of Christian marriage; 1c) Christians, by their behavior, must refute the calumnies of the world.]

# CHAPTER IV.

### THE MESSIAH AND HIS WORK.

### § 75. *Jesus the Messiah.*[1]

At the end of the times, Christ, who was from the beginning foreknown in the counsel of God as the Redeemer, was manifested and made known as such to men (1 Pet. 1:19, 20). It is no longer necessary for Peter to prove to the believers in Israel that Jesus of Nazareth is the Messiah promised by the prophets; the office of the Messiah, with the idea of His being the Mediator of salvation, has already passed over so completely to the Historical Person Jesus, that the term Messiah has become a proper name.

When it is said in 1 Pet. 1:11 that the Spirit of Christ, speaking in the prophets, testified beforehand the sufferings of Christ, we have here presented unto us the doctrine of the pre-existence of Christ as the eternal Son of God. The Spirit with which Christ was anointed at His baptism, according to His human nature, and which was His from eternity according to His Divine nature, was already active in the prophets.

[ANALYSIS: 1) Peter takes for granted that Jesus is the Messiah; 2) the pre-existence of Christ.]

### § 76. *The Saving Significance of the Suffering of Christ.*[2]

Peter, in his First Epistle, repeatedly speaks emphatically of the sufferings of Christ (2:23; 3:18; 4:1,

---

[1] Compare *Weiss*, § 48. This section bears on the doctrine of the Person of Christ, or Christology.

[2] Compare *Weiss*, § 49. This section treats of the Work of Christ, or Soteriology.

## THE SUFFERING OF CHRIST.

13; 5:1). According to 3:18, He suffers as the Righteous One; and, since a saving purpose is ascribed to Him in that suffering, it is plain that it is conceived of as a suffering which was undertaken voluntarily, and therefore also borne willingly and patiently. This is implied also in the image of the lamb, the symbol of quiet patience (1:19), which is borrowed from Isa. 53:7. When this Lamb is described as being "without blemish," the explanatory words "and without spot" show that this is meant, not only in the ritual sense (Lev. 1:10), but in the sense of moral blamelessness, so that the peculiar value of His suffering can be clearly set forth in the innocence and patience of the Suffering One. Although this suffering was voluntary, still it was already foreordained for Christ in Messianic prophecy (1:11).

The peculiar aim of this suffering was to take away from sinners the guilt of sin, inasmuch as, when He died on the Cross, Christ bore the punishment which was incurred by our sins. This suffering was of such a unique kind that, from the nature of the case, it cannot be repeated (3:18). Our access to God was rendered impossible by our sins, but Christ has suffered once for sins, that by this suffering in death He might atone for the guilt of the unrighteous which was caused by sin, and bring us to God. How this has taken place is already indicated when it is said that He has suffered as the righteous for the unrighteous (3:18); but it is from the leading passage in 2:24 that it first of all becomes perfectly clear. By its language, as well as by its whole context, this verse points so plainly to Isa. 53, that it is only by means of this chapter that it can be explained. What is here said is that Christ has borne our sins (Isa. 53:12); that He has suffered for the Divinely appointed consequence of sin; that He has borne our punishment. When Christ, the Innocent One, bears the consequences of the sins which should have fallen upon the guilty (Isa. 53:11), He bears these sins as a burden laid upon Him. It is plain that Peter regards this sin-bearing of Christ in behalf of sinners as the means whereby sin has been removed from them, and by which the stain of guilt has been effaced.

In consequence of the last testament (Mark 14:24), the death of Christ can be represented as if the Church had been sprinkled with the atoning blood of a covenant sacrifice. This saving significance of the death of Christ appears clearly from 1 Pet. 1:2. As God concluded the old covenant with the children of Israel at Sinai, after they had bound themselves to obedience, by the sprinkling with the atoning blood of the covenant sacrifice (Ex. 24:7, 8), so believers are here described as being elect unto obedience and sprinkling with the blood of Jesus Christ—*i. e.*, the people of God, who by obedience are to become true servants of God, are to be cleansed by the sprinkling of blood from the stain of guilt, which hinders them from enjoying perfect fellowship with God. And the death of Christ is regarded by Peter as this atoning covenant sacrifice.

Christ Himself had called His death the ransom whereby He would deliver the souls of men from death (Mark 10:45), and in 1 Pet. 1:18, 19 Peter names the price paid, the ransom — not anything corruptible, however valuable, as silver and gold, but something costly and precious, the blood of Christ. The Apostle describes the suffering of Jesus in ascending gradation: 1) as innocent (2:22); 2) as patient (2:23); 3) as vicarious and expiatory (2:24). Peter also designates as the aim of the death of Christ, moral renovation and sanctification (1:18; 2:24); but this moral effect is conditioned by His vicarious, atoning death. While Peter characterizes this vicarious act of Christ more definitely as "bearing our sins upon the tree," he seems to regard the wood of the Cross on which the body of Jesus was lifted up, and to which it was fastened, as the altar on which Jesus placed His body as a sacrifice laden with our sins, so that He appears in the character of a priest, and His death on the Cross is a priestly act. So that Peter does not simply speak here of a vicarious suffering and death, but in particular of a vicarious sacrificial death on the Cross, which is represented as that act of Christ by which reconciliation was made, whose aim is the reconciliation of sinners, and with it their moral renovation.

In a similar way the reconciling and sanctifying elements in the death of Christ are put together in 3:18 ("Christ suffered for sins once, the righteous for the unrighteous, that he might bring us to God"). The bringing back of those who were estranged and separated from God by sin, and their effectual transference into near communion with God, was the object of the death of Jesus. But since Jesus alone, who is free from sin and holy, may draw nigh to God, the medium of reunion with God is the vicarious, guilt-cleansing and reconciling death of Christ, endured once for all.[1]

[ANALYSIS: 1) Christ's suffering voluntary; 2) He bore our guilt and our punishment; 3) our sins were laid upon Him as a burden; 4) the death of Christ an atoning covenant sacrifice; 5) the ransom paid was the precious blood of Christ; 6) His death vicarious; 7) His death has a twofold aim—*a)* to bring about our reconciliation with God; *b)* to sanctify us.]

---

[1] Compare *Lechler*, vol. 2, pp. 142-145.

## § 77. *The Descent of Christ into Hades.*[1]

In 1 Pet. 3:18, the Person of Christ is looked at from two different sides, one of which is designated flesh, and the other spirit. The spirit here referred to cannot denote the spiritual nature of man in general, as in 1 Pet. 4:6, but the Divine nature of the God-Man, and being truly Divine, Christ could not remain in death, like every other man—*i. e.*, He could not remain in the incorporeal condition of Hades, but must be made alive, and raised from the dead. If in Acts 2:24 Peter grounds the necessity of the resurrection upon the circumstances that it was foretold in prophecy, in 1 Pet. 3:18 it is referred to the unique personal union of the Divine and the human natures of Christ in One Divine-human Personality. There is a contrast between His human nature, flesh, in which he was put to death, and His Spirit, His Divine nature, by which He was restored to life.

In order that we may fully understand the Petrine doctrine of the descent of Christ into Hades, we must examine very carefully three passages of Peter. The first is recorded in Acts 2:24–31, the second in 1 Pet. 3:18–20, the third in 1 Pet. 4:6.

We enter here, indeed, upon a difficult topic, and it behooves us to approach with all reverence the mysteries of God's revelation. Peter unveils to us what Christ has wrought for our redemption in the kingdom of death, and how He has overcome the power of death and of Satan, for all who are members of the Kingdom of God. The wonders of Christ's redemption are greater than many of us conceive; for His re-

---

[1] Compare Delitzsch's *Psychology*, pp. 477-490. Also Goeschel's *Der Mensch nach Leib, Seele und Geist, diesseits und jenseits*, pp. 85-111. Also *manuscript* lectures of Dr. Krauth.

demption, in certain aspects, has a bearing upon the whole universe. It bears a relation to the lower world, known in Scripture as Hades, the place of departed spirits; it bears a relation to this earth, as the middle part of the universe; and it bears a relation to Heaven, the Paradise of God.

Our Lord Jesus Christ truly died. His Soul was separated from his body, His body was laid in the grave. His Soul, separated from the body, went into the invisible world, where all departed souls of the dead went. This invisible world into which all souls went at death, *before* Christ's resurrection, is known in Scripture as Hades. It embraces two parts, the place or state of bliss, and the place or state of misery. Its generic name is Hades, and the soul going into either part would be in Hades. We have already seen, from the Parable of the Rich Man and Lazarus (Luke 16:19-31), that Hades is the name specifically given to the place or state of misery, and Paradise to the place or state of bliss; but both of these places or states belong to the invisible world, and make up the generic Hades. The Soul of Christ, separated at death from the body, went into the invisible world, and into the generic Hades, but into that part of the generic Hades called Paradise, where Abraham was, where Lazarus was in Abraham's bosom, and where the soul of the thief on the Cross met Jesus that very day (Luke 23:43). This descent of the Soul of Christ into Hades was the result of death, the last stage of Christ's humiliation. If Christ was a true man, if Christ's Soul was a true human soul, it was necessary that His Soul should pass through all the states that every true human soul passes. And in this discussion we must distinguish between a twofold descent of Christ into Hades, as taught by Peter.

Peter declares (Acts 2:22-36) that David prophesied of Christ when he said: "Thou will not leave my soul in Hades, neither wilt thou give thy Holy One to see corruption" (*ver.* 27), and that he "spake of the resurrection of the Christ, that neither was He left in Hades, nor did His flesh see corruption" (*ver.* 31), "for God did raise up this Jesus, whereof we all are witnesses" (*ver.* 32). That is, the soul of Christ was not forsaken or abandoned to Sheol, to Hades (Ps. 16:10; Acts 2:27-31). Christ had voluntarily given up His life for our sakes, of His own free-will had subjected Himself to the power of death and of Satan, because He took upon Himself our sins, our guilt and punishment—for by His stripes we are healed (1 Pet. 2:21-25). Christ was sinless 1 Pet. 2:22), and the sting of death which He bore was our sin, and He thus subjected Himself to Satan and unto death "that through death He might bring to nought Him that had the power of death—that is, the Devil" (Heb. 2:14).

But God loosed the pangs of death, because it was not possible that Christ should be held under the power of death or Satan (Acts 2:24). His resurrection was proof that He triumphed over death and Satan. He met death: His Soul as that of a true man passed over under the power of death and Satan, but He was not forsaken to it. He was more than mere man: He was also true God. He came forth victorious from Hades. The thought is not simply that He was not abandoned to Hades, but that He was its Conqueror. As His body was not simply free from corruption, but was triumphant over corruption, which seemed to threaten it, so His Soul was not only not overcome by Hades, but overthrew its gloomy power. His Soul was not left in Hades, not abandoned to the hand or power of death and Satan. Death did not, as with men, thwart Christ's plans, but promoted them; it did not, as with earthly kings, destroy His Kingdom, but was the means of establishing His Kingdom. Hades did not hold Christ's Soul back from this world, but He overcame the gates of Hades, and He returned from its gloomy prison.

The very fact that the Soul of Christ was not abandoned to Hades was preliminary to another great triumphal act of Christ. It foreshadowed to the Prince of Evil the fatal blow he was about to receive in the heart of his dominion. Satan was beaten in the battle which he had struck at the life of Christ, and now the Son of God was about to act on the offensive. Now Christ would manifest Himself as Victor to the powers of evil, making a show of them openly, triumphing over Satan and his angels in it (Col. 2:15). It is to this great triumphal act, which followed after Christ's restoration to life and revivification, that 1 Pet. 3:18-20 and 1 Pet. 4:6 refer.

Three days and three nights, according to biblical phraseology, did the body of our Lord lie in the grave, but, on the third day, the Soul, bursting through the gates of Hades, returned to His body. In the body thus raised to life, revivified, and glorified, before His visible resurrection and manifestion to His disciples—*i. e.*, before His resurrection proper—our Blessed Lord, in His whole Person, Divine and human, revealed Himself to the whole world of the dead. By this supernatural and triumphant manifestation He proclaimed and proved Himself the Lord of vanquished death, of

Hades, and of Satan. This was the first act of Christ's exaltation; and it is to this descent of Christ, *as the God-Man* into Hades, that Peter refers in 1 Pet. 3:18–20, and in 1 Pet. 4:6. In the first passage (1 Pet. 3:18–20), we have a revelation of Christ's manifestation to the whole realm of lost spirits, human and angelic, in Hades proper, or Hell; and in the second passage (1 Pet. 4:6) we have a revelation of Christ's glorious manifestation to all the souls of the believing dead of the Old Testament, who in Paradise awaited the Advent of the Christ.

I grant that we are here treading on debatable ground, and that the passages under consideration are very difficult of interpretation; but if we follow the direct and exact words of Peter, and bring to our aid the analogy of faith, we will find revealed to us deep truths of great importance. It is also well to bear in mind that this manifestation to the underworld did not depend for its power or effect upon the length of time it occupied. What we call a moment may, in that realm, unfold as much as years or ages do with us here. If the Devil with his limited power could cause the kingdoms of this world with their glory to pass before the Saviour in a moment of time, much more could our Omnipotent Lord, radiant now with the fresh glory of triumph, cause His Kingdom with all its glory, involving unspeakably vast issues, to pass before the gaze of fallen angels and lost men, if need be, in a moment of time.

Let us carefully trace the thought in 1 Pet. 3:18–20. 1) A fact is stated—"Christ suffered for sins once, the righteous for the unrighteous." 2) The object of Christ's death was "that He might bring us to God." 3) Peter draws a contrast between the death of Christ

## CHRIST'S DESCENT INTO HADES.

and His being made alive. He was "put to death in the flesh, but quickened in the Spirit." That is, by means of His human nature He was put to death, but by means of His Divine nature, and because He was Divine—because He was also true God—He was made alive, restored to life, raised from the dead. 4) Peter makes a positive assertion of Christ, thus quickened, made alive, with soul and body reunited. Christ, the God-Man, being made alive, performed a certain act. "Quickened in [by] the Spirit, in which [condition] also He went and preached" (*ver.* 19). The "in which" does not designate that "in the Spirit," according to the Spirit, "He went;" nor does it so much describe, that by the power of the Spirit "He went," although this is not excluded, but it rather defines the condition in which He went. He, the Christ, the God-Man, the quickened and living Christ, having overcome death, went and preached. No matter to what mystery this may lead us, this is what Peter says. He is speaking of Christ as made alive: "He went" and performed a certain act. 5) Peter further states whither He went. "He went and preached unto the spirits in prison" (*ver.* 19). This prison was the place where the souls of men, which aforetime were disobedient were confined (*ver.* 20). We have a right to infer it was the Hades in which the rich man found himself in torments and anguish immediately after death (Luke 16:23)—where "the unrighteous are kept under punishment unto the day of judgment" (2 Pet. 2:9); where also "the angels which kept not their own principality, but left their proper habitation, are kept in everlasting bonds under darkness until the judgment of the great day" (Jude 6)—"the Tartarus into which the angels which sinned, were cast, and committed to pits of darkness to be reserved unto judgment" (2 Pet. 2:4); the place in which the souls of all the ungodly of the ancient world found themselves, for God "spared not the ancient world," but only preserved Noah with seven others (2 Pet. 2:5). We believe that we are fully warranted by Scripture in affirming that the prison to which Christ went, according to the statement of Peter, is Hades proper—the home of Satan and his evil angels, the place of misery unto which all the souls of the godless, since sin entered into the world, descended. 6) Peter further states what took place in that prison: Christ "preached unto the spirits." From the context we learn that these spirits are the souls of men which aforetime were disobedient. The time of their disobedience is especially mentioned as being during the last days of Noah, when the long-suffering of God was waiting, while the Ark was preparing (*ver.* 20). Noah's contemporaries are here especially named, possibly with reference to the words of Jesus in Luke 17:26,[1] and in consideration of the exceeding depravity and obduracy of that age, without intending to limit this proclamation to them exclusively. The context in 2 Pet. 2:3-9[2] establishes the same point. The ungodly of the ancient world are especially referred to, but

---

[1] "And as it came to pass in the days of Noah, even so shall it be also in the days of the Son of Man. They ate, they drank, they married, they were given in marriage, until the day that Noah entered into the Ark, and the flood came, and destroyed them all."

[2] "Whose sentence now from of old lingereth not, and their destruction slumbereth not. For if God spared not angels when they sinned, but cast them down to hell, and committed them to pits of darkness, to be reserved unto judgment; and spared not the ancient world, but preserved Noah with seven others, . . . for the Lord knoweth how . . . to keep the unrighteous under punishment unto the day of judgment."

others are not excluded. We must interpret the passage by means of the whole context, and with the aid of parallel passages. The unrighteous of 2 Pet. 2:9, which are kept under punishment unto the Day of Judgment, are also included.

Peter says Christ "preached." The Greek word originally meant "to discharge the office of a herald." In the New Testament the word is used to designate the proclamation of the message of salvation. It is the making known, the proclaiming, the announcement of the facts of salvation. It differs from the Greek word "evangelize," in that this latter characterizes the contents as "good news." The word that Peter here uses does not in itself define the nature of the preaching, nor the effect it may have on the hearer. It may refer to the announcement of pardon to penitents, or of destruction to rebels. It is but a begging of the question to maintain that we have here an example of a probation after death, that Christ here offered an opportunity to the spirits in prison to repent. It does not say so, and it cannot be inferred from this passage. And even if it were, an offer of forgiveness, which we deny, it would not follow that any would repent. The effect of the preaching of the Gospel depends, humanly speaking, on the condition of those who hear. Christ's work of Redemption was potentially finished when He was made alive; He had met death and overcome the power of Hades; and now Christ descended into the very hold of Satan, into the very center of His dominion, there to herald forth His victory, and make manifest His triumph over the power of Satan; and then occurred that wondrous scene to which Paul refers, when Christ "put off from Himself the principalities and the powers, and made a show of them openly, triumphing over them in it" (Col. 2:15).

Doubtless, in connection with this revelation of Christ in Hades as the place of misery, great changes took place in the kingdom of Satan. Satan and his evil angels, and the souls of the ungodly, beheld Christ in majesty and glory as their Conqueror. There no doubt was a real curbing in of the power of Satan; for it is evident that the invisible world, as well as the visible, has its eras of history. Hades remains now as the fore-hell, into which all the souls of the unrighteous go, to be reserved "under punishment unto the day of judgment" (2 Pet. 2:9). And though the full meaning and significance of this passage may never be fully understood by us here on earth, we believe that the exegesis as given above is in strict accordance with the words of Peter, in harmony with the analogy of faith, and opens to us a deeper insight into the wonders of redemption.

The second passage (1 Pet. 4:6) is possibly still more difficult of interpretation. For a true exegesis of the passage we must give the same meaning to the word "dead" in this verse as in the preceding verse. It cannot mean "those that were dead in sins," nor that it was "preached in their lifetime to those now dead." A true exegesis, no matter how difficult the solution may be, requires that we refer this verse to the same event spoken of in 3:19—to an occurrence taking place after Christ's revivification, and that these dead are the departed souls of men.

Peter is speaking of unbelievers (*vers.* 3, 4), who walk in all kinds of excess, who practice abominable idolatries, and who speak evil of Christians; and he says all these "shall give account to Him that is ready to judge the quick and the dead" (*ver.* 5)—that is, they shall give account to Christ. But believers will live not to fulfill the lusts of the flesh, but the will of God (*ver.* 2); for "Christ has suffered in the flesh" (4:1), "has suffered for sins once, the righteous for the unrighteous, that He might bring us to God" (3:18). But since Christ has suffered for sins, and has suffered in the flesh, and is the one to whom judgment has been given over the living and the dead, and since Christ has brought all believers unto God (3:18), the saints of the Old Testament who are dead, who also lived at one time here on earth in the flesh, who in Paradise with Abraham were awaiting the Coming of the Messiah in whom they believed, were also entitled to hear the good news that Sheol and Satan and death had been overcome; and since Christ was also their Judge, therefore "were the good tidings preached even to the dead, that they might be judged according to men in the flesh, but live according to God in the Spirit" (4:6). That is, we maintain that the true interpretation of this passage opens to us a still deeper insight into the wonders of God's saving work through His beloved Son, Jesus Christ. Peter here unveils another mystery belonging to the great work of redemption. He again refers to the manifestation of Christ in the world of departed spirits, that took place at the same time as the event recorded in 1 Pet. 3:18–20; but the reference is now to what took place in the upper part of Hades in Paradise, where the souls of the Old Testament saints were still held under the power of death, of Hades, and Satan. Unto them Christ also manifested Himself after His revivification, and to them His appearance was also one of triumph and glory; but He appeared to them as their glorified and Risen Lord and Redeemer, the Conqueror of Satan, of Hades, and of the power of death. He also heralded forth His victory, and His proclamation and preaching was not simply an announcement of His victory—it was also a preaching of good tidings. The Greek word is different, and the whole context is in perfect agreement with this latter interpretation. It was a message of good tidings, and it brought joy and peace to the Old Testament saints. The Gospel was preached unto them "that they might be judged according to men in the flesh, but live according to God in the Spirit" (1 Pet. 4:6).

There is much in the Scriptures that warrants us in believing and teaching that at Christ's glorious descent into Hades, as the God-Man, great changes were wrought in the condition of the souls of the saints. On the one hand, Hades as such remained the abode of all evil angels, including the souls of the ungodly dead (Rev. 20:13), and it is reserved as the fore-hell into which all the souls of unbelievers enter until the Day of Judgment, and will finally become the Gehenna, the Hell, where body and soul, reunited, shall suffer. On the other hand, that part of Hades which had been known as Paradise before Christ's descent in triumph, has now yielded up its captives, held by the power of Satan and death—for the Lord Jesus hath led captivity captive;[1] He has opened the prison-house of death for the believer, which for man had no exit until Christ overcame death. Christ burst the brazen gates and crushed the iron bolts; He gained the victory over death, Satan, and Hades; and the Old Testament saints were released from the power of Hades.

Paul refers to this great triumphal act in Eph. 4:8, 9, and the gifts which the exalted Christ gave to the saints

---

[1] Eph. 4:8, 9: "When he ascended on high, he led captivity captive, and gave gifts unto men."

of the Old Testament, when He manifested Himself in Paradise, were freedom from the power of Satan and Hades, and from the kingdom of darkness; and when Christ at His ascension into Heaven led captivity captive, He took with Him into Heaven itself those souls who in Paradise had welcomed Him as the Redeemer, and from this time forward Paradise is above the earth, in Heaven itself (2 Cor. 12:1–4); and the souls of the blessed dead, ever since Christ's resurrection and ascension, according to the constant testimony of the New Testament Scriptures, are in Heaven with Christ, under the throne of His glory. But the fuller presentation of this thought belongs more properly to the Pauline Eschatology.

[ANALYSIS: 1) Being truly Divine, Christ's Soul could not remain in Hades; 2) Christ's descent into Hades a difficult topic; 3) Christ's work of redemption had a bearing on the whole universe; 4) we must distinguish between a twofold descent into Hades; 5) at death, Christ's Soul went into Hades; 6) into that part of Hades known as Paradise; 7) this the last stage of Christ's humiliation; 8) Peter's teaching in Acts 2:22–36; 9) Christ subjected Himself to the power of death voluntarily; 10) He could not be holden by death; 11) He was made alive and arose from the dead; 12) Peter's teaching in 1 Pet. 3:18–20; 13) the Risen and glorified Christ descends into Hades; 14) first, into that part of Hades where the godless are; 15) where He made proclamation of His victory; 16) no example of a probation after death; 17) changes may have taken place in the kingdom of Satan; 18) it remains the fore-hell; 19) Peter's teaching in 1 Pet. 4:6; 20) this refers to Christ's manifestation in Paradise, the upper part of Hades; 21) great changes wrought in the condition of the souls of the saints; 22) there are now no saints in Hades; 23) they were taken to Heaven, the Paradise above the earth, at the time of Christ's ascension; 24) believers now enter immediately into Heaven, into the presence of Christ.]

## § 78. *The Resurrection as the Ground of Christian Hope.*[1]

Peter lays special stress on the resurrection of Jesus, since His resurrection is the foundation of faith; for through Christ we believe in God, who raised Him up (1:21). Christ has been exalted and is now at the right Hand of God, in possession of Divine honor and dominion, so that angels, and authorities, and powers are made subject unto Him (3:22). As in 1:12, the angels appear as a higher order of creatures, so by His exaltation over them the universal sovereignty of the Exalted Christ is plainly indicated. Accordingly, Christ is not only called "our Lord," but also "the Lord," like God Himself (1:25; 2:13; 3:12).

Peter says that they were begotten again unto a living hope by the resurrection of Jesus Christ (1:3). Not till it took place was the Crucified Jesus manifested with absolute certainty as the Messiah, or exalted to full Messianic glory. Now for the first time could there open up to the Apostles a new life of hope. The Risen and Exalted Christ could and must make perfect the Messianic consummation (1:21).

Christian hope attaches itself to the expected Second Coming of the Messiah. Not till then will the still invisible Christ be revealed (1:7, 8) in His true character and in His full Messianic glory (4:13; 5:1). Then can the completion of salvation be looked for. The elect have an inheritance surely appointed for them (1:4), incorruptible and undefiled, unfading, which is reserved in Heaven for them, and which is therefore conceived of as heavenly, just as in the discourses of Jesus the perfected form of the Kingdom of God conceived as

---

[1] Compare *Weiss*, § 50.

an inheritance appears also as heavenly. Wherein this blessing consists appears from 3:7, where Christian women are called joint heirs of the grace of life (Acts 3:15). In 4:6 this life is more particularly described as being such a life as God lives—*i. e.*, an eternal and blessed life. In 5:10, however, the characteristic expression for this blessing is the eternal Divine glory in which the believers will yet participate along with their glorified Lord (4:13; 5:1, 4).

The Messianic consummation does not come without the Messianic judgment. The souls of unbelievers are not yet delivered over to final destruction. Christ has made proclamation of His work to the lost spirits (3:19) —even to all the dead (4:6), in order that not only the living but also the dead might be judged in the final Messianic Judgment. And although, after the manner of the Old Testament, God Himself is still regarded as the Righteous (2:23) Judge of the world, who impartially judges according to each one's work (1:17), still in 4:5 Christ seems to be meant as the One to whom the living and the dead will have to give an account (Acts 10:42). And because Christ, as the Judge of the world, has the final decision at His disposal, He can also deliver His own at the Messianic Judgment. Now, since it is through His resurrection and the exaltation which followed, that He has attained to the Divine glory, it is said that the salvation which baptism in His name brings (3:21) is secured through the resurrection of Jesus Christ. This deliverance from the terrible end which awaits those who are disobedient to the Gospel of God (4:17, 18) is the Messianic salvation which was already foreknown by all the prophets, and has been a subject of their investigation (1:10).

[ANALYSIS: 1) The resurrection of Christ the foundation of the Christian faith; 2) Christ exalted to universal sovereignty; 3) by His resurrection Jesus was manifested as the Messiah; 4) His full Messianic glory will be revealed at His Second Coming; 5) then the saints shall receive their heavenly inheritance; 6) the Messianic Judgment; 7) the Messianic salvation.]

## § 79. *The Apostle of Hope.*[1]

With Peter, hope forms the real central point of Christian life. From this standpoint the Apostle describes himself as a partaker of the future glory of Christ (5:1). The new life to which believers have been begotten again he calls a life of hope (1:3). That which makes the Christian wives equally honorable with their husbands is that they are joint heirs of life (3:7). The specific element of Christianity, regarding which the Christian should be able to give a reason to every man (3:15), is his hope and its ground in Christ.

This hope appears in him in the greatest energy, according to which the hoped-for consummation already appears as immediately at hand. The appearance of the Judge is near at hand (4:5). The end of all things is at hand (4:7). Just as, according to the teaching of Christ, the Messianic Judgment brings about a separation, so, according to Peter, the judgment has begun at the House of God (4:17). In the afflictions that try them there is brought about the separation between the genuine and spurious members of the Church, and therewith also the judgment over those who fall away during these temptations (4:17). But because this testing time, in which even the righteous is scarcely saved (4:18), cannot possibly last long (Mark 13:20), the afflictions of the present time can only be for a little while (1:6; 5:10).

[1] Compare *Weiss,* § 51.

So perfect and strong is this hope that the consummation of salvation is already anticipated as if it were present, and felt with blissful joy (1:3-12). In *ver.* 8, this exultant joy is not only described as unspeakably great, but as a joy which is already transfigured by the splendor of the future glory. In 3:14 it is said that Christians are already blessed in their affliction, and the reason of this is assigned in 4:14, because the Spirit of God, which has been given in baptism (3:21), rests upon them. This Spirit of God is more particularly described as the Spirit of Glory, and that, too, of the same Glory in which Christ will be revealed at His return (4:13, 14). Christians, therefore, in the possession of this Spirit, have already a kind of participation in the future glory.

This hope is also a living hope, which influences the whole moral life. It must be a *living* hope (1:3), since a real birth can bring forth only something living; and hope, if it is of the right kind, exerts an active influence over the whole moral life of man. According to 1:9, faith receives a reward. There shall be a proper analogy between the service and the reward; for he who humbles himself shall be exalted at the appointed time (5:6); he who suffers with Christ will partake of His glory (4:13); and blessing can be received only where blessing has been bestowed (3:9). In 5:4 this reward appears as the unfading crown of glory which faithful pastors shall obtain. Life in God is indeed a gift of Divine grace (3:7), and eternal glory is bestowed upon all believers; nevertheless, we shall be rewarded according to our works.

[ANALYSIS: 1) Peter the Apostle of Hope; 2) the consummation of salvation is anticipated as present; 3) this hope must be a *living* hope; 4) faith has its reward.]

## § 80. *Lechler's Presentation.*[1]

The *doctrine* of the Epistle moves round its practical aim, which is to strengthen the Christian Churches in Asia Minor. The peculiar leading idea of the Epistle appears to be the indissoluble connection and succession *of suffering aud glory* in the life of the believing Christian as in that of Jesus. In close connection with this thought is contained an abundant wealth of truths, both as regards the Person of Christ and His redeeming work, and respecting the appropriation of salvation, Christian faith and Christian hope.

The *appropriation of salvation* in Christ, and the treading of the way through suffering to glory, are the result of the calling, regeneration, and continual growth. We are *called* by God, according to His mercy (2:9, 10, 21), out of darkness into His marvelous light (2:9), to inherit a blessing (3:9), even unto His eternal glory. The *New Birth* is effected by God's power *through* the Gospel—the Word of God, which lives and abides forever (1:23, 25).

Entrance into a state of grace and salvation is effected, according to Peter, through *baptism*. He mentions it in connection with the Flood (3:20, 21), as that by which souls are saved. From this incidental expression we see clearly—1) the undoubted *aim* and *efficacy* of baptism; it "doth now save" us from future judgment and destruction, and makes us partakers of salvation; hence it is not merely a symbolical, but an efficacious act—a means of grace; and 2) the *moral nature* and *significance* of baptism. It is not a purification from bodily filth, but we are freed from an evil conscience (Heb. 10:22, 23), since baptism secures to us that which we

[1] Compare his *Apostolic and Post-Apostolic Times*, vol. 2, pp. 135-162.

desire with God—a good conscience, a purifying of the conscience, even the forgiveness of sins (Acts 2:38).

The new-born children of God must *grow* (2:2) unto salvation, in faith (1:5, 8, 9), in obedience to Christ and the truth (1:2, 14, 22), in sanctification, with a pure, God-fearing conduct (1:2, 15). For this purpose there is required, on the one hand, a laying aside of all vice (2:1; 3:10, 11), and abstaining from fleshly lusts (1:14; 2:11; 4:1–4, 15), self-control and sobriety (1:13; 4:7; 5:8); on the other hand, the fear of God (1:17; 3:14, 15), love to Jesus, and communion with Him as the Corner-stone and Chief Shepherd (1:8; 2:4, 5; 5:4); finally, constant brotherly love, which covers a multitude of the sins of others (1:22; 2:17; 3:8; 4:8).

[ANALYSIS: 1) The leading idea of the Epistle; 2) Peter's view of the appropriation of salvation; 3) of the New Birth; 4) of the aim and significance of baptism; 5) of growth in sanctification.]

# SECTION III.

## THE EPISTLE OF JAMES.

### CHAPTER V.

#### CHRISTIANITY AS THE PERFECT LAW.

§ 81. *The Word of Truth.*[1]

Among the good gifts, all of which come from above, from God, James names as the chief, the Word of Truth, by means of which God has made Christians what they are (1:17, 18). This Word is able to save our souls (1:21), because of the revelation of the truth which it contains. This Word of Truth appears as a word which is not only to be heard, but also to be done (1:19–23); and in 1:25 it is even called the Perfect Law, because in it there is given the perfect revelation of the Will of God, and by this term the law of the Old Testament is adjudged as imperfect.

This Word is implanted in Christians (1:21), written in their hearts (Jer. 31:33). By means of it they are begotten again, so that they can now fulfill the perfect law of freedom (1:25; 2:12). The new life of the converted is nothing less than a new birth, the implantation of an essentially new life—a second creation of God. The medium of it is the Word, the Gospel of Christ, which is thus a life-producing, creative Word. The object of this new birth (1:18) is that we should be the

---

[1] Compare *Weiss*, § 52.

first fruits dedicated to God—the sanctified, peculiar people of God. The original ground of it is the free, good, gracious will of God, so that regeneration is solely God's gift and boon (1:17).

Christianity is called a law of *liberty* (1:25; 2:12), because it does not burden with a yoke and enslave with enactments, but, by virtue of regeneration and renewal (1:18-25), it fulfills the law of God spontaneously in a condition of internal liberty, through the union of the human with the Divine will, in grace and love (2:18).[1]

That which characterizes Christians, as such, is their faith (2:5). That James thinks very highly of faith may be clearly seen from 1:3, 6; 2:1, 5; 5:15; particularly that he views faith in internal union with patience (1:3) and work (2:1), as well as with prayer (5:15), and that faith is to him something great and glorious, elevating man and enriching him inwardly (2:5).[2] As regards the *nature* of faith, it is in its inner form a *confidence devoid of doubt* (1:6), excluding all weakness and double-mindedness (1:8). It embraces in itself a moral unity and steadfastness, the result of trials. Faith is therefore *practical* (2:1-4). It is not merely a believing knowledge, as demons have (2:19), but it manifests itself as living (1:3). It cannot be separated from works without becoming in itself something dead (2:17, 26)—being, on the contrary, an active principle and impelling power in man. The *object* of faith is the One God (2:19), our God and Father (1:27; 3:9), and more especially Jesus Christ as the Exalted and glorified Lord (1:1; 2:1), whose coming as Judge of the world is near at hand (5:7, 8).[3]

[1] Compare *Lechler*, vol. 1, pp. 294, 301.
[2] *Lechler*, vol. 1, p 302.
[3] *Schmid*, § 57.

[ANALYSIS: 1) The Word is able to save our souls; 2) is the perfect revelation of the Will of God; 3) by means of it Christians are born again; 4) the object and ground of the new birth; 5) Christianity a law of liberty; 6) the nature of faith; 7) the object of faith.]

### § 82. *Justification.*[1]

The relation of faith to justification (2:14–26) forms an important element in the doctrine of this Epistle. The idea of justification, according to James, is contained in *to save* as the general designation of salvation (2:14; 1:21), and is explained by the expressions, "to be reckoned for righteousness," and "to be called a friend of God" (2:23). In this, James, like Paul (Rom. 4:3), has reference to Gen. 15:6, and understands by justification *to declare righteous*, to treat as righteous, and to place in a friendly relation to God.

In this Epistle, James maintains that justification is conditional, not *on faith alone, but on works* (2:21, 24, 25). But when James says *by works, faith* is not excluded. The works are those of faith, not works simply as such. He merely opposes the delusion that justification was conditional on bare faith, which is without works, and therefore dead (2:26). The whole treatment shows that James is speaking of works by which faith may manifest its vitality and activity; but they are fruits of, and not identical with, faith. A man cannot show faith without works; but where works exist, faith may be proved by them. A merely theoretical belief without works is the faith of devils, not of Christians (2:19)—a dead and empty faith (2:17, 20, 26). Whoever depends on a faith of this kind is "a vain man" (2:20). While James lays so much stress on prac-

[1] Compare *Weiss*, § 53; *Schmid*, § 57; *Lechler*, vol. I, pp. 302–308.

## JUSTIFICATION.

tical and living faith, which brings forth works, he will acknowledge no works as Christian and justifying before God but those in which faith is shown (2;18), and is perfected (2:22).

James makes justification conditional on works effected by virtue of faith, and not on faith in itself. Paul, on the other hand, makes justification dependent on faith alone. There need, however, be no real difference between these views. Both are true, if rightly understood. James and Paul agree, in a negative assertion, in a twofold way. 1) Both teach that justification *is not dependent on the works of the law.* 2) Both agree, in principle, that justification *is not made conditional on a dead faith.* On first examination it seems as if, in positive doctrine, there was a difference—as if Paul said, "Faith, so long as it is without works, does justify;" but James, "does not justify." But this sharp line of distinction is not quite a correct one. The deepest ground of difference lies in this, that James looks at the Christian life as it is shown forth, and he regards faith without works as dead; while Paul dwells on the vitality of faith in itself, before even it has produced works—that it may be, and is, a principle of life in so far as it embraces Christ; and exactly so far a condition of justification, apart from the fact whether it has been developed in works. When James says, that "as the body apart from the spirit is dead, even so faith apart from works is dead" (2:26), we are not to misunderstand James. He certainly does not mean that the works were the soul, and faith the body. He does not mean that God would by works only recognize the genuineness of faith; for to Him, the Omniscient, the true nature of faith is plainly evident ere it has had time to show itself in works. If James had been asked whether a faith, in itself living, can justify the subject, although no time were allowed for this faith to prove itself by works, he certainly could not have denied it; for his view of faith and regeneration show that. He had to do with those who contented themselves with, and boasted in, a merely theoretical, historical faith; with those who, being void of love and despising poor and lowly brethren (2:1-4), presumed to be teachers of others. He calls their attention to the useless nature of a dead faith.

The thought clearly lying at the presentation of James is, that faith, to quote the words of Luther, is "a living, powerful, active thing;" but that its attestation in obedience, in active love to God and one's neighbor, is indispensable to its growth and full maturity. Hence, faith and works do not stand *side by side*, but are connected in a living, organic way; so that works grow out of faith, and in their turn react on faith, which thus attains its completion. (*Lechler.*) Both James and Paul teach that we are justified by faith; but James, to meet a specific perversion that had ignorantly or wickedly been made of that doctrine, shows that the faith that justifies is the one that also works out righteousness. We are justified by faith in the sight of God, and faith is demonstrated before the eyes of men to be a just and true faith by works. My justification does not depend on my works or my sanctification. My certainty of reconciliation requires a more steadfast and immovable foundation. This is Christ, the Perfect One, appropriated by faith.

[ANALYSIS: 1) The idea of justification, according to James; 2) dead faith will not justify; 3) theoretical belief will not justify; 4) the apparent discrepancy between Paul and James; 5) both teach that justification is not dependent on the works of the law; 6) both agree that justification is not made conditional on a dead faith; 7) the real difference is that James looks at the manifestation of the Christian life; 8) while Paul dwells on the vitality of faith in itself; 9) James does not teach that God recognizes the genuineness of faith by works; 10) but that the faith which justifies also works out righteousness.]

## § 83. *Election.*[1]

That which believers are, they do not owe to themselves, but to God alone, who has chosen them (2:5). In contrast to those who preferred the rich, unbelieving Jew to a poor Christian brother (2:1–4), God has chosen the poor to be a people of His possession (2:5), because it was among them that He found those who love Him (1:12; 2:5).

The historical act through which God has accomplished this election is by the new birth wrought by the Word of Truth (1:18). This act is explicitly traced back to the free-will of God (1:18). In 2:5 it is stated that the end of election is that Christians should be rich in faith. According to James, faith is not at all the condition of election; rather God has worked faith in the elect in order that He might enable them to obtain the riches given in faith; or we can regard the historical act of election as consisting in the working of faith, as well as in regeneration by the Word. Since the Exalted Messiah both can and will carry out the work of salvation which He has begun, the believer knows himself to be an heir of the Kingdom of God (2:5).

[ANALYSIS: 1) The elect; 2) the historical act through which the election is accomplished; 3) the ground of it; 4) its aim.]

---

[1] Compare *Weiss*, § 54.

## CHAPTER VI.

#### THE DIVINE CLAIM AND THE DIVINE RECOMPENSE.

§ 84. *The Divine Claim.*[1]

God desires that the spirit of man, which derives its origin from Him, should belong to Him exclusively with all its love (2:5). The friendship of the world is enmity with God, because He wishes to have exclusive possession even of the inclination of the heart (2:4). According to 1:27, there proceeds from the world a staining influence, against which true religion has to guard itself. The less one has of earthly goods, so much the less will this influence be, and therefore it is that the "poor as to the world" love God, and are therefore chosen by Him (2:5).

God claims the most central point of man, the soul, and with it the heart, in which the one has its seat, because if the soul is divided between God and the world there results only an instability of the moral walk (1:8), which cannot be pleasing to God. Every transgression against an individual commandment makes man guilty, as if he had sinned against them all (2:10). Every turning of the heart to that which is worldly is opposed to the exclusive claim of God, and is described as pride (4:6, 7), as a violation of man's dutiful subjection to God. Again, subjection to God, which is meant to hinder man from loving the world, stands parallel with resistance to the Devil (4:7). The Devil is regarded

[1] Compare *Weiss*, § 55.

as the God-resisting power which is dominant in the world—the power which gives to the heart of man its sinful bent to worldly things, and to whose will man subjects himself, when he allows himself to be seduced by the charm of worldly things. Alongside of the Devil mention is also made of demons, or the angels of Satan, who as such are delivered over to the unavoidable judgment (2:19). The wisdom which is selfish is described as earthly, sensual, and of demoniac origin (3:15). Since the demons are delivered over to the judgment, *Ge-henna* is the abode which is appointed to them for the future ; and, since this place is thought of here also as a hell of fire, it is said in 3:6 that sinful passion is kindled by hell. Hell is therefore thought of as even already the characteristic sphere of demoniac power, and this latter is regarded as the active principle in sin. In order that there be an undivided surrender to God, there is required also a trust in God which is free from doubt (1:6-8), and which proves itself by enduring patience in the midst of trial (1:2, 3, 12).

As means of gaining the victory over these trials of affliction, James mentions prayer (5:13), and the intercession, to which we are to invite others (5:14, 16). If prayer is to be heard, it must be a prayer of faith (5:15), and of a righteous man (5:16). Without prayer we cannot receive anything of which we stand in need (4:2); but it must not be for ungodly purposes (4:3). It is only by means of prayer that we can obtain the wisdom which we need (1:5); and God, the Giver of all good gifts (1:17), gives liberally and without upbraiding the earnest supplicant (1:5). Bodily deliverance and recovery are promised as the result of believing prayer and anointing with oil in the name of the Lord ; in close connection with which follows the forgiveness of any special sins which may have stood in a peculiar relation to the state of sickness (5:14, 15).

[ANALYSIS: 1) God wants the whole heart; 2) the world must be resisted; 3) the Devil must be resisted; 4) sinful passions are kindled in hell; 5) for consecration to God deep trust in God is required; 6) the importance of prayer.]

### § 85. *Human Sin.*[1]

It is quite in harmony with the prevailing moral and practical character of the Epistle that James treats so often and so emphatically of sin in a tone of admonition and warning. He pursues it in all its manifestations in lust (1:13, 14; 4:2), in word (3:2, 6–9; 5:12), and in work (2:9, 11), in doing and not doing (4:17). But he rises also to the ultimate origin of sin within the personal life and consciousness, repudiating the error which would attribute to God the authorship of evil. James does this by setting forth the history of sin in every man, in its three stages of development—of *lust*, *sin*, and *death* (1:13, 15). (*Lechler.*)

The first is the *lust* that draws away and entices to evil (1:14), dwelling within man himself and working from within outwards, and not inwards from without. This lust, when it has conceived through the action of the will, brings forth *sin;* and sin, when it is finished, brings forth *death*—spiritual, bodily, and eternal. James's doctrine of the individual man being the free causality of sin, is a correct expression of the moral consciousness in man. How deeply men are entangled in sin is evident from his statement that men are in need of redemption (1:21; 5:20), and that they must be born again through the Word of Truth, so as to belong to the first-fruits of God's creatures.

[1] Compare *Weiss*, § 56; *Schmid*, § 58; *Lechler*, vol. I, pp. 298-301.

## HUMAN SIN.

Intimately connected with this exposition of sin is what James says of sins of the tongue (3:6–8). He perceives that they are so manifold, and have so great an influence on the conduct, character, and destiny of man that he calls the tongue a whole "world of iniquity," ascribes to it an importance in respect to the entire man equal to that of the rudder by means of which a great ship is guided (3:4, 5), or to a little fire which may kindle a whole forest (3:5). He asserts that the tongue may defile the whole body with sin, that it is the impelling power of human nature, the wheel of life (3:6), and that it is set on fire by hell. Hence he describes the tongue as ungovernable, an unruly evil, full of deadly poison (3:8). The universality of sin is very strongly presented: "in many things we all stumble" (3:2).

James does not by any means treat of sin and death merely with respect to the individual man; but in this visible world, as James believes and confesses, sin is connected with a kingdom of darkness in the invisible world. The tongue may be set on fire of hell (3:6), and then kindle the whole body. Ungodly wisdom is not only earthly and sensual, but also demoniac (3:15). He that will be a friend of God must withstand the *Devil* (4:7), which the Christian can do, and with such success that the Devil must flee. (*Lechler.*)

[ANALYSIS: 1) Sin in its three stages of development; 2) the origin of sin; 3) the sins of the tongue; 4) the universality of sin; 5) sin is connected with the kingdom of darkness.]

### § 86. *Recompense and Judgment.*[1]

Those who have patiently borne suffering are called blessed, because they shall receive the crown of life

---
[1] Compare *Weiss*, § 57.

(1:12; 5:11). James supports his warnings by pointing to the judgment (5:9, 12).

The recompense is an equivalent one, and for that very reason the merciful can look also for a merciful judgment (2:13). The more God demands, so much the more does He also give (4:5, 6); the more responsibility one takes upon himself, so much the heavier a judgment has one to expect (3:1). Those who humble themselves shall be exalted (4:10).

In a certain sense there is already an earthly recompense. James assumes that bodily sickness may be a consequence of sin (5: 15, 16). But the Great Day of Recompense is near at hand, because the Advent of the Messianic Judge of the world is near (5:3, 7, 9). The miseries which will then befall the ungodly are already in the act of coming upon them (5:1); already the day of their destruction is imminent, which will indeed be for them "a day of slaughter" (5:5). The Messiah will soon appear (5:8), who as the Judge of the world is alone able to save and to destroy (4:12).

The reward of sin is death, the promise for which Christians look is life and the Kingdom. The judgment shall consume the flesh of the godless as fire (5:3); but the judgment shall especially overtake the soul (5:20); for the body and soul of the godless, after the resurrection, shall remain in eternal torment. The opposite of this eternal death is the crown of life (1:12), which is promised to those who love God.

Not only does judgment threaten ungodly men of the world (5:1–6), but also believers, if they are only hearers and not doers of the Word (1:25); if they know to do good and do it not (4:17); if their worship of God is internally empty and hypocritical (1:26); if they set themselves up as teachers without being called (3:1); if they do not practice merciful love (2:13)—in which case a judgment all the more severe awaits them (2:13 ; 4:12). (*Lechler.*)

[ANALYSIS: 1) There is a recompense coming; 2) which shall be equivalent; 3) there is a partial recompense already on earth; 4) but the great Day of Recompense is near at hand; 5) the wages of sin is eternal death.]

# SECTION IV.

## The Second Epistle of Peter and the Epistle of Jude.

### CHAPTER VII.

#### CHRISTIAN HOPE AND CHRISTIAN STRIVING AFTER VIRTUE.

§ 87. *The Object of Christian Knowledge.*[1]

In the Second Epistle of Peter,[2] Christianity is presented mainly on its subjective side, as knowledge of the grace of God. By it, the Christians have escaped from the pollutions of the world (2:20); by it, grace and salvation are multiplied to them (1:2); in it, their Christian life increases (3:18), because through it everything which pertains to the new life is given (1:3). In conformity with this, the Christian life is said to be the way of truth (2:2), corresponding to the truth given to us (1:12); and Jude speaks of his readers as having once for all known all things (*ver.* 5). This knowledge is the knowledge of the grace of God, who hath called us in the new relation of children, and has given us great and precious promises (1:4).

These promises are those especially contained in the words of the holy prophets of the Old Testament (3:2,

---

[1] Compare *Weiss*, § 127.

[2] For a full development of the Theology, Soteriology, and Eschatology of this Epistle, see my "Studies in the Book," vol. 1, pp. 87–89.

13); for these, being moved by the Holy Spirit, have spoken what they received of God (1:21). These promises have received new light and new security for their fulfillment by the manifestation of Christ (1:17-21).

This knowledge, therefore, is called a knowledge of our Messianic Lord and Saviour Jesus Christ (1:8; 2:20; 3:18). Jesus is acknowledged as our *Lord* (1:2, 8, 14, 16; Jude 4, 17, 21, 25), as the *only* Lord (Jude 4; *cf.* 2 Pet. 2:1). As such, He is praised by a doxology (3.18; Jude 25), and is described as our Messianic Saviour (1:1, 11; 3:2, 18), who, with Divine power (1:3), has given us all things necessary for salvation; and by the cleansing (1:9) and deliverance (2:1) from sin secured by Him has guaranteed to us the consummation of salvation.

With the knowledge of the promises (1:3, 4), there is connected *faith* (1:5), which is regarded essentially as confidence in the fulfillment of the promise. Faith is regarded as a blessing (2 Pet. 1:1), and as a most precious blessing—one to be protected with the holiest earnestness, which cannot be replaced by any other of equal value. Faith is called *most holy* (Jude 20). If it is here designated as the foundation on which the whole Christian moral life is built, there is in this implied only the fundamental thought of the whole Epistle, according to which knowledge and faith, for the sake of their objects, are the impelling motives for all striving after Christian virtue.

[ANALYSIS : 1) Christianity is knowledge of the grace of God; 2) prophecy has received new light by the manifestation of Christ; 3) Christianity may be defined as a knowledge of our Saviour Jesus Christ; 4) joined with faith.]

## § 88. *The Striving After Christian Virtue.*[1]

He who lacks zeal in developing his moral life (1:5) proves himself to be idle and unfruitful in reference to the knowledge of Christ (1:8); like an unfruitful tree, twice dead (Jude 12). True knowledge must, therefore, bear fruit for the moral life. Whoever gives himself up to the false doctrine of liberty has denied the Lord, as though he had never known that He had delivered him from the dominion of sin (2:1). As the preaching of the Gospel, with its promises, produces this fruitful knowledge, these promises may be designated as that by which we are born again, and so made partakers (1:4) of the Divine nature—of Gods peculiar holiness.

Through the preaching of the Gospel, and the knowledge thus imparted, Christians have escaped the defilements of the world (2:20; 1:4). They know themselves to be called and elected from the total mass of sinful men; but their calling and election has to be made sure (1:10) by zeal in the manifestation of fruitful knowledge (1:5). After one has, by the power of God, been once made partaker of His Divine nature (1:4), it is necessary to keep oneself holy and unspotted (3:11, 14; Jude 21). If this keeping is referred to the power of God (Jude 1, 24), then we must understand this as of the work of God by His Word. In the knowledge of Christ (2:20) we have received a holy command, which points out to us the way of righteousness (2:21). This commandment of Christ has been delivered to us by the Apostles (3:2), has been enjointed by Paul in all his Epistles (3:15, 16), and requires us to keep ourselves unspotted, in view of the expected final consummation (3:14).

Godliness forms the deepest root of Christian moral-

[1] Compare *Weiss*, § 128.

ity. In it is comprehended the nature of the true life (1:3). Every form of natural knowledge and moral energy is of no avail without this God-fearing mind of true piety, as it alone gives to moral effort its true worth (1:6). But brotherly love (1:7) is peculiar to Christianity, as also that general love (1:7) which goes beyond the circle of Christian brethren.

The Epistle of Jude is especially directed against a form of heathenish godlessness[1] (*vers.* 4, 15, 18; *cf.* 2 Pet. 2:6; 3:7), whose peculiarity is the walk in the defiling lusts of the flesh (Jude 7, 8, 16, 18, 23), and in covetousness (2 Pet. 2:14). With this Godlessness is conjoined a moral license—a libertinism which is characterized as a despising and a denying of the Lordship of Christ (Jude 4, 8); and in so far as it at the same time brings men under the power of the Devil, is described as a shameful despising of demoniac powers (Jude 8–10). In the Second Epistle of Peter, this libertinism appears expressly as the preaching of a false liberty (2:17–19) which seeks support from misunderstood or perverted passages of Paul and the Old Testament (3:16).

[ANALYISIS: 1) True knowledge must bear moral fruit; 2) is produced by the preaching of the Word; 3) we must make our calling and election sure; 4) by keeping ourselves unspotted from the world; 5) Godliness, true piety, the deepest root of Christian morality; 6) brotherly love; 7) all heathenish godlessness and libertinism must be resisted.]

## § 89. *The Destruction of the World and the Consummation of Salvation.*[2]

Every Divine judgment of the past is but a type of the Final Judgment, which, on the great Day of the

---

[1] In my "Studies in the Book," vol. 1, pp. 104, 105, I have fully developed Jude's remarkable description of the different aspects of sin.
[2] Compare *Weiss*, § 129.

Lord, brings eternal destruction upon all the godless, even those of the past. Prophecy of old (Jude 4; 2 Pet. 2:3) has set forth unto condemnation and destruction all the ungodly (Jude 14, 15). An emblem of this destruction is found in the perishing of Sodom and Gomorrah (2 Pet. 2:6; Jude 7); and, in conformity with this, destruction is regarded under the symbol of eternal fire as a judgment of God. This Divine judgment does not spare even the evil angels, who are kept in the prison of Hades, bound with everlasting chains and covered with deep darkness (Jude 6; 2 Pet. 2:4). This destruction is regarded as the thickest darkness, the deepest misery, as loss of eternal life, as perdition (Jude 13). The great Day of Judgment (Jude 6; 2. Pet. 2:9; 3:7), when the Lord shall come as the Judge of the world (Jude 14, 15), will bring this judgment to its final decisive crisis.

As the old world perished by the waters of the Flood (2 Pet. 3:6; 2:5), and the present form of the world is protected by God's Word of Promise against a second destruction by water (Gen. 9:11; 2 Pet. 3:7), there remains now only fire as the element to bring about this destruction (2 Pet. 3:7). On the great Day of the Lord the heavens will be dissolved in fire, and the earth, with all its works, will be burnt up; and the new heavens and the new earth, wherein dwelleth righteousness, shall appear (2 Pet. 3:10–13). It does not follow, however, that the destruction which shall come upon ungodly men (*ver.* 7) shall consist of a blotting out, or of annihilation; but the godless shall be handed over to a destruction, and eternal misery, from which there is no deliverance (Jude 7).

The Day of Judgment and of the destruction of the world is also at the same time the day of Christ's Coming (1:16; 3:12). And although men shall arise who will mock at the delay of the promise of the *Parousia*, or Coming of Christ (2 Pet. 3:3, 4), this delay is but an act of God's long-suffering, as He would lead even those Christians who had fallen away to repentance (2 Pet. 3:9), and thus save them from the punishment of eternal fire (Jude 7).

With the *Parousia*, the eternal Kingdom of Christ begins, into which Christians who have made their calling and election sure (2 Pet. 1:10) shall enter, there to live for ever (1:11). This eternal Kingdom of Christ begins in the new Heaven and the new earth, in which righteousness dwells (2 Pet. 3:13), and the gift bestowed to believers is eternal life (Jude 21). This perfect Kingdom is therefore no earthly one, as the present form of the world has passed away.

[ANALYSIS: 1) The Day of Judgment brings eternal destruction upon the godless; 2) this destruction described under the symbol of eternal fire; 3) the world shall be destroyed by fire; 4) but the ungodly shall not be annihilated ; 5) the destruction of the world will take place at the *Parousia* of Christ; 6) at which time the eternal Kingdom of Christ begins ; 7) which Kingdom is not earthly.]

# SECTION V.

## THE EVANGELISTS MARK AND MATTHEW.

### CHAPTER VIII.

#### THE MESSIAH OF THE JEWS.

§ 90. *The Gospel of Mark.*[1]

According to the oldest tradition, the Gospel of Mark is based upon the oral Gospel of Peter. It proclaims itself to be the glad tidings of Jesus Christ, the Son of God (1:1)—*i. e.*, of the Messiah, the Christ (14:61). It shows at the very beginning how John prepared the way for Him by his baptism of repentance (1:4–8), and then immediately it introduces Jesus Himself as anointed in baptism, witnessed to by God Himself as His Beloved Son, and proved in temptation by Satan to be the Messiah (1:9–13).[2] Jesus begins his Messianic activity with

---

[1] Compare *Weiss*, § 136.

[2] "The Second Gospel begins immediately with the baptism of John, to end with the resurrection and exaltation of Jesus, and moves thus precisely within that circle which had been marked out by Peter himself (Acts 1:21, 22), for the witness of the Lord." (*Van Oosterzee.*)

"Like St. Peter, Mark is contented to lay the foundation of the Christain faith, and leave the superstructure to others. It is enough that Christ should be presented in the most vivid light, unfolding the truth in acts rather than in words. . . . Everything centres in the immediate facts to be noticed without drawing a complete history. St. Mark frames a series of perfect pictures. . . . The chief point for study in Mark's Gospel is the vividness of its details,

the proclamation of the approach of the Kingdom of God (1:14, 15); and He proves Himself the Promised Messiah, just as in the sermon of Peter (Acts. 10:38), by at once healing the sick, and especially by driving out devils, who knew and feared Him as the Messiah (1:24, 34; 3:11, 12; 5:7). The more clearly He reveals His Messianic calling in His power to forgive sins (2:10), as also in deeds of even greater power,[1] the less do even His chosen Twelve understand Him (4:13; 6:52; 7:18; 8:17–21), until Peter in their name confesses Him as the Messiah (8:29).

These details point clearly to the impression produced upon an eyewitness, and are not such as would suggest themselves to the imagination of a chronicler. At one time we find a minute touch which places the whole scene before us (4:37, 38; 6:38, 48; 9:3, 14-16; 10:50; 15:44); now there is a phrase which reveals the feeling of those who were witnesses of some mighty work (6:52; 8:32; 9:10; 10:24, 32; 11:10); now a word which preserves some trait of the Saviour's tenderness (6:31, 34; 8:3; 9:21, 25, 27; 10:3, 4); or some expressive turn of His language (1:15; 7:8; 8:38; 9:39; 11:17, 24). There are some additions which indicate very distinctly the Apostolic source of the peculiarities of Mark. He alone describes, on several occasions, the look and feeling of the Lord (3:5, 34; 5:32; 6:6; 10:21, 23; 11:11), and preserves the very Aramaic words which He uttered (3:17; 5:41; 7:11, 34; 14:36). . . . St. Mark, more than any other Evangelist, records the effect which was produced on others by the Lord's working. From the beginning to the end he tells us of the wonder and amazement and fear with which men listened to the teaching of Christ." (*Condensed* from Westcott's *Introduction to the Study of the Gospels*, pp. 362-368, Amer. ed.)

[1] 1. The unclean spirit cast out (1:21-28); 2. The fever healed (1:29-34); 3. The leper cleansed (1:40-45); 4. The palsy healed (2:1-12); 5. The withered hand restored (3:1-5); 6. Various miracles (3:10, 11); 7. The tempest stilled (4:35-41); 8. The legion cast out (5:1-17); 9. The woman with issue healed (5:25-34); 10. Jairus's daughter raised (5:35-43); 11. The feeding of the 5,000 (6:35-44); 12. The walking on the water (6:48,49); 13. Various miracles (6:54-57); etc.

From this time Jesus begins to prepare His disciples for His death (8:31 ; 9:12, 31 ; 10:33, 34, 38), while He adds the prophecy of His resurrection, and at last explains the mystery of His death by referring to its saving significance (10:45). At the same time the announcement of His Second Coming in glory begins (8:38), which in the Transfiguration scene (9:2–8) receives its Divine confirmation in the same sense as in 2 Pet. 1:16-18. He finally goes to Jerusalem (11:9, 10), is greeted by the people as the Messiah, declares Himself in the presence of the Sanhedrim as the Beloved Son of God (12:6), and announces to the disciples His coming again (13:3–37)—a coming which is to finish what His earthly activity had left unfinished. He goes with the disciples to the Last Supper, at which He institutes the New Covenant (14:24), and before the judgment seat acknowledges His Messianic dignity (15:2) by an appeal to His exaltation and Second Coming (14:62). At His death the Veil of the Holiest was rent (15:38), by which His Messianic work on earth, as our High Priest, was finished, and by the loud triumphal cry with which He expired the heathen centurion acknowledged Him to be the Son of God (15:39). The Gospel closes with the glad tidings of the resurrection, of the appearance of the Risen One (16:6, 7, 9, 12, 14), and he follows out the Messianic progress up to the exaltation of Christ to Heaven (16:19)—facts which confirm His Messiahship.

It is clear, therefore, from the Gospel of Mark, that during His earthly life Jesus had already shown Himself to be the Messiah both by word and deed, and that this was fully confirmed by His exaltation, and shall be completely perfected at His Second Coming.

[ANALYSIS: 1) The Gospel of Mark is Petrine; 2) proves that Jesus is the Messiah; 3) argument of the Evangelist.]

## § 91. *The Gospel of St. Matthew.*[1]

The First Gospel, in a more artistic and scientific way than the Second, furnishes proof that Jesus is the Messiah promised by the prophets.[2] It begins, therefore, to set forth Jesus, who from His Messianic dignity has the surname of CHRIST (1:1,16,18 ; 2:4; 27:17, 22), as the lawful Heir of the royal house of David, in whom the whole Divinely appointed history of this house is to be closed (1:17). Even in the history of the birth and childhood of this King of the Jews (2:2), the fulfillment of Messianic prophecy is shown throughout (1: 23 ; 2:5, 6, 15, 17, 18, 23). When Jesus is described as a Preacher of the Kingdom of Heaven, and as a healer of the sick (4:23), it is referred to as a fulfillment of prophecy, both in His appearance as a teacher (4:14–16), of which chapters five to seven give an example, and in His healing work (8:17), which chapters eight and nine depict. In the story of His sufferings the fulfillment of prophecy is pointed out in the Messianic entrance into Jerusalem (21:4, 5, 16), in the fate of the betrayer (27:9,10), and in the representation given of the Crucifixion (27:34, 39–43). Finally, He appears in the fare-

[1] Compare *Weiss*, § 136.

[2] Tradition is constant in affirming that St. Matthew wrote his Gospel in Judea, for the use of Jewish converts, and in Aramaic. At the same time all early writers equally agree in accepting the *Greek* Gospel of Matthew, without noticing the existence of any doubt as to its authenticity. There can be no question that an authorized Greek representative of the Hebrew Gospel existed in the generation after the Apostles. There was a Hebrew archetype, and yet the present Greek Gospel bears no marks of being a translation. The true explanation is that an oral Gospel probably existed from the first, both in Aramaic and in Greek, and that St. Matthew originally wrote his Gospel in Aramaic, and then also in Greek. (For a clear presentation of the characteristics of this Gospel, see Westcott's *Introduction to the Study of the Gospels.*)

well scene in Galilee as the Exalted Messiah, who has received the Messianic government of the world (28:16–18).

Matthew loves to set forth prominently how Jesus, in the way of the old prophets, puts more value on compassionate love than on sacrifice (9:13; 12:7), and sets His Person above the Holy Place of the Old Covenant (12:6). The commands which the Exalted Christ lays on His followers to keep (28:20) are no longer the Mosaic, but His own.

A Jewish-Christian tendency belongs to the Gospel of Matthew as well as to the Epistle of James, and there is a close relation between these two Apostles. The Gospel as well as the Epistle of James was written exclusively for believers in Israel. We find James's idea of God the same as that which meets us in the Sermon on the Mount, as the Holy and the Perfect One (5:48)—the Judge who can both save and destroy (5:22–30); as He, who full of love, gives every good and perfect gift (5:45; 7:9–11), especially the Holy Spirit, to them that ask Him (Matt. 7:7–11; James 1:5–7, 17). The Sermon on the Mount presupposes rather than displays the Messiahship of Jesus; and this feature, too, we find in James's treatment. As James sets forth Christianity as righteousness, and the Sermon on the Mount presents this righteousness to be a doing of the Divine Will (7:21), or of the law (5:19), in contrast to the mere saying, "Lord," "Lord!" so also James lays stress on faith being perfected in works;—for faith may be recognized through works, as a tree by its fruits (Matt. 7:16–10).[1]

---

[1] See *Schmid's Biblical Theology*, § 60, in which he gives us a very full comparison between James's system of doctrine and that of the Gospel of St. Matthew.

It is worthy of remark that the precedence of Peter over the other Apostles appears in none of the Evangelists so prominently as in Matthew. In this Gospel Peter is called before all the other Apostles (4:18). He is designated "the first" (10:2), which is not the case in the parallel passages. In 16:18, 19, he receives the weighty promise, which is absent both from Luke and Mark. These circumstances, the prominence given to the precedence of Peter in connection with the book's unmistakable design for churches formed out of Israel, and the fact that the eye of the author is especially directed to the Old Covenant and the union of Christianity with the Old Testament, place the Gospel of Matthew in the rank of the Jewish-Christian Scriptures belonging to the Canon, an example of the Petrine type of doctrine,[1] while the presence of many passages respecting the Divine dignity of the Person of Jesus, the founding of the New Covenant by His atoning death (26:26), the necessity of regeneration to righteousness in the Kingdom of God, and the teaching with reference to the world—embracing destination of Christ's Church,

---

[1] "Whatever we may think as to the intricate questions which this Gospel presents to us, this much is evident: that it bears a purely Palestinian type of character, and that the author is, to that extent, rather allied to Peter than to Paul or John. The manifest tendency of the First Gospel to present Jesus in the light of prophetic Scripture as the Promised Messiah, is entirely in the spirit of our Apostle. As Peter, in his proclamation of Christ (10:38), attaches special value to the miracles of the Lord, so here also a number of His miracles are grouped together (chapters 8 and 9); and as Peter, so also Matthew, proclaims the Lord as Israel's Messiah, while excluding the Gentiles just as little as does Peter. Nowhere, finally, are the eschatological discourses of the Lord, which are of such priceless value for Peter, related so fully and in such order as in the first Gospel." (*Van Oosterzee*, § 31.)

must prevent us from ascribing a narrow, low, or legal standpoint to the First Gospel. (*Lechler.*)

[ANALYSIS: 1) The aim of the Gospel; 2) written for Jewish Christians, in both Aramaic and Greek; 3) argument of the Apostle; 4) close relation between the Gospel of Matthew and the Epistle of James; 5) The Gospel of Matthew clearly Petrine in doctrine.]

# SECTION VI.

## SUMMARY OF PETRINE TEACHING.

### CHAPTER IX.

#### THE PETRINE CHRISTOLOGY.

§ 92. *The Pre-Incarnate Existence of Jesus.*

Peter recognizes the pre-existence of Christ in his first letter (1:11), when he declares that the Spirit which resided in and moved the Old Testament prophets was the Spirit of Christ. From 1:20, we also learn that Christ had an actual personal subsistence before the world's foundation,[1] and was an object of the Divine knowledge, and at the end of the ages was manifested and appeared as a historical person. This can also be seen from Peter's reference to the Three Persons of the Trinity (1 Pet. 1:2), and the designation in the Second Epistle of Jesus Christ as our God and Saviour (2 Pet. 1:1, 2); as also in the ascription to Him of two doxologies, one in each Epistle (1 Pet. 4:11; 2 Pet. 3:18).

We can also infer from the fact that James calls Jesus the Lord (1:1; 2:1; 5:14, 15), and associates Him with the Father (1:1) on manifest terms of equality, and calls Him the Lord of Glory (2:1), that he also believes in Christ's pre-existence.

[ANALYSIS: 1) Peter teaches the pre-existence of Christ; 2) so does James.]

---

[1] 1 Pet. 1:20, "Christ: who was foreknown, indeed, before the foundation of the world, but was manifested at the end of the times for your sake."

## § 93. *Christ Truly Divine.*

Both in the Acts and in his two Epistles, Peter takes it for granted that Christ is truly God—in all essential respects co-ordinate with the Father. In his Sermon on the day of Pentecost, Peter maintains that God hath made "this Jesus, whom ye crucified," "both Lord and Christ" (Acts 2:34, 36). In his First Epistle he ascribes to Him Divine names (1:3; 3:15) and attributes (2:3, 4, 6, 7); and in his Second Epistle Christ is directly called God (1:1).

[ANALYSIS: 1) Christ is truly Divine; 2) Peter ascribes to Him Divine names and attributes.]

## § 94. *Christ Truly Human.*

Peter everywhere ascribes a true humanity to Jesus Christ. This is not only recognized in such texts as where Peter speaks of the suffering of Christ (1 Pet. 1:11, 19; 2:21, 23, 24; 3:18; 5:1), but is likewise expressly asserted in the declarations that Christ "bore our sins in *His body*" (1 Pet. 2:24); that "Christ suffered in the flesh" (1 Pet. 4:1), and that Christ was even "put to death in the flesh" (1 Pet. 3:18). This same truth is taught in Acts 2:30, where Christ is described as being "of the fruit of David's loins."

But Peter describes the *humanity* of Jesus as *sinless*. He was like men, and truly man, yet He was utterly unlike sinful man, in that He "did no sin, neither was guile found in His mouth" (1 Pet. 2:22); and though He died, it was "as a lamb without blemish and without spot" (1 Pet. 1:19); as "the righteous for the unrighteous" (1 Pet. 3:18). This corresponds with what Peter urges with so much emphasis in his early addresses (Acts 3:14; 4:27, 30).

[ANALYSIS: 1) Christ is truly human; 2) human attributes are ascribed to Him; 3) the sinless man.]

# CHAPTER X.

### THE PETRINE ESCHATOLOGY.

§ 95. *Method of Presenting the Petrine Eschatology.*

In our discussion of the Petrine doctrine of the Last Things, we will follow, in general, the same order as we did in the presentation of the teaching of Jesus. Instead, however, of presenting the doctrines of each of the different Apostles belonging to the Petrine type separately, we will combine their views under each special topic, and thus simplify the presentation.

§ 96. *The Teaching Concerning Death.*

Both Peter and James regard death as the punishment of sin, and clearly distinguish between spiritual, bodily, and eternal death. Sin, when it is full-grown, bringeth forth death (James 1:15)—first spiritual, then bodily; and, if spiritual death is not overcome, eternal death. To save us from spiritual and eternal death, Christ bore our sins in His body upon the tree (1 Pet. 2:24), but God raised Him up, having loosed the pangs of death; because it was not possible that He should be holden of it (Acts 2:24). All are subject to bodily death, the good as well as the evil (2 Pet. 1:14), for all flesh is as grass (1 Pet. 1:24). He who converteth a sinner from the error of his way, not only saves a soul from spiritual death but from eternal death (James 5:20). Eternal death is "the blackness of darkness" reserved for the wicked (2 Pet. 2:17), even the destruction which shall overtake the ungodly men (2 Pet. 3:7).

[ANALYSIS: 1) Death a punishment of sin; 2) spiritual death; 3) bodily death; 4) eternal death.]

### § 97. *The Conversion of Israel.*

Does the Word of God teach us that, in connection with the Coming of Christ, the Jews, as a race, shall be converted to faith in Christ? Our Lord Himself, briefly but very clearly, foretells the rejection and the future restoration of Israel. In Matt. 23:38, 39, he says: "Behold, your house is left unto you desolate. For I say unto you, ye shall not see me henceforth, till ye shall say, Blessed is he that cometh in the name of the Lord." Their house was to be left desolate: Christ was to remain long hidden to them; but the time was to come when they should joyously hail Him as coming in the name of the Lord; and with this was to be connected the beholding of Christ again. So also in Luke 21:24, Christ says: "And they shall fall by the edge of the sword, and shall be led captive into all the nations: and Jerusalem shall be trodden down of the Gentiles, until the times of the Gentiles shall be fulfilled." Our Lord here foretells the slaughter of a large part of the nation. He speaks of their captivity; of their dispersion among the nations; of the down-treading of Jerusalem by the Gentiles, and yet of the coming of a time when all this shall have reached its termination—when the times of the Gentiles shall be fulfilled.

Peter also regards the conversion of Israel necessary to render the return of Jesus, and therewith the coming of the consummation of all things possible.[1]

It is evident that the Apostles still hope that the

---

[1] Compare § 68, on *The Conversion of the Whole of Israel.*

whole of Israel will be converted, and this hope is the soul of their missionary labors. It is not, however, thereby said that every individual will be converted and become a believer; for those individuals who refuse to listen to the great Messianic prophet, and to attest their repentance by baptism in Christ's name (Acts 2:38), will be rooted out from among the people (Acts 3:22, 23).

It seems as if the Apostles originally had looked for an earthly restoration of the kingdom of Israel (Acts 1:6), but it cannot be shown that this was their hope after the gift of the Holy Ghost had been bestowed on them on the Day of Pentecost. By the slaying of the Messiah, the earthly consummation of the kingdom of Israel was forever forfeited, and the restoration of all things promised in Acts 3:21 is that same heavenly consummation of the Kingdom of God which will take place at the coming of Christ.

[ANALYSIS: 1) Christ speaks of the rejection of Israel; 2) as well as of the future restoration of Israel; 3) Peter also speaks of the conversion of Israel; 4) but he knows of no earthly restoration.]

§ 98. *The Second Coming of Christ.*

With the first coming of Christ, in the flesh, have commenced "the last days" (Acts 2:17), "the end of the times" (1 Pet. 1:20), the Messianic time to which all the prophets have pointed (Acts 3:24). His resurrection on the third day was a decisive proof of His Messiahship (Acts 2:32; 3:15), and by His exaltation at the Right Hand of God, Jesus has not only become King of Israel (Acts 2:33–36), but has ascended the throne of the world, for "He is Lord of all" (Acts 10:36). The time will come when God will send this Christ, even Jesus, once more, to bring to Israel seasons of refreshing, when shall dawn the times of the Messianic consummation (Acts 3:19–21), for "he is ordained of God to be the Judge of quick and dead" (Acts 10:42).

Christian hope everywhere looks forward to this expected Second Coming of Christ. Then will the Invisible Christ be revealed (1 Pet. 1:7, 8), in His true character and in His full Messianic glory (1 Pet. 4:13; 5:1). Then the completion of salvation can be looked for—because "at the revelation of Jesus Christ grace is to be brought" unto the self-denying (1 Pet. 1:13); "and when the Chief Shepherd shall be manifested," faithful pastors "shall receive the crown of glory that fadeth not away" (1 Pet. 5:4). It is at this last time that the heavenly inheritance shall be revealed (1 Pet. 1:4).[1] The inheritance and salvation which the saints are to look forward to at the Second Coming of Christ is not an earthly one, but, in marked contrast to the inheritance once promised to the children of Israel, is a heavenly one.

James beholds the Messiah coming as a Judge. He exhorts the brethren to be patient, "for the coming of the Lord is at hand" (James 5:7, 8); they are not to murmur one against another, that they be not judged; "behold, the judge standeth before the doors" (5:9).

In his second epistle, Peter asserts that the doctrine of the power and coming of our Lord Jesus Christ is no cunningly devised fable (2 Pet. 1:16); and though His coming is delayed, still the Lord is not slack concerning His promise, for the day of the Lord will come as a thief (2 Pet. 3:4), when the consummation of all things shall take place.

---

[1] "An inheritance incorruptible, and undefiled, and that fadeth not away, reserved in heaven for you, who by the power of God are guarded through faith unto a salvation ready to be revealed in the last time."

Jude likewise speaks of a coming of the Lord "with ten thousands of His holy ones, to execute judgment upon all" (*vers.* 14, 15), and of a "looking for the mercy of our Lord Jesus Christ unto eternal life" (*ver.* 21); and he ascribes glory, majesty, dominion and power to God, who is able to set us "before the presence of His glory without blemish in exceeding joy" (*vers.* 24, 25).

[ANALYSIS: 1) Christ will come again, as Judge; 2) when the heavenly inheritance will be revealed; 3) James beholds the Messiah coming as a Judge; 4) teaching of 2 Peter; 5) teaching of Jude.]

## § 99. *The Resurrection of the Dead.*

From Acts 2:25–31, we infer that the resurrection of Christ consisted in this, that the soul, which was in Hades after its separation from the body, was again clothed with the body. That the flesh did not see corruption, but was immediately changed into its heavenly state, was the prerogative of the Messiah, who was raised up on the third day; while our bodies, passing over into decay, will not be raised until the Last Day. It is only after the resurrection that believers attain the eternal Divine glory in Christ (1 Pet. 5:10; 4:13; 5:1, 4), and that the Lord "executeth judgment upon all, convicting all the ungodly of all their works of ungodliness which they have ungodly wrought, and of all the hard things which ungodly sinners have spoken against him" (Jude 15).

[ANALYSIS: 1) The resurrection; 2) is universal.]

## § 100. *The Day of Judgment.*

The Messianic consummation does not come without the Messianic judgment. The Day of the Lord, that great and notable day, will come (Acts 2:20), when He which is ordained of God will judge the quick and the dead (Acts 10:42). The souls of unbelievers are not yet delivered over to final destruction. Christ has made proclamation of His victory to the lost spirits (1 Pet. 3:19), even to all the dead (1 Pet. 4:6), in order that not only the living but also the dead might be judged in the final Messianic judgment. And, although after the manner of the Old Testament, God Himself is still regarded as the Righteous Judge of the world (1 Pet. 2:23), who impartially judges according to each one's work (1 Pet. 1:17), still, in 1 Pet. 4:5, Christ is named as the One to whom the living and the dead will have to give an account (Acts 10:42). And because Christ, as the Judge of the world, has the final decision at His disposal, He can also deliver His own at the Messianic judgment.

James likewise warns the godless of the terrors of the judgment, of the miseries that are coming (James 5:1). He speaks of the fire of judgment as eating the flesh of the godless (5:3), and of a day of slaughter (5:5). Then shall all men appear before the Judge, "who is able to save and to destroy" (4:12). This topic of the Messianic judgment is still more fully presented in the Second Epistle of Peter and in the Epistle of Jude. Every Divine judgment of the past is but a type of the Final Judgment, which, on the Great Day of the Lord, brings eternal destruction upon all the godless, including those of all ages (2 Pet. 2:9; Jude 14, 15). Prophecy of old (Jude 4; 2 Pet. 2:3) has set forth unto condemnation and destruction all the ungodly (Jude 14, 15). An emblem of this destruction is found in the perishing of Sodom and Gomorrah (2 Pet. 2:6; Jude 7); and in conformity with this, destruction is regarded, under the symbol of eternal fire, as a judgment of God.

This Divine judgment does not spare the evil angels, who are kept in Tartarus or Hades, bound with everlasting chains and covered with deep darkness (Jude 6; 2 Pet. 2:4). This destruction is regarded as "the blackness of darkness" (2 Pet. 2:17; Jude 14), as the deepest misery; "this condemnation" (Jude 4) as the loss of eternal life (Jude 21). The judgment of the Great Day (2 Pet. 2:9; Jude 6), when the Lord shall come as the Judge of the world (Jude 14, 15), will bring the final decisive crisis.

With the *Parousia* and the judgment accompanying it, the eternal Kingdom of Christ begins, into which believers, who have made their calling and election sure, shall enter, there to live with Christ in eternal glory (2 Pet. 1:10, 11). This eternal Kingdom of Christ has its consummation in the new heavens and the new earth, wherein dwelleth righteousness (2 Pet. 3:13), and the gift bestowed to believers is eternal life (Jude 21). This Perfect Kingdom is therefore no earthly one, as the present form and state of the world will have passed away.

In the Petrine Eschatology five great events of the Last Day are closely connected: 1) the Second Coming of Christ; 2) the resurrection of the dead; 3) the Last Judgment; 4) the end of the world; 5) the manifestation of a new heavens and a new earth.

[ANALYSIS: 1) The Messianic judgment; 2) Christ will be the Judge; 3) teaching of James; 4) of 2 Peter; 5) of Jude; 6) the order of events at the Last Day.]

§ 101. *The End of the World.*

As the ancient world perished by the waters of the Flood (2 Pet. 3:6; 2:5), and the present world is protected by God's Word of Promise against a second destruction by water (Gen. 9:11; 2 Pet. 3:7), there remains now only fire as the element to bring about this destruction, for "the heavens that now are, and the earth, by the same word, have been stored up for fire, being reserved against the day of judgment and destruction of ungodly men" (2 Pet. 3:7).

A vivid description of the end of the world is given in 2 Pet. 3:10–13.[1] Note, first, the certainty of this great event. "The Day of the Lord," "the Day of God," the Day of Judgment and the end of the world, *will come.* Whatever else in the future is uncertain, this is sure and inevitable.

Note, secondly, that the writer does not describe the different stages and events of the Second Coming of Christ minutely. He does not enter into all the details describing the transformation of this present world into the new heavens and the new earth of the future. He does not here speak of the signs that precede and accompany the Second Advent, although in Acts 2:19, 20, Peter speaks of "the wonders in the heavens above, and signs on the earth beneath;" he says nothing about the resurrection of the dead, though it is implied when, in 2 Pet. 3:7, the Apostle speaks of the Day of Judgment and the destruction of ungodly men. Peter, in his prophetic vision, sees the whole history of the end

---

[1] "The day of the Lord will come as a thief; in the which the heavens shall pass away with a great noise, and the elements shall be dissolved with fervent heat, and the earth and the works that are therein shall be burned up. Seeing that these things are thus all to be dissolved, what manner of persons ought ye to be in all holy living and godliness, looking for and earnestly desiring the coming of the day of God, by reason of which the heavens being on fire shall be dissolved, and the elements shall melt with fervent heat. But according to His promise, we look for new heavens and a new earth, wherein dwelleth righteousness."

in one glance; it is consummated in one Great Day of the Lord. The coming of the Day of God and the end of the world are to him one event.

Note, in the third place, what shall follow this coming of the Day of God. "By reason of which the heavens being on fire shall be dissolved, and the elements shall melt with fervent heat." In 2 Pet. 3:10, the additional thought is added: "the heavens shall pass away with a great noise," "the earth and the works that are therein shall be burned up."

Fire is the element by which the world is to be purified. And there is nothing incredible in this. The sciences of geology and astronomy, in modern times, contribute to natural evidence of the probability of a burning up of the world. What these sciences affirm as probable, the Bible teaches as most certain and sure. The mystery is not so much that the earth is some day to be burnt up, as that it does not burn up at once. The world is being kept from being burnt up only by a wonderful repression of existing forces. Our earth is a mere shell of solid matter, holding a vast internal sea of elements fused by intense heat—a sea whose tides mark their mysterious pulse in earthquakes, volcanoes, and tidal eruptions of the ocean. Our earth is a world at this moment on fire, and all that is necessary for its destruction is that the power which the earth itself holds be allowed free range. We are sweeping through space on a chariot of fire, and are sustained upon it by the same Arm which was around Elijah when, with the chariot of fire and horses of fire, he arose to Heaven.

Note, in the fourth place, that although we cannot positively determine the extent of this catastrophe, whether the heavens here mentioned are the heavens belonging to our earth—that is, our surrounding atmosphere, or whether they include the heaven of stars—still it is better to regard this great event as affecting the whole solar system, and possibly the whole universe.

Note, fifthly, that the destruction here spoken of does not involve actual annihilation. It involves rather a change of the forms and qualities of the earth, and not the blotting out of the substance. It is a transmutation, a transformation, the regeneration of which Christ speaks in Matt. 19:28. Burning is not annihilation, but involves only a change of form, and the melting of the elements leaves their substance untouched. The fire here spoken of is to be thought of as a fire of purification, and not one of annihilation. There is no foundation for the theory of the annihilation of this world in the analogies drawn from Nature, in the deductions of science, or in the teaching of Scripture.

We note, finally, that this world, thus destroyed and purified by fire, shall be transfigured and transformed into a new world, for "we look for new heavens and a new earth, wherein dwelleth righteousness" (*ver.* 13).

[ANALYSIS: 1) The world shall be destroyed by fire; 2) the teaching of 2 Pet. 3:10–13; 3) the certainty of the destruction of the earth; 4) all the details are not given; 5) the heavens shall pass away; 6) fire shall purify the earth; 7) this destruction will affect the whole solar system; 8) it is not annihilation; 9) but a transformation; 10) the new heavens and the new earth.]

# BIBLICAL THEOLOGY

OF THE

# NEW TESTAMENT

BY

REVERE FRANKLIN WEIDNER,

*Doctor and Professor of Theology, Author of "Studies in the Book," "Commentary on Mark," "Biblical Theology of the Old Testament," "Theological Encyclopædia," "An Introduction to Dogmatic Theology," "New Testament Greek Method," "Christian Ethics," Etc.*

VOL. II.

PART III. THE PAULINE TEACHING.
PART IV. THE TEACHING OF JOHN.

# CONTENTS.

## PART III.—PAULINISM.

### INTRODUCTION.

| SECTION | | PAGE |
|---|---|---|
| 102. The Apostle Paul | | 11 |
| 103. Sources of Paulinism | | 16 |
| 104. Previous Works on Paulinism | | 22 |

### SECTION I.

#### THE EARLIEST TEACHING OF PAUL AS AN APOSTLE TO THE GENTILES.

#### CHAPTER I.

##### THE GOSPEL AS THE WAY OF DELIVERANCE FROM THE JUDGMENT.

| | |
|---|---|
| 105. The Ground of Salvation | 25 |
| 106. The Demands of the Gospel | 29 |
| 107. Summary of Paul's Teaching According to the Acts | 31 |

#### CHAPTER II.

##### THE PAULINE ESCHATOLOGY.

| | |
|---|---|
| 108. Method of Presenting the Pauline Eschatology | 35 |
| 109. The Teaching Concerning Death | 36 |
| 110. The State of the Soul After Death | 37 |
| 111. The Pauline Apocalypse | 41 |
| 112. Antichrist | 41 |
| 113. The Fullness of the Gentiles | 45 |
| 114. The Conversion of Israel | 48 |
| 115. The Second Coming of Christ | 50 |
| 116. The Resurrection of the Dead | 52 |
| 117. The General Judgment | 59 |
| 118. The Final Consummation | 63 |

## CONTENTS.

119. Eternal Life . . . . . . . . . 66
120. Eternal Death . . . . . . . . . 68

## SECTION II.

### The Doctrinal System of the Four Great Doctrinal and Controversial Epistles.

#### CHAPTER III.
##### Universal Sinfulness.

121. Human and Divine Righteousness . . . . 70
122. The Impossibility of a Righteousness of Our Own . . 72
123. The Transgression of Adam and its Consequences . 75
124. The Pauline Anthropology . . . . . . 84

#### CHAPTER IV.
##### The Pauline Doctrine of God.

125. The Doctrine of the Trinity . . . . . 88
126. The Doctrine of Predestination . . . . . 91
127. The Gospel and the Apostleship . . . . . 96
128. The Calling of the Gentiles . . . . . . 99
129. The Hardening and Conversion of Israel . . . 100

#### CHAPTER V.
##### Heathendom and Judaism.

130. The Apostasy of Heathendom . . . . . 104
131. Heathendom and the Divine Training . . . 105
132. Judaism and its Law . . . . . . . 107
133. The Law and the Promise . . . . . . 109

#### CHAPTER VI.
##### Prophecy and Fulfillment.

134. The Prophecy of Scripture . . . . . . 113
135. The Use of the Old Testament . . . . . 115
136. The Time of Grace . . . . . . . . 117

#### CHAPTER VII.
##### The Christology of Paul.

137. The Lord of Glory . . . . . . . . 120
138. The Son of God . . . . . . . . 122
139. The Human Nature of Christ . . . . . 127

## CHAPTER VIII.

### REDEMPTION AND JUSTIFICATION.

140. The Saving Significance of the Death of Christ . . 131
141. The Death and Resurrection of Christ . . . 136
142. Justification by Faith . . . . . . . . 139
143. The Teaching Concerning Sonship . . . . 147

### CHAPTER IX.

### THE NEW LIFE.

144. The Doctrine Concerning Baptism . . . . 150
145. The Lord's Supper . . . . . . . . 154
146. Sanctification . . . . . . . . . . 158
147. Freedom from the Law . . . . . . . 162

### CHAPTER X.

### THE DOCTRINE OF THE CHURCH.

148. The Church and the Gifts of Grace . . . . . 167
149 Church Duties . . . . . . . . . . 169

## SECTION III.

### THE DEVELOPMENT OF PAULINISM IN THE EPISTLES OF THE IMPRISONMENT.

### CHAPTER XI.

### THE FIRST PRINCIPLES OF DOCTRINE.

150. The Doctrine of Justification . . . . . . 174
151. The Doctrine of Salvation . . . . . . 176
152. The Doctrine of Wisdom . . . . . . . 180

### CHAPTER XII.

### THE MORE DEVELOPED DOCTRINES.

153. The Cosmical Significance of Christ . . . . 183
154. The Realization of Salvation in the Church . . 188

## SECTION IV.

### THE DOCTRINE OF THE PASTORAL EPISTLES.

### CHAPTER XIII.

### CHRISTIANITY AS DOCTRINE.

155. The Sound Doctrine . . . . . . . . 191

## CONTENTS.

156. The Paulinism of the Pastoral Epistles . . . 193
157. The Church and Church Government . . . . 196

### SECTION V.
#### LUKE THE EVANGELIST.

#### CHAPTER XIV.
##### PAULINISM IN THE WRITINGS OF LUKE.

158. The Writings of Luke . . . . . . . 200
159. The Paulinism of Luke . . . . . . . 202

### SECTION VI.
#### THE EPISTLE TO THE HEBREWS.

#### CHAPTER XV.
##### THE OLD AND THE NEW COVENANT.

160. The Imperfection of the Old Covenant . . . . 204
161. The Promise of the New Covenant . . . . 206
162. The Realization of the New Covenant . . . . 207

#### CHAPTER XVI.
##### THE HIGH PRIEST OF THE NEW COVENANT.

163. The Messiah as Son . . . . . . . . 209
164. The Messianic High Priest . . . . . 210
165. The High Priest in the Most Holy Place . . . 213
166. Lechler's Presentation . . . . . . . 214

#### CHAPTER XVII.
##### THE SACRIFICE OF THE NEW COVENANT.

167. The Sacrificial Death of Christ . . . . . 216
168. The Necessity of the Sacrificial Death of Christ . . 219
169. The Effects of the Sacrificial Death of Christ . . 220

#### CHAPTER XVIII.
##### THE BLESSINGS AND DUTIES OF THE NEW COVENANT.

170. The New Testament Covenant People . . . . 223
171. Life in the New Covenant . . . . . . 225
172. The Fulfillment of the Covenant Promise . . . 227

## PART IV.

### THE TEACHING OF JOHN.

#### INTRODUCTION.

173. The Apostle John . . . . . . . . 231
174. Sources of Johannean Theology . . . . . 232
175. The Character of Johannean Theology . . . 234
176. Previous Works on John . . . . . . 236

### SECTION I.

#### THE TEACHING OF JOHN ACCORDING TO THE GOSPEL AND THE EPISTLES.

#### CHAPTER I.

##### THE DOCTRINE OF GOD.

177. The Doctrine of the Father . . . . . . 240
178. The Doctrine of the Logos . . . . . . 242
179. The Doctrine of the Holy Spirit . . . . . 245

#### CHAPTER II.

##### THE WORLD AND THE PRINCE OF THIS WORLD.

180. The World in its Alienation from God . . . 246
181. The Prince of this World . . . . . . 248

#### CHAPTER III.

##### JESUS CHRIST THE SAVIOUR OF THE WORLD.

182. The Incarnation of the Logos . . . . . 249
183. The Work of Jesus Christ . . . . . . 250

#### CHAPTER IV.

##### FELLOWSHIP WITH THE FATHER AND THE SON.

184. Fellowship with Christ, and through Him with the Father 252
185. The Fellowship of Believers . . . . . . 254

### SECTION II.

#### THE TEACHING OF JOHN ACCORDING TO THE APOCALYPSE.

#### CHAPTER V.

##### THE DOCTRINE OF GOD.

186. The Name and Nature of God . . . . . 256

## CONTENTS.

| | | |
|---|---|---|
| 187. The Doctrine of the Holy Spirit | | 258 |
| 188. The Works of God | | 260 |
| 189. The Doctrine Concerning Satan | | 262 |

### CHAPTER VI.
#### THE PERSON AND WORK OF CHRIST.

| | | |
|---|---|---|
| 190. The Person of Christ | | 267 |
| 191. The Work of Christ | | 268 |

### CHAPTER VII.
#### THE SAINTS AND THEIR WORKS.

| | | |
|---|---|---|
| 192. The Christian Life in its Origin | | 272 |
| 193. The Christian Life in its Significance | | 273 |
| 194. The Christian Life in its Activity | | 275 |
| 195. The Christian Life in Relation to its Promises | | 277 |

### CHAPTER VIII.
#### THE ESCHATOLOGY OF JOHN.

| | | |
|---|---|---|
| 196. The Method of Presenting the Johannean Eschatology | | 280 |
| 197. Concerning Death in General | | 281 |
| 198. The State of the Soul After Death | | 282 |
| 199. The Universal Preaching of the Gospel | | 287 |
| 200. The Future of Israel | | 289 |
| 201. The Great Apostasy and the Great Tribulation | | 292 |
| 202. The Antichrist | | 294 |
| 203. The Second Coming of Christ | | 297 |
| 204. The Millennium | | 312 |
| 205. The First Resurrection | | 316 |
| 206. The General Resurrection | | 321 |
| 207. The Final Judgment | | 322 |
| 208. The End of the World | | 323 |
| 209. The Second Death | | 324 |
| 210. The New Heaven and the New Earth | | 326 |
| 211. Eternal Life | | 328 |
| INDEX | | 333 |

# PART III.

PAULINISM.

# PART III.

## PAULINISM.

### INTRODUCTION.

§ 102. *The Apostle Paul.*[1]

The reason why the Apostle Paul has written a larger number of letters than the other Apostles is, not only because his extensive missionary activity gave him greater occasion, but also because he of all the Apostles had been best prepared for literary activity by his early education. He was the most scholarly of the Apostles, and his rabbinical education supplied him with the dialectic art of defending his views in controversial discussion, of meeting objections, of expressing his ideas in a sharp and definite manner—of elucidating his statements by means of thesis and antithesis; and, when a principle was thus established, of showing the applicability of its consequence in all directions. It is in his writings, accordingly, that Christian truth first appears as a compact whole, whose leading propositions are sharply formulated and exhibited in their necessary connection with one another.

Before his conversion, Paul had distinguished himself by his zeal for the Pharisaic doctrine of the law, and by his most exact observance of it. Still, according to his own confession (Rom. 7), he found herein no perfect

---

[1] Compare *Weiss*, § 58.

satisfaction, inasmuch as he always remained painfully conscious of the contrast between the demand of the law and man's fulfillment. His conversion was a sudden one. In the midst of his fanatical persecuting zeal he was, by an unparalleled gracious act of God, vouchsafed a special manifestation of Christ, which entirely changed his opinion of the persecuted Nazarene. He was even called to be His Apostle, and qualified for the most extensive labors in His service.

Paul had not enjoyed the personal intercourse with Christ by means of which the religious ideas of the original Apostles had been gradually shaped and transformed. It is possible that he had seen Him at Jerusalem, although this cannot be proved from 2 Cor. 5:16. In the disputation with Stephen (Acts 6:8; 8:1), Saul, who was consenting to his death, naturally must have heard many details of the life and sayings of Christ; that he had to die and be raised again according to the Scripture (1 Cor. 15:3, 4). But it is the express aim of Paul's account in the first chapter of Galatians to show that his whole attitude to Christianity previous to the event at Damascus excluded the possibility of any human influence in the forming of his Gospel (Gal. 1:11, 12). Paul's conversion dates from the time of Christ's manifestation to him. Before his eyes always stood the Exalted Christ in the splendor of Divine glory, just as He had appeared to him and changed the whole of his previous life, by condemning it as illusion and sin. To him this Heavenly Lord was no longer mainly the Messiah of the Jews, who was to bring about the complete consummation of the theocracy; but to him Christ was the Mediator of Divine grace to the sinners who had awakened to the consciousness of their guilt. Christ had come to him, not as a Jew, but as a lost sinner, and had called him to be an Apostle to the Gentiles, who, like himself, were sunk in the irremediable destruction of sin.

It is wrong to think of the Apostle Paul as from the first having no connection with the primitive Christian tradition. No doubt it is but seldom that he expressly quotes sayings of Jesus (1 Cor. 7:10, 11; 9:14; 1 Thess. 4:15); but that many other words of Jesus were known to him is shown by many an echo of them in his writings. It is true, he was conscious that he had not learned from men the Gospel which he proclaimed, but had received it by Divine revelation (Gal. 1:11, 12), and the whole of his subjective assurance of salvation rested upon this direct attestation of the Divine Spirit. But it does not follow from this that, in his exhibition of saving truth, he did not, from the first, attach himself in many ways to the views and forms of doctrine which were current within the primitive Christian circles, as a member of which he unreservedly regarded himself. And when the Mother Church praised God because its previous persecutor was now proclaiming its faith (Gal. 1:23, 24), it cannot but have been aware that he had become altogether one of its members. His calling, indeed, led him to devote himself more and more exclusively to the mission to the Gentiles; and here the form of his teaching must naturally have become more and more a peculiar one when compared with that in the Jewish-Christian circles. For if he was to convert the Gentiles as such, he must proclaim to them a Gospel which declared them free from the rule of life laid down by the Jewish law. In this, his activity as an Apostle to the Gentiles, he must, however, have learned also to present Christianity as the satisfaction of a common human need.

Lechler maintains[1] that the foundation for the character, work, and teaching of Paul was laid in the revelation of Jesus Christ to him at the time of his conversion, and he draws the following conclusions from the three accounts given respecting his conversion, as given in Acts 9:3–19; 22:6–16; 26:12–18:

1) It was not his own act, but an act of God. Paul declares as strongly as possible that his conversion was an *act of God*, resting on God's determination and gracious choice—not on *his own* consideration or determination; that it was an act of compassionate grace and undeserved favor (Gal. 1:12–16).

2) We learn from the utterances of Paul in what God's influence upon him at the time of that event consisted: viz., in *the revelation of Jesus Christ* the *Son of God* (Gal. 1:12, 15, 16). By Divine illumination of his soul, Paul was convinced that Jesus was the Son of God—convinced not merely of His Messiahship, but also of His Divine majesty. The mystery that Christ was the Redeemer of the world was made known to him by *this revelation*, and his call to be an Apostle to the Gentiles was the *object* of this revelation (Acts 26:16–18).

3) The Apostle Paul declares that at his conversion, which he characterizes in Gal. 1 as the revelation of the Son by the Father (1:15, 16), and as the self-revelation of Jesus Christ (1:12), Christ, who had risen, appeared to him in a visible form (1 Cor. 15:8). With this utterance we also connect the question put forward in the same Epistle (9:1): "Am I not an Apostle? Have I not seen Jesus our Lord?"

Lechler further maintains that the nature of the pro-

---

[1] See his *Apostolic and Post-Apostolic Times*, vol. 1, pp. 312–317.

cess which effected the conversion of Paul consisted in the following particulars:

1) Jesus, who had risen from the dead and was exalted to Heaven, did *actually reveal* Himself to Paul as the Living and Glorified One, in Divine majesty and glory. He sees Him bodily (1 Cor. 9:1), in majesty and glory (1 Cor. 9:1, "our Lord"), so that he is as certain as of his own existence that Jesus lives, although He was dead; He is risen again (1 Cor. 15:4, 8); He lives, and is the Anointed of God, the Messiah and Lord. This self-revelation of Jesus was coincident with the revelation actually imparted to Paul by God, that Jesus is the Son of God.

2) This vision was directly connected with the *call to be an Apostle*. In all three passages—Gal. 1:16; 1 Cor. 15:8; 1 Cor. 9:1—both are inseparably joined together in thought and word.

3) But in the fact that this self-revelation of Christ was vouchsafed to him at the moment when he was persecuting the Church of God, Paul must have perceived unmerited grace, compassionate, redeeming love for the blinded and mistaken sinner. This is very strongly and forcibly expressed in 1 Cor. 15:8–10, where this confession is uttered with the deepest humility and emotion: "By the grace of God I am what I am."

What Christ, by His revelation and calling, effected in Paul remained permanent in his soul, and in particular gave to his Apostolic preaching and teaching its unique character. The Apostle, however, did not at once attain to this peculiar conception in all its purity and fullness, but step by step, and under the influence of experiences made in the pursuit of his calling, and under the guidance of the Holy Spirit, he penetrated more and more into its depths, and built up his doctrinal system in growing fullness and independence.

[ANALYSIS: 1) Paul specially fitted for his work; 2) the scholar and dialectician among the New Testament writers; 3) his Pharisaic zeal before his sudden conversion; 4) had not enjoyed personal intercourse with Christ; 5) must have known many of the facts of Christ's life before his conversion; 6) but this knowledge had no influence upon the Gospel he preached; 7) it was the Exalted Christ who appeared to him in the splendor of Divine glory; 8) though he does not often quote the sayings of Christ, his Gospel is one with the original Apostles; 9) its peculiarities arise from his mission to the Gentiles; 10) the foundation of the character of his teaching laid in the revelation of Jesus Christ to him at the time of his conversion; 11) inferences drawn from the threefold account of his conversion; 12) the particulars of this conversion; 13) this conversion gave to his Apostolic preaching and teaching its unique character.]

§ 103. *Sources of Paulinism.*[1]

Of the missionary preaching of the Apostle, we have but very brief accounts. In the Acts of the Apostles we have one example of the Synagogue sermons (13:16–41) with which he sought to gain the Jews and proselytes. The discourse at Athens, in the midst of the Areopagus (Acts 17:22–31), gives us a lively picture of the manner in which Paul, in his missionary activity, was wont to find points of contact with the consciousness of the Gentiles, and shows, also, from what point he was wont to start with his Christian sermon. All the utterances of Paul as related by Luke in the Acts can be used as illustrations of Pauline views. The two Epistles to the essentially Gentile Christian Church at Thessalonica, which were composed during his stay for a year and a half at Corinth (Acts 18:11), about the year 52, are written so short a time after the planting of the Church at Thessalonica that they are, in many

[1] Compare *Weiss*, § 59.

ways, connected with his original missionary preaching there. The circumstance that the moral life of the Church was still manifestly unstable compels him to enter, in an elementary manner, into its Christian aspects; and the excitement which eschatological questions had caused in the Church not only shows with what emphasis Paul had set forth this point in his missionary preaching, but also compels him to discuss the matter still more thoroughly. In both Epistles there is not much stress laid on Anthropology or Christology, or on the doctrine of Justification; but there is a peculiar interest in seeing the shape taken by the teaching and exhortation of the Apostle in their elementary forms.

For all practical purposes, it is best to consider the Epistles of Paul as written at four different periods, five years apart.[1] We find the teaching of the Apostle most richly developed in the four great Epistles to the Galatians, Corinthians and the Romans, but in a form which was essentially conditioned by the controversies with the Judaistic party. The Epistle to the Galatians is the first monmuent of these controversies. The First Epistle to the Corinthians introduces us to the concrete circumstances of a Church which was rich, but which had also serious defects; and in this letter almost all the points of saving truth are incidentally discussed, and, for a special reason, the fifteenth chapter is devoted to a detailed exposition of the doctrine of the resurrection. Although the Second Epistle to the Corinthians is for the most part a personal explana-

---

[1] 1) About 52 A. D., 1 and 2 Thess.; 2) about 57 A. D., Gal., 1 and 2 Cor., Romans; 3) about 62 A. D., Col., Eph., Philemon, Philippians, Hebrews (?); 4) about 67 A. D., 1 Tim., Titus, 2 Tim. (See my "Studies in the Book," vols. 2 and 3).

tion with reference to His Judaistic opponents in the Church, it is none the less rich in discussions, from which we can gather his apprehension of the truths of salvation. It is, however, the Epistle to the Romans which gives us the most complete and systematic presentation of the doctrine of Paul. If the leading import of his preaching is briefly described in Rom. 1:16, 17, then the whole dogmatic part appears to be a well-arranged carrying out of this theme; for, in 1:18–3:20, we have the *negative* proof that we are not justified by works, *because all men are sinners*, and in 3:21–5:21, the *positive* proof that we are *justified by faith* apart from the works of the law; in chapters 6:1–8:39 the new life of the Christian, or the doctrine of sanctification, is discussed, while in chapters 9:1–11:36 we have the realization of salvation in Gentiles and Jews. Even the practical part of the Epistle (12:1–15:13) does not refer so much to the individual concrete needs of the Roman Church, but we have rather a sketch of Christian ethics in outline.[1] The four Epistles written during St. Paul's first imprisonment at Rome have a peculiar character of their own, in not referring to the opposition to Judaism. Although the three letters to the Colossians, Ephesians, and to Philemon were sent at the same time, it is highly probable that the Epistle to the Colossians was written first. Its external occasion was the disquieting of the Churches of southwest Phrygia by a Jewish-Gnostic movement, which professed to lead the Church to a higher stage of Christian knowledge by means of theosophic doctrines, especially regarding the higher spiritual world, and to a

---

[1] The farewell discourse at Miletus (Acts 20:18–35) stands next to these Epistles in point of time, and then the two apologies in Acts 22:3–21; 24:10–21.

## SOURCES OF PAULINISM. 19

higher perfection of Christian life by means of ascetic rules. This movement did not directly proclaim any fundamental heresy; but the Apostle perceived that it nevertheless ultimately threatened the dignity of Christ and His work of salvation, as well as the healthiness of the development of the Christian life.

The thoughts which were stirred up in his mind by this movement Paul has developed to a greater extent, and with a more general reference to the further consequences and dangers of this heresy, in the contemporary circular letter to the Churches of Asia Minor, which now bears the name of the Epistle to the Ephesians. The autograph letter to Philemon has scarcely any special importance for the teaching of the Apostle. The sayings of the Apostle contained in Acts 26:1–28:31 stand nearest these Epistles in point of time. The Epistle to the Philippians was probably written at a later period of his imprisonment. Notwithstanding the more personal character of this Epistle, it unfolds a great wealth of teaching and admonition, and gives us the deepest glimpses, from various sides, into the religious consciousness of the Apostle.

The appearance of the new doctrine of wisdom made it necessary to develop further those sides of the truth of salvation in which are opened up the unfathomable depths of a wisdom which satisfies every true striving after knowledge, and this is especially seen in these four Epistles of the first captivity. It is possible that the situation of the Apostle in his imprisonment gave him more occasion, than his restless and active missionary life had permitted, to penetrate meditatively into the ultimate reasons of the saving truth which he had proclaimed. The new needs of the life of the Church may also have compelled him to enter more thoroughly into the concrete relations of its moral life, and by means of a healthy criticism and regulation of these relations from the standpoint of the Gospel, to oppose the fruitless asceticism to which the Jewish-Christian theosophy was inclined.

The three Pastoral Epistles form a group by themselves, and represent the last stage of the Apostle's life and labors, with his parting counsels to his beloved disciples and co-workers. They show us the transition of the Apostolic Church from primitive simplicity to a more definite system of doctrine and form of government. They contain Paul's pastoral theology and his theory of Church government. The chronology of the Epistles is uncertain. We accept St. Paul's second Roman imprisonment, and believe that 1 Timothy and Titus were written shortly before his final imprisonment, after he had made certain journeys, which are not recorded in the Acts of the Apostles. The second Epistle to Timothy was written while in prison for the second time at Rome, and appears to be the last of Paul's Epistles.

The influence of Paul may also be perceived in the writings of Luke, in his Gospel as well as in the Acts of the Apostles. They must therefore also be regarded as a source of Pauline doctrine. The spiritual analogy between the third Gospel and the Apostle Paul was already observed by Christian antiquity. Irenæus expressly designates the Gospel of Luke, as a copy of the Gospel which Paul preached. In fact, the universalism of Christianity and the doctrine of unmerited grace toward sinners, as those who are justified by faith, not by works, are so clearly imprinted on the third Gospel that we cannot fail to recognize in it the Pauline spirit. The same may be said of the Acts of the Apostles,

## SOURCES OF PAULINISM.

which is but the continuation of the Gospel, written also by Luke, the companion of Paul.[1]

The Epistle to the Hebrews occupies a peculiar position in the New Testament. The author, if not St. Paul himself, undoubtedly belonged to the Pauline school. To all appearance the writing is addressed to Palestinian Jewish Christians, probably to the Christian Church at Jerusalem, having for its object the preservation of Jewish Christians from the threatening danger of apostasy from Christ and complete relapse into unbelieving Judaism (10:25, 29; 6:6). The Epistle is eminently Christological,[2] and resembles the Epistle to the Colossians in this respect. The authorship of the letter will probably never be decided with absolute certainty; but, taking all things into consideration, it is highly probable that Luke wrote it in the name and under the instruction of Paul. As to the time of composition it probably belongs to the period between 62 A. D. and 67 A. D., and the internal evidence is strong that the letter was written before the destruction of Jerusalem (70 A. D.)—even before the outbreak of the Jewish war (66 A. D.); possibly in Italy, about 63 A. D.

[ANALYSIS : 1) We have but brief accounts of Paul's missionary sermons ; 2) our earliest source of Pauline doctrine are the Acts of the Apostles and the two letters to the Thessalonians ; 3) his teaching most fully developed in the four great controversial Epistles (Gal., 1 and 2 Cor., Rom.; 4) then come the four Epistles of the first captivity (Col., Eph., Philemon, Phil.) ; 5) the Pastoral Epistles form the last group of Epistles ; 6) the writings of Luke also Pauline (Gospel and Acts of the Apostles); 7) as also the Epistle to the Hebrews.]

---

[1] Compare *Lechler*, vol. 2, pp. 115-119.

[2] For a special development of the teaching of the Epistle to the Hebrews, see my "Studies in the Book," vol. 3, pp. 52-81.

§ 104. *Previous Works on Paulinism.*[1]

While the earlier writers on the subject still represent the teaching of Paul according to the customary dogmatic categories, Neander and the more recent theologians have attempted to arrange their representation of his doctrinal system more according to its peculiarity.

Neander begins his presentation—1) with developing Paul's idea of *righteousness* and its relation to the *law*, as forming the central point of his doctrine; 2) as the central point of Pauline anthropology he discusses his idea of human nature as alienated from the Divine life and in opposition to the law; 3) then follow Paul's views as to the preparatives for redemption—Judaism and Heathenism; 4) the work of redemption, its accomplishment by Christ, both actively and passively—the results of the work of Christ—reconciliation with God, redemption and salvation, justification; 5) the appropriation of salvation by faith; 6) the new life proceeding from faith; 7) the church and the sacraments; 8) the Kingdom of God, its idea and extent, the doctrine of the Logos, the kingdom of evil opposed to the Kingdom of God, the development of the Kingdom of God till its final completion; 9) the doctrines of the resurrection, state of the soul after death till the resurrection, and the final consummation.

Schmid first discusses Paul's conception of Christianity in general; and then, starting with the basis that Paul's fundamental idea of *righteousness* has its root in the teaching of Jesus, he maintains that the Pauline representation of Christian truth may be divided into two sections, the first relating to the lack of righteousness in all men, and the second referring to the bring-

[1] Compare *Weiss*, § 60.

ing about of righteousness by means of faith in Jesus Christ. This leads to the discussion of the doctrines of Jesus Christ as the Redeemer, His person and work, righteousness and life through Jesus, justification, the completion of salvation in individuals, the kingdom of Christ and the power of darkness, and the consummation of salvation.

Van Oosterzee discusses the Pauline Theology under two headings—1) humanity and the individual man before and out of Christ; 2) humanity and the individual man through and in Christ. Under this last division he treats of—1) the plan of salvation; 2) the Christ; 3) the work of redemption; 4) the way of salvation; 5) the Church; 6) the future.

Lechler deviates from the plan followed by these writers. He discusses the doctrinal system of St. Paul in three chapters with the following titles: 1) The original preaching of the Apostle Paul, according to the discourses in the Acts, and according to the Thessalonian Epistles; 2) The doctrine of the Apostle Paul in its mature form; 3) The doctrine of the Pastoral Epistles. Under the second chapter we find the matter very fully presented. The first doctrinal part has, for its general topic, *Sin*—1) Sin and death as regards individual man; 2) sin and death in general, and the revelation of God in the pre-Christian world. The second doctrinal part has, for its subject, *Grace and Salvation*—1) Jesus Christ, and redemption through the death and resurrection of Christ; 2) salvation and its realization—justification by faith, the Church of God, the final consummation.

Bernhard Weiss, whose system in part we follow, begins with a representation, in its outlines, of the earliest preaching of Paul as the Apostle to the Gentiles, as it is to be discovered, partly in the discourse at Athens, partly in the Epistles to the Thessalonians. The main doctrinal system of the Apostle, however, he develops in his second section, where he treats of the four great doctrinal and controversial Epistles. The topics which are here represented are—1) Universal sinfulness; 2) Heathenism and Judaism; 3) Prophecy and fulfilment; 4) Christology; 5) Redemption and Justification; 6) The New Life; 7) The doctrine of Predestination; 8) The doctrine of the Church; 9) Eschatology. In his third section he discusses the peculiarities of the Epistles of the imprisonment, and lastly the characteristic teaching of the Pastoral Epistles is presented.

[ANALYSIS: 1) Method of Neander's treatment; 2) that of Schmid; 3) of Van Oosterzee; 4) of Lechler; 5) of Bernhard Weiss.]

# SECTION I.

THE EARLIEST TEACHING OF PAUL AS AN APOSTLE TO THE GENTILES.

## CHAPTER I.

THE GOSPEL AS THE WAY OF DELIVERANCE FROM THE JUDGMENT.

§ 105. *The Ground of Salvation.*[1]

The fundamental thought of the preaching of the Apostle as a missionary to the Gentiles is essentially a proclamation of the nearness of the Messianic Judgment. But it was not the promising, but only the threatening aspect of this judgment, which was at first set before the Gentiles, in order to startle them out of their sinful life. The mission speeches of Paul are invaluable models of missionary preaching to this day. Take as an illustration the discourse of the Apostle in Athens—how, attaching itself to what remains of the Gentile consciousness of God, Paul proclaims, in the first place, the One true God (Acts 17:22–29). Then follows the proclamation of the approaching judgment of the world, supported by the fact that God has already appointed a Man who will execute this judgment, and that he has given the strongest reason to believe in it, by raising this One from the dead (17:31).

---

[1] Compare *Weiss*, § 61. This section bears on Soteriology and Ecclesiology.

Upon this message Paul bases his demand that they repent (17:30); and this repentance will consist in their turning away from vain idols to the living God (Acts 14:15), and in serving Him, in view of the impending judgment, according to the will of God as it is proclaimed by His ambassadors. Their fate in the judgment will depend upon their attitude to this demand; for God is willing to overlook the past as the time of ignorance (17:30).

In fact, to sum up, the declarations respecting the Gentiles contained in Acts 14:15–18 and Acts 17:22–31 are remarkable.[1] They consist in the following propositions:

1) The living God, who made and sustains the world (14:15; 17:24, 28), who has distributed man on the face of the earth according to His will (17:26), who has revealed Himself to all, even the heathen (17:23, 27, 28), bears witness of Himself.

2) He will have men worship Him in a becoming manner; He does not desire that they, who are the offspring of God, shall think that the Godhead is like unto *images* made by themselves (14:15; 17:27, 29).

3) God formerly allowed the times of ignorance to pass unpunished (14:16; 17:30).

4) He now requires all men to turn aside from the vain worship of idols, to serve Him, the Living God (14:15; 17:30).

5) For the Day of Judgment is already appointed, the Judge is ordained and accredited (17:31).

That Paul's missionary preaching at Thessalonica had not been different appears from his own retrospect of it (1 Thess. 1:9, 10). The motive which had led the

---

[1] Compare *Lechler*, vol. 1, p. 325.

Thessalonians also to turn from idols to the service of the Living and True God was the proclamation of the impending judgment, which must bring Divine punishment (2 Thess. 1:8) upon all who, without knowing the true God, walked in their lusts (1 Thess. 4:5). They had learned that Jesus, who was raised from the dead, was to be looked for as the Judge of the world coming from Heaven, and that therefore also He alone could deliver from the wrath of God (1 Thess. 1:10; 2 Thess. 1:7–10). It is only as their Divine Lord, who had been exalted to Heaven, and who comes from Heaven, that Jesus can save the Gentiles in the coming judgment (2 Thess. 1:12).

God comes graciously to the Gentile world, which is sunk in sin, and therefore irremediably lost in the approaching judgment, through "the word of salvation" (Acts 13:26), in which he causes Christ to be proclaimed to them as the Mediator of salvation, in order that they may be saved (1 Thess. 2:16; 2 Thess. 2:10). For it is of Christ that the glad tidings treat (1 Thess. 3:2; 2 Thess. 1:8); and it is Christ Himself who sends forth the messengers (1 Thess. 2:6), in order that they should bear witness to His Divine glory, which Paul himself has seen (2 Thess. 1:10, "our testimony"). Through this message the call to salvation is now addressed to them (2 Thess. 2:14), and those who have received it (1 Thess. 1:6), know themselves **as** chosen by God out of the mass of the Gentile world (1 Thess. 1:4). It is the message itself, in its quality as the *Word of God* (1 Thess. 1:8; 2 Thess. 3:1), which works upon the heart with Divine power and begets faith, and faith is expressly traced back to the work of the Spirit of God which is operative in the preaching (1 Thess. 1:5). As many will not believe this message, "for all have not the faith" (2 Thess. 3:2); those in whom the Spirit through the Word worketh faith, thereby know their election (1 Thess. 1:4). Now they know that they are beloved of God (1 Thess. 1:4; 2 Thess. 2:13; 3:5), and may call God their God (2 Thess. 1:12; 1 Thess. 2:2) and Father (2 Thess. 2:16; 1 Thess. 1:3; 3:11, 13). To such as believe He gives, through grace, an eternal comfort and good hope (2 Thess. 2:16) and perfect peace of mind (1 Thess. 5:23; 2 Thess. 3:16) to their conscience, which was terrified at the prospect of the approaching judgment. God has not appointed them to wrath, but that they should obtain salvation through Christ (1 Thess. 5:9).

According to 2 Thess. 2:13 election is accomplished in a historical act, in which God takes individuals out of the world to Himself. He does this, however, "in sanctification of the Spirit"—*i. e.*, by bestowing upon them through His Spirit, the necessary consecration. As in 1 Pet. 1:2, it is only baptism that can be thought of; in it believers receive the Spirit, which puts them into the condition of being consecrated to God (Acts 16:15, 33; 18:8; 19:5; 22:16). Since nothing can be consecrated to God, which is stained with guilt, and therefore unclean, it is self-evident that the consecration by the Spirit in baptism makes him, who receives it, also assured of complete forgiveness of sin (Acts 22:16). Now, however, among adults it is only believers that receive baptism; hence the subjective moment of faith is named alongside of the objective moment of "sanctification of the Spirit" (2 Thess. 2:13). This faith, it is true, is also a work of God for the Word of God worketh faith (1 Thess. 2:13), and the refusal to receive and obey this Word is described as a disobedience which is worthy of punishment (2 Thess. 1:8), and is traced back to an unsusceptibility to the love of the truth, which is rooted in pleasure in unrighteousness (Thess. 2:11, 12). Those whom God has taken to be His possession in consecration by the Spirit and in faith in the truth (2 Thess. 2:13) now form His Church (1 Thess. 2:14; 2 Thess. 1:4).

ANALYSIS: 1) Nearness of the Messianic Judgment the fundamental thought of Paul's missionary preaching; 2) his sermons models for missionaries; 3) method pursued in the sermons in Acts 14:15-18 and Acts 17:22-31; 4) Paul also lays stress on the impending judgment in his letters to the Thessalonians; 5) through the " word of Salvation " faith is wrought; 6) and they who believe are assured of their election; 7) if they are consecrated to God by the Spirit through baptism; 8) and such constitute the Church.]

§ 106. *The Demands of the Gospel.*[1]

As Christians live in the midst of the sinful world, there is always danger that they be defiled anew with sin. This very fact implies that there must be an ever-progressive sanctification (1 Thess. 4:3), and that they must therefore guard themselves against the lusts and sins of the Gentiles—especially against unchastity (1 Thess. 4:3, 6), as well as against every form of evil (1 Thess. 5:22), which defiles men. Christians must be unblamable in holiness before God (1 Thess. 3:13), and their condition of being consecrated to God must be more and more completely realized in them, the spirit, soul and body being preserved blameless (1 Thess. 5:23). It is the will of God that believers lead holy lives (1 Thess. 4:1-3), and the ambassadors of Christ are authorized to proclaim these precepts of the Lord Jesus Christ (2 Thess. 3:6, 12; 1 Thess. 4:1).

[1] Compare *Weiss*, § 62. This section treats mainly of **Christian Ethics**, and the Work of the Holy Spirit, or **Pneumatology**.

Alongside of faith, which must also be more and more established and perfected (1 Thess. 3:2, 10), it is love which characterizes the gratifying continuance (1 Thess. 1:3; 3:6) and the healthy growth of the Christian life (2 Thess. 1:3). If the question arises as to the weapons with which Christians must be equipped as children of the day, in order that they may maintain the watchfulness and the sobriety which secure them against the impure motives of sinful inclinations (1 Thess. 5:5-8), the Apostle names, along with the faith which appropriates the enlightening truth of the Gospel, the love which fulfills the fundamental commandment of the Gospel. This love is, in the first place, love of Christians to one another, or brotherly love (1 Thess. 4:9, 10; 2 Thess. 1:3); and, secondly, toward all men (1 Thess. 3:12), even to those who have done one evil (1 Thess. 5:15). In addition to faith and love, hope of salvation in the approaching judgment of the world (1 Thess. 5:8), or in Christ, through whom they have to look for this salvation (1 Thess. 1:3), appears to be characteristic of Christians as distinguished from the Gentiles, who have no hope (1 Thess. 4:13). Because Christians have in this good hope an eternal comfort (2 Thess. 2:16), with which they can also encourage the fainted-hearted (1 Thess. 5:14), the Apostle can exhort them to rejoice always (1 Thess. 5:16), notwithstanding all the afflictions which they suffer and must suffer (1 Thess. 3:3, 4; Acts 14:22). This joy which arises from hope will show itself in the patience (1 Thess. 1:3) which endures affliction after the example of Christ (2 Thess. 3:5). With this patience there is also connected faithfulness under the persecutions and afflictions which believers have to endure for the sake of the Kingdom of God (2 Thess. 1:4, 5). The Christian stands fast in the Lord (1 Thess. 3:8), and maintains his faith (2 Thess. 2:15) against all the temptations of the Devil (1 Thess. 3:3, 5).

If God makes these demands of His children, He however gives them the needed strength in answer to their prayers. Believers are urged to pray (1 Thess. 5: 17, 18), and we have the assurance that God will also lead the Christian to the salvation which He has made him hope for (1 Thess. 5:24), by strengthening him for the fulfillment of the necessary conditions, and guarding him from the Evil One (2 Thess. 3:3), or by helping him to attain to the completion of his sanctification (1 Thess. 5:23). God does this by continuing His calling activity through the preaching of the Word (1 Thess. 2:11, 12), which begets still more faith and works in them that believe (1 Thess. 2:13), to the encouragement, strengthening and development of the Christian life. In 1 Thess. 4:8 God is described as the One who is continually bestowing His Holy Spirit upon Christians. This Spirit, which accompanies the Word of God, urges men to sanctification (2 Thess. 2:13).

[ANALYSIS: 1) There must be an ever-progressive sanctification; 2) the weapons with which believers must be equipped are faith, love, and hope; 3) the possession of these brings joy, patience, faithfulness; 4) God will strengthen and complete His work of grace; 5) through His Word and Spirit.]

### § 107. *Summary of Paul's Teaching According to the Acts.*[1]

The Acts give a mere summary indication of the first utterances of Paul after conversion, in the synagogues

[1] Compare *Lechler*, vol. 1, pp. 318–325. For a full analytical development of the doctrinal teaching of Paul according to his two Epistles to the Thessalonians, see my "Studies in the Book," vol. 2, pp. 25–32.

at Damascus (Acts 9:20, 22), next a short reproof addressed to Elymas the sorcerer in Cyprus (13:10, 11), proceeding to record two missionary discourses, a longer one delivered in the synagogue of Antioch in Pisidia (13:16-41, 46, 47), and a shorter one addressed to the Gentile inhabitants of Lystra (14:15-17). Then follow brief notices of discourses to the new converts of Asia Minor (14:22), of the missionary report in Antioch (14:27), of the address of Paul and Barnabas at the Apostolic convention (15:12), and of the dialogue with the jailor at Philippi (16:31), succeeded by the sermon on Areopagus in Athens (17:22-31). The farewell discourse to the elders of the Church at Ephesus, delivered at Miletus (20:18-35), is unique of its kind. When a prisoner Paul made several speeches in self-defense; in Jerusalem, partly before the people (22:1-21), partly before the Sanhedrim (23:1-6); in Cæsarea before Felix (24:10-21, 24, 25); lastly, before Festus and Agrippa (26:2-29). The discourses to the Jews at Rome (28:17-20, 23, 29) form the conclusion of the Book. At this period of Paul's activity, however, we can only take into consideration the discourses recorded in the first eighteen chapters of Acts.

The Gospel which Paul preaches, in conformity with this evidence, is the Gospel of *Jesus* as the *Lord* and Saviour. Immediately after his conversion he preaches in the synagogues at Damascus "that Jesus is the Son of God" (Acts 9:20). From this time forward Paul constantly presents Jesus as the Redeemer and Glorified Lord, whether he speaks in the synagogue of Antioch in Pisidia (Acts 13:23, 32), or points out the way of salvation to the jailor at Philippi (16:31).

Paul also emphasizes the fact that Jesus is a descendant of David in accordance with the promise (13:22, 23);

but in the same discourse he declares Jesus to be also the Son of God (13:33; see also 9:20), in whom the promise (Ps. 2:7) of the theocratic Ruler is fulfilled. In proof of his confession that Jesus is the Messiah, the Son of God, he appeals to the fact of His *resurrection* (13:30, 33, 34, 37; 17:31). Hand in hand with this Divine ratification, Paul appeals to the fulfillment of the prophecies of the Old Testament. This is especially seen in the Pisidian discourse (Acts 13:16–41), where 1) the Davidic descent (13:23); 2), the death on the Cross (13:27–29), and 3) His resurrection 13:30–34) are set forth as the fulfillment of God's promise. This certainly corresponds to the primitive Christian preaching, Paul giving prominence to the redemptive death of Christ, His burial, resurrection on the third day, with the appearances of the Risen One, as facts in the history of salvation, which he announces in common with the other Apostles.

Next to the resurrection, the crucifixion of Jesus appears as the principal fact in these discourses, not only as being quite unmerited (Acts 13:28), but also as foretold by the prophets (13:27, 29).

It is to Jesus to whom we owe *salvation* (13:23, 26; 16:31). The grace of God coming through Jesus Christ consists above all in the forgiveness of sins: "Through this man is proclaimed unto you remission of sins, and by Him every one that believeth is justified from all things—from which ye could not be justified by the law of Moses" (Acts 13:38, 39). In this passage an absolute distinction between the Law and the Gospel is set forth. It states—1) *negatively*, no actual forgiveness of sins and justification are given in the law; 2) *positively*, forgiveness and justification from all guilt and punishment, on account of our sins, are proclaimed, offered, and bestowed upon believers through Christ.

[ANALYSIS: 1) We can only here take into consideration Acts 1–18; 2) Jesus is our Lord and Saviour; 3) a descendant of David, in accordance with the promise; 4) the Messiah, as proved by His resurrection; 5) to Him we owe our salvation; 6) there is a difference between the Law and the Gospel.]

# CHAPTER II.

## THE PAULINE ESCHATOLOGY.[1]

§ 108. *Method of Presenting the Pauline Eschatology.*

That Paul in his early missionary preaching already presented the leading truths regarding the doctrine of the Last Things, can be seen from his speeches recorded in the Acts of the Apostles, and especially from his Epistles to the Thessalonians.[2] The excitement which these eschatological questions caused in the Church at Thessalonica not only shows with what emphasis Paul had set forth these topics in his preaching, but also forces him to discuss the matter still more fully.

Although, in a logical point of view, it would be best to delay the presentation of the Pauline Eschatology until we had outlined more fully the teaching of the four great Doctrinal Epistles, still this is the most suitable place for the discussion, as the Epistles to the Thessalonians are so strongly eschatological. In our presentation, we will follow the same order as we did in outlining the teaching of Jesus.

[ANALYSIS: 1) In his early preaching, Paul lays stress on the Last Things; 2) so also in his Epistles to the Thessalonians; 3) method of presentation.]

---

[1] Compare *Weiss*, §§ 64, 96–99. *Lechler*, vol. 1, pp. 333–339; vol. 2, pp. 87–102.

[2] See my "Studies in the Book," vol. 2, pp. 29–32.

§ 109. *The Teaching Concerning Death.*

Through Adam's sin, spiritual[1] as well as bodily[2] death came upon all men, "for the wages of sin is death" (Rom. 6:23)—spiritual, bodily, and eternal. But Christ has overcome death,[3] and believers are now delivered from spiritual and eternal death;[4] but all men, believers as well as unbelievers, are subject to bodily death,[5] but the time shall come when even this also shall be abolished.[6]

To the Christian, bodily death brings no terror or fear; it cannot separate him from the love of God

---

[1] Rom. 5:15, "By the trespass of the one the many died."

Rom. 5:17, "By the trespass of the one, death reigned through the one."

Rom. 8:6, 7, "For the mind of the flesh is death; . . . because the mind of the flesh is enmity against God."

Eph. 2:1, "And you did he quicken, when ye were dead through your trespasses and sins."

Col. 2:13, "And you, being dead through your trespasses."

[2] Rom. 5:12, "As through one man sin entered into the world, and death through sin; and so death passed unto all men, for that all sinned."

1 Cor. 15:21, "By man came death."

[3] 2 Tim. 1:10, The grace of God "has been manifested by the appearing of our Saviour Jesus Christ, who abolished death, and brought life and incorruption to light through the Gospel."

[4] Rom. 5:17, "For if, by the trespass of the one, death reigned through the one, much more shall they *that receive the abundance of grace and of the gift of righteousness* reign in life through the one, even Jesus Christ;" . . . *ver.* 21, "that, as sin reigned in death, even so might grace reign through righteousness unto eternal life through Jesus Christ our Lord."

Eph. 2:5, 6, "Even when we were dead through our trespasses, God quickened us together with [in] Christ (by grace have ye been saved), and raised us up with Him, and made us to sit with Him in the heavenly places, in Christ Jesus."

[5] Heb. 9:27, "It is appointed unto men once to die."

[6] 1 Cor. 15:26, "The last enemy that shall be abolished is death."

(Rom. 8:38, 39), nor from the life in fellowship with Christ (Rom. 8:13, 14). It is but the gate, the door, by which he passes out of this earthly life into a spiritual life—by means of which he enters upon a state of blessed rest—a being "at home with the Lord" (2 Cor. 5:8).

[ANALYSIS: 1) Death the result of Adam's sin; 2) spiritual, bodily, and eternal death; 3) Christ has overcome death for the believers; 4) yet all men are still subject to bodily death; 5) bodily death brings no terror to the believer.]

§ 110. *The State of the Soul After Death.*

Paul does not think of the soul of the believer as, going into Hades immediately after death, but as going unto the Lord, to be with the Exalted Christ in Heaven in the Paradise above the earth, the special dwelling-place of God (2 Cor. 12:2, 4). Paul's testimony as to the immediate entrance of the redeemed at death on their Heavenly state is very explicit.

This is implied already by the view that Paul has of the effect which Christ's death and resurrection wrought in the lower world. He also knows that there were two divisions in Hades, as taught by Christ in the Parable of the Rich Man and Lazarus (Luke 16:19-31), before Christ overcame death and Satan. He also knows of the results which followed Christ's descent into Hades, when, immediately after His restoration to life as God-Man, with body and soul reunited, He manifested Himself as Victor and Lord in the lower world. He accepts and knows the same doctrine which Peter presents in 1 Pet. 3:18-20 and 1 Pet. 4:6.[1] What Paul reveals to us in Col. 2:15 corresponds to the teaching of Peter in 1 Pet. 3:18-20; for it was on this occasion that Christ " put

[1] See the full discussion under the Petrine Eschatology, vol. 1, § 77.

off from Himself the principalities and the powers and made a show of them openly, triumphing over them in it." So, likewise, Eph. 4:8, 9 refers to the same event indicated by Peter in 1 Pet. 4:6; for the effect of Christ's manifesting Himself to the saints of the Old Testament was, that "when He ascended on high He led captivity captive, and gave gifts unto men" (Eph. 4:8).

With Paul, Hades still exists as the abode of Satan and his evil angels, and as the fore-hell into which all the souls of unbelievers enter, awaiting the Day of Judgment; but the Paradise of which Paul speaks is no longer under the earth, in Hades, but above the earth, in Heaven itself—even in the third Heaven (2 Cor. 12:3, 4). That part of Hades known as Paradise before Christ's resurrection and descent in triumph (Luke 23:43) has now yielded up its captives, the saints of the Old Testament, who had been held by the power of Satan and death, for the Lord Jesus "hath led captivity captive;" He has snatched all believers from Hades, and has conquered Satan and Hades; and the gifts which the Exalted Christ gave to the saints of the Old Testament, when He ascended on high and entered upon His Kingly and Heavenly throne, were freedom from the dominion of Satan and Hades, and the blessedness and glory of being with Him in Heaven. When Christ ascended on high into the Heaven of Glory, to sit at the Right Hand of God, He led captivity captive; He took with Him into Heaven—snatching them out of the power of Satan, out of the upper part of Hades— those souls who in Paradise had welcomed Him as the Redeemer; and from this time forward Paradise is not regarded as a place or condition of joy *on* the earth, as it was before the Fall, nor *under* the earth as the upper part of the place of the departed souls, as it was between the Fall of man and the resurrection of Christ, but as *above* the earth, in Heaven itself. And ever since Christ's resurrection from the dead and ascension into Heaven, the souls of the blessed dead, according to the constant testimony of the Apostles, enter immediately into Heaven, to be with Christ in joy and glory—there in blessedness to await the Second Coming of Christ and their glorious resurrection bodies, when, with body and soul reunited, they shall enter upon their full joy in the Lord.

In 2 Cor. 5:6-8,[1] Paul speaks as if the Christian had two homes, and could not leave the one without entering on the other. The one home is where the body is; the other home is where the Lord is; and our Lord is surely not now, in His glorified Presence, in the under world, in Hades, but in the Heaven of Glory. So, also, in Heb. 12:22-24,[2] it is implied that there is no intermediate condition in Hades, between the believer's state here on earth and Mount Zion, the city of the living God, the New Jerusalem, the city of angels. It is implied that the spirits and souls of the saints are with Jesus, the Mediator of the New Covenant. Believers are represented here as actually having come to these, and only needing the supernatural opening of

[1] "Being therefore always of good courage, and knowing that, whilst we are at home in the body, we are absent from the Lord (for we walk by faith, not by sight); we are of good courage, I say, and are willing rather to be absent from the body, and to be at home with the Lord."

[2] "But ye are come unto Mount Zion, and unto the city of the living God, the heavenly Jerusalem, and to innumerable hosts of angels, to the general assembly and church of the first-born who are enrolled in Heaven, and to God the Judge of all, and to the spirits of just men made perfect, and to Jesus the Mediator of a New Covenant."

the vision which takes place at death to realize the glory of their estate. Very explicit, likewise, is the testimony given by Paul in Phil. 1:23, when he says: "I am in a strait betwixt the two, having the desire to depart and be with Christ; for it is very far better."

1) Note that the immediate state of dying saints is an object of desire—a most ardent longing.

2) Note, that to depart and to be with Christ involve each other. There is no Hades, neither place nor state between the two. The ardent longing of the Apostle is not to depart from this life and enter on an intermediate state, or to enter Hades—a state or condition which is to close at the Second Coming of Christ and the general resurrection—but his desire is to depart in order at once to be with Christ.

3) Note, that the state of the departed saint is one in which he is with Christ. This agrees with the teaching of Jesus. "Father, that which thou hast given me, I will that, where I am, they also may be with me; that they may behold my glory" (John 17:24). Paul does not long to be in Hades, but his desire is for that peculiar presence with Christ which is found only in Heaven.

[ANALYSIS : 1) The soul of the believer, after death, does not go into Hades; 2) but into Heaven, into the presence of Christ; 3) Paul also knows of the results of Christ's descent into Hades; 4) Col. 2:15 refers to the same event as 1 Pet. 3:18-20; 5) Eph. 4:8, 9 refers to the same event as 1 Pet. 4:6; 6) with Paul, Hades still exists as the fore-hell for the souls of unbelievers; 7) but the Paradise of God is no longer in Hades, but in Heaven; 8) this change in the condition of the souls of the saints took place, as the result of Christ's descent, at His ascension; 9) the souls of all believers, since Christ's resurrection, enter immediately into Heaven; 10) there to await the glorious resurrection of their bodies, at the Last Day; 11) the teaching of 2 Cor. 5:6-8; 12) of Heb. 12:22-24; 13) of Phil. 1:23.]

## § 111. *The Pauline Apocalypse.*

Paul starts with the fundamental thought of apocalyptic prophecy, that while the end of the development of the world is brought about by a supernatural interposition of God, yet the moment of this catastrophe is conditioned by the development of the world itself, and especially by mankind having made full the measure of its guilt, and having thus become ripe for judgment. Hence the Great Day of the Lord, which brings at once the consummation and the judgment, will not come until evil has reached its fullest development.[1] The fullest information that Paul gives with reference to the point of time when the Second Advent of Christ will take place is given in 2 Thess. 2:3–10, in connection with the presentation of his doctrine of Antichrist.

## § 112. *The Doctrine of Antichrist.*

The passage in 2 Thess. 2:3–10, in which Paul presents the doctrine of Antichrist, is certainly one of the most extraordinary portions of the New Testament. The obscurity in which this passage is seemingly involved has its foundation partly in the fact that the Apostle takes for granted an acquaintance with his previous oral instruction, of which *we* have no knowledge (2 Thess. 2:5, 6). This is not the place to make a critical examination of the endlessly diverse explanations which have been given of the words of the Apostle, from the Fathers down to the present day;[2] and all we

---

[1] 2 Thess. 2:3, "For it will not be, except the falling away come first, and the man of sin be revealed."

[2] It is best not to endeavor to clear up the obscurity in an arbitrary way. Of the various interpretations, that of Weiss—in making the apostasy an unbelieving Christ-opposing Judaism, and "the man of sin," or the pseudo-Messiah, the hero of the Jewish revolution which

can do is simply to follow the words of Paul, and examine what he really does say.

The Apostle here refers to an idea which had found acceptance with many Christians in Thessalonica, and had given rise to some uneasiness of mind (*ver.* 2)—the idea that the Day of the Lord was at hand.[1] Paul does not say that the Lord may not come shortly, but what he does say is, that they were mistaken in believing that He was coming at that very time; that although His coming was imminent, and "as a thief in the night," still the Lord will not come "except the falling away come first, and the man of sin be revealed, the son of perdition (*ver.* 3).

On a careful examination of this whole passage, we find that it teaches:

1) That the adversary (Antichrist) of which Paul speaks, and which is Antichrist by pre-eminence, though not to the exclusion of all others, has his apocalypse or revelation ("he shall be revealed," *vers.* 3, 6, 8). Antichrist is not a mere principle.

2) That this revelation of this "man of sin" will not take place "except the falling away come first" (*ver.* 3). Great apostasies from God have occurred; but here is painted the greatest of all apostasies, without parallel and without equal—"*the* apostasy," "*the* falling away."

3) That the revelation of "the lawless one" will not take place until a certain obstacle to his coming is removed (*vers.* 6–8). There is a definite obstacle in the

---

ended in the destruction of Jerusalem—is probably the most unsatisfactory.

[1] This disquietude had arisen from three causes—1) some professed to have a teaching of the Spirit—"neither by Spirit"; 2) others falsely interpreted Paul's oral teaching—"neither by word"; 3) while still others circulated a forged letter of Paul—"neither by epistle."

way—"there is one that restraineth now, until he be taken out of the way. And then shall be revealed the lawless one." What this restraining influence is, whether it is the restraining power of political government or the influence of human law, it is not necessary for us here to decide.

4) That one of the marked characteristics of this "man of sin" is open opposition to God and religion (*ver.* 4). In him sin and enmity to God reach their highest point. He is an opposer of God, and of all that is the object of reverence in the world.

5) That this "lawless one" lays claim to the incommunicable attributes of God, "so that he sitteth in the sanctuary of God, setting himself forth as God."

6) That this adversary is noted for his iniquity, sin, and lawlessness. He is "the man of sin," "the son of perdition." The perdition which he brings is the most fearful, even the eternal ruin of souls; and the perdition he suffers is to be of the most awful kind.

7) That he shall come "with all power and signs and wonders of falsehood" (*ver.* 9). As Christ came with the power of truth, and with miraculous signs and wonders of truth, so the Antichrist will come with the power and signs and wonders of falsehood.

8) That "his coming is according to the working of Satan." As Christ has His appearing, so Antichrist has his appearing. As the coming of Christ is according to the working or energy of God, so the coming of Antichrist is according to the working or energy of Satan.

9) That "this mystery of lawlessness," which would mature in the gigantic power of evil which is here depicted, was already at work at the time that Paul was writing (*ver.* 7).

10) That this mysterious adversary is unmistakably a person, or, what is the same, this mystery of lawlessness will culminate in a personal Antichrist ("the man of sin," "the son of perdition," "the lawless one").

11) That the downfall of this adversary will occur at the Second Coming of Christ—"for the Lord Jesus shall slay the lawless one with the breath of His mouth, and bring to naught by the manifestation of His coming" (*ver.* 8).

It does not belong to our science, but more properly to the sphere of Dogmatics, to decide whether or not the characteristics of Antichrist here depicted by Paul have their counterpart in the system of the Papacy and the Pope.

It is also generally agreed that Paul refers to the times of Antichrist when in his letters to Timothy he describes how "in later times some shall fall away from the faith" (1 Tim. 4:1–3), and how "in the last days grievous times shall come" (2 Tim. 3:1–5).

There is no conflict between Paul's description of the events of the last days and that given by Christ in His prophecy on Mount Olivet (Matt. 24:3–31). Our Lord does not refer to Antichrist; He does not speak of any one individual or polity, but rather of those forerunners, false Christs, and false prophets, who are the servants of Antichrist and actuated by his spirit. Christ's prophecy does not elucidate for us the characteristics of the Antichrist, nor does it give us any information on this point.

[ANALYSIS: 1) The seeming obscurity of 2 Thess. 2:3–10; 2) Antichrist has his apocalypse or revelation; 3) this revelation will not take place until "the falling away come first;" 4) until a certain obstacle to His coming has been removed; 5) this "man of sin" is in open opposition to God and religion; 6) he lays claim to the incommunicable attributes of God; 7) he is noted for his iniquity and lawlessness; 8) he shall come with the power and wonders of falsehood, 9) according to the working of Satan; 10) this "mystery of lawlessness" was already at work in Paul's time; 11) is undoubtedly a person, an individual; 12) his downfall will occur at the Second Coming of Christ; 13) references to Antichrist in the Pastoral Epistles; 14) this description agrees with the prophecy of Christ in Matt. 24.]

§ 113. *The Fullness of the Gentiles.*

The promise of Jehovah to Abraham was, that in him should all the families and all the nations of the earth be blessed (Gen. 12:3; 18:18). In the great prophecy of Gen. 49:10, it is declared that Shiloh shall come, "and unto Him shall the obedience of the peoples be." Accepting, as the just interpretation of Shiloh, that it refers to the great Prince of Peace (Isa. 9:6), the passage teaches when, in general, the promise to Abraham is to be fulfilled. It is to be after the coming of Shiloh, the Prince of Peace, and He is to be the center of this gathering of the peoples. The *peoples* are the nations, the Gentiles, over against Israel as one people.

The commission given by our Lord to His Apostles embraced all nations—in fact, every creature;[1] and He Himself expressly says that "this Gospel of the Kingdom shall be preached in the whole inhabited earth for a testimony unto all the nations; and then shall the end come" (Matt. 24:14).[2] He also speaks of the rejection of Israel, and the calling of the Gentiles, for "the kingdom of God shall be taken away from you, and shall be given to a nation bringing forth the fruits thereof" (Matt. 21:43).[3]

[1] Matt. 28:19, "Make disciples of all the nations, baptizing them . . teaching them to observe all things."

[2] He does not say that all the Gentiles shall be converted before the end, but that the Gospel shall be preached in the whole inhabited earth for a testimony unto all the nations.

[3] Compare Matt. 22:1-10.

In the prophecy of the calling of the Gentiles, there was, however, the presupposition throughout that Israel should first participate in the Messianic salvation, and that through them it should come to the Gentiles. Salvation, in the historical order, was offered first to the Jew, and then to the Greek (Rom. 1:16). And yet the position of Jews and Gentiles to salvation is not the same. The promise was given by grace to the Jews (Gal. 3:18); but after God had once given this promise, His truthfulness binds Him to a fulfillment of His promise (Rom. 15:8). Towards the Gentiles He had bound Himself by no similar promise; they could but praise the mercy of God if He pitied their need (Rom. 15:9). His calling of the Gentiles is but a richer evidence of His mercy, which from its very nature is free and unconditioned (Rom. 9:15).

By the unbelief of Israel, it was necessary that the natural historical order should be broken. The Gospel should have been embraced *first* by the Jews as a nation, and through them, as a nation of priests and ministers of God, by the rest of mankind. But as the Jews as a race broke the normal, Divine order by their rejection of Christ, the reception of salvation on a large scale took place first among the Gentiles. And Paul, in his great argument of Rom. 9–11, speaks of "the fullness of the Gentiles coming in" (Rom. 11:12, 25), and after this has taken place the hardness of Israel is to cease. Paul speaks of the rejection of Israel and the calling of the Gentiles as a mystery—one of those insoluble, moral mysteries which, after explanation is exhausted, still lies heavy on the heart.[1]

---

[1] Rom. 11:25–27, "For I would not, brethren, have you ignorant of this mystery, lest ye be wise in your own conceits, that a hardening in part hath befallen Israel, until the fullness of the Gentiles be

## THE FULLNESS OF THE GENTILES.

It is God's will that by the apostasy of Israel salvation is come unto the Gentiles (Rom. 11:11, 12). When the gap made in the Kingdom of God by the fall of Israel is filled up,[1] when the fullness of the Gentiles be come in, then shall all Israel be converted (Rom. 11:25, 26). Paul also seems to imply that after the conversion of the Jews a still more powerful converting influence over the Gentile world shall go forth, for "if their fall is the riches of the world, and their loss the riches of the Gentiles, how much more their fullness?" (Rom. 11:12; also compare 11:15).

That a complete picture of the final development of God's Kingdom upon earth, arranged in chronological order, was seen by Paul, is not to be supposed. The Spirit disclosed to him different vistas and features as circumstances made necessary. It is for us, who study his Epistles, to combine these separate features and form them into a harmonious whole. Seven things, at least, Paul takes for granted in his presentation: 1) that Israel has been rejected for a time; 2) that salvation is now being offered to the Gentiles; 3) that the Gentiles may be cast off again on account of unbelief (*vers.* 20-22); 4) that the time will come when the fullness of the

come in; and so all Israel shall be saved: even as it is written. There shall come out of Zion the Deliverer; he shall turn away ungodliness from Jacob; and this is my covenant unto them, when I shall take away their sins."

[1] Some maintain that Paul teaches a universal conversion of the Gentiles before the conversion of Israel, but the true meaning of *fullness* (*pleroma*) in this connection is, "that by which a thing is filled," "the complement," "the full number of the Gentiles." The Gospel is to be preached unto all nations, and, on the one hand, Gentiles shall continue to be saved; but, on the other hand, evil shall also increase until its development into Antichrist (2 Thess. 2:3-10), but at the time when the full number of Gentiles has been converted, then shall all Israel be saved.

Gentiles be come in (*ver.* 25); 5) that then all Israel shall be converted; 6) that then a still larger conversion among the Gentile world shall take place; 7) that all this shall take place at the Coming of Christ, and at the end to which that return is the introduction.

[ANALYSIS: 1) The promise to Abraham; 2) the prophecy of Gen. 49:10; 3) Christ foretells the rejection of Israel and the calling of the Gentiles; 4) salvation was first offered to the Jews, and then to the Gentiles; 5) the calling of the Gentiles an evidence of the mercy of God; 6) the historical order of salvation was broken by the unbelief of the Jews; 7) the fullness of the Gentiles shall first come; 8) then the hardening of Israel shall cease; 9) the teaching of Rom. 11:25, 26; 10) Paul does not teach a universal conversion of the Gentiles before the conversion of Israel; 11) by the fullness of the Gentiles is meant "the full number of the Gentiles," sufficient to fill up the gap made in the Kingdom of God by the fall of Israel; 12) Paul does not give us a description of the last times in a chronological order; 13) seven things which Paul takes for granted.]

§ 114. *The Conversion of Israel.*

Paul clearly teaches that there is to be, before the end of the world, a great national movement of the Jews towards Christianity. God hath not cast off his people which he foreknew (Rom. 11:2). His doctrine on this point is in strict harmony with the prophecy of Hosea,[1] and as that prophet speaks of a national restoration of Israel, in the latter days, in connection with the reception of the Messiah, so also does Paul.

The teaching of Paul also agrees with that of Christ, for our Lord clearly presents the same great facts in regard to Israel's future rejection and restoration. Their

---

[1] Hos. 3:4, 5, "For the children of Israel shall abide many days without king, and without prince, and without sacrifice, and without pillar, and without ephod or teraphim : afterward shall the children of Israel return, and seek the Lord their God, and David their King; and shall come with fear unto the Lord and to His goodness in the latter days."

house was to be left desolate ; Christ was to remain long hidden to them ; but the time was to come when they should joyously hail Him as coming in the name of the Lord ; and with this was to be connected the beholding of Christ again.[1] So also, in Luke 21:24,[2] our Lord prophesies of the slaughter of a large part of the nation, of their captivity, of their dispersion among the nations, of the down-treading of Jerusalem by the Gentiles—and yet of the coming of a time when all this shall have reached its termination, when the times of the Gentiles shall be fulfilled.

This whole subject is most fully discussed by Paul in Rom. 11:11–32. From this passage we learn:

1) That the reference is not to the spiritual Israel—the Israel of God as in Gal. 6:16—but to the national Israel.

2) That Paul refers not simply to individual Israelites, but that this passage can be understood of nothing else than the people of Israel as a nation (*vers.* 26–32).

3) That the hardening in part which has now befallen Israel will cease at a certain definite time in the future (*ver.* 25).

4) That this conversion of Israel will occur when the fullness of the Gentiles shall have come (*ver.* 25).

Paul does not know of any *temporal* restoration of the Jewish nation to Palestine, nor of any renewal of the Temple service in Jerusalem.

[ANALYSIS : 1) God has not cast off his people Israel ; 2) the prophecy of Hos. 3:4, 5 ; 3) the teaching of Jesus ; 4) of Rom 11:

---

[1] Matt. 23:38, 39, " Behold your house is left unto you desolate. For I say unto you, Ye shall not see me henceforth, till ye shall say, Blessed is he that cometh into the name of the Lord."

[2] " And they shall fall by the edge of the sword, and shall be led captive into all the nations: and Jerusalem shall be trodden down of the Gentiles, until the times of the Gentiles be fulfilled."

11–32 ; 5) Paul knows of no temporal restoration of Israel to Palestine.]

### § 115. *The Second Coming of Christ.*

According to the teaching of Paul in his earliest Epistles, Christ comes down from Heaven in Divine glory, accompanied by angels as He Himself has prophesied. The description which Paul gives of the return of Christ is plainly based upon Christ's discourse concerning His Second Coming.[1] He teaches the Thessalonians to look for the Son of God from Heaven (1 Thess. 1:10 ; 4:16), and it is assumed that He comes in the clouds of Heaven (1 Thess. 4:17). The glory of His might in which He is then glorified (2 Thess. 1:9, 10), is none other than the glory of His Father (Mark 8:38), in which he is to appear on the occasion of His return. This *Parousia* is called "the revelation of the Lord Jesus from Heaven" (2 Thess. 1:7), and the angels of His power accompany Him as the executors of his commands. According to 1 Thess. 4:16, the archangel calls together the angels to form the retinue of Christ, and the trump of God (see Matt. 24:31) announces to the whole world the coming of the Great Day of the Lord.

In the four great Doctrinal Epistles, the coming of the Lord also comes into the foreground.[2] With the

---

[1] 1 Thess. 4:16, "For the Lord Himself shall descend from heaven, with a shout, with the voice of the archangel, and with the trump of God."

[2] 1 Cor. 4:5, "Wherefore judge nothing before the time, until the Lord come."

1 Cor. 1:7, "Waiting for the revelation of our Lord Jesus Christ."

1 Cor. 11:26, "For as often as ye eat this bread, and drink the cup, ye proclaim the Lord's death till He come."

1 Cor. 16:22, "If any man loveth not the Lord, let him be anathema. Our Lord cometh."

*Parousia* of Christ comes the end in the absolute sense (1 Cor. 15:23; 1:8; 1:13, 14),[1] and therewith the moment for the realization of the Christian hope.

With respect to the *time* of the Second Coming, Paul constantly refers to the event as "the day of Christ" (1 Cor. 1:8; 5:5; 2 Cor. 1:14). How near the Apostle regarded the Lord's coming is very clear from 1 Cor. 7:29; 10:11; Rom. 13:11, 12.

According to the Pastoral Epistles, there will be in the last times a great falling away from the faith (1 Tim. 4:1; 2 Tim. 4:3, 4), and "grievous times shall come" (2 Tim. 3:15). To Paul these signs are already appearing (2 Tim. 3:5, 6), and he charges Timothy to "keep the commandment, without spot, without reproach, until the appearing of our Lord Jesus Christ, which in His own times He will show" (1 Tim. 6:13, 14), and he exhorts him to preach the Word "in the sight of God, and of Christ Jesus, who shall judge the quick and the dead, and by His appearing and His kingdom" (2 Tim. 4:1, 2). With this Second Coming of Christ comes "that day" (2 Tim. 1:12, 18; 4:8), the Day of Judgment, on which Christ, as the Judge of the living and the dead (2 Tim. 4:1, 8), will render to the wicked according to their works (2 Tim. 4:14); and to the righteous, even to all who love His appearing, shall He assign the crown of righteousness (2 Tim. 4:8).

In the Epistle to the Hebrews the Day of Judgment is regarded as coincident with the day of the Second Advent, when He again bringeth in the first-born into

---

[1] 1 Cor. 15:23, "Then cometh the end, when he shall deliver up the kingdom to God." Meyer's view, that Paul, by the statement "then cometh the end," means "the end of the resurrection," is to be rejected. The end to which Paul here refers is "the end of the present age of the world," "the final consummation."

the world (Heb. 1:6).[1] It is at hand (Heb. 10:37); believers are to make ready for the end (3:14; 6:11), because their salvation is near (6:9). They wait for the Second appearance of Christ, not to come into judgment, but to receive salvation (Heb. 9:28) from the perdition which overtakes those who have not faith unto the saving of the soul (Heb. 10:37–39).

[ANALYSIS: 1) Teaching of Paul in his Epistles to the Thessalonians; 2) in his four great Doctrinal Epistles; 3) in the Pastoral Epistles; 4) in the Epistle to the Hebrews.]

## § 116. *The Resurrection of the Dead.*

The death of believers in the Church at Thessalonica had given rise to the fear that these would either not at all partake in the glory and salvation of Christ's coming, or not in the same manner as the survivors, but that those who would be alive would rather have some advantage over those that had fallen asleep (1 Thess. 4:13). Paul refers them to the word of Christ (*ver.* 15), according to which *all* His elect will be gathered together around Him at His return.[2] To this end the Christians who are dead will then rise first (1 Thess. 4:16). The first is by no means meant to contrast this resurrection with a second general resurrection which would be separated from the first by a thousand years. Of this Paul teaches nothing.[3] It seems from the context that, by this resurrection, the dead in Christ will be placed on a level with the survivors, before the hour of blessedness has struck for

[1] This passage undoubtedly refers to the Second Advent of Christ.

[2] Matt. 24:31, " And he shall send forth his angels with a great sound of a trumpet, and they shall gather together His elect from the four winds, from one end of heaven to the other."

[3] Phil. 3:11 seems, however, to refer to a special resurrection of the righteous.

the latter, and that therefore those that are alive can in nowise precede them that are fallen asleep. Then the survivors, along with the dead who have been thus raised up, will be caught up in the clouds and borne into the air, in order to meet the Lord who is descending from Heaven (1 Thess. 4:17). Thus, then, there is effected that gathering together of the elect into Christ (2 Thess. 2:1), with which their salvation from the world, as well as their greatest blessedness, begins.

So certainly as we believe that Jesus has risen again from the dead, will God through this Jesus, who through this resurrection has been exalted to be the Mediator of salvation, one day bring with Him those who are fallen asleep in Jesus (1 Thess. 4:14). Where God will bring them is not said. It is best to understand 1 Thess. 4:17 to mean that they will be brought to meet the Lord, not for the purpose of fetching Him down to earth, but to be led home by Him. And since the dead and the living believers are one day to live together with Him (1 Thess. 5:10), the former being raised up by a resurrection which is of the same nature as that of Christ (1 Thess. 4:14), and therefore not to an earthly, but to a heavenly life, every thought of an earthly reign of Christ is excluded. The completed Kingdom of God, to which believers are called (1 Thess. 2:12; 2 Thess. 1:5), is plainly conceived of as a heavenly kingdom, such as Christ had spoken of.

In the four great Doctrinal Epistles, the doctrine of the Resurrection is more fully presented. In 1 Cor. 15, Paul discusses two leading points: 1) the fact of a future resurrection (*vers.* 12–34), and 2) the manner of it (*vers.* 35–38). He establishes the fact or the certainty of the resurrection, in opposition to those by whom it is denied, by the resurrection of Christ (*vers.* 12–19).

But now Christ being risen from the dead, His resurrection guarantees and involves the future resurrection of all men (*vers.* 20–22).

Before the coming of the final consummation, death, as the last of all enemies, is overcome and robbed of all power, in that the dead are raised (*ver.* 26). This resurrection takes place in a moment, on the signal given by the last trumpet (*ver.* 52), which, according to 1 Thess. 4:16, announces at the same time the Second Coming of Christ. The believers, who are alive, who have a body which has not yet been delivered from the bondage of corruption (Rom. 8:21, 23), and which is therefore mortal (Rom. 8:11) and not fitted for participation in the perfected Kingdom of God (1 Cor. 15:50), shall be changed at the same moment in which the dead are raised (*vers.* 51, 52), so that their corruptible and mortal bodies immediately put on incorruption and immortality (*ver.* 53), and are clothed with glorified bodies, the habitations which are from Heaven (2 Cor. 5:1, 2).

As Paul mainly speaks of the resurrection of believers, of those who are Christ's (1 Cor. 15:23), who have fallen asleep in Jesus (1 Thess. 4:14), some have maintained that he knows nothing of the resurrection of unbelievers. But Paul distinctly speaks of the Judgment which shall overtake the world, and we frequently find the judgment of wrath on the ungodly associated with the redemption of the pious, by way of contrast.[1] This judgment naturally presupposes a *universal* resurrection, including the ungodly; and although Paul only once makes express mention of the resurrection of the ungodly; still his testimony is very

[1] 2 Thess. 1:6–10; Rom. 2:5–13, 16; 9:22; 2 Cor. 5:10; Gal. 6:7, 8.

explicit and clear.¹ The passage in 1 Cor. 15:20-23 does not exclude the fact that Christ is also the Raiser of the dead for the unbelieving, for the Risen Christ is the beginning of the history of the end. Certainly no one shall be made alive except by Christ and His power, but this will happen to all. Meyer, in his note on 1 Cor. 15:22, puts this very clearly: "Christ, when He appears in His glory, is not simply the Giver of life for His believing people, . . . but His life-giving power extends also to the other side—that is, to the unbelievers who must experience the necessary opposite of the completed redemption; these He awakes to the resurrection of condemnation. Paul thus agrees with John 5:28, 29;² Matt. 10:28;³ and thus His declaration recorded in Acts 24:15,¹ finds its confirmation in our text." The same Almighty power that has raised Christ will raise also all men (1 Cor. 6:14), that each one may receive the things done in the body, according to what he hath done, whether it be good or bad (2 Cor. 5:10), "for we shall all stand before the judgment-seat of God" (Rom. 14:10-12).

According to Paul all shall arise, "but each in his own order" (1 Cor. 15:23), which does not mean so much an order of succession, but rather "in his own

[1] Acts 24:15, "There shall be a resurrection both of the just and unjust." Compare also 2 Cor. 5:10, "For we must all be made manifest before the judgment seat of Christ, that each one may receive the things done in the body, according to what he hath done, whether it be good or bad."

[2] John 5:28, 29, "For the hour cometh, in which all that are in the tombs shall hear his voice, and shall come forth; they that have done good, unto the resurrection of life; and they that have done ill, unto the resurrection of judgment."

[3] Matt. 10:28, "Be not afraid of them which kill the body, but are not able to kill the soul; but rather fear him which is able to destroy both soul and body in hell."

division or class," as of an army. Paul here distinguishes three stages or divisions: 1) the resurrection has begun already with Christ Himself as the firstfruits; 2) at His coming to judge the quick and the dead "they that are Christ's" shall be raised up; 3) "then cometh the end," the absolute consummation, which presupposes or involves the universal resurrection and judgment. How soon or how long after the *Parousia* it is not said, but at the same time of Christ's putting all his enemies under his feet (*ver.* 25), the resurrection of unbelievers shall take place. These too shall be judged (1 Cor. 6:2; 11:32), of which their resurrection is the prelude. Paul certainly does not state that a period, longer or shorter, intervenes between the resurrection of believers at the Second Coming of Christ and the end itself (the Last Judgment); but, on the other hand, he says nothing to exclude this idea. Ellicott, in his commentary on 1 Corinthians, gives us the results of the most exact exegesis of this passage: "Whether any, and, if any, what interval is to be supposed to exist between this *Parousia* and 'the end' of the following verse—in fact, between the *epeita* (*then*) and the *eita* (*then*)—the sober interpreter cannot presume even to attempt to indicate. This only may be said, that the language *seems* to imply a kind of interval; but that there is nothing in the particles or in the passage to warrant our conceiving it to be longer than would include the subjugation of every foe and every power of evil, and all that may be immediately associated with the mighty '*end*' which is specified in the succeeding verse . . . It must be carefully remembered that the Apostle is here dealing with a single subject, the resurrection of the dead, and not with the connected details of Eschatology. These must be gathered from other passages and other portions of Scripture."

The resurrection to which Paul looked forward is by no means a simple restoration of the present body. His views are especially explicit with reference to the resurrection bodies of the believers. He illustrates the *manner* and the details of this resurrection by the similitude of the seed-corn (1 Cor. 15:36-38). It is the body of the particular individual which has decayed, which is quickened at the resurrection, and yet it is, so far as its properties are concerned, an entirely new one. The Apostle seeks to make manifest, by different contrasts, the specific quality of the resurrection body. Instead of the corruption which comes into sharpest manifestation by the decay of the body in the grave, there comes *incorruption* (1 Cor. 15:42), which Paul also describes as the redemption of our body from the bondage of corruption (Rom. 8:21, 23). Instead of dishonor, which belongs essentially to the weak body, and affects in the most shocking way the decaying corpse, there comes, according to 1 Cor. 15:43, *glory;* instead of weakness, which in the corpse appears as complete powerlessness, comes full *power* (*ver.* 43). But all is comprehended in the fundamental contrast (*ver.* 44), according to which the body sprung from Adam, made of the dust of the ground, was earthly (*vers.* 47, 48), and therefore a physical or natural body (*vers.* 45, 46), while that springing from the heavenly Second Adam will be heavenly (*vers.* 47, 48), and therefore, like the glorified body of the Risen Christ (*ver.* 45), spiritual.

In 1 Cor. 15:22, we read : " In Christ shall all be made alive." The *shall* points out the time of the universal resurrection as future. "Christ the first-fruits; then they that are Christ's, at His coming. Then cometh the end" (*vers.* 23, 24). This seems to mark Christ as the only Risen One, and seems to fix the time of every other rising at His coming. There is no warrant, therefore, for the idea that any true resurrection, except that of our Lord, has ever taken place, or that any will take place until His coming, which is to be followed by the Judgment, and the end of all things. To this sole instance of complete resurrection, which is presented by Christ as the first-fruits, conjecture has added the risen saints spoken of in Matt. 27:52, 53.[1]

The opinion of some of the ancients and of a number of the moderns is, that these risen saints went into Heaven with our Lord in glorified bodies. But there is no warrant for this in the words of the text. There is nothing about the glorification of their bodies, nothing about their entering into Heaven with the Lord; and it seems to be the express doctrine of the New Testament that none but Christ has experienced a proper resurrection—*i. e.*, a permanent immortal restoration from death—and that He is the only one who has so far assumed the glorified body.[2] The miracles spoken of in Matt. 27:52, 53, were miracles not of the glorifying resurrection, but of restoration to the natural

---

[1] "And many bodies of the saints that had fallen asleep were raised; and coming forth out of the tombs after his resurrection they entered into the holy city and appeared unto many."

[2] "Each dispensation has had an actual passing of the whole man into eternal life. Under the pre-Mosaic dispensation, Enoch was translated (Gen. 5:24), attesting the doctrine that man has a home beyond this world; under the Mosaic, Elijah was borne to Heaven, undying; and, last and highest, our Lord, the first to rise from the dead in the full sense of rising, and still the only one who has entered on the glorious condition of the resurrection, ascended on high." (*Manuscript Lectures of Dr. Krauth.*)

life. The miracles restored the soul to the body, but did not glorify the body, and those thus restored died again.

The events here recorded are simply an exhibition on a grander scale of the same miraculous power as shown in raising the daughter of Jairus, the son of the widow of Nain, or of Lazarus.

[ANALYSIS: 1) The resurrection will take place at the Second Coming of Christ; 2) those who have fallen asleep in Jesus will rise first; 3) then the believers who are alive at the Coming of Christ; 4) all the saints shall be gathered together with Christ; 5) to what place God will bring them is not said; 6) the completed Kingdom of God is a heavenly Kingdom; 7) the teaching of 1 Cor. 15; 8) Paul teaches the resurrection of the wicked; 9) he distinguishes three stages of the resurrection; 10) the manner of the resurrection; 11) the nature of the resurrection body of believers; 12) the universal resurrection is still future; 13) Christ is the only one that has as yet risen from the dead; 14) the saints of Matt. 27:52, 53.]

§ 117. *The General Judgment.*

The resurrection is not yet the judgment itself, but only the preparation for it. According to the two Epistles to the Thessalonians, written about 52 A. D., the day of the *Parousia* is the Day of the Lord, when the Divine judgment of wrath brings "punishment, even eternal destruction from the face of the Lord and from the glory of His might" upon all the godless, "rendering vengeance to them that know not God, and to them that obey not the Gospel of our Lord Jesus" (2 Thess. 1:8, 9). It is on account of this coming destruction that Paul everywhere urges the sanctification of his readers (1 Thess. 3:13; 5:23; 2:19). The slaying of Antichrist (2 Thess. 2:8) is nothing else than the first act of this judgment. Christ appears on that Last Day "with the angels of his power," "in flaming fire"

(2 Thess. 1:8), which last symbolizes the Divine Judgment of wrath (1 Thess. 1:10; 5:9), as the one who takes vengeance upon the godlessness and wickedness of the Gentiles (2 Thess. 1:8; 1 Thess. 4:6), on account of their carelessness and worldliness (1 Thess. 5:3; see Matt. 24:37-39), and their unbelief and hostility to the Gospel (2 Thess. 1:8; 2:12). As the Judge of the world, he brings an eternal destruction upon all the godless (2 Thess. 1:9; 1 Thess. 5:3)—a destruction which is also called perdition (2 Thess. 2:3), as in the discourses of Christ (Matt. 7:13). Once it is described, in general, as affliction (2 Thess. 1:6, 7).

According to the four great Doctrinal Epistles, salvation is regarded as a salvation from the wrath of God (Rom. 5:9), from death (2 Cor. 7:10), and from the destruction which comes to all who do not attain to righteousness (1 Cor. 1:18; 2 Cor. 2:15). The official decision with reference to those who fall into condemnation, and to those who are saved from it, takes place at Christ's Second Coming.[1]

Paul lays stress on the fact that the day of the *Parousia* is at the same time the Messianic Day of Judgment, when God, by Christ, will decide who is found approved, and who is not (1 Cor. 1:7, 8; 5:5; 2 Cor. 1:14). For even those who profess faith, on account of various sins may fall under the judgment of God (1 Cor. 11:29, 32; Rom. 13:2), or into utter ruin (1 Cor. 10:5-12; 8:11; Rom. 14:15); all heathenish sins simply exclude from the Kingdom of God (Gal. 5:19-21; 1 Cor. 6:9, 10). On those who love not Jesus (1 Cor. 16:22),

---

[1] 1 Cor. 4:5, "Wherefore judge nothing before the time, until the Lord come, who will both bring to light the hidden things of darkness, and make manifest the counsels of the hearts; and then shall each man have his praise from God."

as well as on those who teach false doctrine (Gal. 1:9), Paul utters an anathema.

Each individual, if he wishes to be saved, must participate in the salvation offered in the Gospel (1 Cor. 9:23, 24); therefore, all must appear before the Judgment-seat of God, in order that "each one of us may give account of himself to God" (Rom. 14:10, 12).

The rule by which judgment shall be passed is the righteousness required by God, for God "will render to every man according to his works"—to them that by patience in well-doing seek for glory and honor and incorruption, *eternal life;* but unto them that are factious, and obey not the truth, but obey unrighteousness, *shall be wrath and indignation, tribulation and anguish,* upon every soul of man that worketh evil" (Rom. 2:6–9). "For we must all be made manifest before the Judgment-seat of Christ; that each one may receive the things done in the body, according to what he hath done, whether it be good or bad" (2 Cor. 5:10). There is here no conflict with the doctrine of grace, for believers are saved by faith (Rom. 3:28), but judged and rewarded according to their works. Unbelief and impenitence condemns (Rom. 2:5, 8), and unbelievers shall also be judged and punished according to their works. This equivalence is but the natural correspondence between the harvest and the seed-time (Gal. 6:7, 8).

According to the Epistle to the Hebrews, one of the fundamental doctrines of Christianity is, that there shall be an "eternal Judgment."[1]

---

[1] Heb. 6:1, 2, "Wherefore let us cease to speak of the first principles of Christ, and press on unto full growth; not laying again a foundation of repentance from dead works, and of faith toward God, of the teaching of baptisms, and of laying on of hands, and of resurrection of the dead, and of eternal Judgment."

If believers shall inherit salvation (Heb. 1:14), there is also naturally a retributive punishment to those who neglect so great salvation (Heb. 2:1-3). At the Day of Judgment this retributive punishment shall be visited upon the godless (Heb. 10:30), and his judgment is dreadful [1] and unavoidable.[2] He brings upon those who shrink back,[3] and upon all the adversaries of God,[4] the perdition which according to Heb. 9:27,[5] is not simply bodily death, but something more dreadful, and it is repeatedly represented as a consuming fire (Heb. 10:27; 12:29). This Judgment-day of God (Heb. 10:25) is introduced with the last great shaking of the heaven and the earth,[6]—*i. e.*, with the overthrow of the present world (Heb. 1:11, 12).

The Judgment is held by Christ,[7] but the saints of God also will take part in the Judgment.[8] The state-

[1] Heb. 10:31, "It is a fearful thing to fall into the hands of the living God."

[2] Heb. 12:25, "See that ye refuse not him that speaketh. For if they escaped not, when they refused him that warned them on earth, much more shall not we escape, who turn away from Him that warneth from heaven."

[3] Heb. 10:39, "But we are not of them that shrink back unto perdition."

[4] Heb. 10:27, "There remaineth . . . a certain fearful expectation of Judgment, and a fierceness of fire which shall devour the adversaries."

[5] "It is appointed unto men once to die, and after this cometh judgment."

[6] Heb. 12:26, "Now he hath promised, saying, yet once more will I make to tremble not the earth only, but also the heaven."

[7] Rom. 2:16, "In the day when God shall judge the secrets of men, according to my Gospel, by Jesus Christ."

2 Cor. 5:10, "For we must all be made manifest before the Judgment-seat of Christ."

[8] 1 Cor. 6:2, 3, "Know ye not that the saints shall judge the world? . . . Know ye not that we shall judge angels?"

ment in 1 Cor. 6:2 can best be understood if we suppose that the Apostles and saints of all ages being present at the Judgment sitting on their thrones, participating in the glory of Christ, confirm in their inmost hearts the judgments declared by Christ. The statement in *ver.* 3, implying that believers will hereafter judge not only men but angels, seems to be connected with the idea that Christ will pass judgment upon all hostile powers, even on the spirit-world, when He shall abolish all rule and all authority and power (1 Cor. 15:24), and that the saints in some way shall co-operate and take a part.

But what will become of the ungodly after their resurrection and after the Judgment has been passed upon them? Their lot will be the corruption spoken of by Paul in Gal. 6:8, the destruction of 2 Thess. 1:9; Rom. 9:23, the perdition of Phil. 1:28 and 3:19.[1] What this means we will discuss later.

[ANALYSIS: 1) The resurrection is the preparation for the Judgment; 2) the Judgment accompanies the Second Coming of Christ; 3) the slaying of Antichrist the first act of Judgment; 4) the teaching of the Epistles to the Thessalonians; 5) of the four great Doctrinal Epistles; 6) all must appear before the Judgment-seat of Christ; 7) the rule of Judgment; 8) the teaching of the Epistle to the Hebrews; 9) the Judgment is held by Christ; 10) believers shall take part in it; 11) the lot of the ungodly.]

## § 118 *The Final Consummation.*

We must distinguish between the Kingdom of Christ which begins with the Second Coming and the resurrection of believers, and the consummation itself. The consummation, the end, does not take place until Christ delivers up the Kingdom to God the

---

[1] " They are the enemies of the cross of Christ: whose end is perdition."

Father (1 Cor. 15: 23, 24). It is not for us to decide the times and seasons; but since Christ "must reign till He hath put all His enemies under His feet" (*ver.* 25), it is clear that during the Day of Judgment, which begins with His Second Coming, there still remain enemies to be subdued. The fully achieved victory, the pure, perfect, blessed Kingdom of God, begins with the general resurrection and the judgment of the world, that "day of wrath and revelation of the righteous judgment of God" (Rom. 2:5). As the last enemy that shall be abolished is death (Cor. 15:26), we may infer that the general resurrection immediately precedes.

Paul, however, knows of no earthly consummation. With the resurrection and change of believers there begins immediately the perfected Kingdom of God, when that which is perfect is come, and we see face to face, and know also as we have been known (1 Cor. 13:10–12). From this Kingdom the unbelievers and ungodly are shut out (1 Cor. 6:9, 10; Gal. 5:21). Christ, who as Redeemer has hitherto ruled the Church, after all things have been subjected to Him (1 Cor. 15:28), gives up His dominion to God, even the Father (*ver.* 24), because now the object of the Mediatorial rule has been fulfilled. Henceforward God is all in all (*ver.* 28), in contrast to the Mediatorial rule held by the Son. The whole context of this passage excludes any reference to a restoration or restitution of all things (*Apokatastasis*), for the dominion which God henceforward wields immediately can be no other than that which Christ has received and given up to God the Father; and that does not consist in the fact that all hostile powers are utterly destroyed, *annihilated*, or converted, but in this, that they have become power-

## THE FINAL CONSUMMATION.

less, and are subject to His will. There is no doctrine that contradicts the teaching of Paul in a more unwarrantable manner than that of the so-called *Apokatastasis*, nor is there any foundation whatever to maintain that Paul teaches the final annihilation of the wicked.

As according to Gen. 3:17, 18, the primal curse fell also on the earth, the earth also must share in the promised restoration. This restoration is directly announced in Isa. 11:6–9. Paul, in Rom. 8:19–23, maintains that because irrational creation was involved in the fall, it shall also take part in the restoration. "Creation itself also shall be delivered from the bondage of corruption into the liberty of the glory of the children of God" (*ver*. 21). A new and glorious world shall take the place of the present. This passage, however, does not suggest an absolute annihilation and subsequent new creation, but rather, in harmony with "the redemption of our body" (*ver*. 23), or our bodily resurrection, a transformation and transfiguration of existing nature. It is nowhere said that the *kosmos*, or the world of order, shall pass away, but "the fashion of this *kosmos* shall pass away" (1 Cor. 7:31); and the fire, which shall consume the earth, as we have already seen (2 Pet. 3:10), is to be thought of as a fire of purification, and not of annihilation.

In the Epistle to the Hebrews the final consummation begins in the perfect Kingdom of God "that cannot be shaken" (Heb. 12:28), whose coming presupposes the change (Heb. 1:11, 12) that comes with the final shaking up of heaven and earth (12:26, 27). This Kingdom appears under the image of the city founded by God Himself (11:10), for which even the patriarchs longed as for their heavenly home (11:14–16). And although Christians, even now in a certain sense, are come to this heavenly Jerusalem (12:22), still they long after the abiding city of the future (13:14) as their better possession (10:34). In this Heavenly City of God they will live in immediate nearness to God, seeing His face (12:14); and, being delivered from all their trials, they shall share in His glory (2:10). The final consummation is, therefore, not an earthly one. The contrast between heaven and earth has been removed by the shaking which overtook "not the earth only, but also the heaven" (12:26). It is only after the resurrection (6:2), which is a better resurrection than the simple awakening to earthly life (11:35), which a few individual saints experienced, that believers enter finally into the rest of God. For as God rested on the Seventh day, so they also rest from all their works (4:3–10). The rest which Israel found in the beloved land was but an imperfect copy of this heavenly rest (4:8), as the children of Israel could not enter on the perfect rest (3:18, 19), on account of their unbelief and disobedience (4:6). Now, finally, the Eternal Sabbath of the people of God begins (4:9).

[ANALYSIS : 1) We must distinguish between the Second Coming, the resurrection, and the consummation ; 2) death is the last enemy to be overcome ; 3) Paul knows of no earthly consummation ; 4) Christ gives up His Mediatorial reign to the Father ; 5) Paul knows of no restoration of all things; 6) nor of any final annihilation of the wicked ; 7) the earth also shares in the restoration ; 8) the teaching of Rom. 8:19–23 ; 9) not an annihilation, but a transformation of existing Nature ; 10) the teaching of the Epistle to the Hebrews.]

§ 119. *Eternal Life.*

The state of the believer after his resurrection, according to the Epistles to the Thessalonians, is described as an enduring life in fellowship with the Lord, for risen believers "shall ever be with the Lord" (1 Thess. 4:17). From this it naturally follows that they will then find themselves in a condition which is analogous to that of the Exalted Christ. In this heavenly Kingdom of Christ they attain to participation in the Divine glory (1 Thess. 2:12), even the glory of our Lord Jesus Christ (2 Thess. 2:14).

According to his later Epistles, when the believer receives his glorified body at the resurrection, he has reached the Divine glory which forms the ultimate end of Christian hope, "the hope of glory" (Rom. 5:2), to which the Christian has been appointed (1 Cor. 2:7; Rom. 9:23). Believers, after the resurrection, enter on the possession of their full rights as children of God (Rom. 8:23), so that then only are they perfectly manifested as sons of God (Rom. 8:19), because then they share completely in all that the Son of God has (1 Cor. 1:9). As heirs of God and joint heirs with Christ, in their glorified bodies, they now enter into the full possession of their inheritance (Rom. 8:17). In the fullness of the Kingdom, those redeemed by Christ shall enjoy the perfect freedom of the children of God (Rom. 8:21), and, raised above sin and death, shall lead a blessed life in everlasting happiness (Rom. 2:7, 10; 5:21; 6:22; 1 Cor. 15:54–56). Then shall the finite, imperfect, fragmentary nature of present knowledge be done away, and in its stead shall come the perfect, the actual (2 Cor. 5:7), the immediate vision face to face. Then there shall be a knowing (1 Cor. 13:12), a beholding (2 Cor. 5:7), a triumphant reigning with Christ (2 Tim. 2:12), the glory of which we can here form but a very imperfect conception (1 Cor. 2:9).

No other Apostle describes the blessedness of the future so often as a personal participating in the triumph and dominion of Christ as does Paul (1 Cor. 4:8; Rom. 5:17). Paul, however, distinctly teaches that there are degrees of blessedness and glory in his conception of eternal life (2 Cor. 9:6; Gal. 6:7, 9).

[ANALYSIS: 1) Teaching of Paul according to his earlier Epistles; 2) according to his later Epistles.]

§ 120. *Eternal Death.*

But what will become of the ungodly after their resurrection? Their lot is wrath (1 Thess. 1:10; Rom. 2:5; Eph. 5:6), punishment (2 Thess. 1:9; Heb. 10:29), even eternal destruction (2 Thess. 1:9), and perdition (Phil. 1:28; 3:19); Heb. 10:39), and most unseemly corruption (Gal. 6:8). That this cannot mean hopeless annihilation, a blotting out of existence, irrevocable destruction, is plainly evident from the language of Paul. He teaches, as we have already seen, a resurrection of the ungodly, and everywhere he presupposes the raising up of the wicked unto the Judgment, and the permanent state in which the unrighteous shall forever abide. We can put no other construction upon the explicit testimony of Paul (2 Thess. 1:6–9): "If so be that it is a righteous thing with God to recompense affliction to them that afflict you, . . . at the revelation of the Lord Jesus from Heaven with the angels of His power in flaming fire, rendering vengeance to them that know not God, and to them that obey not the Gospel of our Lord Jesus: who shall suffer punishment, even eternal destruction, from the face of the Lord and from the glory of His might." Rom. 2:5, 8, 9, "But after thy hardness and impenitent heart treasured up for thyself wrath in the day of wrath and revelation of the righteous judgment of God; who will render to every man according to his works: . . . unto them that are

## ETERNAL DEATH.

factious, and obey not the truth, but obey unrighteousness, shall be wrath and indignation, tribulation and anguish, upon every soul of man that worketh evil." Gal. 6:7, "Be not deceived; God is not mocked; for whatsoever a man soweth, that shall he also reap." 2 Cor. 5:10, "For we must all be made manifest before the Judgment-seat of Christ; that each one may receive the things done in the body, according to what he hath done, whether it be good or bad." Heb. 10: 26, 27, "There remaineth no more a sacrifice for sins, but a certain fearful expectation of judgment, and a fierceness of fire which shall devour the adversaries."

There can be no question that Paul teaches the everlasting condemnation of the wicked, and that the final destiny of the godless is eternal punishment.

[ANALYSIS: 1) The portion of the ungodly; 2) Paul teaches the everlasting condemnation of the wicked; 3) their punishment is eternal.]

# SECTION II.

The Doctrinal System of the Four Great Doctrinal and Controversial Epistles.

## CHAPTER III.

### UNIVERSAL SINFULNESS.[1]

§ 121. *Human and Divine Righteousness.*[2]

Even as a Pharisee, Paul had busied himself with the important question, how man could attain to righteousness. This great question of his life was not answered until Christ revealed Himself to Paul at his conversion, on his way to Damascus; and from that time Paul proclaimed salvation as a free gift of Divine grace in Christ Jesus. In all his preaching as an Apostle to the Gentiles, Paul assumes the lost condition of all men in view of the approaching judgment, and that no man can by any human performance do that which is necessary for his salvation. In these four important Doctrinal Epistles (Galatians, 1 and 2 Corinthians, and Romans), he now discusses how such a wretched condition of man's sinfulness has been brought about, and why man does not possess and cannot attain to righteousness of himself; and in what manner salvation is grounded in Christ, and through Christ alone, so as to leave no room for

---

[1] This chapter treats mainly of the doctrine of Man, or Anthropology.

[2] Compare *Weiss*, § 65.

any human performance whatever; and also how through Christ that was effected which men could not effect of themselves.

The origin of the idea of human righteousness is found in the Old Testament, and is that condition of man in which he corresponds with the rule of the truth or of the will of God, which is revealed in the law. So Deut. 6:25 already explains the meaning of the term; in this sense we find it in the teaching of Jesus (Matt. 6:10), as well as in Peter (1 Pet. 2:24; 3:14) and James (3:18). Accordingly, the truth which is revealed in the law states, in conformity with the Divine Will, what is good and evil, in order that, in consequence of its demand, the good may be done. Paul speaks of the doing of that which is good (*tò agathón*, Gal. 6:10; 2 Cor. 5:10; Rom. 2:10; 7:19; 9:11; 13:3) or honorable (*tò kalón*, Gal. 6:9; 2 Cor. 13:7; Rom. 7:18, 21), and of *good works* (2 Cor. 9:8; Rom. 13:3).

When St. Paul, in Rom. 3:5, speaks of the *righteousness* of God, he refers to the fact that God in His judgment of men, and in His bearing toward them, binds Himself to the rule of justice set up by Himself, and that the unrighteousness of men only contributes to the establishing of the righteousness of God; for, without respect of persons, He judges and recompenses man according to his doing. God, in giving judgment, binds Himself by the same rule by which, as lawgiver, He binds man. This is shown—1) negatively, in that He has no respect of persons (Gal. 2:6; Rom. 2:11; *cf.* Lev. 19:15); 2) positively, in that His judgment is *according to truth* (Rom. 2:2)—for not the hearers of the law are righteous in the judgment of God, but the doers of the law will be justified (Rom. 2:13). The righteousness and faithfulness of God will therefore show itself in this, that He bears Himself in one way towards him who is found *righteous* according to this criterion, and in another way towards the *unrighteous;* and it is expressly stated that the very essence of this Divine *righteous judgment* (Rom. 2:5) lies in this, that God renders to every man according to his works (Rom. 2:6). Where this is not the case, as in the history considered in Rom. 9:10-13, the question arises: Is there unrighteousness with God? (Rom. 9:14). Wherever sins are passed by unpunished, and where, therefore, it appears as if God does not deal with the sinner according to the rule of justice, a demonstration of the righteousness of God is required (Rom. 3:25). As, therefore, the righteousness of God recognizes and deals with human righteousness as such, as well as with human unrighteousness, the salvation of man depends upon his attaining a *righteousness* before God.

[ANALYSIS: 1) The great question: How can man attain to righteousness? 2) the answer revealed by Christ to Paul; 3) discussed especially in the four great Doctrinal Epistles; 4) what is meant by human righteousness; 5) by the righteousness of God; 6) there can be no salvation without attaining *a righteousness* before God.]

§ 122. *The Impossibility of a Righteousness of Our Own.*[1]

As the doers of the law are accounted righteous in the judgment of God (Rom. 2:13), and as God has revealed his will to the children of Israel in the law of Moses (Rom. 2:18), and has written the work of the law in the hearts of the Gentiles (Rom. 2:15), all that man has to do to attain salvation is to do and keep this law.

As such a righteousness would be brought about

[1] Compare *Weiss*, § 66.

by the fulfilling of the law, it would be owing to the law (Rom. 10:5), inasmuch as the law, as the revelation of the Divine will, has made it possible; it would also be one's own (Rom. 10:3), inasmuch as it is a righteousness which has been earned by man by his fulfillment of the Divine will (*cf.* Phil. 3:9). Of such a fulfilling of the law man could boast before God, and it would be accounted as merit (Rom. 4:2). But Paul is convinced that no man (not even Abraham) has or can have anything of which he can glory before God (Rom. 4:2), neither can Abraham have been justified by works (Rom. 4:3, 9). He distinctly teaches that Christianity is a dispensation of grace, and that Divine grace excludes all human merit and glorying (Rom. 4:4). If it is by the law that righteousness is brought about, then Christ has died in vain, without reason, unnecessarily (Gal. 2:21). If we are justified on the ground of the law, the bond is broken which connects us with Christ who is the ground of our salvation (Gal. 5:4).

The works of the law might justify, if they only existed, and they should do so, for the law was given unto life (Rom. 7:10), but no one has kept the law; for all have sinned (Rom. 5:12), and fall short of the glory of God (Rom. 3:23), and stand under the curse of the law (Gal. 3:10). The moral corruption of heathendom, as Paul describes it in Rom. 1:18–32, requires no proof, and in a series of Old Testament passages (Rom. 3:10–18) Paul finds a description of the universal sinfulness of man, which, in verse 19, he explicitly declares the Jews must apply also to themselves. According to Gal. 3:22, the Scripture has shut up everything under sin by declaring that all men, Jews and Gentiles, with all that they do, are equally sinful.

The reason why man cannot realize righteousness

Paul finds in the fact that man is dominated by a power which hinders him from fulfilling the law. This is the power of *sin*. Whoever makes himself a servant of sin has thereby freed himself from righteousness (Rom. 6:20), and made his members weapons of *unrighteousness* (Rom. 6:13). So long as man stands under the control of this power of sin (Rom. 3:9; 5:21; Gal. 3:22), so long as it makes him its weak slave (Rom. 6:17, 20), he cannot realize righteousness. This power of sin gives indication of its vitality by exciting evil lust in man (Rom. 7:8), which obtains the mastery of man (Gal. 5:24; Rom. 7:5). When man is thus conquered by sin, he becomes conscious of the power of sin, which dwells in him (Rom. 7:17, 20), as a power which is distinct from his Ego, and which is able to stir up in him something which he does not recognize as his own, in opposition to which he feels himself not free, but dependent, not active, but passive.

In consequence of this subjection to sin, which hinders them from realizing righteousness, men are exposed to the judgment of God (Rom. 3:19, 20), who demands righteousness, and must therefore, in His righteousness, punish its absence. This execution of justice God has reserved to Himself (Rom. 12:19); it is the necessary expression of his wrath (Rom. 13:4) against sin. The law works this wrath, inasmuch as it gives man's sin the character of the transgression of its express commandment (Rom. 4:15); it is revealed, however, against all *unrighteousness* (Rom. 1:8), even where sin is not accounted transgression (Rom. 5:13, 14), or when committed by such as had no positive law which condemns sin as punishable (Rom. 2:12). This judgment of God, from which the evil-doer is not to imagine that he will escape (Rom. 2:3), shall be visited upon him at the day of wrath and revelation of the righteous judgment of God (2:5–9). Then shall the ungodly reap what they have sown (Gal. 6:8 ; 2 Cor. 5:10 ; Rom. 14:10, 12).

[ANALYSIS : 1) To attain righteousness man must keep the law ; 2) but no man can fulfill the law ; 3) for all have sinned ; 4) and are servants of sin ; 5) and therefore exposed to the judgment of God ; 6) which shall surely come upon the ungodly.]

### § 123. *The Transgression of Adam and its Consequences.*[1]

The whole world, because it serves sin, is exposed to the judgment of God (1 Cor. 6:2 ; 11:32 ; Rom. 3:6, 19), and needs reconciliation with God (2 Cor. 5:19 ; Rom. 11:12, 15). Its spirit is opposed to the spirit of God (1 Cor. 2:12); its wisdom is godless (1 Cor. 1:20, 21, 27, 28 ; 3:19); its sorrow leads to death (2 Cor. 7:10). In this term, "the world," is expressed the idea of the sinfulness of the human world. Inasmuch as the sinful human world belongs to this age or *æon* of the world, it is called "this world" (1 Cor. 3:19 ; 5:10). The world, however, which is in the service of sin, stands under the dominion of Satan—whence he is called, "the god of this age" (2 Cor. 4:4), and will yet equip the perfected manifestation of the man of sin, or of lawlessness, with his wonder-working powers (2 Thess. 2:9). It is his spirit which, as it were, animates and moves "the world" (1 Cor. 2:12), and impresses upon it its sinful, ungodly character. With an evident allusion to the narrative of the fall (Gen. 3), it is said, in 2 Cor. 11:3, that the serpent beguiled Eve by his craftiness ; and there is scarcely any doubt that the serpent is

---

[1] Compare *Weiss*, § 67. See also my "Studies in the Book," vol. 1, pp. 46, 84–89; also Lechler's *Apostolic and Post-Apostolic Times*, vol. 1, pp. 341–359.

here conceived of as an organ of the Devil, who thus led the first human beings into sin. But Paul does not explain the universality of sin by tracing it back to the circumstance that it is the power of Satan which moves every individual to commit sin. He has another way of explaining it.

That sin in its "essence" is *enmity against God*, is the prevailing conviction of the Apostle Paul (Rom. 8:7). Sin leads to weakness of will (Rom. 5:6), incapacity for obedience to God and for the performance of that which is good (Rom. 7:19). The depth of Paul's sense of sin proves itself by the fact that he makes sin to consist not merely in *action*, but describes it as a mysterious power dwelling in man (Rom. 7:17, 20).[1] The way in which sins of action arise, he discovers through self-examination.

It is not enough for the Apostle to show that sin is an indwelling power in man, but he goes on to answer

[1] In my "Studies in the Book," vol. 2, pp. 46, 86-89, I have endeavored to develop Paul's teaching with reference to sin, as presented in his four great Doctrinal Epistles. In the Epistle to the Galatians, Paul lays special stress on the *nature* of sin (4:3, 9; 5:13, 16, 17, 19-21), its *universality* (1:4; 2:15-17; 3:22; for no man can keep the law, 3:10, 11, 19), and its *result* (1:6-9; 3:10, 13; 5:21; 6:8). In the Epistle to the Romans alone, Paul uses eleven different Greek words to designate sin. As *hamartia*, sin is regarded as a failing and missing of the true end of our lives, which is God. It is the sin of the world conceived of as a unity, as this was wrapped up objectively in Adam's act (Rom. 5:12), or subjectively dwells in the world (5:13). As sin is present in every man born according to the course of nature, it follows that the law invariably heightens it into *parabasis*, transgression, which word always refers to the breaking of a positive Divine commandment. How this comes to pass Rom. 7:7-13 describes. For sin as an *act*, in its separate deeds, Paul twice (Rom. 3:25; 1 Cor. 6:8) uses the word *hamartema*. By *anomia* (Rom. 4:7; 6:19), lawlessness or iniquity, is designated the condition of one who acts contrary to God's will and law· *adikia*, unrighteous-

the question, What is the actual *seat* of sin in man? Where does the *source* of sin lie in each individual? The answer runs, the source of sin lies in the *sarx*, or flesh—"for I know that in me, that is, in my flesh, dwelleth no good thing" (Rom. 7:18). What, then, does Paul understand by *sarx?* He does not understand *sarx* as something *merely* material and corporeal, for among the works of the flesh (Gal. 5:19–21), together with those sins which certainly spring from sensuousness (unchastity, excess, etc.), he enumerates such also as do not by any means arise exclusively from the flesh or sensual impulses, such as enmities, strife, jealousies, factions, and heresies. Add to this that, in Rom. 8:6, a *mind* is ascribed to the *sarx*—a mode of thinking and moral direction, therefore something spiritual—from which it follows that the *sarx* or flesh is a selfish, ungodly manner of thought and aim, which gives the reins to sensuousness, and allows the members of the body to become a means of enticement to sin, instruments of the flesh (Rom. 6:19).

Paul looks at humanity as a whole, and perceives it to be a world characterized by sin, and therefore fallen under the sentence of God (Rom. 3:19). Every individual has sinned (Rom. 5:12), and all have come short of the glory which God possesses and can bestow (Rom. 3:23). Not only have all committed acts of sin, but all

ness is opposed to righteousness (Rom. 3:5; 6:13), and contrasted with truth (1:18; 2:8); *kakia*, maliciousness (1:29), is the opposite of virtue; *poneria*, or worthlessness, is shown in conduct (1:29); *asebia*, ungodliness, is want of reverence towards God (1:18; 11:26); *paraptoma*, trespass (nine times in Romans, six times in 5:15–20), is sin as a missing and violation of right, almost synonymous with *parabasis*, but not quite so strong; *parakoe*, disobedience (5:19), is rebellious conduct towards the revealed will of God, a failing to hear; *hettema* (11:12; 1 Cor. 6:7) is *loss* as respects salvation.

are likewise subjected to the *power* of sin, as slaves to their masters (3:9).

With Paul, both Jew and Gentile stand on the same moral basis; there is no distinction (3:22). They are both alike sinners, and both have fallen under the Divine judgment. But the Apostle goes still further, and, taking humanity as a living abstract unity, he derives the actual sinfulness of all, together with its consequence and punishment, universal mortality, from *one* beginning; and, appealing to the revelation of the Old Testament, goes back to the first sin of the first man, to Adam's fall. True, there is only one passage (Rom. 5:12–21) in which this argument is fully set forth, but I Cor. 15:21, 22, and 2 Cor. 11:3, also refer with unmistakable clearness, though briefly, to the sin of Adam as the starting-point of the sin and death of all mankind.

The leading thought of the whole section (Rom. 5:12–21) is this: The righteousness of God, destined for all mankind—together with its fruit, eternal life—is due to the one Man, Jesus Christ, and His obedience; just as sin, which reigns in all men, and its effect, death, entered the world by one man, Adam, and was transmitted to all.[1]

The context points clearly—1) to the connection between *sin* and *death*—sin the cause, death the effect (Rom. 5:12, "death through sin;" 6:15, "by the tres-

---

[1] Note the contrast, as developed by Paul in his argument:

| ADAM. | CHRIST. |
| --- | --- |
| The trespass. | One act of righteousness, *ver.* 18. |
| Judgment unto condemnation. | Justification as a free gift. |
| Death unto all | Eternal life to all |
| Because partakers of Adam's nature. | Who receive Jesus Christ. |

(See notes in my "Studies of the Book," on Rom. 5:15–17, vol. 2, p. 85).

pass . . . [they] died; 5:17, 21, "sin reigned in death"). But this is not the main thing with the Apostle. The emphasis lies—2) on the *connection* between the *one* and *all* ("the many" of *ver.* 15), as regards sin and death. The point is, that the sin of the one, Adam, became the *cause* and *source* of the sin and death of all (5:19, "through the one man's disobedience the many were made sinners")—*i. e.*, they were made sinners by the disobedience of Adam, so that they stand as sinners before the eye of God.

Wherein consists the dependence of the sinfulness and death of all on the sin of one? The Apostle answers: 1) In the fact that by one man sin and death first entered the world ; 2) in the fact that sin and death were transmitted from one to all.

Paul takes it for granted that the first man was created sinless after the image of God, and that the first man, before the fall, was without sin. Through the trespass of one man sin entered into the world, and death through sin (Rom. 5:12, 17). By the entrance of sin the nature of man experiences a *moral* change. Before the fall, man was without sin, but after the fall he is infected with it. The condition of man has become different in a moral aspect.

In Paul's conception, too, the first man before the fall was immortal, inasmuch as death in its present actual form would not have entered without sin, for death is the fruit and wages of sin (Rom. 6:23), and sin is the deadly sting by virtue of which death is what it is (1 Cor. 15:56).

Another question arises: What is meant by the *transmission* of sin and death *from one to all?* Paul nowhere gives a definite account of the *manner* of this operation ; for to him it is a question of religious truth for heart and conscience, not of the satisfaction of a scientific need or the solution of a problem of research. It is, however, clear from the progress of Paul's argument that the Apostle affirms an historical and causal connection between the first sin of the first man on the one hand, and the sin and death of all mankind on the other. The context, by its association of the whole human race and its tendency to sin with the *one* progenitor and originator of it, certainly proves that nothing but affinity by nature and transmission by generation, as the ladder for sin and death, can be meant.

We have no indication in this passage, much less any direct statement, that Paul intends to convey the meaning that Adam's sin is *imputed* to us; that in Adam all have sinned. Paul clearly says, "through one man sin entered into the world," and in 1 Cor. 15:22, that in Adam all *died;* but nowhere does he say that in Adam all *have sinned*. And, though Paul most clearly teaches that original sin has been in the world since Adam's fall—that without that fall it would not have been—that our natural descent from him actually is accomplished in every case by the inheritance of the moral nature into which, so to speak, Adam fell, he does not define *how*, *theoretically*, the sin of Adam is related to us.

In a summary, we may say that Paul traces the universal sinfulness of mankind back to the transgression of their common ancestor. To him humanity is an organic human race. This is of such importance in his mind that, in his elementary preaching as a missionary to the Gentiles, he connects with the proclamation of the One God also the proclamation of the descent of the nations from one (Acts 17:26). The universal condition of servitude to sin, which is found throughout the whole human family, can therefore be traced back only to that which constitutes the unity of the race—*i.e.*, to its connection with its ancestor. In Rom. 5:12 it is expressly said that sin has entered into the human world through one man—namely, Adam (*ver.* 14). Paul does not say that the sin of *one* man, but that *through* one man *sin* came into the world, and that, too, according to what follows, *through* his *trespass* (Rom. 5:15, 17, 18). In this verse, *sin*—*i. e.*, the sinful condition of the human world with all sinful acts issuing therefrom—is contemplated as an abstract unity. It is the sin of the world taken as a totality both as to its principle and its manifestation. Sin has now, through the transgression of Adam, come into the world as a principle or as a dominant power, and has therefore become operative, first, in Adam himself and then in the human race, which is organically connected with him. In consequence of this assertion (*ver.* 12), accordingly, Paul assumes in what follows that *all* (without exception) have sinned, and are under the judgment of condemnation (Rom. 5:18).

According to Gen. 2:17, the transgression of Adam was one for which death had been expressly appointed the punishment. This implies, in the first place, bodily death, which is shown by the reference in Gen. 3:3, 19, and Rom. 5:14. Accordingly, death comes upon all men through one man, because the sin which came with Adam's transgression has entered into the human world and all have sinned, and now their sin draws upon them the punishment of death (Rom. 5:12). Thus by the transgression of one the many died (Rom. 5:15, 17); because of *one* man the judgment of God unto condemnation has become a judgment of condemnation unto *all* men (Rom. 5:16, 18). Here we have the plain explanation of what is meant when it is said in 1 Cor. 15:21, 22, that death has come through one man, and that it is owing to him, and their organic connection with him, that all die. Ever since Adam's fall death has become unavoidable for all men. This death does not simply mean *bodily* death, as can be seen by Rom. 5:17, 18, 21, where *life*, eternal life, forms the antithesis of *death*, even *eternal* death. But present *spiritual* death is also involved, which finds its completion in eternal death.

Paul does not express himself directly as to the manner in which the influence of Adam's transgression upon the whole human race, which produces universal sinfulness, is brought about. Since it is only by the process of procreation that Adam stands in a living connection with the whole race, it seems highly probable that Paul conceives this influence as brought about by sexual procreation. This depends, however, upon the fleshly union of the two sexes (Eph. 5:31; Gen. 2:24). In this marriage union there is begotten, primarily, the flesh (John 3:6) as the material substance of the bodily organism, and therefore the relationship which is brought about by procreation is a fleshly one (Rom. 9:3; 11:14). More particularly, however, the substance of the earthly body, which cannot attain to the heavenly kingdom of God, is described as flesh and blood (1 Cor. 15:50); and, according to the Old Testament view, it is in the blood that the soul has its seat (Gen. 9:4; Lev. 17:11). Now, since in the procreation of a living man it is naturally living flesh—*i. e.*, flesh possessed of a soul, which is begotten—the soul is evidently conceived of as being also begotten. While the first man, who was formed out of the dust of the earth, became a *living soul* by the inbreathing of the Divine breath of life (1 Cor. 14:45), every descendant of Adam becomes a living soul by procreation. As the same flesh and blood, so also, we may say, the same soul essence is propagated through the human race. If, therefore, the sin which has become, through Adam's transgression, the dominating power, first of all in himself, has passed ever to all his descendants, it can have done so with the *flesh* only because sin had its seat in the *flesh* and in the *soul*, or because man's flesh, which is possessed of a soul, was the one which was dominated and corrupted by it. In Rom. 7:17, 18, St. Paul indirectly states that the sin which dwells in him is that very evil which dwells in his flesh. And if, according to 1 Cor. 2:14, the psychical man is as unsusceptible to the Spirit of God as, according to Rom. 7:14, the carnal man is: nay, if, according to the connection with 1 Cor. 3:1-3, *psychical* is merely a synonym of *fleshly*, it is clear that, according to Paul, sin has its seat in the flesh, which is possessed of a soul, and is transmitted from Adam to his descendants along with this flesh, which is corrupted by it. How this is to be understood can only appear from a closer examination of Pauline anthropology.

[ANALYSIS: 1) The whole world is under sin, and exposed to the judgment of God; 2) Satan the god of "this world;" 3) the essence of sin; 4) Paul's teaching in Galatians; 5) Paul uses *eleven* different Greek words, in Romans, to designate sin; 6) the source of sin; 7) the meaning of *sarx* or flesh; 8) the universality of sin; 9) Paul traces the universal sinfulness of man to Adam; 10) the passage in Rom. 5:12-21; 11) the first man was created sinless, in the image of God; 12) through the trespass of Adam sin came into the world; 13) original sin; 14) death the punishment appointed for sin; 15) death, spiritual, temporal, and eternal; 16) sin is propagated by sexual procreation; 17) the soul is propagated in the same way as the body; 18) sin has its seat in the soul, which permeates the flesh.]

§ 124. *The Pauline Anthropology.*[1]

According to Paul, the material substance of the body is not evil in itself; nor does he regard sensuality as the principle of all sin, but rather selfishness. In Rom. 7:18, we learn that the flesh (*sarx*) is not itself sin, for Paul thinks of sin as an operative power, the principle of sin; but sin only dwells in the flesh. If sin had its root in the flesh, if the nature of the flesh were evil in itself, then the body could not be for the Lord (1 Cor. 6:13, 15), nor serve righteousness with its members (Rom. 6:13, 19); and, as Paul undoubtedly speaks of a *defilement* of the flesh, the *flesh* (*sarx*) is not conceived as being sinful in itself.

That sensuality is not the principle of all sin can be seen from Gal. 5:19-21, where are mentioned not only sins that have their origin in the sensuous nature, but also sins of uncharitableness; for the works of the flesh include not only reveling and unchastity, but also strife and jealousy (Rom. 13:13, 14). Because of their jealousy and strife the Corinthians are *carnal* (1 Cor. 3:3). The real essence of sin must lie elsewhere than in sensuality; for, according to Paul, the essence of moral renewal consists in man's ceasing to live unto himself (2 Cor. 5:15; Rom. 14:7), and the highest form in which sin appears is the sin which consists in the pride of blasphemous arrogance (2 Thess. 2:4).

What, then, does Paul mean by *flesh* (*sarx*), which he regards as the seat of sin? When he speaks of the flesh or *sarx*, it is thought of in the perfect unity with the soul, or *psyche*, and therefore the materiality of the flesh as body cannot come into consideration at all; for in the soul or *psyche* as the vital principle of the

[1] Compare *Weiss*, § 68.

flesh there is already involved something immaterial—a vital principle, which, according to Matt. 10:28, endures even after its separation from the *sarx*, which has fallen a prey to death. There can also be no question that, according to Gen. 2:7 and 1 Cor. 15:45, this vital principle is conceived of as originally derived from God, and therefore not as standing in an *original* opposition to Him. But since sin has come into the human world through the transgression of Adam, human nature is frequently called flesh, because a radical change of the nature of the soul, which vitalizes the flesh, has taken place. In consequence of the fact that from Adam onwards sin dwells and reigns in the *sarx* or flesh through its vital principle, the soul, the flesh has become sinful, and the natural human being in its relation to God has been perverted into a self-willed opposition. Now man *in the flesh* serves the law of sin (Rom. 7:25), for since sin is the God-opposing principle, the *sarx* or flesh which is dominated by it cannot subject itself to the law of God. Accordingly, they who are in the flesh, and are therefore under the dominion of sin, cannot please God (Rom. 7:5 ; 8:8); and to live after the flesh brings death (Rom. 8:4, 12, 13).

Paul knows also of a side of man which is spiritual; but, in opposition to the power of sin in the flesh, this remains powerless, and is unable to determine man's practical behavior. This is evident from Rom. 7:25, where another side of the human being, in antithesis to the flesh, is distinguished—for Paul expressly says: "With the mind (*noûs*) I serve the law of God, but with the flesh the law of sin." This *noûs* is the organ of the knowledge of good and evil—a knowledge which is lost when the *noûs* is corrupted (Rom. 1:28 ; *cf.* Eph. 4:17)—as well as the organ by means of which man can learn to know God in consequence of his creation (Rom. 1:20). It is this *noûs* (and its *thoughts*) that is hardened and blinded and shuts out the illumination of the Gospel of Christ (2 Cor. 3:14; 4:4). This *noûs* is, therefore, as contrasted with that which is bodily, unquestionably something spiritual in man, and primarily a theoretical faculty;—but it is not the spirit of man in the specific sense. This *noûs* in man is also corrupted (Rom. 1.28), and therefore needs to be renewed (Rom. 12:2).

Some have maintained that Paul only knows of the *sarx* (*flesh*) and *psyche* (*soul*) of the natural man, and that he nowhere speaks of the *pneuma* or spirit of the natural man, and that when he uses the word *pneuma* or spirit as referring to man, it always means the *pneuma* or spirit of the believer—a holy, Divine power, the principle of the new, holy life in the Christian.* But that Paul distinguishes between flesh (*sarx* or *soma*, *body*), soul (*psyche*), and spirit (*pneuma*) in the natural man is not only evident from 1 Thess. 5:23; Heb. 4:12, but also from 1 Cor. 2:11, and Rom. 8:16. That this spirit in the natural man is also corrupted is evident from Eph. 4:23 (*cf.* Rom. 12:2), for it also must be renewed. This *pneuma* is indeed the innermost life in the natural man, in which conscience has its seat, in which dwells especially that image of God which still remains in the natural man. This *pneuma* or *spirit of the mind* (Eph. 4:23), being renewed, seeks to make the *noûs* spiritual again, which has become fleshly (Col. 2:18). The natural man is therefore regarded as flesh, soul, and spirit, and each one of these elements is regarded as corrupted. The flesh is corrupt because its vital principle which endows it with life, even the soul, is corrupt; and the soul, being of the same nature as the spirit, being but the external nature of the spirit, is corrupt, because the spirit of man is corrupted and is at enmity with God, and is incapable of receiving that which comes from the Spirit of God (1 Cor. 2:14).

The heart is the seat of all emotions and feelings, of sadness and anxiety (2 Cor. 2:4; Rom. 9:2), as well as of delight and joy (Rom. 10:1); temptation addresses itself to the heart (Rom. 16:18), and it needs strengthening in holiness (1 Thess. 3:13). It is the seat of consciousness (2 Cor. 3:2), of thought (Rom. 10:6, 8), and of knowledge (1 Cor. 2:9). On the one hand, the heart is the seat of the fleshly lusts (Rom. 1:24); on the other, it is into the heart that the Spirit is shed (Gal. 4:6; 2 Cor. 1:22; 3:3; Rom. 5:5); it is in the heart that Christian enlightenment takes place (2 Cor. 4:6), and in it faith dwells (Rom. 10:9, 10).

[ANALYSIS: 1) The material body in itself is not sin, but sin dwells in the flesh; 2) sensuality is not the fundamental principle of sin, but rather selfishness; 3) the soul is the vital principle of the flesh; 4) by the term "flesh" is meant sinful human nature; 5) the *noûs* or mind of man is also corrupted; 6) Paul also speaks of a spirit or *pneuma* of the natural man; 7) which is also corrupted, for it must be renewed; 8) the natural man in his depraved state consists of flesh, soul, and spirit; 9) the heart.]

# CHAPTER IV.

### THE PAULINE DOCTRINE OF GOD.[1]

§ 125. *The Doctrine of the Trinity.*

Paul speaks only incidentally of the *nature of God*, and in such a way as to show clearly that he takes for granted the doctrine of God given in the revelation of the Old Testament. The God of Israel is the *One* living God, holy and supermundane, the Almighty Creator and Lord of all the earth. This is the fundamental truth of the Old Testament, on which, in Paul's view, everything rests. God is One (Rom. 3:30; Gal. 3:20), the so-called gods are nothing (1 Cor. 8:4-6; Gal. 4:8). He is eternal (Rom. 16:26) and unchangeable (Rom. 1:20; 11:29), the living One (2 Cor. 3:3), but invisible (Rom. 1:20). He is incorruptible (Rom. 1:23), immortal (Rom. 9:6), infinite (Rom. 11:33, 36), omnipresent (Rom. 8:27), and incomprehensible (Rom. 11:33-36). He is the Creator of all things (1 Cor. 8:6; Rom. 1:25; 4:17; 11:36), the Ruler, Almighty (Rom. 1:16, 20; 4:17, 21; 9:21), wise (Rom. 11:33, 34), holy (Rom. 1:18; 2:5; 5:9), true (Rom. 1:9, 25; 3:4, 7; 9:28; 11:1), just (Rom. 1:17, 32; 2:2, 3, 5, 6; 3:5; etc.), and impartial (Rom. 1:11; 9:24). By virtue of His truth (Rom. 3:4), His promise is absolute and His faithfulness everlasting (Rom. 3:3; 4:21; 1 Cor. 1:9; 10:13); but above all He is rich in love (Rom. 5:5, 8; 8:32, 39), grace (Rom.

---

[1] Compare my development of this topic in "Studies in the Book," vol. 2, pp. 45, 46, 97-102.

## THE DOCTRINE OF THE TRINITY. 89

1:2, 7; 9:16), mercy (Rom. 2:4; 9:15, 23; 11:32) and long-suffering (Rom. 2:4; 3:25; 9:22; 10:21). When we take into consideration that the Apostle speaks of these attributes òf God only in the course of developing and expounding other doctrines, each of these utterances gains a peculiar life and force. These truths, in Paul's estimation, appear not as worn-out coins, but fresh from the mint—evidences of a living faith, clearly imprinted.[1]

Although Paul adheres strictly to the monotheism of the Old Testament, knowing only *One* God, still he also speaks comprehensively of a triad in God—the Father, the Son, and the Holy Ghost, of "the grace of the Lord Jesus Christ, the love of God, and the communion of the Holy Ghost" (2 Cor. 13:13). Especially rich is the doctrine of God as presented in Paul's Epistle to the Romans. In various passages the Apostle refers to the Three Persons of the Trinity in such a close connection that no one need be at a loss to arrive at Paul's conception of a Trinity in Unity (Rom. 5:5, 6; 8:9, 11, 15:30).

With reference to the doctrine of God the Father, Paul makes many explicit statements. The Father made a promise concerning His Son (Rom. 1:2), and sent His own Son into the world (Rom. 8:3), and did not spare Him, but delivered Him up for us all (Rom. 8:32), and finally raised Him from the dead (Rom. 4:24; 10:9). It is the Father who is the origin of all grace (Rom. 1:7, 16; 5:15; 6:23; 11:33), who also calls us (Rom. 1:6, 7, 8:28, 30; 9:24), and who declares the believer just for Christ's sake (Rom. 8:30, 33), and will finally glorify the believer (Rom. 8:30).

---

[1] Compare *Lechler*, vol. 2, pp. 3. 4.

That the Father is true God is shown by the fact that to Him are ascribed:

1) Divine Names: Rom. 1:1, 7, 8, 18, 19, 20, 21, 23; etc.

2) Divine Attributes: Incorruptibility (Rom. 1:23), blessedness (Rom. 1:25), eternity (Rom. 16:26), incomprehensibility (Rom. 11:33–36).

3) Divine Works: Creation (Rom. 1:25; 4:17; 11:36), providence (Rom. 11·36), resurrection from the dead (Rom. 4:17, 24; 10:9).

4) Divine Worship (Rom. 1:8, 9, 21, 23, 25; 15:6).

Without encroaching upon the Christology of Paul, which will be developed in a later chapter, it will suffice to state in this connection that Paul in this Epistle (Romans) takes it as a fundamental fact that Jesus Christ is true God, because to Him also He ascribes:

1) Divine Names: Son of God (Rom. 1:3, 4, 9; 5:10; 8:2, 32), Lord (Rom. 1:4, 7; 4:24; 5:1, 21; etc.), God blessed forever (Rom. 9:5).

2) Divine Attributes: Omnipotence (Rom. 9:5; 10:12), Lord of both the dead and the living (Rom. 14:9); etc.

3) Divine Works: Bestows grace and peace (Rom. 1:5, 7; 16:20); Creator and Preserver of all things (Rom. 11:36); redemption (Rom. 8:32); judgment (Rom. 14:9); etc.

4) Divine Worship (Rom. 10:12, 13; 15:30; 16:18).

With Paul likewise the Holy Ghost is not simply an attribute of God, nor a mere energy of influence, but the Third Person of the Holy Trinity—an intelligent agent, possessing personal properties. It is God the Holy Ghost who sheds abroad in our hearts the love of God (Rom. 5:5), who dwells in (Rom. 8:9, 11) and leads believers (Rom. 8:14), who bestows righteousness, peace and joy (Rom. 14:17), helpeth our infirmity and maketh intercession for us (Rom. 8:26, 27), and bears witness with our spirit (Rom. 8:16), working with great power (Rom. 15:13, 19), and sanctifying us (Rom. 15:16). The Holy Ghost proceeds from the Father and the Son, for He is called the Spirit of the Father (Rom. 8:9, 11, 14) as well as the Spirit of Christ (Rom. 8:9). That the Holy Ghost, the Third Person of the Trinity, is truly Divine, true God, of the same essence with the Father and the Son, is proved from the fact that to Him are ascribed:

1) Divine Names: Holy Ghost (Rom. 5:5 ; 9:1 ; 14:17; 15:13, 16, 19), Spirit of God (Rom. 8:9, 14).

2) Divine Attributes: Omnipotence (Rom. 8:11 ; 15:13, 19), omnipresence (Rom. 8:9, 11, 14, 16, 26, 27), omniscience (Rom. 8:27).

3) Divine Works: Resurrection of the dead (Rom. (8:11), bestows righteousness (Rom. 14:17), sanctification (Rom. 15:16).

4) Divine Worship (Rom. 9:1 ; 15:30).

[ANALYSIS : 1) Paul's conception of the nature of God ; 2) the attributes of God ; 3) Paul's teaching concerning the Trinity ; 4) the teaching of the Epistle to the Romans; 5) the doctrine of God the Father ; 6) of God the Son ; 7) of God the Holy Ghost.]

## § 126. *The Doctrine of Predestination.*[1]

The assurance of the individual depends on his calling to the fellowship of the Christian Church, because by this calling the Divine purpose of election begins to be realized towards him. This assurance rests on the faithfulness of God, who alone can strengthen him who is in trial that he continue to stand (Rom. 14:4 ; 16:25), and who will not allow the trial to become too severe

---

[1] Compare *Weiss.* § 88.

(1 Cor. 10:13), but will strengthen the wavering that he remain unreprovable unto the end (1 Cor. 1:8).

Though God continually calls us through His Word, still in these four great Doctrinal Epistles the Calling is regarded more particularly as a visible act done once for all, in which God has, as it were, given to the individual the assurance that He will lead him on in this way to perfect salvation; and this act is his introduction to the fellowship of the Christian Church (1 Cor. 7:17, 18, 20–22). So far as the members of the Christian Church belong to Christ, they are "called to be Jesus Christ's" (Rom. 1:6); so far as they stand in a living fellowship with Christ, they are "called in the Lord" (1 Cor. 7:22); in so far as they are free from the law, they are "called for freedom" (Gal. 5:13); in relation to the sinfulness of this world, they are "called to be saints" (Rom. 1:7).

It is the *universal* will of God that all men, without a single exception, should be saved (Rom. 5:15, 17, 18, 21; 8:32; 11:32). This will may also be called *antecedent*, because it antedates all question as to the manner in which man may treat the offered grace. But the will of God is not *absolute*, for God has clearly revealed what the *conditions* of salvation are (Rom. 3:22; 5:8, 11; 10:12)—to accept the grace and gift of righteousness through Jesus Christ (5:17). It is God's *purpose* to save all who love Him (Rom. 8:28), and all who abide in the love of God which is in Christ Jesus our Lord (Rom. 8:39).

The Divine decree of election becomes clearly manifest in our calling into the fellowship of the Church (1 Cor. 1:26, 28). While God thus takes the first step, so to speak, for carrying out His purpose for the salvation of the individual (Rom. 8:30; 9:23, 24), He also gives them the assurance that He will not allow them to fail in all that follows.

It is implied in the very idea of election or choosing that it is a free act. The mercy of God, on which it rests, can be dependent on nothing else than God Himself as having compassion (Rom. 9:15, 16). In Rom. 9:19–24, Paul is contrasting the supremacy of God with the arrogance of man; and in that passage the Apostle vindicates for God as the Creator the absolute right to make and prepare one man for salvation and the other for destruction; but he does not say that God has done so. On the contrary, when Paul comes to speak of the actual attainment of salvation, by the use of the adversative *de* (*but*),[1] he puts the actual dealings of God at present in express contrast with the absolute right vindicated for God in the abstract (*ver.* 22). Paul does not say that God has "*fitted unto destruction*" "vessels of wrath"— but that although God is Almighty in power, He defers the exhibition of His anger and His avenging power, and till now "*endured with much long-suffering* vessels of wrath fitted unto destruction" (by their own guilt and scornful rejection of Divine grace), in order to lead them to repentance (Rom. 2:4, 5). So also Paul does not say that God has created "vessels of mercy," but that He " afore prepared " them " unto glory," by His preventing grace (Rom. 9:23). Here, indeed, a predestination to *eternal life* is distinctly asserted in express words; but nowhere is a predestination to *condemnation* affirmed, although it is necessarily implied that those who are not of the " election of grace " (Rom. 11:5) shall not attain unto salvation.

In the examination of Paul's teaching on this difficult subject, we must carefully note what he says con-

[1] English Version, *What.*

cerning the *purpose* of God, the *foreknowledge* of God, and the *decree* itself. The *purpose* of God is not grounded in our works (9:11, 16; 11:6), but is of pure grace (Rom. 11:5, 6), after the counsel of the will of God the Father (Rom. 8:28; 9:11, 16, 18). From the *purpose* of God the "calling" follows, hence believers "are called according to His purpose" Rom. 8:28). This *calling* appears in the form of the preaching of the Gospel (Rom. 10:12-15), finds its conclusion in baptism (Acts. 2:38), and has for its goal the fellowship of Christ (1 Cor. 1:9). It by no means follows, however, that because election is of grace that God must act from pure arbitrariness as regards those He chooses to pity, but only that it depends on Himself alone, and not on any human merit, what the conditions are on which He makes election to salvation depend. Independently of all human works and deserts, God determines according to His absolute will to what conditions He will attach His grace.

The condition with which He has connected His election is nothing else than the love which He foreknew in the receptive soul. The passage in Rom. 8:28-30 announces, in the plainest terms, on what the assurance of those predestinated to salvation rests. Those whom God has once foreordained to salvation (*ver.* 29) He conducts with steady hand from the first beginning of the Christian life to its completion (*ver.* 30), so that all that happens to them in this life must work together for their good (*ver.* 28). Now it is here expressly said (*ver.* 29) that He foreordained those whom He foreknew. But this foreknowledge of God, or intimate knowledge which God has from eternity (for with God everything is present, there being no past or future with Him), can refer only to that quality on which God has determined, according to His own free-will, to make election depend; and what this is, is explicitly stated in the connection of *vers.* 28 and 29. Those whom God from all eternity knew would *love Him* and abide in Christ Jesus perseveringly unto the end (9:23, 24; 11:2), He *predestinated, foreordained* unto salvation. The decree made from eternity necessarily finds its temporal realization. The *purpose*, the *foreknowledge*, and the *decree* are to be viewed as *pre-temporal;* on the other hand, the calling, the justification, and the glorification (which, though still future, is so certain that Paul speaks of it as already having taken place), are to be viewed as *temporal* acts of God.

So also, in 1 Cor. 8:3, Paul says that he who loves God is known as such by Him, and according to 1 Cor. 2:9 God has prepared salvation for all who love Him. This love to God is, however, not regarded by Paul as a human act, for anything human cannot possibly be the condition of election. The longing for salvation, the very receptivity of faith, and faith itself, is to be regarded as the work of God in us. The election is, on God's part, simply the outcome of free love, freely choosing its object, and excludes all legal claim or human merit on the part of its object;—depending entirely on the grace and will of God that calleth.

[ANALYSIS: 1) Assurance of salvation; 2) the calling; 3) the universal will of God; 4) not absolute; 5) but conditioned; 6) the purpose of God; 7) the Divine decree of election; 8) is a free act; 9) rests on the mercy of God; 10) there is a predestination to eternal life; 11) but Paul does not affirm a predestination to condemnation; 12) one must distinguish between the purpose, the foreknowledge, and the decree of God; 13) the teaching of Rom. 8:28-30; 14) those who love God and abide in Christ are predestinated to be saved.]

§ 127. *The Gospel and the Apostleship.*[1]

If the Gospel is to work faith, it must carry in itself a Divine power. That it has this Divine power is shown by the fact that it is the glad message come from God (Rom. 1:1; 15:16; 2 Cor. 11:7), in which God Himself speaks, and the salvation provided in Christ is by Him revealed to men (Rom. 1:16, 17; 3:21; 2 Cor. 2:14). For the contents of the Gospel or the Word is the Cross of Christ (1 Cor. 1:18), or the atonement thereby provided (2 Cor. 5:19); and this is incidentally more closely defined as the Divine glory of the Exalted Christ (2 Cor. 4:4), or as faith in Christ as the condition of salvation. As a message coming from God, it stands on the same level with the Old Testament Word of Revelation (Rom. 3:2, 4; 9:6). Inasmuch as God has now to make use of human instruments for the spread of the message, His Word is preached or heralded (Gal. 2:2; 1 Cor. 15:11; Rom. 10:8); it is called "preaching" (1 Cor. 1:21; 2:4; 15:14), "the testimony of Christ" (1 Cor. 1:6), "the mystery" or possibly *testimony* "of God" (1 Cor. 2:1). If God Himself is to speak by His messengers on behalf of Christ (2 Cor. 5:20), then it must be preached without human wisdom of speech (1 Cor. 1:17), "without excellency of speech or of wisdom" (1 Cor. 2:1); much less is it to be corrupted by human additions (2 Cor. 2:17; 4:2). The Gospel must work by its own power simply, by the demonstration or persuasion (Gal. 5:8) which the Spirit of God, working in this Word of God, produces (1 Cor. 2:4). The contents and form of what is preached has to be given to the preacher by the same Spirit (1 Cor. 2:12, 13), so that it becomes a word "in the power of

[1] Compare *Weiss*, § 89.

the Holy Ghost" (Rom. 15: 19). And the inspiration by which the Apostles were moved and directed did not consist simply in the enlightenment by which they knew the truth of the Gospel, but it enabled them also to preach it with the power of God—a power effectual in producing faith. Christ had already, while still on earth, promised His disciples the aid of the Holy Spirit (Matt. 10:19, 20; Luke 21:14, 15; John 15:26–16:4); and this promise was fulfilled in the extraordinary and special gifts which were either given directly to the fellow-laborers of the Apostles, or transmitted to them by the Apostles themselves (1 Cor. 12:4–11, 28; Rom. 12:4–6).

The Apostles are messengers commissioned with the preaching of the Gospel (Gal. 2:7), ambassadors for Christ, by whom God speaks (2 Cor. 5:20). They are ministers of a new covenant (testament) (2 Cor. 3:6), sent exclusively to preach the Gospel (1 Cor. 1:17); and this they are to do in order thereby to produce faith (Rom. 1:15; 1 Cor. 3:5). As the general calling of Christians is now effected by the preaching of Christ, the Apostles who are to preach this Gospel to all others must themselves be called by Christ (1 Cor. 1:17; Rom. 1:5), who has sent them. With great emphasis Paul lays stress on the fact that he is "an Apostle not from men, neither through man, but through Jesus Christ and God the Father" (Gal. 1:1). But this calling was effected by Christ, when Paul saw the Lord on the road to Damascus; and, hence, this occurrence belongs essentially to the conditions of his Apostolic dignity (1 Cor. 9:1; 15:8, 9). It was the good pleasure of God, who called the Apostle to reveal His Son in Him, that he might be able to preach Him (Gal. 1:16). It was not from man that he had received or learned the Gospel, but by the revelation given him by Christ (Gal. 1:12). Christ revealed Himself to Paul, not only when He appeared to him on the way to Damascus, but also when He made known to him, by visions and revelations, the full significance of His person and work (1 Cor. 11:23 ; 2 Cor. 12:1-7), and by His Spirit taught him to know thoroughly the depths of the Divine purposes of salvation. This origin of his Gospel through revelation by no means excludes the claim that Paul received the historical elements of his preaching from tradition, and in many ways appropriated the forms of doctrine offered him; but in all these did not lie the special efficacy of his preaching. His Gospel is certainly not a communication of historical facts as such, or a peculiar system of doctrine; it is nothing else, primarily, than making known the secrets of the saving purpose of God (Rom. 16:25), the contents of which God has revealed to the Apostle by His Spirit (1 Cor. 2:7, 10, 12). What Paul claims as special to himself is, that the knowledge of the saving truth, which all others receive by Apostolic preaching, he has received directly from God through Christ, or through His Spirit, and has thus been made fit to be a minister of the New Testament (2 Cor. 3:5, 6).

In contradistinction from the Twelve, and those who besides them were called to Apostolic activity, Paul is conscious that he has been called to be the Apostle of the Gentiles (Gal. 2:7-9). The object of his Apostleship was to work the obedience of faith among all nations (Rom. 1:5, 14); he was the minister of Christ Jesus unto the Gentiles (Rom. 15:16), the Apostle of the Gentiles (Rom. 11:13). As such he had to preach the Gospel to the heathen, and thereby to lead them into the fellowship of the Church.

[ANALYSIS: 1) The Gospel has Divine power; 2) its contents; 3) must be preached; 4) the inspiration of the Apostles; 5) they were called immediately by Christ; 6) Paul's special call as an Apostle to the Gentiles.]

## § 128. *The Calling of the Gentiles.*[1]

With reference to the want and need of righteousness, there is no difference between Jew and Gentile. They are both without righteousness (Rom. 3:22, 23), because they are both under the dominion of sin (Rom. 3:9), which had its original source in the general descent of all men from Adam (Rom. 5:12). As God Himself must give justification to men without their co-operation, and from free grace, because men of themselves had not and could not obtain righteousness, then the way in which He does this could be only one, as He is Himself but One (Rom. 3:30). The new life, and this justification, must be accomplished in all in the same way, by living fellowship with Christ, in which all differences of pre-Christian life vanish (Gal. 3:8; 1 Cor. 12:13); and the only thing of any avail is faith in Jesus Christ (Gal. 5:6).

God had not bound Himself by a promise to the Gentiles, yet the extension of the calling even to them had been often prophesied in the Scriptures.[2] In this prophecy, however, the presupposition throughout was that Israel should first participate in the Messianic salvation, and that through them it should come to the Gentiles. Paul did not deny this privilege to Israel; but his special work was the mission to the heathen as such, and the result was the formation of a Gentile Church, which before Israel, and in the place of Israel, became a sharer in the Messianic salvation.

[1] Compare *Weiss*, § 90.
[2] See § 113, on *The Fullness of the Gentiles.*

The thought that even those who were not, after the flesh, descendants of Abraham, might come into participation in Israel's salvation, was by no means strange to Judaism. All proselytes entered in this way into fellowship in the blessings of Abraham; but that fellowship was complete, to be sure, only when they accepted circumcision and the law. But that Christianity differs from proselytism into Israel's fellowship the Apostle shows from this, that Justification, on which the promise rests, was given to Abraham when he was yet uncircumcised, simply on the ground of faith; and thus also is salvation made accessible to the spiritual children of Abraham (Rom. 4:9, 10, 11, 13). He sees in this an explicit intention of God to show that Justification, and therewith the obtaining of salvation, does not depend on circumcision, but only on this: that one be like Abraham in faith, and in so far his spiritual child, whether he be circumcised or not (Rom. 4:11, 12). In Gal. 3:2–5 Paul also shows that the Gentile Christains had received the gift of the Spirit on the ground of faith, as Abraham had received Justification (*ver.* 6); that they therefore in respect of their faith are children of Abraham in a metaphorical sense (*ver.* 7).

[ANALYSIS 1) Both Jew and Gentile are under sin; 2) there is only one way of Justification; 3) the calling of the Gentiles prophesied in the Old Testament; 4) but Israel was first to participate in the Messianic Salvation; 5) the distinction between Jewish proselytism and the Gospel.]

§ 129. *The Hardening and Conversion of Israel.*[1]

What may have appeared the most startling fact in connection with the calling of the Gentiles, was that the casting away of Israel, at least of the greater portion, went hand in hand with it. The engrafting of

[1] Compare *Weiss*, § 91.

## THE HARDENING OF ISRAEL. 101

the wild branches implied the breaking away of the natural branches (Rom. 11:19). Paul expressly announces it as a judgment that the preaching of the Gospel, by which the calling is realized, has been turned away from the Jews to the Gentiles (Acts 13:46; 28:28). By the withdrawal of the preaching of the Gospel the way to salvation was shut to them, although they were the natural branches (Rom. 11:24). And yet the promise transmitted from the fathers was the inalienable possession of Israel, and they still continued to be a people beloved of God for the fathers' sake (Rom. 11:28). If God had once chosen them, their unfaithfulness could not remove His faithfulness towards His own promise (Rom. 3:3). God would not withdraw gifts of grace given them, and His calling in particular (Rom. 11:29). The Divine mercy is indeed free in the selection of its objects (Rom. 9:15), but to whomsoever God has once bound Himself by a promise to him He will ever be faithful. This great problem, of which Paul (Rom. 9:1—11:36) so fully treats, was not easy to solve, and lay as a burden upon his heart.

Those shut out from salvation are shut out in consequence of their stumbling at Christ, and on account of their inexcusable opposition to the plan of salvation. The guilt of Israel consisted in this: that they sought after righteousness by works (Rom. 9:31, 32), and so wished to set up their own righteousness instead of submitting themselves to the new rule of righteousness (10:3) after the end of the law had come with Christ, and the righteousness of faith had come in the place of a righteousness by works (Rom. 10:4–13). They could not excuse themselves by saying that they had not heard the message of this new righteousness, for it had gone into all the world (Rom. 10:18); nor by saying that they had not understood it, for even the unintelligent Gentiles had quite well understood it (Rom. 10:19, 20). The cause of their disobedience was that they stumbled at the Messiah (Rom. 9:32), because the crucified One was no Messiah in their view (1 Cor. 1:23); and now hardening had come upon them as a judgment, as the prophets had already described (Rom. 11:7–10). But this hardening, and the exclusion from salvation connected with it, has come to them through their own guilt (Rom. 11:20).

God has made use of their fall to carry out His saving purpose towards the Gentiles; for the Gospel rejected by the Jews has been brought to the Gentiles, and their deliverance thereby rendered possible (Rom. 11:11). In order to make room for the engrafting of the branches of the wild olive tree, the natural branches were broken off (Rom. 11:19), and thus the Divine judgment which is accomplished on Israel by their transgressions has become the riches of the Gentiles (*ver.* 12). The casting away of the one has been the reconciling of the other (*ver.* 15).

The calling of the Gentiles, which became possible through the casting away of Israel, has for its object not only to make the Gentiles partakers of salvation, but also to provoke the Jews to jealousy (Rom. 11:11), and thus to reach in an indirect way God's saving purpose towards His chosen people. As soon as the Jews turn to the Lord, the blinding veil which now lies upon their hearts will be taken away (2 Cor. 3:16), and then they, through the same mercy of God which the Gentiles have now obtained, will obtain mercy (Rom. 11:31). As soon as they cease to be unbelieving, those branches that have been broken off will again be grafted in (11:23, 24). And this ultimate deliverance of Israel is not only possible, but it is to the Apostle certain,[1] because of the Divine promise (11:26–29). When the full number of the Gentiles shall have entered into the fellowship of the Elect people, then shall all Israel be saved (Rom. 11:25, 26). Paul's whole argument is, that the temporary hardening of Israel has brought this about; that salvation has even already come from the Jews to the Gentiles; and that this must finally serve only this end: that salvation will come back from the Gentiles to the Jews, and thus the promise of the Elect Nation will be perfectly fulfilled.

[ANALYSIS : 1) The hardening of Israel a judgment ; 2) Christ a stumbling-block ; 3) they sought a righteousness by works ; 4) by their fall salvation is come to the Gentiles ; 5) when the fullness of the Gentiles be come in, all Israel shall be saved.]

---

[1] Compare § 114.

## CHAPTER V.

### HEATHENDOM AND JUDAISM.

§ 130. *The Apostasy of Heathendom.*[1]

Paul, as the Apostle to the Gentiles, answers the question, How is it that heathendom has come into the irremediable condition in which it is actually found? The Gentiles are sinners (Gal. 2:15), destitute of righteousness, and are without excuse (Rom. 1:20), and are with justice exposed to Divine retribution. It is true, indeed, that the Gentiles had no positive Mosaic law, and in this sense they are "without law" (1 Cor. 9:21); but, as they sin "without law," they shall also perish 'without law" (Rom. 2:12). The Apostle starts with the assumption that the Gentiles originally had a knowledge of God (Rom. 1:21), because, ever since the creation of the world, God has manifested unto them by His works the eternal power and fullness of His Divine attributes (Rom. 1:20); has borne witness of Himself to them by His good deeds, in that He gave them from Heaven rain and fruitful seasons, filling their hearts with food and gladness (Acts 14:17), having distributed the nations over the earth, determining their appointed seasons and the bounds of their habitation (Acts 17:26). God has done His part to lead them to a knowledge of Himself, and in their wisdom they should have found God, but they did not attain to this knowledge (1 Cor. 1:21; Rom. 1:20, 21). The organ which God gave them for this purpose is the *noûs*, the mind ("*being perceived*"), by means of which His invisible attri-

[1] Compare *Wess.* § 69.

butes can be perceived spiritually ("clearly seen") (Rom. 1:20). The Gentiles are a law unto themselves (Rom. 2:14), because, although they have no positive revealed law, they show the work of the law written in their hearts, demanding obedience to God. This is the moral consciousness which was originally implanted in men, and its presence is testified to by conscience (Rom. 2:15). And the Gentiles themselves have also the consciousness that they " who do those things which are not fitting " (Rom. 1:28) are worthy of death, and therefore liable to punishment (Rom. 1:32). Accordingly, the fundamental law of Divine retribution applies to them as well as to the Jews (Rom. 2:9, 10).

In consequence of their practical turning away from God, the Gentiles are delivered up unto darkness (Rom. 1:21 ; 2:19 ; 2 Cor. 6:14), and their wisdom has become foolishness in the judgment of God (1 Cor. 3:19). The climax of their foolishness is idolatry, and the inmost essence of heathenism is this, the deification of the creature, which leads to the deepest degradation. The further consequence of their turning away from God was an unlimited self-surrender to their natural lusts (Rom. 1:24)—a self-surrender which culminated in the unnatural sensual vices (Rom. 1:24, 26, 27), and a complete blunting of the moral consciousness (Rom.1: 28).

[ANALYSIS: 1) The Gentiles are, with justice, exposed to Divine retribution; 2) for they had a knowledge of God; 3) and although they have no positive revealed law; 4) they have the work of the law written in their hearts; 5) their wisdom is foolishness; 6) and their idolatry has brought upon them the deepest degradation.]

§ 131. *Heathendom and the Divine Training.*[1]

In the background of the whole description of the sinful development of heathendom, as given in Rom. 1:

[1] Compare *Weiss*, § 70.

18-32, lies the thought that one object God has in view in leaving the Gentiles to their natural development, which is always leading them to a worse and worse corruption, is that sin by its development should manifest itself in its true nature. But Paul by no means always looks at this development of heathendom from a pedagogic standpoint.

Paul has a very vivid conception of the relation of the Gentile world to the kingdom of evil. According to 1 Cor. 12:2, the Gentiles are under the dominion of a foreign power, which drives them, without will and understanding, unto a degrading idolatry. The idols whom the Gentiles worshiped are the demons (1 Cor. 10: 20), or the evil angels, the servants and organs of Satan; and it is through them, probably, that the Devil has especial dominion over heathendom. The Devil is the prince of this world (2 Cor. 4:4); and Paul assumes (1 Cor. 10:20, 21) that the heathen sacrificial feasts, participation in which was forbidden to the Christians, bring men into a real and polluting fellowship with demons, just as the Lord's Supper brings them into fellowship with Christ. The demoniac powers have drawn heathendom into its godless (2 Cor. 6:14-16) and polluting sinful condition.

And thus there is brought about that dreadful depravity of heathendom, in which the Divine judgment of wrath against its apostasy punishes sin by means of sin. This is especially evident from Rom. 1:18-32, where we see that the wrath of God is revealed against the Gentiles as a judgment for their apostasy. It is quite in keeping with the fundamental law of Divine retribution, according to which guilt demands an equivalent punishment, if God punishes sin by sin, by permitting the sinner to sink deeper and deeper into sin through the process of the development of sin. Thus sinners must receive in their own persons ("in themselves") the equivalent reward ("recompense") of the error of their apostasy from God, which was necessary ("which was due") according to Divine appointment (Rom. 1: 27). God accordingly gives them up to the uncleanness of the unnatural sensual vices (Rom. 1:24, 26). These are, on the one hand, the necessary consequences of their idolatry and of their life in the lusts; and, on the other, they are the righteous punishment through the dishonor which they bring with them.

[ANALYSIS: 1) In the sinful development of heathendom sin manifests its true nature; 2) the idols of the Gentiles are the evil angels; 3) the dreadful depravity of the Gentiles is a punishment for their apostasy from God.]

§ 132. *Judaism and its Law.*[1]

Although the Jews stand on the same level with the Gentiles, in that they are all under sin (Rom. 3:9), still the Jews in many respects have an advantage (Rom. 3:2). The enumeration of their advantages, however, reaches its climax (Rom. 9:5) in the descent from the "fathers," from whom the Jews derive the theocratic title of Israelites (Rom. 9:4). In the fathers they are elected to be God's possession, beloved for the fathers' sake (Rom. 11:28). The people of Israel are the people of God (Rom. 11:1, 2; 15:10); they are the children of God (Rom. 9:4, 7, 8, 25, 26).

In consequence of this advantage which the Jewish nation had over all other nations, it was intrusted with the oracles of God (Rom. 3:2)—*i. e.*, with the Divine revelations which are contained in the Old Testament. In the revealed law the Jews possessed a representation

[1] Compare *Weiss*, § 71.

of the truth, from which they learned to know the will of God and to prove the difference between good and evil (Rom. 2:18, 20). Paul takes it for granted that in the Old Testament we have a true revelation of the nature of God as far as He revealed Himself, and when he is speaking of any of the Divine attributes he repeatedly appeals to the Old Testament. Thus for God's truthfulness he appeals to Ps. 51:4 (Rom. 3:4), for His free mercy to Ex. 33:19; 9:16; Isa. 45:9 (Rom. 9:15, 17, 20), for His unsearchable wisdom to Isa. 40:13 (1 Cor. 2:16; Rom. 11:34), for His righteous judgment to Deut. 32:35 (Rom. 12:19), and for the universality of judgment to Isa. 45:23 (Rom. 14:11).

When Paul teaches that Moses was the giver of the law (1 Cor. 9:9; 2 Cor. 3:15; Rom. 5:14, 20; 10:5, 19), who as mediator received it through the intermediation of angels (Gal. 3:19), there is no intention whatever of denying the Divine origin of the law. This law of Moses (Rom. 7:7) is the law of God (Rom. 7:22, 25; 8:3, 7); it has its origin in the Divine Spirit (Rom. 7:14), and is holy as God is Holy (Rom. 7:12). When Paul speaks of the law, he thinks not only of the Mosaic legislation, but also of all the commandments of God as they are contained in the Old Testament, and therefore also of the development of the law by the prophets (1 Cor. 14:21; Rom. 3:19).

But Scripture (Rom. 3:9–19) as well as experience (Rom. 2:1–3; 21–24) teaches that the Jews do not keep the law, and that they are therefore along with the Gentiles exposed to the judgment of God (Rom. 3:19). If they appeal to the gracious dealings of God towards Israel, they only show that they misunderstand and despise His forbearance and long-suffering, which are leading them to repentance (Rom. 2:4; 9:22), and by their hardness of heart and impenitence increase their guilt (Rom. 2:5).

[ANALYSIS: 1) Although the Jews are all under sin, still they had special advantages; 2) to them were intrusted the oracles of God; 3) especially the law, which is holy; 4) but the Jews did not keep the law; 5) and are therefore exposed to the judgment of God.]

## § 133. *The Law and the Promise.*[1]

It was an advantage to the Jews, as contrasted with heathendom with its moral consciousness (Rom. 2:15), to have the written law as an objective revelation (Rom. 2:27)—an advantage which should have led them to fulfill the law. That which made the law weak, so that it could not work its fulfillment, was not its objectivity, nor any defect whatever in the law, which in itself is good and holy (Rom. 7:12, 16)—but according to Rom. 8:3 it was rather the power of the flesh, or rather the power of sin, which dwells in the flesh. Because sin has dwelt in humanity ever since Adam's fall, the commandment forbidding lust does not suppress lust, but only stirs it up (Rom. 7:7, 8), and awakens the power of sin which is slumbering in man. This is not owing to the law, which cannot possibly be sinful (Rom. 7:7); for the law is spiritual, issuing from the Spirit of God, and holy as He is holy (Rom. 7:12); it is owing to the sin which dwells in the flesh (7:13). So long as man stands under the dominion of the law, the dominion of sin over him cannot be broken (Rom. 6:14; Gal. 3:23). The law only works the wrath of God, inasmuch as it demands the execution of the punishment which is threatened by it to the sinner (Rom. 4:15), and so pronounces its curse upon man (Gal. 3:10). As the law expressly stipulates that death shall be the punishment

---

[1] Compare *Weiss*, § 72.

of sin (Deut. 30:15, 19), the letter of the law pronounces the sentence of death upon man (2 Cor. 3:6).

The same Divine training, which left heathendom to itself, in order that the development of the sinful tendency which it had adopted might come to maturity, reached the same end among the Jews by the interposition of the law; for the "law was added because of transgressions" (Gal. 3:19), "that the trespass might abound" (Rom. 5:20). In consequence of the presence of sin, which is operative in man, the law has made manifest the exceeding sinfulness of sin (Rom. 7:13), and has brought upon man spiritual death as well as temporal death as the punishment of sin. As the law is spiritual and originally was unto life (Rom. 7:10), sin cannot reveal its real nature more clearly than by showing that for man it turns the blessing into a curse (Rom. 7:10, 11). When man, through the law, has experienced the whole destructive power of sin (Rom. 3:20), there arises from him the cry of anguish for deliverance out of this state of death into which it has brought him (Rom. 7:24), and through the awakening of this longing for salvation the law becomes a "schoolmaster to bring us unto Christ" (Gal. 3:24).

From the pedagogic character of the law, Paul deduces its transitoriness. With the coming in of faith, or of Christ as the object of faith, there is involved the end of the law (Rom. 10:4), because God now no longer justifies on the ground of the works of the law, but on the ground of faith. The law was originally only added to the promise until an appointed time (Gal. 3:19), which has come in with the appearing of Christ and faith in Him. As the law was only meant for a definite epoch of the development of humanity, it also belongs to the "weak and beggarly rudiments of the world"

## THE LAW AND THE PROMISE. 111

(Gal. 4:3, 9)—*i. e.*, to the elementary rudiments of religion.

The Jews already possessed a promise, before "the law came in beside" (Rom. 3:20)—a promise which God is bound to fulfill for His truth's sake (Rom. 15:8), seeing that He has solemnly ratified it in the covenants which He entered into with the patriarchs (Rom. 9:4). According to Rom. 4:13, the import of the promise which was given to Abraham and his seed is, that "he should be heir of the world." What this really means we learn more clearly from Gal. 3:16. "The seed" is not a collective term for the descendants of Abraham, but a designation of the Christ, who was descended from the fathers (Rom. 9:5). It is to Him, therefore, as the Lord of the Messianic Kingdom, that the promise of the possession of the world especially refers (Gal. 3:19). With the Messianic Kingdom, however, every Messianic blessing is directly promised to the seed of Abraham (in the collective sense), or through his seed (in the personal sense).

Now God has granted this Messianic possession of salvation to Abraham by promise, as a gift (Gal. 3:18), not as a reward for a definite performance, but on the ground of the righteousness of faith (Rom. 4:13), of which circumcision was the seal (Rom. 4:11), and therefore "according to grace" (Rom. 4:16). From this it follows that the possession of salvation is altogether independent of the law. The covenant by which God had bound Himself to fulfill His promise to Abraham's descendants could not be rendered invalid by the law, which was given four hundred and thirty years later (Gal. 3:17). If the Messianic inheritance were to be attained on the ground of the law, the promise would be altogether done away with (Rom.

4:14); for seeing that sin reigns in man, the law necessarily calls forth transgression of the law, and thereby the wrath of God (Rom. 4:15). Wrath, however, excludes the manifestation of grace which the fulfilling of the promise would involve, and God could no longer fulfill the promise to those under the law, because they are objects of His wrath (Gal. 3:9, 10). Accordingly, the law was only given till the seed should come to whom the promise was given (Gal. 3:19), and in order to convince men of their inability to attain to righteousness by themselves and by the works of the law—as a pedagogue leading them to Christ, causing them to seek justification by the way of faith in Him. Here, then, we stand upon the boundary line of the pre-Christian age, and there is opened up the prospect of the new era of grace and salvation.

[ANALYSIS : 1) The powerlessness of the law is owing to the sin which dwells in man ; 2) the law only works the wrath of God, and pronounces death ; 3) the law was given to make manifest the exceeding sinfulness of sin ; 4) is a tutor to prepare us for Christ ; 5) was given only for a time ; 6) did not supersede the promise ; 7) the true meaning of the promise given to Abraham ; 8) the promise is according to grace ; 9) and the possession of salvation is altogether independent of the law.]

# CHAPTER VI.

### PROPHECY AND FULFILLMENT.

§ 134. *The Prophecy of Scripture.*[1]

Inasmuch as the Old Testament Scripture refers to the Messianic Salvation and its realization, its fullest and deepest significance belongs to those who receive that salvation, and therefore to the Christian present. The import of God's message of salvation, which the Apostle proclaims, God has promised afore by His prophets in the Holy Scriptures (Rom. 1:2), and the specific significance of these writings is now made known unto all who believe in Christ (Rom. 16:25, 26). Thus for example, that the Gentiles should participate in Abraham's salvation was preached beforehand as glad tidings by the *Scriptures* (Gal. 3:8; Gen. 12:3). For whatsoever things were written aforetime were written for our learning (Rom. 15:4) and for our admonition, upon whom the ends of the ages are come (1 Cor. 10:11). Thus, such a prophecy as Isa. 49:8 refers especially to men's behavior in the Christian present (2 Cor. 6:2); and like every other statement regarding the will of God (*cf.* 1 Cor. 14:34), even the Mosaic law may be regarded as prophetic, and as having a direct spiritual bearing upon the regulation of Christian circumstances (1 Cor. 9:9, 10).

Paul finds the import of the Messianic message of salvation directly preached beforehand in Scripture. Christ has died and risen again according to the Script-

---

[1] Compare *Weiss*, § 73.

ures (1 Cor. 15:3, 4; Ps. 22:16–18; Isa. 53:5–12; Dan. 9:26; Ps. 2:7; 16:10; etc.); the reproaches that fell upon Him are foretold in Ps. 69:9 (Rom. 15:3); the dominion which was given Him in Ps. 8:6 (1. Cor. 15:27). The doctrine of the righteousness of faith is witnessed by the law and the prophets (Rom. 3:21; Rom. 1:17, after Hab. 2:4; Rom. 4:6–8, after Ps. 32:1, 2); in particular, witness is borne to faith as the condition of salvation in Isa. 28:16 (Rom. 10:11), and as the source of the preaching of the Gospel in Ps. 116:10 (2 Cor. 4:13). That the Gospel shall be preached throughout the whole world Paul finds in Ps. 19:4 (Rom. 10:18); the destruction of human wisdom by the foolishness of preaching in Isa. 29:14 (1 Cor. 1:19); the calling of the Gentiles in Hos. 1:10; 2:23 (Rom. 9:25, 26); etc. The unbelief of the Jews he sees foretold in Isa. 53:1; 65:2 (Rom. 10:16, 21); the offense which they take at Christ in Isa. 8:14; 28:16 (Rom. 9:33); their obduracy in Isa. 29:10; 6:9; Deut. 29:4; Ps. 69:23 (Rom. 11:8–10); their partial rejection in Isa. 10:22, 23; 1:9 (Rom. 9:27–29); their final salvation in Isa. 59:20; Jer. 31:33, 34 (Rom. 11:26, 27). That the Christian Church is the Temple of God, he finds in Lev. 26:11, 12; Isa. 52:11; Jer. 31:9; 2 Sam. 7:14 (2 Cor. 6:16–18); and the special gift of speaking with tongues in Isa. 28:11, 12 (1 Cor. 14:21). The continual persecution of Christians is foretold in Ps. 44:22 (Rom. 8:36); the final overthrow of death in Isa. 25:8; Hos. 13:14 (1 Cor. 15:54, 55).

Scripture is prophetic not only in its expressions, but also in its typical history. Thus, according to Rom. 5:14, Adam is a type of Him that was to come, inasmuch as in him it is shown how an influence extends from one to the whole race. What happened to the Israelites happened to them *typically* (1 Cor. 10:6, 11)—

*i. e.*, so that we might learn what we have to experience and shall experience, if we conduct ourselves similarly. What Scripture relates regarding the justification of Abraham is not only written in order to describe his justification, but also to instruct us as to the manner of our own (Rom. 4:23, 24). When Christ is represented as a *propitiation* (Rom. 3:25) and as a Paschal Lamb (1 Cor. 5:7; *cf.* Eph. 5:2), when the sacrificial system in general (Rom. 12:1; 15:16) and the rite of the feast of the Passover in particular (1 Cor. 5:7, 8) are given an application to Christian circumstances (*cf.* Col. 2:11; Phil. 2:17; 3:3; 4:18), when the Church is called the true Temple of God (1 Cor. 3:16; 2 Cor. 6:16), when an appointment of the law relating to the priests is used as an illustration of an ordinance of God in the Christian Church (1 Cor. 9:13), and the Jewish sacrificial meal is used as an analogue of the Lord's Supper (1 Cor. 10:18), there lies at the basis of all these allusions the presupposition that these institutions, which were appointed by God, have a typical character.

[ANALYSIS: 1) The Old Testament of the deepest significance to the Christian Church; 2) has a direct spiritual bearing upon the Christian life; 5) the economy of salvation directly foretold in it; 4) the Old Testament is prophetic not only in its language, but also in its typical history.]

§ 135. *The Use of the Old Testament.*[1]

Paul quotes the Old Testament very frequently. It is in our four Doctrinal Epistles, however, that by far the most of his quotations are found. These the Apostle usually introduces with "it is written" (about thirty times), or with the similar formula "the Scripture saith" (Gal. 4:30; etc.). It is seldom, indeed, that Paul introduces the writers as speaking (Rom. 4:6;

[1] Compare *Weiss*, § 74.

11:9; 9:27, 29; etc.). Most of his quotations are from Isaiah and the Psalms; next in order comes the Pentateuch, especially Genesis and Deuteronomy.[1] Paul mainly quotes from the text of the Septuagint, using his quotations with great freedom, often combining different passages (1 Cor. 15:54, 55; 2 Cor. 6:16–18; Rom. 3:10–18; 9:25, 26; 11:26, 27), or freely mixing them together (Rom. 9:33; 11:8), and the passages are often abbreviated or insignificantly changed to suit their Messianic interpretation (1 Cor. 1:31; 2 Cor. 6:16; Rom. 14:11; Gal. 4:30; 1 Cor. 3:20; 15:45; Rom. 10:11; etc.).

In the use that Paul makes of the passages of Scripture he lays no stress on their historical connection, but takes into consideration only the language used in the expressions, on the presupposition that the whole of the Old Testament prophesies of the Messiah and the events of the Messianic time, so that everything which admits of being applied to these circumstances is interpreted in this sense, and that too as a direct prophecy. Thus in Ps. 69:9, the Messiah is conceived of as speaking (Rom. 15:3), and Joel 2:32 is applied by him, as well as by Peter (Acts 2:21), to the Messiah (Rom. 10:13).

In discussing, however, this subject of quotation from the Old Testament we must be careful to distinguish between literal quotation and the homiletical use of Scripture; and it is often impossible to decide with full certainty which of these uses of Scripture we have before us.

[ANALYSIS: 1) Paul quotes the Old Testament very frequently; 2) mainly from the Septuagint; 3) lays no stress on the historical connection; 4) we must distinguish between literal quotation and homiletical use of Scripture.]

---

[1] See especially Appendix III to Westcott and Hort's *New Testament in Greek*, vol. II, pp. 180–182.

§ 136. *The Time of Grace.*[1]

It appears from prophecy that the salvation which is being realized in the present was long ago resolved upon by God, and depended upon a decree of His wisdom, which was formed by Him from all eternity, and hidden, even a mystery (1 Cor. 2:7), absolutely unknowable by human knowledge of itself, and such it remained, even after prophecy, until its fulfillment (Rom. 16:25). Now, however, this mystery (Eph. 3:3), or the individual mysteries which are contained in it, such as the final conversion of Israel (Rom. 11:25), the resurrection and transformation of believers (1 Cor. 15:51), are revealed by God (1 Cor. 13:2) and preached by His stewards (1 Cor. 4:1). This happened with the sending of the Son, when the fullness of time came (Gal. 4:4; Eph. 1:9, 10). This expression presupposes that a definite measure of time had to be filled up before the moment appointed for the execution of that decree appeared. It is this moment of which it is said, in 1 Cor. 10:11, that the ends of the past ages are come upon the generation which is living in the present. That this time is come, is the Pauline expression for the proclamation of Jesus, that the promised Kingdom of God has come, that the Messianic time of the end has commenced, that the completion of the theocracy in which God bestows His graces and the historical epoch, which concludes the whole development of the human race, has begun.

This new epoch of the world is characterized by the sovereignty of grace, which is diametrically opposed to sin and the law, as well as to all human work and merit. In the previous age of the world sin reigned; the principle which rules in the new age is the grace

[1] Compare *Weiss*, § 75.

of God (Rom. 5:21). The dominion of sin was owing to the dominion of law; hence, grace forms the antithesis of the law (Rom. 6:14). The law demands works; grace excludes all human activity; works and grace are directly opposed to each other (Rom. 11:6; *cf.* Eph. 2:8, 9). Human doing acquires merit. Grace, however, is not deserved, but presented *gratis* (Rom. 3:24); grace and merit are also diametrically opposed (Rom. 4:4). Grace is given (1 Cor. 1:4) and received (2 Cor. 6:1; Rom. 1:5); in it we stand (Rom. 5:2) and walk (2 Cor. 1:12); it is the new standpoint upon which the new age is placed. Through it men are called (Gal. 1:15) and justified (Rom. 3:24); it is upon it that the Christian hope is based (2 Thess. 2:16). The Christian is what he is through the grace of God (1 Cor. 15:10); and the Apostle rightly characterizes the Christian time as the time of grace.

*Grace* is not conceived of as a passive Divine attribute or disposition. It is rather the operative principle of salvation—the manifestation of the relation and conduct of God towards sinners; it is the Divine favor thought of in its activity, which for that very reason excludes all human activity; it is the expression for the exclusive Divine causality of salvation (2 Cor. 5:18; 1 Cor. 8:6; Rom. 11:36). It is to be distinguished from the *mercy* of God, inasmuch as the latter has reference more particularly to the Divine behavior towards *wretchedness* and *misery*, not towards *sin*. In the relation of grace to sin, the *freeness* of grace, its *spontaneous inclination*, is especially prominent—a thought which does not lie in *mercy*. Nor is grace the *love* of God, although the death of Christ, upon which the new dispensation of grace rests, can also be regarded as a proof of that love (Rom. 5:8); for it is within the

## THE TIME OF GRACE. 119

dispensation of grace that this love is first restored to man; and in Rom. 5:2-5, we find that the love of God is shed abroad in the hearts of those who stand in grace, and in 2 Cor. 13:14, the love of God comes after grace. Nor is grace the *goodness* of God, which shows itself in the conferring of benefits (Rom. 2:4; 11:22).

As it is through the grace of God that the Christian is what he is (1 Cor. 15:10), so he also owes it to Christ (1 Cor. 8:6). Everything for which he has to thank God has been brought about by Christ (1 Cor. 15:57). It is through His instrumentality that grace, the new principle of His salvation, exercises its rule (Rom. 5:21); it is through Him that we obtain grace or access to it (Rom. 1:5; 5:2), reconciliation (2 Cor. 5:18; Rom. 5:11), peace with God (Rom. 5:1), salvation (Rom, 5:9; 1 Thess. 5:9), life and resurrection (1 Cor. 15:21, 57; Rom. 5:17). It is in Christ that grace is given us (1 Cor. 1:4); in Him rests reconciliation (2 Cor. 5:19), redemption (Rom. 3:24), justification (Gal. 2:17; 2 Cor. 5:21), the love of God (Rom. 8:39) and eternal life (Rom. 6:23). In Him all the promises of God are fulfilled (2 Cor. 1:19, 20), and the blessing of Abraham comes upon us (Gal. 3:14). This new time of grace, which is the Christian dispensation, is therefore the Promised Messianic time.

[ANALYSIS: 1) The plan of salvation rests in the eternal counsel of God; 2) the mystery of salvation revealed to us in Jesus Christ; 3) in the fullness of time; 4) the Christian dispensation the time of grace; 5) grace antithetical to law; 6) to works; 7) to merit; 8) the new standpoint upon which this Christian age is placed; 9) grace is the operative principle of salvation; 10) to be distinguished from the mercy of God; 11) from His love; 12) and from His goodness; 13) this grace of God we all owe to Christ; 14) as well as all the works of grace.]

# CHAPTER VII.

### THE CHRISTOLOGY OF PAUL.

§ 137. *The Lord of Glory.*[1]

For Paul the peculiar dignity of Christ is summed up in the title *Lord*. He describes the sum of his preaching as consisting in this, that he preaches Jesus Christ as the Lord (2 Cor. 4:5); and inasmuch as his preaching is always gaining new confessors of Christ, it ministers to the glorifying of His name (Rom. 1:5). The specific confession, therefore, of the Christian Church declares that Jesus is the Lord (1 Cor. 12:3; Rom. 10:9). In this title is summed up all that Christ is to it; and hence the reverential designation of Christ as the Mediator of salvation is: *Jesus Christ our Lord* (1 Cor. 1:9; Rom. 1:4; 5:21; 7:25); or, as in the Epistles to the Thessalonians (some nineteen times), *Our Lord Jesus Christ*. As in the early preaching of the Apostles, Jesus is acknowlegded to be the Mediator of the expected completion of salvation, because He has proved Himself to be the Promised and expected Messiah, so He can be acknowledged by Paul and the Gentile Christians to be the Mediator of the grace of God, which has been revealed and is operative in Christianity, only if He is confessed as the Heavenly Lord of the Church. To belong to Him as Lord is the characteristic mark of all Christians (Rom. 14:8), since, in order to obtain this sovereignty, He has died and become alive again (Rom. 14:9; 2 Cor. 5:15). His com-

[1] Compare *Weiss*, § 76.

## THE LORD OF GLORY. 121

mand is decisive for believers (Gal. 6:2 ; 1 Cor. 9:14,21); from Him is derived all authority in the Church (1 Cor. 5:4 ; 2 Cor. 10:8 ; 13:10), and He Himself will be their Judge (2 Cor. 5:10).

The name *Lord* describes Christ also as the Divine sovereign of the world (Rom. 10:12), sitting at the Right Hand of God (Rom. 8:34). to whom is given the possession of the word, which was promised to the seed of Abraham (Gal. 3:16). Without any explanation Paul applies to Christ passages in the Old Testament which refer to God (1 Cor. 2:16 ; 10:22 ; Rom. 10:13), and designates Him the Lord in a connection where God has just been designated Lord (Rom. 14:6–9). Moreover, Paul draws the full consequences of this designation of Christ. Divine worship is paid to Him (2 Cor. 12:8 ; Rom. 10:12, 13); and, at His Second Coming, the Exalted Messiah appears with such full Divine omniscience as is possessed only by the Searcher of hearts (1 Cor. 4:5). Accordingly, it is not surprising that Paul in Rom. 9:5 extols Christ as being over all, God blessed forever.

Since it is through His being raised up by God (2 Cor. 13:4 ; Rom. 4:24, 25) that Christ has attained His exaltation, and since God has put all things in subjection to Him (1 Cor. 15:27), it is evident that His whole mediatorial work is only the execution of the will of God the Father. Christ wills what the Father wills. God has transferred to Him, until the completion of the work of salvation, the arrangement, superintendence, and execution of everything necessary for the realizing of the salvation which has been procured by Him. He reigns until the end, till He hath put all His enemies under His feet. Then of His own freewill He delivers up the Kingdom to God, even the

Father (1 Cor. 15:24), and subjects Himself to Him, that God may be all in all (1 Cor. 15:28). This subjection of Himself to the Father has no other aim than to bring about the completion of the sovereignty of God, and is in accordance with God's Eternal counsel. To speculate how the Mediatorial reign of Christ, which shall cease, differs from the government of God in His completed Kingdom is far remote from the mind of the Apostle.

Paul speaks of Christ as *the Lord of Glory* (1 Cor. 2:8). This glory, which belongs only to the incorruptible God (Rom. 1:23; 5:2), the Apostle be held in the face of Christ (2 Cor. 4:6; 3:18); and he therefore proclaims the Gospel of the glory of Christ, who is the image of God (2 Cor. 4:4).

[ANALYSIS: 1) Christ is the Lord; 2) because He has proved Himself the Messiah; 3) Christ is also the Lord of the world; 4) Paul ascribes to Him Divine names; 5) Divine worship; 6) and Divine attributes; 7) the Mediatorial work of Christ is but the execution of the will of God; 8) His Mediatorial reign shall cease; 9) that God may be all in all; 10) Christ is the Lord of Glory.]

§ 138. *The Son of God.*[1]

Because Paul had seen Jesus as the Lord, in the radiant light of Divine Glory, He became to him the true Messiah, who had been promised to His people, and for whom he had also looked. This Messiah is now also to Paul, as in the Old Testament, the Son of God (Rom. 1:3, 4). He who is preached by Paul, and in whom all the promises of God are fulfilled, is called the Son of God (2 Cor. 1:19, 20; Gal. 1:16).

Paul lays so great stress on the truth that Jesus is the Son of God, that His single utterances have great weight. When in Gal. 1:16 the Apostle says, "God has

[1] Compare *Weiss*, §§ 77, 79; *Lechler*, vol. 2, pp. 2–13.

revealed His Son in me," we are not to explain away these words, but to understand them as meaning that, by this very revelation, Paul was brought to the knowledge of Jesus as He is in truth, and he was taught to recognize Him not merely as the Messiah, but as the Son of God. In Rom. 8:3 the Apostle lays special stress on that which is here indicated, using the words: " God, sending *His own* Son,"—where it is clear how close a community of nature between Jesus and God the Father is implied by the reflexive pronoun. Still stronger is the declaration in Rom. 8:32, " He that spared not *His own* Son." There is a special significance of the use of *idios* (*His own*) in this passage, as is shown by the immediate context. The Apostle asserts a close, exclusive community of essence between Jesus and God the Father; in other words, he ascribes to Jesus not merely a theocratic dignity, but the metaphysical Sonship of God. Here belongs also the more difficult passage (Rom. 1:4), where, in two parallel utterances respecting His Person, Jesus is called the Son of God—1) "Who was born of the seed of David according to the flesh;" and 2) " Who was declared to be the Son of God, with power, according to the spirit of holiness by the resurrection of the dead." Though Christ *was* already the Son of God before the creation of the world, and as such was sent (Gal. 4:4; Rom. 8:3), yet it was necessary to instate His human nature into the rank and dignity of His Divine Sonship. He first showed Himself as David's Son, and then by His resurrection was proved to be the Son of God. Of the three clauses which define the participle " declared ;" the first indicates the manner, " with power;" the second, the moral cause, " according to the Spirit of holiness;" the third, the efficient cause, " by the resurrection of the dead."

When in Rom. 8:3 Paul says God *sent* His Son (also Gal. 4:4), this assertion unquestionably presupposes that the Son already existed, and was with God before He came into the world, for the connection incontestably proves that the "sending" refers to an entrance into the visible world, into earthly life. The Redeemer is here regarded as a *Person* before he became man, and was constituted the Son of God before He was born on the earth (Gal. 4:4). This is unmistakably implied in the question in Rom. 10:6, "who shall ascend into heaven? that is, to bring Christ down." This does not refer to His ascension, nor to His sitting at the Right Hand of God, but to His incarnation; and the statement implies that Christ was in Heaven before His incarnation, and as a person could, as it were, be brought down. Moreover, the words of 2 Cor. 8:9 refer to the prehistoric existence of Christ. When Paul here reminds the Corinthians that Jesus, "though He was rich, yet for your sakes He became poor, that ye through His poverty might become rich," he plainly has in view a pre-earthly state of Christ when He was rich in Divine fullness. Further, Paul refers to a Personal activity of Christ in the Old Testament revelation, in leading Israel (1 Cor. 10:4), explaining that the rock giving forth water in the journey through the Desert was Christ, who gave them drink miraculously. Thus the idea is unmistakably implied that it was Christ invisible and yet actual, who had been the agent, and that Christ pre-existed before His historical appearance, and was acting as Mediator of the revelation of God.

The Apostle soars still higher in thought, when in 1 Cor. 8:6 he says: "One Lord, Jesus Christ, through whom are all things, and we through him." The "all things" refers to all existence, to the universe. The

## THE SON OF GOD.

world came into existence through Christ. The expression implies not only a pre-human existence of the Redeemer, but also that He existed before the world was formed—from eternity, inasmuch as He is the Mediator, the instrument of the world's creation, while God is the Primeval Cause of all things (there is One God, the Father, *of* whom are all things, 1 Cor. 8:6). The sense is, therefore, that the Redeemer is eternal, not only existing before His incarnation, but also before the world and time, and that the creation of the world, of which God is the First, Absolute Cause, was accomplished by Christ as the Mediator of the Divine work. Respecting the Person of Christ, according to His Divine nature, we have therefore the following statements: He is the Son of God exclusively and essentially, and as such stands in the closest unity of essence with God the Father, Whose image He is. Before He became man, even before the world was, He existed, not as an unpersonal idea in God, but as a Personality. He is not a creature of God, but, on the contrary, the creation of all that exists is mediated by Him as the instrument of Divine revelation.

St. Paul, however, persistently makes a distinction between God and Christ (1 Cor. 8:6; Rom. 11:36). From this distinction arises their order in subsisting and in operating, and this order is one of origin and relation. Christ is the *Son of God*, His *first-born*. God *sent forth* His Son (Gal. 4:4), raised Him from the dead (Gal. 1:1), exalted Him to the highest glory (1 Cor. 15:27). The head of Christ is God (1 Cor. 11:3), and Christ is God's (1 Cor. 3:23).

Two things, however, must always be kept in view: 1) that Paul invariably starts from the historical Christ and the historical relation of Christ to the Father, even when looking back to the pre-historic time or forward to the future; and 2) that the relation in God between Father and Son is reciprocal.

Christ is the antitype of Adam (Rom. 5:14), because His influence extends to the whole human race in the same manner as that of Adam—*i. e.*, as all human beings born in the course of nature have Adam's nature, and are therefore sinful (Rom. 5:12), so all human beings, becoming partakers of the Divine nature, by being born again of God and receiving the abundance of grace and of the gift of righteousness, have life through the one, even Jesus Christ (Rom. 5:17). As sin and death came into the world through Adam, and all sharers of his nature partake of the same, so righteousness and life have come into the world through Christ, and all sharers of His nature, partake of the same.

In 1 Cor. 15:45, 47 Christ is called "the last Adam," "the Second Man," *the last Adam* in reference to the *first* Adam, whose antitype He is as the head and beginner of the new humanity redeemed and justified through Him, as also with reference to the fact that after Him no other is to follow with an Adamite vocation. Apart from this latter reference, Christ may also be called the Second Man or Adam (*ver.* 47). In 1 Cor. 15:47 it is said expressly that the Second Man was "of Heaven;" and this allusion to His Heavenly origin involves the thought that Christ, according to his Divine nature, must Himself have been an inhabitant of Heaven. His human body He did not bring with Him from Heaven; but after His resurrection it was exalted to Heaven, in which glorified body He is now in Heaven.

[ANALYSIS: 1) The Messiah is the Son of God; 2) is of the same essence as the Father; 3) the world was created through

Him, 5) the Son exists as a Person distinct from the Father; 6) Christ is called "the last Adam;" 7) the Second Man from Heaven.]

§ 139. *The Human Nature of Christ.*[1]

The Twelve look up from the picture of the earthly life of Jesus, which they themselves had seen, to the Divine Glory of the Exalted Lord; but Paul looks back from the radiant light of this Glory, in which Christ had appeared to him, to His earthly life. That Christ was descended from Abraham and the fathers (Gal. 3:16; Rom. 9:5), and, in particular, that he was of the seed of David (Rom. 1:3), was known to Paul from His parentage and history. For the death of Christ and His resurrection on the third day, which form the basis of his preaching regarding Him, he appeals to tradition (1 Cor. 15:3, 4, 11), to the individual appearances of Christ to the Twelve and to the first disciples (1 Cor. 15:5, 7), as well as to himself (*ver.* 8). He knew that, at the feast of the Passover (1 Cor. 5:7), Jesus was crucified by the Jewish and Gentile rulers (1 Cor. 2:8; Gal. 2:20; 3:13; 5:11; Rom. 6:6). That he knows that, on the night when He was betrayed into the hands of His enemies, Christ instituted the Holy Supper (1 Cor. 11:23–25), only shows that he found the custom of breaking bread and consecrating the cup already existing in the Church, and inquired into its origin, and he mentions the fact in order that he may attach to it doctrines regarding the significance of this meal; and these doctrines he himself traces back to a higher origin (1 Cor. 11:23). That he repeatedly lays stress upon the burial of Christ (1 Cor. 15:4; Rom. 6:4), is closely connected with the circumstance that this guar-

---

[1] Compare *Weiss*, § 78.

antees the reality of Christ's death as well as that of His resurrection, and is therefore equally important for both the great saving facts of his system. He regards Christ as being immediately exalted to Heavenly glory by means of the resurrection, and he does not think of any special intermediate condition between the resurrection and the exaltation to Heaven. Only once does Paul set forth the sinlessness of Christ in a dogmatic manner (2 Cor. 5:21), because to him it is self-evident in the case of the Messiah, who is exalted to Heaven, and who had, by His death, redeemed the world from sin. It is highly significant how he, in order to set up the sacrificing love of Christ as a pattern, contrasts His pre-temporal state of existence with His earthly life (2 Cor. 8:9). As Paul says that Christ was born of a woman (Gal. 4:4), born of the seed of David *according to the flesh* (Rom. 1:3), we have a right to infer that Mary was descended from David; and we need no more reliable authority than Paul, although we have other testimony in favor of this view in Scripture.

If we inquire as to the idea which Paul has formed to himself of the Person of Christ during His earthly life, it appears from Rom. 1:3; 9:5, that in Him the *flesh* (*sarx*) is regarded as only one side of His being. The contrast is not so much between body, soul and spirit, as rather between the whole human nature of Christ as distinguished from a higher Divine nature which he possessed (Rom. 1:4). Now in all men the *flesh* is the seat of sin, and under the dominion of sin, not because the *flesh* is sinful in itself, but because, with the transgression of Adam, sin has come into the world, and by generation sin is propagated. Although the *flesh* of Christ is not a *flesh of sin*, which it cannot

## THE HUMAN NATURE OF CHRIST.

be, as he did not know sin (2 Cor. 5:21), He is nevertheless man in the fullest and truest sense (1 Cor. 15:21. Rom. 5:15)—true man such as Adam was before sin began to dwell and reign in him. And as, according to Pauline anthropology, flesh in the living man cannot be thought of otherwise than as possessed of a soul, Christ must also have had a human soul; and, as soul cannot be thought of otherwise than as ruled by spirit, Christ must have possessed a human spirit and human will.

We will now be better able to understand Rom. 8:3, where Paul states that God sent His own Son *in the likeness of sinful flesh*. Here Christ's Personality is conceived of as pre-existing; and the Son of God, when He became incarnate, appeared not "in the flesh of sin," which is an Ebionite conception, nor "in the likeness of flesh," which leads to Docetism, but "in the likeness of sinful flesh," which is the Pauline view. And the word *flesh* here manifestly refers to the entire nature of man, as in Rom. 1:3; 9:5. Christ could appear indeed "in the flesh," but not in the flesh of sin; for he must, of necessity, be "without sin" (2 Cor. 5:21). This expression, therefore, in Rom. 8:3 does not in any way call in question the actual humanity of Jesus, but only denies that He is tainted with sin.

Now if Christ, although a true man, had no sin in Him, had not the principle of death in Him, how was it possible for Him to die? According to Paul Christ died on account of sin (Rom. 6:10; 2 Cor. 5:21); but it was not on account of sin in Himself, but because our sin was laid upon Him. He bore our penalty—even the penalty of sin.

[ANALYSIS: 1) Christ was of the seed of David; 2) was crucified; 3) instituted the Holy Supper in commemoration of His death; 4) was buried; 5) was raised from the dead; 6) exalted to

Heaven ; 7) His sinlessness ; 8) in the fullness of time born of a woman ; 9) therefore a true man, though sinless ; 10) we must distinguish between the human and the Divine nature of Christ ; 11) the flesh of Christ not the seat of sin ; 12) Christ possessed a human body, a human soul, a human spirit and will ; 13) the meaning of Rom. 8:3 ; 14) this passage does not deny the reality of His human nature ; 15) His death brought about by our sin.]

# CHAPTER VIII.

### REDEMPTION AND JUSTIFICATION.

§ 140. *The Saving Significance of the Death of Christ.*[1]

If we ask whereby Christ in His manifestation upon earth has become the Mediator of Salvation, there is only one answer that can be given according to the Pauline view; and that answer is, by His death. Hence this death forms the real central-point of his preaching (1 Cor. 1:17, 18)—"the word of the Cross." He preaches Christ as crucified (Gal. 3:1 ; 1 Cor. 3:2). This death was one which Christ took upon Himself of His own free-will, for the cause of His death was different from that of all other men. It is only because all have sinned that death reigns over all the descendants of Adam (Rom. 5:12); yet Christ was not rendered subject to death simply because he was a true man, for He knew no sin. To the Incarnate Son of God death was by no means a necessity of Nature, not to speak of the shameful and painful death upon the Cross. It was an act of free obedience—a willing fulfillment of the purpose of God. He gave Himself for our sins, that He might deliver us out of this present evil world, according to the will of our God and Father (Gal. 1:4)—a manifestation of His great love to us (Gal. 2:20; 2 Cor. 5:14, 15).

Whether the death of Christ is regarded as a sacrifice of love on the part of God or on the part of Christ, it

---

[1] Compare *Weiss*, § 80 ; *Lechler*, vol. 2, pp. 34–50 ; *Schmid*, § 80.

took place in behalf of men (1 Cor. 11:24; 2 Cor. 5:15). How this is to be understood appears from Rom. 5:8, according to which Christ has died for us, inasmuch as we were sinners (Rom. 5:6), or on account of our sins (Rom. 4:25; Gal. 1:4; 1 Cor. 15:3). Now, since the evil which sin has brought upon men is death, the death of Christ, which was suffered for the salvation of men and because of their sin, can only have had the design of removing from them the miserable consequences of sin—*i.e.* the punishment of sin, which consists in death. If Christ, however, who did not as a sinless man need to die the death, dies in order to free sinners from death, His death is a vicarious one. Paul presents the idea of substitution without any reference to the Old Testament prophecy of the sin-bearing of the Servant of God, and connects it with the working out of our righteousness. God has made Him who did not know sin to be sin in our behalf, and has looked upon and treated Him as if He were a sinner, in order that we might become the righteousness of God in Him—*i. e.* that, on the ground of what happened to Him, we could be looked upon and treated as such as God declares to be righteous (2 Cor. 5:21). Here it is expressly asserted that the treatment of the Sinless One as a sinner was the means whereby the treatment of sinners as sinless was rendered possible, and so the new righteousness upon which the salvation of man depended was wrought out. Accordingly, the death of Christ, which was suffered for the salvation of men, stands vicariously for the death of all. His being treated as a sinner makes it possible that they should be treated as righteous, so that they need no longer die the death which He has died in their stead; and it is in this supreme act of kindness which He has shown men that the constraining power of His love towards them lies (2 Cor. 5:14, 15). When Paul says: "because we thus judge, that one died for all, therefore all died" (2 Cor. 5:14), this cannot refer to the ethical dying with Christ, as if therefore all are partakers of the benefits of Christ's death, for this ethical death is by no means the consequence of the death of Christ *in itself*—for the unbeliever, in spite of the sacrificial death made for all, is still in his sins; but this ethical death results from the fellowship of Christ's death, which is involved in the living fellowship with Him, the basis of which is laid in baptism (Rom. 6:4). Nor is this ethical death the consequence of Christ's death *for all*, since only believers enter into living fellowship with Christ, whereas His death has certainly taken place for all, and in itself stands for the death of all, whether or not men appropriate the salvation which is thereby provided. The *objective* matter of fact which Paul here affirms, that when Christ died the redeeming death for all, all died, has its *subjective* realization in the faith of the individual so soon as he becomes a believer.

According to Gal. 3:13, the painful and shameful death which Christ suffered on the Cross, in order that sinners might not die the death, is represented as the curse which was pronounced by the law against its transgressors (Gal. 3:10), and which now rests upon Him who is hanging upon the Cross. If Christ has become a curse in order to redeem us from this curse, then this passage says, only in a form which is conditioned by the context, exactly the same as 2 Cor. 5:21—that God has treated the Sinless One as a sinner, in order that He need not treat sinners as such.

It is Christ who has redeemed us (Gal. 1:13), and the price which was paid for this redemption from the curse of the law was His death on the Cross; and in 1 Cor. 6:20; 7:23, it is similarly said that we have been bought with an actual redemption-price, even *by His blood* (Rom. 3:25). In 1 Cor. 1:30 Christ also appears as the Author of our redemption, the underlying thought being that guilt holds man captive—in prison, as it were (*cf.* Eph. 1:7; Col. 1:4). For if the redemption which is found in Christ is the means whereby justification by grace is rendered possible (Rom. 3:24), it must be thought of as a redemption from the state of *guilt;* for it is the guilt which rests upon the sinner that hinders his justification. With the guilt of sin we are at the same time delivered from the *penalty* of sin, from the wrath of God (Rom. 5:9), as well as from spiritual and eternal death (Rom. 5:17, 21).

It is also in Rom. 3:24, 25, that Paul states more particularly in how far this redemption from the state of guilt rests in Christ. It is said that God has openly "set forth Christ Jesus, by His blood, to be a *propitiation* through faith." Here too, just as in Gal. 3:13, His death, and that, too, the violent, bloody death which He suffered on the Cross, is thought of as the redemption price. Christ, as our High Priest and sacrifice, is the *propitiation*, the *kapporeth*.[1] Sprinkled with His own blood, Christ was truly that which the cover, or *kapporeth*, or "mercy-seat," had been typically. Scripture also distinctly says that Christ presented Himself to God an expiatory sacrifice (Heb. 9:14, 28; Eph. 5:2) for the sins of mankind. This expiation or atonement by Christ is only appropriated *subjectively* through *faith*,

---

[1] The Greek word for *propitiation* is the same which in the Septuagint translation of the Old Testament is used for the *cover* of the Ark of the Covenant—the *kapporeth*, "the lid of expiation," translated in English "the mercy-seat."

and on its *objective* side it only has value in the *blood* of Christ.

God has, therefore, appointed the blood which was shed in the death of Christ to be the means of propitiation, which makes atonement for the sins of men, and therefore renders their redemption from the state of guilt possible. God willed to show His righteousness in the present time of salvation in such a manner that He might be at once just and righteous, and yet able to justify the believer (Rom. 3:26). Accordingly, in the blood of Christ He set forth to the world a means of propitiation through faith.

By means, then of the death of Christ, the world can become reconciled with God, who now no longer condemns those who accept the message of salvation. So long as man is under the bondage of sin, the wrath of God rests upon Him,[1] "because the mind of the flesh is enmity against God" (Rom. 8:7), and the wrath of God threatens the sinner with His punitive judgment (Rom. 5:9, 10). We can be saved from the wrath of God only through Jesus Christ, being justified by His blood (Rom. 5:9.)

[ANALYSIS: 1) Christ became our Mediator through His death; 2) which was voluntary; 3) He gave Himself for our sins; 4) to remove from believers the consequences of sin; 5) His death a vicarious one; 6) He was made sin in our behalf; 7) our salvation has not its ground in our ethical dying with Christ; 8) but in the death of Christ on the Cross; 9) He is our redemption price; 10) the propitiation; 11) even the true *kapporeth*; 12) He who made atonement for sins; 13) this atonement is only appropriated *subjectively* through faith; 14) has value only objectively in the *blood* of Christ; 15) only through Christ can men become reconciled to God.]

---

[1] God is a jealous God (Ex. 34:14; Deut. 6:15), and the Divine zeal is but the energy of the *Divine Holiness*. It turns itself avengingly against every violation of the Divine will, and manifests itself

§ 141. *The Death and Resurrection of Christ.*[1]

According to Rom. 8:3,[2] sin, which always drew a *condemnation* upon men (Rom. 5:16, 18) by the dominion which it had over them, has now, through the incarnation and death of the Son of God, received a condemnation itself by being robbed of its power and dominion. For there is now no longer any *condemnation* to them that are in Christ Jesus (8:1), because the Son of God has appeared in the flesh, and by Him the judgment on sin was carried out in the flesh. But the question here arises, In what way was the *condemnation* of sin carried out? Some would refer this condemnation exclusively to the *blotting out* of sin by Christ's holy life; but the truer meaning is that Christ condemned sin at some definite moment in His life, when an actual *condemnation* in the proper sense of the word took place. This is the moment of death (Rom. 5:16, 18). The whole doctrine of redemption as taught in the Epistle to the Romans points to the fact that the condemnation of sin is to be conceived of as carried out in the death of Christ. The sin of mankind lay upon Christ, their surety and representative (" Him who knew no sin He made to be sin on our behalf," 2 Cor. 5:21), and in Him was condemned. And this condemnation was really carried out in the penalty of death. The powerlessness of the law was the work of the *flesh*, because sin in human nature, condemned by the law, could not be blotted out, but only inflamed to so much

as *Divine wrath*. For the wrath of God is the most intense energy of the Holy will of God, the zeal of His wounded Love.

[1] Compare *Weiss*, § 81; *Lechler*, vol. 2, pp. 50–56.

[2] "For what the law could not do, in that it was weak through the flesh, God sending His own Son in the likeness of sinful flesh and for sin, condemned sin in the flesh."

the greater intensity. On the other hand, when our sin was laid on the Holy humanity of Christ, sin was blotted out and reduced to naught, for sin was condemned. Expiation was made in the death of Christ, and of that expiation His resurrection bears witness.[1] They who are in Christ Jesus, with the remission, at the same time have the power to overcome sin—both blessings subsisting in Christ in inseparable unity.

The resurrection of Christ is the proof not only of His Messiahship, but also of that saving significance of His death which has made Him the Mediator of salvation. And although the resurrection of Christ by no means stands on the same footing with His death in the work of procuring salvation, it is nevertheless, according to 1 Cor. 15:3, 4, 14, one of the principal articles of evangelical faith. It is the fact of His resurrection which should lead men to believe in Jesus as the Messiah (Acts 17:31), and according to 1 Cor. 15:12–15 the faith of Christians rests upon the proclamation of His resurrection; for by means of that resurrection He is exalted to His Messianic sovereignty at God's Right Hand (Rom. 1:4; 8:34)—in consequence of which sovereignty He has become the Mediator of salvation. This function of Mediator of salvation is, however, grounded solely upon His death. To Paul Christ's resurrection proves that His death was not the death of a sinner, but the vicarious death of the sinless Mediator of salvation, who is exalted to Messianic sovereignty, and which death is therefore the ground of our redemption and reconciliation. If Christ has not risen, our faith is vain—we are yet in our sins (1 Cor. 15:17). If that were the case, there would be no reason to assume that by His death the guilt of our sin is taken away

[1] Compare *Philippi* on Rom. 8:3.

from us. Accordingly, the assurance that God does not condemn those that are in Christ Jesus is owing, primarily, it is true, to the death of Christ, but still more to His resurrection and exaltation to God's Right Hand (Rom. 8:34), inasmuch as these events prove that His death was the death of the Mediator of salvation, who has redeemed us from condemnation. Hence the righteousness which is of faith bids us, not first of all to seek to bring up Christ from the dead, but to believe that God has raised Him up, and therefore made Him Lord and Mediator of salvation (Rom. 10:7, 9). It is in Rom. 4:25 that the Apostle gives the clearest expression to this relation of the death and the resurrection, according to which the former is the means of procuring salvation, the latter the means of appropriating it. Christ was delivered up (to death) for our trespasses, and was raised for our justification. The *objective* atonement was accomplished by means of the death of Christ; but the appropriation of it in justification is only possible if we believe in the saving significance of His death, and we can attain to faith in that only if it is sealed by means of the resurrection[1] (compare Phil. 3:9, 10).

[1] According to Paul, the resurrection of Jesus from the dead is as essential to the work of salvation as His death on the Cross (1 Cor. 15:4; Rom. 4:25). We may present Paul's teaching under two heads—1) the importance of the resurrection in relation to the Person of Jesus, and 2) its importance to believers.

I. With respect to the *Person of Jesus*, His resurrection is of the greatest importance—1) because by it He is proved to be the Son of God (Rom. 1:4). This attestation took place with (in) power—*i. e.* it was an act of Divine omnipotence, characterized by power and energy. Paul, therefore, asserts that in Christ's resurrection from the dead we have the strongest proof that He is actually the Son of God.

2) In Rom. 6:9 Paul also refers to the effect that the resurrection

[ANALYSIS: 1) The Son of God condemned sin in the flesh; 2) at the time of His death; 3) this the true meaning of Rom. 8:3; 4) the resurrection of Christ the proof of His Messiahship: 5) the assurance of our justification rests on Christ's resurrection; 6) the importance of the resurrection in relation to the Person of Jesus; 7) He is attested to be the Son of God; 8) He now possesses an absolute, eternal, Divine life; 9) He is now Lord of the dead and of the living; 10) the significance of the resurrection of Christ to believers; 11) it is the basis of their justification; 12) the foundation of the new life; 13) the pledge of their own resurrection.]

## § 142. *Justification by Faith.*[1]

Salvation for the world of sin has been given in the Person of Christ, in His death, resurrection, and exaltation. But this salvation must be appropriated by the individual, who by God's agency is placed in a state of grace by means of the word and of baptism, whereby he is grafted into Christ and becomes partaker of His mediatorial death (2 Cor. 5:18–20; Rom. 6:3–5). Hence arises a new life, the new creature, the growth of a new

had on Christ Himself: by virtue of His resurrection Christ dieth no more, but lives an absolute, eternal, Divine life ; 3) In Rom. 14:9 the aim and result of the resurrection life of Jesus are made to consist in the fact that He is Lord, and, by virtue of His death and resurrection, Lord of both the dead and the living.

II. On the other hand, the resurrection of Jesus has, in Paul's estimation, just as important a *significance for believers.* 1) It is the basis of justification (Rom. 4:25 ; 1 Cor. 15:17). If Christ be dead but not risen, then His death has no reconciling and justifying efficacy : in so far faith is without validity ; but the resurrection is the Divine seal of the work of atonement. 2) It is the foundation of the new life in believers (Rom. 6:4). Accordingly, the new life of the Christian is the image as well as the fruit of the raising of Christ from the dead (2 Cor. 4:10–12). 3) It is the beginning, ground, and pledge of the future resurrection of believers (1 Cor. 6:14). This is expressed more clearly in Rom. 8:11 (*dia* with the genitive being assumed as the right reading) and 1 Cor. 15:20. (After *Lechler.*)

[1] Compare *Weiss*, § 82; *Lechler*, vol. 2, pp. 63–67; *Schmid*, § 82.

man (2 Cor. 5:17; Gal. 6:15). The human will, by the grace and power of God, must cease its resistance against the Holy Ghost, and receive His grace, surrender to the love of God, apprehend the precious message of salvation, and obey the will of God. The life of the new man then passes through manifold stages of development closely connected one with another—namely, justification, sonship or adoption, sanctification and hope.[1]

[1] Paul takes it for granted in all his Epistles that there is an order of grace—that the Holy Spirit works in the hearts of men according to some spiritual law. With him God the Father is the source of grace (Gal. 1:3; 2:21; 5:8), Christ the Mediating imparter (Gal. 1:3, 6; 6:18), and the Holy Spirit the person who applies the gifts of grace and redemption to the heart of sinful man (Gal. 3:2, 5, 14; 4:6). Paul also implies that the grace of God through the *Word* acts *before* conversion in a three-fold way: 1) by *prevenient* grace, the implanting of the first holy thought and godly desire; 2) by *preparative* grace, which prepares the heart; 3) by *exciting* grace, which works in the heart. In the *act* of conversion, which is brought about by the Holy Spirit through the Word as an instrument, we may distinguish between—1) *operating* grace, which works *a*) the knowledge of sin, and *b*) compunction of heart; and 2) *completing* grace, which works faith and confidence in Christ, which is the final act of conversion, and takes place instantaneously. *After* conversion we may speak of the grace of the Holy Spirit as—1) *co-operating* grace, which preserves him in the faith, and assists and strengthens him; and 2) *indwelling* grace, which dwells in the heart of man and changes it spiritually, enabling him to grow in grace and sanctification.

As the acts of applying grace follow one another in certain relations and connections, we may arrange the "Order of the Works of Grace" (Acts 26:17:18) somewhat as follows: 1) The calling or vocation (Gal. 1:6–8); 2) the illumination (Gal. 1:3, 4, 6; 2:16, 21; 3:22–24); 3) regeneration (Gal. 2:20; 3:2; 6:15); 4) conversion (Gal. 1:13, 14, 24; 4:3, 9), which consists of—5) repentance (Gal. 1:23; 5:13, 16, 22), and 6) faith (which consists of three elements: knowledge, Gal. 4:9; 3:23, 2:2; assent, Gal. 1:6,8, 11, 12; 2:14; confidence or trust, Gal. 2:16, 3:26); 7) Justification (which consists of

The new righteousness which the Gospel proclaims is a gift of God, who justifies man through grace, by not imputing to him his sins, on the ground of the suffering and death of Christ, and by imputing to him the righteousness which was obtained for the believer by the complete fulfillment of the law by Christ. The fundamental doctrine of Justification by Faith is most fully discussed in the Epistles to the Galatians and to the Romans. In the last Epistle it is the leading theme (Rom. 1:16, 17). After the Apostle has shown that it is impossible of oneself, by means of the works of the law, to attain to a righteousness that avails before God, he continues in 3:21, 22, thus: "But now apart from the law a righteousness of God hath been manifested— even the righteousness of God through faith in Jesus Christ unto all them that believe."

This is not a righteousness of our own, which we have earned ourselves, but a righteousness which is of God, because He alone bestows it (Rom. 10:3), and He alone procured it for us (1 Cor. 1:30). It is a gift, a free bestowment of God's grace (Rom. 3:24; 6:23). It is this righteousness which is now proclaimed in the Gospel (Rom. 1:16, 17), as being brought about by means of the death of Christ (2 Cor. 5:21). It is guaranteed through *Christ* as the *Mediator*, His death and resurrection forming the condition (Rom. 4:24, 25; 5:9).

But four questions here come under consideration:

two things—*a*) remission of sins, Gal. 1:4; 3:13, 22; and *b*) the imputation of Christ's righteousness, Gal. 2:21; 3:27); 8) the mystical union with God (Gal. 2:20; 3:27, 28), 9) adoption as sons of God (Gal. 3:26; 4:4, 5, 6, 7); 10) sanctification (which consists of—*a*) of renovation or the putting off of the old man, Gal. 5:13, 17, 19-21; and *b*) of sanctification proper, the putting on of the new man, a walking by the Spirit, Gal. 5:16, 25). (See my "Studies in the Book," vol. 1, pp. 14, 15; vol. 2, pp. 47-52).

1) what is the meaning of the expression *to justify*; 2) in what does *justification* itself consist? 3) what is the condition of justification? and 4) what is the true nature of faith?

1) It is evident that Paul always uses the word *dikaioun*, "to justify," in the sense of *esteeming, pronouncing, accounting, treating as righteous*, both according to the measure of the law (Rom. 2:13; 3:20), and also according to grace.[1] And in the whole discussion of the Epistle to the Romans (and Galatians) the justification of the sinner before God is the theme —that man, although not justified by the law, is esteemed and treated as righteous by God. In all these passages, the fundamental meaning of *to justify* is the *forensic* and *juridical* signification, *to account as righteous*. It is, moreover, unquestionable that *to justify* is explained by Paul as an *imputation of righteousness* ("to reckon righteousness," Rom. 4:6, 22), to a person who is not righteous in himself (Rom. 4:5); and this imputation includes also the *forgiveness of sins* (Rom. 4:6–9), man thus having peace with God (Rom. 5:1), and standing in a friendly relation with Him, being no longer his enemy, but reconciled to Him (Rom. 5:9; 10:11). The contrast of "to justify" is therefore "to accuse" (Rom. 8:33). The antithesis of justification is condemnation (Rom. 5:18). Whosoever is not justified is liable to punishment, and under the curse (Gal. 3:10, 11; Rom, 10:13). From all this there can be no doubt as to the forensic character of the words "to justify" as used by Paul.

The opposite interpretation, which understands "to justify" as *making righteous*, has been brought forward by the Rationalists, by the Roman Catholic Church, and by such Protestants as blend *justification* with sancti-

[1] See the able discussion of *Schmid*, § 82.

## JUSTIFICATION BY FAITH. 143

fication, and connect the former not with faith, where it rightly belongs, but with love and good works. Not only is the signification of the word itself, but the context everywhere, opposed to this view.

2) If we examine more closely the Divine act of *justification* we find that it involves two things—*a*) that *sin is not imputed to the sinner as guilt*, or *forgiveness of sins* (Rom. 4:5-8; Gal. 3:11, 13; *cf.* Acts 13:38, 39). Since it is in consequence of sin that man becomes unrighteous, God can justify him who is not righteous in himself only by not reckoning unto him his sin (2 Cor. 5:19), or by forgiving him his sin (Rom. 4:7). *Before* justification man is under sin, under bondage, under the curse of the law (Gal. 3:13, 22, 23); *after* justification the sinner's relation to God is changed, for he is in a state of grace (Gal. 1:6; 2:21; 3:2, 5, 14), and freed from the bondage and curse of the law (Gal. 2:4; 3:25; 4:31; 5:1, 13). We may call this the *negative* side of justification.

The second part in justification consists—*b*) *in the imputation to the believer of the righteousness obtained by Christ through His fulfilling the law*. A righteousness has been obtained by Christ (Gal. 2:21) which is reckoned unto the believer as if he possessed it (Gal. 3:21, 27; Rom. 4:11). We may say, therefore, that the imputing or reckoning of righteousness unto the believer is the *positive* side of justification, for faith is counted to the sinner as righteousness (Rom. 4:5; *cf.* Phil. 3:9).

Our *peace* (Rom. 5:1) is conditioned on these two points, and thus the relation between God and man is constituted so that we have access to God (Rom. 5:2). We are thus reconciled to God (Rom. 5:10, 11; 2 Cor. 5:20), and have the assurance of the Divine love to us, this love being spread abroad in our hearts (Rom. 5:5).

Enmity has departed, and we know ourselves to be sons of God (Rom. 8:14–17; Gal. 4:6, 7). Justification is, therefore, the atonement rendered subjective and brought to consciousness. Whom God thus justifies no one can any more accuse; for He will no longer reckon the sins on account of which one could be accused.

3) God has appointed the condition under which He justifies the sinner. This condition is faith. His righteousness is revealed only unto believers ("unto all them that believe," Rom. 3:22; "to every one that believeth," Rom. 10:4); "every one that believeth is justified" (Acts 13:39). The righteousness of God is attained and appropriated *by* faith (Rom. 1:17; 5:1), even *through* faith (Rom. 3:22, 22, 25, 30). To speak more accurately, faith is the condition of justification or righteousness (Rom. 9:30; 10:6); or, to express it in another way, justification is attained upon the occasion of faith; the new righteousness is a righteousness which is of faith (Rom. 4:11, 13; 10:10). Accordingly, the act of justification can also be so described as that faith is reckoned by God as righteousness (Rom. 4:5, 24). This, however, is a pure act of Divine grace, accomplished immediately and at once, as soon as faith is given. It is not a gradual process, in which there are stages;—believers *are* justified (1 Cor. 6:11; Rom. 5:9, 1).

The act of God in the matter of justification is by no means an absolutely new one. It is not only borne witness to prophetically in the Old Testament, but it has already found its typical precedent in the history of Abraham. According to Gen. 15:6, Abraham believed, and his faith was reckoned unto him for righteousness (Gal. 3:6; Rom. 4:3).

4) But it is still a matter of dispute as to what is the positive Pauline conception of faith. In Paul's view

faith is the confident grasping and holding fast of Jesus Christ, which presupposes a renunciation of one's own sufficiency, and is an entry into the fellowship with Christ. The righteousness which is of faith forms the antithesis of the righteousness which is of the law (Gal. 3:11; Rom. 10:5, 6); the law and faith are mutually exclusive opposites (Gal. 3:23, 25; 5:4, 5; Rom. 4:13, 14). He who is justified *by faith* is justified "apart from the works of the law" (Rom. 3:28). Faith, first of all, generally refers to Christ or to the Gospel (Rom. 1:16, 17); it is the subjective origin of *righteousness* or justification, and it is continuously that to which the latter refers (Rom. 3:22). The Pauline faith is not a mere honesty of conviction. In a few passages, like in Rom. 3:3, *pistis* has, indeed, the signification of faithfulness; yet in most passages this idea is not contained in it, but only that of *conviction* and *trust*. The idea of moral conviction is involved in Rom. 14:22, 23. Again, faith is not a mere theoretical and sure belief in the Gospel, or an historical knowledge of Christ, but a lively inward apprehension of Christ and His Gospel. Abraham trusted in the Divine promise under circumstances which contradicted all human expectation (Rom. 4:18), and did not allow himself to be perplexed in his trust by these circumstances (Rom. 4:19, 20). The faith of Christians is a similar absolute trust; and, accordingly, it is characterized in *ver.* 24 as a trust in Him who has raised up Jesus our Lord from the dead. Now, since justification is brought about by means of the atoning death of Christ, faith can equally be described as a faith which is grounded upon Christ (Rom. 10:14; *cf.* Col. 2:5; Phil. 1:29), or as a faith which rests in Christ (Gal. 3:26; *cf.* Col. 1:4; Eph. 1:15); or, lastly, as a trust in Christ (Rom. 3:22, 26; Gal. 2:16; 3:22).

This trust is evinced by their calling upon His name (1 Cor. 1:2) as the Mediator of salvation (Rom. 10:14). Faith is, therefore, the trustful acceptance of the gift of Grace offered by God. It is the key-note of religious feeling, not the normal disposition of the moral will. In faith the soul lays hold on Jesus, thus entering into life communion with Him;—by faith Christ dwells in the heart, so that He lives in man (1 Cor. 1:9; Rom. 8:10; Gal. 2:20).

Where there is true faith, all three elements of faith (knowledge, Gal. 4:9; 3:23; 2:2; assent, Gal. 1:6, 8, 11, 12; 2:14; and trust, Gal. 2:16; 3:26) must be present: but confidence or trust in Christ is the principal part of faith. The power and energy of faith are two-fold, receptive and operative. *Receptive* faith passively receives Christ and everything obtained by his merit (Gal. 3:14, 22; 2:16), while *operative* faith manifests itself actively by works of love (Gal. 5:6, 14, 22; 6:10). Faith, so to speak, has two hands. One, which it extends upwards to embrace Christ with all His benefits, and by *this we are justified;*—not, however, as the *ground* of our justification, for this is the atoning death of Christ; nor as the *cause* of our justification, for this is the abounding mercy of God; nor as the *means* by which grace is *conferred* upon us, for this is done by means of the Word and Sacraments, but simply as the means whereby forgiveness of sins is *accepted*. The other hand reaches downward to perform the works of love, and by this we *prove the reality of faith*, but are not thereby justified.

[ANALYSIS: 1) Salvation must be appropriated by the individual; 2) the new life; 3) there is an order of the works of grace; 4) the work of grace in conversion; 5) the order of the works of grace; 6) the righteousness by faith a gift of God; 7) the great theme of the Epistle to the Romans ; 8) not a righteousness of our own ; 9) four questions must be answered ; 10) the meaning of " to justify ;" 11) it has the forensic and juridical signification ; 12) the antithesis of justification ; 13) the error of the interpretation "to make righteous ;" 14) in what justification consists ; 15) forgiveness of sins the negative side of justification ; 16) imputation of Christ's righteousness the positive side ; 17) the condition of justification is faith ; 18) the nature of faith ; 19) the Pauline conception of *pistis* ; 20) the three elements of faith ; 21) the two-fold power of faith ; 22) the ground of our justification ; 23) the cause of our justification ; 24) the means used by God for conferring justification ; 25) faith but the means for accepting it.]

§ 143. *The Teaching Concerning Sonship.*[1]

If the believer is justified by faith, on the ground of the atoning death of Christ (Rom. 5:1), he has peace, and the love of God is shed abroad in his heart through the Holy Ghost which is given unto him (5:5). God who has given him the greatest proof of His love in the delivering up of His Son at a time when he was still His enemy on account of his sin, can now, when He is reconciled to him, and when God has justified him (*vers.* 6–9), only show him His love more richly (*ver.* 10). Nothing can any longer separate the Christian from the love of God, which is bestowed upon him in Christ Jesus (Rom. 8:32, 38, 39). The Christian is beloved of God (Rom. 1:7 ; 2 Cor. 13:13). This new relation to God is represented as the relation of a son, being brought about by a juridical act, described as adoption (Gal. 3:26 ; 4:4,5), by means of which man is put into a relation to God which is opposed to his previous servile relation. Man is no more in himself a child of God than he is righteous in himself ; it is a deed of His grace through which God adopts him as His child. As man is declared righteous by God, so is he also received

[1] Compare *Weiss*, § 83; *Lechler*, vol. 2, pp. 70–72.

as a child through the declaration of God. To the apostle adoption is a legally valid relation, into which man is translated. Like justification, adoption takes place immediately in consequence of faith (Gal. 3:26); yet it appears in Rom. 8:23 as something which believers have still to wait for—seeing that, like Christ Himself, it is not till after their earthly life that they enter into the full rights of children, and therewith into that position in which their sonship is perfectly revealed (Rom. 8:19). Believers, indeed, already possess a part of these rights of children. As sons of God they call upon Him as their Father with a childlike trust, which excludes all fear (Gal. 4:6; Rom. 8:15), and hence they are heirs of God (8:17).

The sum of all the blessings that the believer has received through grace in his new filial relationship, the apostle describes as *peace*, and as derived throughout from God *our Father*. But, with Paul, *peace* does not simply denote *peace with God*, but that inner feeling, that inner satisfaction which the possession of salvation begets, and which the Christian accordingly possesses in faith (Gal. 5:22; Rom. 15:13). Peace with God is the ground of this inner peace of soul. This peace, along with righteousness, characterizes the Christian's new state of salvation (Rom. 14:17). Along with these there stands here in Rom. 14:17, as in Gal. 5:22; Rom. 15:13, joy. Outward afflictions cannot do away with this joy (2 Cor. 6:10; 8:2).

In itself adoption is an altogether objective transaction, a pure act of Divine grace, which can first receive its significance for our consciousness, when the inner assurance of it is worked in us. This, however, can only take place by God Himself giving us the Spirit of adoption (Rom. 8:15), which testifies that we are God's children (*ver.* 16), by teaching us to call upon the Father with childlike confidence (Gal. 4:6). Through the Spirit the love of God has been shed abroad in our hearts (Rom. 5:5), and has become an object of our consciousness, and this assurance of the love of God is identical with the consciousness of adoption. The fruit of the Spirit is, accordingly, also *joy* and *peace* (Gal. 5:22), which can naturally only be found when we have become certain of our state of grace. This peace is a peace of God (Phil. 4:7), which He gives through His Spirit, and this joy is a joy in the Holy Ghost (Rom. 14:17; 15:13).

[ANALYSIS: 1) The believer has peace; 2) nothing can separate the Christian from the love of God; 3) this new relation is described as adoption; 4) is also a forensic action; 5) it takes place immediately; 6) nevertheless on earth we possess but a part; 7) the inner peace of the soul is the result of peace with God; 8) the three characteristics of the Christian's state of salvation; 9) adoption an act of Divine Grace; 10) the assurance of it is wrought in us by the Spirit; 11) peace and joy are closely related to each other.]

## CHAPTER IX.

### THE NEW LIFE.

§ 144. *The Doctrine Concerning Baptism.*[1]

Reception into the Christian Church took place through baptism into the name of Christ (1 Cor. 1:13-16). But Paul never treats of baptism merely as an external act, but as a spiritual-corporeal act. "For in one Spirit were we all baptized into one body" (1 Cor. 12:13). Baptism is a "putting on of Christ" (Gal. 3:27), "a washing away of sins" (Acts 22:16; 1 Cor. 6:11), a baptism into the death of Christ (Rom. 6:3). Paul refers to baptism as that act by which the Christian has been taken into communion with Christ (Rom. 6:3-5). It is the sacrament of initiation into this communion (Gal. 3:27; *cf.* also Col. 2:11, 12). The communication of the Spirit, which first makes the believer assured of his justification, and must therefore be directly connected with the bestowal of forgiveness of sins in baptism, takes place also according to him in baptism, in which we are baptized with one Spirit, into one body (1 Cor. 12:13), which is also in the same verse represented in another way, as a having been made to drink of one Spirit. And, indeed, it is the *Holy* Spirit which is then poured out into the heart (Rom. 5:5; 1 Cor. 6:19; 2 Cor. 6:6); or, what is, according to 1 Cor. 12:3, identical therewith, the Spirit of *God* (1 Cor. 3:16; 6:11; Rom. 8:11, 14). This Spirit is now the principle of a new life in the Christian.

[1] Compare *Weiss*, § 84. This section properly belongs under the Doctrine of the Church, or Ecclesiology.

The Spirit of God which is communicated to Christians in baptism is, according to Rom. 8:9, none other than the Spirit of Christ (Gal. 4:6; 1 Cor. 2:16; 2 Cor. 3:17). Christ is in man through His Spirit, just as God also Himself in His Spirit dwells in man (1 Cor. 3:16). Paul confesses of himself that he no longer lives, but Christ lives in him (Gal. 2:20). A man does not become a true Christian until Christ is formed in him (Gal. 4:19). In this most intimate living fellowship, Christ and the believer become one spirit (1 Cor. 6:17). This living fellowship with Christ commences in baptism, when His Spirit is communicated to us. The word that goes before offers to all collectively the gracious gift which baptism conveys to the particular definite individual. In Rom. 6:3, Paul says that those who were baptized "were baptized into Christ." We must take this in the sense of a being baptized into Him, whereby one is put into a real fellowship of life with Christ (Gal. 3:27). And the consequence of their having put on Christ, is that they are now in Him (Gal. 3:28). If the Christian feels himself in a real fellowship with Christ, he has been crucified with Him (Gal. 2:20; *cf.* 6:14 ; Rom. 6:6), and has died with Him (Rom. 6:8; Gal. 2:20). Baptism, which has translated him into this fellowship, is, accordingly, not merely a being baptized into Christ, but more especially a being baptized into His death (Rom. 6:3). The Apostle describes a psychological event, mysterious indeed, but real and certain, although conceivable only by *experience* of the new birth. As the death of Christ is the crown and chief element of His redemptive work, baptism above all introduces into union with the *death* of Christ. If by baptism we are brought into fellowship with Christ's death, it follows that we are also buried with Him, inasmuch as burial is the attestation of the truth and reality of death (Rom. 6:4). But as incorporation into Christ's death is the death of the old man, so is incorporation into Christ's resurrection the resurrection of the new man. We can live in Christ only as He lives in us; and from Gal. 2:20 we learn that, as a consequence of our being baptized—of our being crucified with Christ—He lives in us; His spiritual, holy life takes the place of our natural sinful life by His receiving us into the fellowship of His resurrection life. Paul lays stress on the fact that in baptism we become assured of the beginning, in principle, of the new life. That which brings salvation in this dying and rising up again with Christ in baptism does not consist in the saving efficacy of His death and resurrection being thereby appropriated *by us*, which takes place only through faith, but it consists in this, that a new life is implanted in us—we are ingrafted into Christ. Paul nowhere speaks of what Christians *did*, but of what *was done* in them in baptism. It is only in appearance that it seems, according to Gal. 5:24, as if man accomplishes anything himself. Moreover, this very passage shows that the "crucifying" takes place in baptism when one becomes a member of Christ (*cf.* 1 Cor. 1:12, 13).

If in the communication of the Spirit in baptism the believer experiences a dying and a resurrection through his being translated into the fellowship of life with Christ, then nothing less has happened to him than a new creation—the new birth wrought by the Holy Spirit through the Word. If any man is in Christ he is a new creation; the old things are passed away—behold, they are become new (2 Cor. 5:17). It appears also, from the connection of Gal. 6:14, 15, that with the crucifying to the world the Christian has become a new creation. With Paul all baptized Christians are *saints*, holy—(1 Cor. 1:2; 6:1, 2; 14:33; 2 Cor. 1:1; 8:4; 9:1; Rom. 1:7; 8:27; etc.)—for they belong neither to any other man (1 Cor. 7:23) nor to themselves (1 Cor. 6:19, 20), but to God alone, who has bought them with a price, and are thereby become His exclusive possession. This consecration to God extends even to everything which belongs to Christians as Christians; and Paul traces this consecration back to the working of the Holy Ghost, which they have received in baptism. He who has died unto sin in baptism is freed from the dominion of sin, and therewith made a servant of righteousness, even to God Himself (Rom. 6:18, 22).

The real aim of the dispensation of Grace which is found in Christianity is to work out the righteousness of man. God works out this righteousness in two ways: 1) by the new creation, the implanting of the new life, which has its beginning in baptism, and which develops through growth in sanctification, and therewith into actual righteousness and holiness of life; and 2) by justification, which is an individual, completed act, in which God daily, for Christ's sake, forgives the believer all his sins, and regards him as possessing the righteousness of Christ. Justification does not presuppose holiness; nor, truly speaking, is holiness (active righteousness) the necessary consequence of justification. Holiness is the fruit of the Spirit, the development of the new life implanted in the believer at his baptism; and the way to it is through sanctification. As there is, therefore, a beginning of the new life, this new life is not only capable of development, but requires it. This leads us to consider Paul's presentation of the doctrine of the Lord's Supper.

[ANALYSIS: 1) Baptism is the sacrament of initiation into communion with Christ; 2) in it the Holy Spirit is bestowed; 3) which is the Spirit of God and of Christ; 4) now fellowship with Christ begins; 5) the meaning of Rom. 6:3; 6) we are brought into fellowship with Christ's death; 7) and with Christ's resurrection; 8) the beginning of the new life; 9) with Paul all baptized Christians are saints; 10) and are consecrated to God; 11) God works out the righteousness of man in two ways; 12) there is a distinction between the new birth (regeneration), justification, and sanctification; 13) the new life develops through sanctification.]

### § 145. *The Lord's Supper.*[1]

If the ground of the new life of the Christian is laid in baptism, the Lord's Supper serves to its further nourishment. In 1 Cor. 10:1–4 Paul gives us an undoubted right to put together baptism and the Lord's Supper as the means of grace, which serve the grounding and nourishment of the new and higher life of the Christian. He there represents Israel's experiences of grace in the Wilderness as types of the experiences of grace which Christians have had. Christian baptism is regarded as the antitype of the baptism which the Israelites had under the cloud and in the sea (*vers.* 1, 2); and the manna (the bread from heaven) and the water that issued from the rock are regarded as spiritual food and spiritual drink (*vers.* 3, 4)—types of the Lord's Supper. As these gifts supported redeemed Israel during its journey through the Wilderness, so the Lord's Supper is regarded as the Church's means of spiritual nourishment.

The Lord's Supper was instituted by the Lord (1 Cor. 11:20), and is distinctly spoken of as His cup and His table (1 Cor. 10:21; 11:27). Paul gives us the earliest account of its institution (for his Epistle to the Corinthians was written in A. D. 57—earlier than any of the Gospels);

---

[1] Compare, *Weiss*, § 85. This topic properly belongs to the doctrine of the Church, or Ecclesiology.

## THE LORD'S SUPPER. 155

and he, no doubt, received his information either directly or indirectly from the other Apostles. When Paul appeals (1 Cor. 11:23) to a communication which had been made to him personally by the Lord, this does not refer to the narrative itself regarding the institution of the Supper, which had been delivered by the original Apostles to all in the same manner, but to its *design*, and the consequent demands that are made upon those who celebrate it.

The essential significance of the Lord's Supper is, that it brings us into a real fellowship with Christ, and therefore supports and strengthens (although from a peculiar side) the fellowship which is established in baptism, and which is the ground of the new life. The Lord's Supper is the communion of the body and blood of Christ (1 Cor. 10:16). In its nature it is not limited to an act of remembrance (1 Cor. 11:24, 25)—in which case it would be simply a commemoration, inasmuch as believers show the Lord's death till He come (1 Cor. 11:26), but it is a *communion of the blood and body* of Christ (10:16)—*i. e.*, it brings us into actual communion with Christ, real participation in His body and blood. Just as those who offer sacrifice to idols, and partake of the flesh of the offerings, put themselves by this means in actual communion with demons (1 Cor. 10:20), so the table of the Lord is an actual communion with the body and blood of Christ. For this reason, whoever taketh the bread and the cup unworthily, not discerning the Lord's body, sins against Christ—eats and drinks condemnation to himself, and makes himself guilty of the body and blood of the Lord (1 Cor. 11:27-30).

In conformity with the meaning which Christ Himself had given to the bread and wine in the Supper

(Matt. 26:26–29; Mark 14:22–25; Luke 22:15–20), to Paul the real fellowship with Christ, which the Supper specifically brings about, is owing to the participation in His body and in His blood, which is brought about by the partaking of the consecrated bread and cup (1 Cor. 10:16). The participation in His body cannot possibly merely denote that believers belong to the Church; for 1 Cor. 10:17 expressly adduces the union of the many into an organic unity, which is brought about by the one bread, as an evidence that the bread is not common bread, the partaking of which in common by no means produces such a unity, but is such a bread as brings about participation in a third person, who can become a bond of such a unity. If now, according to Rom. 12:4, 5, this third person is Christ Himself, then here it is the body of Christ that is truly, but in a supernatural manner, received in the Supper. Similarly the communion of the blood of Christ (1 Cor. 10:16) cannot be merely an expression for the reconciliation which it provided, and in which the believer participates directly in faith (Rom. 3:25). As to the manner in which Christ can make us partake of His body that was given up to death for us, and of His blood that was then shed, Paul has certainly not speculated, but he has, on the contrary, confined himself to the words of the institution; and in these words he has found the assurance that in the Lord's Supper we become participants of the body and blood of Christ.

Even those who partake unworthily receive the body and blood of the Lord; but they are thus guilty of them, for which they are punished. At Corinth abuses had occurred in connection with the celebration of the love feast, with which the Church was wont to connect the celebration of the breaking of bread instituted by the Lord (1 Cor. 11:20–22). The rich separated themselves from the poor, and reveled in the abundance they had brought with them. This desecration of the Lord's Supper, which had thus become a profane feast, made a real celebration of it impossible (*ver.* 20). If one partook of the bread or the cup of the Lord in this mood, one did so unworthily, and became guilty of the body and blood of the Lord (*ver.* 27). Even the unworthy partaker has therefore become a participant of the body and blood of the Lord; but he has sinned against the Lord, because he has not discerned the body in which he has participated through the Supper; he has not appreciated it in its significance as the bearer of a blessing, and so he has eaten and drank judgment unto himself (1 Cor. 11:29). By such a sin man brings upon himself a judgment of God (*ver.* 29), which can naturally be thought of only as a punishment (*ver.* 34), just as Paul saw, in the numerous cases of sickness and death which had at that time befallen the Church, a Divine punishment of the profanation of the sacred meal (*ver.* 30). Accordingly, he demands earnest self-examination before partaking of the Supper (1 Cor. 11:28), in order that they should become, not worse by the misuse of this means of grace, but better by the right use of it (1 Cor. 11:17), by being strengthened and furthered by it in their faith in the atoning efficacy of the death of Christ. How this is required for a healthy development of the Christian life, we shall show in what follows.

[ANALYSIS: 1) The sacrament of baptism is the **initiation**, the sacrament of the Lord's Supper the nourishment of the new life; 2) the meaning of 1 Cor. 10:1–4; 3) the institution of the Lord's Supper; 4) Paul in 1 Cor. 11:23 speaks of a revelation concerning the *design* of this sacrament; 5) the significance of the Lord's Supper;

6) not simply an act of remembrance ; 7) it brings us into real participation with Christ ; 8) unworthy partaking.]

§ 146. *The Process of the Development of the New Life, or Sanctification.*[1]

The more the Spirit that is bestowed in baptism becomes the determining rule of the whole Christian life, so much the more the antagonistic power of the flesh and of sin is broken, and righteousness and holiness are realized in man. If the Spirit has become the impelling power of a new life, the Christian becomes "spiritual"—one who is determined by the Spirit in his whole being and character (1 Cor. 2:15 ; 3:1). This being "in the Holy Ghost" characterizes his speaking and confessing (1 Cor. 12:3), his praying and his rejoicing (Rom. 8:15 ; 14:17). His whole walk is determined by the rule of the Spirit which leads him to strive after that which is of the Spirit (Rom. 8:4, 5); fervent in the Spirit, he suffers himself to be led by it to the fulfilling of every duty (Rom. 12:11).

The *sarx* or flesh, however, is by no means destroyed once and forever, and robbed of all its power over believers in the death of Christ. There is a continual conflict between the flesh and the Spirit, each of which seeks to hinder the Christian from obeying the other (Gal. 5:17 ; Rom. 8:6, 7). So far as the Christian surrenders himself to the determining influence of the one or the other, he will "mind the things of the flesh" or "the things of the Spirit" (Rom. 8:4, 5 ; Gal. 5:16: 6:8). If he still walks after the manner of the natural man, he is still carnal (1 Cor. 3:3); and in 1 Cor. 3:1 the Apostle represents even the "babes in Christ," who nevertheless still have the Spirit, because without it

[1] Compare *Weiss*, § 86.

they could not be "in Christ," as still carnal. Sin, it is true, with its dominion, is thrust back mainly upon the outer sphere of the sensuous corporeity; but, for that very reason, Christians must still be admonished not to let sin reign in their body, so that lest they should obey its lusts (Rom. 6:12, 13). In those, however, who walk after the Spirit and not after the flesh, the requirement of the law is, in fact, realized (Rom. 8:4), and therewith the quality of the life which is well-pleasing to God is restored (Rom. 8:10); their members enter into the service of righteousness (6:13), so that sanctification is now brought about in them (*ver.* 19), to the furthering of which all their fruits must minister (*ver.* 22).

To Paul the new life manifests itself in a two-fold manner—negatively as renovation, and positively as sanctification. Sin still dwells in the believer after justification (Rom. 7:17, 20, 23; Gal. 5:16–18), and the old leaven of the sinful nature must be continually purged out (1 Cor. 5:7). Our renovation, the cleansing from every sinful defilement, progresses from day to day, and is to be continued throughout life (2 Cor. 4:16; 7:1). We are to die unto sin continually (Rom. 6:11);—we are not to let sin reign in our bodies (6:12–14);—we are continually to present our bodies as a living sacrifice (12:1, 2), and daily mortify our members which are upon earth (Rom. 8:13). Renovation is the putting off of the old man and of the dominion of sin, in order that we may be renewed in the image of God.

Paul regards sanctification a positive surrender to the service of God—a putting on of the new man; the obtaining of *inherent* holiness of mind and heart (Rom. 6:19, 22). The thought is expressed in various ways by him. It is a putting on of the Lord Jesus Christ (Rom. 13:14); it is a transformation by the renewing of the mind (12:2); it is an abounding in the work of the Lord (1 Cor. 15:58)—a perfecting of holiness in the fear of God (2 Cor. 7:1). This life of sanctification is to extend to everything; for whether we eat or drink, or whatsoever we do, all is to be done to the glory of God (1 Cor. 10:31).

If through the communication of the Spirit in baptism the Christian has been put into a fellowship of life with Christ, the new life, which is therewith constituted in principle, can be realized only by that living fellowship being now also continually and completely realized in the further life of man. Although the believer has put on Christ in baptism (Gal. 3:27), he must nevertheless be ever exhorted anew to put on Christ (Rom. 13:14). He is still a babe in Christ (1 Cor. 3:1), and he can become a full-grown man in Christ (*cf.* Col. 1:28) only by gradually learning to perform all the functions of his life in Christ (1 Cor. 4:17). When this is the case believers ground their conviction (Rom. 14:14) and confidence (Gal. 5:10) on the fellowship of life with Christ, speak in Christ (2 Cor. 2:17; 12:19; Rom. 9:1), labor in Him (Rom. 16:12), love one another (Rom. 16:8; 1 Cor. 16:24), receive one another (Rom. 16:2), greet one another (Rom. 16:22; 1 Cor. 16:19), marry one another (1 Cor. 7:39), and at last fall asleep, in Christ (1 Cor. 15:18).

This living fellowship with Christ, however, shows itself in its progressive realization, not only by the overcoming of the whole of one's old life, but also by this: that, as the believer has died and risen again with Christ, so he now also suffers with Him (Rom. 8:17). The specific characteristic of such suffering as appertains to fellowship with Christ is the patience (2 Cor. 6:4; 12:12; Rom. 8:25) with which it is borne (Rom. 12:12).

## DEVELOPMENT OF THE NEW LIFE.

Although the Christian is and remains responsible for his growth in sanctification, yet it is from first to last a work of Divine Grace, which, however, throughout presupposes faith. If faith is the sole condition of the Divine act of grace which makes the beginning of the new life, then it alone can be also the condition of every furthering of that life. The ultimate aim of every exhortation can only be to strengthen faith—*i. e.* to strengthen absolute trust in Divine Grace, which can and will do everything itself in man; its final aim can only be to lead man to give up his own working, and willing, and allow grace to work in him (*cf.* Phil. 2:12, 13), because it is in this way alone that he becomes susceptible to the operation of grace, which God or Christ is carrying on by His Spirit in them, with whom He has entered into a living fellowship through the communication of the Spirit. The Apostle, accordingly, calls upon his readers to try themselves whether they are in the faith, and whether in consequence of it Christ is working in them (2 Cor. 13:5), in order that they may stand in the faith (1 Cor. 16:13; 2 Cor. 1:24).

One has received the grace of God in vain (2 Cor. 6:1), and has fallen away from it again, as soon as one seeks salvation in another way than through faith (Gal. 5:5), which must therefore be continually strengthened afresh in the Lord's Supper. Throughout the whole course of his Christian life, the Christian is directed to the grace of God. That which applies to his work as an apostle applies essentially to every activity of the Christian. It is not Paul that does what he does, but the grace of God does it in operative helping fellowship with him (1 Cor. 15:10). Only in the power of Divine

Grace, which makes him capable of it, can the Christian walk as he ought to walk (2 Cor. 1:12).

[ANALYSIS: 1) The Christian must become spiritual; 2) he must be led by the Spirit; 3) the flesh is not overcome all at once; 4) the Christian life manifests itself in a two-fold manner; 5) the negative side we may describe as renovation; 6) the positive side as sanctification; 7) there must be a growth in the Christian life; 8) and a suffering with Christ; 9) of which the specific characteristic is patience : 10) growth in sanctification a work of Divine Grace.]

§ 147. *Freedom from the Law.*[1]

In order to attain to the filial relationship, Christians have been redeemed by Christ from the bondage of the law, in the place of which the Spirit urges them from within to fulfill the will of God after they have died with Christ unto the law. The condition under the law was in keeping with the immature childhood of humanity, during which it had still to be kept in a state of guardianship (Gal. 4:1–3). If, therefore, a real filial relationship was to be brought about, there must first be a deliverance from this bondage. This deliverance was wrought by Christ, and is appropriated by faith in Christ. When the fullness of time came, God sent His Son, who, by voluntarily subjecting Himself to the law, redeemed those who stood under the law from this bondage, in order to make them capable of receiving the adoption of sons (Gal. 4:4, 5). There was required a substitution similar to that which took place when redemption was made from the curse of the law, by the vicarious death of Christ—*i. e.* by His *passive* obedience. Paul does not discuss how Christ's obedience to the law could have the effect of releasing us from it. He confines himself to the fact of which he was certain,

[1] Compare *Weiss*, § 87.

that with the sonship brought through Christ the bondage of the law has ceased, and that if Christ, who, as the Son of God, did not stand under the law, was nevertheless made subject to it during His earthly life, this could only have a vicarious significance, in the same manner as the death, as a sinner, of Him who was sinless. In this sense we can and must, according to the Pauline view, speak of a *vicarious* fulfilling of the law, or of the *active* obedience, on the part of Christ.

Christ has set us free from the law (Gal. 5:1);—we are called unto freedom (Gal. 5:13); and in Christ's state of exaltation He bestows His Spirit upon believers, and where the Spirit of the Lord is, there is liberty (2 Cor. 3:16, 17). Those who are led by the Spirit are no longer under the law (Gal. 5:18); for what the law with its requirement strove after, and yet could not reach (Rom. 8:3), that the Spirit really attains to (Rom. 8:4). The power of the Spirit, which is operative within the believer, has taken the place of the law, which is outwardly fixed in the letter (Rom. 2:29). Through our redemption from the law the old condition of the letter has given place to the new condition of the Spirit (Rom. 7:6). But freedom from the law is not a license to sin (Rom. 6:15). We were freed from the law, not that we might hand over the sovereignty to the flesh (Gal. 5:13), but that we might henceforth live unto God (Rom. 2:19; Rom. 7:4), and fulfill His will—only no longer on the ground of the outer requirements of the law, but at the inner instigation of the Spirit. Materially, nothing else is aimed at by means of the Spirit than by the law; for the love, which the Spirit works, is the fulfilling of the law (Gal. 5:13, 14; Rom. 13:8–10).

The Apostle also discusses the question, How is the emancipation of the individual from the law to be legally justified? He starts from the fact that death looses the bond of every legal obligation (Rom. 7:1), taking as an example the marriage bond (Rom. 7:2, 3). Man in his pre-Christian condition stands under the dominion of the law, but when he becomes a Christian the old man dies with Christ and the new man chooses for itself a new Lord, which is none other than Christ. As being dead we have been discharged from the law, in whose power we were hitherto held (Rom. 7:6); and, since this dying is brought about by the fellowship of life with Christ, we have freedom from the law in Christ Jesus (Gal. 2:4).

The Spirit teaches Christians what they have to do according to the will of Christ: but Paul furthers the knowledge of that will by pointing them to his own example (Gal. 4:12; 1 Cor. 4:16, 17; 11: 1) and that of the mature Christians, as well as to the word and example of Christ, and by his own precepts (1 Cor. 11:1, 2). Now, as a "law of the Spirit" is spoken of in Rom. 8:2, inasmuch as the Spirit is the normative power in the life of the Christian, this principle dwelling and ruling in man's heart can also be called "the law of Christ" (Gal. 6:2), inasmuch as that Spirit is the Spirit of Christ, and therefore makes known His will, which the Christian is bound to obey, and in this sense Paul calls himself "under law to Christ" (1 Cor. 9:21).

There is no doubt that the Old Testament was read in the assemblies of the Gentile-Christian Churches for the purpose of worshiping God. This was so much the more necessary, as everything in Scripture had been written for the instruction and admonition of Christians (1 Cor. 10:11; Rom. 15:4). As a revelation of God, Scripture in all its parts makes known His will, and must in so far even now still instruct Christians as to that will. But Scripture, which on one side has a thoroughly legal character (law in contradistinction to Gospel), is not thereby received as law. Of course, if the Christian stood under the exclusive dominion of the Spirit, he would no more stand in need of being referred in this way to the revelation of the will of God in the Old Testament; nor would he require to be exhorted by the Apostle. The Spirit would then enlighten him sufficiently through the Gospel as to that which is the will of God, as well as impel him to fulfill it. But as the Christian must still be in conflict with sin, the knowledge as to that which is the will of God must in many ways be brought to him by means of the Scriptures of the Old and New Testaments.

This subject of freedom from the law is fully set forth in the Epistle to the Galatians, as also in that to the Romans. In a summary we may say, by faith, *Christ Himself* is the principle which lives in believers, and brings about in them an organic unity of life with Him, and not the law. The rule of the law has ceased, because the position of man for which the law was prescribed is come to an end (Gal. 4:1-7; Rom. 7:1-3). Another cause of the freedom from the dominion of the law is, that now a higher dispensation, instead of the power of the law, has actually presented itself to man (Gal. 4:4, 5). He is become the property of another; he has passed from the law into the life of the Spirit; he walks in the Spirit; the new man has been created in righteousness; the life of the Spirit has become an actual power of life in him, as the law of the Spirit (Rom. 8:2), as freedom (2 Cor. 3:17), and as sonship (Gal. 4:4-7; Rom. 8:15, 16). This new freedom is at the same time an inward moral obligation (Rom.

6:18, 19); and thus a life is developed, which manifests itself outwardly in "faith, hope and love" (1 Cor. 13:13).

[ANALYSIS: 1) Christians have been redeemed from the bondage of the law; 2) this deliverance wrought by Christ; 3) by His vicarious fulfillment of the law; 4) those who are led by the Spirit are no longer under the law; 5) the power of the Holy Spirit takes the place of the law; 6) but this freedom from the law is not a license to sin; 7) the meaning of the passage in Rom. 7:1-6; 8) the meaning of the expressions "the law of the Spirit" and "the law of Christ;" 9) the will of God must still be made known to us through the Word; 10) summary.]

## CHAPTER X.

THE DOCTRINE OF THE CHURCH, OR ECCLESIOLOGY.

§ 148. *The Church and the Gifts of Grace.*[1]

Of the Jews and Gentiles that have been called there is formed a new community, which is expressly designated as "the Church of God" (1 Cor. 10:32), in which God dwells by His Spirit, and which, in virtue of its really living fellowship with Christ, forms His body. With Paul the word *Ekklesia*, or Church, means the assembly of Church members (1 Cor. 11:18; 14:28, 35), as these are to be met with in any definite place (1 Cor. 16:19; Rom. 16:5). A single congregation or the collective body of Christians in any definite city is called an *Ekklesia* (1 Cor. 1:2; 2 Cor. 1:1; Rom. 16:1), and Paul speaks of "the churches of Galatia" (Gal. 1:2); yet the expression *Church* is also used to denote the collective community of Christians (1 Cor. 12:28).

Paul naturally looks upon all the members of the Church as elected and called, but this by no means excludes the idea that they may yet fall away. Were a member of the Church to become guilty of gross sins, or of persistent disobedience to the apostolic commands, then every fellowship with him is to be broken off (1 Cor. 5:11). By participation in the Spirit through baptism (Gal. 3:27, 28), all the individual members of the Church are put into a real living fellowship with Christ (1 Cor. 1:2), and are become one (Gal. 3:28). By this living fellowship all are equally connected with the

[1] Compare *Weiss*, § 92.

living center (Christ), and so have become one organism or body (Rom. 12:5, "so we, who are many, are one body in Christ, and severally members of one another;" 1 Cor. 6:15, "Know ye not that your bodies are members of Christ?"). Paul presents this union and unity as being brought about in a two-fold way: 1) By baptism we are transplanted into this loving fellowship, "for in one Spirit were we all baptized *into one body*, whether Jews or Greeks" (1 Cor. 12:13); 2) in another way the organic unity of the many is continued by the partaking of the Lord's Supper, which also unites us into fellowship with Christ (1 Cor. 10:16, 17). One may even say that Paul sees in the Lord's Supper, as he does also in baptism, a constitutive moment for the true nature of the Church. As the natural body is a unity and yet has many members, but all the individual members, although they are many, yet form a single body, so is it with Christ (1 Cor. 12:12). He also has many members, but these many members form but one body; and thus far the organic unity of the Church may be designated as the body of Christ, whose members are individual Christians (1 Cor. 12:27).

It is implied, in the nature of the Christian Church, that it must continually be extending externally more and more; and that in each individual member of it the new life, quickened at his baptism, must be ever more perfectly realized in him. In this respect it is a field belonging to God, in which Paul and his fellow-laborers work continually—a building belonging to Him, on which they have continually to build (1 Cor. 3:9). The foundation stone of this building has been laid once for all by God (*ver.* 11), in that He has made Jesus to be the Messiah, and therefore the corner-stone; but this corner-stone is ever laid afresh as the foundation of each individual church by the preaching of Christ, which works faith and founds churches (1 Cor. 3:10; Rom. 15:20). Every advance of the Church in her extension, or in the development of life, is an upbuilding or edifying (1 Cor. 14:4, 12, 26; 2 Cor. 10:8; 13:10). As, now, the founding of the Church is brought about only in this way: that God, by His Spirit, works in the Apostles the gifts of grace needed for the preaching of the Gospel, so her upbuilding also can be brought about only by a similar working of God; and this likewise comes from the Spirit, which the individual member of the Church has (1 Cor. 12:7). The single object of all these gifts is the upbuilding of the Church (1 Cor. 12:28; 14:26).

[ANALYSIS: 1) The word *Ekklesia*; 2) the meaning of "the Church;" 3) believers are members of Christ; 4) the two-fold way in which this union is sustained; 5) the upbuilding of the Church; 6) the gifts of grace.]

§ 149. *Church Duties.*[1]

If the diversity of gifts in the service of the Church is to co-operate beneficially, there is need of Christian modesty. No one is to think more highly of himself than he ought to think (Rom. 12:3), nor to set his mind on high things (12:16). Above all things, no one is to overestimate the value of his own gifts; for without love, which puts them entirely at the service of the Church, and turns them to the best account, they are all worthless (1 Cor. 13:1-3); they may even become dangerous if they puff up the individual (1 Cor. 8:1). Christian modesty, moreover, grows out of humility, which will not be wise in its own conceits (Rom. 12:16; 11:25), which does not imagine itself to be something

[1] Compare *Weiss,* § 93.

(Gal. 6:3), and knows that it has nothing which it has not received (1 Cor. 4:7). Humility is with Paul, as in the teaching of Jesus and of Peter, one of the cardinal virtues—only that it is here presented in the form of modesty as a duty to the Church.

But the first and most fundamental virtue continues to be love—not only to the brethren (Rom. 12: 9, 10; 1 Cor. 16:14), but towards all men (Gal. 6:10), and even towards enemies (Rom. 12:19, 21 ; 1 Cor. 4:12, 13). Love is the source of all the virtues (1 Cor. 13:4–7), the first-fruits of the Spirit (Gal. 5:22), by which faith, which conditions participation in the Spirit, proves itself effectual (Gal. 5:6). Love, even love unfeigned (2 Cor. 6:6), stands first (Rom. 12:9) among all the exhortations, and comprehends them all (1 Cor. 16:14).

A special exercise of Christian love is required (in Paul's time as well as in our own), when differences of opinion arise about certain questions which some hold to be matters of difference, while others assign to them a religious significance. A point of this sort was the partaking of meat sacrificed to idols, in which one saw defilement as from idol-worship (1 Cor. 8:4–7), while another ate the meat without scruple (1 Cor. 8:4, 8, 9,10 ; 10:25, 26). So there were some in the Church who, from ascetic grounds, believed they ought to forego the use of all kinds of flesh and wine (Rom. 14:2, 20, 21), and who considered themselves bound to keep sacred certain days, apparently fast-days (Rom. 14:5). Paul designates such as weak in faith (Rom. 14:1), because their confidence in the salvation given in Christ was not strong enough for them to acknowledge that the possession of salvation could not be endangered by such things. He starts from the fundamental principle that neither the use nor the denying oneself of any food, which, like the organ for which it is appointed, is transitory (1 Cor. 6:13) can determine the worth of a man before God (1 Cor. 8:8).

Paul knows that the Kingdom of God does not consist in eating and drinking (Rom. 14:17); and hence he agrees with those who have the faith to regard everything to eat, and every day, as alike (Rom. 14:2, 5; 1 Cor. 10:25, 26). He is persuaded that in itself no food is unclean (Rom. 14:14, 20), but each is alike good so long as it is taken with thanksgiving towards God (1 Cor. 10:30, 31; Rom. 14:6); and he makes clear the fundamental principle that all things, not sinful in themselves, are lawful to the Christian (1 Cor. 6:12; 10:23; 3:22).

The Apostle likewise expressly acknowledges that for him who regards anything as unclean, it is unclean (Rom. 14:14), because he cannot eat without having his weak conscience stained with the consciousness of guilt (1 Cor. 8:7). If such a man eat, his conscience taking offense at his indulgence (Rom. 14:20), then this act, not proceeding from the assurance of faith, is sin, by which he falls under the Divine condemnation (Rom. 14:23); his conscience is wounded in the deepest roots of his religious life (1 Cor. 8:12), and this very act of indulgence tends directly to lead him unto destruction (1 Cor. 8:11; Rom. 14:15, 20).

Paul does not pretend to remove the existing differences of opinion, but only desires that each be thoroughly persuaded in his own mind (Rom. 14:5), so that he wavers not hither and thither doubtfully (14:23); and whatever view the Christian adopts, he is to employ it in the service of Christ (Rom. 14:6, 7).

But this is, by no means, the end of the matter. If, however, these differences of opinion in the Church cannot be removed (they have existed since the Apostles' time, and are at the present time more antagonistic and intolerant than ever before), Paul lays down the principle by which the peace of the Church and the advancement of its members (Rom. 14:19) may best be promoted. We are to make brotherly love the highest law of our conduct (Rom. 14:15). The stronger—that is, the more liberal-minded—is not to despise the weaker on account of his scruples; and, again, the latter is not to condemn the former as one who, by his freer conduct, has forfeited salvation (Rom. 14:3, 10). Both are to receive each other in brotherly love (Rom. 15:7), without the stronger subjecting the scruples of the weaker to his criticism (14:1). The stronger, however, has a special duty of love to discharge; for to him alone is the matter in dispute a matter of indifference. He alone can give up the indulgence which he holds to be permitted without surrendering in any way his conviction (Rom. 14:22), and without forfeiting anything thereby in the eye of God (1 Cor. 8:8). Love also requires that he give no offense to his weaker brother (1 Cor. 8:9, 13; 10:32; Rom. 14:13, 21). For if by his freer conduct he should influence his weaker brother to do the same things, without there being any change in the latter's deepest convictions, then he would be the means of leading the weak brother to destruction (1 Cor. 8:10). For the sake of another's conscience, he who is more liberal-minded must give up enjoyments which in themselves are lawful (1 Cor. 10:28, 29); and in this case the self-denial will be to him morally praiseworthy (Rom. 14:21). The strong must, therefore, bear the infirmities of the weak (Rom. 15:1; Gal. 6:1), and not simply seek to please himself (Rom. 15:1)—maintaining indeed, and defending his more free convictions, but nevertheless not carrying them into practice, seeking to pleasing one's neighbor while he helps him in his Christian life (Rom. 15:2; 1 Cor. 10:33). For true love seeks not its own (1 Cor. 13:5), but that which is another's, good (1 Cor. 10:24).

[ANALYSIS : 1) The virtue of Christian modesty; 2) of humility; 3) love is the fundamental virtue; 4) the source of all virtues; 5) love must aid in solving difficult religious questions; 6) the question of eating flesh sacrificed to idols; 7) the fundamental principle laid down by Paul; 8) the state of the weak brother with a tender conscience; 9) Paul does not remove the difficulty; 10) the solution lies in brotherly love; 11) the duties of the stronger; 12) of the weaker; 13) the solution of the problem lies with the stronger.]

# SECTION III.

The Development of Paulinism in the Epistles of the First Imprisonment.

## CHAPTER XI.

### THE FIRST PRINCIPLES OF DOCTRINE.

§ 150. *The Doctrine of Justification.*[1]

Although in the Epistles of the first captivity (Colossians, Ephesians, Philemon, Philippians) the doctrine of Justification does not come into prominence, still it does not entirely disappear. These Epistles proceed not only on the same fundamental principles, but also on the same anthropological ideas as the earlier ones. The idea of righteousness is conceived of in the same way. Righteousness and truth are synonymous ideas (Eph. 5:9; 6:14; Phil. 4:8). God's Righteousness appears as impartiality (Col. 3:25; Eph. 6:9); the manifestation of Divine Holiness appears as wrath which comes upon the children of disobedience (Col. 3:6; Eph. 2:2, 3; 5:6), and brings destruction upon them (Phil. 1:28; 3:19). Righteousness cannot be attained by the law, because no one can keep the law (Phil. 3:9).

Paul gives us in these letters a very vivid representation of the condition of the Gentiles apart from Christ. They walk "in the vanity of their mind" (Eph. 4:17), because they have emptied it of its true contents by their departure from God (compare Rom. 1:21), and

[1] Compare *Weiss,* § 100.

## THE DOCTRINE OF JUSTIFICATION.

their hearts have become thereby even harder; and thus they have become the victims of an ignorance which is the result of their own guilt (Eph. 4:18, "alienated from the life of God, because of the ignorance that is in them, because of the hardening of their heart"), by which they are darkened in their understanding (Eph. 4:18). They are "dead through trespasses and sins," walking "according to the course of this world"—"according to the prince of the power of the air, of the spirit that now worketh in the sons of disobedience," living "in the lusts of the flesh," "doing the desires of the flesh and of the mind" (Eph. 2:1–3), "separate from Christ," "strangers from the covenants of the promise," "having no hope and without God in the world" (Eph. 2:12).

"But now in Christ Jesus the Gentiles that once were far off are made nigh in the blood of Christ" (2:13). God has made known His purpose of salvation, "the mystery which hath been hid from all generations" (Col. 1:26; Eph. 3:9). All is of Divine grace. By it we are saved (Eph. 2:5), and redeemed (1:7), and grace forms the very contents of the Gospel, "the word of His grace" (Acts 20:32). According to Eph. 4:7, it is Christ who, by the distribution of His gifts, brings about the possession of grace. By Him is everything mediated for which the Christian has to thank God (Col. 3:17)—atonement (Col. 1:20), sonship (Eph. 1:5), access to God (2:18), the fruits of righteousness (Phil. 1:11);—in Him it is that God has admitted us to share in His grace (Eph. 1:6; 2:7);—in Him we have redemption (1:7), the forgiveness of sins (4:32), reconciliation with God (2:16);—in Him we receive every blessing (1:3; Phil. 4:19); and hence all praise to God is grounded in Christ (Eph. 3:21).

It is this Jesus Christ who is preached as our Lord and Redeemer (Eph. 1:3, 17; 5:20; 6:24; Col. 1:3); and He has become such by His death (Col. 1:22)—even by His death on the Cross (Col. 1:20; 2:14; Eph. 2:16; Phil. 2:8). It is through Christ that we obtain forgiveness of our sins (Col. 1:14; Eph. 1:7); for He has made reconciliation between God and man, satisfying the justice of the Father (Col. 1:20); and the price paid for our redemption was the blood of the Son of God (Col. 1:20; Eph. 1:7). It is Christ who fulfilled the law for us, bore its penalty (Col. 2:14), and overcame the power of death and Satan (Col. 2:15).

The Pauline doctrine of Justification as developed in the Epistles to the Galatians and Romans is also expressed very precisely in these Epistles. "I count all things to be loss for the excellency of the knowledge of Christ Jesus my Lord, . . . that I may gain Christ, and be found in Him, not having a righteousness of mine own, even that which is of the law, but that which is through faith in Christ, the righteousness which is of God by faith" (Phil. 3:8, 9). So, in Eph. 2:8, 9, we find the true Pauline antithesis. "Through faith" . . . "not of works," refers to the deliverance resulting from grace—a deliverance which presupposes Justification.

[ANALYSIS: 1) The idea of righteousness; 2) the condition of the Gentiles apart from Christ; 3) salvation alone in Christ Jesus; 4) who is our Lord and Redeemer; 5) Justification by faith alone.]

## § 151. *The Doctrine of Salvation.*[1]

The doctrine of a living fellowship with Christ, resting on the gift of the Spirit in baptism, by which a condition of righteousness is produced, is the same in

[1] Compare *Weiss*, § 101.

## THE DOCTRINE OF SALVATION. 177

these Epistles as in the earlier ones. Baptism is bestowed on the recipient on the ground of faith in the one Lord (Eph. 4:5, " one Lord, one faith, one baptism "), and brings with it a cleansing from the stains of guilt (Eph. 5:26, 27, " having cleansed the Church by the washing of water with the Word, that he might present it to Himself a glorious Church, not having spot or wrinkle or any such thing, but that it should be holy and without blemish ").[1] The Christian is, from the very beginning of his Christian life—that is, from his baptism—in living fellowship with Christ (Eph. 2:13 ; 5:8). The result of his appropriation of Christ by faith (Phil. 3:9) is, that he is found in Christ, and in Him is filled with the fullness of all the blessings of salvation (Col. 2:10). The Christian is dead with Christ (Col. 2:20), and is buried with Him in baptism (Col. 2:12)—only that here the being quickened and raised with Him comes expressly into prominence (Col. 3:1 ; 2:12 ; Eph. 2:6).

Christ dwells by His Spirit (Phil. 1:19) in the heart (Eph. 3:17), so that the life of the Christian is only a life of Christ in him (Phil. 1:21). In the believer a new creation takes place, which is perfected in this living fellowship with Christ (Eph. 2:10 ; 4:24). Christians are saints or holy ones (Col. 3:12; 1:2, 4, 12, 26; Eph. 1:1, 15, 18 ; 2:19 ; etc.) ; and this on the ground of their living fellowship with Christ (Phil. 1:1 ; Eph. 2:21, " each several building groweth into a holy temple in the Lord "), and righteousness is actually wrought in them (Eph. 4:24 ; 5:9 ; Phil. 1:11).

The healthy development of Christian life depends on the ever fuller realization of that living fellowship with Christ, and on the unrestrained activity of the

[1] Compare also Acts 22:16, " Arise, and be baptized and wash away thy sins, calling on his name."

Spirit in believers, by whom the Divine work of grace is effected. The new principle of life implanted in baptism must ever be realized more and more; and although each believer is in Christ, and Christ in him, Christ must ever anew make His abode in their hearts (Eph. 3:17) till He becomes all in all (Col. 3:11). Believers have to be kept in living fellowship with Christ (Phil. 4:7), and to continue to stand (4:1); from babes in Christ they have even to grow until they become "perfect in Christ" (Col. 1:28), rooted firmly in Him (Col. 2:7), continuing to walk in Him (2:6). He in whom Christ dwells is constantly strengthened (Eph. 3:16, 17) and renewed (4:23) by His Spirit. Only by the help of this Spirit can one receive all things which one requires for the preservation of the Christian life (Phil. 1:19)—only by Him can one really serve God (3:3).

A progressive renewal is also here required. Although "the body of the flesh" is put off in baptism (Col. 2:11), yet the old man needs ever again to be put off, and the new man ever more to be put on (Col. 3:9, 10; Eph. 4:22, 24); the holiness which the Christian possesses must be ever more perfectly realized (Eph. 5:26, 27; 1:4), until he becomes without blemish before Him, filled with the fruits of righteousness (Phil. 1:11). On this account the Christian must ever anew prove the difference of good from evil (Phil. 1:10), and learn to recognize the will of God (Col. 1:9; 4:12; Eph. 5:10, 17). To this the Apostle leads him on by referring to his own example (Phil. 3:17; 4:9), also to the pattern of Christ (Eph. 5:2; Phil. 2:5). The Apostle also draws motives from the fundamental facts of salvation: they are to forgive as they have been forgiven (Eph. 4:32); they are to walk worthy of their Christian calling

## THE DOCTRINE OF SALVATION.

(4:1), or of the Lord (Col. 1:20), and of the Gospel of Christ (Phil. 1:27); they are to remember that they have been created for good works, which God has before appointed as the element of the new life, in which they are to walk henceforth and bear fruit (Eph. 2:10; Col. 1:10). And although the Apostle makes the believer himself answerable for the progress of his Christian life (Phil. 3:12, 13), it is nevertheless the Divine grace which, after all, works all in him (Phil. 2:12, 13). He who has begun the good work in them will also perfect it (Phil. 1:6). It is the surpassing greatness of the power of God which helps believers to the completion of their salvation (Col. 1:11; Eph. 1:19); and it is God who arms them with all weapons needful for victory in the Christian fight (Eph. 6:10–13), and for the fulfillment of their calling (Col. 1:29).

In these Epistles the doctrine of hope, so far as it is more definitely stated, is the same as that of the earlier Epistles. Hope is the principal moment in the subjective life of the Christian (Col. 1:4, 5); Christ is its Author and contents (Col. 1:27), and the Holy Spirit is its pledge (Eph. 1:4) and seal (4:30). The object of hope is salvation (Eph. 1:13) from perdition (Phil. 1:28), even eternal life (Phil. 2:16; 4:3)—a possession which shall be perfectly realized in the perfected Kingdom of God (Col. 4:11; Eph. 5:5). The reward which Paul specially expects for his work is the glory he will share on the day of Christ (Phil. 2:16; 4:1).

[ANALYSIS: 1) Paul's teaching concerning baptism; 2) the believer is in living fellowship with Christ; 3) the growth of the Christian life; 4) a progressive renewal is required; 5) motives for growth in sanctification; 6) all the work of grace; 7) the doctrine of hope.]

## § 152. *The Doctrine of Wisdom.*[1]

According to the teaching of the earlier Epistles the message of salvation, in contrast to all human wisdom, contains the *true* wisdom, in that it brings no mere theoretical knowledge of God's nature and of Divine things, but shows the way of salvation given in Christ (1 Cor. 1:18–31 ; 2:6–16). This Heavenly wisdom has nothing in common with the wisdom of the world, but is a deeper insight into the hidden saving purpose of God (1 Cor. 2:7), which He has revealed by His Spirit to the Apostles (*ver.* 10), and which can only be understood and judged of by the spiritual man (*vers.* 14, 15).

Special attention is given to the doctrine of wisdom or philosophy in the Epistles of the first captivity. The reason of this is the appearance in the churches of Asia Minor of a new philosophy, which offered to conduct believers to a higher state of knowledge, but which Paul regards as a relapse into "the rudiments of the world," because it has to do with theosophic traditions, and therefore with a *philosophy* (Col. 2:8) in the sense of human wisdom. In opposition to all this, Paul maintains that in the Gospel we have all the riches of wisdom (Col. 1:28 ; 2:2), the perfect knowledge ; and that the contents of this knowledge is no sort of theosophic doctrine, but the mystery of salvation, even of Christ, in whom are all the treasures of wisdom and knowledge hidden (Col. 2:2, 3).

The contents of this mystery, by whose disclosure God has most richly shown His grace in all wisdom and knowledge which He has bestowed on us, is according to Eph. 1:8, 9, His will purposing our salvation ; according to Eph. 5:9, the institution of salvation, which makes known the Gospel, and which, by its realization

[1] Compare *Weiss*, § 102.

## THE DOCTRINE OF WISDOM. 181

in the Church, makes known the manifold wisdom of God (*ver.* 10); according to Col. 1:26, it is the promise of God, which is fulfilled by the preaching of the Word (Col. 4:3 ; Eph. 3:4); according to Col. 2:2, 3, even *Christ* Himself. It is also the peculiarity of our Epistles that every prayer for the further development of Christians is concentrated in this: that the Spirit of wisdom and revelation may lead them to the knowledge of God (Eph. 1:17)—a knowledge which teaches to what a hope God has called us (*ver.* 18), and how great His power is by which He conducts us to this goal (*ver.* 19).

But this Christian knowledge has a pre-eminently practical issue. The Gospel is indeed the Word of truth (Col. 1:5; Eph. 1:13) ; but this truth is also a practical principle, the rule of righteousness, directing to the renewing of the life (Eph. 4:20, 21). Right doctrine is thus a teaching, a tradition of Christ (Col. 2:6, 7 ; Eph. 4:20, 21), as well as a doctrine of the life of Christian virtue (Phil. 4:9). The activity of the Apostles (Col. 1:28), as of the Church herself, if the Word of Christ dwell in her richly (Col. 3:16), is thus practical correction as well as instruction ; and both of these advance her in true wisdom. Christian wisdom and intelligence is, therefore, on the one hand a knowledge of the Divine way of salvation (Eph. 1:9); on the other, a knowledge of the Divine will (Col. 1:9), by which one brings forth fruit in good works and makes increase (*ver.* 10), or walks strictly according to the will of the Lord (Eph. 5:15, 17); and thus wisdom (Col. 4:5) stands directly for the practical rule of righteousness.

In these Epistles, therefore, Christian wisdom is especially regarded as having moral duties in view. The doctrine of wisdom is regarded as penetrating into the deeper grounds and into the more comprehensive results of the great facts of Christian salvation—even of carrying saving truth into practical life, with the varied riches of its concrete relations.

[ANALYSIS : 1) The Gospel as contrasted with the wisdom of the world ; 2) a special discussion of the doctrine of wisdom in the Epistle to the Colossians ; 3) the contents of the true wisdom, the mystery of salvation ; 4) Christian wisdom or knowledge has preeminently a practical tendency.]

## CHAPTER XII.

### THE MORE DEVELOPED DOCTRINES.

§ 153. *The Cosmical Significance of Christ.*[1]

The eternal purpose of salvation (Eph. 3:11), on which the redemption of the world depends, was made in Christ, who, as the first-born Son of Love, was before all creatures (Col. 1:15-17). In the heavenly world God has blessed us with every spiritual blessing, in that He hath chosen us in Christ before the foundation of the world (Eph. 1:3, 4); and the calling by which this election is realized, because it proceeds from God, is a heavenly calling (Phil. 3:14). And if, as is said in Eph. 3:9, the mystery of salvation was hidden from eternity in God, who created all things, it is indicated by this characteristic of God, that the purpose of salvation is connected in the closest way with the plan of the world, which began to be realized in creation; and that purpose, having been formed by the Creator before the creation of the world, was regulative even in its creation.

If Christians are chosen in Christ before the foundation of the world (Eph. 1:4), and are thereby already blessed in Him in the heavenly world (*ver*. 3), then the Mediator of salvation, in whom the election and the blessing could be grounded at a time when the objects of these did not exist, must have Himself existed before the world. For Paul there is an eternal Divine exist-

---

[1] Compare *Weiss*, § 103. This section treats mainly of Christology. For a full development of the special doctrines of these Epistles, see my "Studies in the Book," vol. 3, pp. 9-49.

ence of the Christ who in His earthly life has become the Mediator.

Col. 1:15–20, together with Eph. 1:20–23, and Phil. 2:6–11, are the three most important passages in the Epistles of the first captivity, in which the doctrine of the Person of Christ is most fully unfolded. In Col. 1:15–17 the reference is specially to the *Pre-incarnate* Son of God in relation to God and to His own creatures. Christ is the original Image of God (Heb. 1:3; 2 Cor. 4:4), in perfect equality with the Father in respect of His essence, nature, and eternity; with reference to *every* created thing, the Son is here solemnly defined as "*first-born*" "before all things" (*ver*. 17)—the word *Only-begotten* (John 1:14, 18; 1 John 4:9) defining more exactly His relation to the Father. Paul here declares the absolute pre-existence of the Son. It is a false interpretation to infer that the Son was a created being, though the earliest; for, in *vers*. 16, 17, we have an explanation by Paul in what sense the Son of God is "the first-born of all creation." The wonderful statement is made that the Eternal Son of God according to His Divine nature has the same relation to the universe as the Incarnate Christ (*ver*. 18), the God-Man, has to the Church.[1] According to this passage the Son of God, *i. e.* Jesus Christ, according to his Divine nature, is the *conditional* Cause of creation (*i. e.* the act of creation depends on Him, "for *in* Him were all things created"). He is the *instrumental* Cause of creation (*i. e.* "all things have been created *through* Him"). He is also the *ultimate* Cause of creation (*i. e.* "all things have been created *unto* Him" to enhance His glory). When Paul in *ver*. 17 so emphatically says: "He is before

[1] Compare my "Studies in the Book," vol. 3, on the passages cited from Colossians, Ephesians and Philippians.

all things," the *He* emphasizes the Son's *personality*, and the *is* His *pre-existence*.

In Col. 1:18-20 the reference is specially to the *Incarnate* and now glorified Son in His relation to His Church. He, the same Person, the Creator of the world, having assumed human nature, the Incarnate and glorified God-Man, is the Head of the body, the Church. In relation to the Church the Incarnate Christ is *the beginning*—1) in that He was the first-fruits of the dead (*ver.* 18; 1 Cor. 15:20, 23), and 2) also the source of life (Acts 3:14). He rose first from the dead, that others might rise through Him. And in Col. 1:19; 2:9, the Apostle lays especial stress on the fact that the whole fullness of God, the totality of the Divine powers and attributes, was pleased to dwell in Christ. Christ our Mediator is, therefore, both divine and human. It was necessary that in Him should all the fullness of the Godhead dwell, and also that He should be born into the world, and through the blood of the Cross suffer as a man for us and make atonement for us (Col. 1:19, 20).

According to Paul the fact that all creation was grounded in Him (Col. 1:16) includes the two-fold idea— 1) that not only were all things created *by* Him, but also 2) that all was created *for* Him (Col. 1:16), who also is to bring to completion both the saving purpose of God, as also the whole development of the world. How this goal of the world is conceived of, Eph. 1:10 shows, where it is mentioned as the final goal of the institution of God's grace, that all things pertaining to the Kingdom of God shall be gathered together in Christ as in a center. In this passage Paul does not teach the ultimate restoration of the wicked. The words, strictly interpreted with reference to the context, do not signify any such idea. The whole context has reference to believers, and to Christ's relations with His Church on earth and in heaven. Christ is, indeed, the Head of the universe; and all, wicked spirits as well as wicked men, shall finally acknowledge His power and authority (Eph. 1:20-23; Phil. 2:10, 11). But it is questionable whether Paul has reference even to this great truth in the passage before us, to say nothing of the false doctrine of the restoration of all things in Christ.

Christ has been appointed to be this central point of the Kingdom of Christ and God (Eph. 5:5); and, although this world has now become the abode of sin, there will come a time when all this shall be changed, and all things be subject to Christ. "For, according to His promise, we look for new heavens and a new earth, wherein dwelleth righteousness" (2 Pet. 3:13; Isa. 65:17).

In order to lead the world created in Him to the goal appointed for it in the pretemporal purpose of salvation, the Son of God had to assume human nature, and become man—in which form alone He could perform the office of a Redeemer. Christ Jesus, the Incarnate Son of God, although He took the form of a servant and was made in the likeness of men (Phil. 2:6, 7), was nevertheless "in the form of God"—*i. e.* He still truly *possessed* at the same time a Divine nature, and did not *lay aside* His Divine attributes. When the Son of God assumed the human nature, He did not cease to subsist in His Divine nature; and as the God-Man, by His own peculiar pre-eminence itself as Lord, it was entirely in His power "to be on an equality with God," to adopt a mode of life and outward distinctions which would correspond to His dignity, that He might be received and treated by all creatures as their Lord. But He chose otherwise;—to come as the humble

Jesus of Nazareth. It would not have been "robbery," "a prize," "a thing to be grasped," if He had used His own right; yet He abstained from doing so, just as if it had been robbery, because He became Incarnate for the purpose of making reconciliation for the sins of men (Phil. 2:6–8). He "emptied Himself, taking the form of a servant, being made in the likeness of men; and, being found in fashion as a man, He humbled Himself, becoming obedient even unto death—yea, the death of the Cross" (*vers.* 7, 8). In His state of humiliation Christ abstained from the full, universal use of the Divine Glory and majesty which He possessed. For our sakes He bore Himself in the same way as if He were *empty*. He pleased not Himself (Rom. 15:3); for our sakes He denied Himself and abstained from His rights. In the great fact of Christ's humiliation Paul lays stress upon three points: 1) He emptied Himself; 2) By taking the form of a servant; 3) By becoming obedient even unto the death of the Cross.

As the reward for this, Christ has been exalted, according to His human nature, to the full participation in the Divine honor and dominion of the world (Phil. 2:9–11), which according to His Divine nature He always possessed, so that He, the God-Man, in whom all the fullness of the Godhead dwelt here on earth (Col. 1:19), now is the head of all principality and power (Col. 2:10). According to Col. 3:1; Eph. 1:20, God, after raising Christ from the dead, has set Him at His own Right Hand in the Heavenly world, "that in all things He might have the pre-eminence" (Col. 1:18). This position of dignity, equal with God, Christ, the God-Man, now possesses, also according to His human nature. The summit of exaltation, to which the God-Man has been raised, according to His human nature, is expressly described in Phil. 2:9–11. God has "highly exalted Him, and given unto Him the Name which is above every name; that in the Name of Jesus every knee should bow—of things in heaven, and things on earth, and things under the earth; and that every tongue should confess that Jesus Christ is Lord, to the Glory of God the Father."

[ANALYSIS: 1) The eternal purpose of salvation; 2) believers are chosen in Christ before the foundation of the world; 3) the pre-existence of Christ; 4) the meaning of Col. 1:15–17; 5) of Col. 1:18–20; 6) Christ the God-Man; 7) the meaning of Eph. 1:10; 8) of Phil. 2:6–8; 9) Christ's state of humiliation; 10) the meaning of Phil. 2:9–11; 11) Christ's state of exaltation.]

§ 154. *The Realization of Salvation in the Church.*[1]

The ultimate end of the world appointed by God, which is to be reached by the execution of the Eternal purpose of redemption, has begun to be realized in the Church,[2] in so far as Christ has been given her by God as Head (Eph. 1:22). Christ is the head (Eph. 4:15), the Church is His body (4:12; Col. 1:24); both are, as the head and the body, inseparably united (Col. 1:18). Marriage is presented as the earthly type of this relation (Eph. 5:23). As the body of Christ, the Church must increase. This increase, wrought by God, proceeds organically from Christ (Col. 2:19; Eph. 4:16).[3]

[1] Compare *Weiss*, § 105.

[2] In our Epistles *Ekklesia* occurs most frequently for the whole community—*i. e.* the Church; but it is also used for local churches (Col. 4:16; Phil. 4:15), and even for single meetings within these (Col. 4:15; Phil. 2). In the Epistle to the Ephesians Paul especially develops the doctrine of the Church, or Ecclesiology. See my "Studies in the Book," vol. 3, pp. 35–38.

[3] Col. 2:19, "Holding fast the head, from whom all the body, being supplied and knit together through the joints and bands, in-

Christ became the Peace-maker (Eph. 2:14) when He came and proclaimed an equal salvation to those "that were far off," and to them "that were nigh" (Eph. 2:17)—*i. e.* to Gentile and Jew. And thus those who were once foreigners, and were "strangers from the covenants of the promise, having no hope and without God in the world" (Eph. 2:12), become now, according to 2:19, "fellow-citizens with the saints, and of the household of God."

The complete union of Gentiles with Jews in the Church depends not only on the fact that the former share now in what the latter formerly enjoyed, but also on this, that there has been taken away that which formerly prevented fellowship between them, and which, like a dividing wall, kept the two portions of pre-Christian humanity apart (Eph. 2:14, 15). Now Christ has abolished, in the flesh, the law of commandments consisting in ordinances. With the abolition of the law the dividing wall between Gentiles and Jews has been taken away, and nothing now prevents the complete union of the two. So long as the law was in force the Jews were bound to a different rule of life than the Gentiles; but both are now made one new man in the fellowship of life with Christ (Eph. 2:15). They have but one rule of life, in which every difference that separated pre-Christian humanity falls away, because Christ is all in all (Col. 3:11). The law gave to the Jews a way appointed for them to attain reconciliation with God by means of the institution of sacrifice. Both

creaseth with the increase of God." Eph. 4:16, " Christ, from whom all the body fitly framed and knit together, through that which every joint supplieth, according to the working in due measure of each several part, maketh the increase of the body unto the building up of itself in love."

Jew and Gentile are now united in one body, the Church (Col. 3:15), and in this union are reconciled to God in the same way by the Cross (Eph. 2:16, Col. 1:20); both have access to the Father through Christ in one Spirit (Eph. 2:18).

The law, according to its real meaning, is fulfilled in Christianity, because it typically pointed to Christ. All the legal institutions were but "a shadow of the things to come" (Col. 2:17). They picture the outer form, but do not contain the essence. The body itself, the concrete realization, belongs to Christ, inasmuch as He is their Author, and all point to Him. His atoning sacrifice, given of His free-will, is the real atoning sacrifice acceptable to God (Eph. 5:2). The circumcision wrought by Him, which consists in the putting off in baptism of the *body*, ruled by the *flesh*, completed in the fellowship of His life, is the true circumcision not made with hands (Col. 2:11). Christians are therefore those really circumcised. Their worship, wrought by the Spirit of God, is the true service of God (Phil. 3:3; *cf.* Rom. 12:1); and the exercise of Christian love (Phil. 4:18) and the discharge of one's heavenly calling (2:17) are the real sacrifices. In this way the law in its deepest sense is fulfilled in Christianity, so far as its ordinances typify in a shadowy way the nature of the law of Christian life.

[ANALYSIS: 1) The Church in her relation to Christ; 2) usage of the word *Ekklesia*; 3) in Christ Jew and Gentile are united in one body, the Church; 4) the real meaning of the law is fulfilled in Christianity.]

# SECTION IV.

THE DOCTRINE OF THE PASTORAL EPISTLES.

## CHAPTER XIII.

### CHRISTIANITY AS DOCTRIN

§ 155. *The Sound Doctrine.*[1]

The two Epistles to Timothy, along with that to Titus, form a closely connected, inseparable group—inseparable not only in substance, but also in form, aim, and character. These three Epistles are rightly described as pastoral. They are much less occupied with the mission and *planting* of Churches than most of the Pauline Epistles. Their aim is rather to turn the training of the Churches into the right path, and to keep them from error. Consistently with this aim the Gospel of Christ takes the form of *doctrine* (1 Tim. 4:6; 6:1, 3; Tit. 2:10.) If Christianity is regarded objectively as the doctrine of the truth, it can be regarded subjectively only as the knowledge of the truth (2 Tim. 2:25; 3:7); and this, along with faith, is mentioned as the distinguishing mark of the Christian (1 Tim. 4:3; Tit. 1:1).

The reason why our Epistles regard Christianity mainly as doctrine lies in the circumstances of the time. Some had turned away from the truth (1 Tim. 6:5; Tit. 1:14; 2 Tim. 2:18). There had arisen a *gnosis*, a knowledge, falsely so called (1 Tim. 6:20), which, to be

[1] Compare *Weiss*, § 107; *Lechler*, vol. 2, pp. 103—105.

sure, did not appear as an error uprooting the foundations, but as an unhealthy tendency (1 Tim. 6:4)—a being occupied with empty, unprofitable, foolish, even profane questions of controversy (1 Tim. 1:6; 6:20; Tit. 1:10; 3:9; 2 Tim. 2:16, 23), which gendered only contention and discord (1 Tim. 1:4; 6:4; etc.).

In opposition to such errors these Epistles emphasize *sound doctrine* (1 Tim. 1:10; 6:3; Tit. 1:9; 2:1, 8; 2 Tim. 1:13; 4:3); and this finds its firm abode only in a heart which has become sound in sincerity of faith (Tit. 2:13), keeping the conscience pure (1 Tim. 1:5; 2 Tim. 1:3).

The Pastoral Epistles are characterized by an unmistakable tendency to insist upon honest piety—a heart morally sound, the only guarantee of genuine faith and sound doctrine.

Not only does true faith depend on piety, but our Epistles also bring into the strongest prominence the inner relationship of sound doctrine with godliness. The "mystery of godliness" is, even as to its contents, nothing but the truth (1 Tim. 3:15, 16)—just as the doctrine which proclaims this truth is "according to godliness" (1 Tim. 6:3). Every kind of sin, which in its deepest roots is ungodly and unholy (1 Tim. 1:9), contradicts wholesome doctrine (1 Tim. 1:10). The turning away from sound doctrine goes hand in hand with a longing for such teachers as please the ear, while they teach only such things as correspond to the sinful inclinations of their hearers (2 Tim. 4:3, 4).

[ANALYSIS: 1) The peculiarity of the Pastoral Epistles; 2) the Gospel of Christ takes the form of doctrine; 3) the reason lies in the circumstances of the time; 4) special emphasis is laid on sound doctrine; 5) the inner relationship between sound doctrine and godliness.]

§ 156. *The Paulinism of the Pastoral Epistles.*[1]

The doctrine which incidentally appears in the Pastoral Epistles is none other than that which Paul, the teacher and Apostle of the Gentiles, has been accustomed to preach. It centers in the great truth that Jesus Christ is the Saviour of sinners, given to us by God as the Author of salvation (1 Tim. 2:3–7). *Universal sinfulness* forms the background of all evangelical preaching (1 Tim. 1:15 ; Tit. 3:3). This last verse (Tit. 3:3) presupposes that all men need deliverance, and without it fall into "destruction and perdition" (1 Tim. 6:9). Sound doctrine points the way to deliverance, and he who abides by it saves both himself and his hearers (1 Tim. 4:16; 2 Tim. 2:10 ; 3:15).

In these Epistles God the Father is designated as our Deliverer (Tit. 3:4). It is from the Father that Christian doctrine comes (Tit. 2:10); it is by His command that the Gospel is preached by the Apostle (1 Tim. 1:1 ; Tit. 1:3); it is He who wills the salvation of all men (1 Tim. 2:3, 4), and on whom therefore the hope of the Christian rests (1 Tim. 4:10; 5:5; 6:17). But Christ is also designated as our Deliverer and Saviour (Tit. 1:4 ; 3:6), who appeared as such on earth (2 Tim. 1:10) "to save sinners" (1 Tim. 1:15), and appears again at His Epiphany, or Second Coming (Tit. 2:13), and on this account deliverance rests on Him (2 Tim. 2:10), and the Gospel testifies of Him (2 Tim. 1:8 ; 2:8).

The deliverance of sinners is given in Christ, the one Mediator between God and men—the *Man* Christ Jesus (1 Tim. 2:5). Paul particularly emphasizes the word *man* in connection with the one Mediator, probably in opposition to heretical doctrine, as though angels or other higher beings were mediators of salvation. The

[1] Compare *Weiss*, § 108 ; *Lechler*, vol. 2, pp. 107–114.

descent of Jesus from David is made prominent in 2 Tim. 2:8, in order to point out the fulfillment of the Old Testament promises and the connection between the Old and New Testaments. On the other hand, the Deity of Christ is strongly attested and intimated in the expression in 1 Tim. 3:16, "He who was manifested in the flesh," in which the real pre-existence of Christ before His incarnation and historical appearance is unmistakably involved.

The redemption which Christ has brought us is attached to His death and resurrection; for Christ "gave Himself a ransom for all" (1 Tim. 2:6; Tit. 2:14)—an expression which can only refer to His vicarious atoning death. The essence of the salvation mediated by Christ consists, according to 2 Tim. 1:10, in the fact that He destroyed the power of death, abolished it, and brought life and incorruption to light. In Tit. 2:14 the aim of the redemption is said to be that Christ might redeem us from all iniquity (as a power under which we had fallen by guilt), and purify unto Himself a people for His own possession, zealous of good works.

Paul in greeting Timothy as his "true child in faith" (1 Tim. 1:2) designates *faith* as the element in which alone the spiritual life of a Christian can originate and continue. Moreover, when Timothy (1 Tim. 6:12) is admonished to fight the good fight of faith, and to lay hold on eternal life to which he is called; and, in like manner, when the author says of himself (2 Tim. 4:7) that he has fought the good fight, finished the course, and kept the faith, the idea again is that faith is the fundamental state of the heart toward God—to obtain and keep which, in spite of all temptation and hostility, is the life problem of the child of God. The same conception of faith manifestly lies at the foundation of the passage in 1 Tim. 1:5, where faith unfeigned is joined with purity of heart and a good conscience.

The deliverance of sinners accomplished by Christ is appropriated by individuals through God's mercy, through faith by means of baptism, which is a washing of regeneration and the renewing of the Holy Ghost (Tit. 3:5). In these words Paul unmistakably designates baptism as an actual and operative means of grace, since God delivers souls through it, and makes them partakers of salvation. Regeneration and renewal through the Holy Spirit are here associated directly with the sacramental act of baptism.[1]

The Pastoral Epistles are distinguished by their insisting upon the maintenance of a good conscience—the manifestation of faith in genuine piety and a pure, virtuous walk. It is not the form, but the power, of piety on which stress is laid (2 Tim. 3:5). The end of the Gospel is love out of a pure heart (1 Tim. 1:5); "the grace of God hath appeared, bringing salvation to all men, instructing us to the intent that, denying ungodliness and unworldly lusts, we should live soberly and righteously and godly in this present world" (Tit. 2:11). The peculiar people of Christ are redeemed and purified, to the end that they may be "zealous of good works" (Tit. 2:14). The man of God must be complete, thoroughly furnished unto every good work (2 Tim. 3:17).

The hope of eternal life is based not on works, but on God's mercy in Christ, and we are justified by

---

[1] So sanctification and justification, as the effect of grace, are in 1 Cor. 6:11 ascribed to baptism, which is certainly included in the "washing." Similarly in Rom. 6:3-5, we find baptism described as a planting and a uniting into Christ, into His death and resurrection. Compare also Gal. 3:27

faith alone; "we believe on Jesus Christ unto eternal life" (1 Tim. 1:16), for it is He who "saves me unto His heavenly kingdom" (2 Tim. 4:18). Faith, which leads to eternal life, is confidence resting on Christ as the Mediator of salvation (1 Tim. 1:16)—a confidence which gives the full assurance of salvation (1 Tim. 3:13). To trace all salvation, as is done in the earlier Epistles, to the grace of God, does not exclude the idea that the perfecting of salvation continues dependent on men's conduct. It is the remaining in the faith, perseverance in the Christian life (1 Tim. 2:15), the faithful discharge of the special calling given to the individual (1 Tim. 4:16), and in particular, patience in suffering (2 Tim. 2:10), by which salvation is attained.

[ANALYSIS: 1) The doctrine of the Pastoral Epistles; 2) the universality of sin; 3) God the Father is represented as the Deliverer and Saviour; 4) as well as Christ; 5) Christ the one Mediator between God and men; 6) truly human; 7) and truly Divine; 8) Christ's vicarious atoning death; 9) the aim of the redemption; 10) the teaching concerning faith; 11) concerning baptism; 12) concerning a holy life; 13) salvation does not depend on works; 14) it is of grace through faith.]

## § 157. *The Church and Church Government.*[1]

An important doctrine of the Pastoral Epistles is that of the Church. The Church of the living God, in 1 Tim. 3:15, is characterized as the "pillar and ground of the truth." God is the Master of this Holy household (2 Tim. 2:21); its stewards are the bishops or pastors (Tit. 1:7). The members of God's family are all such, and only such, as God has chosen and acknowleged as His own (Tit. 1:1; 2 Tim. 2:19).

[1] Compare *Weiss*, § 109.

It is evident that in the last passage (2 Tim. 2:19)[1] a distinction is drawn within the Church. In it there are true believers, who actually belong to God, "according to the faith of God's elect" (Tit. 1:1), and who give evidence of their faith by departing from unrighteousness (2 Tim. 2:19). It likewise contains such as "name the name of the Lord," but are guilty of unrighteousness. The latter are, indeed, members of the Church externally; they profess to belong to the Lord, but without any just claim. As a matter of fact they have not renounced iniquity. In 2 Tim. 2:20 they are compared to vessels of dishonor, such as are to be found in a great house, while even between the vessels unto honor there still exists a relative distinction like that between vessels of gold and silver on the one hand, and vessels of wood and earth on the other hand—according as Christians of moral purity or virtue strive to do good work in the service of God (*ver.* 21).

In these Epistles the disciples of Paul appear as leaders of the Churches. As such they receive from him instructions how they are to exhort old and young, male and female, on the ground of sound doctrine (Tit. 2:1–6; 1 Tim. 5:1, 2). Directions are also given with reference to the different orders in the community, as the rich (1 Tim. 6:17–19), and the slaves (Tit. 2:9, 10; 1 Tim. 6:1). But, above all, Paul exhorts Timothy (and all teachers and pastors) concerning the *teaching* (1 Tim. 4:13, 16; 6:2; Tit. 2:7; 2 Tim. 4:2). On the ground of the gift given him (1 Tim. 4:14; 2 Tim. 1:6), Timothy is exhorted to preach the Word (2 Tim. 4:2),

---

[1] ' Howbeit the firm foundation of God standeth, having this seal, The Lord knoweth them that are his: and Let every one that nameth the name of the Lord depart from unrighteousness."

to do the work of an evangelist, to fulfill his ministry (2 Tim. 4:5). It is required throughout that he follow the doctrines of the Master, and be guided by them in all his teaching (1 Tim. 4:6; 2 Tim. 3:10,14).

The most important interest of our Epistles is how doctrine is to be kept pure for the future in the Church, which is the pillar and ground of the truth (1 Tim. 3:15). The disciples are to look out for trustworthy men; and these they are to commission with the work of teaching, just as the Apostles had commissioned their disciples with it (1 Tim. 6:20; 2 Tim. 1:14), that these may be capable of bearing the burden of the further development of the truth (2 Tim. 2:2). What the qualifications are that the Church must demand of her ministers, Paul very clearly defines in 1 Tim. 3:1–7; Tit. 1:5–9; 2 Tim. 2:24, 25.

The right government of the Church depends, above all, on the right appointment of office-bearers, which consists of bishops and deacons, and in the administration of proper discipline. That the elders of the congregation are those who in the Pastoral Epistles bear the Pauline name of *bishops* (Phil. 1:1) is plainly proved by Tit. 1:5, 7, compared with Acts 28:17, 28. The teachers and overseers of the Church, in so far as they discharge the duties of their office by way of a calling, are to be supported by the Church (1 Tim. 5:17, 18).

In the appointment of deacons, there is also a careful scrutiny necessary (1 Tim. 3:8–13). The deacon had to deal primarily with the temporal needs of the Church; but his office gradually developed into that of an assistant to the presbyter. The deaconesses possibly had the oversight of the female portion of the congregation (1 Tim. 3:11). It is also highly probable that there was an order of widows belonging to the officials of the Church, and for their appointment directions are given in 1 Tim. 5:9–16.

[ANALYSIS: 1) The doctrine of the Church; 2) the visible and the invisible Church; 3) the leaders of the Church; 4) they are to give attention to the teaching or doctrine; 5) doctrine must be kept pure; 6) qualifications of the ministers of the Church; 7) the office-bearers of the Church; 8) bishops or presbyters; 9) deacons; 10) deaconesses.]

# SECTION V.

## LUKE THE EVANGELIST

### CHAPTER XIV.

#### PAULINISM IN THE WRITINGS OF LUKE.

§ 158. *The Writings of Luke.*[1]

It is universally agreed that the Third Gospel was written by Luke, the friend and companion of Paul, "the beloved physician" of Col. 4:14, the "fellow-laborer" and faithful friend who attended on the Apostle in his last imprisonment (2 Tim. 4:10, 11). From Col. 4:11, 14 we may infer that Luke was a Gentile, his conversion evidently having taken place before he joined Paul at Troas (Acts 16:11). From Acts 16:16–17:1, in comparison with Acts 20:5, 6, we may infer that Luke remained at Philippi during the second and third missionary journeys of Paul (52–57 A. D.), probably preaching the Gospel in Philippi and its neighborhood. From the time when he joined Paul again at Philippi, at the end of the third missionary journey (Acts 20:5, 6), to accompany him to Jerusalem, Luke was in constant attendance on the Apostle. He sailed with him to Rome (Acts 27:1), was by his side during his first imprisonment (Col. 4:14; Philemon 24), and was also with him during his second imprisonment (2 Tim. 4:11). Of Luke's later life we have no trustworthy account.[2]

The distinctive characteristic of Luke's life lies in the

[1] Compare *Weiss*, § 137; *Schmid*, § 89.
[2] Compare my "Studies in the Book," vol. 1, pp. 54–56, 67–71.

one certain fact of his long companionship with Paul. The earliest writers insist on this with uniform and emphatic distinctness.[1] It is also the unanimous testimony of the Early Church that the Gospel of Luke is based upon the "Oral Gospel" preached by Paul. Although it is not definitely known when Luke wrote the Acts (possibly about 63 A. D.), we have the right to infer that the Gospel was shortly written before that period, either during Paul's imprisonment at Rome (60-63 A. D.) or probably during his imprisonment at Cæsarea (58-60 A. D.)—for Luke was with him in both these imprisonments.

Since the Gospel of Luke openly acknowledges the intention to confirm doctrine, and especially, as we shall see in the next section, Pauline doctrine (Luke 1:4), it is certainly significant that in its early history the Messiah is praised as the Light of the Gentiles (2:32), and that His genealogy is traced back to Adam (3:23–38). But, above all, it is occasioned by this doctrinal intention, that the representation of His Galilean activity opens with the scene in the synagogue of Nazareth, which not only indicates beforehand the rejection of Jesus by His people (4:24), but also at the same time points prophetically to this: that the salvation of which Israel had shown themselves unworthy must come to the Gentiles (4:25–27).[2]

[1] Compare Westcott's *Introduction*, pp. 239-241.

[2] A careful analysis of the Gospel (abridged from Westcott) is very suggestive:

1. Introduction. Luke 1:1–2:52.
2. The Preparation. Luke 3:1–4:13.
3. The Announcement. Luke 4:14-44.
4. The Future Church. Luke 5:1–9:43*a*
    *a*) Its universality. Luke 5:1–6:11.
    *b*) Its constitution. Luke 6:12–8:3.

Luke, however, has not omitted either the Messianic character of Jesus's appearance, or the historical signification of His salvation for Israel.

The Acts of the Apostles show how, by explicitly Divine indications, the transference of the Gospel from the Jews to the Gentiles was effected, till Gentile missions reached in their progress the capital of the world. The careful analysis of the book manifests this in a striking manner.

[ANALYSIS: 1) Luke the constant companion of Paul; 2) his Gospel based upon the "Oral Gospel" of Paul; 3) also the author of the Acts; 4) The Gospel is Pauline in its doctrine; 5) as well as the Acts.]

§ 159. *The Paulinism of Luke.*[1]

The real groundwork of the Acts of the Apostles is to be found, not only in the aim of representing the Apostle Paul as the divinely authorized Apostle of the Gentiles, but also in the idea of the universality of Christianity, which is so pre-eminently set forth by Paul. In the Gospel, likewise, truly Pauline is the selection which Luke makes of the parables which set forth God's

 *c*) Its development. Luke 8:4-56.
 *d*) Its claims. Luke 9:1-43*a*.
5. The Universal Church. The Rejection of the Jews foreshown. Luke 9:43*b*—18:30.
 *a*) Preparation. Luke 9:43*b*—11:13.
 *b*) Lessons of warning. Luke 11:14-13:9.
 *c*) Lessons of progress. Luke 13:10-14:24.
 *d*) Lessons of discipleship. Luke 14:25-17:10.
 *e*) The coming end. Luke 17:11-18:30.
6. The Sovereignty claimed. Luke 18:31-21:38.
 *a*) The journey. Luke 18:31-19:27.
 *b*) The entry. Luke 19:28-48.
 *c*) The conflict. Luke 20:1-38.
7. The Sovereignty gained by death. Luke 22:1-24:53.

[1] Compare *Weiss*, § 139.

love to sinners (Luke 15), and which illustrate the undeservedness of men (Luke 17:7–10). To this belongs also the way in which he brings forward the forgiveness of sins as the specific saving blessing (Luke 7:47, 48; 24:47). So likewise Luke makes the Apostle himself briefly describe the Pauline doctrine of justification in one of his discourses (Acts 13:38, 39).

The importance which, in the writings of Luke, is laid on the activity of the Spirit is also in strict agreement with Pauline doctrine. For both Paul himself (1 Cor. 12:1–3; Gal. 3:2–14), and Luke in the Acts (2: 16–18, 23; 8:15–17; 10:44–47; 19:1–6) similarly represent the communication of the Spirit and the gifts of the Spirit as the essential signs of Christianity. A careful study of the Acts proves that Luke has reproduced the specific peculiarities of the Pauline method of doctrine.[1]

[ANALYSIS: 1) Luke lays stress on the universality of the Gospel; 2) the doctrine of forgiveness of sin; 3) the work of the Holy Spirit; 4) the Apostles' Creed clearly taught by Paul and in the Acts.]

---

[1] It may be of interest to note that all the doctrines of the Apostles' Creed, which may be illustrated so fully from the writings of Paul, are also clearly taught in the Acts. We only add a few references to each prominent thought: I believe (Acts 16:31) in God the Father Almighty, Maker of heaven and earth (4:24; 17:24); and in Jesus Christ (3:20; 2:36), His only Son, our Lord (2:36; 9:17, 20); who was born of the Virgin Mary, suffered under Pontius Pilate (1:14; 2:23; 13:28); was crucified (2:23, 26; 4:10), dead and buried (2:24); he descended into Hades (2:31); the third day he rose again from the dead (2:31; 4:10), ascended into heaven (1:11; 2:34); and sitteth on the Right Hand of God the Father Almighty (2:33), from thence he shall come to judge the quick and the dead (1:11; 10:42). I believe in the Holy Ghost (2:4; 5:3,4); the holy Christian Church, the Communion of saints (2:39, 42, 47; 20:28); the forgiveness of sins (2:28); the resurrection of the body (4:2); and the life everlasting (5:20; 11:18; 13:46). (See my "Studies in the Book," vol. I, pp. 70, 71).

# SECTION VI.

## The Epistle to the Hebrews.

## CHAPTER XV.

### THE OLD AND THE NEW COVENANT.[1]

§ 160. *The Imperfection of the Old Covenant.*[2]

The Epistle to the Hebrews presents the relation of Christianity to Judaism under the aspect of a New Covenant, which is to bring the promise given in the Old to fulfillment. The first covenant (Heb. 8:7, 13; 9:15) has given place to the covenant or testament recently made (12:24), which as to its nature is new (9:15), and as to its continuance is eternal (13:20). The object of this New Covenant, under which we inherit after the manner of a testament or will, is to bring to actual fulfillment the promise which the Old Testament was meant to fulfill, but could not. In the Gospel which presents the fulfillment of the promise, we have received the same glad tidings as the people of the Old Testament (4:2, 6); and the aim of the New Testament is the fulfillment of the Old, because it alone realizes the conditions thereto.

The fulfillment of the promise in the Old Testament depended on the fulfillment of the law. Every transgression of this law was a breach of the covenant, which released God from His obligation towards the people, and rendered the fulfillment of the covenant promise

[1] Compare *Lechler*, vol. 2, pp. 120–128.
[2] Compare *Weiss*, § 115.

impossible. As transgressions were constantly occurring (9:15), and the fathers continued not in the Old Covenant by the fulfilling of the law, God must promise a new Covenant, if He would yet fulfill the covenant promise (8:9; after Jer. 31:32).

On account of transgression, there was given indeed the atoning institution of sacrifice, by which the people were to be put into the position of perfection necessary for obtaining the fulfillment of the covenant promise. If now through the Old Testament priesthood perfection could have been really attained, there would naturally have been no need of a New Covenant with a new priesthood (7:11). But, as a matter of fact, the law brought nothing to perfection (7:19), and thus gave evidence of its weakness and unprofitableness (7:18). It set up priests who had infirmities themselves, and on that account required atonement (7:27, 28); it assigned the priesthood to mortal, and therefore to changing men (7:8, 23). These priests served, to be sure, in the Holy Place, but only in that made with hands (9:11, 24)—a mere copy of the true heavenly Holy Place (9:23, 24; 8:5). The sacrifices could not effect what they ought to have effected to make the worshiper perfect (9:9), as the need of their continual repetition shows (10:1);—the conscience was not purified from the consciousness of guilt by them (10:2, 3), because the blood of animals could not take away sin (10:4, 11; 9:12); they could only effect Levitical purification (9:13).

The atoning work of the Old Testament ritual, therefore, had only this one object in view: prefiguratively to set forth as a typical prophecy the perfect atonement of the New Covenant (10:1).

[ANALYSIS: 1) The New Testament is the fulfillment of the Old; 2) in the Old Covenant the fulfillment of the promise depended on the fulfillment of the law; 3) transgressions rendered the fulfillment of the promise impossible; 4) the office of the atoning sacrifices; 5) they served as a type of the perfect atonement of the New Covenant.]

§ 161. *The Promise of the New Covenant.*[1]

The Old Testament itself points to the transitory character of the law, and of the whole covenant resting on it, while it presents to view a new one with better promises. A new priesthood is already spoken of in the Old Testament (7:21, 28; Ps. 110:4), and in Ps. 40:6–8 the imperfect offerings of the law are set aside (Heb. 10:8, 9). What these better promises are, the prophecy of Jeremiah (31:31–34), quoted in 8:8,12, tells us. In three things especially the New Covenant shall differ—1) the law of God shall be written on the heart of the people (8:10); 2) the knowledge of God shall become general, including also the Gentiles (8:11); 3) there shall be complete and perfect forgiveness of sins (8:12). And all these things have come to pass, because now we have a *real atonement*, and not a typical one, through which we draw nigh to God (7:19).

The writer of the Epistle to the Hebrews believes in the identity of the revelation of God in the Old and New Covenants. In the Old Covenant God has often and in many ways[2] spoken to the fathers in the prophets, as His organs (1:1), as now in His Son; and if, according to 2:2–4, the despising of Christ is reckoned more culpable than the despising of Moses, this is made to depend on the richer gifts which are received from Christ. It is the same revelation, but in the Son, God

---

[1] Compare *Weiss*, § 116.

[2] The "divers portions" and "divers manners" of Heb. 1:1 does not have any reference to the *defect* of prophecy, but rather expresses the riches and fullness of Divine revelation.

has made the last and highest revelation, and it demands most stringently a hearing and a reception, because it offers to men the highest salvation.

In the view of the author of the Epistle, the period which prophecy has in view for the transitional duration of the Old Testament institution of atonement is past. The ordinances of the Divine service of the first covenant belong to the past (9:1); with the entrance of complete forgiveness of sins the offering for sin has ceased (10:18); and the thank-offering, which is well pleasing to God, is no longer that of the Old Testament (13:12, 15). The exhortation of the Epistle culminates in the demand to abandon fellowship with the worship of the Old Testament (13:13), and he presupposes that the Levitical worship has lost every claim upon his readers (13:9; 9:9, 10).

[ANALYSIS: 1) The Old Testament itself bears witness to the transitory character of the law; 2) Jeremiah prophesies already of better promises; 3) there is an identity of revelation in the Old and New Testaments; 4) in the Son, God has made the last and highest revelation; 5) Christianity has now superseded the Levitical worship.]

§ 162. *The Realization of the New Covenant.*[1]

All the members of the Old Covenant people are called to the attainment of the promise (9:15); but those only who confess Jesus as the Apostle of God and the High Priest (3:1; 4:14) are really partakers of the heavenly calling. It follows then, of itself, that all that part of Israel remaining in unbelief are shut out from the fellowship of the family of God. The writer, who is seeking to deliver the Jewish Christians from the bonds of fellowship with their countrymen in matters of worship, takes it for granted that the Gentiles are

[1] Compare *Weiss*, § 117.

now partakers of salvation. By the grace of God Jesus tasted death for every man (2:9), and He became unto *all them that obey Him* the Author of eternal salvation (5:9).

But only believing Israel has a share in the New Covenant, as those Israelites who abide in unbelief fall under the righteous punishment of their apostasy. God has spoken to us in His Son "at the end of these days" (1:1)—*i. e.* the days of the pre-Messianic age; and at the end of the period belong thereto (9:26) is the perfect sacrifice offered which really takes away sin. The sacrificial death of Christ forms, therefore, the dividing point of the two ages; for with Him the Messianic age has come. Christians have already tasted its powers ("the powers of the age to come," 6:5); they have already received its blessings (9:11; 10:1).

The perfected salvation promised is, indeed, still future; but, as it is guaranteed by the introduction of the New Covenant, to the Christian consciousness it seems to be already present.

[ANALYSIS: 1) All the members of the Old Covenant are called; 2) but the greater part of Israel remains in unbelief; 3) the writer takes for granted that salvation is also for the Gentiles; 4) even for *all* that *obey* Him; 5) distinction between the pre-Messianic age and the Messianic age; 6) the final consummation still future.]

# CHAPTER XVI.

### THE HIGH PRIEST OF THE NEW COVENANT.

§ 163. *The Messiah as Son.*

Christ is the perfect, unique Mediator, not only of Divine revelation (1:1), but also of the reconciliation and the fulfillment of all the promises, because He is the *Son of God*, the first-begotten (1:6)—*i. e.* above all creatures infinitely exalted, even above the angels (1:4); for He is "the effulgence of the glory of God, and the very image of His substance" (1:3)—*i. e.* the absolute image of God, in whom His essence is fully expressed; in other words, He is the same nature with the Father. This harmonizes with the fact that the Son Himself is addressed as God (1:8), that all the angels worship Him (1:6), and that the very same Divine honor is paid to Him as it is customary throughout the Scriptures to ascribe to God the Father (13:21). In short, the Godhead of Christ is attested in this Epistle as clearly and unequivocally as possible. We cannot wonder that eternity and pre-existence are attributed to Him. The very expression "when he cometh into the world" (10:5), used of Christ's incarnation, implies His pre-existence; and eternity is still more clearly ascribed to Him when, as the type of Melchizedek, He is said to have " neither beginning of days nor end of life" (7:3). He, the eternal Son of God, is the Instrument not only of the creation of the world (1:2), but also of its preservation (1:3). To Him, by Divine appointment, belongs the sovereignty of the world—the inheritance of all things (1:2).[1]

[ANALYSIS: 1) Christ is described as the Son of God; 2) of the same nature with the Father; 3) Christ is truly Divine; 4) because to Him are ascribed Divine Names; 5) Divine Attributes; 6) Divine Works; 7) and Divine Worship.]

## § 164. *The Messianic High Priest.*[2]

If Christianity is essentially a new covenant, it requires also a new Mediator (Heb. 9:15; 8:6; 12:24). Such is Christ, by whom God pre-eminently speaks to His people at the end of the pre-Messianic age (1:1), to announce to them the deliverance prepared in the New Covenant (2:3). This Mediator must also be the

---

[1] Compare *Lechler*, vol. 2, pp. 123, 124. In my "Studies in the Book," vol. 3, Study IX, on "The teaching of the Epistle to the Hebrews," I have fully developed all points bearing upon the Person and work of Christ. The writer of the Epistle regards Jesus Christ as the God-Man, truly *Divine* and truly *human*. That He is truly *Divine*, can be seen from the fact that he ascribes to Him:

1) *Divine Names.* He is the Son of God (1:2, 5, 8; 4:14; 5:5; 6:6; 7:3; 10:29), the first-born (1:6), the Lord (2:3; 7:14; 13:21), the Author of eternal salvation (2:10; 5:9), the Author and Perfecter of our faith (12:2), the Great Shepherd of the sheep (13:20).

2) *Divine Attributes.* He is the effulgence of the glory of God (1:3), the very image of the essence of God (1:3), has pre-existed from all eternity (1:2, 3), is righteous (1:8, 9), is heir of all things (1:2), sovereign of the world to come (2:5), glorious (1:3), omnipotent (1:3, 13), and unchangeable (1:12; 13:8).

3) *Divine Works.* Through the Son, God made the world (1:2, 10; 11:3), the Son upholds all things by the word of His power (1:3, 12), He rules over all (2:5–8), is the Author of the salvation of men (2:10; 5:9; 7:25); it is He who sanctifies (2:11; 9:13, 14; 13:12), who delivers us from the power of death (2:14, 15), who overcame the Devil (2:14, 15), and who obtained eternal redemption for us (9:12).

4) *Divine Worship.* For He is worshiped by the angels (1:6), and worshiped and adored by the saints (13:20, 21).

[2] Compare *Weiss*, § 119.

High Priest of the New Covenant. Jesus is not simply "the Apostle" or Messenger of God, but He is at the same time the High Priest of our confession (3:1 ; 4:14). According to 5:1, 2, it is essential and necessary that the High Priest be taken from among men, and be a partaker of human nature and human infirmity, that he may properly discharge the duties of His office and be a merciful and faithful High Priest (2:17). This was accomplished by the Son of God, whose very name characterizes Him as a Divine Being, exalted above the angels (1:5–14), because for a little while He was made lower than the angels, on account of the sufferings which He endured (2:9, 10), and took upon Himself the infirmities of our nature (2:10, 14).

Christ's humiliation does not consist so much in the fact that He became incarnate, for even now in His State of Exaltation He is still incarnate, the God-Man, having all authority ; but it lies rather in the nature of the earthly human life which the Son of God assumed as the Son of Man—a humiliation which He assumed of His own free-will, with a view to His Messianic calling (2:10). In order that He might be a sympathizing High Priest, He was in all things made like unto His brethren (2:17), yet without sin (4:15); and this could only be if He was tempted (tried) in all points, because thus only could He have sympathy with their infirmities (4:15). This happened in His suffering (2:10, 18), for which He was so susceptible that, in the days of His flesh, He offered up prayers and supplications with strong crying and tears (5:7).

The High Priest of the New Covenant, in contradistinction to that of the Old, was a Perfect Priest. He needed not for Himself to offer for sins (5:2, 3). Christ was tried, but without sin (4:15)—which means not only that He conquered every trial and temptation, but also that no sinful impulses of His own moved Him. On His entrance into the world He declared it to be the fundamental principle of His life to do the will of God (10:7, 9; after Ps. 40:8, 9); and though He was the Son, yet He learned obedience, according to His human nature by the things which He suffered (5:8), while He patiently bore the even harder trials which the sin of the world imposed on Him (5:7, 9). He was faithful to His calling (2:17; 3:2), and trusted in God (2:13); for, as the Leader of the company of believers, as the Captain and Perfecter of our faith, He has carried faith to perfection in His life, while He endured the shame of the Cross, bearing His reproach (6:6; 13:12, 13), in view of the joy that was set before Him (12:2, 3).

In Heb. 5:1–10, the writer of the Epistle explains the office of the High Priesthood. Christ fulfilled the two great requisites for the office. He was not only able to sympathize with men, but He was also appointed of God. And then the author begins to unfold the way of human sorrow, of godly fear, of suffering, and of submission to the Divine will, by which Christ, according to His human nature, attained His exaltation, and how that now He sits enthroned in Heaven as High Priest forever, after the order of Melchizedek.

In Heb. 7:1–10, we have a discussion of the glory of this priesthood of Melchizedek (*vers.* 1–3), and of its superiority to the Levitical priesthood (*vers.* 4–10). The actual historical Melchizedek lived and died, but there is no record of the beginning or end of his priesthood, as in the case of the Levitical priesthood;—for the priesthood of Melchizedek is continuous, unbroken by transmission or inheritance. Birth had nothing to do with his priesthood; death is not alluded to as depriving him of it; he passes it to no one else;—the Melchizedek of the Scripture narrative does nothing but live.

Now Jesus is the true High Priest after the order of Melchizedek—not of the race of Aaron (7:11-14); not by carnal descent of any kind, but through the absolute dignity of His own Person (7:15-19), appointed with a Divine oath (7:20-22), with an unchangeable priesthood, ever living to make intercession for us (7:23-25). Christ then being the true High Priest, He is superior to the Aaronic priests not only in the nature of His Priesthood, but also in the nature of His ministration (7:26-28). The superiority of the administration of the High Priesthood of Christ is manifest from the Divine and heavenly sphere in which both His high priestly and kingly offices are now discharged (8:1-6), as well as from the superiority of the New Covenant under which He acts (8:7-13), as by the eternal validity of the New Covenant (9:1-12).

[ANALYSIS: 1) Christ is the true High Priest; 2) His state of humiliation; 3) the Perfect High Priest; 4) He fulfilled the two great requisites for the office; 5) the argument of Heb. 5:1-10; 6) of Heb. 7:1-10 7) of Heb. 7:11-28; 8) of Heb. 8:1-13; 9) of Heb. 9:1-12:]

§ 165. *The High Priest in the Most Holy Place.*[2]

What specifically distinguished the high priest of the Old Covenant from the other Levitical priests, was that he alone went once a year into the Holy of Holies, in order to effect the purification of the people (9:3, 6, 7, 25). As Jesus has become our real High Priest, He too has gone within the veil (6:19, 20); has, through His own blood, entered in once for all into the Holy Place, having obtained eternal redemption (9:12). But the Most

[1] Compare my "Studies in the Book," vol. 3, pp. 64-69.
[2] Compare *Weiss*, § 120.

Holy Place of the Tabernacle was but a copy of God's heavenly dwelling, which He had shown to Moses on the Mount (8:5 ; 9:23). Our High Priest has not entered a holy place made with hands, but into Heaven itself, now to appear before the face of God for us (9:24), where He is now a great Priest over the house of God (10:21).

By His entrance into Heaven, the Mediator of the New Covenant has become a dweller in the Heavenly City of God, in which is the Most Holy Place (12:22, 24). There dwell with Him the innumerable hosts of angels, and all the souls of believers awaiting their resurrection from the dead (12:22, 23).

As the Heavenly Holiest is at the same time the Throne-room of God, where He as the Universal Ruler has His seat (4:16), the entrance of Christ into it is at the same time His elevation to the Throne of God (8:1 ; 12:2), and He now rules with royal, Almighty power over the Heavenly dwelling of God (10:21).

[ANALYSIS: 1) The duties of the High Priest ; 2) Christ as our High Priest has entered within the veil ; 3) this Most Holy Place is Heaven itself ; 4) where, as our High Priest, He also rules as King.]

### § 166. *Lechler's Presentation.*[1]

We may summarize the whole teaching of the Epistle to the Hebrews on the High Priesthood of Jesus as follows:

The Mediator of the New Covenant is Jesus Christ as the *High Priest* without a parallel (4:14; 10:21). He is this in two respects—1) by virtue of His mild and merciful disposition towards sinners, His brethren, for whom He intercedes before God (2:17 ; 4:15, 16), and

[1] Compare his *Apostolic and Post-Apostolic Times*, vol. 2, pp. 127–129.

2) by virtue of His relation to God, who called and appointed Him (5:5, 10).

Jesus Christ is the true and absolutely Perfect High Priest:

1) Because He is sinlessly holy, so that He had not, like a Levitical high priest, to present an offering first for His own sin (7:27).

2) Because He no longer performs His office on earth, but in Heaven, in the invisible sanctuary not made with hands, of which the Mosaic Tabernacle is a mere shadow (8:2–4; 9:24).

3) Because He did not offer a sacrifice of animals, but Himself as a sinless offering, and entered into the sanctuary through His own blood (9:12; 10:10).

4) By His redeeming death He established the New Covenant, and effected the forgiveness of sins and an everlasting, all-sufficient redemption for all who believe on Him (5:9), since He entered for us into the Presence of God once for all (9:12, 23, 24; 10:12, 14).

5) The heavenly, high-priestly ministration of Christ (8:2, 6) has an infinite superiority over the priestly performances of a Levitical kind, because it takes place in the true sanctuary, the Holy of Holies in Heaven, and Christ presents Himself to God for us (9:24). The Exalted Mediator exercises an everlasting, uninterrupted activity on our behalf by His intercession (7:25), and by His love applying to us full salvation.

[ANALYSIS: 1) Christ is the Great High Priest; 2) in two respects; 3) the absolutely Perfect High Priest.]

## CHAPTER XVII.

### THE SACRIFICE OF THE NEW COVENANT.

§ 167. *The Sacrificial Death of Christ.*[1]

The specific duty of the priesthood is the offering of sacrifice (5:1 ; 8:3). As the sacrifices of the Old Covenant were imperfect, the New Covenant required better sacrifices (9:23). The Messiah had already announced, in Ps. 40:7–9, that He would come not to offer the ordinary sacrifices, which are not well-pleasing to God, but to do God's will (Heb. 10:5–7), and He has therefore taken away the imperfect animal sacrifices (10:4) of the Old Testament law (10:8, 9). According to the meaning which the author gives to the passage from the Psalm, God has prepared for the Messiah a body (10:5), in order that He may offer it in sacrifice. This offering of Himself by the Messiah is hence the sacrifice which is really well-pleasing to God; and the highest demand of the Levitical sacrifice, blamelessness (9:14), was not wanting to it, because He presented Himself as the sinless One. If in Heb. 9:14, it is said that Christ offered Himself "through the eternal Spirit " without blemish to God, it is evidently meant that Jesus through the medium of His own eternal Spirit—*i. e.* through His Divine inward being as the God-Man, through His Divine eternal personality—of His own accord offered His life to God in sacrifice. This inward being of Christ is called here *eternal Spirit*, because absolute, Divine, and purely self-determined. This act of self-sacrifice *through this eternal Spirit* is an ethical one of

---
[1] Compare *Weiss,* § 121.

absolute validity and worth. Being a fully conscious and absolutely free act of obedience and love, made in the energy of His eternal Spirit, it is productive of a real atonement before God. It is the self-surrender of a pure and sinless, and, at the same time, infinite and ever-enduring life, and a work of infinite intensity and saving power commensurate to the need, not of individuals only, but of all mankind.[1]

But this perfect sacrifice, according to its nature, is offered once for all, because it renders any repetition of it unnecessary and impossible (10:18). But Christ, by His offering once for all, or by the offering of His body on the Cross (10:10, 14), by which He made sacrifice for sin (Heb. 10:12), has attained that purpose which the Old Testament sacrifices could not attain (9:9; 10:1); and there is hence no more need forever to repeat this self-offering, as the high priests of the Old Covenant offered theirs (7:27). It cannot be also on this account, since each man dies but once (9:27), and therefore the offering presented by His death (9:26) can never be repeated (9:28). It is clear, moreover, from the connection of 10:14 with 10:10, 12, as from 9:26–28, that the single act of self-offering was conclusively perfected by His death on the Cross (7:27).

The death of Christ more especially corresponds to the sacrifice on the great Day of Atonement, the blood of which the high priest carried into the Most Holy Place. As this sacrifice, accordingly to Lev. 16:15, had to be killed by the high priest himself, so the Perfect High Priest had freely to offer Himself on the Cross and as the high priest, once a year, entered the Holy of Holies, " not without blood " (9:7), so Christ "through His own blood entered in once for all into the Holy

[1] Compare *Delitzsch*, on Heb. 9:14.

Place, having obtained eternal redemption" (9:12). But this Holy Place into which Christ entered is one not "made with hands, like in pattern to the true, but Heaven itself" (9:24).

As in the Old Covenant the atoning point of the sacrificial act lay in the outpouring of the blood, and the presentation of the blood on the altar and in the Most Holy Place, so the presentation of the blood of Christ in Heaven makes valid before God for our comfort the salvation obtained by the shedding of His blood on the Cross (9:12, 16; 12:2). The author of the Epistle to the Hebrews shows very fully how that Christ in His death was the true antitype of the ritual of the great Day of Atonement. He lays stress, even, on the fact that as the bodies of the animals whose blood the high priest brought into the Most Holy Place were burned without the camp, even so Christ suffered without the gate (13:11, 12).

The only sacrifice in the Old Covenant which really could not be repeated (9:19, 20; *cf.* Ex. 24:6–8) was the one offered at the institution of that covenant. If now Christianity is set forth as a New Covenant, which is to be grounded on the setting up of a perfect atoning sacrifice, nothing is easier to see in the perfect sacrifice on which it is based the covenant sacrifice of the New Covenant. Wherefore, because Christ with the blood of a perfect atoning sacrifice has entered once for all into the Holy Place (9:12), He is the Mediator of a New Covenant (9:15); and in 9:19–25, the author expressly makes the blood with which Christ entered into Heaven parallel with the blood of the Old Testament sacrifice.

[ANALYSIS: 1) The sacrifices of the Old Testament were imperfect · 2) the perfect sacrifice of Christ; 3) the meaning of Heb.

9:14 ; 4) Christ's offering once for all ; 5) it cannot be repeated ; 6) the ritual of the Day of Atonement a type ; 7) Christ's death the covenant sacrifice of the New Testament.]

## § 168. *The Necessity of the Sacrificial Death of Christ.*[1]

The death of Christ was necessary for the setting up of the New Covenant, whether one look upon it as a will of Christ's (9:15–17), which came into force only by the death of Him that made it, or as a relation of fellowship with God, which was hindered by the guilt of the covenant people (9:23). When the writer designates the blood of Christ as "the blood of the covenant" (10:29), evidently thinking of the words of Christ at the institution of the Lord's Supper, he looks at the covenant established by Christ as a will, by which Christians are become possessors of the covenant promise. Now, as a will comes in force only after the death of the testator (9:16, 17), so the death of Jesus was necessary in order that Christians may really take possession of the promise bequeathed to them by the New Covenant.

If the blood of animal sacrifices could not remove sin (10:4, 11), then that arose not from the impossibility of an atonement really removing sin by means of sacrificial blood, but only from the imperfection of the Old Testament means of atonement, which was only shadowy and typically prophetic. Through the offering of Christ there is effected an actual putting away of sin (9:26). Sin has lost the right and power to stain believers with guilt, and thus to separate them from God, because it is atoned for.

The believer by this atonement has been delivered from the guilt of sin in that Christ by His death has

[1] Compare *Weiss*, § 122.

representatively borne the punishment of his guilt (9:15). In 9:28 we have a statement of the Divine purpose to which Christ's death on the Cross was made subservient. "He was offered to bear the sins of many." The reference in the sacred writer's mind is to Isa. 53:12. He died in order to take upon Himself—*i. e.* to make atonement for, and bear the penalty of, the sins of many. The writer here refers to the vicarious endurance of punishment for the sins of others.

[ANALYSIS: 1) The death of Christ was necessary; 2) a testament is of force only after the death of the testator; 3) the sacrifices of the Old Testament were but types; 4) the efficacy of Christ's death; 5) He bore the punishment of our sins.]

§ 169. *The Effects of the Sacrificial Death of Christ*.[1]

As the Old Testament covenant people were sprinkled with the cleansing blood of the covenant sacrifice (9:19, *cf.* Ex. 24:8), so are believers sprinkled with the blood of Christ (9:22, 23; 10:29); but here also this sprinkling is more exactly referred to the heart, and the deliverance produced thereby is from an evil conscience (10:22), for the blood of sprinkling proclaims the perfected atonement (12:24). By this sprinkling the hearts of believers are purified from the stains of guilt, and their consciences delivered from the consciousness of guilt. This is clear from 9:22 and 10:22. The thought can here be only of a deliverance from sin—a cleansing from the stains of sin, not a cleansing and expelling of its unholy power.

That the idea of *sanctifying* stands in very close connection with that of cleansing is seen from Heb. 9:13, 14. What cleansing is to the subjective consciousness of the man, that sanctification is for his objective rela-

[1] Compare *Weiss*, § 123.

tion to God. Because believers have once for all been consecrated by the sacrifice of the body of Christ (10:10; 12:12), or by the cleansing blood of the covenant (10:29), they are called saints, holy brethren (3:1; 6:10; 13:24). And the Christian, after he has once for all been put in the position of one cleansed from sin—a position which fits him to be of the family of God—has now laid on him the task of keeping himself in this position by avoiding fresh defilement from sin; for we are to follow "the sanctification without which no man shall see the Lord" (12:14).

If those who have been sanctified by the sacrificial death of Christ have been forever perfected by one offering (10:14), it is clear that by the *perfection* of the Christian here referred to, cannot be understood moral perfection as we speak of the moral perfection or sinlessness of Christ. The idea here expressed by the writer of the Epistle to the Hebrews closely corresponds with the Pauline idea of *justification*, with this characteristic difference: that the latter refers to the putting into a state or relation to God required by the law, while the perfection here spoken of refers to the putting into the state or relation which was aimed at by the whole atoning agency of the Old Covenant, but never reached (9:9; 10:1; 7:11, 19)—the state of perfection necessary for perfect covenant relationship. As, therefore, with Paul, *justification* is essentially identical with the not-reckoning or the forgiveness of sins, so, according to the connection of 10:14 with 10:11, 18, *perfection* is identical with the taking away or the remission of sins.

By the appropriation of the salvation and perfection wrought by Christ (10:14, 18), believers are put in the position of being well-pleasing to God, in which alone they can draw near to Him; and this drawing near to God (11:6) is the condition of all true worship of God. By means of the Perfect High Priest only can we draw near to God (7:25); through Him alone can we offer sacrifices well-pleasing to God (13:15, 16); only in consequence of the cleansing perfected by Him can we worship the living God (9:14) in the way well-pleasing to Him (12:28). On the ground of the blood of His atoning sacrifice (10:19, 20) have we confidence to enter into the Holy Place. Christ Himself has gone as our High Priest into the Holiest of the heavenly dwelling of God to make his atoning sacrifice effectual by His blood, and thus to become the forerunner, who has not only opened the way thither, but has first trod it (6:20), and has thereby consecrated it for us (10:20). Christians may now be encouraged (4:14; 10:21) to approach with boldness the throne of grace (4:16), which is in the Holy Place (10:19, 22). The author can even designate Christians as those who have already come to the Heavenly City of God (12:22), where the Judge as their covenant God dwells (12:23), with the Mediator of the New Covenant, whose blood testifies to the perfected atonement (12:24).

[ANALYSIS: 1) Believers are sprinkled with the blood of Christ; 2) what this signifies; 3) its relation to sanctification; 4) the *perfection* of which the writer of the Epistle speaks; 5) the effects of the sacrificial death of Christ.]

## CHAPTER XVIII.

### THE BLESSINGS AND DUTIES OF THE NEW COVENANT.

§ 170. *The New Testament Covenant People.*[1]

If by the sacrifice of Christ the people of the Old Covenant are put in the position of being well-pleasing to God, then only now can that be realized which was intended from the first in the covenant relation, but which could be perfectly realized only in the New Covenant in conformity with the promise (Heb. 8:8–12; Jer. 31:33). He has become their God, and they are His people (8:10). The Israel of the New Covenant are the true family of God (3:6); for those only really belong to God who, having been perfected by purification and consecration (10:14), now draw near to Him in fullness of faith (10:22), and obey the Author of eternal salvation (5:9). The people of the New Covenant, whether Jew or Gentile (5:9), may come to the throne of God, as to the throne of grace (4:16), with assured confidence, there to receive mercy and to find grace. Every one who falls away from Christ turns away from this grace of God (12:15). It is grace which establishes the heart (13:9), and which gives the Spirit (10:29).

As Christ appears among the heavenly Sons of God as the first-born (1:6), so the Christian Church is called "the Church of the first-born" (12:23); and the words added, "who are enrolled in heaven," show unequivocally that to those who are already enrolled as citizens in the Heavenly City of God, though they yet wander

---

[1] Compare *Weiss*, § 124.

on the earth, the final consummation is therewith secured in virtue of this right of the first-born.

Among the six subjects of elementary instruction, mentioned in Heb. 6:1, 2, is reckoned instruction with reference to "washings and of laying on of hands." The Christian catechumen coming out of Judaism had to be instructed how New Testament baptism in the name of Jesus, or the Triune God, is distinguished by its sacramental, inwardly transforming, and mysterious character from the "divers washings" of the law (9:10), as well as from the preparatory baptism of John, which paved the way for the coming kingdom.

In the "laying on of hands," the writer refers (at least primarily and principally) to the imposition of hands which in the Apostolic age was connected with baptism, and which followed it either immediately, as at Acts 19:5, 6, or at a later period (Acts 8:15–17). The writer evidently draws a distinction between Christian baptism and the imposition of hands. Baptism brings the man as a person into the state of grace, and the imposition of hands qualifies him for bearing witness; the former translates him out of the world into the fellowship of Christ; the latter, by means of the marvelous gifts which were so richly poured out in the Early Christian Church, enables him to serve Christ in the world; the former ministers to him the Divine *Grace*, the latter the manifold Divine *charismata*, or spiritual gifts.[1]

If now, in accordance with the promise of the New Covenant (Jer. 31:33), the law is written on the heart (Heb. 8:10; 10:16), this implies that believers have received a new mind, and are drawn and led on by God to holiness and righteousness (12:14; 13:4, 5). In this God Himself helps, while He establishes the heart

[1] Compare *Delitzsch*, on Hebrews, 6:1.

by His grace (13:9), and accompanies the believer in every way (13:25); but, in particular, while by His Fatherly chastisements in times of trial He draws His true children to an ever fuller participation in His holiness (12:5–10), and so works in them the peace-bringing fruits of righteousness, which are well-pleasing to God (12:11). So that God Himself makes the Christians ready for every good work, to do His will, while He works in them what is well-pleasing to Him through Christ (13:21).

To the blessings already given to believers belongs also enlightenment by the Word of God—a knowledge of God which shall be alike and common to all (8:11). The writer is evidently thinking of the perfect revelation of God made in the Son (1:1), and which ought to have already fitted even the readers of this Epistle to be able to be teachers (5:12). They had already obtained the knowledge of the truth (10:26), and were therefore enlightened (6:4; 10:32). But there are different stages in the revelation of the New Testament Word of God, as there are in the knowledge wrought by it. The enlightenment brought by the Word is to be ever advancing and to be ever becoming more perfect (6:1, 2).

[ANALYSIS: 1) The blessings of the New Covenant; 2) the Christian Church is called "the Church of the first-born;" 3) the teaching of "baptisms;" 4) and "of laying on of hands;" 5) the "new mind" of the believer; 6) growth in knowledge necessary.]

§ 171. *Life in the New Covenant.*[1]

A two-fold condition is required for entrance among the people of God: 1) A *change of mind—i. e.* a turning away from dead works (6:1), which is a work of God's

[1] Compare *Lechler*, vol 2, pp. 129–132.

grace, transforming and renewing the inmost mind of man (6:6). Next to repentance and change of mind, 2) *faith* is a condition of entrance into the New Covenant (6:1). The axiom that it is impossible to please God without faith is clearly laid down in 11:6 and 10:38. This already implies that faith is not mere thought and knowledge, but a moral turning and attitude of the mind, full of confidence and joyful trust (11:1). It is steadfast confidence regarding the things that are hoped for—an evidence, an assurance, of things not seen; therefore, a matter of the heart. Unbelief, on the contrary, is a thing of the mind and will; disobedience towards God's Holy will—mistrust, infidelity to God—on the other hand, proceeds from an evil heart (4:6; 3:12).

If the preaching of the Gospel finds a willing hearing (2:1), with change of mind and faith (6:1), there is, after baptism has taken place (6:2), a full entrance into all the blessings embraced in the life of the New Covenant. Having tasted the good Word of God, and having become enlightened and made partakers of the Holy Ghost, having tasted of the heavenly gift of reconciliation with God (6:4, 5), believers receive the eternal, unchangeable kingdom of God, which cannot be shaken (12:28). It is the certainty of reconciliation through faith which assures the heart of God's favor (11:6), and of a righteousness through faith (11:4).

The author loves to describe the life in the New Covenant as a joyful approach to God (4:16; 7:25; 10:1), as a continual service of the living God (9:14; 12:28), with priestly offering up of sacrifice in word and deed—*i. e.* in thanksgiving and praise to God; in joyful confession (13:15), as well as in pious beneficence (13:16; 10:24). The *duties* of believers are thus indicated, the most essential of which are constancy of faith, steadfast trust in God and His promises, enduring strength of spirit—even under trials, reproaches, and persecutions (6:11; 10:36).

The practical aim of the Epistle is to strengthen the minds of the readers, to fortify them against indolence and moral deadness, and to preserve them from apostasy and covenant-breaking, which lead to fearful judgment. Instead of relapse and apostasy, believers are rather to strive after moral growth, to change their state of childish minority for the maturity and perfection of manhood (5:11-14), to lay aside the first principles of Christian knowledge, and to rise to a fuller and more independent understanding and discernment; to attain to the full assurance and strength of hope (6:11), and in the power of Christ to strive after holiness (12:10; 13:20, 21).

[ANALYLIS: 1) Repentance and faith the conditions of entrance into the Kingdom of God; 2) the blessings of the New Covenant; 3) description of the life in the New Covenant; 4) the duties of believers; 5) the practical aim of the Epistle.]

§ 172. *The Fulfillment of the Covenant Promise.*[1]

While the patriarchs (11:13), and all believers of the Old Covenant (11:39), did not really receive the promise, as they had first to be perfected by the one sacrifice of Christ (11:40), the members of the New Covenant have this advantage over them, that they are fitted and destined to receive directly the perfect salvation promised. Believers have now the perfect realization of the Divine promises, and can even now be designated as "heirs of the promises" (6:12, 17). They are heirs of salvation—that perfect blessedness which we can only attain through the mediation of Christ, the Author and

[1] Compare *Weiss*, § 126.

Perfecter of our faith (12:2). This ultimate aim of salvation the author represents, in colors drawn from the Old Covenant (Ps. 95:11), as the blessed rest of the people of God (3:7–11; 4:1, 9)—in the heavenly home, the Jerusalem above, the City which is to come (12:22; 13:14).[1]

[ANALYSIS: 1) Believers are now heirs of salvation; 2) the final consummation, however, still future.]

---

[1] Compare § 118, on *The Final Consummation.*

# PART IV.

THE TEACHING OF JOHN.

# PART IV.

## THE TEACHING OF JOHN.

### INTRODUCTION.

§ 173. *The Apostle John.*

To the Apostle John, the brother of James, the son of Zebedee, belongs the memorable distinction of being the disciple whom Jesus loved, and to whom He committed the care of His mother (John 19:26, 27). The passionate love of John for his Saviour seems to have found satisfaction in exclusive devotion to Him, and he grew ever more and more into the likeness of Him whom he so truly loved. Of the first thirty and the last fifty years of his life we have scarcely any trace. Only one portion of his life, the fifteen years following his call to the discipleship, stands out before us in the clearness of broad daylight. We have no record of any independent missionary work on his part. He was still in Jerusalem about 50 A. D., and took part in the settlement of the controversy between the Jewish and Gentile Christians (Acts 15:6); and his position and reputation was such that in this connection Paul speaks of him, in co-ordination with James and Peter, as one of the pillars of the Church (Gal. 2:9). His special work during the next twenty years of his life may have been that of teaching and organizing the Churches of Judea, and in the fulfillment of this charge his life may have been one of loving and reverent thought rather than one of conspicuous activity. Early tradition, however, unanimously points to Asia Minor, and to Ephesus in particular, as the scene of the later activity of John. The time of his removal from Jerusalem to Ephesus is uncertain, but it must have been after the death of Paul. It is generally agreed that he was banished to Patmos during his stay at Ephesus, but the time of his exile is also uncertain. It is also allowed on all hands that John was released from exile, that he returned to Ephesus, and that he lived to an extreme old age.

[ANALYSIS: 1) The disciple whom Jesus loved; 2) we have no record of his missionary work; 3) Ephesus the scene of his later activity.]

§ 174. *Sources of Johannean Theology.*[1]

For the presentation of the doctrinal system of the Apostle John, we have at our command two different sources—1) the Fourth Gospel and the three Epistles of John; and 2) the Apocalypse. It does not belong to our province to establish the genuineness of the Apocalypse, or of the Gospel and the three Epistles—for this proof belongs to Biblical Introduction. The history of this discussion, however, is very interesting, and teaches a good lesson to modern critics. Thirty years ago De Wette very tersely expressed the general result of the higher criticism of his day when he said: "In New Testament criticism nothing is so firmly established as that the Apostle John, if he be the author of the Gospel and the Epistles, did not write the Apocalypse; or, if the latter be his work, that he cannot be the author of the other writings." The school of Schleiermacher ascribed the Gospel and the Epistles to the Apostle John, but denied his authorship of the Apocalypse, and this view prevailed generally thirty years ago. Then

[1] Compare *Weiss*, § 140.

the opposite view gained the ascendency, that of the Tübingen school, that the Apocalypse was a genuine Johannean production, but that John was not the author of the Gospel and the Epistles. For ourselves, we abide firmly by the unity of authorship, and recognize both the Apocalypse and the Gospel as well as the Epistles as apostolic and Johannnean.

Even apart from the question of the time of composition, scientific thoroughness requires that the doctrinal contents of the Apocalypse should be examined and developed separately from those of the Gospel and the Epistles. For our purpose, it is not necessary to discuss the date of the composition of the Apocalypse, although the majority of modern critical historians and commentators, diverse as may be their views on other points, agree in this, that the Apocalypse, no matter by whom written, was composed between the death of Nero (June 9, 68 A. D.) and the destruction of Jerusalem (August 10, 70 A. D.)[1] But this question has not been finally settled, because the internal evidence, upon which the main stress is laid in proof of an early date, is not sufficiently convincing to overcome the clear and weighty testimony of the Early Church that John wrote the Apocalypse, in his old age, at the end of Domitian's reign (95 or 96 A.D.),[2] at about the same time that he wrote the Gospel and the Epistles.

[ANALYSIS: 1) The writings of John; 2) the question of the genuineness of the Gospel and of the Apocalypse settled by Biblical Introduction; 3) the date of the several writings.]

[1] So Neander, Gieseler, Lücke, Bleek, Ewald, De Wette, Reuss, Düsterdieck, Renan, Weiss, Auberlen, Stier, Gebhardt, Davidson, Cowles, Bishop Lightfoot, Stanley, Schaff, Westcott.

[2] So also the great majority of older commentators, and among moderns, Ellicott, Alford, Hengstenberg, Ebrard, Lange, Hofmann, Godet, Lee, Van Oosterzee, and others.

§ 175. *The Character of Johannean Theology.*[1]

As one of the disciples who had been constantly in fellowship with Jesus from His very first appearance; as one of the three confidential disciples (Mark 5:37; 9:2; 13:3; 14:33); as he whom Jesus had counted worthy of a special love (John 13:23; 20:2, 21:20), John must have felt himself drawn by the Person of Jesus, even more directly and more powerfully than the other disciples, and must have been influenced by it in his entire spiritual life. How this came about depended on his spiritual individuality. As he appears in his Epistles, he was eminently intuitional and contemplative. His whole spiritual work is a contemplative sinking of himself in a small circle of great truths, which unveil ever new sides to him, and disclose ever new depths in them. If we think of this contemplative nature brought face to face with Jesus, then it could not be any one thing Jesus taught, but His own Person itself, which seized his spiritual life, and concentrated on itself his undivided regard. To sink himself ever deeper into its whole height and significance; to seek and find in it on all sides the highest salvation; to become ever more sure and more joyful in the ever-more complete surrender to this possession, must have been the goal of all his spiritual struggles and life. Thus the whole view of the Person of Jesus, so full of life, and the saving significance of it, grew on him, and became the animating and blessful center of his whole spiritual life. This complete view of the Person of Christ and its saving significance, forms, therefore, the starting-point of his whole doctrinal view. Therein rests the peculiar character of John's theology. It is a knowing immediately, a living looking on the highest revelation of God, given

[1] Compare *Weiss*, § 141.

in and with the Person of Christ—an ever-sinking of himself in fathomless depths of that Revelation which had been manifested in Christ.

A fruit of this contemplation, as it corresponded to the spiritual individuality of the Apostle, we find in the great comprehensive first principles which are peculiar to the Johannean theology. They are not abstract ideas got from reflection, but forms of intuitive perception, in which the highest things, about which his spiritual life was occupied, ever afresh presented themselves to his mind. He sees throughout the comprehensive contrasts of God and the Devil, of light and darkness, of truth and falsehood, of love and hatred, of sin and holiness, which trace all phenomena back to their deepest reason, their ultimate principle. And therefore he announces so generally what is the norm in the deepest nature of things, untroubled by the thought how many exceptions and deviations may occur in practical experience. He often takes no apparent notice of the different stages of development, because in each ease he looks mainly at the essence. Truth is truth, whether it be the imperfect Old Testament truth or the perfected and eternal truth of the New Testament. Faith is faith, knowledge is knowledge, from its germinal beginnings to its fullest completeness. Life is eternal life, even in this world. This tendency may be called the idealism of John's view of doctrine.

On this stand-point there can be no contrast between the theoretical and the practical, between knowing and doing, between faith and life. John does not know of this contrast, and he will not acknowledge it; for him there is but a knowledge of the full revelation of God in Christ, which brings about as its result the doing of what is good. The knowledge of God and Christ is a being in God and Christ, and a being of God and Christ in us. This is the Johannean mysticism, which does not consist in a soaring in indefinite and confused views and feelings, but in an effort to get at the one central point of the spiritual life, in which everything that is to have real value is traced back to the deepest foundation of the being to the personal life itself—which, moreover, finds as the religious element its deepest satisfaction in the direct relation of person to person. This mysticism is begotten of the innermost need of the emotional life, is comprehended in feeling and self-surrender, in finding in love the foundation and the object and the goal of all living and life-giving knowledge. Thus John, with all in whom love to God has been quickened, has found in Christ the full revelation of the love of God; and in this sense he may be called the Apostle of Love.

[ANALYSIS: 1) John's relation to Christ; 2) the contemplative Apostle; 3) the Person of Christ the center of his doctrinal views; 4) he meditates upon the deep contrasts in life, and their ultimate principles; 5) to him there is no contrast between theory and practice; 6) the mysticism of John; 7) the Apostle of Love.]

§ 176. *Previous Works on John.*

Neander[1] gives us a full discussion—1) of the Apostle John and his ministry as the closing point of the Apostolic Age; and 2) of the Doctrine of John. He makes John's central-point of doctrine to consist in the thought of "Divine Life in Communion with Christ," and in successive paragraphs discusses the original estrangement of man from God, the susceptibility of redemption, the Person and Work of Christ, the import of the

[1] In his *History of the Planting and Training of the Christian Church.* Edited by Robinson. New York: 1864. See pp. 354-379, 508-531.

sufferings of Christ, faith as the principle of a new life, progressive sanctification of believers, harmony of John's doctrine with Paul's, the resurrection and judgment, the Second Coming of Christ, the idea of the Church, and the Sacraments. He gives us many deep glimpses into the peculiarity of the Johannean theology, but still there is much that must be criticised.

Schmid[1] has pursued the right method, in that he maintains that we can develop a Johannean system of doctrine as distinguished from the teaching of Jesus as recorded by John. He rightly holds that the history and the discourses of Jesus belong to the Messianic period, and must be presented under the teaching of Jesus. According to Schmid, John takes Christ as his groundwork and however much he may set forth His death he dwells upon His Person more clearly than upon His works. The distinctive character of John's system is constituted by his assuming a *theological* and *Christological*, and not an *anthropological* standpoint, as Paul. He therefore discusses John's teachings under the following heads: 1) God in Christ; 2) the Word, the Only-begotten Son; 3) the Father and the Holy Spirit; 4) the world and mankind in their original relation to God; 5) the world in its alienation from God; 6) the fellowship of the world with God through Christ; 7) fellowship with Christ, and through Him with the Father; 8) the effect of this fellowship on believers; 9) consummation of the fellowship with Christ, both for individuals and the Church.

Van Oosterzee,[2] in general, follows Schmid. He maintains that the doctrinal teaching of John can be recog-

[1] In his *Biblical Theology of the New Testament*, §§ 90-100. English edition, pp. 519-548.

[2] In his *Theology of the New Testament*, pp. 372-437. London, 1871.

nized from the Apostle's own utterances, preserved partly in the Gospels and Epistles, and partly in the Apocalypse. In the contemplation of the Gospel as a source of knowledge for the Johannean doctrine, we must by no means take into account the utterances of the Johannean Christ, but exclusively those in which the Evangelist himself appears as witness or defender.[1]

Van Oosterzee then discusses the teaching of the Gospel and the Epistles under the three general headings: 1) The world out of Christ; 2) the appearance of Christ on earth—the Incarnation; 3) life in Christ. This is followed by a brief presentation of the teaching of the Apocalypse.

Lechler[2] gives us a very satisfactory presentation. He first develops the teaching of the *Apocalypse*, and then passes to the *Gospel* and *Epistles* of John. But he does not confine the sources of John's doctrine to the Epistles and to those parts of the Gospel in which John himself speaks, but uses also the discourses of Jesus as a means to discover the Apostle's doctrine. According to Lechler,[3] John's fundamental view is this: "Jesus the Christ and Son of God, in whom is life."

In addition to these, we must make special mention of the presentation of the Johannean theology as given

[1] John 1:1-18; 2:21, 22; 6:64-71; 7:39; 11:51, 52; 12:14-16, 33, 36-43; 13:1-3; 19:28, 35-37; 20:30, 31; 21:23.

[2] In his *Apostolic and Post-Apostolic Times*, vol. 2, pp. 163-213. Edinburgh, 1886.

[3] Analysis of Lechler's Presentation:
I. The Doctrine of Jesus Christ, the Son of God.
   A. God; B. The world and the Prince of this world.
II. Jesus Christ the Son of God, in whom is Life.
   A. Jesus Christ the Only-begotten Son of God.
      1) His Person; 2) His work.
   B. Fellowship with the Father and the Son. 1) Its origin; 2) its condition and development; 3) its completion.

by Messner,[1] Gebhart,[2] and Bernhard Weiss.[3] The latter also gives us a very complete discussion of the theology of John in his " Biblical Theology of the New Testament," but, in his peculiar way,[4] includes the speeches of Christ, as recorded by John, as sources for the Johnnean theology.

[ANALYSIS: 1) The presentation by Neander; 2) by Schmid; 3) by Van Oosterzee; 4) by Lechler; 5) by Bernhard Weiss.]

---

[1] In his *Lehre der Apostel.* Leipsic, 1856.

[2] In his *Doctrine of the Apocalypse*, and its relation to the doctrine of the Gospel and Epistles of John. Edinburgh, 1878. We have made constant use of this suggestive work.

[3] In his *Johanneische Lehrbegriff*, in seinen Grundzügen untersucht. Berlin, 1862.

[4] The following paragraph will enable the reader to get an idea of the peculiar position which Weiss holds with reference to the historical accuracy of the Gospels:

"John was conscious to himself that he had reproduced the speeches of Jesus not in verbal accuracy, but by a free reproduction conformable to the laws of memory, which must, moreover, at any rate be assumed, considering the length of time after which he wrote it all down. That this now really took place is confirmed by the undeniable uniformity between the doctrinal terms and the development of thought in the Epistles, and the speeches and dialogues in the Gospel." [§ 140 (c.)]

In answer to this it is sufficient to say, that John at times records certain utterances of Jesus with the remark that they were at that time not rightly understood by the Apostles (John 2:19–22; 7:37–39; 12:33), thus clearly distinguishing between the thoughts of Jesus and those of the Apostles, and consequently from his own personal ideas. The length of these discourses is no argument against their authenticity. If in the form, tone, and style of Jesus's discourses we find a harmony with John's form, tone, and style, this only goes to prove that the Disciple had thoroughly adopted and elaborated in his own mind the teaching of his Master, and can afford no argument for throwing doubt on the essential faithfulness of the record, and for removing all distinction between the teaching of Jesus as historically recorded by John and the latter's own personal ideas. (See also my presentation in § 12.)

# SECTION I.

The Teaching of John According to the Gospel and the Epistles.

## CHAPTER I.

### THE DOCTRINE OF GOD.

§ 177. *The Doctrine of the Father.*[1]

John does not anywhere give us any direct teaching as to God in general; but, whenever he speaks of God, or specially of the Father, a reference also to the Son is always evident. This is the case in the prologue to his Gospel (John 1:1–18), as well as in his first Epistle. In both the name *Theos* is that most frequently used for God the Father (John 1:13, 18; 1 John 4:9, 10, 12). In distinguishing Him from the Son, the word *Father* is also used (John 1:14, 18; 1 John 1:2, 3; 2:1; 3:1; 4:14; etc.). This God is, moreover, described as the *One true* God (1 John 5:20; *cf.* John 17:3), in contradistinction to all idols (1 John 5:21). No man hath seen Him (John 1:18; 1 John 4:12, 20); the Only-begotten Son has declared Him (John 1:18).

John affirms of God, positively, that He is *light*, perfect and *holy*, and unstained by sin, for "in Him is no darkness at all" (1 John 1:5, 6). *Light* is a figurative expression, which may mean, generally, every kind of spiritual perfection; but the context shows that the idea of *holiness* is here involved.

[1] Compare *Schmid*, § 93; *Lechler*, vol. 2, pp. 181–183.

## THE DOCTRINE OF THE FATHER. 241

As the *invisible* God, He is *eternal life* (1 John 5:20; *cf.* John 5:26), absolutely perfect, having eternal life in Himself, the origin and source of all material and spiritual life of the creature. In this conception of light and life, not only is the idea of God as a spirit contained, but all the other predicates which John attributes to Him are to some extent based on it; and among them especially the attributes of knowing and understanding everything; also that He is the true, faithful, and righteous God (1 John 3:20). The Father is pure as the nature of light, but He is also the All-wise Father; and both conceptions of Him, of His omniscience and His love, flow in equal measure from the contemplation of His nature as light.

Finally, John lays special emphasis on the conception of God as *love* (1 John 4:8). His very nature is love. He is the absolute *personality*, whose nature and will consist in love. Love is of God (1 John 4:7), and the love of God was manifested in this, that He sent His Only-begotten Son into the world to be the propitiation for our sins, that we might live through Him (1 John 4:8–10). The true idea of love flows from the self-sacrifice of Christ. From this idea of God it also naturally follows that God is true, faithful, and just.

John lays stress on these moral attributes of God. He is *true*, and in Him is truth (1 John 1:10). God is *faithful*, as being true to His word, and because He fulfills His promises; He is just and righteous, because, in conformity with His promise, He forgives those who confess their sins, and allots to every one his due. For this reason, and with reference to His promise, His faithfulness and justice involve the forgiveness of sins and the cleansing of the sinner (1 John 1:8,9). Along with the omniscience of God we have, in 1 John 3:20, the statement, "God is greater than our heart." By virtue of its connection with *vers.* 19 and 21, this cannot mean that God is greater in holy severity, but must have a comforting sense. God is greater than our hearts in consequence of His perfect power of forgiving sins, and because, as the omniscient God, He knows our innermost thoughts, and displays that mercy which is in full harmony with His holiness and justice.

[ANALYSIS: 1) John carefully distinguishes between the Father and the Son; 2) there is one true God; 3) invisible; 4) God is light; 5) God is life; 6) God is love; 7) God has made manifest this love; 8) God is true; 9) faithful; 10) and just; 11) the meaning of 1 John 3:20.]

### § 178. *The Doctrine of the Logos.*[1]

The idea of Jesus Christ as the *Incarnate Divine Word* is set forth by John in the prologue to his Gospel (1:1-18), with which we must compare the brief hints given in the first Epistle (1 John 1:2). Everywhere his eye is directed to the Divine glory shining forth in the human life of Jesus. He is eternal life made manifest; He is the *Logos* made flesh. The *idea of this Logos* must be derived from the prologue to the Gospel. Some external cause may have influenced John to make use of this designation in describing the Divine nature in Christ; but the basis of the peculiarity of John's prologue, and the whole of his teaching as to Christ, lies much deeper—in the disposition of the Apostle himself to view the Divine nature of the Son in its eternal and original existence.

It is the Apostle who first presents the truth in its purity and fullness, its genuineness and depth, to rectify the current ideas of his time. In this prologue,

[1] Compare *Schmid*, § 92; *Lechler*, vol. 2, pp. 189-192.

## THE DOCTRINE OF THE LOGOS.

John gives the result and the quintessence of all that, as a faithful witness of Jesus, he had to relate as to His life and discourses. At the same time he states the point of view from which they are to be regarded. The synoptists Matthew and Luke preface their account of Christ's public appearance with the history of His earthly origin, and also with a *human* genealogy, and thus manifest the character peculiar to them of keeping to the historical side of His appearance. John, on the other hand, traces back Christ's appearance to that which is eternal—giving, as it were, a *divine* genealogy.

The Apostle, in John 1:1–5, unquestionably has in mind Gen. 1:1–3. He here treats of the Logos *before* the Incarnation. In John 1:1 he declares the relation of the Logos *to God*, and in John 1:2–5 he defines His *relation to the world*.

1) The Logos was *in the beginning*, before all creation, *pre-mundane* and *before time*, consequently eternal. The statement does not indeed go beyond the beginning of the world; but, since it certifies that the Word did not originate when the world began, but already existed, the implication is that the Logos did not *become*, but *is*, eternal.

2) The Logos is *God*, of one substance with the Father. The word *God* must be taken as the predicate, meaning that the Logos is *true* God, not merely "godlike, divine." This unity is to be understood in such a way that the Logos may be distinguished from God the Father, but not divided from Him.

3) The Logos is *personally distinguished* from the Father—"the Word was with God." He was God with God, more accurately; toward (*pros*) God, so that His direction tended toward God; His look ("in the bosom of the Father," 1:18) was directed to God; His fellow-

ship was a communion with God. Thus the personal distinction between the Logos and God is stated as definitely as His unity of essence with God. In short, *the personality* of the essential Word, the Son of God, is here most distinctly attested.

We must now consider the relation of the Logos to the world.

1) The Logos is the *Mediator of creation*, "all things were made *through* Him" (1:3); the negative antithesis, "without Him was not anything made that hath been made" (1:3), purposely excludes eternity of matter. The *"through (dia) Him"* (1:2, 10) must not be overlooked; the Logos is the *instrument* of the world's creation, while the Father is the original Author of creation.

2) With respect to the world of humanity, the Logos is *the source of life and light* (1:4, 5). In John 1:9–18, the Apostle goes on to describe still further the operation of the Logos among mankind. *a*) The first point is, that the Logos had been at all times the principle of spiritual enlightenment ("there was the true light," 1:9). *b*) The second stage of the manifestation is intimated in 1:9, 10, the light *came into the world;* but although "He was in the world, and the world was made by (through) Him," nevertheless the world knew Him not. *c*) Now follows the third stage of His agency. Not only does the Logos produce spiritual enlightenment among men, but He has appeared and dwelt among men, so that they could behold His glory (1:14–18).

[ANALYSIS: 1) The idea of the Logos must be derived from John 1:1–18; 2) the reason of this prologue; 3) in John 1:1–5 the Apostle treats of the Logos *before* the incarnation; 4) he first defines His relation to God; 5) and then His relation to the world; 6) and closes with a description of the work of the Logos among mankind.]

§ 179. *The Doctrine of the Holy Spirit.*

John's teaching as to the *Holy Spirit*, like his teaching as to God generally, is not of an independent, detailed, and complete character. It is remarkable that the name never occurs with the epithet "holy" in the Epistles or Apocalypse. He speaks, however, often of "the Spirit of God" (1 John 4:2), "His Spirit" (*i. e.* of God) (1 John 4:13), "the Spirit" (1 John 3:24; 5:7, 8). He looks upon the Spirit, first of all, as the Spirit communicated to man (1 John 2:20, "ye have an anointing from the Holy One;" 3:24; 4:6, 13), and all he says on this point shows clearly that he considers that this communication is brought about by the Son, following the idea expressed by him in his Gospel (7:39).

In 1 John 5:7, 8,[1] we have the statement that "it is the Spirit that beareth witness," now and uninterruptedly, and that this "witnessing" is the peculiar office of the Spirit (*cf.* John 14:26; 15:26; 16:8–11). By this it is that men are enabled to pierce beneath the external phenomena and the external rites to their innermost meaning. Just as Christ is the Truth (John 14:6), so the Spirit sent in Christ's name is the Truth.

In *ver.* 8, the Spirit is regarded both as a power and as a person. In this whole passage there is a striking parallelism between the office of Christ and the office of the Spirit. *Jesus is He that came*, once for all fulfilling the Messiah's work; and the *Spirit is He who bears witness*, ever applying and interpreting His mission and His gifts.[2]

[ANALYSIS: 1) The names given to the Spirit by John; 2) sent by the Son; 3) office of the Spirit; 4) personality of the Spirit.]

---

[1] *Critical* Greek text, the same as in *Revised* Version.

[2] Compare *Westcott* on 1 John 5:6–8.

## CHAPTER II.

#### THE WORLD AND THE PRINCE OF THIS WORLD.

§ 180. *The World in its Alienation From God.*[1]

The world in all its parts was created by God through the Logos (John 1:3, 10). But the world in its existing state is at enmity with God, so that he who loves the world cannot love God. By the world (*kosmos*) John understands the whole sphere of earthly creation so far as it is estranged from God, and subject to the dominion of evil (1 John 2:15–17). It is this *love of the world*, as opposed to God, which forms the contrast to the love of God and to eternal life. God is Light, the world darkness; God is Life, in the world death reigns (1 John 1:5, 6; 2:9; 2:16; 3:14).

Sin is *lawlessness*, the transgression of the law—estrangement from the holy will of God (1 John 3:4). The transgression of the law by sin consists—1) partly in separation *from the truth;* 2) partly in separation *from love*. The first is shown in *lying* (1 John 1:6, 8; 2:21, 22); it is the opposition to God's truth and action, showing that the truth is not in us (1 John 1:8). This separation from the *truth* is also expressed in *unbelief* (1 John 5:10). He who believeth not God believeth not on Him in His Son; and thus, by his contradiction of God's truth, shows openly his opposition to it (1 John 5:9). The separation *from love* manifests itself in wrath, hatred, and bloodthirstiness (1 John 2:9–11; 3:12–14). The latter passage points out the inward cause of the hatred which is based on alienation from God.

[1] Compare *Schmid*, § 95; *Lechler*, vol. 2, pp. 184, 185.

The sin of man ultimately *blinds* him. This gives rise to the conception of *darkness*, which fills such an important place in the prologue to John's Gospel—its moral root and character being most clearly expressed in 1 John 2:8–11. Hatred results in darkness, because it blinds the heart. That is to say, darkness is nothing else but alienation from God—an idea which may also be inferred from 1 John 3:10; 4:6; 2:16. This darkness goes on to increase to an inward condemnation (1 John 3:14).

Sin, moreover, is universal among mankind. Because the principle of sin is a false love of the world; it is conceived of as being organized into a system, and is called simply *the* world (*kosmos*); "for all that is in the world, the lust of the flesh, and the lust of the eyes, and the vainglory of life, is not of the Father, but *is of the world*" (1 John 2:16). It is the *kosmos* which does not know the disciples (1 John 3:1), indeed hates them (3:13), from which the enemies of Christianity take their rise, and of which they speak (1 John 4:5). Man cannot free himself from it by his own power, without the Son he has not life, but remains in death (1 John 5:12). If we deny or undervalue this power or hold of sin, we shall only become deeper and deeper entangled in its toils (1 John 1:6–10). But this community of sin is not original among men; human sin has a mighty antecedent in the Devil, the wicked one, who is the beginner of sin (1 John 3:8). It is of this one that we must now treat.

[ANALYSIS: 1) John's conception of the *kosmos;* 2) the love of the world; 3) definition of sin; 4) its two-fold manifestation; 5) the result of sin; 6) John's conception of darkness; 7) sin is universal; 8) is conceived of as organized in a system; 9) man cannot free himself by his own strength; 10) sin had its origin in the will of the Devil.]

## § 181. *The Prince of this World.*[1]

It is an essential element in the conception of the world's estrangement from God that whoever commits sin is of the *Devil* (1 John 3:8). This being, Satan, is the author of all evil, "for the devil sinneth from the beginning" (3:8; *cf.* John 8:44). Sins are the *works* of Satan, and those who do evil are his children, morally dependent on him as the author of the evil within them (1 John 3:8, 10, 12). The whole evil world lies in the wicked one—*i. e.* under the power of the wicked one (1 John 5:19). He is the one "that is in the world" (1 John 4:4; *cf.* John 10:31, "the prince of this world"). Satan is the personal principle of evil, "for the Devil sinneth from the beginning. To this end was the Son of God manifested, that He might destroy the works of the Devil" (1 John 3:8). This, however, does not mean that the Devil is originally and by nature an evil being; for if the Devil be "a murderer from the beginning" (John 8:44), this "beginning" can only coincide with the creation of man and his fall, and not with the *existence* of the Devil himself. John certainly does not speak of a fall of the Devil, nor does he make mention of the fall of the first men. On the contrary, he describes the nature and work of Satan as it is, making no statement as to the origin of his hostile disposition towards God, but rather taking it for granted, on the basis of Old Testament revelation.[2]

[ANALYSIS: 1) Satan is the author of all evil; 2) the personal principle of evil; 3) not originally and by nature an evil being; 4) John describes the nature and work of Satan as he now exists.]

---

[1] Compare *Lechler*, vol. 2. pp. 185–188.
[2] For a special study on the teaching of the New Testament concerning *Satan*, see my "Studies in the Book," vol. 1, p. 103.

## CHAPTER III.

### JESUS CHRIST THE SAVIOUR OF THE WORLD.

§ 182. *The Incarnation of the Logos.*[1]

As Logos, the Son of God was a purely spiritual being, but "the Logos became flesh, and dwelt among us" (John 1:14). In becoming flesh, the Logos entered upon a new and essentially different state. Setting out with the heavenly existence of the Logos, John goes on to say that the Life, which was with the Father, was manifested (1 John 1:2); and we have heard, seen with our eyes, looked up, and our hands handled, this very Word of Life (1 John 1:1). When John says "the Word became flesh" (John 1:14), there is no reason for understanding this to mean anything else than that the Son of God assumed the whole true human nature in all its fullness and reality, sin alone excepted. With equal emphasis John ascribes to Jesus a true human body (John 19:34, 35), a true human soul (1 John 3:16), and a true human spirit (John 13:21). A denying that Jesus Christ is truly come in the flesh is the spirit of the Antichrist (1 John 4:2, 3; 2 John 7). The Word *became* (*egeneto*), in John 1:14, must be taken in a strict sense, not merely as a coming and appearing in the garb and form of the *flesh*, but as an actual passing over on the part of the Logos, which is Spirit, into the *flesh* (*sarx*), so that by virtue of this assumption of the flesh the heavenly *doxa* or *glory* itself might be made perceptible, for "we beheld His glory."

[1] Compare *Lechler*, vol. 2, pp. 192–195.

[ANALYSIS: 1) The Word became flesh; 2) Jesus had a true human body; 3) a true human soul; 5) a true human spirit.]

## § 183. *The Work of Jesus Christ.*[1]

The work of Jesus Christ dwelling among us in the flesh is thus summarized by John: "We have beheld and bear witness that the Father hath sent the Son to be the Saviour of the world" (1 John 4:14); "to this end was the Son of God manifested that He might destroy the works of the Devil" (1 John 3:8).

1) He is the *personal truth;* by Jesus Christ grace and truth came (John 1:17); the Only-begotten Son, which is in the bosom of the Father, has declared the truth (John 1:18; 1 John 1:5). As He was, even so should we be in this world (1 John 4:17); as He walked so should we also walk (1 John 2:6).

2) He is the *propitiation* for the sins of the whole world (1 John 2:2; 4:10). The most general expression is, He laid down His life *for us* (1 John 3:16)—*i. e.* in our stead; His blood shed for us has power to cleanse from sin (1 John 5:6; 1:7). In 1 John 1:7, the Apostle bears witness to the purifying effect of the blood of Jesus which was shed on the Cross, declaring that the cause and power of the purification, its efficacy, is not in us, nor in our conversion and moral walk in the light, nor yet in Christian fellowship, but is in fact in the *blood* of Jesus—*i. e.* in his bloody death on the Cross, Jesus being the God-Man, true man (being able to die) and true God (the Son of God). This cleansing efficacy was not exerted once for all, but is represented as present and always continuing—it *cleanseth* us. But in what this cleansing essentially consists is a matter of dispute. It is better to take the *cleansing* as purification from *guilt,*

[1] Compare *Lechler*, vol. 2, pp. 195-198.

in the sense of forgiveness of sins and justification, and not as deliverance from the *dominion* of sin, which is rather wrought by the Holy Spirit in the power of the new life which is implanted in us at our regeneration in baptism. From 1 John 2:2; 4:10, we must infer that John has in view a propitiatory sacrifice, offered to make possible the removal of the state of guilt and punishment. As the Advocate with the Father (1 John 2:1), He makes good before the Father the forgiveness obtained by His blood in His death on the Cross (1 John 1:7; 2:2). Believers have forgiveness of sins for His name's sake (1 John 2:12; 1:9).

[ANALYSIS: 1) The object of the incarnation; 2) Christ the personal truth; 3) the propitiation for the sins of the world; 4) the meaning of 1 John 1:7; 5) Christ is our Advocate with the Father.]

## CHAPTER IV.

### FELLOWSHIP WITH THE FATHER AND THE SON.

§ 184. *Fellowship with Christ, and through Him with the Father.*[1]

He who hears the Word (1 John 2:7; 2:24; 1:2,3), and believeth in the witness that God hath borne concerning His Son (1 John 5:10), and believeth on the name of the Son of God (1 John 5:13), that Jesus is the Christ, is begotten of God (1 John 5:1). Born of the Spirit, the believer has become a child of God (1 John 3:1, 2), and has been translated into fellowship with the Father and the Son (1 John 1:3; 5:20). As a child of God he is permitted to have the consciousness of it (1 John 3:1, 2; 2:29; 5:14); his sins are forgiven (1 John 1:9; 2:12), and power is given him of doing righteousness and of being able to keep God's commandments (1 John 2:3; 3:7,10; 5:3), especially of loving God and the brethren "in deed and in truth" (1 John 5:1, 2; 4:20, 21; 3:16–18), and consequently of knowing God (1 John 3:6; 4:8; 5:20; 2:20; 3 John 11).

John speaks much of knowing, indeed of seeing, God; but both are made entirely conditional on faith and love (1 John 2:13; 3:16; 4:7, 16; 5:20). And being in possession of the love of the Father (1 John 3:1; 1:7–10), a joyful, fearless confidence in God is finally given us (1 John 4:17, 18), the *boldness* in the future day of judgment, which in the perfection of love casteth out fear (1 John 2:28; 3:19), and, moreover, gives

[1] Compare *Schmid*, § 97.

us an assurance that our prayers will be heard (1 John 5:14; 3:22). We have therefore perfect joy (1 John 1:4), and the sure hope of the consummation of salvation, namely, the fellowship with Christ (1 John 3:2, 3). But if we abide in the Son, we abide also in the Father, and He abideth in us, and His love is perfected in us (1 John 2:24; 1:3; 4:12; 5:20).

Even when the believer is in fellowship with Christ, we are not to regard this relation as excluding every sinful emotion and action; for the believer, even when in a position of faith, must retain the consolation of the propitiation (1 John 2:1, 2). Jesus is the Advocate for the sins into which even believers may fall (1 John 3:19); but believers can be preserved through the fellowship with Christ, which is made certain to them by the consciousness that they have received the Spirit (1 John 3:24). For this Spirit is the very Spirit of Jesus, of whose fullness He has Himself imparted to us (1 John 4:13). Believers are, moreover, preserved from sin by the power of constantly purifying themselves (1 John 3:3), and of keeping themselves so that "the evil one toucheth him not" (1 John 5:18; 3:9; 2:13, 14); for this immunity from the attacks of the Evil One constitutes the chief victory over sin and the freedom from its dominion. He that is born again, that is begotten of God, doeth no sin, because His seed abideth in him; and he cannot sin, because he is begotten of God (1 John 3:9). We show that we really know Christ by following Him and keeping His commandments (1 John 2:3–6). This is no difficult task to him who is born of God and remains actually united to Christ, the Sinless One. He does not sin and cannot sin in so far as the new life is in union with Christ (1 John 5:3; 3:6, 9). We must here observe that John represents this impossibility of sinning as consequent upon and conditioned by the Divine life present in the regenerate man. There is no conflict between John's teaching of the sinfulness even of believers (1 John 1:8, 9) and this ideal view. The fundamental thought is, the believer in his new life, in the new man united to Christ, cannot sin; but the remnant of sin that is still left in the old man continues to exercise such power that the believer is compelled again and again to have recourse to the Advocate, who has, indeed, become the propitiation for our sins and the sins of the whole world (1 John 2:1, 2). Careful watch over oneself is therefore necessary, and constant moral purification (1 John 3:3; 5:18); in addition to honest, active, self-sacrificing brotherly love (1 John 3:14-17, 23; 4:7-12; 5:1), and victory over the world (1 John 5:5).

[ANALYSIS: 1) The believer has become a child of God; 2) receives forgiveness of sins and power unto a holy life; 3) a true knowledge of God is conditioned on faith and love; 4) fellowship with the Son includes fellowship with the Father; 5) the believer needs a continual growth in sanctification; 6) John regards the sinner from a two-fold view; 7) there is no conflict in John's teaching on this point.]

### § 185. *The Fellowship of Believers.*[1]

Fellowship with the Son and the Father is the means of producing a fellowship among believers (1 John 1:3, 7). Believers, because they are believers, have become *brethren* in a higher sense of the term, in virtue of being joint partakers in the new birth from God (1 John 4:20, 21; 5:1, 2). It is the power of love (1 John 3:16-18), and of a right confession of faith (1 John 2:23; 4:2, 3; 2 John 7, 9-11) which causes this fellowship to be both inward and outward; and thus those who are as-

[1] Compare *Schmid*, § 98.

sociated together in one place join together to form a Church (3 John 6, 9).

This fellowship of believers forms, moreover, a contrast to the world as the whole body of unbelievers subject to death, including also those of heterodox views, among whom false prophets and antichrists are specially mentioned as seducers (1 John 4:1–6; 2:18, 22, 26). Against these it is necessary for believers to be on their guard, by trying the spirits whether they be of God (1 John 4:1, 2, 6), and also by strictly abstaining from any participation in their wicked course of action (2 John 8, 10, 11). But, on the other hand, believers are to be of good courage in the face of these adversaries, knowing that they have already overcome them in virtue of their fellowship with Christ, who is greater than he that is in the world—*i. e.* than the Evil One (1 John 4:4; 5:18, 19).

But the *world* is not to be sought for only among unbelievers; for even among the brethren (1 John 5:16, 17), within the Christian community itself, a sin is mentioned which "is a sin unto death." Whosoever is burdened with this sin belongs to the world, although he may be externally numbered among believers. Such an one is absolutely severed from the inward fellowship and sphere of life in Christ—so much so, indeed, that believers can no longer pray for him with a hope that their prayer will be granted. This "sin unto death" is doubtless the blasphemy against the Holy Ghost, by which the germ of Divine life is radically expelled from the man committing it;—it is therefore a sin which cannot be forgiven.

[ANALYSIS: 1) Believers have become brethren in a special sense ; 2) there is an inward and outward fellowship ; 3) which is in contrast to the world ; 4) the sin unto death.]

# SECTION II.

## The Teaching of John According to the Apocalypse.

### CHAPTER V.

#### THE DOCTRINE OF GOD.

§ 186. *The Name and Nature of God.*[1]

The prophetic character of the Apocalypse renders it difficult to estimate its biblical theological value, but it does not lessen that value. In conformity with the whole plan of the book, many views, full of significance, are presented only in images, whose interpretation is not easy, and often it is difficult to draw the distinction between literal fact and the prophetic coloring. Nevertheless, we are able to examine the objective contents of the book—its doctrines, its direct and indirect statements—in their theological significance.

The *name* of Him who is feared by the devout (Rev. 11:18), blasphemed by the beast (13:6) as well as by men when they suffer from the plagues (16:9), is God. It is highly probable that the name of God, which Christ will write upon those who overcome (3:12), and which the 144,000 who are with the Lamb (14:1), and which the servants of God bear upon their foreheads (22:4), is that of *Jehovah;* but the name of God is expressed in many ways: "He which is and which was

[1] Compare *Gebhardt*, pp. 19–32.

and which is to come" (1:8; 4:8; 11:17; 16:5), "the Alpha and the Omega, the beginning and the end" (21:6; 1:8), "He that liveth forever and ever" (4:9; 10:6; 15:7).

In the doctrine of the Apocalypse concerning God, it is especially prominent that He is the "only Holy One" whom all must fear and adore; that He created the whole world by His will (4:11; 10:6); and that in opposition to the false gods of the Gentiles ("which can neither see, nor hear, nor walk" 9:20), God is living and eternal (7:2; 4:9), the All-powerful Creator (4:11; 10:6; 18:8).

God is called "the Lord" (4:11; 11:15; 15:4; 6:10),[1] as well as "the Lord God" (1:8; 4:8; 11:17; 18:8; 21:22). This latter name is synonymous with the Old Testament Adonai Jehovah, or Jehovah Elohim, and is more solemn and emphatic than the simple term "God." There can scarcely be any doubt that John, in his formula expressing the living and energetic eternity of God ("the Almighty, which is, and which was, and which is to come," 1:4, 8; 4:8; 11:17; 16:5), intends to represent and interpret the sacred and incommunicable name of Jehovah (Ex. 3:13–15).

With reference to the judgments depicted in this book it is emphatically asserted that God is holy, just and true (6:10; 15:4; 16:5). Everywhere stress is laid on the ethical perfection and absolute goodness of God (4:8; *cf.* Isa. 6:3). His ways are "righteous and true" (15:3); His judgments "true and righteous (16:7; 19:2). What the writer understands by God's justice we learn from 13:10; 14:9–11; 18:6–8; 22:12. It is retribution, strictly and accurately corresponding to desert; and

[1] In all these passages by "the Lord" is not meant Christ, but God.

the individual acts in which He exercises His justice are called His "righteous acts" (15:4).

[ANALYSIS: 1) It is difficult to develop the doctrine of the Apocalypse; 2) the name of God; 3) the only Holy One; 4) the Lord God; 5) His judgments are true and righteous.]

§ 187. *The Doctrine of the Holy Spirit.*[1]

John at one time speaks of the "Seven Spirits of God" (1:4; 3:1; 4:5; 5:6); at another of "the Spirit" (2:7, 11, 17, 29, etc.); and then again of "the Spirit of prophecy" (19:10), and of being "in the Spirit" (1:10). The question arises, How are these various expressions related to each other? By "the Seven Spirits of God" John wishes to represent the Spirit of God in the whole fullness of His nature. Seven is the number of perfection, and denotes multiplicity. By the Seven Spirits of God is to be understood the Holy Ghost sevenfold in His operations (not only of seven, but as the Author of all spiritual gifts). John speaks of the "Seven Spirits" when he speaks of the Holy Ghost independently of God the Father or of Christ (1:4; 4:5), and also when he considers Him as the Spirit which Christ has (3:1; 5:6). In 2:7; 14:13, he speaks solely of the Spirit, and understands thereby what he expressly says in 19:10, and unmistakably points out by the association of the Spirit and the Bride in 22:17, that the Holy Spirit is the Spirit of prophecy, and reveals Himself to and through the prophets. The Spirit of prophecy also affirms itself in manifold variety in the individual prophets, hence the Apostle speaks of "the spirits of the prophets" (22:6), which God subjects to Himself and inspires and instructs by His own Spirit.

[1] Compare *Gebhardt*, pp 128–138.

From what has already been said, we see that John decidedly distinguishes the Spirit as a Being distinct from God the Father, from Christ, and from Christians (1:5 ; 4:5). When, in 22:17, the Spirit and the Bride say to Christ, "Come!" we need no further proof that the writer conceives the Spirit as independent of the Son and of the Church. But what is the relation of the Spirit to *God*, to *Christ*, and to *believers?* Though the Spirit is expressly distinguished from the Bride, the Church (22:17), and speaks to the churches (2:7, 11, etc.), the Spirit does not, therefore, stand outside the Christian, "for the testimony of Jesus is the spirit of prophecy" (19:10), and that testimony is possessed by believers (19:10); and the spirits of the prophets (22:6) are the witnessing acts of the Holy Spirit to the individual prophets. In like manner, though the Spirit's independence in relation to Christ is clearly expressed in 22:17, the Spirit does not stand outside, and with Christ, but he *has* the Seven Spirits of God (3:1); the Lamb has the seven eyes, which are the Seven Spirits of God (5:6), and the testimony of Jesus is the Spirit of prophecy (19:10). The prophet only becomes "in the Spirit" (1:10) while Christ *has* the Spirit; it belongs to His nature—they are His eyes (5:6). The prophet is the instrument of the Spirit, or the Spirit witnesses through him (22:18); Christ speaks or testifies continually through the Spirit (19:10).

Keeping, therefore, in mind John's conception of the Spirit of God, it will not surprise us when, in 1:4, 5, the Apostle thinks and speaks in a *Trinitarian* sense, where the expression, "He which is, and which was, and which is to come," refers to the Father.

[ANALYSIS: 1) The meaning of "the Seven Spirits of God;" 2) John distinguishes between the Holy Spirit, God the Father, and the Son; 3) the spirit dwells in believers; 4) proceeds from Christ; 5) the doctrine of the Trinity.]

## § 188. *The Works of God.*

God *created* the world   The elders say, "Thou didst create all things, and because of Thy will they were, and were created" (4:11).  The angel swears "by Him that liveth forever and ever, who created the heaven and the things that are therein, and the earth and the things that are therein, and the sea and the things that are therein" (10:6).  The angel having the Eternal Gospel cried "Worship Him that made the heaven, and the earth and sea, and fountains of waters" (14:7).

God *governs* the world.   He sits on the throne (4:2). He is *King*, in the full meaning of the word, over all things which He has made.   But certain as it is that God is truly King of all the earth, it does not yet so appear in the existing condition of the world, nor in the acknowledgment of men.   The cause of this is the Devil, who deceives the whole world (12:9).

The aim of the Divine government is opposed to Satan and his kingdom, bringing to men deliverance or salvation (12:10), and to God Himself the real kingship over the world.   It is this glorious completion of the kingdom of God which is "the mystery of God," the good tidings which He declared through the prophets (10:7).   At every stage of its development this completion is, by anticipation, celebrated in heaven (12:10; 11:15, 17; 19:1, 6).

By what means does God work out this salvation and the establishment of His kingdom (11:15)?  By His "true and righteous judgments" (16:7; 15:3).  This is symbolically represented to us in 4:5, 6.  The "light-

[1] Compare *Gebhardt*, pp. 33-42.

nings and voices and thunders" represent God's avenging justice or manifestations of wrath in the world (*cf.* Ex. 19:16; Ps. 18:8-10; 29:3, 4), and correspond to the red *sardius* in the picture of the Divine majesty (4:3), which symbolizes the ardor of the Divine wrathful judgment. The seven lamps of fire are the Seven Spirits of God which, according to 5:6, are "sent forth into all the earth," through the mediation of Christ, and correspond to the green *emerald* (4:3), the image of grace in the representation of God; and, finally, the "glassy sea like unto crystal," which appears in 15:2 mingled with fire, is a representation evidently originating in a combination of the symbols occurring in Ex. 24:10 and Ezek. 1:22-28. As a sea represents immeasurableness and profundity (Ps. 36:6), and a sea of glass the holiness of God (Rev. 21:11), so a "glassy sea mingled with fire" is the symbol of holiness manifesting itself in wrath. This symbol, therefore, reminds us of the righteous deeds of God, resulting on the one hand from the avenging judgments of God, and on the other from the Spirit's work, and so the "glassy sea like unto crystal" of 4:6 corresponds to the bright *jasper* of 4:3—an image of the Divine holiness and unclouded glory.[1]

To the doctrine of God and His works belongs also the doctrine of the Angels. John most decidedly believed in the existence of angels in the sense of supernatural personal beings—concrete spirits, engaged in the service of God. Opposed to the Great Dragon and his angels are Michael and his angels (12:7-9); and

[1] The fundamental meaning, therefore, of these symbols is, that the final glorious and blessed completion of the Kingdom of God will be brought about by the true and righteous judgments of the holy, righteous and gracious God.

Christ is represented as speaking of the angels of His Father (3:5), who are also described as "the holy angels" (14:10). To the seer the *multitude* of the angels serving God seems to be innumerable (5:11 ; *cf.* Dan. 7:10). Their office in heaven seems to consist in never-ceasing adoration of God (5:11, 12 ; 7:11, 12). At the same time they are represented as the instruments of the Divine activity among men. They present the prayers of the saints before God (8:3–5), and bring about in many ways the Divine revelations, while they show the visions to the prophet (17:1) and explain them (17:7), or effect the symbolical actions which represent the future (7:2 ; 10:2, 5 ; 18:21). They also appear (14:17–19) as those who help Christ to execute judgment, in that they gather together the objects of it. They are fellow-servants with God's servants on the earth (19:10; 22:9), who worship God as their God (7:3, 12) on their faces (7:11). As with Paul so with John, there are also grades among them. Mention is made of the seven angels which stand before God (8:2), and of strong angels (5:2 ; 10:1 ; 18:21)—by which, doubtless, angels of a higher order are meant. Michael appears to be the leader of the heavenly host in God's name and strength contending for the Kingdom of God against the power of Satan (12:7).

[ANALYSIS: 1) God created the world; 2) and governs it as King; 3) the aim of the Divine government of the world; 4) the means by which the glorious completion of the Kingdom of God is brought about; 5) the meaning of the imagery in Rev. 4:3–6; 6) the teaching of John concerning holy angels; 7) their office.]

### § 189. *The Doctrine Concerning Satan.*[1]

It is in this connection that it is best to discuss the

---

[1] Compare *Gebhardt*, pp. 52–57; *Weiss*, § 133.

doctrine of Satan, for it is evident that the Devil must once have belonged to the good angels. We have a right to infer this from 12:4, 7–9, and 9:1,[1] where it is taken for granted that the Devil originally belonged to the inhabitants of heaven, but fell, and in his fall carried with him a part of the angels, who are designated as "his angels" (12:7, 9).

In the Apocalypse the personal principle of evil is called "the devil" (2:10; 12:9, 12; 20:2, 10), and "Satan" (2:9, 13, 24; 3:9; 12:9; 20:2, 7), "the Old Serpent" (12:9; 20:2), "the Serpent" (12:14, 15), "the Great Red Dragon" (12:3; *cf.* 12:4, 7, 9, 13, 16, 17; 13:2, 4; 16:13; 20:2). The name *Devil* (*diabolos*) denotes the enemy of men, because he is the disturber of their union with God. He is the antagonist of *men*, their *accuser* before God (12:10), the deceiver of the whole world (12:9; 20:10). The word *Satan* refers to him as the *adversary* and *antagonist* of men and of God. The two words (Devil and Satan) mean about the same thing, the first being from the Greek and the second being from the Hebrew.[2] The Devil is called the *Old Serpent*, or, more briefly, the *Serpent*, because of the manifestation which he has given of himself in the history of the fall of man as the Tempter (Gen. 3:1–5). The idea of the Devil as a *Dragon* (12:3, 9) is based upon Gen 3:1–5, to which the connection of "the Great Dragon" with "the Old Serpent" (12:9), and the interchange of the expressions "the Dragon" and "the Serpent" (12:13–17), clearly refers.[3] Gebhardt, however,

[1] It is probably best to identify the "star" of 9:1, and "the angel of the abyss" of 9:11, with Satan.

[2] *Cremer*, in his *Lexicon*, rightly remarks that a distinction between the two words cannot be pointed out in the New Testament. So also *Gebhardt*.

[3] *Duesterdieck* on Rev. 12:3.

would refer us to Isa. 27:1 ; Ezek. 29:3. The Dragon is called "great" on account of his power, and "red" to characterize him according to his raging, murdering and persecuting disposition.

As Satan, the old Serpent, seduced our first parents, so does he still seduce and deceive the whole world (12:9; 20:8). His special sphere of dominion is among the nations of the earth, who worship him with his angels (13:4; 9:20). As the ruler of the world, he appears with seven crowned heads (12:3). He is therefore the old enemy of God, who hinders the realization of the Kingdom of God on the earth. When, therefore, Christ was born, it was Satan who attempted to devour him; but He was caught up unto God and unto His throne, and thereby delivered from his power (12:4, 5). By Christ's exaltation the victory over Satan is won, and the Kingdom of God and His Messiah shall be surely established, because by this exaltation of the Messiah lies the security for the completion of the Kingdom of God (12:10). By the death of Christ and His ascension into heaven the right of the Devil to accuse believers of their guilt, and his power over them, has been lost (12:10). But his activity among them is as yet by no means destroyed. Just because he has been cast down to earth with his angels (12:9), which took place at the ascension and exaltation of Christ (12:7-12), he has for "a short time" (12:12) power to let loose his wrath on men.

This naturally leads us to consider that difficult and mysterious question as to Satan's *relation* to heaven. Although Satan and his angels had been cast out of heaven at some time previous to the fall of man (2 Pet. 2:4; Jude 6), yet it seems that he was still permitted, in the counsel of God to enter into His presence (Job

1:6–12; 2:1–7; 1 Kings 22:21; Zech. 3:1, 2). No matter how mysterious the passage in Rev. 12:7–12 may seem, it is evident that the casting down of Satan from his office of accuser in heaven is connected with the great justifying work of redemption. John here gives us a glimpse into the world of spirits which can be compared with what Christ reveals to us in Luke 10:17, 18, John 12:31; with what Peter unfolds in 1 Pet. 3:19, 20, and with the revelations of Paul in Col. 2:15; Eph. 4:8–10. We have a right to infer that Satan, when he found himself unable to overcome Christ here on earth by subtlety, carried his war into heaven itself, returning thither with his angels, with the vain hope of supplanting Christ on the throne of heaven—God permitting it, in His eternal counsels, for the sake of the glory of His Son. But "Michael and his angels went forth to war with the Dragon. . . . And the Great Dragon was cast down to the earth, and his angels were cast down with him" (12:7–9). Henceforth Satan no longer returns to heaven. His sphere of activity is now confined to earth and Hades. He is now the persecutor of the Church (12:13–17). Hence unbelieving Jews, who persecute the Christians, are called Satan's synagogue (2:9); by them he has thrown the believers into prison (2:10), and where such persecution exists there has he his throne (2:13). But he works also by seduction; for the false prophets, who profess to have known the depths of God, have known in truth "the deep things of Satan" (2:24). In particular, however, he manifests himself as the special enemy of the Church of God, in that he equips the two beasts against her. To the first beast he will give his power (13:1, 2), represented by the ten horns (12:3; 13:1); and to the second beast he will give the power of working miracles, by which Satan misleads the inhabitants of the earth (13:14). Only after the binding of Satan can the glorious period of the Church on earth begin (20:1-3). After his release from prison (20:7), he will make one more great attempt, and his final one, to oppose Christ in person (20:7-9); but he will then be *finally* overthrown and cast into the lake of fire and brimstone (20:10)—" into the eternal fire which is prepared for the devil and his angels " (*cf.* Matt. 25:41). After he has been awarded his punishment, then the heavenly consummation begins, and the new heavens and the new earth appear (21:1).

[ANALYSIS: 1) Satan originally was a good angel; 2) significance of the name "Devil;" 3) of the name "Satan;" 4) of the title "the Old Serpent;" 5) of the title "the Great Red Dragon;" 6) the deceiver of the world; 7) the ruler of this world; 8) the meaning of 12:7-12; 9) its great significance; 10) Satan is now the persecutor of the Church; 11) at his binding the Church shall enter upon her glorious state on the earth; 12) after his release he makes a final attempt to oppose Christ; 13) is finally overthrown and cast into the lake of fire.]

## CHAPTER VI.

### THE PERSON AND WORK OF CHRIST.

§ 190. *The Person of Christ.*[1]

Most commonly Christ is called by His historical personal name, *Jesus* (1:9; 12:17; 14:12; 17:6; 19:10; 20:4; 22:16); twice the *Lord Jesus* (22:20, 21); thrice *Jesus Christ* (1:1, 2, 5); twice *the Christ* (20:4, 6); and twice *the Christ* of God (11:15; 12:10).

With reference to His *person* we find the union of the human with the Divine clearly indicated. He is the Lion of the tribe of Judah, the Root of David (5:5; 22:16), and therefore of human descent, of the lineage and race of Israel, to whom the Messianic promise was given. But to Him likewise are ascribed everywhere Divine names, Divine attributes, Divine acts and Divine worship. He is "the first and the last" (1:17; 2:8), "the Alpha and the Omega," "the beginning and the end" (22:13), the "holy" and "true" (3:7), "the Word of God" (19:13). As God alone in the Old Testament tries the heart and reins (Ps. 7:9), so is this attribute ascribed to Christ (2:23), and this heart-searching glance is described in this way, that His eyes are like flames of fire (1:14; 2:18; 19:12). As the "Ancient of Days" (Dan. 7:9), His white hair (Rev. 1:14) points to His eternity. He has the seven spirits of God (3:1), by which as the Omniscient and Omnipresent One, He operates throughout the world;—because by them, which,

---

[1] Compare *Gebhardt,* pp. 77–105; *Weiss,* § 134; *Lechler,* vol. 2, pp. 168, 169.

according to 5:6 (*cf.* Zech. 4:10), are sent forth into all the earth, He appears everywhere present. The angels of God are His angels (1:1; 22:16); the four living creatures and the twenty-four elders fall down before Him as before God Himself (5:8,14); and this is here all the more significant, as *worship* is declined by the angels as being a specific prerogative of God (19:10; 22:9). The angels praise Him not otherwise than God Himself (7:12; 5:12, 13), and repeated doxologies are ascribed to Christ (1:6; 7:10). Throughout the book the reverence paid to Christ is divine—such as can only be paid to God.

[ANALYSIS: 1) Names given to Christ; 2) a unique Person, consisting of two natures; 3) regarded as truly human; 4) as well as truly Divine; 5) because to Him are ascribed Divine names, Divine attributes, Divine works, and Divine worship.]

§ 191. *The Work of Christ.*[1]

The *work* of Jesus Christ proceeds from His love to us (1:5). According to the doctrine of the Apocalypse the work of Jesus Christ consisted:

1) In His testifying the Word of God. Christ is called "the faithful witness" (1:5), "the Amen, the Faithful and True witness" (3:14). Believers "hold the testimony of Jesus" (19:10). Christ is the absolutely Faithful Messenger of the Divine will and the Divine truth; the Revealer of the truth, and the Word Himself.

2) In the next place, He overcame the Devil. In 12:3–9 we have a representation of this conflict. In 12:3, 4 the Dragon is represented as standing before the woman, ready to devour her child as soon as it is born.

[1] Compare *Gebhardt*, pp. 106–128; *Weiss*, § 134; *Lechler*, vol. 2. pp. 170, 171.

## THE WORK OF CHRIST.

That the Devil really attacked Christ, and that Jesus really entered into conflict with him, is expressed in the statement that Jesus *overcame* (5:5 ; 3:21). According to outward appearances, Christ was overthrown by the Devil in this struggle, for He was crucified (11:8); and of this crucifixion it is implied that the Devil is the author (11:7). But the overthrow of Christ was only in appearance—really, He had overcome ; for "the child was caught up unto God, and unto His throne" (12:5). And note, too, that the slain Lamb of 5:6 is the Lion of the tribe of Judah, which "hath overcome" (5:5). However, by this victory of Christ the Devil is not yet "cast into the lake of fire and brimstone" (Rev. 20:10); it did not even result in "the binding" of Satan for a period, and in "his being cast into the abyss" (20:3); but it ended in the expulsion forever of Satan from heaven, and in his casting down, with his angels, to the earth (12:9, 12). This victory of Christ over Satan is but the beginning of the final victory, which will take place at the consummation of the Kingdom of God.

3) Again, the Apocalypse continually sets forth Jesus as the *crucified* One, under the figure of the Lamb that was slain (5:6, 12 ; 13:8; "the blood of the Lamb," 7:14 ; 12:11). The use of the diminutive *arnion*, "a little lamb" (twenty-nine times) may serve to sharpen the contrast between the announced Lion of the tribe of Judah (5:5), and the "Lamb standing, as though it had been slain" (5:6). The figure of the lamb in this book, as well as in I Pet. 1:19, evidently is derived from the paschal Lamb, while the passage in Isa. 53:7 was also at the same time uppermost in the Apostle's mind. It is implied that the death of Jesus on the Cross was of an atoning and sacrificial character. Hence a sin-redeeming (5:9, "thou wast slain, and didst purchase

unto God with thy blood, men ") and cleansing power (1:5; 7:14)[1] is attributed to His blood. If the Christians have washed their robes and made them clean in the blood of the Lamb (7:14; 22:14), this blood is regarded as the means of purification which removes from them the stains of the guilt of sin. If this purification is at the same time designated as a "loosening from sin" (the better reading in 1:5), then the blood shed by Christ in His voluntary death is the ransom for which men are delivered from the guilt of sin.

4) Great stress is also laid on the *resurrection* of Christ (1:18; 2:8). He is "the first-born of the dead" (1:5). He is now alive for evermore, and has the keys of death and of Hades (1:18). He now sitteth with the Father in His throne (3:21), which is the throne of God and of the Lamb (22:1, 3).

5) We have also a description of the work of the *Exalted* Christ. *a*) He is now God's Anointed, sharing with God the lordship over His kingdom (11:15; 12:10). He is "the Ruler of the kings of the earth" (1:5), "the Lord of lords, and King of kings" (17:14). *b*) He has "the key of David," and therefore complete power over the Messianic Kingdom (3:7, after Isa. 22:22). As such He is the Lord of believers (11:8; 14:13; 22:20, 21), and they are His servants (1:1; 2:20), and bear His name (14:1; 3:12). It is certainly not without meaning that the Lamb is represented as being "in the midst of the throne" (5:6; 7:17). By this evidently is meant the efficacy of Christ's sacrificial death and His priestly intercession for His people. But John also sees "one

---

[1] Rev. 1:5, "Unto him that loveth us, and loosed [some ancient MSS. read "washed"] us from our sins by his blood."

Rev. 7:14, "They washed their robes, and made them white in the blood of the Lamb."

like unto a Son of man" in the midst of the seven golden candlesticks (1:12, 13), " holding the seven stars in his right hand" (2:1). This represents that He is also ever present with His Church on earth, and always active among believers. It is He who searcheth the reins and hearts, and giveth unto each one according to his works (2:23). *c*) Finally, as the Son of Man of Daniel (1:13; 14:14), He will *come again* (1:7; 20:22), in great glory, accompanied by an army of saints (19:11–19).

[ANALYSIS: 1) The work of Christ has its origin in His love to us; 2) He is the true prophet; 3) He overcame the Devil; 4) He is represented as the Lamb slain for us; 5) He was raised from the dead; 6) exalted to heaven; 7) the King of kings; 8) the Lord of believers; 9) our High Priest; 10) and He shall come again in glory.]

## CHAPTER VII.

#### THE SAINTS AND THEIR WORKS.

§ 192. *The Christian Life in its Origin.*[1]

It is God's will that all men should repent and be saved (3:10; 9:20, 21; 16:9, 11, "and they repented not to give him glory"). It is everywhere implied that the righteous judgments of God have the tendency either of leading the world to turn to God or wholly against Him. Salvation is offered to the penitent and the impenitent (14:6, 7), and men have the opportunity of accepting or rejecting the Eternal Gospel. God is not unfaithful; He does everything to help the world, and if men are not saved their ruin is self-caused.

In 17:14 Christians are described by the three-fold designation as "called, and chosen, and faithful." The believer has been *called*, by the grace of God, through the Gospel, which has invited him to become a partaker of the Messianic salvation. Then he who has obeyed the gracious call, and accepted the offered salvation, and believed in Jesus Christ, has been *chosen* out of the world—elected, received by God as his own child, and appointed or ordained to salvation (13:8; 17:8). Finally, the believer must make "his calling and election sure" (*cf.* 2 Pet. 1:10) by remaining *faithful*, by holding fast the offered and communicated grace in his continual struggle with the world and the flesh (2:7, 10, 17; 3:5, etc.). But the Christian owes his deliverance from sin and destruction, his sanctification and heavenly blessed-

[1] Compare *Gebhardt*, pp. 143-153; *Weiss*, § 135.

ness, not to himself, but to God and Christ. It is Christ who "gives unto him that is athirst of the fountain of the water of life freely" (21:16; 22:17). Christians have paid no price, have no claim or merit that they should be saved. Salvation has its origin in God alone (7:10, 12; 12:10; 19:1).

In the Apocalypse *faith* is also the fundamental condition for appropriating salvation. " Here is the patience of the saints, that they keep the commandments of God, and the faith of Jesus" (14:12). It is on this account that the keeping of the word of Christ goes hand in hand with the confession of His name (3:8). That true conversion consists of *repentance* and *faith* can also be seen from the earnest exhortations to repentance given by Christ Himself (2:5, 16, 21, 22; 3:3, 19). Compare also 9:20, 21; 16:9, 11.

[ANALYSIS: 1) God wishes that all men should be saved; 2) believers are those who are called; 3) and chosen out of the world; 4) and who shall attain salvation if they remain faithful.]

## § 193. *The Christian Life in its Significance.*[1]

When the sinner becomes a Christian he turns from the works of his hands, and no longer worships idols; he also ceases from murder, sorcery, fornication and theft (9:20, 21). He is washed from his former uncleanness (3:4; 7:14; 21:27); from wretchedness he passes to gladness, from misery to joy, from poverty to riches, from blindness to sight, and from nakedness to being clothed in white garments (3:17, 18); from death he rises to life (3:1-3). He is redeemed from slavery to the Devil, and from the bondage of sin (1:5; 5:9; 14:3, 4).

What it implies to be a Christian can also be seen

[1] Compare *Gebhardt*, pp. 153-163; *Weis*, § 135.

from the *names* given to believers. They are uniformly called "saints" (5:8; 8:3, 4); and often, which name as "the holy" implies both their consecration to God, as well as their separation from the world. Next to the designation of saints the most frequent name applied to Christians is that of "servants of God" (7:3; 19:2,5). Christians are sometimes called the servants of God or of Christ, because they have been redeemed unto God and the Lamb (5:9; 14:4; 6:10), and thus properly belong to God (7:3; 19:2; 22:6). In other places they are called servants of God, because they keep His commandments (12:17), or wait upon Him in priestly service (7:15; 22:3). In 18:4 the saints are called "the people" of God, and in 11:18 and 19:5 they are described as those that "fear" Him. Again, in 1:6 and 5:10, the redeemed of Christ are called "priests unto God." The priesthood of believers lies in this, that they can personally draw near to God, through Jesus Christ, without any other mediator, offer their prayers and thanksgivings, and devote themselves as a peculiar people to God in holy obedience and spiritual service. With this priestly kingship (1:6; 5:10) of Christians is also closely associated the idea of their being *firstfruits* (14:4). If Christians are servants of God and of Christ in relation to one another, they are *fellow-servants* and *brethren* (6:11; 12:10; 19:10).

The Christian religion is represented in three main aspects—1) as tribulation or suffering in Jesus (2:9, 10; 7:14); 2) as authority or kingship in Jesus (1:6, 5:10); and 3) as steadfastness or patience in Jesus (2:2, 3; 3:10; 13:10; 14:12). Christians have these three features in common, and are sharers therein.

[ANALYSIS: 1) The results of conversion; 2) believers are called "saints;" 3) "servants of God;" 4) "the people" of God; 5) "priests unto God;" 6) "the first-fruits;" 7, the Christian religion in its three-fold manifestation.]

§ 194. *The Christian Life in its Activity.*[1]

According to the Apocalypse Christians continually need the grace, mercy, and love which God shows to the sinner, and only thereby can the spiritual life be maintained in them and by them progressively toward perfection (1:4; 22:21; *cf.* also the "freely" of 21:6; 22:17). In each of the letters to the seven churches the Lord speaks of the *works* of Christians (2:2, 5, 19, etc.). The dead are judged according to their works (20:12, 13); and the Lord, when He shall come, will render to each man according as his work is (22:12). The Apostle speaks almost exclusively of the works of Christians according to their activity, development, and manifestation.

But in what do the works of Christians consist? The Christian leads a holy life, and does righteousness (22:11); the Lamb's Bride, the Church, shall be arrayed in "fine linen, bright and pure; for the fine linen is the righteous acts of the saints" (19:8). If the Christian life is true and real, then there is growth and progress; there is an increase in works, in love, in faith, in ministry and in patience, and the last works are more than the first (2:19). Special stress is laid on *love* (2:4), which is love to God and Christ manifesting itself in love to the brethren. Frequent reference is also made to "the prayers of the saints" (5:8; 8:3, 4). We learn the contents of Christian thanksgiving and prayer, not merely from the few words of 22:17, 20, but also from the petitions to which expression is given in heaven. We need only compare the adorations of the four living

[1] Compare *Gebhardt*, pp. 163-178.

creatures (4:8, 9), of the twenty-four elders (4:10, 11; 5:9, 10; 11:16, 17), of the angels (5:12), of the victors (7:10; 15:3, 4), and of the heavenly inhabitants (12:10, 11; 19:1–7). The prayers, as the passages quoted show, are sometimes addressed to God, sometimes to the Lamb, and sometimes to God and the Lamb at the same time.

The Apostle is well acquainted with the dangers and difficulties of the Christian life, both with the temptations which are found in the believer himself in his own flesh and mind, and those which have their origin outside of the believer. The latter come partly from the Jews (2:9), and partly from the Gentiles (2:14), Satan being the secret author (2:9, 13), and consist not merely in *persecutions* by word and deed, but also in temptations to *doctrinal errors* (2:14, 15; 2:20). The tribulations which believers have to endure for the sake of Christ become inducements to apostasy. There are such who will be afraid of the things they shall suffer (2:10); some will not keep the word of Christ, but deny His name (3:8); there will be many who will worship the beast and receive his mark upon their foreheads and upon their hands (13:8; 20:4); there will be those who are cowardly and faithless (21:8).

But what must the Christian *do in order that he may overcome?* Believers must remain steadfast in their faith, and not permit themselves to be led astray by false teachers (2:2, 3, 20, 25). With respect to persecution in word and deed, believers must remain faithful unto death (2:10, 13; 3:8, 10, 11). The remnant of the woman's seed, with which the Dragon went to make war, is described as consisting of those "which keep the commandments of God, and hold the testimony of Jesus" (12:17). "Here is the patience of the saints,

## THE CHRISTIAN LIFE—ITS PROMISES. 277

that they keep the commandments of God, and the faith of Jesus" (14:12). With reference to the temptations which come from the flesh, the Lord says, "Blessed is he that watcheth, and keepeth his garments, lest he walk naked, and they see his shame" (16:5 ; *cf.* 3:3, 4, 17, 18); so also we read, "Come forth, my people, out of Babylon, that ye have no fellowship with her sins, and that ye receive not of her plagues" (18:4).

[ANALYSIS: 1) Christians continually need the grace, mercy, and love of God; 2) in what the works of Christians consist; 3) the prayers of the saints; 4) the difficulties of the Christian life; 5) how the believer may overcome.]

### § 195. *The Christian Life in Relation to its Promises.*[1]

It is evident, from a careful examination of the promises of the Apocalypse, that while these reach to the heavenly state, and refer principally to the final consummation of the kingdom of God, they refer also to life on earth. Those who are in heaven wear white robes (7:9–13), and so do the saints who are yet on earth (3:4). In heaven they stand "before the throne of God, and serve him day and night in His Temple" (7:15); but in the earthly life they are already servants of God and of Jesus (2:20; 7:3). The heavenly inhabitants bear the name of God and of the Lamb on their foreheads (14:1 ; 22:4), and also on earth they have on their foreheads the seal of the Living God (7:2, 3). The promise of Christ is, "I will give thee the crown of life" (2:10); but He also gives the admonition, "Hold fast that which thou hast, that no one take thy crown" (3:11). The works of Christians follow them into heaven (14:13); but Christ says that

[1] Compare *Gebhardt*, pp. 178–184.

true Christians are rich even here (2:9). The Apostle, in strict analogy with the teaching of the New Testament respecting the triumphs of Christians, regards the promises as being on the one hand *fulfilled*, while on the other hand the believer is regarded as acquiring a gradual victory over evil. The promises are continuously fulfilled—in this life, amid struggle and conflict with the external reality ; in heaven, immediately after death, in the ideal hidden reality ; and in the final perfect state, after the resurrection, in ideal manifest reality. The contents of the promises are everywhere the same ; but the measure of their fulfillment in the different stages is various, yet always more complete and glorious.

If we were to enter upon more particular statements with reference to the meaning of the promises given to believers, we might possibly explain them as follows: By the promise in 2:7, that to him that overcometh will be given "to eat of the tree of life, which is in the Paradise of God," is meant that the believer shall have eternal life in blessed communion with God ; in 2:10 eternal life is spoken of as "the crown of life," the reward of victory ; in 2:11, the thought is that the opposite of eternal life—condemnation, misery and perdition—the second death, can do no harm to the Christian; in 2:17, the hidden manna is the heavenly bread in distinction from the manna in the Wilderness; the new name is the ideal glory of believers ; in 3:4, 5, the white garments symbolize purity, holiness, or righteousness; being written in the Book of Life describes the Divine election to eternal life; in 3:12, the inscription of the three names evidently relates to three aspects of the life of the Christian—his consecration to God, his citizenship in the New Jerusalem, and his belonging to Christ, with all its deep significance (*cf.* 14:1; 22:4); from 3:21 we learn that the Christian shall share the Divine power and authority with Christ, as Christ does with God.

[ANALYSIS: 1) The promises of God are continuously fulfilled; 2) already on earth; 3) immediately after death; 4) at the final consummation; 5) meaning of the promises.]

# CHAPTER VIII.

## THE ESCHATOLOGY OF JOHN.

### § 196. *The Method of Presenting the Johannean Eschatology.*

In our presentation of the Johannean doctrine of the Last Things, we will follow in general the same plan that we did in the discussion of the Pauline Eschatology. Instead, however, of presenting the doctrine of the Apocalypse separately, we will add the teaching of John according to his Epistles, thus simplifying the discussion. In this outline we need not enter upon a full exposition of the Apocalypse, nor upon a criticism of the different systems of interpretation,[1] because Biblical Theology has to do mainly with the ideas and doctrines underlying the book. As, however, this book bears directly upon the Last Things, the writer will have to indicate what he believes to be the significance and object of the Apocalypse, and also what he regards the teaching of John to imply.

---

[1] There are three principal systems of interpretation, according to which the Apocalypse has been expounded: 1) The Preterist; 2) the Continuous or Historical; 3) the Futurist.

According to the *Preterists*, these prophecies apply chiefly to the destruction of Jerusalem, and the history of Pagan Rome. Among the most eminent expounders of this view we may mention Grotius, Bossuet, Calmet, Hug, Herder, Ewald, Lücke, De Wette, Düsterdieck, Bleek, Renan, Reuss, Samuel Davidson, Moses Stuart, Cowles, Desprez and Weiss. Some refer it chiefly to the overthrow of Jerusalem, others chiefly to the fall of the Roman Empire, and still others to both

[ANALYSIS: 1) Method of the presentation; 2) there will be no attempt made to expound the book fully; 3) three principal systems of interpretation; 4) the Preterists; 5) the Continuous or Historical expositors; 6) the Futurists.]

§ 197. *Concerning Death in General.*

John in all his writings clearly distinguishes between spiritual death (Rev. 3:1 ; 1 John 3:14),[1] natural death (Rev. 2:10, 23 ; 9:6 ; 12:11 ; 13:3 ; 18:8 ; 21:4), and eternal death (Rev. 2:11 ; 20:6, 14 ; 21:8 ; 1 John 5:16).[2]

Spiritual death is the state in which man is, as condemned through sin. It is the opposite of life as blessing and salvation; he who would not abide under condemnation must pass out of death into life (1 John 3:14), and this life can only be found in the Son of God.[3]

Natural death, the end of earthly life, is the punishment pronounced by God upon sin (Gen. 2:17), and over-

The *Continuous* or *Historical* expositors regard the Apocalypse a progressive history of the fortunes of the Church from the first century to the end of time. This school includes the great majority of the Protestant commentators, but they differ widely among themselves in chronology and the application of details. Here we may mention Luther, Gerhard, Bengel, Mede, Vitringa, Faber, Elliott, Gaussen, Wordsworth, Alford, Lee, Auberlen, Hengstenberg, Philippi, Ebrard and Hofmann.

The *Futurist* expositors maintain that the whole book, with the exception of the first three chapters, refers principally to events which are immediately to precede, or immediately to follow, the Second Advent of Christ. The writers of this school usually interpret prophecy literally. Many of those who lay stress on the *Continuous* interpretation of the book reach in many points the same conclusions as the *Futurists*.

[1] 1 John 3:14, "We know that we have passed out of death into life. . . . He that loveth not abideth in death."

[2] 1 John 5:16, "There is a sin unto death; not concerning this do I say that he should make request."

[3] 1 John 5:12, "He that hath the Son hath the life; he that hath not the Son of God hath not the life."

takes all men, but for believers the power of death has been overcome by Christ, because He was dead, and behold now He is alive for evermore, and has the keys of death and Hades (Rev. 1:18)—*i. e.* He has power over death and Hades. In this passage, as well as in Rev. 6:8; 20:13, 14, Hades appears in close connection with death—in fact, as a consequence of death. But in these passages we must distinguish between them. In Rev. 1:18 death is personified and regarded as a possessor of gates. Strictly speaking, death is not to be regarded as a *place*. The *place* of death, which appears closed in with gates, is Hades. In Rev. 6:8 Hades, the place belonging to death, is represented like death itself as a person, following death. In Rev. 20:13, 14 death and Hades appear personified as demoniacal powers, and for believers are abolished (1 Cor. 15:26). They are cast into the lake of fire, and become identical with it—into which also all unbelievers, whose names shall not be found written in the Book of Life, will be cast (Rev. 20:14, 15). In the new heaven and the new earth death shall find no place (Rev. 21:4). Natural death, as the end of this earthly life, is the *first* death, in contradistinction to eternal death, which is the *second* death (Rev. 20:14).

[ANALYSIS: 1) John distinguishes between spiritual, bodily, and eternal death; 2) spiritual death; 3) bodily death; 4) difference between death and Hades; 5) the first and second death.]

### § 198. *The State of the Soul After Death.*[1]

John conceives of the universe as consisting of three great regions—heaven, earth, and Hades (Rev. 5:3, 13),[2]

[1] Compare *Gebhardt*, pp. 42-52, 250-252, 318.

[2] Rev. 5:3, "And no one in the heaven, or on the earth, or under the earth, was able to open the book."

and in this he agrees with Paul (Phil. 2:10).[1] Heaven is above the earth, and is conceived of as the ideal sphere of existence; earth is the sphere of the development of the struggle between heaven and hell; and the lower world, or Hades, is the antithesis to heaven, the home and center of the power of death and of the Devil.

With John the place of death is *Hades;*—it is the realm of death where sinners find the result of their life. As with Paul so with John, no believer is represented as entering after death into Hades. For Christ, as the Redeemer, has conquered Hades, and He preserves His own from its power (Rev. 1:18). The true interpretation of Rev. 6:8[2] is that the judgments therein mentioned are visited upon unbelievers alone. So likewise in Rev. 20:13–15,[3] those who are raised are unbelievers who are delivered over to the second death. In fact the testimony of the New Testament is explicit, that after Christ's death and resurrection the souls of believers do not enter into Hades, but into heaven, and that the souls of unbelievers alone come under the power of death and Hades.

But John also speaks of this lower world as the *abyss*[4] (Rev. 9:1, 2, 11; 11:7; 17:8; 20:1, 3). It is the

[1] Phil. 2:10, "That in the name of Jesus every knee should bow, of things in heaven, and things on earth, and things under the earth."

[2] Rev. 6:8, "And I saw, and behold, a pale horse: and he that sat upon him, his name was Death; and Hades followed with him. And there was given unto them authority over the fourth part of the earth, to kill with sword, and with famine, and with death (pestilence), and by the wild beasts of the earth."

[3] Rev. 20:13, 14, "And death and Hades gave up the dead which were in them; and they were judged every man according to their works. And death and Hades were cast into the lake of fire. This is the second death, even the lake of fire."

[4] Compare *Gebhardt*, pp. 57–59.

same place as Hades, but is regarded as the present abode of the Devil and his angels, as distinguished from "the lake of fire," which shall become their abode after the judgment (Rev. 20:10).[1] Out of the smoke arising from this abyss come forth the locusts (Rev. 9:1-3), which have over them as king "the angel of the abyss" (Rev. 9:11), which angel, if it is not Satan himself, is one of Satan's chief angels. Out of this *abyss* likewise comes the beast (Rev. 11:7; 17:8), which is the concrete representation of the anti-Christian world-power, and into the abyss the Devil is cast, having been bound for "a thousand years" (Rev. 20:1-3). This abyss is the seat of Satan, where his power centers, where he properly belongs, and from which all his demoniacal powers emanate. It is his true home, where his angels are, from which he proceeds to work upon earth. "As Christ during his sojourn on earth was at home only in heaven, though he had not his residence there, so the Devil abides until the end not in his own place, but on the earth among men; indeed, we may say, that according to the doctrine of the Apocalypse, the whole course of the history turns upon the fact that he is not where he belongs, but at length must be banished thither" (*Gebhardt*). Satan is active on earth now, and will remain so until he shall be bound for "a thousand years" (Rev. 20:1-3), and at the end of this period he shall be loosed out of his prison for a time (Rev. 20:8), and then shall receive his final sentence (Rev. 20:10).

This abyss, which is the home of Satan and his king-

---

[1] Rev. 20:10, "And the devil that deceived them was cast into the lake of fire and brimstone, where are also the beast and the false prophet; and they shall be tormented day and night for ever and ever."

## STATE OF THE SOUL AFTER DEATH. 285

dom, is identical with Hades, and is the invisible but real world where the souls of the ungodly and the evil angels abide. Here Satan wields his power, and into this kingdom passes the soul of every unbeliever at his death.

On the other hand, it is the definite teaching of John that true believers enter heaven at death. They do not immediately receive their full and final glory, which they do not attain until after the resurrection, but the souls of believers enter immediately into heaven and are with God. This is distinctly implied in Rev. 6:9–11 [1] and Rev. 20:4–6.[2] In this last passage the prophet sees two classes of dead believers taking part in the first resurrection: 1) the martyrs, not only those whose souls are under the altar and cry for vengeance (Rev. 6:9–11), but also those additional ones who have for the Gospel surrendered their lives (Rev. 6:11; 13:7, 10, 15; 16:6; 17:6; 18:24); and 2) all other believers who have died in the Lord, whether a natural or violent death (Rev. 14:13, 16). Among these souls are included the innumerable multitude standing before the throne and before the Lamb (Rev. 7:9–17), who were purchased from among men to be the first-fruits unto God and the Lamb (Rev. 14:1–5), who sing the song of Moses and of the Lamb (Rev. 15:2–5). All these passages only prove that according to John all those who die in the Lord, at death immediately enter into

---

[1] Rev. 6:9, " I saw underneath the altar the souls of them that had been slain for the word of God."

[2] Rev. 20:4, " And I saw the souls of them that had been beheaded for the testimony of Jesus, and for the word of God, and such as worshiped not the beast, neither his image, and received not the mark upon their forehead and upon their hand; and they lived and reigned with Christ a thousand years. The rest of the dead lived not until the thousand years should be finished."

heaven, and are with Christ now, awaiting the hour of His visible return and of their glorious resurrection.

"They have now the salvation which God, through Christ, has imparted to Christians, as is implied in their grateful ascription (Rev. 7:10). And this salvation or blessedness in heaven has a negative and a positive side. On the negative side it consists in freedom from the sufferings of the earthly life. They come out of the great tribulation (Rev. 7:14); they rest from their labors (14:13; 6:11); they shall hunger no more, neither thirst any more; neither shall the sun strike upon them, nor any heat; and God shall wipe away every tear from their eyes (7:16, 17). But while Christians in death leave their sufferings behind them—and here we come to the positive side of their heavenly happiness—"their works follow with them" (14:13). Not the reward of their works; still less do their works follow them to judgment to secure their justification; but "their works," that is, what constitutes them Christians, their Christian nature, which subjectively makes them fit for objective blessedness. It appears also as a positive element of this blessedness, that Christians have palms in their hands (7:9) and are arrayed in white robes. As here on earth they became sanctified or saints, so they are recognized and honored as such in heaven. They stand before the throne and the Lamb (7:9); they are before the throne of God, and and serve Him day and night in His temple (7:15). . . . But to this blessed state in heaven there will yet follow a higher and highest" (*Gebhardt*).

[ANALYSIS: 1) The three regions of the universe; 2) the souls of unbelievers enter Hades; 3) after Christ's resurrection the souls of believers do not enter Hades; 4) Hades is the abyss; 5) it is the seat of Satan's power; 6) the invisible but real world. where the evil angels are, as also the souls of the ungodly; 7) believers, at death, immediately enter heaven; 8) the blessedness of believers in heaven, in their intermediate state, has a negative and positive side.]

§ 199. *The Universal Preaching of the Gospel.*

It is the distinct teaching of Christ that "the Gospel of the Kingdom shall be preached in the whole world for a testimony unto all the nations, and then shall the end come" (Matt. 24:14). With this John also agrees: "And I saw another angel flying in mid-heaven, having an eternal Gospel to proclaim unto them that dwell on the earth, and unto every nation and tribe, and tongue and people; and he saith with a great voice, Fear God and give Him glory, for the hour of Judgment is come" (Rev. 14:6, 7).

It is the common opinion that this universal preaching of the Gospel brings about the conversion of the whole world before the personal coming of Christ. The question is not whether God is not able to bring about this glorious result by the preaching of the Word, but the question is purely and simply what the Word of God teaches as to the result of the preaching of the Gospel to the whole world at the time of Christ's Coming in Glory. The Bible gives us a very explicit answer, and no doubt whatever need rest in our mind. When Christ shall make His visible appearance in glory the wickedness of the earth shall be great. There is not a single passage in the whole Bible where it is stated that the whole world shall be converted before Christ's Second Coming. The Apocalypse everywhere implies that supreme wickedness shall exist on the earth until the very end. Let any one read the terrible descriptions given of the end of the world in Rev. 6:12–17; 11:15–19; 14:18–20; 16:17–21; 19:11–16, and ask himself what is thereby implied. And all this is in perfect harmony with the teaching of Christ, of Peter, and of Paul. Christ does not say in Matt. 24:14 that the whole world shall be converted before the end, but he does say that the Gospel shall be preached—1) "in the whole world;" 2) "unto all the nations;" 3) "for a testimony." That is, all shall have an opportunity to accept the Eternal Gospel, but it does not follow that all will accept it. It will be a witness against those who reject it. It will bring on a crisis of either life or death. In perfect agreement with this is the statement of John in Rev. 14:6, 7.

That evil and unbelief shall increase and be on the earth until the end, until Christ comes in glory, is also in harmony with the doctrine of the manifestation of Antichrist, whom Christ shall slay at His coming. This also agrees with the doctrine of Antichrist as taught by John in his Epistles (1 John 2:18, 22; 4:3; 2 John 7).

In a summary we may state that John distinctly teaches—1) that the Gospel must be preached throughout the *whole* world as a testimony before the end comes; and 2) that the effect of the preaching of the Gospel will be a dividing of the inhabitants of the earth into two great camps—*a*) that of the saints, who keep the commandments of God, and the faith of Jesus (Rev. 14:12); and *b*) that of the worshipers of the beast and his image (Rev. 14:9, 10).

In other words, the two great signs of the Coming of Christ are—1) the universal spread of the Gospel; and 2) the great apostasy of the latter times.

[ANLYSIS: 1) There must be a universal preaching of the Gospel before the Coming of Christ; 2) this does not imply that the whole world shall be converted before His Coming; 3) supreme wickedness shall exist until the very end; 4) the teaching of Matt. 24:14;

5) this is in harmony with the teaching concerning the manifestation of Antichrist; 6) the two great signs of the Coming of Christ.]

## § 200. *The Future of Israel.*

The doctrine of the Apocalypse can be developed without attempting to expound its meaning in detail, and without entering into a discussion of the various interpretations, Preterist, Continuous Historical, or Futurist. But the perspective and aim of the book, as viewed by the student, will vary according to the system of interpretation followed. The writer holds that the book itself already decides for us how we are to view its contents. It is "the Revelation of Jesus Christ, which God gave unto him to show unto his servants, even *the things which must shortly come to pass*" (Rev. 1:1); "Write, therefore, the things which thou sawest, and *the things which are,* and *the things whcih shall come to pass hereafter*" (Rev. 1:19); "Come up hither, and I will shew thee *the things which must come to pass hereafter*" (Rev. 4:1).

In general we may say that, from Rev. 4:1 onward, we have a description of what was future not only in John's time, but also of that which now still largely lies in the future; for these visions and prophecies mainly refer to the end of all things. It is also important to make up our minds whether the visions themselves represent one consecutive series of events, or whether they are to be divided into groups, each of which extends to the end of time. For the purpose of Biblical Theology it matters very little whether the seventh seal is suppposed to contain within it as sub-divisions the seven trumpets, and the seventh trumpet to comprehend in like manner the seven vials, or whether we accept the *recapitulation* theory, that each group of visions contains a prophecy reaching from the prophet's time to the end of the world. The writer, however, cannot but come to the conclusion that the prophet at least five times gives us a description of the end (Rev. 6:12-17; Rev. 11:15-19; Rev. 14:18-20; Rev. 16:17-21; Rev. 20:11-15), and this would favor the view that the five groups of visions (Rev. 5:1—8:1; 8:2—11:19; 12:1—14:20; 15:1—16:21; 17:1—20:15) contained in the main body of the book (Rev. 4:1—22:5), in a general way, refer to events parallel to one another, each one culminating in a vivid description of the final end.

Another important question, separate from the symbolical character of the book, must be settled. In our method of interpreting this prophecy of the end, are we to insist on the grammatico-historical meaning and teaching of the Apocalypse, or are we to spiritualize all its statements? Are the promises and statements concerning "Israel" to be taken spiritually as referring to the Christian Church composed of true believers, whether Gentiles or Jews, or do these promises when given to Israel in particular refer to the national Israel, to the Jews as a separate people? If we are to be guided by the fulfillment of the prophecies of the Old Testament concerning the Messiah and consider how in every case, referring to the first Advent, they have been *literally* fulfilled, surely no fault ought to be found with those who believe that the direct and positive assertions of God's Word concerning the Second Coming of Christ, as recorded in the Old and New Testaments, will also be literally fulfilled, in so far as they do not come in conflict with the nature of God's Kingdom as presented in the New Testament. There is a bare realism which would restore "the beggarly elements" of Judaism, but of which the Apocalypse knows nothing.

A careful study of all the references to Israel in the Apocalypse, especially Rev. 7:1—8 and 11:1–13, leads us to the conclusion that John, like Paul, takes it for granted that in close connection with the Coming of Christ, Israel as a nation shall be converted. It is evident that we need not to lay too much stress in Rev. 7:1–8 on the literal number of 144,000, but this vast multitude represents the Jewish believers, which form the nucleus of the Christian Church during the great apostasy, and which must endure the trials of the day of Antichrist. This company of sealed servants of God are regarded as being on earth, in contradistinction to the innumerable multitude of Rev. 7:9–17, which are conceived of as in heaven. This final conversion of the Jews probably will take place at the time of the great tribulation (Rev. 11:1–13), after which follows the Messianic Judgment and the end of the world (Rev. 11:14, 15). There are others, however, who maintain that this "conversion of the Jews" will be brought about by the Coming of Christ, and that this event will be one of the features of the Millennium.

[ANALYSIS: 1) The aim of the Apocalypse; 2) its prophecies are mainly unfulfilled; 3) the book is not to be interpreted as if the events are to follow each other in chronological order; 4) the visions in the main run parallel to one another; 5) we have at least five descriptions of the final end; 6) we are not to spiritualize all its statements; 7) nor to insist on too literal an interpretation; 8) all the prophecies, however, in the Old Testament, referring to the first Advent of Christ, have been literally fulfilled; 9) John takes it for granted that in connection with the Coming of Christ, there shall be a national conversion of the Jews.]

§ 201. *The Great Apostasy and the Great Tribulation.*

The Church, before the end, is not only to have a large external development and to be spread over the whole earth, as depicted by Christ in the Parable of the Mustard Seed (Matt. 13:31, 32), but it is also to have an inner development of faith, as indicated by the Parable of the Leaven (Matt. 13:33). The external development is brought about by the preaching of the Word (Matt. 24:14), and although the Gospel everywhere will bring about a separation between the Kingdom of God and the Kingdom of Satan, and the larger number shall reject the Gospel, still believers shall be found among all the nations of the earth. The inner development consists of a deeper apprehension of the contents of revelation, a firmer reliance upon the promises of God's Word, a more earnest zeal, and a closer communion with God; and although the Word of God alone can work such a deep faith and consecration to God, it shall be brought about, as the end draws near, by the great apostasy and the great tribulation.

In the Apocalypse it is everywhere implied that there shall come before the end a great apostasy. Not only shall "the whole earth wonder after the beast," "and all that dwell on the earth worship him, every one whose name hath not been written from the foundation of the world in the Book of Life of the Lamb that hath been slain" (Rev. 13:3, 8), but it is also implied that many believers shall become cowardly and faithless (Rev. 21:8), shall be deceived (Rev. 13:14–16), and shall receive the mark of the beast upon their forehead and upon their hand (Rev. 20:4). Christians shall be tried and many believers shall not only be overcome by the pressure of false doctrines, but also by the temptations of the flesh (Rev. 16:15). So likewise, in his first Epistle, John regards apostasy as a sign of the last times (1 John 2:18, 19), and this also agrees with the teaching of Christ, "howbeit when the Son of Man cometh, shall he find faith on the earth?" (Luke 18:8). Compare also Luke 17:26–30; Matt. 24:37–39; Matt. 24:24; and the Parable of the Ten Virgins (Matt. 25:1–13). Of this apostasy Peter speaks (2 Pet. 3:3, 4), and Paul in prophetic vision sees the evils of the last days coming upon the world (2 Thess. 2:1–12; 1 Tim. 4:1–3: 2 Tim. 3:1–9; 4:3, 4).

But the time of the great apostasy is also the time of the great tribulation for the saints. If we follow closely the history of the development of the end, as given in the Apocalypse, we find that believers are tried by Satan through false doctrines and grievous persecutions; but these temptations appear greatly intensified in the visions of the two beasts as recorded in Rev. 13:1–18. So great is this tribulation that John foresees that all that dwell on the earth, save those whose names are written in the Book of Life, will worship the beast (Rev. 13:8).

We are not to understand the sealing of the servants of God in Rev. 7:3, 4, to signify that believers shall not experience the calamities coming upon the world, but this sealing designates the unchangeable firmness of their election (Matt. 24:21–24), which is not affected by the trial of the last great tribulation. The sealing does not designate preservation from tribulation, but victory over tribulation.

That believers will have to endure such great tribulation can also be seen from John's description of those who have overcome the trials of the Last Day. In his Vision of the Glassy Sea (Rev. 15:2, 3), John sees those "who had come victorious from the beast" standing by the glassy sea, having harps of God, singing the song of Moses and of the Lamb. He also sees "the souls of them that had been beheaded for the testimony of Jesus, and for the Word of God, and such as worshiped not the beast, neither his image, and received not the mark upon their forehead and upon their hand." Everywhere it is implied that believers will have to endure great tribulation in the last times (Rev. 7:14), and in this "is the patience and the faith of the saints" (Rev. 13:10).

[ANALYSIS: 1) The teaching of the Parable of the Mustard Seed; 2) of the Parable of the Leaven; 3) the Great Apostasy; 4) which is also the time of the great tribulation; 5) believers will have to endure this great tribulation.]

§ 202. *The Antichrist.*

In the last times there shall develop a trinity of evil, the Dragon (Rev. 12:3, 9, 17), the beast with ten horns (Rev. 13:1–10), and the beast with two horns (Rev. 13:11–18), the last known also as the false prophet (Rev. 16:13; 19:20; 20:10). The dragon is Satan, the Anti-God; the beast is Antichrist; and the false prophet is the opponent of the Holy Spirit, the anti-Spirit, bearing witness to the first beast as the Holy Spirit bears witness of the Son.

The beast of Rev. 13:1–8 is the same one that is referred to in 11:7, and more fully described in 17:3, 7–18, and is evidently identical with the beast of Dan. 7:7, and seems, in the first place, to designate some anti-Christian world-power, either political or spiritual, possibly as Gebhardt maintains, "a definite individual empire, the latest and most extreme, reproducing in itself all earlier phases of the world's enmity to God; or, the last and most remarkable of all empires, the climax and complement of all that had existed before it." But from a careful study of the description of the beast in Rev. 17:7–18, it is equally clear that John does not so much conceive of an empire as of an *individual person*. That explanation which finds everywhere only an empire, fails as much as that which finds everywhere only an individual person. As the individual forms of the anti-Christian world-power finally culminate and unite in one empire, which is called "the Beast," so likewise, in the development of this empire, the anti-Christian world-power shall culminate finally in one King, the eighth, the personal Antichrist, which John also describes as "the Beast," which "goeth into perdition" (Rev. 17:11), recalling the language of 2 Thess. 2:3.

The beast of the two horns (Rev. 13:11–18), known also as the false prophet (Rev. 16:13; 19:20; 20:10) has no direct counterpart in Daniel, but has much in common with "the little horn" of Dan. 7:8, although there are some who would identify the first beast with "the little horn" of Daniel. This second beast possibly represents anti-Christian prophecy in the last times, converging finally into an individual person (Rev. 13: 13; 19:20), who shall prepare the way of Antichrist and assist in carrying on his work. In fact, it seems as if the idea of Antichrist in the Apocalypse is represented under two figures—those of the beast and of the false prophet—the first representing the *political* anti-Christian world-power, and the second the *spiritual* anti-Christian world-power, and that both have Satan as their source. To the first beast Satan intrusts all his power and dominion over the world, and the second beast seduces the inhabitants of the earth by its lying wonders to worship the first beast (Rev. 13:12, 14, 16). There is but one outcome to all this anti-Christian development of the last days: "And the beast was taken, and with him the false prophet that wrought the signs in his sight, . . . they twain were cast alive into the lake of fire that burneth with brimstone" (Rev. 19:20).[1]

So likewise, in his Epistles, John speaks of the last day as being recognized by the coming of Antichrist (1 John 2:18). He takes it for granted that the Second Coming of Christ cannot come until the God-opposing and Christ-hating power (1 John 2:22, 23) has become concentrated in the highest degree in an historical appearance. His readers have heard from him that Antichrist comes (1 John 2:18; 4:3). Corresponding to the two-fold form of anti-Christianity as described in the Apocalypse, of a God-hostile, worldly power and of false prophecy, John lays special stress on false prophecy as one of the marks of the Antichrist (1 John 4:1, 3; 2:22; 2 John 7). In his Epistles John, however, gives us rather a practical application of the doctrine of Antichrist than a formal statement of it. He warns his readers that the spirit of Antichrist was then already existing, although his coming was still future, and that all who denied the Messiahship and Sonship of Jesus were antichrists, as being types of the final Antichrist who was to come.

[ANALYSIS: 1) The trinity of evil; 2) the beast with ten horns is Antichrist; 3) Antichrist is conceived of as a political or spiritual world-power; 4) as well as an individual person; 5) the beast of the

---

[1] Lechler regards the first beast of Rev. 13:1–8 as 'the world-power at enmity with God, the whole kingdom of the world as opposed to the Kingdom of God," and the second beast or the false prophet (Rev. 13:11–18) as "wisdom and intellect at enmity with God."

two horns or the false prophet represents anti-Christian prophecy, 6) also developing into an individual person; 7) both beasts have Satan as their source; 8) the outcome; 9) John also speaks of this two-fold form of anti-Christianity in his Epistles.]

§ 203. *The Second Coming of Christ.*

The Second Coming of Christ in glory is the great theme of the Apocalypse. Christ indeed speaks of every great visitation upon the Church or the individual as a Coming of the Lord, whether at one time it is a manifestation of chastisement (Rev. 2:5, 16; 3:3), or at another of gracious blessing (Rev. 3:20); but it is unanimously agreed that the great theme of the Book of Revelation is the Second Advent.

John gives us certain intimations as to the *time* of Christ's final appearance, but he is faithful to the eschatological principle, expressed in Christ's prophecy of the Last Times as recorded by the Synoptists, and as taught by Paul in his Epistles to the Thessalonians. The time and hour of Christ's coming is known to God only, and the prophet simply describes the times of the end immediately preceding the glorious appearance of Christ. The Holy City shall be trodden under foot by the nations forty-and-two months (Rev. 11:3); the two witnesses shall prophesy a thousand two hundred and three score days (Rev. 11:3); the woman (the Church) is to be nourished in the place prepared for her in the wilderness for the same period (Rev. 12:6), even "for a time, and times, and half a time" (Rev. 12:14), and power is given the beast from the sea or Antichrist "to continue forty-and-two months" (Rev. 13:5). All these periods seem to be synchronous, and the same as "the time, the times and half a time" spoken of by Daniel (7:25; 12:7). Probably it is best to regard this period as the time immediately before the end, when the enmity of the world has increased to its highest intensity, when the persecution of the righteous have reached their utmost limit, when the Divine plagues attain their most terrible development, during which time the proclamation of the Gospel, with a view to repentance, will become universal (Rev. 14:6, 7).

The Apocalypse contains a threefold representation of Christ's Advent. In the first place, it is an unquestionable fact that the coming of Christ is described as a visible thing in connection with great events taking place on the visible world. "Behold, he cometh with the clouds; and every eye shall see him, and they which pierced him; and all the tribes of the earth shall mourn over him" (Rev. 1:7). His coming "with the clouds" (Dan. 7:13 ; Matt. 24:30 ; 26:64) does not denote so much the glory of His coming as the terror of that Great Day (Rev. 11:12, 13 ; 14:14–16).

John gives us another representation of the Second Advent in Rev. 14:14–20. It is highly probable that the Harvest here spoken of (Rev. 14:14–16) refers to the ingathering of the saints (compare Mark 4:26–29), to the reaping of the fruit of the preaching of the Eternal Gospel mentioned in Rev. 14:6, 7; while the vintage and the treading of the wine-press refers to the ingathering of the wicked (Rev. 14:17–20).

But the Advent is placed before us in the most concrete and definite form in Rev. 19:11–21, the beginning of the passage which describes the final consummation, the history of which is given in consecutive order in Rev. 19:11—22:5. This representation of the coming of the Lord for the final struggle with his enemies, and of the struggle itself, rests upon a combination of Old Testament descriptions of the Judgment, as given in Isa. 63:2, 3 and Ezek. 39:17–20.

The returning Christ will first of all make vigorous war upon all his enemies, and will victoriously overcome them. As Babylon, the great world-city, already had been judged and destroyed (the actual overthrow is assumed to have taken place between the events recorded in Rev. 18:24 and Rev. 19:1), so Christ himself at His appearing will execute the merited judgment upon all who oppose Him. The Antichrist and the false prophet shall be taken and cast alive into the lake of fire that burneth with brimstone (Rev. 19:20), and their adherents shall be killed (Rev. 19:21).

The great question to be decided respecting the Second Coming of Christ is whether it will *precede* " the thousand years," spoken of in Rev. 20:1–9, or not. The answer to this question depends on the view we take of the relation of the twentieth chapter to the preceding one. Those who maintain that the twentieth chapter takes up and continues in historical order the narrative of the nineteenth chapter hold that the Second Advent of Christ is to precede the Millennium. This seems to be the most natural interpretation of this much controverted question. To avoid this conclusion others maintain that in Rev. 20:1–9 we have simply a recapitulation of events dating from the First Advent of Christ, and that "the thousand years " here spoken of are already past, or refer figuratively to the long duration elapsing between the First and Second Advent.

We here come to certain theological problems pertaining to the events of the Last Day, which cannot be definitely solved by the light and insight which the Church now has. These much-discussed topics refer, in general, to the time and circumstances of Christ's Coming, the length of the Last Day, the nature of the

Millennium, and of the First Resurrection. Most diverse views are held by the most reverent and earnest seekers after the truth. This diversity of views arises partly from the fact that the perspective of prophecy is not clearly understood, and partly because of the various methods of interpretation in vogue.

The questions upon which the most diverse views are held are these:

1) Is the Millennium past or future?

2) If future, shall Christ come before the Millennium spoken of in Rev. 20:4–6, or after?

3) If His coming is pre-millennial, shall we expect a two-fold coming of Christ—one to set up His Kingdom, and another to Judgment?

4) If Christ comes before the Millennium, is the Resurrection spoken of in Rev. 20:4–6, literal or spiritual?

5) If literal, does it include *all* believers, or only the special class spoken of in Rev. 20:4?

6) Are the thousand years to be taken literally, or does this period of time designate only an indefinite period?

7) Shall the risen ones reign with Christ over the earth *from* heaven, or shall Christ and these risen ones dwell *on* earth?

8) Does the Last Day cover a long prophetic period, and are we to distinguish between two resurrections, with the Millennium intervening, or not?

9) Does the second resurrection spoken of in Rev. 20:13–15 consist of believers and unbelievers, or of unbelievers alone?

10) What is the nature of the Millennial reign of Christ over the earth simply spiritual, or is an earthly kingdom to be set up with its center at Jerusalem?

11) Are we to take the whole passage, Rev. 20:1-10, in a spiritual and symbolical sense, or in a literal sense?

There are those who deem it of the most vital importance to make a definite answer to all these questions, and pronounce harsh judgments on every one that does not hold exactly the same opinions that they have on these speculative topics. But to all such we can only say that although God by means of His prophecies would in advance prepare us for the great events that shall yet come to pass, still we are unable to form to ourselves an exact and perfectly clear idea of them until their accomplishment. The great central facts are most definitely revealed:—Christ shall come again in glory and with great power; there shall be a resurrection of believers and unbelievers; there shall be a judgment; men shall receive reward or punishment according to their works; there shall be a new heaven and a new earth; believers shall inherit eternal life; eternal death shall be the lot of unbelievers;—but as to the exact order of events, and the nature of the Millennium, and the time it takes for the carrying out of God's plan with reference to His kingdom,—on these and the other much disputed points, it is best if with patience and faith we await the times of the fulfillment of the words of prophecy, for we need not doubt their fulfillment: "Heaven and earth shall pass away, but my words shall not pass away" (Matt. 24:35); "These words are faithful and true; and the Lord, the God of the spirits of the prophets, sent His Angel to show unto his servants the things which must shortly come to pass" (Rev. 22:6); "I testify unto every man that heareth the words of the prophecy of this book. If any man shall add unto them, God shall add unto him the plagues which are written in this book: and if any man shall take away from the words of the book of this prophecy, God shall take away his part from the tree of life, and out of the Holy City" (Rev. 22:18, 19).

As the time of the fulfillment of these events draws nearer, the Church and individual believers may be able to understand and comprehend more fully than now.

As introductory to the next two sections, we will quote a few eminent commentators to show how they interpret the events recorded in Rev. 19 and 20:

*Godet:* "We approach the moment when Christ shall arrive and free His Church from the hands of the enemy. It is described in all its magnificence in Rev. 19:11-21. It is this event which St. Paul announces in 2 Thess. 2:8. . . . This supreme act is accompanied with the resurrection of those among the faithful who have died, and the glorification of those who are still alive; and it is followed by a state of affairs in which the reign of God can be perfectly realized among mankind, and Christianity develop all its blessings, spiritual and terrestrial. It is the reign of a thousand years—the Sabbath of humanity on earth—after its long week of work. Nothing in this apocalyptic picture compels us to assume that the Lord shall be visibly present on earth during this whole epoch; it is His Spirit that shall reign and glorify Him. At the end of this period Satan, who as yet is only bound, shall try once more to destroy the work of God, but he shall only give the signal of his own final punishment, which is accompanied by universal judgment (Rev. 20:7-10, 11-15). The terrestrial state founded on the day of Creation (Gen. 1) now gives place to the new heaven and the new earth (Rev. 21), in which God is all and all." At another place he says: "In Rev. 20: 1-10, before the mention of the general resurrection and the Final Judgment

(Rev. 20:11–15), we are told of a special resurrection of the martyrs and of those who had not received the mark of the beast, also of a judgment which shall be committed to them, and of their reigning with Christ a thousand years. This crisis in human history is brought on by a glorious appearance of the Lord and of the armies of heaven, of which we have a splendid description in Rev. 19:11–16. All this seems to imply that, before the general resurrection and the Final Judgment, there will be a visible appearance of Christ on the earth, and a resurrection of believers; after that a period of extraordinary blessing to the world. In Rev. 20:7–10, we read that a last revolt will take place before the glorious Final Coming of the Judge." Again, "The teaching of the Apocalypse is exactly the same under a dramatic form as that of Paul under a didactic form. Both alike present the following order of things to come: A visible appearance of the Lord accompanied by the resurrection of the faithful, and followed by the reign of believers and the judgment of visible powers (here 1 Cor. 6:2, 3). At the close of this reign and of this judgment exercised by the faithful will come the general resurrection and the Final Judgment. We find this identical conception in both the Sacred writers. It places the Millennium between a visible *Parousia* of the Lord and the general resurrection followed by the Final Judgment."

*Delitzsch:* "The New Testament Apocalypse represents 'The Last Things' in their future successive temporal order and relations. It is, in this respect, the key to the entire prophetic word—for example, in the beautiful prediction in Isa. 24–27, which lifts itself up even to the destruction of death through victory. The triumph and the glory of that time form the Millennial age. I believe in the literal reality of this apocalyptic picture without pressing slavishly the letter (1 Cor. 13:12). I am, therefore, a Chiliast; but the *Damnamus* in the seventeenth article of the Augustana does not hit me."

"According to Rev. 19:11-21, the *Parousia* of our Lord precedes the Millennium (Rev. 20:1-6). He comes and destroys the Antichrist (Rev. 19:19, 20; 13:1, 6, 7; 2 Thess. 2:8; Isa. 11:4). Then Satan is bound and a Sabbath-time, a "Sabbatismos" (Heb. 4:9), begins which is the prelude to a blessed eternity. But even this blessed time of peace is interrupted and declines. Once again the power of the wicked one rages against the Kingdom of Christ on earth; and now, finally, all temporal history closes with the judgment of fire upon God, and with the general resurrection. At this point the Apocalypse says nothing of the *Parousia* of the Lord; but we know that the Final Advent of the Lord, as Judge of the world, connects itself with what we read in Rev. 20:9-15."

With reference to Rev. 20:4-6, Delitzsch says: "Is it conceivable that the Glorified Lord will permanently dwell upon the old unglorified earth? Is it conceivable that the Risen One will continuously associate Himself with men who still have 'flesh and blood,' which cannot inherit the Kingdom of God? Bengel could not conceive of that; and as little could Jacob Boehme, the German philosopher, whose tendency was realistic, and whose mind was also given to mystery. I have always preferred the exegesis of Bengel, according to which Rev. 20:4, "they lived, and reigned with Christ a thousand years," indicates a reigning of ascended saints who rule, with Christ, from heaven. The view that our Saviour will set His throne in the Jerusalem of the old unglorified earth, and rule from there, seems to me a crass Chiliasm. And, although I am a friend of Israel, yet Christ, exalted to the Right Hand of God, is to me so much a supernatural Son of Man that I believe in no reproduction of the Old Testament earthly national theocracy."

*Auberlen:* "When the security of the world-power, and the distress of the people of God, have reached the highest point, then, as a thief in the night, *the Lord Jesus Christ shall appear from heaven*, put an end to the whole course of this world, and establish His kingdom of glory upon earth. This coming of Christ must be carefully distinguished form His coming to the Final Judgment. . . . The expression *Parousia* of Christ denotes, in the New Testament, this advent, and it alone; and this Second Coming of Christ, viewed in connection with the kingdom established by it upon earth (the Millennial) occupies a much more prominent position in the biblical mode of conception than in that of the modern church. . . . This appearance, which shall be accompanied by corresponding powerful natural phenomena, is described in Rev. 19:11–16; and then follows in verses 17–21 the destruction of the *anti-Christian power of the beast and of the fasle prophet*. . . This judgment puts an end, for all times, to the beast; it is destroyed from off the earth; the world-kingdoms, in the form they had previously, now cease forever; the history of the world assumes now a character totally different from its character hitherto. In place of the kingdom of the beast comes the Kingdom of the Son of Man, and His saints. . . .

"The first thing the Apocalypse tells us concerning the Millennial Kingdom is the binding of Satan, and that he is cast into the bottomless pit, and shut up (Rev.

20:1-3) . . . Humanity will be freed, as it were, from a nightmare, which weighed on it. Everything good will develop freely; and though sin will not be absolutely abolished—for men will be still living in the flesh upon the earth—sin will no longer be a universal power. . . . And this leads us to the second point. The Apocalypse states, as a characteristic feature of the Millennium, that the earth *is governed by Christ and His transfigured Church*. . . .

"Among the saints who are called to reign with Christ, the martyrs of ancient and modern times are mentioned first; they became most like to the Lord Jesus in their suffering and death, and are, therefore, nearest Him in His life and reign. . . . Next to the martyrs are mentioned all who had not worshiped the beast, be it in more remote times or in the last days. Our passage refers, indeed, to the whole congregation of believers, who are born of God, even all the children of God (Rom. 8:17) . . . These have been with Christ in heaven, but appear now with Him, and are then no longer invisible (2 Thess. 1:7-10; Rev. 17:14). But in order that they may become visible, they are clothed in the moment of their appearance with their bodies, which are pervaded by heavenly spirit and life-power, and are spiritual bodies, and thus they pass completely into the perfect life of transfiguration. This is the *first* resurrection (Rev. 20:4-6) as distinguished from the second, or general resurrection (Rev. 20:12). . . . Those who are thus raised are ordained to be a blessing to their brethren who are still in the flesh. They do not only live in the highest sense of the word, but they likewise reign with Christ a thousand years (Rev. 20.4). After having gathered His Church, and after having taken His Bride to Himself, Christ returns with her to heaven. Earth is not yet transfigured, and can, consequently, not be the locality meet for the transfigured Church. But from heaven the saints now rule the earth, whence we may conclude that one of the glories of the Millennium shall consist in the much freer and more vivid communion of the heavenly and earthly churches in particular, and the lower and higher world in general; a type of which state may be seen in the forty days of the Risen Saviour, during which He appeared to His disciples. . . .

"It is, then, that Christianity will pervade the world and all relations of life in spirit and in truth; the union of the royal and priestly office in the ruling saints will be mirrored in the kingdom upon earth in the union of Church and State—that is, in the *Kingdom* of God, as distinguished from the mere Church, which is at present still the form under which Christianity exists."

*Luthardt* takes a somewhat bolder position. In his brief commentary on Revelation (Rev. 20:3), he says: "The thousand years of the binding of Satan cannot lie in the past — say, for example, in the time of the German Empire, from Charlemagne 800 A. D. to 1806; for Satan was not then bound, but loose in Rome and elsewhere, and Luther himself caused the Church to sing:

"And check the stroke of Pope and Turk."

Consequently, here a period of the future is meant, in which no longer Sin, but Christ and His Word, shall be the controlling power in history, although the obedience shown by all may not be the inner obedience of the heart."

On *ver. 4*. "*They sat upon them*"; "to take part in the rule of Christ"; "*and judgment was given to them;*"

"that is, power of judging, as the Judges of Israel had, also dominion over the earth (Ps. 2:10; compare Matt. 19:28); "*And I saw the souls of them that had been beheaded;*" "that is, the martyrs. Satan may kill, but Christ will raise to life;" "*And they lived;*" not spiritually in bodily life, for the expression refers to dead believers. . . . The words can only be understood of a bodily resurrection, but of course in a glorified body;" "*And reigned with Christ a thousand years;*" "This is consequently a great era of the rule of Christ and of His faithful ones, raised from death and glorified —a rule on earth, an era of the Church triumphant."

*Ver. 5.* "*The rest of the dead lived not;*" "This is consequently not the general resurrection of the dead;" "*This is the first resurrection;*" "of faithful believers, which precedes the general resurrection of the dead, so that between the two lies the era of the Church triumphant."

*Ver. 6.* "*And they shall reign,*" "regally on earth, over the rest who live upon earth;" "*With him a thousand years:*" "Here consequently is taught the so-called Chiliasm—*i. e.* the rule of Jesus Christ and His glorified Church of faithful confessors over the rest of mankind . . . which is to follow the present course of the world and the resurrection of the righteous. By the thousand years is meant a great world-day. Not a fleshly rule (compare *Augsburg Confession*, Art. XVII), but a spiritual, heavenly reign of peace and state of blessedness on earth—of which, indeed, inasmuch as it does not pertain to the present order of things, we have no conception, nor can we frame any idea. But we may be satisfied that we shall ever be with Christ, and that He will glorify His Church before the world—a doctrine which in the first three centuries be-

## THE SECOND COMING OF CHRIST. 309

longs to orthodoxy, but was allowed to decline subsequently. For, as Bengel says: 'When Christianity had attained through Constantine the upper hand in the world, the hope of the future became greatly weakened by the enjoyment of the present.' The doctrine thereby fell into the hands of the fanatics, and was basely perverted."

*Düsterdieck*, who is a Preterist, in his Commentary on Revelation, says: "With respect to what is said in Rev. 20:1-10, we must distinguish between the unprejudiced establishment of the exegetical results and the theological judgment of what is found based upon the analogy of Scripture; and only from the former can we arrive at the latter. The exegetical comprehension of *vers.* 1-10, as a whole and in its details, has its most essential condition in the recognition of the fact that what is here described lies immediately *before* the proper judgment of the world (Rev. 20:11-15), and *after* those judicial acts of the final catastrophe which are described in Rev. 19:19-21—*i. e.* in other words, every exposition must utterly fail which in *vers.* 1-10 maintains a *recapitulation*, which can occur only if the interpretation here be also allegorical."

We will close this citation of different interpretations of Rev. 20:1-10, by quoting some passages from Starke's *Synopsis:*

"The thousand years of the binding of the Dragon and the reign of Christ and His saints are properly years. There is no reason why we should deviate from a literal interpretation. If we explain them of the past, we shall involve ourselves in inextricable difficulties. Still less can they be referred to eternity, because verses *seven* and *eight* indicate their completion, and show what will occur after the thousand years are expired." Then follow three reasons why we should abide by the literal interpretation.

"These thousand years are not past, but still future. If we date them from the Birth of Christ, or from the Resurrection of Christ, or from the transition of the Gospel to the Gentiles, or from the destruction of Jerusalem, or from Constantine, etc., we are involved in inextricable difficulties." Then follows a discussion under five heads proving that such a view is contrary to the Scriptural teaching.

"But the thousand years are *still future;* for in them Satan is to be bound, no longer to deceive the nations; for no period can be shown in which the Church was thus free from the persecution and deception of Satan, and enjoyed such distinction as the reign of the saints for a thousand years demands. The fall of Babylon and Antichrist, which immediately precedes this (Rev. 19:21), has not yet occurred." . . .

"The Literalists understand a literal resurrection as here spoken of. This resurrection is shown:

1) By the text (Rev. 20:6), for although John saw only *souls*, yet this was the reason that the souls, which hitherto had been in a certain degree of heavenly joy, now united with their bodies, are, by such union, to be transplanted into still greater joy and glory. He does not say the *souls* lived and reigned, but he speaks of the *whole* person. They became alive by union of the soul with the body, and reigned with Christ a thousand years. That the Greek word used means 'they came to life' is clearly seen from Rev. 2:8."

2) By what follows the text, for it is not said, *ver* 6. " Blessed and holy is the *soul* that hath part in the first resurrection," but speaks of the *whole person,* consisting of soul and body, which has part therein;" . . .

3) "By other passages of Scripture." Here follows a long discussion, and among other passages, the writer especially expounds Luke 24,14; John 5:28; 6:39, 40, 44, 54; 1 Cor. 15:23-26.

4) "By the exposition of the oldest Church Fathers, who lived nearest the time of the Apostles." He then appeals to the views of "Papias, Justin, Irenæus, Tertullian, Victorinus, Lactantius—orthodox men, who, according to the testimony of Justin, understood this passage to refer to a proper bodily resurrection." Among others, he also refers to the views of Dannhauer and Selneccer among the Lutherans.

Then follows a clear presentation of the objections urged by Preterists and Allegorists to this literal interpretation, and the writer closes the exposition in these words:

"Thus, the reader has the various expositions, with the reasons *for* and *against*. He who thinks he can make the Preterist and Allegorist interpretations agree with the text and parallel passages, it is to be hoped, *will have at least so much Christian modesty* as not to accuse a man, who prefers the literal interpretation—that of the Church Fathers, of a bodily resurrection of the martyrs to the kingdom of glory—*as guilty of heresy in doctrine.*"

[ANALYSIS: 1) The Second Coming of Christ is the great theme of the Apocalypse; 2) the time is known to God alone; 3) John describes mainly the times immediately before the end; 4) the Apocalypse contains a three-fold representation of Christ's Advent; 5) the most concrete and definite description is given in Rev. 19:11-21; 6) this Coming seems to be pre-Millennial; 7) certain questions pertaining to the Last Day cannot be definitely settled; 8) most diverse views are held by most reverent theologians; 9) eleven disputed points; 10) many points, however, pertaining to the Coming of Christ, the resurrection, and the judgment, are clear; 11) as the times of fulfillment draw nearer we may be better able to understand; 12) Godet's interpretation of the events of the Last Day; 13) the views of Delitzsch; 14) of Auberlen; 15) of Luthardt; 16) of Düsterdieck, 17) explanation given in Starke's *Synopsis*.]

§ 204. *The Millennium.*

When Christ comes in glory as King of Kings and Lord of Lords (Rev. 19:16), His appearance brings destruction to His enemies, and glory to His saints. All the enemies of Christ shall be overcome (Rev. 19: 19–21). Antichrist and the false prophet shall be cast alive into the lake of fire (Rev. 19:20), and immediately after this the author and prince of all evil, the Dragon, the old serpent, which is the Devil and Satan, is cast into the abyss, where he is confined and bound during "a thousand years," in order that he may not be able to deceive the nations during this period (Rev. 20:2, 3).

At the resurrection of Christ and His exaltation to the Right Hand of God, the kingdom of Satan received a great blow; and Satan, the deceiver of the whole world, was cast down to the earth, and his angels with him, and their place was no longer found in heaven (Rev. 12:7–10). And although Satan has been overcome, and the believer is free from his dominion, still Satan is the prince of this world; and though his home and the seat of his kingdom is in Hades, he still exercises his power largely on earth, and in this our present dispensation it can truly be said: "Woe for the earth and for the sea: because the Devil is gone down unto you, having great wrath, knowing that he hath but a short time" (Rev. 12:12). But at Christ's coming in glory, Satan and his power shall be banished from the earth until "the thousand years" shall be finished (Rev. 20:7).

It is at the beginning of "the thousand years" that the believing and faithful ones shall take part in the glory of their Lord's return. John in perfect agreement with 1 Thess. 4:15-17; 1 Cor. 15:51, 52, takes it for granted that believers shall be living on the earth at Christ's Second Advent (Rev. 16:15). Christ Himself says: "Hold fast till I come. And he that overcometh, and he that keepeth my words unto the end, to him will I give authority over the nations" (Rev. 2:25, 26).

When John says: "And I saw thrones, and they sat upon them, and judgment was given unto them" (Rev. 20:4), we are not to think so much of judicial thrones as of royal thrones—these thrones referring to the beginning of the authority of the saints; and it is highly probable that the saints who live to see the Second Advent shall be among the number of those transfigured and glorified ones who sit upon these thrones (compare Dan. 7:9, 10, 22, 27; Matt. 19:28; 1 Cor. 6:2, 3; 1 Tim. 2:12). For John like Paul (1 Thess. 4:17; 1 Cor. 15:52; Phil. 3:21) expects a change of the living, and they are included among the risen saints who share in "the thousand years" reign. But not only shall the saints who are alive at the Coming of Christ partake in the glory of our Saviour's Kingdom, but John particularly says: "And I saw the souls of them that had been beheaded for the testimony of Jesus, and for the Word of God, and such as worshiped not the beast, neither his image, and received not the mark upon their forehead and upon their hand; and they lived, and reigned with Christ a thousand years. The rest of the dead lived not until the thousand years should be finished. This is the first resurrection. Blessed and holy is he that hath part in the first resurrection: over these the second death hath no power; but they shall be priests of God and of Christ, and shall reign with him a thousand years" (Rev. 20:4-6).

John here mentions two classes of the believing dead:

1) "The noble army of martyrs"; and 2) all other believers who have not worshiped the beast, neither his image, nor received his mark. These two classes of dead believers are especially referred to, but believers who have died in the Lord before the conflict in the last time are not excluded.

The *first* resurrection is of believers alone, and must be understood in a literal sense, of a resurrection with glorified bodies, and is called the *first* in distinction from the resurrection to judgment *described* in Rev. 20:11–15.[1]

John here speaks of the risen saints as "priests of God and of Christ," and as "reigning with Christ a thousand years" (Rev. 20:4–6), a state of glory which is described in pure and Scriptural language without the admixture of sensuous traits.

It is a question much discussed whether this reign of Christ with His saints *over* the earth shall be exercised *on* the earth, or *from* heaven. It is not the province of Biblical Theology to discuss these topics in their dogmatic relations; but this passage gives us no foundation for the view that the Lord Himself with His risen saints shall be visibly present on earth during this period. The reigning of the saints with Christ over this earth takes place from heaven. The "thrones" which the Apostle saw are not on earth, but in heaven. Twice before, in his visions, has the Apostle seen

[1] This is even granted by *Zezschwitz*, that most conservative of Lutheran theologians. His exact words are worth quoting: "Die Schrift lehrt, auch nach meiner Einsicht, klar eine sogenannte 'erste Auferstehung' von Glaübigen vor der allgemeinen Todtenauferstehung. Was darüber (Apoc. 20:4, 5, *cf.* 13) zu lesen ist, kann nicht wol anders gedeutet werden." (See his *Christenlehre*, vol. 2, p. 375. Second edition, Leipsic, 1884.)

"thrones" in heaven. In Rev. 4:4, we read, "round about the throne were four-and-twenty thrones." In this fourth chapter the throne is the throne of heaven; the scenes and surroundings are those of heaven, of the angelic world. It is a scene of heaven, not of earth. In Rev. 11:16, we have the same scene repeated. The scenes and surroundings are again those of heaven. Rev. 3:21: "He that overcometh, I will give to him to sit down with me in my throne, as I also overcame, and sat down with my Father in his throne," helps us to determine the place of Christ's throne;—it is in heaven; it is with the Father's throne. It is a throne shared by all who overcome; the language is explicit, and this throne in heaven. It is best, therefore, to regard these thrones which John saw as in heaven, and the risen saints reign with Christ *from* heaven. Furthermore, this earth will not be transformed until after the Millennium, and therefore during the Millennium it is not yet the proper home for the risen and transfigured saints; the earth hath not yet been prepared for the Glorified Church, nor for the heavenly Kingdom of God. During "the thousand years" there is still a separation between heaven and earth, between humanity glorified and humanity still living in the flesh.

It is implied that during this period the nations which have not taken an active part in the conflict against Christ and His army (Rev. 19:19–21) are still living on the earth (Rev. 20:7-10). John does not enter upon a detailed description of the events of the Millennial period; nor is it wise for us to do so.

The writer has taken special pains to examine the most important interpretations attempted by the different schools of commentators and dogmaticians

(Preterist, Continuous-Historical, and Futurist); and although in following the distinct teaching of Scripture it seems that it is safest to take these events of the twentieth chapter in their simple, plain sense, and regard all these things as still future, still he must confess that with his present knowledge he cannot understand this description, much less would he attempt, as some do, positively to explain and define what the order and glory of the events of the Last Day will be.

[ANALYSIS: 1) The events following Christ's Coming; 2) the binding of Satan; 3) believers are on the earth when Christ comes; 4) being transfigured they shall share in the reign of Christ; 5) the believing dead shall be raised; 6) the first resurrection is of believers alone; 7) Christ's reign over the earth shall be exercised *from* heaven; 8) the thrones which the Apostle saw are in heaven; 9) the earth not yet the proper abode for the glorified saints; 10) the earth shall not be transformed until after the Millennium; 11) we cannot describe the nature of the Millennium in detail.]

§ 205. *The First Resurrection.*

If we lay stress on the clear and distinct teaching of Scripture in Rev. 20:4–6, 11–15, and interpret literally, we must conclude that John speaks of two resurrections, with the Millennium intervening—the first of believers alone, and the second of the general resurrection to judgment. The topic here under discussion is the *first* resurrection. Much stress has been laid on the fact that there seems to be a conflict between the teaching of John in Revelation and the teaching of Jesus and of Paul—that both Jesus and Paul take it for granted that there is but one resurrection, and that this resurrection takes place at one and the same time, on the Last Day, and includes both believers and unbelievers; while, in Revelation, John speaks of two resurrections "a thousand years" apart, the first of believers only, and the second of the general resurrection to judgment.

We are willing to grant that this passage in Rev. 20:4-6 is the clearest prediction we have with reference to this subject, and we are even ready to concede that without this definite prophecy we would have no sure guide in Scripture concerning this important question of the first resurrection; but it by no means follows from this that this doctrine so clearly taught by John is in conflict with or contrary to the teaching of Jesus or of Paul. There is a progress in revelation, and we have a right to expect that He who was divinely chosen to reveal "the things which shall come to pass hereafter" (Rev. 1:19, 4:1) would give us revelations that are in advance of all others, especially as Christ Himself says: "I have yet many things to say unto you, but ye cannot bear them now. Howbeit when he, the Spirit of truth, is come, he shall guide you into all the truth: . . . and he shall declare unto you the things that are to come" (John 16:12, 13).

When Christ in Luke 14:14 says: "Thou shalt be recompensed in the resurrection of the just," it does not follow that Christ here draws a distinction between two resurrections—the one of the just exclusively, and the other of the rest of the dead; but neither does He exclude this view. In Luke 20:35, 36, "they that are accounted worthy to attain to that world, and the resurrection from the dead, neither marry, nor are given in marriage: for neither can they die any more: for they are equal unto the angels; and are sons of God, being sons of the resurrection," Christ evidently refers to the resurrection of believers, and the remarkable expression "they that are accounted worthy to attain . . . the resurrection from the dead," has a peculiar significance, and can best be explained, if we regard it the teaching of Jesus that this resurrection here referred to is a special privilege granted only to the faithful believers. But even here we would not lay too much stress on this interpretation; for it is sufficient to agree that this saying of Christ does not exclude the view that there is a first resurrection, and that of believers exclusively. So also, when Christ in John 5:28, 29 says: "Marvel not at this: for the hour cometh in which all that are in the tombs shall hear his voice, and shall come forth; they that have done good, unto the resurrection of life; and they that have done ill, unto the resurrection of judgment," it does not follow that Christ here teaches that all shall be raised *at the same time*, any more than that all the spiritually dead spoken of in John 5:25 ("The hour cometh, and now is, when the dead shall hear the voice of the Son of God; and they that hear shall live") shall be quickened simultaneously. The teaching of John in Revelation makes it clear to us that there is a period designated by "the thousand years" between the resurrection of believers unto life and the resurrection of unbelievers. Nor does the doctrine of John as presented in the Apocalypse come in conflict with Christ's repeated statement that he will raise the believer "at the last day" (John 6:39, 40, 44, 54); for the resurrection of believers does take place at the Last Day, but it is at the beginning of the Last Day, while the general resurrection takes place at the end of the Last Day, for it is the peculiar teaching of John that the Last Day is a longer period than is generally conceived—that it has a beginning and an end. Nor does this doctrine of the first resurrection come in conflict with Christ's description of judgment as recorded in Matt. 25:31-46; for this last description is in

## THE FIRST RESURRECTION. 319

harmony with Rev. 20:11-15, for all the risen saints shall be present at the Final Judgment, although they do not come into the judgment (John 5:24), and shall even in some way take part in the judgment (1 Cor. 6:2, 3). And it is only after the final judgment recorded in Rev. 20:11-15 that the saints shall enter upon their complete and full glory and inheritance in the new heavens and the new earth (Rev. 21:1).

So likewise the doctrine as taught in the Apocalypse does not conflict with the teaching of Paul. In 1 Thess. 4:16, 17, when Paul says: "And the dead in Christ shall rise first: then we that are alive, that are left, shall together with them be caught up in the clouds, to meet the Lord in the air: and so shall we ever be with the Lord," it is a false exegesis to say that Paul here draws a distinction between the *first* resurrection of believers and the *second* resurrection of unbelievers. He may have in view as such the *first* resurrection, in contradistinction to the second; but this we cannot infer from his words, and such forced exegesis does more harm than good. All we can say is that Paul does not exclude such a distinction between the first resurrection of believers and the second or general resurrection.

In 1 Cor. 15:22-26, " In Christ shall all be made alive. But each in his own order: Christ the first-fruits, then they that are Christ's, at His coming. Then cometh the end, when he shall deliver up the kingdom to God, even the Father; when he shall have abolished all rule and all authority and power. For he must reign, till He hath put all enemies under his feet. The last enemy that shall be abolished is death." If we had no hint given us in Rev. 20:4-6, we could not presume to indicate what time would elapse between the resurrection of those that are Christ's at His coming, and " the end," when He shall deliver up the kingdom to God, even the Father. All we could say is that the language seems to imply some interval, and as we know that the interval marked by the "then" between the rising of Christ as the first-fruits, and the rising of those "that are Christ's, at His coming," is for certain more than eighteen hundred years, we ought not to be staggered if John in the book of Revelation tells us that there is an interval of a period described as "a thousand years" between the resurrection of believers at the Coming of Christ and the end of the Last Day, or the time of the resurrection of unbelievers unto judgment. If it were not for this passage in Revelation we should not know of this period of "a thousand years," but Paul's teaching does not in any way conflict with the teaching of John, for he does not exclude the idea of a second resurrection of unbelievers at a period later than the resurrection of believers.

The only passage in Paul's writings where possibly there is a reference to the first resurrection in contradistinction to the second, as a resurrection of special honor and glory, is Phil. 3:11 "If by any means I may attain unto the resurrection from the dead." This peculiar expression suggests the *first* resurrection, which includes only true believers; and although there is no reference whatever to the time between the resurrection of the believers and the unbelievers, this passage surely is not in conflict with the teaching of John that a longer or shorter period elapses between the two resurrections.

[ANALYSIS: 1) John seems to speak of two resurrections; 2) is there a conflict between the teaching of John on the one hand, and of Jesus and Paul on the other? 3) there is a progress in revelation; 4) a difference does not necessarily imply a conflict; 5) the examination of the saying of Jesus in Luke 14:14; 6) of His saying in Luke 20:35, 36; 7) of John 5:28, 29; 8) of John 6:39, 40, 44. 54; 9) of Matt. 25:31-46; 10) the examination of the saying of Paul in 1 Thess. 4:16, 17; 11) of his saying in 1 Cor. 15:22-26; 12) of Phil. 3:11.]

§ 206. *The General Resurrection.*

The description of the Final Judgment in Rev. 20:11-15 presupposes the presence of all men in their risen bodies: "I saw the dead, the great and the small, standing before the throne; and books were opened: and another book was opened, which is the book of life: and the dead were judged out of the things which were written in the books, according to their works" (*ver.* 12). Nothing is said in this passage of the resurrection of the saints, for it is taken for granted that they already have arisen in the *first* resurrection. This second resurrection, from a close study of the context, appears to consist of unbelievers alone. But all, believers and unbelievers, are present at the judgment; the believers shall even participate in it (1 Cor. 6:2, 3), and each one will receive his final reward or punishment according to his works done on earth. Gebhardt truly says: "When, on this occasion, the book of life is opened, the saints collectively (Rev. 11:18) are interested in it; but since, by the first resurrection, they are already recognized as registered in the book of life, they are not now judged according to their works; for them the general judgment can be nothing else than the declaration of what they are, the solemn confirmation of what was assured to them by their sharing in the thousand years' reign (Rev. 20:6), Christ's acknowledgment of them as His before His Father, and before the holy angels (Rev. 3:5), the distribution of reward in the highest degree, the completion of that which came to them at the Coming of Christ (Rev. 1::18; 22:12). On the other hand, all the rest of the men, without distinction or exception, are judged according to their works."

[ANALYSIS: 1) At the judgment all men shall be present in their risen bodies; 2) believers shall in some way participate in the judgment; 3) but shall not come *into* judgment; 4) in Rev. 20:13-15 we have a description of the resurrection of unbelievers.]

§ 207. *The Final Judgment.*

In the five different descriptions of the end as given by John (Rev. 6:12-17; 11:15-19; 14:18-20; 16:17-21, 20: 11-15), we have different aspects of the Divine judgments which shall be visited upon the Godless world at the Last Day. All these passages have reference to that great day of wrath (Isa. 13:13; Ezek. 7:19; Zeph. 1:15; Rom. 2:5, 6), that great day of God (Jer. 30:7; Joel 2:11; 3:14; Zeph. 1:14; Mal. 3:2, Acts 2:20; Jude 6), that *final catastrophe* in which God will fulfill to the world His threatenings and promises in manifest reality. And yet some of these passages (Rev. 6:15-17; 14:18-20; 16:17-21) refer more particularly to the events that take place at the beginning of the Last Day, corresponding to Rev. 19:11-21, while Rev. 11: 15-19,[1] and 20:11-15 refer particularly to the great event known as the Final Judgment, which occurs at the completion of the Last Day.

From Rev. 20:11, "And I a saw a great white throne, and him that sat upon it, from whose face the earth and the heaven fled away; and there was found no place

[1] Rev. 11:18, "And the nations were wroth, and thy wrath came, and the time of the dead to be judged, and the time to give their reward to thy servants the prophets, and to the saints, and to them that fear thy name, the small and the great, and to destroy them that destroy the earth."

for them," we can infer that in connection with this judgment, and just preceding it, we have the end of the world; that this whole *present visible world* shall then be transformed. As has already been stated all believers shall be present at this judgment, but shall not come under its power, because this judgment is for "the rest of the dead," for unbelievers. All those whose names are not written in the Book of Life, all whose works are evil, will now manifestly, as the rejected of God, receive their merited doom,—for they will be "cast into the lake of fire."

[ANALYSIS: 1) In the Apocalypse we have five different descriptions of the end ; 2) the Last Day has its beginning and its end; 3) the Final Judgment occurs at the completion of the Last Day, 4) is closely associated with the end of the world; 5) refers especially to unbelievers.]

§ 208. *The End of the World.*

When John saw the great white throne, and Him that sat upon it, he beheld and "the earth and the heaven fled away; and there was found no place for them" (Rev. 20:11). The Apostle does not here give us a description of the destruction of the world ; but, in Rev. 6:12-14, where we also have a prediction of the end of the world, we have a most vivid description: "And there was a great earthquake; and the sun became black as sackcloth of hair, and the whole moon became as blood ; and the stars of the heaven fell unto the earth, as a fig tree casteth her unripe figs, when she is shaken of a great wind. And the heaven was removed as a scroll when it is rolled up; and evey mountain and island were moved out of their places." From this passage and Rev. 16:20, "And every island fled away, and the mountains were not found," we can infer that

John's conception of the end of the world was similar to that of Peter's (2 Pet. 3:7, 10, 12).

[ANALYSIS: 1) The vivid description of the end of the world given in Rev. 6:12-14; 2) John's conception is similar to that of Peter's.]

§ 209. *The Second Death.*

The Apostle does know of any *apokatastasis* or final restoration of the unbeliever. The great conflict between heaven and hell, between God and the Devil, finally comes to an end, and is forever closed;—but it ends in an *absolute dualism*.[1] God and heaven have obtained the victory. The Devil and hell have been defeated and overcome. But the Devil is not changed, hell is not purified, nor are they destroyed in the sense of ceasing to exist. The wicked are not annihilated, but after the Day of Judgment continue eternally in the lake of fire and brimstone. Two places of abode are most graphically contrasted: the one is the lake that burneth with fire and brimstone, and the other is the new heaven and the new earth. Heaven and hell have now become, in visible reality, what they were in hidden reality.

"This is the second death, even the lake of fire. And if any was not found written in the Book of Life, he was cast into the lake of fire" (Rev. 20:14,15). There is a second death, for "he that overcometh shall not be hurt of the second death" (Rev. 2:11). "Blessed and holy is he that hath part in the first resurrection: over these the second death hath no power" (Rev. 20:6). This second death, the intensified death, is the coming of sinners in their risen bodies to the eternal death, from which there is no resurrection or change. It is the

[1] On this section, compare especially *Gebhardt*, pp. 290, 291.

awful coming or going to perdition (Rev. 17:8, 11), which consists not in the "destruction or annihilation of the wicked," but in the definite loss of happiness, in eternally restless pangs, and perpetual consciousness of consummated death. Antichrist and the false prophet, their time having expired, shall be cast alive into the lake of fire that burneth with brimstone at the Coming of Christ (Rev. 19:20); then after the last suppression of Satan's outbreak, he also shall be cast into the same place (Rev. 20:10), and the Devil, together with the beast and the false prophet, shall be tormented day and night for ever and ever (Rev. 20:11). It is also in this lake of fire that we must look for Babylon, the great city (Rev. 18:21), for "her smoke goeth up for ever and ever" (Rev. 19:3); "If any man worshipeth the beast and his image, and receiveth a mark on his forehead, or upon his hand, he also shall drink of the wine of the wrath of God, which is prepared unmixed in the cup of His anger; and he shall be tormented with fire and brimstone in the presence of the holy angels, and in the presence of the Lamb: and the smoke of their torment goeth up for ever and ever; and they have no rest day and night, they that worship the beast and his image, and who so receiveth the mark of his name (Rev. 14:9-11), "But for the fearful, and unbelieving and abominable, and murderers, and fornicators, and sorcerers, and idolaters, and all liars, their part shall be in the lake that burneth with fire and brimstone, which is the second death" (Rev. 21:8).

[ANALYSIS: 1) The Apostle knows of no *apokatastasis* or universal restoration, ) the conflict between heaven and hell ends in absolute dualism; 2) God is the victor, but hell is not destroyed; 4) the wicked are not annihilated; 5) there are two places of final abode, heaven and hell, 6) the second death; 7) punishment is both negative and positive; 8) the awful description given by the seer.]

§ 210. *The New Heaven and the New Earth.*

With the Day of Judgment comes the end of the world (Rev. 20:11), and a new world takes its place. "And I saw a new heaven and a new earth: for the first heaven and the first earth are passed away" (Rev. 21:1); "The first things are pased away. . . . Behold, I make all things new" (Rev. 21:4, 5). From this presentation we cannot infer that the new earth will arise from the old, as from a seed; nor, on the other hand, does it teach that the old world shall be annihilated, and a new heaven and earth newly created. It is best, however, in accordance with Scripture teaching, to regard the new earth as renewed, refined, transfigured, and that it is related to the old as gold which has passed through the purifying fire is related to the unrefined ore. We may Compare Rom. 8:18-21; 2 Pet. 3:13.

We must distinguish between the new heaven and the new earth on the one hand, and the New Jerusalem on the other; for upon this new earth the New Jerusalem comes down from God. "And I saw the holy city, New Jerusalem, coming down out of heaven from God, made ready as a bride adorned for her husband. And I heard a great voice out of the throne saying: Behold, the tabernacle of God is with men, and He shall dwell with them and they shall be His peoples, and God Himself shall be with them, and be their God" (Rev. 21:2, 3). This New Jerusalem is ever only a part of the new earth—though, according to its meaning as well as in its representation, it almost entirely occupies the foreground. It means the people of God, the multitude of the saints, the Church, the Kingdom of God, in the stricter sense of its completion (compare Heb. 11:10; 12:22; 13:14; Gal.

4:26).[1] The people of God are described under a twofold representation. The first is a *personal* resting upon such Old Testament passages as Isa. 54:1-3; Hos. 2:19, 20; Ezek. 16:7-14; and especially Solomon's Song, and regards the Messiah as the Bridegroom, and the Church as the Bride; the final consummation is the time of the marriage; the happiness of the heavenly state appears under the image of a marriage feast; and the saints are those who are called to it, the marriage guests (Rev. 19:6-9; 21:2, 9,10; 22:17).

The second representation is the *general* picture of the perfected people of God as the *New* Jerusalem (Rev. 3:12). It is this New Jerusalem which John saw coming down out of heaven from God, adorned as a bride for her husband (Rev. 21:2, 9, 10). In keeping with this general representation, John depicts the perfect state of the Church by a description of the New Jerusalem in its *architecture*, after the type of Ezek. 48:30-35 (Rev. 21:9-21). And Gebhardt adds: "The New Jerusalem is therefore, in extent and amplitude, in beauty of material and form, indeed in every respect, a perfect building; and this perfect building is the image of the final state of the Church as a perfect one, whether considered in its universal importance, in the number of its members, in its inviolability and peace, or in its magnificence and glory." It is this New Jerusalem, the holy city, which shall abide forever on the new earth.

[ANALYSIS: 1) At the Day of Judgment the old world passes away, 2) a new world takes its place; 3) which is a transformation of the old; 4) we must distinguish between the new earth and the New Jerusalem; 5) the New Jerusalem is only a part of the new

---

[1] Compare *Gebhardt*, pp. 290-295.

earth; 6) the New Jerusalem represents the people of God; 7) is described as a bride; 8) and as the holy city.]

## § 211. *Eternal Life.*

John presents *eternal life* under three aspects. It belongs already to the believer—*a*) here *on earth;* *b*) is his inheritance in the heavenly *state* before the resurrection; and *c*) is his glorious possession in the *New Jerusalem.*

1) The moment we become Christians we become members of the Kingdom of God, and are made priests of God (Rev. 1:6; 5:9, 10;) the prayers of the saints on earth rise to heaven (5:8); the name of the believer is written in the Book of Life (3:5), and the promises of God are His inheritance (2:7, 10, 11, 26; 3:12, 21). This agrees with the saying of Christ as recorded by John: " He that believeth on the Son hath eternal life" (John 3:36); " He that heareth my word, and believeth him that sent me, hath eternal life, and cometh not into judgment, but hath passed out of death into life" (John 5:24).

2) Immediately after death believers are in heaven, in the presence of God and Christ, and are clothed with white robes (Rev. 6:9–11), and have palms in their hands (Rev. 7:9,10). They are before the throne of God, and have entered upon rest (Rev. 7:15–17; 6:11; 14:13). Heaven is conceived as the abode of God's presence and glory, and where, that which earth has lost, is reserved for the children of God. The Paradise of God with the Tree of Life (2:7), once on earth, is now in heaven, and there are the "fountains of waters of life" (Rev. 7:17). The New Jerusalem (3:12), which one day is to descend from heaven (21:2), is even now there. We may even say that John regards heaven as the

region of all that is beautiful, and sublime, holy and pure, in contrast to the actual and visible world of sin and sorrow, and that the doctrine of the Apocalypse is, that this heaven is to become a visible world of perfection when the new heaven and the new earth take the place of this present world of sin.

3) But John also describes the eternal blessedness of the Godly in the New Jerusalem, and he does this in a three-fold manner.[1]

1) As he saw the New Jerusalem descend, he "heard a great voice out of the throne saying: Behold, the tabernacle of God is with men, and he shall dwell with them, and they shall be his peoples, and God himself shall be with them, and be their God: and he shall wipe away every tear from their eyes; and death shall be no more; neither shall there be mourning, nor crying, nor pain, any more: the first things are passed away. . . . I will give unto him that is athirst of the fountain of the water of life freely. He that overcometh shall inherit these things; and I will be his God, and he shall be my son" (Rev. 21:3-7). Now are fulfilled the great promises given in Lev. 26:11, 12; Ezek. 37:27, 28; Jer. 24:7; 30:22; 31:33; 2 Cor. 6:16, Heb. 8:10. Then is fulfilled also the prediction of Isa 25:8; 65:19; for with the first earth all suffering connected with it, and even death itself, pass away; it is a new and blessed state, corresponding to the new earth.

2) In the closer description of the New Jerusalem, John sees the holy city, coming down out of heaven, "having the glory of God; her light was like unto a stone most precious, as it were a jasper stone, clear as crystal" (21:11). He sees "no temple therein: for the Lord God the Almighty, and the Lamb, are the temple

[1] Compare *Gebhardt*, pp. 292-303.

thereof, and the city hath no need of the sun, neither of the moon, to shine upon it, for the glory of God did lighten it, and the lamp thereof is the Lamb. And the nations shall walk amidst the light thereof; and the kings of the earth do bring their glory unto it" (Rev. 21:22–24). It is further said: "And there shall be night no more; and they need no light of lamp, neither light of sun; for the Lord God shall give them light" (Rev. 22:5).

The glory of God is the revelation of His nature as light, and so in the New Jerusalem the prediction of Isa. 60:19, 20 is also fulfilled. Instead of earthly light there is in the heavenly life "the glory of God," and by it the noblest of all night; the glory of God so shines that there is "no more light," and the Light-bearer, the Mediator, the Revealer of the Divine glory is the Lamb, Christ our Redeemer (Rev. 21:23).

There are some who stumble at Rev. 21:24–26, "And the nations shall walk amidst the light thereof; and the kings of the earth do bring their glory into it," etc. By this nothing more is meant than the glorious statement that the Gentiles, just as the Jews, receive full citizenship in the New Jerusalem, and in like manner participate in the blessed glory of the holy city (Rev. 22:2). John here describes the people who are to find entrance into the future city, and he uses the language of the ancient prophets (Isa. 60:3, 11; Ps. 72:10). The Gentiles are expressly designated as those who, according to ancient prophecies, are to find admission into the city.

3) The angel shows John "a river of water of life, bright as crystal, proceeding out of the throne of God and of the Lamb, in the midst of the street thereof. And on this side of the river and on that was the Tree of

Life, bearing twelve manner of fruits, yielding its fruit every month; and the leaves of the tree were for the healing of the nations. And there shall be no curse any more: and the throne of God and of the Lamb shall be therein: and his servants shall do Him service; and they shall see his face; and his name shall be on their foreheads. . . . And they shall reign forever and ever" (Rev. 22:1–5). Thus that great prophecy of Ezek. 47:1–12, concerning a stream of living water and healing trees is fulfilled; also that of Zech. 14:11, that no one shall again fall under the destroying curse of the Lord. "They shall see His face"—*i. e.* they shall enjoy immediately God's bliss-giving presence and absolute self-revelation (Matt. 5:8). By the side of the river of water of life is "the Tree of Life," for in eternity, the continually growing fruits of the Tree of Life serve the blessed for food; and by the words "the leaves of the tree were for the healing of the nations" John emphasizes the eternal refreshment and glorification of believing heathen, just as in Rev. 21:34, 26.

[ANALYSIS: 1) John presents eternal life under three aspects; 2) believers have eternal life already on earth; 3) possess it immediately after death in heaven; 4) but receive it in a special sense after the judgment in the new heaven and the new earth; 5) eternal blessedness is described in a three-fold manner in the New Jerusalem; 6) God shall dwell with his people; 7) the glory of God shall lighten the city; 8) there shall be in it the Tree of Life bearing twelve manner of fruits.]

UNTO HIM THAT SITTETH ON THE THRONE, AND UNTO THE LAMB, BE THE BLESSING, AND THE HONOR, AND THE GLORY, AND THE DOMINION, FOR EVER AND EVER. AMEN.

# INDEX TO SUBJECTS.

Abiding in Christ, I. 133-135
Abraham's bosom, I. 99
Absolution, I. 142
Abyss, II. 283, 284
Active obedience of Christ, II. 163
Acts of the Apostles,
  discourses of Peter in, I. 149-151;
  doctrine of discourses of Peter in, I. 156-170;
  discourses of Paul in, II. 16, 17;
  doctrine of discourses of Paul in, II. 25-40;
  Luke the author of, II. 20,
  teaching of Luke in, II. 200-203
Adam, consequences of transgression of, II. 75-83
Adoption, II. 147-149
Advent, the Second:
  teaching of Jesus, I. 102-107
  time of, I. 102-105; II. 297
  signs of, I. 105, 106; II. 288
  object of, I. 106;
  manner of, I. 107
  teaching of Peter, I. 196, 197, 218, 219, 231, 232
  teaching of James, I. 232
  teaching of Jude, I. 233
  teaching of Paul, II. 50-52

teaching of John. II. 297-311
threefold representation of, II. 298
is pre-millennial, II. 299-311
*Aeon*, meaning of the, I. 115
Age, consummation of the, I. 114-116
*Aionios*, I. 119, 120
Allegorists, II. 311
Angels, evil, I. 67, 68, 77, 187, 189; II. 106, 264
Angels, good, I. 77; II. 261, 262
  shall take part in the Judgment, I. 114
Annihilation of the wicked, there is no, I. 99, 122; II. 64, 65, 325
  of the earth, I. 238
Anointed One, Christ the:
  I. 55-57, 157, 180.
  II. 33, 120, 121
Antecedent will of God, II. 92, 93
Anthropology, doctrine of:
  teaching of Jesus, I. 77-81
  teaching of Paul, II. 70-87
  teaching of John, II. 246-248
Antichrist, teaching concerning, II. 41-41, 288, 294-296
Apocalypse, date of the, II. 233
  doctrine of, II. 256-331
Apocalypse of Christ, according to Paul, II. 41

*Apokatastasis*, I. 146; II. 64, 65, 185, 324

Apostasy of the Gentiles, II. 104–106

Apostasy, the Great, II. 42, 43, 292, 293

Apostles' Creed, doctrine of illustrated in the Acts, II. 203 (*note*)

Apostolic council, I. 167

Apostles, the Twelve, I. 89, 140, 141;

office of, I. 163, 164

Appropriation of Salvation, I 64–66, 132–135

Ascension of Christ, I. 58, 59, 128, 158, 168; II. 38, 39

Assurance of salvation, II. 91

Atonement for sin:
teaching of Jesus, I. 54, 55.
teaching of Peter, I. 181–183
teaching of Paul, II. 131–139, 193, 194, 210–222
teaching of John, II. 250

Attributes of God, II. 88, 89, 241

Auberlen, with reference to the Last Times, II. 305–307

## B

Babylon, II. 299

Baptism:
teaching of Peter, I. 161, 168, 169, 171, 172, 176, 200.
teaching of Paul, II. 28, 150–153, 154, 176, 177, 195, 224

Bauer, I. 22

Bearing sin. See Atonement.

Beast, the first, II. 265, 284, 294, 295

the second, II. 265, 295

Beck, I. 25

Bengel, I. 21; II. 304

Bernard, on characteristics of the Gospels. I. 35–37 (*note*)

Believer, the true, is certain of his salvation, I. 88, 89,

at death the soul of, enters heaven, I. 194, 195; II. 37–40, 282, 286, 328

resurrection of, I. 108, 109, 233; II. 52–54, 57, 300, 313, 314, 316–320

Biblical Dogmatics as distinguished from Biblical Theology. I. 18

Biblical Theology, definition of the science, I. 13;
relation to other branches, I. 14, 15,
divisions of, I. 16–18;
sources of, I. 19;
origin of science of, I. 20, 21;
earlier works on, I. 22;
recent works on, I. 22–25;
auxiliary works to, I. 25–27.

Birth, new. See Regeneration.

Bishop, office of, I. 178; II. 198

Blessedness, eternal, II. 329

Blood, I. 78, 79

Blood of Christ:
teaching of Jesus, I. 54, 55, 66, 131
teaching of Peter, I. 181–183
teaching of Paul, II. 131–139, 220–222
teaching of John, II. 250

Bodily death, I. 78–81, 91, 92, 94, 95, 118–123, 210, 211, 229; II. 36, 37, 281, 282
a particular judgment at time of, I. 96–98
no probation after, I. 96–98

## INDEX TO SUBJECTS

Body of man,
  teaching of Jesus, I. 78–81
  glory of, in eternal life, I. 118
  teaching of Paul, II. 70–87
  teaching of John, II. 246–248
Boehme, II. 304
Bread of Life, Christ is, I. 129, 130

### C

Calling, doctrine of the,
  teaching of Jesus, I. 82, 83
  teaching of Paul, II. 92
Captivity, Epistles of the first, II. 18–20
  teaching of, II. 174–190
Character, no change of, after death, I. 96, 97, 100, 101
Chiliasm, II. 304, 305, 308
Christ, is the Son of Man, I. 48–50, 126–128, II. 127–129;
  the Son of God, I. 50–53, 125–128, II. 122–124, 194, 242;
  the Messiah, the Anointed One, I. 55–57, 157, 180; II. 33, 120, 121;
  the Son of David, I. 57, 58; II. 33, 127, 128;
  the Exalted Messiah, I. 58, 59, 128, 156, 158, II. 270;
  the life, I. 63, 64, 129, 130, 168;
  works salvation, I. 64–66, 131, 180–183; II. 33, 249;
  overcomes Satan, I. 67, 68, 137–140; II. 268;
  the Judge, I. 97, 112, 158, 159, 169; II. 61, 62;
  Second Coming of, I. 102–107, 196, 197, 218, 219, 231, 232; II. 50–52, 297–311;
  the Light of the world, I. 130, 131
  the Lord of glory, II. 120–122
  the Saviour of the world, I. 131, 168; II. 32, 33.
  sends the Holy Ghost, I. 143–145;
  is the Nourisher of the new life, I. 176;
  descent of, into Hades, I. 184–195;
  is the Second Adam, II. 126;
  significance of, to the world, II. 183–188
Christology,
  according to Jesus, I. 48–59; 125–128;
  to Peter, I. 156–158, 167, 168, 180, 184, 185, 227, 228,
  to Paul, II. 120–130, 183–188, 210 (*note*),
  to John, II. 242–244, 249, 267
Church, doctrine of the:
  teaching of Jesus, I. 41–49, 89, 90, 140–142, 145, 146;
  teaching of Peter, I. 161–164, 173–175;
  teaching of Paul, II. 150–158, 167–173, 188–190, 196–199;
  teaching of John, II. 242–244, 249–251
Church government, II. 197–199
Colossians, Epistle to the, II. 18
  teaching of, II. 174–190
Coming, Second. See Advent.
Commandment, the greatest, I. 72, 73
Commandments of God, I. 134, 135
Condition, no change of, after death, I. 96, 97, 100, 101
Consummation, of the age, I. 114–116, 235–238;
  of salvation, I. 198, 199;

the final, II. 63–66, 323
Continuous historical expositors, II. 281
Conversion, I. 61–63, 82, 83, 160, 168; II. 225;
  works of grace in connection with, II. 140 (*note*)
Conversion of the Gentiles, II. 45–48, 102
Conversion of Israel, I 164, 165, 230, 231; II. 48, 49, 100–103, 289–291
Conversion of Paul, II 11–16
Corinthians, two Epistles to the, II. 17–18;
  teaching of, II. 70–173
Covenant, imperfection of the Old, II. 204, 205.
  promise of the New, II. 206, 207
  realization of the New, II. 207, 208
  sacrifice of the New, II 216–222,
  blessings and duties of the New, II. 223–228
Creation of the world, II. 124, 125, 184–186, 244
Cremer's Greek Lexicon, I. 27

## D

Darkness, as a symbol of punishment, I. 121, 122,
  John's conception of, II. 247
Davidic descent of Christ never questioned, I. 57, 58
Deacon, office of, I. 162, II. 198
Deaconess, II. 198
Dead, resurrection of the. See Resurrection.

Death of Christ:
  teaching of Jesus, I. 54, 55, 65, 66, 131,
  teaching of Peter, I. 180–183, 184–192,
  teaching of Paul, II. 127–129, 131–139, 216–222
Death, I 78–81;
  teaching of Jesus, I. 91, 92, 94–101, 118–123,
  teaching of Peter, I. 229;
  teaching of James, I. 210, 211;
  teaching of Paul, II. 36, 37, 81, 82;
  teaching of John, II. 281
  the Second Death, II. 324
Decree, the Divine, II. 92–95
Degrees of punishment, I. 100, 122
  degrees of reward, I 99, 100
Delitzsch, on the Last Times, II. 303–305
Demons, I. 67, 68; II 106
Descent of Christ into Hades, I. 184–195, II. 37–40
Destruction of the world. See World.
Devil. See Satan.
Discipleship, I. 84, 85
Divine, Christ truly. See God.
Doctrinal systems to be distinguished in N T., I. 17, 18
Doctrine. See Teaching.
Dogmatics, in Biblical Theology no distinction between Ethics and, I. 13
Dogmatic Theology as related to Biblical Theology, I. 15
Dragon, the red, II. 263–266, 294
Duesterdieck, on the Last Things, II. 309

Duties. See Ethics.

### E

Earth, destruction of the, I. 236–238; to be transformed, II. 63–66, 327; the new, II. 326
Ecclesiology,
  according to Jesus, I. 41–47, 89, 90, 140–142, 145, 146
  according to Peter, I. 161–164, 173–175
  according to Paul, II. 150–158, 167–173, 188–190, 196–199;
  according to John, II. 242–244, 249–251
*Ekklesia*, II. 167, 188 (*note*)
Elder, office of, I. 163; II. 198
  duties of, I. 177, 178
Elect, the, I. 85–89, 140, 141, 171, 172
  according to James, I. 207
Election, teaching of Paul, II. 28, 92–95, 183
Ellicott, on characteristics of the Gospels, I. 34, 35 (*note*)
End of the world. See World.
Ephesians, Epistle to the, II. 18; teaching of, II. 174–190
Epistles of John, II. 232, 240–255
Epistles of Paul, written at four different periods, II. 17
Eschatology, doctrine of:
  teaching of Jesus, I. 91–123
  teaching of Peter, I. 229–238
  teaching of Paul, II. 35–69
  teaching of John, II. 280–331
Eternal death, I. 91, 92, 118–123, 212; II. 68, 69, 282, 324

Eternal fire I. 99, 218; II. 324
Eternal life, I. 116–118, 129–131; II. 66, 67, 328
Eternal punishment, I. 99, 118–122, 212, 218; II. 324, 325
  degrees of, I. 109, 122
Ethics:
  teaching of Jesus, I. 72–76, 86
  teaching of Peter, I. 173, 174, 177–179, 216, 217
  teaching of James, 204–206, 208, 209
  teaching of Paul, I. 29, 30, 169–173, 226, 227
Evil angels. See Angels, evil.
Exaltation of Christ, I. 58, 59, 128, 158, 159, 168, 196; II. 187, 188
Exegesis, as related to Biblical Theology, I. 15

### F

Faith is trust in God, I. 84, 85, 132, 133
  has its reward, I. 199
  teaching of James, I. 203–206, 208, 209
  and knowledge, I. 215
  teaching of Paul, II. 28, 30, 139–147, 194, 225, 226
  teaching of John, II. 252–254
False prophet, the, II. 294, 295
Father, doctrine of the, I. 51–53, 125–128; II. 89, 90, 193, 240–242
Fellowship with Christ, I. 132, 133, II. 177, 252–254
  with God, I. 134
  of believers, I. 145, 146; II. 254, 255
Fidelity, I. 86, 87

Final judgment, I. 96–98, 111–114, 212, 218; II. 321, 322
Fire as a symbol of punishment, I. 121, 122
Flesh:
  teaching of Jesus, I. 77–79
  teaching of Paul, II. 77, 82, 83, 84–87, 158–162
Foreknowledge of God, II. 94, 95
Forgiveness of sins:
  teaching of Jesus, I. 64–66, 90
  teaching of James, I. 204–206
  teaching of Peter, I. 159, 168
  teaching of Paul, II. 137–147, 174–176
  teaching of John, II. 252–254
Freedom from the law, II. 162–166
Fulfillment of prophecy, II. 113–115
  of the promises, 227
Fullness of the Gentiles, II. 45–48, 102, 103
Futurists, the, II. 281

## G

Gabler, I. 21
Galatians, Epistle to the, II. 17, 18
  teaching of, II. 70–173
*Ge*, this world as, I. 115
Gebhardt, II. 239
*Gehenna*, I. 95, 99, 120, 121
Gentiles, Jesus taught the calling of the, I. 83, 84
  teaching of Peter concerning, I. 165–167, 169, 172
  teaching of Paul, II. 25–28
  the fullness of the, II. 45, 47, 102
  the calling of the, II. 99, 100, 102

apostasy of the, II. 104, 105
Divine training of the, II. 105–107
Gnashing of teeth, I. 122
God, Christ is true:
  teaching of Jesus, I. 50–53, 58, 59, 125, 126
  teaching of Peter, I. 158, 184, 186, 228
  teaching of Paul, II. 90, 121–126, 184–186, 210 (*note*)
  teaching of John, II. 242–244.
God, doctrine of:
  teaching of Jesus, I. 70–76, 88, 143–145
  teaching of Peter, I. 171, 172
  teaching of Paul, II. 26, 88–103
  teaching of John, II. 240–245, 256–266
Godet, on the Last Times, II. 302
Godliness and sound doctrine, II. 191, 192
Gospel, doctrine of:
  teaching of Jesus, I. 63
  teaching of Paul, II. 29–31, 96–98
  and law, II. 33, 109–112
  preaching of, II. 287, 288
Gospels, the characteristics of the, I. 34–37 (*note*)
Government of the world, II. 260
Grace of God may be lost, I. 87, 88
  teaching of Paul, II. 117–119
  antithetical to law, II. 118
  to works, II. 118
  order of works of the, II. 140 (*note*)
Growth in grace, necessary, I. 86, 201; II. 158–162, 177, 178
Guilt, I. 93, 94

## H

*Hades*, I. 94-101; II. 37-40, 265, 283
  descent of Christ into, I. 184-195; II. 37-40
*Haima*, I. 78.
Hardening of heart, I. 139
Harvest of the world, I. 114
Hearing of the Word, I. 84, 132
Heart, the I. 75, 80, 81; II. 87
Heathendom, II. 104-107
Heaven, degrees of dignity in, I. 99
  saints are in, I. 194, 195; II. 37-40, 285
  the new heaven, II. 326
Hebrews, Epistle to the, II. 21
  teaching of, II. 202-228
Hell, I. 95, 99, 120-122
Highest good, I. 74, 75
High Priest, Christ the true, II. 210-215
Hofmann, I. 25, 26
Holy Ghost, doctrine of the Person of, I. 143-145, 168; II. 90, 91, 245, 258, 259
Holy Ghost, doctrine of the work of:
  teaching of Jesus, I. 82, 85, 144
  teaching of Peter, I. 175, 176
  teaching of Paul, II. 29-31, 96-100, 117-119, 139-149, 158-162, 167-169, 174-176
Holy Ghost, sin against the, I. 65; II. 255   [214
Holy Place, the most, II. 213,
Hope, I. 198, 199; II. 30, 179
Horn, the little, of Daniel, II. 295
Human nature of Christ. See Man.

Human righteousness, II. 70-75
Humiliation, Christ in the state of, I. 127, 128, 185; II. 186, 187, 211   [170
Humility, I. 73, 74, 177; II. 169,

## I

Idolatry, results of, II. 105
Immer, I. 25
Imprisonment. See Captivity.
Imputation of Christ's righteousness, II. 142-147
Incarnation, purpose of the, I. 54, 55
  teaching of Jesus, I. 48-50, 125-128
  teaching of John, II. 249
Inheritance of the saints, I. 197, 232
Inspiration, of the Bible, I. 14, 15
  of the Apostles, II. 97, 98
Interpretation, biblical, I. 15
  literal, II. 290, 310
Israel, conversion of, I. 164, 165, 230, 231; II. 48, 49, 100-103, 289-291
  chosen as a peculiar people, I. 173, 174
  hardening of, II. 100-102
  future of, II. 289-291

## J

James, Epistle of, I. 152, 153
  doctrine of Epistle of, I. 202-213
  teaching of, as contrasted with Paul, I. 204-206
Jerusalem, the new, II. 326, 327
Jesus, teaching of, I. 31-146

sayings of, historical, I. 32
the foundation of all Apostolic teaching, I. 33
the very essence of Christianity, I. 33
sources for representation of, I. 33, 34
discourses of, in John's Gospel, I. 38, 39
general divisions of teaching of, I. 40, 41
on the Kingdom of God, I. 41–47
testimony to Himself as the Messiah, I. 48–59
as to the Messianic activity, I. 60–68
concerning the righteousness of the kingdom, I. 70–76
teaching concerning anthropology, I. 77–81
the Messianic Church, I. 82–90
eschatology of, I. 91–123
christology of, I. 125–128
soteriology of, I. 129–131
pneumatology of, I. 132–135
teaching concerning salvation, I. 136–146
See Christ.
Jewish proselytism, II. 100
John, characteristics of Gospel of, I. 35–37 (*note*)
discourses of Jesus as given by, I. 38, 39
the Apostle, II. 231, 232
sources of theology of, II. 232, 233
character of theology of, II. 234–236
previous works on theology of, II. 236–239

teaching of, according to the Gospel and Epistles of, II. 240–255
teaching of, according to the Apocalypse, II. 256–331
Joy, II. 30
Judaism, II. 107, 108
Jude, Epistle of, I. 153, 154
doctrine of, I. 214–219
Judge, the, is Christ, I. 97, 112, 158, 159, 169
the Triune God, I. 111–114
Judgment, doctrine of:
a particular one at death, I. 96–98
an internal one in this life, I. 97
both these differ from the final, I. 98
the Last or Final, I. 96–98, 111–114, 212, 218; II. 321, 322
is universal, I. 112, 212
principle of, I. 113, 114
the rule, I. 114
teaching of Peter, I. 234, 235
teaching of James, I. 234
teaching of Jude. I. 234, 235
teaching of Paul, II. 26, 59–63
Judgments of God, II. 257
Justification:
teaching of James, I. 204–206
teaching of Paul, II. 137–147, 174–176
teaching of John, II. 252–254

## K

*Kapporeth*, II. 134
Keys, office of the, I. 89, 90

Kingdom of God, doctrine of, as taught by Jesus, I. 41-44, 129, 130
 founded by Christ, I. 61
Knowledge and faith, I. 215
Kosmos, this world as the, I. 115, 116
 teaching of John, II. 246, 247
Kuebel, I. 26

## L

Lake of fire, II. 266, 324, 325
Lamb, the, II. 269
Last Day, events of, I. 102-123; II. 292-323
 meaning of, I. 114, 115
 questions with reference to, II. 300, 301
Last Things, doctrine of the:
 teaching of Jesus, I. 91-123
 teaching of Peter, I. 229-238
 teaching of Paul, II. 35-69
 teaching of John, II. 280-231
 order of, II. 47, 48, 300, 301
Last Judgment, I. 96-98, 111-114, 212, 218; II. 321, 322
Law, doctrine of the:
 teaching of Jesus, I. 70, 71, 136, 137
 teaching of James, I. 204-206
 and Gospel, II. 33, 109-112
 of Judaism, II. 107, 108 [190
 teaching of Paul, II. 109-112,
 freedom from the, II. 162-166
Lechler, I. 24, 167-170, 200, 201
 on Paul's conversion, II. 14, 15
 on Paulinism, II. 23
 on the resurrection of Christ, II. 138 (*note*)
 on the high priesthood of Christ, II. 214, 215
 on the theology of John, II. 238
Life, the Christian, in its origin, II. 272
 in its significance, II. 273
 in its activity, II. 275
 in relation to the promises, II. 277
Life. See New Life.
Light of the world, I. 130
Likeness to God, I. 72
Literal fulfillment of prophecy, II. 290
Literalists, II. 310
Logos, doctrine of the, II. 242-244, 249
Lord's Prayer, the, I. 176 (*note*)
Lord's Supper:
 teaching of Peter, I. 162
 teaching of Paul, II. 154-157
Love, elements of, I. 72, 73, 132-135, 146; II. 30
 Jesus, the example of, I. 73
 brotherly, I. 177; II. 30, 170-172
Luke, characteristics of Gospel of, I. 35, 36 (*note*); II. 20 (*note*)
 writings of, Pauline in tendency, II. 20, 21, 202, 203
 teaching of, II. 200-203
Lust, I. 210
Luthardt, on the millennium, II. 307

## M

Man, Christ is true, I. 48-50, 57, 58, 126-128, 184, 185, 228; II. 127-129, 243
Man of Sin, the, II. 41-44
Man, doctrine of:
 teaching of Jesus, I. 77-81

teaching of Paul, II. 70–87
teaching of John, II. 246–248
Mark, characteristics of Gospel of, I. 35, 36 (*note*)
the Evangelist, I. 155
doctrine of, I. 220–222
Marriage, Christian, I. 178
Matthew, characteristics of Gospel of, I. 35, 36 (*note*)
the Evangelist, I. 155
doctrine of, I. 223–226
Mediator, Christ is our. See Atonement.
Meekness, I. 177
Melchizedek, II. 209, 212, 213
Messiah, Jesus is the, I. 42–44, 48–59, 136, 137, 156–160, 167, 198, 221, 222; II. 33, 120, 121, 209, 210
Messianic time, coming of the, I. 159, 160, 196, 197
Methodology of Biblical Theology, I. 16–18
Michael, II. 261, 262, 265
Millennium, questions with reference to, II. 299–301, 312–316
Luthardt, on the, II. 307–309
Mind of man is corrupted, II. 86
Ministry, qualifications of the, II. 197, 198
Missionary sermons, of Peter, I. 150
of Paul, II. 16, 25, 26
Modesty, Christian, II. 169, 170
Mysticism of John, II. 235, 236

## N

Name of God, II. 256
Natural man, the, II. 70–87
Neander, I. 22

presentation of Paulinism, II. 22
on theology of John, II. 236
New Life, doctrine of:
teaching of Jesus, I. 63, 132–135
teaching of Peter, I. 175, 176, 200
teaching of James, I. 202, 203
teaching of Paul, II. 139, 140, 150–166, 225–227
*Noûs*, the, is corrupted, II. 85, 89

## O

Obedience of Christ, passive, II. 162, 163; active, II. 163, 164. See Suffering of Christ.
*Oikumene*, this world as the inhabited, I. 115, 116
Old Testament, fulfilled in Christ, I. 136, 137
significance of, II. 113–115
use of, II. 115, 116
Only-begotten Son, Christ is the, I. 50–53, 125–128; II. 184
Oracles of God, II. 107, 108
Order of works of Grace, II. 140 (*note*)
Original Sin, II. 80, 81

## P

Parables expounded:
of the Sower, I. 45, 83
of the Mustard Seed, I. 46; II. 292
of the Leaven, I. 46; II. 292
of the Tares, I. 46
of the Draw-net, I. 46

of the Prodigal Son, I. 64, 65
of the Unmerciful Servant, I. 65
of the Compassionate Samaritan, I. 72
of the Treasure, I. 74
of the Pearl, I. 74
of the Great Supper, I. 83
of the Laborers in the Vineyard, I. 92, 93
of the Rich Man and Lazarus, I. 94-101, 185
of the Foolish Man, I. 96
of the Pounds, I. 100
of the Talents, I. 100
of the Ten Virgins, II. 293
Paraclete. See Holy Ghost.
Paradise, I. 95-101, 185, 194, 195; II. 37-40
*Parousia*, time of, I. 102-105, 115, 218, 219, 235; II. 303, 304
signs of, I. 105, 106
object of, I. 106
manner of, I. 107
Passive obedience of Christ, II. 162
Pastoral Epistles, II. 20
teaching of, II. 191-199
Patience, I. 178; II. 30, 31, 160
Paul and James, on faith, I. 204-206
Paul, life and conversion of, II. 11-16
Epistles of, II. 17, 18
sermons of, II. 16, 25, 26, 31, 32
Paulinism, II. 11-228
sources of, II. 16-21
works on, II. 22-24
earliest teaching, II. 25-69
teaching of four great Doctrinal Epistles, II. 70-173

teaching of the Epistles of the first captivity, II. 174-190
teaching of the Pastoral Epistles, II. 191-199
teaching of Luke, II. 200-203
of the Epistle to the Hebrews, II. 204-228
Peace, II. 148, 149
Person of Christ. See Christology.
Peter, discourses of, in Acts, I. 149, 150
doctrine of, in Acts, I. 156-170
first Epistle of, I. 151, 152
doctrine of first Epistle, I. 171-201
second Epistle of, I. 153, 154
doctrine of second Epistle of, I. 214-219
the Apostle of Hope, I. 198, 199
Petrine teaching, the, I. 149-238
teaching of Peter, I. 149-154, 156-170, 171-201, 214-219
teaching of James, I. 152, 153, 202-213
teaching of Jude, I. 153, 154, 214-219      [222
teaching of Mark, I. 155, 220-
teaching of Matthew, I. 155, 223-226
Philippians, Epistle to the, II. 19
teaching of, II. 174-190
Philosophy, II. 180
Plenary inspiration, I. 14
*Pneuma*, I. 79, 80; II. 86
Pneumatology, doctrine of:
teaching of Jesus, I. 82-85, 132-135, 144
teaching of Peter, I. 175, 176
teaching of Paul, II. 29-31, 96-100, 117-119, 139-149, 158-162, 167-169, 174-176

Prayer, I. 86, 87, 141, 209; II. 31
the Lord's, I. 176 (*note*)
Preaching to the spirits in prison, I. 189-192
Preaching of the Gospel, the universal, II. 287, 288
Predestination, doctrine of, I. 171-172; II. 91-95
Pre-existence of Christ, I. 51, 52 (*note*), 126-128, 180, 227; II. 184-186, 243
Presbyter, office of, I. 163, 177, 178; II. 198
Preterists, II. 280, 311
Priests, believers are, I. 174, 175
Prison, spirits in, I. 189-192
Probation ends at death, I. 96-98, 191, 192 [227
Promise, the, II. 111, 112, 206, 207,
Propagation of sin, II. 82, 83
of the soul, II. 82, 83
Prophecy, I. 136, 137, 156, 214; II. 113, 115
Propitiation, II. 134, 135, 250
*Psyche*, II. 84-87
Punishment, doctrine of, I. 93, 94, 99, 212; II. 63, 68, 69
degrees of, I. 100
Purpose of God, II. 94, 95

## Q

Quickening of Christ, I. 186-189
Quotations from Old Testament, II. 115, 116

## R

Ransom. See Blood of Christ; Death of Christ; Atonement for Sin; Sacrifice of Christ.

Recapitulation theory, II. 290
Recompense, doctrine of, I. 92-94, 211, 212
Reconciliation, I. 182, 183
Redemption, doctrine of:
teaching of Jesus, I. 54, 55, 65, 66
teaching of Peter, I. 158-160, 180-183, 184-195
teaching of Paul, II. 131-139, 193, 194
Regeneration, doctrine of:
teaching of Jesus, I. 63, 132-135
teaching of Peter, I. 161, 168, 169, 172, 175, 176, 200
teaching of James, I. 202, 203
teaching of Paul, II. 139, 140, 151, 152
Reigning of saints, with Christ, II. 314
Renovation, II. 159, 178
Repentance, doctrine of:
teaching of Jesus, I. 61-63, 82, 83
teaching of Peter, I. 160, 168, 169
teaching of Paul, II. 140, 225
Restoration, no universal, I. 146, 164, II. 64, 65, 185
Resurrection of believers, I. 108, 109, 233, II. 52-54, 57
of unbelievers, I. 109, 110, 233; II. 54, 55
Resurrection of Christ, I. 58, 139, 141, 158, 167, 186-195, 196, 233; II. 137-139, 270
Resurrection, the first, II. 300, 313, 314, 316-320
Resurrection, the general:
teaching of Jesus, I. 108-110
teaching of Peter, I. 233

teaching of Paul, II. 52–59
teaching of John, II. 321, 322
Reuss, I. 24
Revelation, progressive, I. 13, 14,
    Jesus the Mediator of the
    Highest, I. 60, 61; prepara-
    tory, I. 136, 137
Reward, doctrine of, I. 93, 94
    degrees of, I. 99, 100
Righteousness, doctrine of:
    teaching of Jesus, I. 70–76, 92
    teaching of Paul, II. 70–75, 101,
    141–147, 174–176
Right Hand of God, I. 158
Romans, Epistle to the, II. 17, 18
    teaching of, II. 70–173

## S

Sacrifice of Christ:
    teaching of Jesus, I. 54, 55, 131
    teaching of Peter, I. 180–183
    teaching of Paul, II. 131–139,
    216–222
Saints, the inheritance of, I. 197
    after death enter heaven, I. 194,
    195; II. 37–40
    reigning of, with Christ, II. 314
Salvation, doctrine of:
    teaching of Jesus, I. 64–66, 132–146
    teaching of Peter, I. 160, 200
    teaching of Paul, II. 25–29, 117–119, 131–149, 174–190
    teaching of John, II. 249–251
Sanctification, I. 183, 216, 217
    is progressive, II. 29, 30
    teaching of Paul, II. 158–162,
    178, 179
    teaching of John, II. 253, 254
*Sarx*, I. 78, 79; II. 77, 82–87, 158
Satan, doctrine of:

teaching of Jesus, I. 67, 68, 92,
    137–140
teaching of John, II. 262–266
Christ has overcome, I. 184–192
must be resisted, I. 208, 209
the god of this world, II. 75,
    247, 248, 284
Saviour, Christ the, I. 64–66, 131,
    137, 138, 168
Schmid, I. 23; II. 22, 237
Sealing of the servants of God,
    II. 293, 294
Second Coming. See Advent.
Self-denial, I. 74, 75, 86
Selfishness, II. 84
Self-righteousness, II. 72–75
Self-sacrifice, I. 74, 75
Sensuality, II. 84
Serpent, the old, II. 263–266
Seven spirits of God, II. 258
*Sheol*, I. 100
Sin, doctrine of:
    teaching of Jesus, I. 62, 134,
    135, 138
    teaching of James, I. 210, 211
    teaching of Paul, II. 70–87
    in Galatians, II. 76 (*note*)
    in Romans, II. 76 (*note*)
    in Pastoral Epistles, II. 193
    teaching of John, II. 246, 247
Sin against the Holy Ghost. See
    Holy Ghost.
Sinfulness, universal, II. 70–87
Sinlessness of Christ, I. 186, 228;
    II. 128, 129
Sleep of soul, I. 94, 95, 98, 99
Social life, Christian, I. 177–179
Son of God, Christ is the:
    teaching of Jesus, I. 50–53, 125–128     [186, 228
    teaching of Peter, I. 158, 184,

teaching of Paul, II. 90, 120–127
teaching of John, II. 242–244
Son of Man, Christ is the:
teaching of Jesus, I. 48–50, 126–128
Sonship, II. 147–149
Soteriology, doctrine of:
teaching of Jesus, I. 64–66, 129–131
teaching of Peter, I. 158–160, 180–183, 184–195
teaching of Paul, II. 25–29, 117–119, 131–149, 174–190
teaching of John, II. 249–251, 268–271
Soul of Christ, I. 185
Soul, doctrine of the:
teaching of Jesus, I. 77–8.
state of soul after death, I. 95–101; II. 37–40; 282–286, 328
a particular judgment of, at time of death, I. 96–98
glory of, in eternal life, I. 118
teaching of Paul, II. 37–40, 82, 83, 84–87
Soul-sleep, I. 94, 95, 98, 99
Sound doctrine and godliness, II. 191, 192
Spener, I. 21
Spirit, Holy.   See Holy Ghost.
Spirit of Man, doctrine of the, I. 78–81; II. 86, 87
glory of, in eternal life, I. 118
Spirits in prison, I. 189–192
Spiritual death, I. 91, 92; II. 82, 281
Starke's *Synopsis*, quoted, II. 309–311
State, the, I. 178
Stephen, speech of, I. 165
Strong, duties of the, II. 170–173

Suffering, I. 200; II. 160, 161
Suffering of Christ, significance of, I. 180–183, 188; II. 131–139
Supper, the Lord's.   See Lord's Supper.
Synoptists, teaching of Jesus according to the, I. 40–123

T

Tartarus, I. 189, 190, 235
Teaching of Jesus, I. 31–146 Compare Jesus.
Teaching of John, II. 231–331
Teaching, the Petrine, I. 149–238. See Petrine Teaching.
Teaching of Paul. See Paulinism.
Testament, imperfection of the Old, II. 204, 205; promise of the New, II. 206, 207; realization of the New, II. 207, 208; sacrifice of the New, II. 216–222; blessings and duties of the New, II. 223–228
Thayer's Greek Lexicon, I. 27
Theology of the Church, I. 20
Thessalonians, two Epistles to the, II. 16, 17
teaching of, II. 25–69
Thousand years, the, II. 299–301, 307–309, 310
Tongue, sins of the, I. 211
Transgression of Adam, II. 75–83                                [294
Tribulation, the Great, II. 293,
Trichotomy of man, I. 78, 79
Trinity, doctrine of the, II. 89, 259

# INDEX TO SUBJECTS. 347

Trust, I. 209
Types of doctrine, I. 17, 18
Typical character of Old Testament, II 115

## U

Unbelievers shall arise from the dead, I. 109, 110, 233; II. 54, 56, 321-323
  shall be judged, I. 112-114; II. 62, 63, 322
  punishment of, I. 93, 94, 99, 212; II. 63, 68, 69, 324
Universal restoration, there is no, I. 146, 164; II. 64, 65, 185, 324
Universal sinfulness of man, II. 70-87
Universal will of God, II. 92, 93

## V

Van Oosterzee, I. 24; on Gospel of John, I. 38 (*note*)
  on the Kingdom of God, I. 44 (*note*)
  on the Gospel of Matthew, I. 225 (*note*); on Paulinism, II. 23
  on the theology of John, II. 237, 238
Vicarious death of Christ, I. 54, 55, 181-183; II. 131-139; 193, 194
Vicarious fulfillment of the law, II. 163

## W

Watchfulness, I. 86, 87
Weak, duties to the, II. 170-173

Weeping and gnashing of teeth, I. 122
Weiss, I. 25; II. 23, 239
Wicked, no annihilation of the, I. 99, 218; II. 64, 65, 325
  punishment of, I. 93, 94. 99, 212; II. 63, 68, 69, 282, 324
Wickedness shall exist on the earth at the end, II. 287, 288
Will of God, universal or antecedent, II. 92, 93
  not absolute, but conditioned, II. 92, 93
Wisdom, doctrine of, II. 180. 182
Word of God, supernatural character of, I. 175, 176
  teaching of James, I. 202, 203
Work of Christ. See Soteriology.
Works of God, II. 260-262
Works of the law do not justify, I. 205, 206
Works on Biblical Theology, I. 22-27
World, the end of the, I. 114-116; 235-238; II. 63-66
  must be resisted, I. 208, 209
  teaching concerning, by John, II. 246, 247, 323
  prince of this, II. 248
  creation of, II. 260
  government of, II. 260
Worship of O. T abolished, I. 171
Wrath of God, the law works, II. 109, 110

## Z

Zezschwitz on the first resurrection, II. 314

# INDEX TO TEXTS.

*Only those passages of Scripture are referred to which are specifically discussed. Citations from Scripture simply to prove a statement made are not given, as such a list would cover nearly the whole of the New Testament.*

## OLD TESTAMENT.

### GENESIS.

2:17, II. 81.

### LEVITICUS.

11:44, I. 72

### ISAIAH.

11:6–9, II. 65.

### DANIEL.

7:13, 14, I. 42, 48, 49, 58.

### HOSEA.

3:4, 5, II. 48.

## NEW TESTAMENT.

### MATTHEW.

7:26, 27, I. 96.
8:22, I. 91.
10:23, I. 103.
10:28, I. 95, 99
10:45, I. 66.
11:25–27, I. 51, 60.
12:31, 32, I. 65.
13:3–9, I. 45, 83.
13:24–30, I. 46.
13:39–41, I. 115.
13 44–46, I. 74.
13:47–50, I. 46.
16:13, I. 48.
16:18, I. 90.
18:23–27, I. 65.
19:28, I. 238.
20:1–16, I. 92.
22:31, 32, I. 99
22:45, I. 52.
23:38, 39, I. 230, II. 49.
24:14, II. 288.
24:34, I. 103, 104.
25:41, I. 119.
25:46, I. 118, 119.
26:64, I. 53.
27:52, 53, II. 58, 59.
28:19, I. 53.

### MARK.

1:14, 15, I. 41, 42.
2:17, I. 62.
4:2–20, I. 83.
9:43–45, I. 120.
12:37, I. 52.
13:32, I. 53.
14:24, I. 66.

### LUKE.

1:1–4, I. 37.
10:21, 22, I. 51.

14:14, II. 317.
14:16-24, I. 83.
15:11-32, I. 64, 65.
16:19-31, I. 94, 95-101, 185.
20:35, 36, II. 317.
20:44, I. 52.
21:24, I. 230; II. 49.
23:43, I. 98, 185.

### JOHN.

1:1-5, II. 243.
1:9-18, II. 244.
1:14, II. 249.
3:18, I. 97, 109.
5:24, I. 97, 109.
5:28, 29, I. 108, 109; II. 318.
6:29, 40, II. 318.
8:44, I. 138.
12:32, I. 146.
16:8-11, I. 144.
16:12, I. 32.
20:30, 31, I. 39.

### ACTS.

2:24-31, I. 184-187, 233.
2:39, I. 169.
3:20, I. 158.
3:21, I. 164, 231.
6:2, I. 162.
9:3-19, II. 14.
13:38, 39, II. 33.
14:15-18, II. 26.
17:22-31, II. 16, 26.
22:6-16, II. 14.
26:12-18, II. 14

### ROMANS

1-4, II. 123.
1:18-32, II. 106.
2:6-9, II. 61, 68, 69.
3:5, II. 71.
3:24, 25, II. 134.
4:25, II. 138

5.8, II. 132.
5:12-21, II. 78-81, 126.
6:3, II. 151.
6:23, II. 36.
7:1-6, II. 163, 164.
7:18, II. 77, 84.
7:25, II. 85.
8:3, II. 123, 129, 136.
8:6, II. 77.
8:19-23, II. 65.
8:28-30, II. 94, 95.
8:32, II. 123.
9:11-36, II. 101-103.
9:19-24, II. 93.
10:6, II. 124.
11:11-32, II. 49.
11:12, II. 46.
11:25-27, II. 46, 47.

### I. CORINTHIANS.

6:2, II. 63.
10:1-4, II. 154.
10:16, II. 155.
12:23-25, II. 127.
11:27-30, II. 155.
15:12-34, II. 53, 54.
15:20-23, II. 55.
15:22, II. 55, 57, 58.
15:22-26, II. 319, 320.
15:23, II. 51, 55, 56.
15:24, II. 64.
15:27, II. 121.
15:28, II. 64.
15:35-38, II. 53, 57.
15:45, II. 85.
15:45-47, II. 126.

### II. CORINTHIANS.

5:6-8, II. 39.
5:14, II. 133.
5:21, II. 132, 136.
8:6, II. 124.
8:9, II. 124.

11:3, II. 75.

### GALATIANS.

1:16, II. 122, 123.
3:13, II. 133.
5:19–21, II. 84.

### EPHESIANS.

1:10, II. 185.
1:20–23, II. 184.
2:1–3, II. 175.
4:8, 9, I. 194, 195; II. 38.
4:18, II. 175.
5:26, 27, II. 177.

### PHILIPPIANS.

1:23, II. 40.
2:6–8, II. 186, 187.
2:9–11, II. 187.
3:8, 9, II. 176.
3:11, II. 320.

### COLOSSIANS.

1:15–20, II. 184–186.
2:15, I. 187, 191, 192; II. 37.

### I THESSALONIANS.

4:16, II. 50, 319.

### II. THESSALONIANS.

1:6–9, II. 68.
2:3–10, II. 41–44.

### HEBREWS.

5:1–10, II. 212.
6:1, 2, II. 224.
7:1–10, II. 212.
7:11–28, II. 213.
8:1–13, II. 213.
9:1–12, II. 213.
9:13, II. 220.
9:14, II. 216, 220.
9:28, II. 220.
10:14, II. 221.
12:22–24, II. 39.

### JAMES.

1:13–15, I. 210.
1:25, I. 202.
2:21–25, I. 204–206.
3:6–8, I. 211.

### I. PETER.

1:2, I. 182.
1:11, I. 180.
2:24, I. 181.
3:18, I. 181.
3:18–20, I. 184–195; II. 37.
3:20, 21, I. 200.
4:6, I. 184, 192–195; II. 38.

### II. PETER.

3:10–13, I. 218, 236–238; II. 324.

### I. JOHN.

3–8, II. 248.
5:7, 8, II. 245.

### REVELATION.

1:7, II. 298.
2:7, II. 278.
2:10, II. 278.
217, II. 278.
3:4, 5, II. 278.
3:12, II. 278.
4:3–6, II. 261.
6:8, II. 283.
6:12–17, II. 322, 323.
7:1–8, II. 291.
7:3, 4, II. 293.
11:1–13, II. 291.
11:15–19, II. 322.
12:3–9, II. 268, 269.
12:7–12, II. 265.
13:1–10, II. 294, 295.
13:11–18, II. 295, 296.
14:6, 7, II. 287.
14:14–20, II. 298.
14:18–20, II. 322.

15:2, 3, II. 293, 294.
16:17–21, II. 322.
16:20, II. 323.
17:7–18, II. 294, 295.
17:14, II. 272.
19:11–21, II. 298, 305.
20:1–9, II. 299, 302, 309.
20:4–6, II. 285, 304, 306, 307, 308, 313–315, 317.

20:11, II. 322, 323.
20:11–15, II. 321, 322.
20:13–15, II. 283, 316, 319.
21:2, 3, II. 326.
21:3–7. II. 329.
21:11, II. 329.
21:23, II. 330.
21:24–26, II. 330.
22:1–5, II. 331.

www.ingramcontent.com/pod-product-compliance
Lightning Source LLC
Chambersburg PA
CBHW071216290426
44108CB00013B/1200